NEW YORK UNIVERSITY SERIES IN SELECTED ECONOMIC WRITINGS

BOOKS IN THE SERIES

Selected Economic Writings
of William J. Baumol
Edited by Elizabeth E. Bailey

•

Selected Economic Writings
of Fritz Machlup
Edited by George Bitros

•

Selected Economic Writings
of Oskar Morgenstern
Edited by Andrew Schotter

•

Selected Economic Writings
of Abba P. Lerner
Edited by David C. Colander

•

Selected Economic Writings
of W. Arthur Lewis
Edited by Mark Gersovitz

Selected Economic Writings of W. Arthur Lewis

Edited by
Mark Gersovitz

Research Economist and Public Affairs Analyst
Department of Economics and Woodrow Wilson School
of Public and International Affairs
Princeton University

New York • New York University Press • 1983

Library of Congress Cataloging in Publication Data

Lewis, W. Arthur (William Arthur), 1915-
Selected economic writings of W. Arthur Lewis.
(New York University series in selected economic writings)
Bibliography: p.
Includes index.
1. Economic development—Addresses, essays, lectures. 2. Economic development—Effect of education on—Addresses, essays, lectures. 3. Underdeveloped areas—Addresses, essays, lectures. 4. Industrial organization (Economic theory)—Addresses, essays, lectures. 5. International economic relations—Addresses, essays, lectures. I. Gersovitz, Mark. II. Title. III. Series.
HD82.L4154 1983 338.9 82-18819
ISBN 0-8147-2984-3

Manufactured in the United States of America

Preface

W. Arthur Lewis is best known for his writings on economic development. Yet the first paper on development in this volume appeared when Lewis was almost forty years old. By that time, Lewis already had won recognition as a specialist in industrial organization and had begun his research into the international transmission of economic growth. The analysis of economic development is thus the third phase of his career as an economist.

This volume collects papers representing Lewis' work in these three areas of economics. The essays are organized into five sections by theme, and within each section by date of publication. While I shall focus mostly on the papers in this volume, Lewis has authored many books and monographs which complement these papers. Elsewhere, Jagdish Bhagwati (1982) and Ronald Findlay (1982) have provided a broader, more thematic discussion of Lewis' contributions as well as some biographical information.

Part I presents a number of papers on industrial organization. The first paper originates the theory of the two-part tariff. Interestingly, many development economists borrowing this tool from another area of economics for use in project evaluation are probably unaware of yet another debt to Lewis. "The Economics of Loyalty" discusses ideas of implicit contracting and reputation that are only now of concern to a large group of researchers. Similarly, "Competition in Retailing" presents notions of spatial competition that received little attention in the next decades but are the subject of a wide contemporary literature.

The second group of papers discusses the international influences on a country's economic growth. Along with the books *Economic Survey 1919–1939* and *Growth and Fluctuations 1970–1913* these papers form an integrated program of research encompassing theory, measurement and empirical verification. The first paper is primarily an initial attack on the difficult problem of assembling the requisite statistics. This effort is continued in appendices to "Aspects of Tropical Trade" and "The Rate of Growth of World Trade"; the latter appendix is omitted from this printing.

This research stresses that the growth of the developing world has depended on the growth of world trade for the past century. This latter growth rate has been determined by the growth of output in the developed world. The first part of this linkage is the focus of the Wicksell Lecture. The second relation is analyzed most recently in "The Rate of Growth of World Trade". Finally in the Nobel Lecture, Lewis asks "Is this linkage inevitable?" and discusses prospects and strategies for self-sustaining growth by the developing. The second and third papers in this section apply this mode of thinking about the engine of growth to the prospects of the British economy.

Lewis' papers on the dual economy have received the largest audience of any of his work. In the first part of "Economic Development with Unlimited Labour" he sets out a small, general equilibrium growth model. The strategic assumption of a horizontal supply of labor from agriculture to industry allows the decomposition of a complex interdependent system in an almost inconceivably simple way. This representation of the economy serves as an organizing framework for an analysis of many of the most important questions in development and of their relations to each other. Savings behavior and capital accumulation, choice of technique and technological change, population growth, urban and rural labor markets, the labor force participation of women, migration and unemployment, the terms of trade between agriculture and industry, and the distribution of income and more all have their place in Lewis' scheme of things. It is no wonder that a model capable of making all these different parts into a whole plays a central role in the theory of economic development. Three of the other essays in this section extend and defend the concepts introduced in "Unlimited Labour". The remaining three papers investigate in detail two problems, income distribution and unemployment, that are particularly susceptible of analysis using this model.

As though this is not enough, "Unlimited Labour" also contains a model of the terms of trade between industrial and primary producers, further elaborated in the Wicksell Lectures. This model is quite distinct from that of the dual economy. In this case, the simplification is the assumption that of three goods, food, a primary product and an industrial product, only the first is produced and traded by both types of country. As a result the relative well-being of the citizens in the two economies is determined by their relative efficiencies in food production. Technological advance in primary production will be passed on to industrial economies via the terms of trade. It is only improvements in their food production that raise the living standard of the primary producers.

Part IV comprises five papers on the role of education in development. The first, second and fourth discuss the requirements for good educational planning during the development process. Lewis sharply rejects constant-coefficient manpower planning. Instead, he emphasizes the substitution of educated for non-educated labor and the consequent compression in relative earnings at different stages of development. "Secondary Education and Economic Structure" presents empirical estimates of educational requirements at different levels of the proportion of population outside agriculture, a favorite Lewis index of development. This paper includes an interesting graphical relation fitted by eye of the type now estimated by nonlinear methods. The last essay discusses roles for the university in LDC's in the broadest possible terms: as a bearer of culture, as a trainer of skills, on the frontiers of knowledge and as a service agency. These essays nicely illustrate Lewis' interest in economic issues and their wider social significance.

The last group of papers addresses a varied menu of topics in development. Some of these essays are broad in scope, others are narrowly focused. The Ely Lecture and "The Gap Between Rich and Poor Nations" provide an optimistic assessment of what has been achieved by the LDC's and what can be expected for them. The notion of a shortage of entrepreneurship as a stumbling block is skillfully dismissed. Especially noteworthy given the year of the Ely (1965) is the discussion of unemployment emphasizing the attraction of possible employment at high wages and the importance given to promoting agriculture. This latter topic is considered in the even earlier "Shifting Fortunes of Agriculture" and "Thoughts on Land Settlement".

"Patterns of Public Revenue and Expenditure" has the announced purpose of seeing how patterns of expenditure and sources of revenue vary with economic development, in the hope of discovering what patterns are appropriate. It provides a meticulously assembled set of data on sixteen countries in an area of inquiry that, given the latitude in budgetary classification available to governments, is surely one of the most difficult. The effort expended in consistently distinguishing capital from current expenditure, for example, is clear witness to the Lewis credo that properly organized data are the foundation of analytical progress. I leave the reader to savor the vast array of analytical insights abstracted from these data. Lewis' views on inflation (his closing remarks to the inflation and growth conference and "Unlimited Labour") are closely related to the concerns of public finance since he emphasizes inflation as a way of financing government capital formation.

Two of the papers in this last section relate to international influences on development. "The Evolution of Foreign Aid" reviews the recent development record and asks what can be attributed to foreign aid. The major trends in aid-giving are set out, as are principles for effective aid design. "The Less Developed Countries and Stable Exchange Rates" begins with the "General Motors principle": the LDC's need an exchange regime that is good for the developed countries so world trade can expand. Lewis then considers the factors relevant to an LDC's decision to float or peg.

Both "Industrialisation and Social Peace" and "Socialism and Economic Growth" build on Lewis' views of economic development to explain aspects of social development. In the first essay he discusses how changes in the organization of production, in the spatial distribution of economic activity and in the distribution of incomes yield new classes and changes in the status and power of individuals. As a consequence, economic development means social tension, but as development proceeds far enough these tensions abate. "Socialism and Economic Growth" contrasts the objectives of democratic socialism with the requirements of economic growth and discusses the resolution of conflicts created by a desire for socialist growth.

References

Bhagwati, Jagdish N., 'W. Arthur Lewis: An Appreciation' in M. Gersovitz et al (eds.), *The Theory and Experience of Economic Development: Essays in Honor of Sir W. Arthur Lewis* (London: George Allen & Unwin, 1982), pp. 15–28

Findlay, Ronald, 'On W. Arthur Lewis' Contributions to Economics' in M. Gersovitz et al (eds.), *The Theory and Experience of Economic Development: Essays in Honor of Sir W. Arthur Lewis* (London: George Allen & Unwin, 1982), pp. 1–14.

Acknowledgments

Grateful acknowledgment is made to the following for permission to use essays which appear in their publications:

Academic Press, Inc.
American Economic Review
Daedalus, Journal of the American Academy of Arts and Sciences
District Bank Review
Economica
George Allen & Unwin
Holmes & Meier Publishers, Inc.
International Council for Educational Development
Journal of Agricultural Economics
Macmillan Company
National Westminister Bank Limited
North Holland Publishing Company
Oxford University Press
Per Jacobsson Foundation
Social and Economic Studies
St. Martin's Press, Inc.
The Institute of Chartered Accountants in England and Wales
The London School of Economics and Political Science
The Manchester School
The Wicksell Lectures Society
The World Today
University College, Cardiff
UNESCO and the International Institute of Educational Planning
Yale University Press

I would also like to thank Ms. Joan Grant and The Elmer Holmes Bobst Library and Study Center, New York University and Ms. Susanne McNatt of the Princeton University Library for their assistance in lending us original books from their respective collections for the purpose of reproduction in this volume.

CONTENTS

PART ONE

INDUSTRIAL ECONOMICS

[1]

CHAPTER II

THE TWO-PART TARIFF

The essence of two-part charging is that the consumer is required to pay two charges, one which varies directly with the amount of the commodity consumed, and another which does not. Thus the Post Office charges for the use of the telephone (1) a quarterly rental, payable whether any calls are made or not, plus (2) a charge for each call. Similarly for electricity one may be asked to pay a fixed charge depending on e.g. the size or rateable value of one's house, plus a charge per unit of actual consumption.

This system of charging has made steady progress in this country since it was first suggested in the later years of the nineteenth century. In the electricity industry, where it was first adopted, the two-part tariff is now almost universal; it has been adopted by the Central Electricity Board, which controls wholesale distribution, and strongly recommended to retail distributors by two committees reporting to the Electricity Commissioners. In 1921 it was applied to the telephone system, where it is now the principal method of pricing. Gas legislation has been specially altered to permit undertakings to use the system, and they were adopting it with some zeal in the years immediately preceding the outbreak of war. In industry at least one well-known concern has been using the system for some forty years. Yet, despite this progress the principles of two-part charging are not widely known or understood, and it is the purpose of this essay to elucidate them.

First we shall examine the incentives to two-part charging, and then we shall enquire how it serves the public interest.

There are five possible incentives to two-part charging. First, where in consequence of periodical fluctuations in demand there are regular periods when equipment is standing idle, it is often suggested that the only "scientific" way to allocate costs to consumers is to use a two-part tariff. Secondly, even where there are no such fluctuations regularly foreseeable, an entrepreneur with fixed costs may find it profitable to use a two-part tariff in order to escape the risks of unforeseeable change. Thirdly, the two-part tariff may enable an entrepreneur to extract more revenue from his customers, in given demand conditions, than would a single pricing system. Fourthly, it is a form of price discrimination. And fifthly, it is very appropriate where "customer costs" are large. We shall examine each of these in turn.

I

THE ANALYSIS OF THE PEAK

Most industries are subject to some degree of regular fluctuation in the demand for their products; at some times business is brisk, at others it is slack. The cycle may be diurnal—restaurants, buses and shops have regularly each day hours of peak demand and hours almost of idleness—or it may be weekly, or seasonal, or like the trade cycle it may extend over several years. Where the product can easily be stored, these fluctuations in demand need not induce similar fluctuations in production; the plant can work continuously throughout the year, storing in the slack period the excess output which will be required at the peak. If the product cannot be stored, or the cost of storing is prohibitive, the result is different; the plant must be large enough to meet the maximum demand, and when demand slackens equipment lies idle.

If the idle hours are all needed by the plant for overhauling, repairs or rest, there is no real off-peak excess capacity, and no special problem of peak costing. Again, if we are dealing with equipment which wears out proportionately with use, there is no problem. The cost of the equipment enters directly into marginal cost, which is therefore the same for all units of output. Our problem is best isolated by assuming that the equipment will have to be scrapped on account of technical obsolescence long before it has worn out, and that there is no element of user cost entering into the marginal cost of production. It is also further simplified by assuming that prime costs of operation are zero, so that we may concentrate all attention on the capital costs.

A diagram may help. Fig. 1 shows the number of units consumed at different hours of the day, time being measured on the horizontal and quantity on the vertical axis. It is assumed that consumers take a quantity of one unit marked A throughout the day, a quantity of one unit per hour marked B for four hours, and a quantity of three units per hour marked C for a later four hours. Since the product cannot be stored there must be a total capacity of four units per hour, equal to 96 units a day. Since, however, only 40 units are consumed, there will be 56 units of unused capacity. The problem is now to allocate costs between A, B and C.

Many solutions have been suggested. The simplest is to treat all units of demand alike, dividing the total cost by 40. Assuming that the daily cost of the capital required to produce one unit per hour throughout the day is £24, and that capital costs are constant so that the daily cost of the four units installed is £96, then cost per unit of capacity used is £96 ÷ 40, i.e. £2·4 per hour. Another solution makes each hour of the day contribute the same amount, irrespective of capacity used. The amount required for four units installed is £4 per hour. So, following Fig. 1, for the first five hours

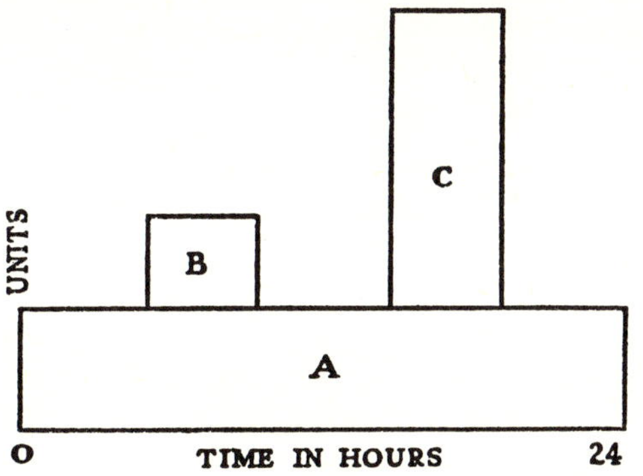

Fig. 1

A is charged £4 per unit per hour; in the next five hours A and B each pay £2 per unit per hour; then A pays £4 per unit per hour; and then A and C pay £1 per unit per hour. In a third solution each piece of equipment used must earn its £24 a day. The first unit supplies A throughout the day and charges £1 per unit. The next supplies B for four hours and C for four hours, and charges £3 per unit per hour. The other two supply C for four hours and charge £6 per unit per hour.

These three are only a small selection from the wide variety of published solutions which is already at our disposal.[1] There is, in fact, hardly any limit to the number of plausible solutions that can be suggested. Equity, from which they mostly start, will

[1] A very useful summary and classification of the published solutions is the monograph by P. Schiller, *Methods of Allocating to Classes of Consumers or Load the Demand-Related Portion of the Standing Costs of Electricity*, published by the British Electrical and Allied Industries Research Association.

support anything. For example, the first solution can be supported on the ground that it is equitable to charge the same price for all units; the second on the ground that it is equitable to make each hour's customers pay for the amortisation of the equipment during that hour, irrespective of how much they use it; and the third on the ground that it is equitable to charge the full cost of each unit of equipment to those who use it. In this field equity is the mother of confusion.

Economists are interested not in equity but in costs. They are predisposed to the view that the most equitable charge is that which corresponds to cost, but their first business is not charges but costs. Economic cost is concerned with the value of resources in alternative uses; it is measured by asking how total expenditure is affected by increasing or by reducing output. Cost is therefore a function of change. It can be found only by enquiring how expenditure is altered if output is altered. Once we start from this point only one solution is possible, that which corresponds to the facts of change, and all others must be rejected.

In terms of the case in hand, the undertaking must compute its costs by asking how its expenditure is affected if demand alters; e.g. if it is asked to supply an extra unit of product. A little reflection will show that the question cannot be answered unless the hour at which the extra unit is to be taken is specified. If it is to be taken at the peak, when the plant is already fully utilised, new plant must be installed, and cost is high. If it is to be taken other than at the peak it may be possible to supply using existing idle equipment, and without extra cost. Peak and off-peak marginal costs are different.

In the early days of electricity supply the problem was simple. The plant was used mainly for lighting purposes, at night, and lay idle during the day. The peak period was clearly definable, and sharply marked off from the off-peak. The cost analysis was simple. Extra supplies at the peak involved additional equipment, and extra off-peak supplies involved none. The whole cost was chargeable to peak supplies, and the cost of off-peak supplies was zero.

This simplicity disappeared when a second peak began to develop. Basing their prices on the cost analysis, undertakings had sold off-peak supplies at very low rates. These had stimulated the demand for electricity for purposes other than lighting, and the consumption for these uses grew steadily until in many undertakings the peak situation altered. In some the morning demand came to exceed evening demand. In others they were about equal. This change created great confusion. When there were two peaks should costs be divided equally between them? If the morning peak exceeded the evening peak should the latter now be disregarded and all costs now be loaded on to the morning peak? Such dramatic changes in price policy were bound to provoke protests, and how should these protests be answered?

The correct policy emerges only if we put the problem into its correct analytical framework. What we are dealing with here is the general problem of amortisation. When an entrepreneur is installing plant, he looks forward through the years and knows that its output will fluctuate with demand. In some years (days or hours) it will be very great, in others small. He cannot allocate the cost of the plant individually between the hours; he hopes only that the profits of all hours taken together will cover the total cost. If we treat the output of each hour as a separate product, the result is exactly as if he were engaged in joint production. The theory of amortisation is a part of the theory of joint costs, and if we take the classical joint cost example of cotton production it helps us to understand the analysis of the peak.

Suppose to begin with that there is no demand for cotton seed whatever; it follows that the whole cost of the plant must be recouped from the sale of lint. Then suppose that there springs up a demand for seed which increases steadily. At first the quantity of seed already being produced in consequence of the demand for lint will exceed the demand for seed. In a competitive market the seed will be sold at a price which only just covers the special costs of recovering it, which for convenience let us assume to be zero. Despite the fact that some seed is being sold, the entire cost of cultivation falls to be contributed by lint; and this must be so as long as the demand for seed at a zero price does not exceed the quantity being produced in consequence of the demand for lint. This corresponds to the simplest peak situation, where there is only one clearly defined peak. The whole cost is attributable to it.

Now let us continue. As the demand for seed grows there comes a point where at zero price the demand just equals the supply available. At that point there ceases to be excess capacity in producing seed. If the demand continues to increase, we can no longer attribute the entire cost of the plant to lint. In a competitive market the price of seed will rise and the price of lint simultaneously fall; the contribution of each to costs will depend solely on demand. In terms of electricity this means that when the morning demand reaches equality with the evening demand, and threatens to exceed it, the proper policy is to raise the morning price and lower the evening price, in an effort to keep the two peaks of equal height. As with lint and seed, the appropriate relation between prices is that which disposes fully of both outputs, eliminating excess capacity. No dramatic price change is called for; the whole cost is not suddenly to be transferred from one peak to the other. As the morning demand grows, the price is raised against it; not at the start to equality with the evening price, but only to such extent as will keep its growth in check, and in line with that of the evening demand, whose further growth is now stimulated by correspondingly reducing its price. If new plant is installed, at this stage, the effort must be to keep it occupied morning and evening, and the appropriate charges are those which secure this result.

But suppose that the morning demand refuses to be kept in check even with this treatment. Let us return to our cotton example. In the situation that we left all the lint and all the seed were finding a market. Now suppose that the demand for seed continues to increase, the seed price rising and the lint price falling. There will come a point where the price of lint falls to zero because the amount of lint produced to satisfy the demand for seed exceeds the demand for lint. At that point and thenceforward the price of seed must cover the whole cost of the plant. There are three stages to the process; a stage where the whole cost is attributable to lint, a stage where the whole cost is attributable to seed, and an intermediate stage where cost allocation depends on demand.

The fact that there is this intermediate stage is usually ignored, but it solves all the problems. Every effort should be made to keep within it, i.e. to keep morning and evening peaks equal. It is only if one demand is so much more powerful than the other that even a zero price for the other cannot equate them that we are in a true peak and off-peak situation where all the cost must be allocated to the peak and none to the off-peak.

Now in practice it is seldom possible to make frequent changes in public utility prices, and so in changing conditions prices cannot be adjusted constantly to the appropriate levels. The main

D

error has been to base prices on the current situation instead of on estimates of future demands. For example, a particular type of electricity load may now be small and definitely off-peak. But if the undertaking charges a very low price based on the existence of excess capacity, and works up the load, it may well grow so enormously as to convert off-peak into peak, as power loads have done. In quoting a price, therefore, the undertaking must have its eye on future possibilities, and not just on present circumstances, and must try to find a mean between a price so high that the load remains altogether undeveloped, and a price so low that a peak emerges—at any rate until such time as the next change in prices becomes feasible.

II

THE PEAK AND THE TWO-PART TARIFF

The home of the two-part tariff is electricity supply. There it was applied long before the peak became a complex problem. In the early days electricity was used primarily for lighting, and the peak was single and clearly defined. Large demands were made on the plant in the evening, while during the day most of the equipment lay idle.

The suggestion that in these conditions the appropriate method of charging is to use a two-part tariff we owe to an English engineer, Dr. John Hopkinson, who became consulting engineer to the first Edison electric power stations in this country, and subsequently Professor of Electrical Engineering at King's College, London. For his presidential address to the Junior Engineering Society in 1892 he chose as subject "The Cost of Electric Supply."[1] The paper begins by stressing the fact that costs are determined by peak demand, goes on to analyse the various elements of fixed and variable cost, and concludes:

> "The ideal method of charge then is a fixed charge per quarter proportioned to the greatest rate of supply the consumer will ever take, and a charge by meter for the actual consumption."[2]

According to this principle it is necessary to discover for each consumer not only how much he consumes during the quarter,

[1] First published in the *Transactions* of the Society, Vol. III. Reprinted with other papers by Hopkinson in his *Original Papers*, Vol. I.

[2] *Original Papers*, p. 261.

but also what is his maximum rate of consumption, defined as the largest amount taken in any small period, e.g. half an hour. Since the equipment of the concern depends on its maximum output in a short period, the consumer is made to pay a fixed charge depending on his maximum in a short period. A similar idea underlies the "Wright" rates offered by some concerns—a type of quantity discount whose gradations depend upon the maximum rate of consumption of the individual consumer.

This conclusion was hailed as a great discovery, and made the basis of many tariffs. Unfortunately it was based on a simple confusion. It is true that it costs a station more to supply 1,000 units if they are all to be taken in one minute than if they are to be spread over a longer period; but this applies to the aggregate output of the station, and not to supplies to the individual consumer. What is true of the individual consumer is that the cost of selling to him is greater if he buys during peak periods than if he buys during slack periods (unless there is excess capacity even at the peak). If therefore he takes 24 units all in one minute during the slack period it may cost less to supply him than if he takes 24 units at the rate of one unit per hour, because in the latter case he adds to capital costs at the peak. The maximum rate at which the individual consumer takes is irrelevant; what matters is how much he is taking at the time of the station's peak.

This point is now generally accepted among the better writers on the subject, but it is not yet fully realised in tariff making. Thus a recent survey of the tariffs of the larger electricity undertakings show 34 per cent offering to industrial consumers two-part tariffs based on individual maximum demand, and a smaller percentage offering such tariffs to domestic consumers.[1] They have also been recommended by a committee reporting to the Electricity Commissioners,[2] and adopted by the Central Electricity Board. Gas engineers, indeed, have gone so far as to suggest for their product two fixed charges based on individual maximum demand, one to take account of the production peak, and one for the distribution peak. Since gas can be stored, the two peaks do not coincide. The volume of output produced varies not from hour to hour, but from season to season, the size of the plant being determined by the greatest demand in any 24 hours. But the

[1] D. J. Bolton, *Costs and Tariffs in Electricity Supply* (1938), pp. 117 and 136.

[2] *Report on Uniformity of Electricity Charges and Tariffs*, by a Committee appointed by the Electricity Commissioners (1930), paras. 119, 136.

calls on the distribution system vary from hour to hour. Two fixed charges to cover the standing costs of production and distribution, a third to cover "customer" costs (discussed in Section IV of this paper), and a variable to cover prime costs, would give the industry a four-part tariff—such are the heights to which this sort of analysis leads!

Hopkinson himself seems to have been a little uneasy about all this, for he added:

> "In fixing the rates of fixed charge it must not be forgotten that it is improbable that all consumers will demand the maximum supply at the same moment, and consequently the fixed charge named might be reduced or some profit be obtained from it."[1]

This, however, merely added to the confusion. For subsequent writers professed to meet the difficulty by introducing the concept of the "diversity factor." Since all consumers are not taking at their maximum rates at the same time, the sum of the individual maximum demands is greater than the total demand on the station at the time of its peak. The diversity factor is defined as the ratio of the sum of the individual demands to the total demand at the time of the peak. There are many theories as to the way in which this diversity factor should be used to "correct" cost allocations based on individual maximum demand; the subject has a vast literature. The latest English work on the subject, D. J. Bolton's *Costs and Tariffs in Electricity Supply* (1938), contains a thirty-page chapter on the diversity factor, full of mathematical symbols, curves and principles deduced from the laws of probability, though from the tentativeness with which he puts them forward, the author himself does not seem to have much faith in them. This is as well, for no amount of correction can alter the fact that the standing costs of the undertaking are related not to the maximum rate at which the individual consumer takes, but to the amount he takes at the time of the station peak. Both the Hopkinson two-part tariff and the Wright quantity discount, based on the maximum demand of the individual consumer, are fallacious in so far as they claim to be exactly allocating to each consumer the costs he causes the undertaking to incur.

As we have already seen, the true essence of the problem is that

[1] *Original Papers*, p. 261.

marginal costs are greater at the peak than at other times. To put the matter loosely, capital costs are to be allocated exclusively to consumers taking at the peak, and in proportion to the amount each takes at that time. It is not uncommon to find cases where prices are for this reason higher at the peak than in slack times. Thus transport undertakings frequently offer cheap tickets in the middle of the day, the telephone system has its cheap night rates, and there are seasonal fluctuations in shipping freights and in hotel charges. Such price differentiation is not price discrimination, or charging what the traffic will bear, for those terms in their proper meaning relate to differentiation based on differences in elasticity of demand, while the differentiation here is due to differences in marginal cost, and is just as likely, if not more so in perfectly competitive conditions as in cases of monopoly.

Nevertheless, while we may say that the "normal" way to allocate standing charges where there are peaks is simply to charge different prices at the peak and in slack periods, it is theoretically possible to achieve the same result with a two-part tariff. If the fixed charge is based not on individual maximum demand but on individual consumption at the time of the station peak, the total charge to any consumer will be the same as it would be if he were charged different prices at different times for a consumption with the same time pattern. This method of allocating standing charges need not be confined to electricity. The season tickets offered by transport undertakings are of the same kind; the holder is expected to travel to and from work at the peak, and makes his contribution to expenses in a lump sum; he is then allowed to travel free at all other times, since the cost of carrying the marginal traveller at other times is negligible. Even the long fluctuations associated with the business cycle could be dealt with in this way, the consumer paying at the beginning of say every ten years a fixed sum based on his consumption during the boom.

In the early days of electricity it was not possible cheaply to record individual consumption according to the time of day, and therefore peak and off-peak consumption could not be charged separately. In these circumstances some early concerns were content to make a charge which did not vary with the hour; but this was clearly inappropriate not only because it allocated part of the standing charges to units consumed in slack periods, but also because the result of so doing was to discourage consumption in the off-peak period when costs are low. The adoption of the two-part tariff in these circumstances was a definite advance on previous practice.

But, if the two-part tariff is to work satisfactorily, the fixed charge paid by each individual really must bear a fairly close relation to the costs that he imposes on the undertaking at the time of the peak. In the early days when peak consumption was confined to lighting demand, the indices on which the fixed charge is usually based—rateable value of the consumer's house, size of the house, capacity of meters, maximum demand—were fairly acceptable guides to the costs imposed by different individuals. But in these days this is no longer the case. The peak is no longer associated with lighting, as far as domestic consumption is concerned; it is associated rather with the use of electricity for heating, whether space heating, water heating, or cooking, and the costs imposed by a consumer who uses electricity for these purposes are several times as great as those imposed by a consumer who uses electricity only for lighting. Size of house and rateable value are useful indices only when all houses use electricity for the same purposes; but in a period, such as the present, when different houses make very different demands, they are most misleading indices for a fixed charge. Even individual maximum demand is now a better guide than size of house, because the persons with high maximum demands are almost certainly using electricity for heating, and almost certainly all coming on to the peak.

The best theoretical solution is still to charge different prices for peak and off-peak consumption. Failing this, the next best would be a two-part tariff with the fixed charge based on appliances in use, so that persons using electricity for heating could be made to bear their full cost, as compared with persons using it only for lighting. A two-part tariff with the fixed charge arbitrarily determined, as at present (e.g. based on rateable value), is both uneconomic, because it overstimulates the peak demand, and unfair because persons who impose high costs on the undertaking pay no more than those who impose low costs. It would be better to have no fixed charge, and to base payments solely on consumption than to have an arbitrary two-part tariff, because consumption is at least a better guide to cost imposed than is rateable value.

We may therefore conclude that as a method of cost allocation where there are peaks in demand and supply, the two-part tariff, suitably framed, is superior to having a single undifferentiated price which discourages off-peak consumption, but inferior to charging different prices at different times, though it may sometimes be more convenient than the latter if the measurement and timing of consumption are costly. This may have been the case when electricity was first being developed, but does not seem to be so any longer. According to Bolton:

> "If one were starting *de novo* it would be an easy matter to invent a much more scientific tariff on the costs side, and moreover a perfectly practical one.[1] Undertakings usually know when their peaks will occur, both locally and on the bulk supply. Tariffs would be framed to avoid these times, and for domestic loads they might be, say, 4d. a unit from 4 to 6 p.m. and ½d. all other times. A combined single-phase meter and synchronous clock could be mass produced for about 30s. to 35s., and for another 5s. the makers could probably extend the hands and put it in a bakelite case. It could then hang in the hall and show the time of day (and, incidentally, the rate of charge). An alternative method of changing the timing could be by 'ripple control,' referred to at the end of Chapter VII.
>
> "Such a tariff would require no alternatives and would save all individual assessments and charges whatsoever. It is perfectly easy to understand, particularly after all the publicity recently given to the 'shilling trunk calls' based on exactly the same principle. It represents real costs and at the same time it gives endless scope for heating, cooking, etc., at competitive figures for all times outside the narrow high price zone. However, such ideals (if ideal they are) must be reserved for some brave new world, since the timid old one has chosen other methods and is too fearful of change to be likely to give them up."[2]

III

THE RISK ELEMENT

To conclude that two-part charging, using any of the usual bases for calculating the fixed charge, is an inferior method of

[1] The author adds the cryptic footnote: "I.e. it would work, and in fact has worked. But this is not to say that it would be more satisfactory, in practice, than our present schemes. Experience in Paris suggests that it might not, and anyhow it is far too large a question to be discussed in a sentence."

[2] *Op. cit.*, pp. 208–9.

cost allocation, is not, however, to conclude that it is either an undesirable or an unprofitable method of recovering the standing charges. It may be a method by which a firm protects itself against the risks of unforeseen change.

Let us suppose that an entrepreneur is deciding to invest capital in the form of durable equipment in a certain industry. In doing this he runs the risk that his expectations of the future may be frustrated; if there are new products, new rivals, new inventions, or other unfavourable changes, he may be unable fully to recover the money he is investing. How is he to protect himself against the risk of such changes? From his point of view, the most satisfactory arrangement might be to avoid all risk by getting each potential consumer to pay in advance some proportion of the sum invested. If in the aggregate consumers contributed sums sufficient to cover the capital invested, the entrepreneur would be relieved of all risk of loss. Nevertheless, much as this arrangement might please the entrepreneur, it would be unlikely to please the consumer, who is reluctant to pay in advance for services which he may never use. If this method proved impracticable, the entrepreneur might try as his next best course to get each user to contract to take a minimum quantity of the product, or if payment is by monthly subscription, to subscribe for a minimum number of months—this is a common feature of telephone, gas, electricity and other undertakings. Failing this, the entrepreneur may try to protect himself by securing exclusive contracts, the customer promising not to use the services of any rival undertaking. The list of concerns using such contracts is large; it includes the railway companies, who offer special "agreed charges" to clients who send all their traffic by rail, liner conferences who offer a "deferred rebate," brewers, film distributors, iron and steel concerns, a manufacturer of shoe machinery, and others. Or he may simply offer quantity discounts. All these are methods of tying the consumer to the undertaking, relieving the entrepreneur of the risk of loss due to miscalculations or to changes in demand or supply conditions.

Such devices run counter to the spirit of private enterprise. The essence of that system is that entrepreneurs are the specialists in risk-bearing. It is therefore very difficult to introduce such devices into an industry where entry is unrestricted and easy. There is usually some entrepreneur who is willing to charge the consumer per unit consumed, and to assume himself the risk that over a number of years demand will be large enough for him to recoup all his costs[1]; and where there are such entrepreneurs, consumers are unwilling to be tied by payment in advance or by any exclusive contract. Competitive private enterprise demands that overhead costs shall be recouped not through any fixed charge, as the theory of the two-part tariff suggests, but by inclusion in the variable charge.[2]

The monopolist, too, may meet his overhead costs simply by having a sufficiently high variable charge. But he may choose between doing so and making a fixed charge. He may have a fixed and no variable charge, or a variable and no fixed charge, or some combination of both. The risk of unforeseen change is a strong argument in favour of a fixed charge, which will throw upon the consumer any loss resulting from unfavourable change. Hence unless the entrepreneur is willing himself to bear this risk —and with it the possibility that there may be *favourable* changes —he may seek to impose such a charge. His incentive to insure himself in this way will be particularly great if his product has to face strong competition from other products. For the imposition of a fixed charge in a sense ties the customer to the undertaking, making it worth his while to buy as much as possible from that concern, rather than to divide his purchases, so that his average price may fall as low as possible.

However, the power of the entrepreneur to secure himself in

[1] Sometimes it is suggested that in very risky industries no entrepreneur will come forward unless protected either by a monopoly or by special contracts. For instance, the patent system receives some support on the ground that entrepreneurs would be unwilling to try out new inventions unless protected by a monopoly. Similarly combinations in liner shipping are said to be necessary since shipowners would be unwilling to send their ships on regular voyages unless protected against intermittent competition. There seems to be little ground for this view. In the liner case the combinations emerged because there were too many regular sailings, not because there were too few, and their effect was to reduce, not to increase the number. But this is too large an issue to be developed here.

[2] Sometimes part of the "overheads" can be traced to some particular consumer. For instance, a firm may generate its own electricity, but may also connect itself to the public service as an insurance against breakdowns. Where the public station has to instal extra plant as a reserve against this contingency it will make a fixed charge to the firm whether it takes any electricity or not. But in these cases the "overhead" is not an overhead at all; it is a cost directly attributable to the particular consumer, and would not be incurred but for the undertaking to serve him; it is a "customer" cost, as defined in section IV of this paper.

this way depends on the attitude of consumers and on the strength of his monopoly position. It may well be that if a fixed payment is demanded some consumers who are not certain how large their consumption will be will refrain from buying at all. Thus a recent survey of gas undertakings in Great Britain which offer consumers the alternatives of a two-part tariff and a single variable charge shows that a large percentage of those who would benefit by switching over to the two-part tariff fail to do so. Ignorance of the advantages of the two-part tariff may account for this to some extent, but it is also probable that some consumers prefer to remain on the ordinary tariff because they are uncertain how large their consumption is likely to be, and unwilling to commit themselves to the payment of a fixed charge.[1] Where this is an important element, there must be no fixed charge or only a low one, or alternatively consumers must be permitted to choose between a two-part tariff and an ordinary one. Note however that in some cases the element of risk may work the other way. A potential customer may say, "I am unwilling to take this commodity on the basis of so much per unit because I am uncertain how much my family and I will take from time to time, and I may find at the end of the year that we have run up a tremendous bill; I would prefer you to quote me one lump sum charge, and then let us take as much as we like." If the commodity is a new one, or subject to large and unpredictable variations in demand (e.g. one's demand for medical services) the risk element may well favour the imposition of a high fixed charge with a very low or no variable.

IV

THE CONSUMER'S SURPLUS

Another incentive to having a fixed charge is that this may make it possible for the firm to extract some of the "consumer's surplus." The extent to which this is possible depends on the income elasticity of demand for the commodity. If income elasticity is zero, then when a fixed charge is imposed, so long as it is not so high that the consumer ceases to buy altogether, he will buy the same amount at any given marginal price as he would have bought if there were no fixed charge; he will there-

[1] See P. Chantler, *The British Gas Industry*, pp. 127–130.

fore be paying a higher average price for any given quantity than he would be prepared to pay if there were only a variable charge. The effect of the two-part tariff is as it were to shift his demand curve to the right.[1] But this is only so where income elasticity of demand is low. What it boils down to in practice is that the firm will gain from the two-part tariff if customers keep their eyes on the cost of the marginal unit rather than on the total amount spent on the commodity. If the customer watches the size of his bill rather than the marginal price the demand curve facing the firm will be substantially the same whatever system of charging it may use. This point is not always understood. Thus it is sometimes suggested that the success of the two-part tariff is proved by the fact that sales expand when a firm adopts it.[2] But this view is fallacious. If the fixed charge is small, the effect of adopting a two-part tariff is to lower the average price at which the commodity is sold. But if the firm lowered its average price without adopting a two-part tariff sales would similarly expand. The only relevant question is, if the average price had been lowered to the same extent without adopting a two-part tariff, would sales have expanded to the same or a lesser extent? For the two-part tariff is superior only in so far as it enables the firm to sell more at any given average price than it would if average and marginal prices coincided. In some cases this will be so, in others where the customer concentrates on the size of his bill rather than on the marginal price the two-part tariff has not this advantage.

The fact that two different elasticities are relevant when the two-part tariff is used—income elasticity and elasticity of substitution at the margin—is important where two products are highly competitive with each other, as in the case of gas and electricity. The point is not important if one product is a substitute for the other in all uses, for then even if one industry is offering a two-part tariff with a very low variable charge, the consumer will carefully compare his probable total expenditures in using the one product or the other before he commits himself to the payment of the fixed charge. Here competition is determined not just by the marginal price, but also by the amount of

[1] The two-part tariff shares this characteristic with quantity discounts of the "block" type. Wherever the average charge differs from the marginal charge, the demand curve tends to be shifted to the right.

[2] E.g. J. T. Haynes, giving the results of a two-part tariff at Rotherham, makes this claim. *The Two-Part Tariff as an Aid to Gas Sales*, pp. 23–35.

the fixed charge; it is average price that counts.[1] But the position is different if each product has a use in which it is essential, and competition is limited to certain additional uses, e.g. if electricity is considered essential for lighting, and gas for cooking, but they compete for heating and other purposes. Here since the fixed charge has to be paid anyway, only the marginal price is relevant. Each industry may find it profitable so to reduce its variable charge that it only just covers marginal cost. It is easily shown that it will not pay to go below marginal cost. Thus in the following diagram, if DD is the demand curve, OS the marginal cost, and income elasticity is assumed zero, the maximum consumer's

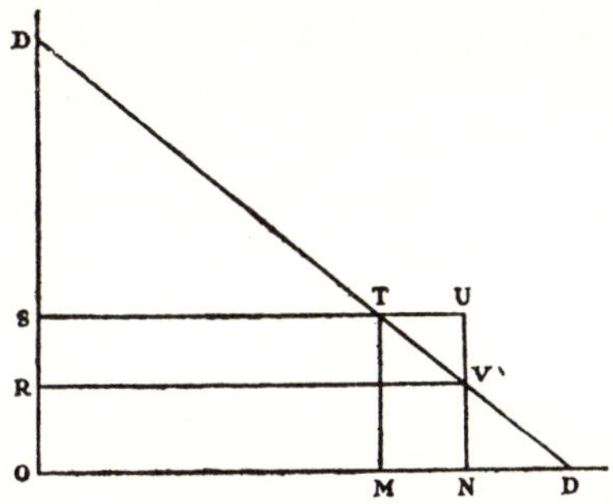

FIG. 2

surplus which can be extracted from this particular consumer by way of fixed charge is the area DST. If the firm made a variable charge less than OS, say OR, the consumer would demand ON, and the firm's net revenue would be a maximum of DST minus TUV, the fixed charge being increased to DRV. If the variable charge is to go below marginal cost, it must be for some reason other than consumer's surplus, such as the reasons already mentioned. Now marginal cost is not the same as prime cost; it includes all costs which vary with output. In the long run most costs, including equipment and expenses of management, vary with output, and this must be remembered in appropriate circumstances. In the limiting case all the firm's costs are marginal costs, to be recouped through the variable charge, and if it is

[1] If after making the comparison the consumer chooses the product using the two-part tariff, he will become tied to the firm, which will then profit if there should be unforeseen change unfavourable to him. But this is a separate point which we have already discussed in the preceding section of this paper.

subject to strong competition the firm will be unable to tap consumer's surplus by levying a fixed charge. In general a fixed charge can only be levied if the firm is in a strong monopoly position, or if marginal cost is less than average cost and firms take account of this in their oligopolistic competition with each other.

V

PRICE DISCRIMINATION

Next we come to two-part charging as a form of price discrimination. The effect of making the same fixed charge to all consumers is to discriminate against the small ones. This will pay only if their demands are on the average less elastic than those of large consumers. This is not usually the case, but may be found in special conditions. Thus the small consumer of electricity may be small because he is using it only for lighting, while the large may be using it for heating, power, or other purposes for which the demand is much more elastic than for lighting. One way of meeting this situation would be not to use a two-part tariff, but to charge different prices for current used for different purposes. The two-part tariff, however, serves the same purpose; it is an alternative to rate classification.

Nevertheless it is unlikely that the ability to bear a fixed charge will be the same among all consumers. To avoid discriminating heavily against small consumers, undertakings sometimes have a different fixed charge for each consumer, varying according to the rateable value of his house, the number of rooms, or some similar index. This has indeed the advantage that the fixed charge can be made to increase so rapidly that in effect larger consumers are made to pay higher average prices per unit than smaller consumers, if the smaller are thought to have the more elastic demands.

To avoid frightening off the smaller consumers it is also customary to offer as an alternative to the two-part tariff a single variable charge, somewhat higher than the variable charge of the two-part tariff; the latter is then used only by larger consumers. Or the firm may offer not a two-part tariff but a "block" quantity discount; e.g. it may say, "for the first 20 units, 6d. per unit; additional units at 1d. per unit." This is not so hard on the small consumer, while for the consumer of more than 20 units it has the same effect as a two-part tariff in that the average price differs from the marginal. Here too the size of the first block may vary from consumer to consumer.[1]

Finally, the whole of this discussion so far has been based on the tacit assumption that price discrimination is practicable. This is, of course, only the case if the commodity cannot easily be transferred from those who pay a low price to those who pay a high price. Suppose, for example, that a department store tried to recoup its overhead costs by using a two-part tariff: it might, for instance, offer a 10 per cent discount to any customer who pays a "quarterly subscription" of £2. It would be unlikely to continue the scheme long, because it would soon find that some people were getting goods through subscribing members without themselves paying a subscription. Unless buyers can be isolated from each other, the two-part tariff is an unprofitable method of pricing.[2]

There is, however, one exception to this rule. If a firm is selling to middlemen, a two-part tariff will enable the large middleman to produce more cheaply than the small, if the fixed charge is the same to both, and perhaps to capture his business. The firm may prefer to have only a few large customers, for it may wish them

[1] It has sometimes been suggested that when a firm first introduces the block quantity discount each consumer should have as his first block an amount equal to his previous consumption. But this is not an easy policy to put into effect. J. T. Haynes, who contemplated introducing it in one undertaking he controlled, explains why it was rejected: "It was then proposed that every consumer should be charged a greatly reduced price for all gas used in excess of his normal consumption. This sounded attractive, but examination revealed a number of difficulties. What was a consumer's normal consumption? A large number of typical meter cards were examined, and adjacent houses were found to have widely different consumptions, affected by the number in the family, periods of sickness, inclination or disinclination to use gas, etc. The application of the proposal in such cases would quickly create a sense of unequal treatment between neighbours, and could not be defended by the undertaking in the light of the equal conditions clauses in the Corporation's Gas Acts." See *The Two-Part Tariff as an Aid to Gas Sales*, p. 13. C. L. Paine's proposal (see his article "Some Economic Consequences of Discrimination by Public Utilities," *Economica*, 1937) would be even more difficult to apply than this, because it involves raising the upper price above the level of the previous price and estimating how much each consumer would have bought if this were the only price.

[2] The department store might meet this difficulty by putting a limit on the amount bought on any one subscription, say £30. But then "membership" ceases to correspond to the true two-part tariff, and becomes a means of charging a special price to those who purchase between £20 and £30.

to be able to form a combine to increase their own charges to the public, so that it in turn may be able to share part of their monopoly gains. Trade unionists sometimes for a similar reason urge their employers to combine. In such circumstances the firm will discriminate heavily against small customers, having a fixed charge which is very high relatively to the variable, or even dispensing entirely with the variable and allowing any customer who pays the fixed charge to take as many units as he likes. On the other hand, it is equally likely that the firm may fear that a reduction in the number of its customers might be harmful, since they may be able to combine to force down its charges. In this case it will pursue the opposite policy, discriminating not against the small middleman but against the large. Or again it may particularly want to discriminate against large purchases if the commodity is trade marked and perishable, and it wishes to maintain a reputation for freshness; or to discriminate against small purchases if it wishes to create a reputation of exclusiveness for its products (e.g. cosmetics). Any argument for reducing the number of one's retail outlets is an argument supporting the use of a two-part tariff; any argument in favour of increasing their number is an argument against having a fixed charge.

VI

CUSTOMER COSTS

We have left to the last the case for two-part charging based on the existence of "customer" costs, because, though it seems the most obvious case, to analyse it is to get a summary of the whole problem. "Customer" costs are those costs which have to be incurred if any given customer is to be served, but which do not vary directly with his consumption; such costs as equipping his house with electric wires and fittings, installing a meter and reading it periodically, keeping his account and so on; costs which vary with the number of customers rather than with output.

Suppose, for example, that an electricity concern is supplying electric current, and undertakes to wire premises and instal all necessary fittings. The cost of the installation is an indivisible item which does not vary directly with the amount of current consumed. At first sight it seems quite reasonable to make a separate charge for this, or to use a two-part tariff, basing the fixed charge on the cost of installation, or at least to offer quantity discounts for current. But this is not necessarily the most profitable policy. In suitable circumstances the firm may prefer to make only a fixed charge, supplying the consumer with as much current as he likes without any additional charge. Or on the other hand it may prefer to instal "free of charge," recouping itself for the cost of installation by having a high variable charge. Its fixed charge may be high, low, zero, or even negative (that is to say, instead of asking the consumer to pay for installation, the firm may actually pay him a "rent" for the privilege of installing its equipment on his premises). Similarly, its variable charge may be high or negative; the firm may not merely supply current free, but it may also undertake to repair the equipment free of charge (this being the equivalent of a variable negative) or pay a refund to the consumer if his consumption is large.

This problem is not confined to public utilities; it appears wherever there are complementary goods like gramophones and gramophone records, razors and razor blades, motor cars and tyres, telephone instruments and a telephone service, or other twin commodities one of which is a durable instrument which must be installed before the other can be used. If conditions were suitable a company might give away gramophones to stimulate the sale of records, or give away records to stimulate the sale of gramophones. This poses the question, what is a commodity? In the former case the company would say that it was selling records, the gramophone being only part of the cost of production; in the latter it would be the record that was part of the cost of selling gramophones. The enjoyment of any satisfaction involves a number of separate costs, some of which are indivisible, and it is a problem to decide how many of these indivisible costs are to be treated as different commodities and charged separately, and how many to be merged into a single variable charge. Nor is the problem confined to cases where all costs are undertaken by the same firm. Even if the gramophone companies are separate from the record companies, it may pay one set of companies to subsidise the other; so also it might pay motor car manufacturers to subsidise the sale of petrol, and so on. Given the complementarity it is always the same problem: how high should the fixed charge be relatively to the variable?

We can also fit into the same category another problem which is really only a limiting case of the first. This is the case where the only cost is an indivisible customer cost. An example of this is a case where a firm leases machinery to manufacturers. There is only an installation cost, the cost of the machine. Yet the firm may charge either a fixed monthly rent, or a monthly rent plus a royalty varying with the output of the machine, or a royalty alone with no fixed rental.[1] Wherever a firm is leasing some durable commodity, the use of which is measurable, it can adopt, if it wishes, a two-part tariff as its charge. How high should the fixed charge be?

In competitive conditions the solution is simple: the fixed charge is no more and no less than the cost of installation. But in an imperfect market this is not necessarily the most profitable policy; then all the arguments for and against a fixed charge which we have discussed in the previous sections are once more relevant. The difference now is that we must take as our base for the fixed charge the amount of the installation cost. Arguments in favour of a fixed charge are to be interpreted as supporting a fixed charge greater than the amount of the installation cost; arguments against a fixed charge are arguments for reducing the fixed charge below installation cost, even to zero or a negative price.

Thus the element of risk may serve to reduce the fixed charge below installation cost: consumers may hesitate to wire their premises because they are not sure that their consumption of electricity will justify the initial sum involved, so the firm may assume that risk for them. Or on the other hand it may be the variable charge which they fear, and so the firm may quote a single fixed charge, allowing them to consume as much as they please. Similarly, if potential purchasers of motor cars are deterred by the high initial cost involved, the gasolene companies might profitably subsidise the motor manufacturers, and raise the price of petrol; but if it is the running cost which deters the purchaser, it will be the motor manufacturer who will profitably subsidise the gasolene company, the tyre company, the repair companies, and so on.

The relevance of the two elasticities is as great here as to the allocation of overhead costs. Sometimes by reducing the variable charge one can increase the amount of consumer's surplus to be obtained through the installation charge. At other times, free installation is justified, because it leads to such a terrific increase

[1] A well-known case is that of the United Shoe Machinery Company, which leases machinery to shoe manufacturers on a two-part basis.

E

in demand for the subsidiary commodity. Discrimination, too, may justify either a high installation and low variable charge, if for instance demand is less elastic in some uses than in others; or a fixed charge less than installation cost and high variable charge, if the firm is selling to middlemen and particularly wants to have a large number of outlets, for example if it is leasing machinery and fears the consequence of a buyers' monopoly. With customer costs, as with standing charges, there is no simple solution; each case must be weighed on its own merits.

Finally, it must be remembered that it may not be worth while making a variable charge at all if the cost of measuring the amount taken by each consumer is high. In the early days of electricity and of the telephone, before simple recording devices were invented, consumers were for this reason charged a lump sum independent of use. Similarly in some countries it is considered that the cost of installing water meters in each house, and reading them periodically, would not be justified. The argument is most forceful where elasticity of demand is not very high, so that consumption is not much greater if unmeasured than it would be if it were measured and charged for. If elasticity of demand is high, and marginal cost high, the argument loses its force.

VII

WELFARE ASPECTS

It remains to consider two-part charging from the standpoint of the public interest. We have seen that from the point of view of the entrepreneur the two-part tariff may frequently be the most profitable method of charging. Can we say that the public interest requires that the fixed charge should be exactly equal to customer cost and that anything more or less is undesirable?

To answer this we must re-examine the incentives to making a fixed charge greater or less than customer cost. The first was that the tariff may be used as a means of allocating overheads where there are peaks in production due to peaks in demand; we saw that it is an inferior method of doing this, even from the standpoint of the entrepreneur, but there is no substantial reason why it should not be adopted if it prove the most convenient. Secondly, a two-part tariff may be a means by which either the entrepreneur or the consumer relieves himself of risk. There is nothing in this inherently contrary to the public interest; but there is some danger of abuse if the consumer is "tied" to one undertaking in competition with others. Especially is this so if the variable charge is reduced below marginal cost, for competition between undertakings must be based on marginal cost if there is to be an "ideal" allocation of resources.

When we come to the two-part tariff as a means of stimulating consumption at the margin the matter is not so simple. It is now generally agreed that the "ideal" output of a concern is such that every consumer is getting every unit for which he is prepared to pay marginal cost.[1] If marginal cost is equal to or greater than average cost, there is no case for a fixed charge; a variable charge equal to marginal cost will cover the total costs of the firm. But if marginal cost is less than average cost, a variable charge equal to marginal cost will not cover total costs. If total costs are to be covered, either the variable charge must be greater than marginal cost, or a fixed charge levied in addition to the variable. It is easily shown that it is better to recoup the difference between average and marginal cost by a fixed charge than to add it to the variable. Consider the following diagram where AD is the demand curve (for convenience a straight line) of a consumer whose income elasticity is assumed to be zero, and ON the marginal cost on the assumption that the cost of supplying this consumer is constant and there is no customer cost. Suppose that the firm was formerly charging a single price OP (average cost), and that it now adopts a two-part tariff with a variable charge ON. This consumer's purchases will then increase from OM to OS, income elasticity being assumed zero. If the amount of the fixed charge is equal to the area PQRN, the consumer will be better off than he was under the previous system since QRT will be added to his consumer's surplus. He will in fact be better off than before so long as the fixed charge is less than PQRN + QRT. This means that two-part charging can benefit both the buyer and the seller better than having a single variable charge, equal to average cost. The danger is that the firm may try to take the whole of the consumer's surplus, ANT, in which case two-part charging becomes the most perfect form of discrimination, and capable of the gravest exploitation. But provided that this danger is guarded

[1] There are difficulties in applying this principle to the use of a two-part tariff by public utilities because marginal cost to the undertaking is not necessarily equal to marginal social cost; on this problem see C. L. Paine, *loc. cit.*, pp. 428–431.

against, two-part charging is clearly better than having only a variable equal to average cost, in cases where marginal cost is less than average cost.

Next, an objection raised against two-part charging is that small consumers may have to go without the commodity because they cannot afford to pay the fixed charge. In so far as the fixed charge is being levied as a contribution to overhead costs, this is easily met by an appropriate adjustment of the fixed charge; it is not in the interest of the undertaking, any more than of the public, that the charge should be so high as to exclude anybody. But where the fixed charge is levied to cover customer costs, the

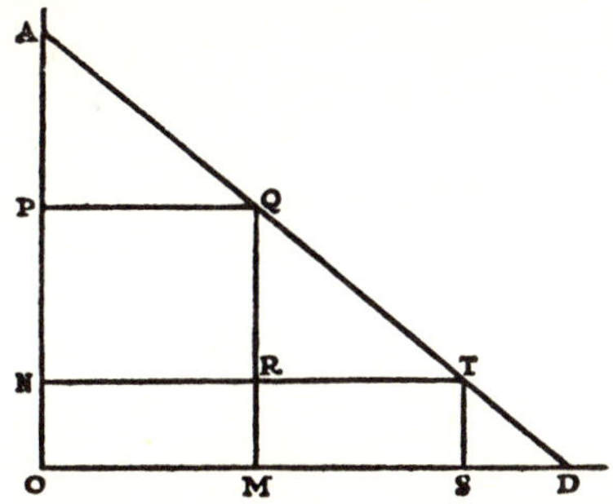

FIG. 3

objection is equivalent to suggesting that some consumers should get the commodity for less than it costs. Thus, in 1933 the Parliamentary Secretary to the Board of Trade explained to representatives of the gas industry why he would oppose any clause permitting a two-part tariff in a forthcoming Bill:

> "I am not attempting to justify the exclusion of the minimum charge from the Bill on any ground of logic or technicality. I am doing it entirely on the political argument that the Government are not prepared to face the opposition that would necessarily come from people in scattered places amounting to millions in total who would never understand the reasons behind a clause of this kind."[1]

An argument like this for compelling the gas industry to supply gas below cost to some consumers and to recover the loss from

[1] *Joint Committee of the House of Lords and House of Commons on Gas Prices* (H.L. 24, 91, H.C. 110), 1937, para. 16.

others does not seem to be strictly within the province of the economist.

Again, two-part charging may be used as a means of increasing or reducing the number of one's retail outlets. For example, it is sometimes alleged that one consequence of two-part charging by the United Shoe Machinery Company has been to maintain an excessive number of small shoe manufacturers. In general we may assume that it is not in the public interest to have a larger or smaller number of outlets than would emerge in conditions of perfect competition. But there is seldom perfect competition either in manufacturing industry or in retail trade. Hence the most that we can say is that the usefulness of two-part charging depends on whether or not it tends to bring about the results which would emerge under perfect competition. For example, if it is used in order to counteract monopolistic tendencies in the outlets it is in the public interest; if it is used to reduce the number of outlets in order to create an illusion of "exclusiveness," it is harmful.

The public's principal safeguard against the abuses of tariff making is competition, which makes exploitation impossible. Where there is little competition, the abuse of two-part charging merges itself into the general problem of the control of monopoly. We cannot take up this subject here in all its ramifications. It is sufficient to point out that in the cases where the two-part tariff is most common there is already some machinery of control. In industry the outstanding case of two-part charging, the shoe machinery case, is based on patent rights; and there already exists under the patent legislation provision for the control of abuses which might well be tightened up. Elsewhere two-part charging is most common in public utilities, the price policies of which are usually subject to regulation in one way or another. Two-part charging can be of great benefit to the public; all that is needed is control adequate to prevent abuse of the power it confers on those who use it.

[2]

CHAPTER III

THE ECONOMICS OF LOYALTY

The desire for loyal patronage is almost universal. Every business man seeks to build up that goodwill which brings the customer back again and again. The quality, design and style of an article; its price; the credit facilities provided; free rest rooms; free delivery; advertising; with these and many other services, real or fictitious, firms try to impress their "personality" upon their customers and secure loyal patronage. What is unusual is not the desire for loyalty, but deliberate discrimination against those who are disloyal; and the purpose of these notes is not to study the economics of goodwill in general, but to examine only those cases where there is some differentiation between the loyal and the disloyal customer, whether in price, or in other conditions of service.

This differentiation does not always meet the eye. If a firm or group of firms announces that it will give a discount to customers who undertake never to buy elsewhere, or in extreme cases will refuse to sell at all without such an undertaking, there can be no mistake. But a firm can secure a similar result without any specific demand for loyalty simply by offering quantity discounts of one shape or another, since these make it cheaper to be loyal than to spread one's purchases over many sellers. The boundary between our field of study and other ways of inducing loyalty lies in this element of price differentiation. Tasteful design, branding, advertisement and other devices help to secure loyal patronage, but do not result in the customer getting a better price from the firm if he is loyal than if he is not.

In the following pages we shall first analyse the incentives to this differentiation; then we shall examine some cases of it; and finally we shall enquire how the public interest is affected.

I

THE EFFECTS OF LOYALTY

There are two reasons why a firm may differentiate between loyal and disloyal customers. One is that the costs of supply may be different; the other, that it may be seeking to maintain or extend a monopoly position. Take cost first. Loyalty affects it in two ways, through the economies of quantity buying, and through the economies of regularity.

As for quantity, the loyalty of a customer may reduce costs because his purchases from any one establishment are larger than they would be if he split his custom. It may be cheaper to sell to a customer who comes again and again than to sell the same quantity during the same period to a number of different customers. If the business is done on credit, only one account needs to be kept, and the cost of preliminary enquiries as to credit status is less for one than for many customers (the risk of bad debts, however, may be affected one way or the other). The customer may, on his first visit, examine all the alternative products on sale, and subsequent sales may involve much less sales effort than if the whole range had to be shown to a new customer on each occasion. In brief, there are indivisible elements in selling. Hence customers who come again and again are cheaper to serve than casual customers. There are, of course, disadvantages as well. The loyal customer may waste one's time in gossip; he may consider himself entitled to special treatment, and so on. But in many cases there will on balance be a gain. The analysis of this case is complicated because we more frequently associate the economies of quantity buying with the customer who buys a large amount at a single purchase, and recognise that such a customer may give rise to greater economies, even though disloyal on other occasions, than will a loyal customer buying in driblets. The true comparison is not between large and small purchases, but between sales of a given size to a constant clientele, and sales of the same size to an ever-changing clientele.

The other saving in cost is a function of regularity. If a seller can count on the loyalty of his customers, he can plan his investment more accurately. He also shifts to others losses associated with the risk of fluctuations in demand. In a market where prices are perfectly flexible, and any seller can always dispose of the whole of his output at the market price, there is no incentive to give any special price to loyal customers. One may enter into a contract now to supply some client for the next two years at a price which is below the current market price, but will only do so if one expects months in which it will be compensatingly above the prices then ruling; the quoted price is not a loyalty price, but simply the average of current and future prices. It is in markets with a price floor that it is important to have affiliations. When prices are low, but not low enough to clear the market, that seller is fortunate who has loyal customers. When prices are high, but supplies still less than demand, it pays him, remembering the lean days that lie ahead, to reserve his supplies for those who will support him during the slump, and even to charge such persons a price below the current price.

These two elements in cost, quantity and regularity, provide an incentive to loyalty discounts wholly unconnected with monopoly power, and may emerge even in highly competitive industries. The other incentive to loyalty discounts is that they may in imperfect markets be a device for maintaining or extending monopoly power. Loyalty and innocence are twin virtues. If one is lucky enough to have customers who are prone to either virtue, one may be able to exploit them.

When a seller attempts in an imperfect market to impose exclusive patronage on a customer without offering a sufficiently attractive inducement, the issue resolves itself into a test of strength. If a seller without strong monopoly tries to impose a stipulation of loyalty without the appropriate discounts, his customers will simply leave him to buy elsewhere. He cannot use such a stipulation to *create* monopoly; he can only enforce the stipulation if he already possesses some legal or natural monopoly which compels customers to give him at least some of their patronage, and therefore enables him to penalise them if they withhold the rest. Such monopoly power may be based on a legal privilege such as a patent, copyright, a trade mark, or a licensing system, on ownership of nearly all the sources of some factor of production such as a mineral, or on membership of a combine, and we shall examine some cases in a later section.

Not always does it pay to use monopoly power to compel loyalty. Take the case where a firm has a monopoly for one of its products, but not for the others. It produces X, which is patented, and Y which is unpatented and sold by many competitors. If the purchasers of X also need some Y, it may be tempted to refuse them X unless they also buy all their Y from itself. This will be very profitable if the demand for X is so strong that it will not be much affected by the stipulation; it will not pay if X, though patented, has close substitutes. This is what the Americans call full-line forcing. In its extreme form X and Y will only be sold together. For instance, suppose that a manufacturer of motor cars secures a patent on a carburettor which reduces fuel consumption by 50 per cent. He may decide to reserve such carburettors exclusively to his own make of car, thus using the patent to push his own make; or he may allow rival manufacturers to use the carburettor on payment of a royalty. This extreme type of full-line forcing will only pay if sales of his own car expand so much as to compensate for the royalties which might have been obtained if other manufacturers were allowed the use of the carburettor.[1]

Given the necessary monopoly power, to stipulate that one's commercial customers buy exclusively one's own products may be an alternative to vertical integration. To compel a distributor to stock only one brand is, from the manufacturer's point of view, just one step short of setting up his own retail shops. It is a much safer step. The risks and costs of vertical integration are too well known to require elaboration here. Though there are cases in which it pays, it results generally in loss of the advantages of specialisation. The manufacturer ceases to be a specialist in production, and has to acquire also the techniques of wholesaling and retailing. He has not the same knowledge of local supply and demand conditions as experts in those branches of distribution. His organisation grows so large that it tends to lose flexibility. His distribution costs may be higher than would be those of

[1] The issue sometimes presents itself to the seller in the form, "What is my product unit? Am I prepared to quote separately for every distinct operation or separable component?" For instance, a furniture firm has to decide whether it will sell only suites, or whether individual tables and chairs can be separately bought; and if it decides to sell them separately, whether to sell suites at a price which represents a discount on the aggregate price of component items. Similarly a gramophone company has to decide whether to sell the individual records of a symphony, or to sell them only in sets. In practice the component items can usually be bought separately, a discount being not infrequently offered. There are also cases where they are not sold separately. His Master's Voice sells the Schnabel recording of Beethoven's Waldstein sonata only in sets, and moreover will sell it only to customers who at the same time take the Opus 26. The company explains this by saying that the two sonatas together make up one "volume" out of the fifteen "volumes" issued by its "Beethoven society." But the terminology does not alter the fact that this is an ordinary case of full-line forcing. Putting all the records together may give them extra value for a few people. But there must be many who want the Schnabel Waldstein but not the Opus 26. Full-line forcing pays only if they want the Schnabel Waldstein so badly that they will take the Opus 26 as well, rather than buy some other artist's recording.

independent distributors, pooling his goods with those of many other manufacturers. His range of products is usually more limited than the range stocked by the retailer; if he integrates he may have to buy complementary (even competitive) products from other manufacturers to sell with his own, and the greater the number of such products, the more his business will assume the characteristics of wholesaling and retailing, and the less will he be a specialist in production. These disadvantages of integration are avoided by exclusive dealing arrangements. The retailer is then tied to the manufacturer, but the manufacturer is not tied to the retailer. The advantages of specialisation are preserved, but the manufacturer shifts some of his risks on to the retailer. This he can do only if he has monopoly power. In its absence the retailer will not pledge loyalty unless he is given adequate compensation. Loyalty stipulations cannot be used to create a monopoly; they can only extend or maintain existing privileges.

II

QUANTITY DISCOUNTS

So much for the incentives to differentiation between loyal and disloyal customers. We come now to examine some cases of such differentiation which were found in Great Britain before the outbreak of war. In this section we shall deal with cases where there is no stipulation of loyalty, but the discounts are such that it pays to be loyal; the next will be devoted to cases where loyalty is a specific condition for earning the discount.

All the devices belonging to this section are variations on the theme of the quantity discount—the season ticket, the return ticket, the two-part tariff, coupon trading, all promote loyalty because the price diminishes with quantity bought.

The effectiveness of a quantity discount in promoting exclusive patronage depends in the first place on whether it is "cumulative" or "non-cumulative."[1] A discount is cumulative if the quantity to which it applies is the aggregate quantity purchased during a given period, without reference to the size of the individual purchase. It is non-cumulative if it applies only to the amount taken at a single purchase. Obviously cumulative discounts

[1] The terminology is from that very useful and not sufficiently well-known article by W. H. Stevens, "Some Laws of Quantity Discounts," *Chicago Journal of Business*, 1929–30.

promote exclusive patronage to a greater extent than non-cumulative, as the latter are effective only when the article is not expensive to store; then it will pay the purchaser to buy a whole season's stocks from a single seller at one purchase.

The effectiveness of the discount depends also on the rapidity with which the average price falls as the quantity bought increases. There is a difference between discounts where the average price falls in jerks, and those where it falls steadily. The price will fall steadily if the discount given when purchases reach a certain size applies only to additional units taken beyond that point; it will fall in jerks if it applies to the original amount as well. If the price falls in jerks, the exclusiveness of the discounts depends on how close the jerks are to each other. Consider for instance the following terms:—

2 per cent discount on purchases between £5 and £12
3 per cent discount on purchases over £12

If all sellers are offering these terms, a person who habitually buys £11 of the commodity gets the same discount whether he buys exclusively from one seller or buys £5 from one, and £6 from another. The discount is most effective when the upper limit of a range is less than twice the lower limit, thus:—

2 per cent discount on purchases between £5 and £9
3 per cent discount on purchases between £9 and £17

If the price falls steadily this question does not arise. Another difference is that if the average price falls steadily there is a difference between the average price and the marginal price which will have promotional effects, similar to those of the two-part tariff.

Finally, the effectiveness of a quantity discount in promoting exclusive patronage depends on the range of commodities covered by the discount. If the buyer earns his discount for each commodity separately, his incentive to complete loyalty is not as great as if the discount applied to aggregate purchases of all commodities from the same firm. A quantity discount can thus be used as a substitute for full-line forcing.

The reasons for granting the ordinary quantity discount are not difficult to understand. Some are based on economies in cost, arising whether in production, in selling, or in transport, to minimisation of risk, or to differences in elasticity of demand.

This does not mean that every quantity discount can be justified on economic grounds; some are due just to custom or other arbitrary factors, a point which is well illustrated by a writer whose analysis of the discounts offered in certain trades reveals unaccountably wide variations of practice.[1]

Railway policy provides interesting examples of quantity discounts which cannot always be explained. Take the season ticket. There is an economy in issuing one ticket instead of several. The season ticket holder's extra journeys are mainly in slack periods when trains are half-empty. The traveller bears the risk that he may not be able to travel, wherefore the discount on a yearly season is greater than the discount on a monthly season. Loyalty to the railway is secured at the expense of competing motor traffic. The season ticket class as a whole is perhaps more sensitive to charges than the ordinary ticket holders, whose demand is more inelastic. The rate also tapers in the sense that the charge per mile diminishes with distance. This is because the long distance season is used less frequently than the short distance; because the elasticity of demand of the long distance ticket holder is higher, though against this must be set the fact that motor competition is more effective on the shorter journeys; and because differential costs of operating the train are somewhat lower per mile. These are understandable reasons. Yet the evidence given by the railway companies on this subject suggests much arbitrariness in fixing the exact fare.[2] And the principle of the tapering rate, though applied to seasons, is not applied to other passenger fares. The discount on monthly returns is also somewhat arbitrary. In 1926 Sir Ralph Wedgwood informed the Railway Rates Tribunal that the companies had come to the definite conclusion, based on pre-war experience, that the discount was uneconomic, and that having suspended it during the war, the railways had no intention of restoring it,[3] but in 1933 the reduction was reintroduced, at first only in the summer months, to stimulate

[1] "The Relation between the Quantity Purchased and the Price per Unit," by Edward L. Thorndike, *Harvard Business Review*, Vol. XVII, pp. 209 *et seq.*

[2] See *Proceedings of the Railway Rates Tribunal*, April, 1926, Questions 18,088–93, 18,107–9, 18,112, 22,052, 22,061, 22,066, 22,069–70, 22,090–101. Sir Ralph Wedgwood gave evidence as Chairman of the rates and charges committee appointed jointly by the railway companies to prepare evidence for the Tribunal, which was approving the "standard charges" to come into operation on the "appointed day" under the Railways Act, 1921.

[3] *Ibid.*, Questions 17,182–9, 17,194.

holiday traffic, but later as a permanent measure. Since 1926 motor competition has become more intense, and the discount helps to secure loyalty on the return journey. Yet, in view of the language used in 1926, a discount of $33\frac{1}{3}$ per cent takes some explaining.

In analysing the economic basis of quantity discounts there is one pitfall to be avoided. The economies which justify a discount are economies in differential and not in average costs. Average prime costs may be falling for output as a whole, but this is no justification for discriminating between large and small purchases. The acceptance of a large order may enable a firm to reach a scale at which, for instance, it can buy its raw materials very cheaply, but this is no case for discrimination. If total costs are the same whether a firm handles one large order or many small ones of the same aggregate amount, there is no reason to offer quantity discounts. The fact that you can get a quantity discount on your purchases is no reason for giving a quantity discount on your sales; it is only an argument for quoting to both large and small buyers a price low enough to extend your output to the point where marginal revenue will equal marginal cost. The popular view that a large purchase deserves a special price because it "reduces overheads" has no economic foundation.

At the same time, even where there are real economies in quantity selling, a firm may nevertheless refuse to offer quantity discounts. One reason may be to avoid arguments over repeat orders; where the economy is one which justifies a non-cumulative but not a cumulative discount, repeat orders sometimes cause trouble, as the customer may expect to get as good a price for a small repeat order as he did for the original large order. Another reason may be to avoid restricting one's outlets. The offer of quantity discounts enables large middlemen customers to drive their smaller rivals out of the market, so that the supplier may find himself at the mercy of one, or a few, large customers. Or the reason may be that some customers exert pressure to prevent discounts from being allowed to rival customers who would otherwise qualify for them, as when wholesalers insist on the "classification" of customers, to prevent large retailers from receiving the same "trade" discounts as wholesalers buying similar quantities. This may also work the other way, large retailers insisting on receiving quantity discounts to the disadvantage of small retailers, where there are actually no substantial economies in quantity selling. Or the firm itself may prefer to give such discounts even in the absence of economies, because it wishes to eliminate small customers (middlemen or manufacturers), either so that its large customers may make monopoly gains in which it can share, or because it believes that restricting the number of retailers handling its product to a few "high class" firms will give its product a reputation for exclusiveness on which a monopoly price policy can be based. In the fixing of trade discounts, political strategy is often the major consideration.

Finally, a note on coupon trading. There is no need to repeat the analysis of the reasons why manufacturers use this form of sales promotion, the types of product suitable for coupon trading, its cost, or the organisational factors already discussed in an extensive literature.[1] Suffice it to note that coupons are very efficient promoters of loyal patronage because the seller must continue with the same brand until he has collected a minimum number of coupons, or the number he requires for redemption in "free gifts." The same applies to trading stamps, which do for the retailer what the coupon does for the manufacturer, and, to a lesser extent, to cigarette cards.[2] [3]

III

LOYALTY CONDITIONS

Cases in which exclusive patronage is specifically demanded as a condition for special treatment are not by any means as common

[1] The fullest report on the position in Great Britain is the *Report of the Committee on Gift Coupons and Trading Stamps*, Cmd. 4385, 1933; two pamphlets, *The Case for Gift Coupon Advertising*, published by the Advertising Manufacturers and Distributors Association, 1933, and *The Case against Coupon Trading*, Anon., 1933, are also useful, especially the former for its statistics not obtainable elsewhere. Useful American articles are I. M. Rubinow, "Premiums in Retail Trade," *Journal of Political Economy*, 1905, and A. R. Sommer, "Premium Advertising," *Harvard Business Review*, Vol. X.

[2] The history of cigarette cards and organisation of the card market are described in I. O. Evans, *Cigarette Cards.*

[3] The dividend paid by co-operative societies resembles the trading stamp, and is often called a loyalty dividend. It does not fall within our scope, however, because there being no minimum set to purchases, as with trading stamps and coupons, the customer does not pay a higher net price to the shop the less loyal he is. Some societies, but not all, do not pay dividends on non-member purchases. The authoritative study of the subject is J. A. Hough, *Dividend on Co-operative Purchases.*

as the quantity discount device. They are mostly cases where a group of firms is trying to crush competitors who have stayed outside the ring; but there are also cases where individual monopolists have felt strong enough to use the device.

A well known case is the "tied" public-house. The licensing system of Great Britain limits the sale of liquor to licensed premises, and is designed to restrict their number. Consequently the brewer is induced to buy up premises. A House of Commons Committee in 1817 reported that already half the houses in the Metropolis were controlled by brewers.[1] By 1899, according to the Royal Commission on Liquor Licensing Laws, 75 per cent of the houses in the country were so controlled,[2] and by 1931 the figure had risen to 95 per cent.[3] Some of these brewer-owned houses are operated by salaried managers, but the majority are leased to tenants, the tenant being the licensee recognised by the law. And in every case the brewer imposes on his tenant a condition that he shall purchase beer exclusively from the lessor. In many cases he goes even further, compelling the tenant to take not only beer but also his wines, spirits and even matches and sawdust through the brewer, who supplies them usually at a price above the market rate. On the other hand, the rent charged for the house is usually below the market rate, so that it is not easy to compare the position of licensees who own their own houses with that of tied tenants. Whether the brewer can exploit the tenant depends on whether that class of person is restricted in his choice of occupation; that he can use the tie to exploit the public is due to the licensing system preventing the building of competing houses.

Another famous case is that of the United Shoe Machinery Company. This company was formed in the United States in 1899 to buy up existing companies, and by 1910 controlled 90 per cent of the shoe machinery industry in that country. Most of its machinery is not sold, but let out on lease to manufacturers, and in 1901 it introduced a new lease with tying clauses; any manufacturer using any of its most important machines had to pledge himself in effect not to use any machinery made by any other firm, and as the company held patents for some of the best and

[1] *Royal Commission on Liquor Licensing Laws*, 1898, Vol IX, p. 116 (Reprint of Committee's Report). [2] Final Report, p. 96.

[3] *Royal Commission on Licensing* (*England and Wales*), 1929–31, Report, para. 295.

most advanced machinery in the industry, it was thus able to compel manufacturers to resort to it exclusively as well for other machines not covered by patents. The company duly extended its activities to the United Kingdom, where, with the help of these leases, it now controls 90 per cent of the trade.[1] Since the Patent Act was revised in 1907, manufacturers must now have the option of free leases, but the rental on these terms is so much higher than the rental on tied terms, that the option is not of much practical value.

A third case is the use of the copyright privilege by American film renters (the wholesalers of the industry) to tie up the outlets. Until the passage of the Cinematograph Films Act in 1927, "block booking" was a common practice; a renter controlling a good film with a popular star would refuse to let an exhibitor have it unless he contracted also for others which he would not otherwise have taken. The large companies controlling chains of theatres could not be exploited in this way, but the one-cinema exhibitor is weak, and renters have kept him so by refusing to recognise exhibitor co-operatives.[2] So firm a hold did the American producers get through this device that Parliament was persuaded in 1927 to prohibit "blind booking" (i.e. the booking of films before they are trade shown), and to restrict advance booking to a period not exceeding six months, thus limiting severely the number of films which can be forced on an exhibitor at any given time. This Act (tightened up in 1937) has reduced the extent of the practice, but it still persists.

Apart from these three cases, all the other important instances of exclusive dealing arrangements are due to pressure by combinations of firms. The pattern is that of the labour market, where many trade unions have long insisted on the closed shop. Trade combinations seem to have started to follow this model after about the 1870's. The best known examples where exclusive terms are, or have once been offered, are the unsuccessful attempts of the

[1] Accounts of the company's activities in the United Kingdom are given in the *Report of the Departmental Committee on the position of the Engineering Trades after the War*, 1917, and the *Report of the Committee on Trusts*, 1919. The company's methods are attacked in *The Growth of a Monopoly*, a pamphlet published in 1918 by the British Boot Machinery Manufacturers' Association, and defended in Richard Roe, "The United Shoe Machinery Company," *Journal of Political Economy*, 1913–14.

[2] On this whole question see *Cinematograph Films Act*, 1927, *Report of a Committee appointed by the Board of Trade*, Cmd. 5320 of 1936.

Birmingham Alliances,[1] the Scotch Boiler Plate Association,[2] the White Lead Convention,[3] and the cotton spinners[4]; and the more successful attempts of the Bradford Dyers Association,[5] the shipping conferences,[6] the National Light Castings Association,[7] the Tin Plate Conference,[8] various other groups in the iron and steel industry,[9] the Greystone Mortar Association,[10] the Midland Pipe Association,[11] the Electric Cable Makers' Association,[12] the Electric Lamp Makers' Association,[13] the Wallpaper Manufacturers,[14] and the railway companies.[15] Space forbids an analysis of each of these cases; we select only those which best illustrate the common problems.

Every trade combination, unless protected by special legislation, is subject to internal and external stresses which threaten to wreck it. The external stress is the competition of firms outside the ring; the internal stress the quarrels of members over quotas and prices. The ring is most secure from outside competition if its members own nearly all the sources of some mineral, or if the optimum technical unit is so large that only firms with large financial resources can hope to establish themselves in the industry; or if the group is protected by some legal privilege such as trade marks, patents or tariffs. If by reason of its special privilege the group can count on each of the buyers in the market having to come to it at some time or other, it can impose such heavy penalties for disloyalty that they all pledge themselves to it. But if outside the group are firms able to supply all the requirements of the market, customers are not at the mercy of the group, and there is little reason to think that the mere adoption of exclusive terms will enable a group to establish and retain a monopolistic position.

Thus in the Lancashire cotton industry attempts have been

[1] H. W. Macrosty, *The Trust Movement in British Industry*, p. 79.

[2] *Ibid.*, p. 67.

[3] P. Fitzgerald, *Industrial Combination in England*, p. 118.

[4] *Infra.*

[5] Macrosty, p. 155; Fitzgerald, p. 20.

[6] A full account of their origins, failures and successes is in the report and evidence of the *Royal Commission on Shipping Rings*, 1906–9; there is an inferior discussion in the *Report of the Imperial Shipping Committee on the Deferred Rebate System*, 1923.

[7] Fitzgerald, p. 48.

[8] *Ibid.*, p. 44.

[9] D. L. Burn, *History of Steel Making*, p. 342, and *infra.*

[10] Fitzgerald, p. 110.

[11] *Ibid.*, p. 112.

[12] *Ibid.*, p. 122.

[13] *Ibid.*, p. 124.

[14] *Ibid.*, p. 155.

[15] See L. A. Carey, *Modern Railway Practice*, Ch. X, G. Walker, *Road and Rail*, Ch. II, and *infra.*

F

made for some years to fix and maintain prices above the competitive level, groups of firms in each section signing agreements not to sell below a given minimum price. One such agreement, signed in 1937, covered nearly 90 per cent of the firms in the Egyptian mule spinning section, and as the position was being undermined by the outside firms, the signatories tried in November 1938 to strengthen their position by offering a discount of 5 per cent to all customers who undertook to patronise the group exclusively. The manœuvre failed; price net of rebate continued to exceed that of the outsiders, who accordingly lost no customers. The offer was therefore withdrawn in April 1939.

The fate of rebates in the iron and steel industry was similar, though this was their home. They flourished in one or two specialised sections, but not in the major ones. The failure of pre-1914 rebates in steel manufacture has already been described by Burn.[1] In 1926 new associations were started in the steel section which included practically all the British steel manufacturers. The competition they had to face was that of the continental producers. In 1927 this was intensified, and in reply to it a rebate varying from 5s. per ton on steel ship plates to between 5s. and 12s. 6d. per ton (a quantity discount) on joists and angles was granted to all buyers who signed an agreement to use only British steel. By the end of 1927 80 per cent of British steel users had signed. To coerce the remaining 20 per cent prices were advanced 5s. per ton in February 1928, and the loyalty rebates simultaneously increased by 5s.; so that loyal buyers paid the same net prices as before, but others were at a disadvantage of from 10s. to 17s. 6d. on all steel bought at home. "So long as foreign supplies were cheap and plentiful," Messrs. Wm. Jacks & Co. comment,[2] "that did not matter." Buyers who depended mainly on British steel pledged loyalty; the others continued to get the bulk of their supplies from abroad. In 1928 and 1929 continental prices rose, and were above British steel prices, which were kept stable; this drove some buyers to sign the pledge. Then in 1930 and 1931 came the real test. British prices were maintained, but continental prices fell below them. To strengthen its hold, the association increased the rebates in January 1931; there was, nevertheless, much fear that the schemes would break down, and

[1] Loc. cit., p. 342.

[2] *Annual Review of the Iron and Steel Trades in 1928*, p. 18. This account is summarised from the pages of the firm's Annual Reviews, 1927–32.

a clamour for a tariff began which was satisfied in 1932. Without this tariff it is doubtful how much longer the rebates would have been effective. The subsequent history of rebates in the industry is interesting, because they have now been put to a new purpose. The Iron and Steel Federation was formed in 1934, and in 1937 had 27 constituent associations. Its hold over these associations being weak, it decided to use loyalty rebates to strengthen it. Each association is encouraged to give a rebate to such customers as pledge themselves (*a*) to purchase exclusively from firms within the Federation and (*b*) to belong to one of the constituent associations of the Federation. The idea is that if any firm breaks away from its own association, all other associations will come to the rescue by withholding from the offender all rebates on all his raw materials. The signal to do this, however, must come from the Federation, which is thus able to withhold support from associations whose policy it disapproves.[1]

In shipping, the amount of capital required to start a new liner service facilitates monopoly. But even here, and despite the particularly onerous terms of the rebate, the conferences have not had it all their own way. In the days before 1914, when the industry was prosperous, many new companies broke into the conferences. The rebate system is most effective in warding off sporadic competition by tramps, but is unable to prevent all competition. Where the commodity is one for which the tramp is most suitable, or one which can be accumulated and sent by tramp, e.g. coal, rice, sugar, the deferred rebate system cannot be applied to it, and the shipper is free to patronise the tramp without forfeiting rebates on other commodities; he is also always free to charter a whole ship without forfeiting rebates though he is penalised if he sends less than a full cargo by tramp. The rebate system strengthens the hands of the conferences, but does not confer unlimited power on them.

A new case of loyalty provisions is the "agreed charge" which railways are allowed to make under the Road and Rail Traffic Act of 1933. The feature of this charge is generally that if the consignor agrees to send all his traffic by rail he gets a special quotation. It is designed to meet motor competition, and the limits to its success depend on the strength of motor competition. Only a small number of consignors have entered into agreements;

[1] See *Import Duties Advisory Committee, Report on the Iron and Steel Industry*, 1937.

and in a number of cases part of their traffic is pledged, but not all, and allowance also made for the consignor to do his own delivery within a specified local range. Another special feature of these agreements is that the freight is calculated per parcel (ton, etc.) without reference to distance carried. The major incentive to this break with all railway traditions is said to be that it reduces clerical work, since the number of parcels has to be counted, but no account need be taken of classification or distance. This system has its dangers. The price quoted per parcel is less than the usual price for long-distance work and greater than the price of short distance. The consignor has, therefore, an incentive to do the short distance work himself, or get other contractors to do it, but this is frustrated by requiring him to send all his traffic by railway, or at least imposing restrictions on the amount not so sent. He is now also able to compete more effectively in distant markets, so there is a progressive tendency for the average length of haul to increase, and the charge has regularly to be revised. From the social point of view the flat rate is undoubtedly uneconomic, because it causes cross-hauling. Having promoted the charge in 1933, the Ministry of Transport has had to cope since the outbreak of war with some of its anti-social results.

IV

IN THE BUYERS' MARKET

We have written so far as if in all exclusive dealing arrangements it is the seller who is seeking to tie the buyer. This is by no means the case. The buyer in many markets has just as great an incentive to tie the seller. The quantity discount is paralleled in agriculture, where higher prices are usually paid for large quantities than for small parcels of produce. Exclusive arrangements are found in the sale of the goodwill of businesses, the training of apprentices, and the grant of exclusive agencies by manufacturers to distributors—to take only a few of the well-known examples. Buyers' combinations are exemplified in the Report of the Board of Trade Committee on Restraint of Trade, 1931, which described the pressure retail trade associations bring to bear on manufacturers to stop supplies to retailers who are cutting prices or infringing distance or other restrictions. The habits of such associations in the grocery trades, tobacco, stationery, newsagencies, motor agencies, cycle trades, and the photography trade[1] need no further description. We shall illustrate their problems from the history of a new association which has emerged since that committee reported.

The retail prices of proprietary drugs are fixed, and any chemist who undercuts them is penalised by having his supplies stopped through the machinery of the Proprietary Articles Trade Association. This association, which is adequately described elsewhere,[2] protects the chemist against price competition, but not against an increase in numbers, one of the consequences of price maintenance itself. He would like to see the number of chemist shops reduced, whether by imposing a distance limit, as in the newsagent's trade, or by tightening up qualifications. So far nothing has been done to limit the number of chemist shops, but steps have been taken to prevent competition with chemists by other retailers. The object of the "Chemists' Friends Association" is to persuade manufacturers to sell medicinal products exclusively through qualified chemists, and to stop selling through grocers, barbers, cafés and other outlets. Manufacturers who undertake to do this are enrolled in the association, on the council of which they are represented. And to ensure control over all outlets, wholesalers are included in the scheme. Where a manufacturer believes that his retailers should have special qualifications, as in the photographic trade, there is little difficulty in persuading him to join such an association. The "Chemists' Friends" has met its full quota of opposition. To coerce manufacturers, retail chemists refuse window display or other sales promotion to the products of manufacturers who refuse to join. Manufacturers of extensively advertised products are able to withstand this pressure, but the losses in the ensuing struggle are frequently severe. At the end of 1939 over 100 manufacturers had already capitulated, and the fall of other big concerns was confidently predicted.

V

WELFARE ASPECTS

Should these exclusive arrangements be tolerated? Is it anti-social to reward the loyal customer with a special price? The

[1] The Joint Council in this trade has been discontinued since the Committee reported, but its functions continue to be performed by the manufacturers' association.

[2] In the Report, and in E. T. Grether, *Resale Price Maintenance in Great Britain.*

official commissions reporting *ad hoc* on specific cases have adopted no consistent view; in shipping, the iron and steel industry and retail trade exclusive arrangements have been blessed; in the liquor trade, the film industry, and engineering they have been condemned.

The first difficulty in answering these questions is the fact that such arrangements are not always harmful. In so far as loyal patronage secures economies, it should be encouraged, and the loyal patron rewarded. The economies are frequently exaggerated. Those who believe that after the war the housewife should have to continue to register with particular shops point out that if each butcher in the street knows every week to expect fifty customers, stocks carried and waste are smaller than if one week one butcher gets a hundred customers and the other none, and the distribution of customers from week to week is completely unforeseeable. This is true, but not very realistic. And yet in so far as loyal patronage facilitates planning, the loyal should be encouraged. There is no case for compulsory loyalty, but there is a case for a loyalty rebate where the economies are real. In such circumstances the consumer should retain his freedom to choose between loyalty and the right to change his seller for whatever reason seems good to him. If he exercises this right he must pay the full cost, in forfeiting the rebate given to loyal customers. To compel loyalty violates consumers' freedom; provided they are prepared to pay the cost of it, this seems to be a freedom which might well be retained, as anyone who has experienced the discourtesies of shopkeepers will appreciate. Let him who wishes to be loyal get a rebate.

The real point is that such rebates only become harmful in the hands of monopolists in a position to exploit them. Even in the hands of monopolists, we can only condemn the rebate if we condemn the monopoly. The commissioners who supported exclusive arrangements in shipping, iron and steel, and retail trade, did so because they believed that in those trades monopoly is more desirable than competition. Whether they were right or not, the principle is accepted that there are a few industries in which monopoly may lead to economies not realised in competition; there exclusive arrangements are clearly desirable.

It follows that exclusive dealing ought to be prohibited, but only in the hands of monopolists, and that provision should be made for excluding desirable monopolists. In England there has been no specific legislation against it,[1] except for an ineffective provision in the Patent Act, and the courts have rather surprisingly decided that it does not violate the common law prohibition of restraint of trade.[2] In the United States, however, section 3 of the Clayton Act declares that:

> It shall be unlawful for any person . . . to lease or make a sale or contract for sale of goods . . . or fix a price charged therefor, or discount from, or rebate upon, such price, on the condition . . . that the lessee or purchaser thereof shall not use or deal in the goods . . . of a competitor or competitors of the lessor or seller, *where the effect of any such lease, sale or contract . . . may be to substantially lessen competition or tend to create a monopoly in any line of commerce.*

The greatest difficulty in enforcing this section has been the words in italics, as it has been left to the courts to determine the line between monopoly and competition. Courts are not competent to do this; the line must be drawn in the Act itself. A monopolist might be defined for legislative purposes as any person who has a patent, copyright, trade mark, brand, licence or other privilege protected by the law; any person whose purchases or sales amount to one-third of the total sales of the commodity in the United Kingdom; or any person acting in combination with other buyers or sellers. Any monopolist who considered it to be in the public interest that competition be suppressed in his industry should have the right to apply to the appropriate minister (say the President of the Board of Trade) for exemption from the provisions of the law, and the Minister, if satisfied that a *prima facie* case existed, should refer it to a commission for public enquiry, and act according to its report; on condition that he must lay down terms regulating the prices, profits and other circumstances of each monopolist to whom he grants exemption.[3]

[1] As a wartime measure the Prices of Goods Act forbids refusal to sell one commodity except on condition that the buyer takes simultaneously some other commodity. This is really an attack on one of the methods of evading price control.

[2] *United Shoe Machinery Co. v. Brunet* (1909), A.C. 330.

[3] Some supervision already exists, but it is inadequate. The Comptroller of Patents has some power to redress abuses; so has the Railway Rates Tribunal; the Import Duties Advisory Committee can bring some pressure to bear on the iron and steel industry; and the Imperial Shipping Committee and the Cinematograph Films Council can give publicity to abuses in their respective industries. More adequate controls need to be established, with fuller powers, but this is not the place to discuss the subject.

In this way desirable monopolies would be supervised, and the undesirable prevented from using loyalty rebates to extend their power. The Clayton Act prohibited only sellers' exclusions; prohibition of buyers' exclusions is also desirable to put an end to trade boycotts.

The other difficulty in enforcing this type of legislation is the fact that there are effective substitutes for loyalty rebates. One is the use of quantity discounts. In America the Robinson-Patman Act has dealt with this, by placing on the person granting such discounts the onus of proving that there really are corresponding economies. Another substitute is to put different commodities together and call them one commodity, thus compelling people who want *x* to buy *y* also. In *Federal Trade Commission v. Gratz et al.*,[1] the Supreme Court allowed this evasion; it would have to be forestalled by specific provision in the Act. Yet another substitute is to use a contract of agency instead of a contract of sale[2]; this means that exclusive agencies must be prohibited no less than exclusive sales and leases. The fourth substitute is not so easily dealt with. It is vertical integration. If a manufacturer is prevented from tying his retailers, he will be tempted to set up his own retail shops; vertical integration has been marked in the cinema industry since the restrictions on block booking, though, of course, other and more important factors were also at work in the same direction. To prohibit loyalty rebates without prohibiting vertical integration is to leave a gap.

The fact is that loyalty rebates are only one weapon in the hands of a would-be monopolist. A law prohibiting them is a useful part of an anti-monopoly programme, but it is only a part. There must be simultaneous revision of the patent law, provision of credit facilities for small firms, prohibition of price and quota agreements and associations, and supervision of industries where monopoly is considered desirable, whether through tribunals like the Railway Rates Tribunal, or through operation by public corporations. We cannot end or control monopoly simply by prohibiting loyalty rebates; but if we wish to end monopoly, such legislation should be an integral part of the programme. Here in Britain we continue to laud the virtues of competitive private enterprise almost without realising the extent to which our

[1] 253 U.S. 421 (1920).

[2] *Federal Trade Commission v. Curtis Publishing Company*, 260 U.S. 568, 574 (1923).

economy has ceased to be competitive. This remains almost the only important country without legislation to keep the market free, or at least a general law to control the activities of trusts. If private groups are not to submerge the public interest, Parliament must take bold anti-trust action after the war, and now is the time to prepare its programme.

[3]

CHAPTER VI

MONOPOLY AND THE LAW

AN ECONOMIST'S REFLECTIONS ON THE *CROFTER* CASE[1]

I

THE EVOLUTION OF THE LAW

How far apart economists and judges have travelled in their attitudes to monopoly: that is one's most striking impression on reading the judgments in this case.[2] There was not always this difference of view. The early judges abhorred monopoly no less than does the economist; where the modern judge smiles beatifically they grew apoplectic. The early history of the common law shows no favour to trade combinations. In the earliest of these cases, *R.* v. *Journeymen Tailors of Cambridge*,[3] the defendants were convicted for criminal conspiracy, the court stressing that this was an offence at common law. This view of trade combinations continued to be expressed for at least a century and a half. Lord Mansfield stated it quite plainly in *R.* v. *Eccles*:[4]

> "Persons in possession of any articles of trade may sell them at such prices as they individually may please, but if they confederate and agree not to sell them under certain prices, it is conspiracy."

So also in *R.* v. *Mawbey*,[5] *R.* v. *Hammond*,[6] *R.* v. *Bykerdike*,[7] *R.* v. *Rowlands*,[8] *Hilton* v. *Eckersley*,[9] and *R.* v. *Druitt*,[10] though the decision did not always turn on the point, judges went out of their

[1] This chapter was originally written for *The Modern Law Review* and published in that journal in April 1943. The preceding issue had contained the reflections of a lawyer on the same case, including a comparison of the facts and legal arguments in this and other cases.

[2] *Crofter Hand Woven Harris Tweed Co., Ltd.* v. *Veitch and Another* (1942), 1 All E.R. 142.

[3] (1721), 8 Mod. 10.

[4] (1783), I Leach 274.

[5] (1796), 6 T.R. 619.

[6] (1799), 2 Esp. 719.

[7] (1832), I Moo. & R. 179.

[8] (1851), 17 Q.B. 671.

[9] (1855), 6 E. & B. 47; dicta of Crompton, J.

[10] (1867), 10 Cox 592

way to make it plain that trade combinations were a criminal conspiracy at common law. We know that at least some would-be conspirators were accordingly deterred; for when in 1852 the booksellers were contemplating a price-fixing association, and asked Lord Campbell's opinion, they disbanded themselves on his advising that such an association would render them liable to prosecution for criminal conspiracy.[1]

This position has now been abandoned. As early as 1815 pressure from trade conspirators for recognition of their agreements began to have its weight with some of the judges. In the criminal division they had little hesitation in pronouncing against conspiracies, because they wanted to leave no loophole for trade unions; in the civil division cases affected mainly business men's agreements, and the civil courts had begun to accept conspiracies between business men while the criminal courts were still rejecting conspiracies between their workers. As the legislature gradually extended its protection to trade unions, the urgency of declaring against trade conspiracies seemed to diminish.[2] By the last decade of the nineteenth century the capitulation was complete. The *Mogul* case[3] is the decisive watershed. Since that case, English judges have decided that business men[4] are to be free to enter into whatever combinations are necessary for the protection and advancement of their private trade interests. The public interest, on which the prohibition of conspiracy had rested, has been dethroned from its original place as the deciding factor. Lord Esher's last stand in the *Mogul* case, affirming the combination to be unlawful as against public policy, was not supported by his colleagues in the Appeal Court or by his superiors in the Lords. In the criminal courts no common law prosecution for trade conspiracy could now succeed. In actions in tort, Lord Cave's two propositions:

> "(1) A combination of two or more persons wilfully to injure a man in his trade is unlawful and, if it results in damage to him,

[1] M. Plant, *The English Book Trade*, p. 439.

[2] Up to 1875 the decisions accepting conspiracies were *Hearn* v. *Griffin* (1815), 2 Chitty 407; *Wickens* v. *Evans* (1830), 3 Y. & J. 318; *R.* v. *Selsby* (1847), 5 Cox 495; *Shrewsbury and Birmingham Railway Company* v. *London & North Western Railway Company* (1851), 21 L.J.Q.B. 89; and *Hare* v. *London & North Western Railway Company* (1861), 2 J. & H. 80.

[3] (1892) A.C. 25.

[4] They had still not finally decided how much protection to give to workmen's combinations (*Quinn* v. *Leathem* (1901), A.C. 495), or to co-operatives (*McEllistrim* v. *Ballymacelligott Co-operative and Dairy Society*, (1919) A.C. 548).

> is actionable. (2) If the real purpose of the combination is, not to injure another, but to forward or defend the trade of those who enter into it, then no wrong is committed and no action will lie, although damage to another ensues"[1]

will exculpate a combination for almost anything it is likely to do. And in the law of contract, practically all their agreements will receive the enforcement of the courts. Public policy is still occasionally mentioned, but how little consideration it receives can be judged from the observation of the Judicial Committee of the Privy Council in *Attorney-General of Australia* v. *Adelaide Steamship Company*[2] that—

> "Their Lordships are not aware of any case in which a restraint, though unreasonable in the interests of the parties, has been held unenforceable because it involved some injury to the public."

The *Crofter* case reveals how far we have now been led. We knew before that a combine could charge whatever prices it saw fit and hold the public to ransom without interference from the courts. We knew that the court would help it discipline its members by compelling them to obey its rules, however anti-social those rules might seem. We knew that it was free to ruin any outside trader who did not accept its dictates. Now we discover new freedoms. Business men seeking to advance their private trade interests may not only combine with each other, but also bring their workers into the scheme, and promise them part of the swag; even this was hardly in doubt after the decision in *Reynolds* v. *Shipping Federation, Ltd.*[3] Now we know that they may use not only their own workers, but workers in any other industry who happen to belong to the same union. The trader or manufacturer who wishes to keep outside the conspiracy may find himself boycotted by every worker in his district. The householder who prefers Danish bacon to British may find that, at the behest of British farmers, the agricultural workers have persuaded the transport workers not to take him to his office, the laundry workers not to wash his clothes, the shop assistants not to sell to him, and so on, provided that they all belong to the same general union.

[1] *Sorrel* v. *Smith*, (1925) A.C., at p. 712.

[2] (1913) A.C. 781.

[3] (1924) 1 Ch. 28.

II

THE CASE AGAINST COMPETITION

Why did the judges go back on their original opinion? It is easy, if disrespectful, to picture them as pawns of the capitalist class, serving their masters' wishes even at the cost of the public good; easy, but not adequate. Doubtless some judges, consciously or unconsciously, have acted in the light of their inner conviction that the business man is the pillar of society and that law must serve and protect his ends. But the language to which they give expression is far more subtle than this. Most of the judgments which most strongly support combination are also those which in the strongest language insist on the freedom of the individual to trade on whatsoever terms he please. What has happened is a confusion of the different meanings of a single phrase. The free trade economists were clear enough what they meant by freedom of trade; to them it meant the absence of restraints on prices, emanating whether from Government or from private agreement, whether directly by price-fixing, or indirectly by curtailment of supplies. To them freedom meant freedom to enter the market and sell; not freedom to prevent others from so doing; or even freedom to barter away one's right of entry (of which the freedom to sell oneself into slavery is only the most extreme form). The judges confused these freedoms; have chosen to support the second and third, and therefore have become powerful agents in restraining the first. Some may have done this with a deliberate desire to advance the interests of their friends and heroes in the world of big business; most seem merely to have been confused; finding themselves called to deliver judgments on subjects they were never equipped to understand, they threw in their lot with what appeared to them to be the most modern developments. We must remember the atmosphere in which these cases are tried; though the decision is supposed to rest on what is or is not in the public interest, the courts admit no evidence on public policy.

> "The question whether a restraint of trade is reasonable either in the interest of the parties or interest of the public is a question for the court, to be determined after construing the contract and the circumstances existing when it was made. It is really a question of public policy and not a question of fact

upon which evidence of the actual or probable consequences, if the contract be carried into effect, is admissible."[1]

As Lord Bramwell commented—

"No evidence is given in these public policy cases. The tribunal is to say, as a matter of law, that the thing is against public policy and void. How can the judge do that without any evidence as to its effect and consequences?"[2]

He is left to work things out for himself from first principles, never having been trained to analyse such economic problems, and it is not surprising that he has gone astray.

Nevertheless, the line of reasoning which began as a defence of freedom has not been content to stay there. By degrees judges came out more and more openly as opponents of competition and supporters of monopoly as a way of life for Britain. There is a long line of *dicta* from the days of Ellenborough, C.J., who upheld a price-fixing agreement on the ground that—

"This is merely a convenient mode of arranging two concerns which might otherwise ruin each other,"[3]

to modern times, when Lord Haldane calmly assures us—

"Unquestionably the combination in question was one the purpose of which was to regulate supply and keep up prices. But an ill-regulated supply and unremunerative price may, in point of fact, be disadvantageous to the public. Such a state of things may, if it is not controlled, drive manufacturers out of business, or lower wages, and so cause unemployment and labour disturbance."[4]

And Scrutton, L.J., says—

"In view of the fluctuating character of the yearly supply of hops I see nothing unreasonable in hop-growers combining to secure a steady and profitable price, by eliminating competition amongst themselves, and putting the marketing in the hands of one agent, with full power to fix prices and hold up supplies, the benefit and loss being divided amongst the members."[5]

[1] Lord Parker in the *Adelaide* case (*supra*), at p. 797.
[2] In the *Mogul* case (*supra*), at p. 45.
[3] *Hearn* v. *Griffin* (1815) (*supra*), at p. 407.
[4] *North Western Salt Co.* v. *Electrolytic Alkali Co., Ltd.*, (1914) A.C. 467.
[5] *English Hopgrowers, Ltd.* v. *Dering*, (1928) 2 K.B. 174.

L

These judges do not merely say that they have no legal power to suppress monopoly; they go rather out of their way to make it clear that they consider monopoly to be in the public interest.

Judges are not unique in holding this view. The fervent belief in the virtues of competition which characterised the Britain of pre-1914 has died. The man in the street, no less than his rulers, has come to believe that competition is outmoded and anti-social, and that its speedy replacement serves the common weal. We have to decide whether this belief is justified or not. If it is acceptable, the judges are to be congratulated for being among the first to recognise a great truth. If it is rejected, a whole programme of legislative reform is needed to cope with the mischief they have done.

It is easy to show how fallacious are some of the arguments used in support of monopoly. Simplest of all is the fallacy that because monopoly benefits some, therefore it benefits all. Even learned judges have succumbed to this; it is implicit in the three passages just quoted; here again is Lawrence, L.J., arguing that the public is not injured if it is asked to pay more—

> "Moreover, even in such a case, the mere intention to raise prices would not establish a case of injury to the public; it would still have to be proved that the intention was to raise prices to an unreasonable extent; for no such intention would be inferred, the reason being that *prima facie* it would be highly improbable that the seller in his own interest would want to fix unreasonable prices."[1]

The fact is that any increase in price makes the consuming public poorer, since it now has less money to spend on other things. As Adam Smith wrote in a classic passage, as long ago as 1776—

> "The interest of the dealers, however, in any particular branch of trade or manufactures, is always in some respects different from, and even opposite to, that of the public. To widen the market and to narrow the competition, is always the interest of the dealers. To widen the market may frequently be agreeable enough to the interest of the public; but to narrow the competition must always be against it, and can serve only to enable the dealers, by raising their profits above what they would naturally be, to levy, for their own benefit, an absurd tax upon the rest of their fellow citizens. The proposal of any

[1] *Palmolive Co.* (*of England*) v. *Freedman*, (1928) 1 Ch. 264.

> new law or regulation of commerce which comes from this order, ought always to be listened to with great precaution, and ought never to be adopted till after having been long and carefully examined, not only with the most scrupulous, but with the most suspicious attention. It comes from an order of men, whose interest is never exactly the same with that of the public, who have generally an interest to deceive and even to oppress the public, and who accordingly have, upon many occasions, both deceived and oppressed it."[1]

This is advice that every judge should take to heart.

There are, however, more subtle fallacies. One is that monopoly substitutes order and co-operation for chaos and antagonism. The view that there is no order in a competitive system appeals to those who, because they cannot actually see the wheels turning round, cannot realise that there are nevertheless powerful controls which operate it, to make it serve the consumer. Indeed, the true meaning of "to compete" is "to offer the public a substitute"; to serve the will of the market is the essence of competition. It involves antagonism in the sense that it allows the man in the street freedom to oppose business men to each other; to choose what he shall have and who shall serve it to him. Business men dislike this; it forces them to be efficient, and to be moderate in their prices. They see that by co-operating with each other they can take away from the man in the street his only means of subordinating them to his will —his freedom to choose between them, which compels them to seek his favours. Competition ended, the masses must take what their masters allow them. Competition has given way to co-operation if you like, but it is only co-operation between the few for the enslavement of the many.

Does not monopoly, however, reduce the insecurity of the economic system? Did not excessive competition characterise those two terrible decades from 1920, when the fear of unemployment hung like a cloud over millions of lives, and its reality broke so many thousands? Monopoly does, indeed, bring security for the few who are inside it; Lord Haldane is quite right to say that in its absence prices in some industries would fall; what he forgets is that the money the public saves in this way it can spend on buying the goods of other industries, thus increasing employment there. Competition cannot cause a slump. Neither can monopoly

[1] *The Wealth of Nations* (Cannan's Edition), Vol. I, p. 250.

either prevent slumps or cure them. It transfers income from poor to rich, and therefore, if anything, reduces employment by withdrawing money from those who would spend it and keep the wheels of industry turning, to those who characteristically save most. It is a complete fallacy to believe that competition causes the standard of living to be lowered; exactly the opposite is true.[1] The lean years were associated with competition, but competition was not their cause. Men swallow the fallacy because they associate slumps with low prices, and booms with high prices. Monopoly may keep prices stable, and may keep them high, but in doing so merely makes some richer and others poorer. There is a world of difference between high prices due to monopoly and high prices due to the great demand of men in employment in prosperous times. We cannot stabilise the demand, the employment and the prosperity simply by stabilising the prices.

The real cause of our difficulties in the past quarter of a century has been the absence of full employment; the real remedy lies not in the suppression of competition but in the maintenance of aggregate demand. Given full employment, everyone has opportunities of making a living, and it is not only desirable but imperative that he should justify the rewards he receives by being made to stand up to the competition of rival suppliers. If business men then combine to eliminate competition they can certainly secure higher earnings than they would otherwise, but they do so only at the expense of the public; to assume that if they profit the public also must gain is the most elementary of fallacies.

The case against competition is not, however, composed entirely of fallacies. All social institutions are imperfect, and competition is no exception.

There are two important classes of circumstance in which the effects of competition may be undesirable.

The first of these is where an industry whose equipment and labour force are highly specialised is suffering from long-term excess capacity. Suppose, for example, that the demand for the products of an industry contracts sharply, as in the British cotton, shipbuilding and coal industries after 1920, and that there is no

[1] If the monopoly is in an export trade it may be in a position to raise the standard of living at home by exploiting the foreign consumer; but few export industries are able to do this since in foreign markets they usually have to face the competition of other foreign exporters. A monopoly in an export industry usually exploits rather the domestic consumer.

prospect, as far ahead as one can see, of the industry's plant being fully utilised. It is then desirable that the surplus resources, men and equipment be transferred to other industries. Competition works to bring this about. Prices, wages, profits and other incomes in the industry fall to low levels, and pressure is thereby exerted on resources to transfer themselves elsewhere. The trouble is that if the resources are highly specialised it is very difficult to make the transfer. Then for years the situation drags on. All associated with the industry are impoverished, and they may try by trade combination to keep prices up as much as possible in order that their incomes should not sink too low. A trade combination for these purposes is obviously not so wicked as one designed simply to secure power to dominate the market. Nevertheless it does not contribute to the basic problem, which is to find employment elsewhere for the surplus resources which are acting as a drag on the market. What is really needed is positive action by the Government to promote industrial mobility. The industry needs a sharp surgical operation which, by adjusting supply to demand, can fit it once more to be restored to normal control by competition. This type of situation, while not remedied by the trade combination, does secure it greater sympathy. But it is the exception, and not the rule; in the cases so far brought before the courts it could seldom be argued that there was a severe and intractable problem of excess capacity to mitigate the offence.

The second case in which competition has undesirable effects is where the market is so limited in relation to the economies of large-scale production that there is really room only for one firm, or at most for two or three. Competition in these cases is not necessarily undesirable; it may, on the contrary, be the means by which one firm gains ascendancy in the market and attains the size at which the full benefit of the economies of scale can be obtained; the revolutionary effects of the entry of Henry Ford into the American automobile industry forty years ago is the standing proof that competition in price is frequently the quickest way to secure the economies of large-scale production. The danger in these cases is the possibility of a stalemate; when the firms, sharing the market in more or less equal portions, compete not by driving prices down to the minimum, in a fight to the death, but by differentiating their products and foregoing the benefits of standardisation, and by multiplying their sales staffs and otherwise adding to selling costs. The truth is that competition works well only where the market is so large relatively to possible economies of scale that there is room for a large number of producers. In other cases it tends to promote waste by multiplying the number of firms, the types of product, and the costs of distribution.

But even here the remedy is not the trade combination. What is needed in this sort of situation is that the number of firms should be reduced, unnecessary costs eliminated, and prices reduced. But what the combination does is to preserve the number of firms, by guaranteeing to each its quota, and to raise the price, or at least to keep it at a level adequate to maintain all the existing firms. If the firms were to amalgamate into a single unit, substantial economies could be achieved; redundant plant could be eliminated, and also duplication of selling costs. But this is quite a different proposition from a combination in which the firms retain their separate identities and merely share the market. Everything here rests on making the right distinctions. There is competition and competition; what is needed is competition in price, which almost always brings desirable results in the end, though the way may be painful; whereas competition in advertising, or in number of salesmen, or in product differentiation is frequently not in the public interest. Similarly there is monopoly and monopoly; the monopoly of a single large firm, securing the economies of scale, is frequently desirable, whereas the monopoly which consists of an agreement between separate firms to share out the market between them is most usually contrary to the public interest.

There is no doubt that this confusion in the public mind secures for monopoly an unmerited support. The impressive performance of monopoly is its technical achievement. We think of monopolists as owners of large factories working on a tremendous scale with wonderful machines with which workers can do in a day what others do in months. There is no doubt that there are industries where the economies of large-scale production are great, and where large monopolistic concerns are therefore able to produce more cheaply than small competitive establishments. This is beyond question; and so is its corollary that any law which tried to make the emergence of these concerns impossible would be a handicap to economic progress.

But what has this to do with trade combinations? We fall into error unless we distinguish sharply between the kind of monopoly where one firm by its size dominates the market, and that other kind where a number of firms enter into agreement to restrict output and maintain prices. The former may be associated with economies of large-scale production; the latter is not. In the sort of arrangement which is typified by the facts in the *Mogul* case, the *Adelaide* case, the *Salt* case, the Motor Trade Association cases,[1] or in *Joseph Evans* v. *Heathcote*,[2] there is no increase in productive efficiency. There may be some small economies in selling costs; but in so far as they result from diminishing the buyer's freedom of choice, they are not necessarily desirable; and they are in any case usually swamped by the loss of efficiency on the productive side. For a trade combination usually reduces productive efficiency, and this not merely because the stimulus to efficiency, competition, is removed. The whole *raison d'être* of such a combination is usually to prevent the firms with low costs from bringing prices down to the detriment of those with high costs; it usually allocates quotas, preventing the expansion of the low-cost firms, and enabling the inefficient to continue in production. It is a device which simultaneously robs the public and protects the inefficient. Whatever there may be to say in favour of the large firm, there is nothing to be said in favour of trade combinations. However well-meaning the judges may have been, they opened a door which could result only in the public detriment.

III

AIDS TO MONOPOLY

So much for trade combinations; what of that other form of monopoly where a firm by its size comes to dominate the market?

It is true that the emergence of such giants sometimes results in increased efficiency; but we must not too easily be deceived. In the first place, we must not conclude that the desirable pattern for all industry is necessarily the industrial giant. The fact is that the economies of large-scale production are greater in some industries than in others. Pig iron is most efficiently produced on a large scale; specialised steels are as cheaply produced by the small firm. The assembly of motor cars calls for large factories; the manu-

[1] *Ware & De Freville, Ltd.* v. *Motor Trade Association*, (1921) 3 K.B. 40; *Hardie & Lane, Ltd.* v. *Chilton*, (1928) 2 K.B. 306; and *Thorne* v. *Motor Trade Association*, (1937) A.C. 797, overruling *R.* v. *Denyer*, (1926) 2 K.B. 258.

[2] (1915) 1 K.B. 418.

facture of most of the parts to be assembled is efficiently done on a small scale. To run a regular liner service in shipping demands size; tramp shipping is easily done with very limited funds. The number of cases in which large firms are notably more efficient than small is not in fact great; over most of industry the small firm can produce as cheaply as the large. Technical economies are not so great as is supposed; very many large firms are using the same machines as small ones; only they are using more of them. And even where there are technical economies they may well be offset by the administrative difficulties involved in trying to co-ordinate the activities of a large concern, and to minimise the ever-present risk of bureaucratic inflexibility. In most industries, then, large scale confers no economies; in these monopoly has nothing to offer which competition would not be much more likely to secure.

Secondly, we must not lightly assume that all firms which grow in size are to be welcomed as torch-bearers of efficiency; nothing of the sort. This would only be the case if efficiency were the sole basis of expansion. But the fact is that many inefficient firms are able to grow by taking advantage of defects in our social organisation. A firm which has grown because it produces cheaply is to be welcomed; but a firm which has grown solely because it has bought up all the deposits of some essential mineral used by its industry, or all the outlets which the State will license, as in the case of breweries, or all the essential patents; or a firm which has grown by using financial strength to strangle its competitors—such a firm is not necessarily deserving of praise. Monopoly is too great a source of power for us to accept its emergence save on grounds of the strictest purity. As the late Professor Allyn Young has written—

> "Most of the more weighty discussion of the economic advantages of monopoly have to do with the effect of monopoly upon the aggregate production of wealth measured in terms either of subjective satisfaction or of objective commodity units. Even from this point of view the case for monopoly is exceedingly dubious, and at best, has a validity that is restricted and conditioned in many ways. Moreover, such considerations are relatively unimportant compared with matters like the effect of monopoly upon distribution, upon the scope for individual initiative, upon economic opportunity in general, and upon a host of social and political relations. In short, it is a question

> less of the relative 'economy' of monopoly or competition than of the kind of economic organisation best calculated to give us the kind of society we want. Until our general social ideals are radically changed, it will take more than economic analysis to prove that it would be sound public policy to permit monopoly in that part of the industrial field where competition is possible."[1]

On the purely economic issues most monopolists hasten to assure us that they intend to keep their undertakings up to the highest pitch of efficiency, and that they will not use their power to exploit the public. But the issue of monopoly is not just a question of whether prices are to be high or low, and output large or small, important as these matters are in a world as poor as ours still is. It is even more a question of opportunity. The spread of monopoly is the spread of privilege; opportunity is denied to those who are outside the ring. In nineteenth-century Britain, men with initiative could rise in industry; in the twentieth century they are locked out, unless they are the sons or favourites of the industrial barons who have assumed control over the country's major industries. A new hereditary industrial aristocracy has replaced the old hereditary landed aristocracy; and the brief vision of democracy which early capitalism seemed to be bringing in the nineteenth century has vanished. The rise of monopoly has meant a concentration of control over great aggregations of wealth in the hands of a few men; in nearly every British industry one man or two, in his own name or that of the ring he represents, can take decisions which may plunge thousands into unemployment, put prices beyond the range of thousands more, suppress new inventions, or ruin all the carefully laid plans of some local authority. The power they possess may be well exercised, but it is arbitrary power. In the nineteenth century we learnt to reject power over society without control by society in the political field; the twentieth is teaching that it is no less vicious in the economic field.

Let us therefore examine more closely some of the steps on which a firm may climb to power without necessarily being efficient. They are not all associated with defects in the law. Thus one of these steps is the superior financial facilities available to large firms. The situation is not as bad here as it is in the United

[1] "The Sherman Act and the New Anti-trust Legislation," *Journal of Political Economy*, Vol. XXIII (1915), p. 214.

States of America. There big business and banking are indissolubly linked, and denial of finance a major means of strangling the small firm. In this country banks are more closely confined to short-term finance; firms are not dependent on them for capital; and their power to strangle is much less. But the small firm does meet unnecessary difficulties in raising capital, compared with the facilities available to large firms. The Macmillan Committee recommended in 1931 that this situation should be remedied. If there were adequate sources of finance for small firms, such as a Government financial corporation might provide, they would keep alive more easily, and the big firm would not so easily gobble them up. Another device for rising to power is mass advertising. It is not a very secure method, since advertised products compete with one another, and have in addition to face the competition of unadvertised products bought by those members of the public who, for a guarantee of quality, rely more on the advice of their regular retailer than on what they read in newspaper advertisements. Advertising is the reason for the existence of some large firms, but the case against it does not rest primarily on its rôle as a source of monopoly power. Rather does it rest on the fact that it does not seem to serve any social purpose useful enough to justify the £100,000,000 a year spent on it. Proposals to confine advertising to trade periodicals certainly deserve sympathetic hearing.

Turn, however, to the defects in the law which aid would-be monopolists. The first of these is in the patent law. The theory underlying the grant of the patent privilege is that it is a reward for the inventor: he is entitled for a number of years to a royalty on any use of his invention. In fact, however, the existing patent law confers a privilege not only on the inventor, but also on the user. A firm may buy the patent, and with it the right to exclude all other firms from using the invention, however willing they may be to pay the inventor his royalty. Thus a rich firm can buy up all the most essential inventions in its industry and dominate the market; those inventions which challenge its invested capital it may suppress. Reform this situation, and a number of monopolies would dissolve. Make all patents "licence of right," giving any firm the right to use the invention on paying a royalty to the inventor. This might mean that some doubtful inventions would not be tried out on a commercial scale, since no firm would sink money in the experiment unless assured that only it would benefit;

but this is not likely to be common, and any social loss through this source would be more than compensated by ending a system under which valuable inventions are suppressed and delayed, and others used to exploit the public. The Patent Acts have tried to prevent the abuse of patents by giving special powers to the Comptroller of Patents; but experience shows that large abuses call for drastic remedies.

A second defect is that the law permits boycotts and insistence on exclusive dealing. If strong enough, a firm may use a boycott to kill a rival, either by threatening its customers, or by threatening its suppliers. An example of the former is the *Shoe Machinery* case,[1] where the firm insisted on exclusive dealing, penalising customers who wanted to do part of their business with its rivals. The courts have not been presented with a case illustrating the use of boycotts on supplies by a single firm, though there are many cases of its use by trade combinations, as in *Sorrel's* case and the Motor Trade Association cases. Could there be any clearer example of an attempt to restrain trade than the use of the boycott? Yet the Privy Council dismissed the *Shoe Machinery* case on the ground that—

> "By virtue of the privilege which the law secures to all traders, namely that they shall be left free to conduct their own trade in the manner which they deem best for their own interests, so long as that manner is not in itself illegal, the respondents are at liberty to hire or not to hire the appellants' machines as they choose, irrespective altogether of the injury their refusal to deal may inflict on others. The same privilege entitles the appellants to dispose of the products they manufacture on any terms not in themselves illegal, or not to dispose of their products at all, as they may deem best in their own interest, irrespective of like consequences. This privilege is indeed the very essence of that freedom of trade in the name and in the interest of which the respondents claim to escape from the obligations of their contracts."[2]

Is not this passage of the very essence of that confusion between freedom to trade, freedom to restrain trade, and freedom to dispose of one's own freedom to trade, to which the judges have proved so prone? And the cases where firms have got suppliers to

[1] *United Shoe Machinery Co.* v. *Brunet*, (1909) A.C. 330.

[2] Ibid., at pp. 342–3.

withhold supplies from a rival, instead of being discussed in terms of the desirability or otherwise of this form of restraint of trade, have been made, by some peculiar legal quirk, to hang on the test of conspiracy; curious exercises have been made to show why a boycott engineered by two in combination is worse than a boycott engineered by one giant—the judgments explaining away *Quinn* v. *Leathem* and justifying *Allen* v. *Flood* would make amusing reading were they not so tragic—and after all this the offenders have got away on the ground that their conspiracy was only to promote legitimate trade interests. There was, indeed, some point in the question whether the restraint involved in tying a customer or supplier to a particular firm is an unreasonable restraint. If X contracts to serve as Y's secretary for a year, and to serve no other person during that time, or if A agrees to sell all his output to B, there is a restraint on the freedoms of X and A to enter their respective markets. But it is not necessarily an undesirable restraint. It becomes such only in the hands of a monopolist, for he alone can use it as a device for strangling rivals. The law might well permit such contracts to firms which cannot exploit them, while denying them to others in a monopolistic position. The attempt to apply this principle to one kind of monopolist, the possessor of a patent, failed because when the Bill passed from the House of Commons to the House of Lords, their Lordships so mutilated the relevant section as to render it practically useless. What we need now is a well-drafted clause applying to all monopolists.

A third defect in the law is that it permits price discrimination. Would-be monopolists flourish by extorting special prices and rebates from their suppliers to the detriment of smaller rivals; and they conquer small markets often by temporarily lowering the price there until the local firm is driven out of business; the use of "fighting ships" in the *Mogul* case was an example of this. Price discrimination is another device which, though harmless in the hands of small firms, can be deadly in the hands of monopolists. Parliament has recognised this, and in most cases where it creates monopoly it controls price discrimination—on the railways, in electricity supply and in the hands of other public utilities. What is lacking is the realisation that monopolies which do not emerge with Parliamentary backing are even worse than those which do, and that therefore their actions need even greater control.

These defects in the law all point in one direction. If it is accepted that the giant concern can only be tolerated where its size is based on efficiency, and that monopoly on any other basis is bad, then it follows that the law ought positively to remove all undesirable aids to size. In the nineteenth century it was taken for granted, more or less, that the market could look after itself. This was obviously untrue of some markets, like transport or gas, but these were taken as exceptions, and special provision was made for them as public utilities. What is now clear is that all markets have to work within a certain legal framework, and that unless the framework is adequate, the market will cease to be free. To keep the market as free as possible should be a positive task of the law. How far is this possible?

IV

LESSONS FROM AMERICA

It is now commonly believed that American experience has proved the futility of any attempt to control monopoly by law. "See," we are told, "America is the country with the most determined anti-trust legislation, and yet nowhere else are there more powerful monopolistic corporations." On this there are several things to be said.

The first is, that if American experience proves anything, what it proves most is that no law can succeed unless the means are provided for enforcing it. When the Sherman Act was passed it seems to have been expected to operate largely through private parties bringing suits against monopolies. Business men injured by combinations would set it in motion for the recovery of triple damages. Accordingly only very small sums were set aside for public enforcement. In Theodore Roosevelt's day the anti-trust division had only five lawyers; in the 1920's the number never exceeded twenty-five; not until 1938 did it reach fifty. Private enforcement has proved inadequate—apart from anything else it is much too expensive a procedure. Accordingly in 1939 the other Roosevelt multiplied the sums at the disposal of the division; its staff of lawyers reached two hundred; for the first time the division was able to prepare its cases properly and to make a wide assault on monopoly. The results of this action leave no doubt that anti-trust legislation can be a most effective deterrent of monopolists, and save the public millions of dollars. The first lesson for us, therefore, is that, desirable as it may be to encourage actions in tort to compensate for injuries inflicted, major reliance should be placed on enforcement by a Government department with adequate funds. Rather a special kind of Government department is required: our traditional repository for powers of this kind, the Board of Trade, has not the machinery. It must be a department with police powers, including men capable of nosing out restraints from the conflicting evidence of witnesses and files of complicated papers; a department with economists trained to analyse the pattern of an industry and the effects of its peculiar restraints; and a department with lawyers, able to present a good case. We need a special "Department of Monopoly Control."[1]

That is the administrative side of American experience. What of the legal side? Can the law really maintain competition? The answer to this is in two parts, corresponding to the two different types of monopoly, the single giant and the trade combination.

American experience does indeed prove that it is useless to try to prevent rival firms from merging into big corporations. Much of the confusion, and most of the disappointment associated with American anti-trust experience, have been due to the fact that the Sherman Act did not make plain whether such fusion was to be penalised or not. The Act prohibited monopolies and attempts to monopolise. At first the Supreme Court interpreted this in such a way as to forbid mergers that promoted monopoly; then it changed its mind. The Clayton Act was more specific, prohibiting big concerns from purchasing each other's shares, or even having interlocking directorates—but the corporation lawyers got round this: now one company buys not the shares but the physical assets of the other. If two concerns do not want to compete with each other, no law can compel them to, and it is futile to try to stop them from merging.

But while this is true of two big concerns determined to co-operate, it does not quite apply where a giant is trying to swallow a number of smaller rivals. It is a lot to ask the public to stand by and watch some magnate buying up all the cinemas, or all the pubs, with intent to create a monopoly, and to take no steps to

[1] Far and away the best appraisal of the administrative problems involved is the monograph by W. H. Hamilton and I. Till, for the Temporary National Economic Committee, *Anti-trust in Action*, 1940; it contains also a valuable discussion of such problems as penalties and the enforcement of judicial orders. See also T. W. Arnold, *The Bottlenecks of Business*, New York, 1940.

stop him. Sometimes he will have a clear case in his favour, where the resulting reorganisation under a single control can bring substantial economies and lower costs and prices. But frequently there is no such case. There ought to be powers entitling the government to stop a monopolist from making further acquisitions where it cannot be shown that substantial economies will result. It is proposed, under Town and Country Planning legislation, that every time land use is to be changed a licence must be sought from public commissioners. It is not therefore too much to require—a much less frequent occurrence—that any firm which controls (or any large shareholder in a firm which controls) say one-third of the trade in any line of business should be prohibited from buying the assets or shares of rival concerns except under a licence, which would be granted only where substantial economies were expected to result.

This is the most difficult part of monopoly control, and is the part where American anti-trust legislation has clearly failed, through omitting provision for the exercise of administrative discretion. (A law which does not provide for the reasonable exceptions always breaks down.) In other important directions, however, anti-trust legislation has been amply successful. The Clayton Act (now reinforced by the Robinson-Patman Act) forbade exclusive dealing, boycotts and price discrimination, which, as we have seen, are important tools for monopoly-building. These prohibitions have been very effective despite defects in the drafting. One defect was that, since the Acts prohibit these devices "where the effect . . . may be to substantially lessen competition or tend to create a monopoly in any line of commerce," the courts were left to decide when this condition was fulfilled, and had to plunge into a mass of economic material which judges are not usually trained to interpret. The difficulty could be got round by denying these devices to monopolists, and defining a monopolist as "any person who has a patent,[1] copyright, trade mark, brand, licence or other privilege protected by the law; any person whose purchases or sales amount to one-third of the total sales of the commodity in the United Kingdom; or any person acting in combination with other buyers or sellers."[2] Another defect was that while the Clayton Act applied the prohibition to leases and to contracts

[1] If all patents were "licence of right," patentees could be omitted.

[2] Trade combinations need not be included if their formation is prohibited under some other clause.

of sale it omitted agency,[1] which thereby unnecessarily gave scope for evasion. A third defect was that instead of refusing to sell a commodity X unless the buyer bought also Y, an act forbidden by the law, a seller could put X and Y together, call them one commodity, and refuse to sell them apart;[2] this is another evasion which might easily be stopped up.

If in Britain we were to enact similar provisions to those in the Clayton and Robinson-Patman Acts directed against boycotts, exclusive dealing and price discrimination, and if we were simultaneously to revise the patent law, the market would take a new lease of freedom. Concerns would then have to rely primarily on efficiency as a means of growth. They would be surrounded almost always by numerous smaller rivals, with free and fearless access to supplies (except where these are limited mineral deposits) and to markets; the large firm could not boycott, and could make few gains not wholly deserved on the basis of efficiency. In many cases no further control would be needed to prevent exploitation. But in some cases, where the economies of large scale are marked, no small rivals could survive. Then the market would be at the mercy of one or two large giants, and more positive controls would be needed. They lie easy to hand; Parliament controls some monopolies by regulating their prices, e.g. electricity concerns, others by limiting their profits, e.g. gas concerns. In other cases there is operation by municipal authorities, by Government departments, or by specially created public corporations like the London Passenger Transport Board. Wherever the scale of production is too large for competition to survive, there should be machinery for public control. This is a well-established tradition in Great Britain, only we have limited its application to a narrow field that we choose to call "public utility," and to one or two other special cases, such as the rather inadequate supervision of the Import Duties Advisory Committee over iron and steel prices; what we need now is to extend the principle of public utility control to all cases where the economies of scale must supersede competition.[3]

So much for the giant concern. What does American experience

[1] *Federal Trade Commission* v. *Curtis Publishing Co.*, 260 U.S. 568 (1923).

[2] *Federal Trade Commission* v. *Gratz et al.*, 253 U.S. 421 (1920).

[3] If all these large concerns were controlled as to profits and prices or publicly operated they might perhaps be excluded from the prohibition of exclusive dealing, since this method of trade is sometimes beneficial, and is only harmful in the hands of uncontrolled monopolies.

teach about the attempt to prevent rings and combinations between the smaller fry? This, after all, is the type of monopoly much more common in the United Kingdom than is the industrial giant, though of those we have also our share. Here the interpretation of the law provided little difficulty; the Supreme Court wavered only once,[1] and not for long. The experience is overwhelmingly conclusive that trade combinations are easy to smell out, and that their suppression presents little practical difficulty.

Properly to understand what is possible, we must begin by analysing markets into three types. At one extreme are those where the scale of operation is so small that the number of firms is very large, e.g. in this country cotton spinning, road haulage, or retail trade. In such markets no voluntary agreement is stable; the numbers concerned are too large; and a minority will always blackleg and spoil the fun. Experience has proved that an agreement will survive only if the legislature intervenes to impose it on all firms. Competition in such cases has disappeared only because the State has prohibited it; even after war-time concentration, repeal of a dozen Acts would usually restore it in full vigour.

At the other extreme are markets which are so small, or where the scale of operations is so large, that agreement is inevitable and no law can prevent it. With these we have already dealt; anti-trust measures are futile; what is required are positive controls, whether price or profit limitation, or public operation.

The intermediate cases are the most difficult. Here the number of firms is large, but not too large for agreement. There is the inevitable minority which would ruin the agreement, but it can be boycotted. This is also where an anti-combination law is most useful. It can make the agreement a criminal conspiracy; refuse the enforcement of contracts; and give to injured minorities full damages (triple damages under the Sherman Act) at law. American experience shows that the existence of such a law makes it extremely difficult for such combinations to hold together effectively. They have of course sought means of evading it. Not all the acts of trade associations are vicious, and not all are prohibited. Those which need to be prohibited are the fixing of prices, the restriction of output, allocation of quotas, imposition of distance limits, compilation of stop lists or agreements express or implied with suppliers to withdraw supplies from outside firms. There are, however, legitimate activities—research, compilation of statistics,

[1] *Appalachian Coals, Inc.* v. *U.S.*, 288 U.S. 344 (1933).

M

promotion of standardisation, representation on public committees, etc. The difficulty arises where legitimate activities are used for illegitimate purposes, as when an association circulates information as to current prices or orders placed or output which its members tacitly accept as indications what prices they should charge or how far to restrict their output. The existence of this possible loophole, however, is not very dangerous unless the group is small enough to exclude blacklegs, or is able to penalise them and get away with it in the courts. So also with that other evasion, "price leadership." This is found where there is some large firm dominant in an industry, surrounded by a number of smaller rivals. There is no price agreement, but all firms take their cue from the leader, and he, by virtue of his strength, exercises the function of bringing recalcitrants into line. If all large firms were publicly controlled this might solve the problem of "price leadership," but even without this the situation can be kept in hand, provided there is an enforcing authority with its eyes open for cases of boycott, exclusive dealing, or price discrimination, since these are the weapons with which price leadership is enforced. If agreement is prohibited, the wings of the large firm clipped, and the small firm encouraged, the market will keep free without much difficulty.

What are the alternatives? Given that business men cannot be left free to do as they please, there are two. One is the German system; to recognise cartels with their quotas and minimum prices, but to take power to supervise them, as under the *Kartellverordnung* of November 1923. It is well known that this decree was never seriously applied; but assuming that such a decree could be enforced, and that it were possible adequately to supervise the prices and quotas fixed by every single trade association, is this the desirable alternative? To hold this view is to forget that monopoly is not primarily a question of prices; it is even more a question of efficiency, of initiative, of opportunity and of freedom from concentrated power; these are the ends which competition secures more effectively than any other form of organisation. To reject competition and choose price regulated cartels is to miss altogether the meaning of the problem. The other alternative, some socialists would suggest, is nationalisation. Is it really an alternative? Leaving out workers on their own account, there are over a million separate commercial establishments in this country. Is it a practical proposal for a Labour Government simultaneously to take over every one of them? Surely, leaving aside the very big question whether such action would be desirable on its own merits, do not at least the administrative difficulties compel concentrating nationalisation on the most urgent cases, which, apart from industries nationalised for reasons of political strategy, are the cases where large-scale economies make monopoly inevitable? However distasteful he may find it, the Labour Prime Minister is bound to leave whole sectors of the economy to private enterprise while he concentrates his energies on key industries. He has therefore to decide whether it is to be monopolistic or competitive private enterprise. He may well want to keep the trade associations because their existence makes it easier to deal with the producers in an industry and to issue them their orders. But this does not mean that they must retain monopoly powers. Let them negotiate with Government, publish statistics, and do all the other legitimate activities of trade associations; but boycotts, price-fixing, quotas and all the other paraphernalia of monopoly must go. Private enterprise can only be retained in so far as it is competitive; in so far as it is retained it must be made to compete.

V

CONCLUSION

"If the monopoly established by the appellants and their mode of carrying on their business be as oppressive as is alleged (upon which their Lordships express no opinion) then the evil if it exists may be capable of cure by legislation or by competition, but in their view not by litigation"; thus the Privy Council in the *Shoe Machinery* case.[1] This article has sought to indicate the sort of legislation that is needed to carry on the good work which the judges so unfortunately abandoned. It may be summarised as follows:

(*a*) The maintenance of free markets is a positive task to which the police power of the State should be applied; this requires a special department, amply staffed.

(*b*) The Act under which such department operates should prohibit trade combinations, specifying the acts which are outlawed; and should deny to monopolists the right to buy up competitors and the use of boycotts, exclusive dealing

[1] *Supra* at p. 344.

and price discrimination, specifying what is meant by a monopolist.

(*c*) The patent law should be revised to make all patents "licence of right"; and

(*d*) The principles of public utility regulation or public operation should be extended to all industries where the economies of large-scale production necessarily result in the market being dominated by a few large concerns.

We cannot produce complete economic democracy simply by adopting this programme; there are many other points at which business needs to be regulated in the public interest. We need these provisions, however, at least as part of the programme if such private business as is retained after the war is to be made not the master but the servant of the public. This remains almost the only important country without legislation to keep the market free, or at least a general law to control the activities of monopolists. If private groups are not to submerge the public interest, Parliament must take bold action to control monopoly, and now is the time to decide what lines it should follow.

[4]

CHAPTER V

COMPETITION IN RETAIL TRADE

"The prejudices of some political writers against shopkeepers and tradesmen are altogether without foundation. So far from it being necessary either to tax them or to reduce their number, they can never be multiplied so as to hurt the public though they may be so as to hurt one another. The quantity of grocery goods, for example, which can be sold in a particular town, is limited by the demand of that town and its neighbourhood. The capital, therefore, which can be employed in the grocery trade, cannot exceed what is sufficient to purchase that quantity. If this capital is divided between two different grocers, their competition will tend to make both of them sell cheaper than if it was in the hands of one only; and if it were divided among twenty, their competition would be just so much the greater and the chance of their combining together, in order to raise the price, just so much the less. Their competition might, perhaps, ruin some of themselves; but to take care of this is the business of the parties concerned, and may be safely left to their own discretion."

Thus spake the old master in 1776.[1] His conclusion has never been widely accepted. Retailers have always claimed that competition hurts the public no less than themselves and sought public support for their elaborate efforts to restrain it. Even the classical writers were unsure.[2] Modern economists feel more confident to tackle the problem, using as tools the newly shaped theory of monopolistic competition, but a combined knowledge of theory and of the structure of retailing is all too rare, and attempts at a synthesis all too infrequent. A further venture does not therefore seem superfluous. Neither is the moment untimely. In November 1941 the Board of Trade made an Order prohibiting any person from opening a new retail business in this country except under licence. This was purely a wartime measure, and the President of the Board pledged himself to withdraw it after the war. But its enactment raised some hopes that permanent restrictions would

[1] Smith, A.: *The Wealth of Nations* (Cannan's Edition), Vol. I, pp. 341–2.

[2] Cf. the extracts from the classical economists gathered together in H. Smith, *Retail Distribution*, Ch. IV.

follow, and recent fortunes at the polls have helped to revive these hopes. Meanwhile, some town planning authorities are already using, or planning to use, their powers in such a way as drastically to reduce the number of shops. This article may, perhaps, help to clarify the issues involved.

The procedure adopted is to analyse first the effects of competition in prices and in services. The third section deals with certain special forms of competition which have been denounced as unfair, and the fourth section tries to reach conclusions on the main issues in the debate.

I

THE NUMBER, SIZE AND LOCATION OF SHOPS

1. In the contemporary approach, the earliest doubts of the effectiveness of competition in retailing are associated with the name of Hotelling. In a stimulating article[1] he argued, on certain special assumptions, that the effect of competition would be to cause sellers to cluster together, instead of dispersing at equal distances, and showed that this undesirable result in location causes transport costs to be excessive. Various writers interested themselves in the problem, but the outstanding advance is the contribution of Lerner and Singer eight years later, in an article[2] which generalises Hotelling's case, and is the most convenient starting point.

The basic assumption is that the customers are strung out at equal distances along a road. Then, on the further asumptions (*a*) that no two shops can be on the same spot; (*b*) that each end of the road is a cul-de-sac; (*c*) that each customer pays his own transport costs; (*d*) that the number of shops is given; (*e*) that the price is fixed; and (*f*) that there are no economies of scale, Lerner and Singer show that in equilibrium (i) there cannot be more than two shops together, and (ii) there must be two shops together at each end of the road. They also imply that each shop must have the same number of customers, unless there is an odd number of shops, when one may have more than the others; but this is not so. The third condition of equilibrium is only that no shop may have less customers than half the number between any two other shops, or less than the shops at the end. Shops may be

[1] Hotelling, H.: "Stability in Competition," *Economical Journal*, June 1929.

[2] A. P. Lerner, and H. W. Singer, "Some Notes on Duopoly and Spatial Competition," *Journal of Political Economy*, April 1937.

equidistant, but need not be, and as in any case the end shops must be paired, transport costs must be above the ideal.

Removing some of these assumptions brings the equilibrium conditions nearer to the ideal. Assumption (*a*) makes a negligible difference. Removing assumption (*b*) destroys conclusion (ii); if the road connects say two big market centres, the first shop at either end of the road may stand alone. As for assumption (*c*), Lerner and Singer themselves reach the important conclusion that if transport costs are paid not by the customers but by the sellers, shops will be located at equal distances from each other, which is the ideal situation.

2. To advance the analysis beyond the Lerner-Singer stage it is necessary to remove the remaining assumptions. If the number of shops is not given, and prices are not fixed, and there are no economies of scale, the number of shops will be as great as the number of customers. This odd conclusion brings into the open the odd assumption underlying the whole analysis that transport cost from wholesaler to retailer can be neglected, but not transport cost from retailer to customer, an assumption which becomes the more unreasonable the greater the ratio of shops to customers. Nevertheless, the conclusion serves to remind us that the convenience of customers requires that there should be as many shops as possible, each small, and that it is only economies of scale which prevent this. The assumption of constant costs is incompatible with equilibrium in retailing, given dispersal of customers. For if a reduction in the size of shops will not increase costs, it will pay some seller to insert himself between two existing shops.

Should shops, then, be of "optimum" size, meaning the minimum size consistent with minimum average cost, or should they be smaller, and if so, how much smaller? If we can assume that the inconvenience of not having a shop nearby can be translated into monetary terms as a function of the distance of the shop, the problem is capable of precise solution.

Let us assume (1) that all shops have the same costs; (2) that there are no prime costs, but only an overhead, so that the average cost curve is a rectangular hyperbola (marginal costs are assumed away only for convenience of exposition; what matters is the assumption of falling average cost); (3) that the customers are strung out along a road on either side of each shop, one customer for each unit of distance; (4) that each customer buys one unit (money value) of merchandise; and (5) that the inconvenience of distance can be expressed as one unit of money per unit of distance, paid by the customer. Then the following diagram shows the position.

AC is a rectangular hyperbola, representing the average cost curve of any shop, varying with the number of its customers (and therefore sales). MTC is the curve of marginal transport costs; the first two customers, one on either side, incur one unit each, the next two customers incur two units each, and so on; the curve can thus be drawn for simplicity as a straight line with a slope of 0·5. Total transport cost is the area lying beneath it, and average transport cost per customer will be a line with a slope of 0·25.

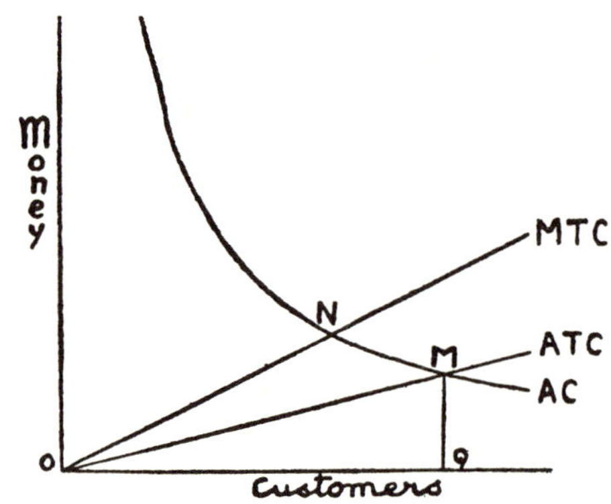

The ideal number of shops (or number of customers per shop) is such that, given the total number of customers to be served, the sum of shop costs and transport costs is at its minimum. This condition is fulfilled when for each shop the sum of average shop costs and average transport costs is minimised. Since for each new customer the former falls and the latter rises, the condition is fulfilled when the negative slope of AC equals the positive slope of ATC. AC being a rectangular hyperbola and ATC a straight line from the origin, this will be at the point where they meet. M gives us the ideal size of shop. It cannot correspond with the point where average shop cost would be minimised; since ATC is rising and AC is falling, the minimum point of ATC + AC must be to the left of the minimum point of AC. In other words, it is desirable that shops should be of less than "optimum" size.

Will competition bring about the right size? If there is free entry, and if there cannot be abnormal profits, the price charged by each shop (its gross margin) must lie somewhere along AC. If a shop reduces its price by one unit it will attract two customers, one on either side, who transfer their custom from its rivals. It pays therefore to lower the price by one unit if getting two more customers will reduce AC by more than one unit. Its equilibrium is therefore at the point N where the slope of MTC equals the slope of AC.[1] Thus shops will not cut their prices low enough to bring the right size. In competition, there will be too many shops, each too small.

The result can be generalised by assuming that consumers do not live along a road, but are distributed over an area, one in each unit of space. It remains desirable that shops should be

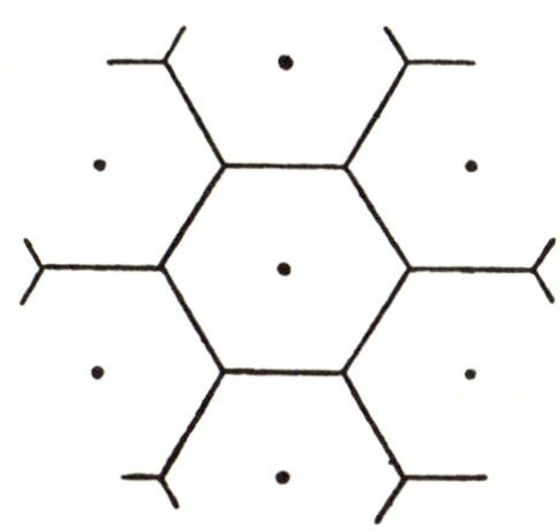

equidistant, and this condition can only be fulfilled if each is at the centre of a hexagon. How many shops there should be, and what should be the size of each, is then determined if we know how large the hexagon should be. Retaining our previous assumptions, the solution is as follows: If we write r for the length of the radius of the inscribed circle, the length of each side will be $1 \cdot 15r$. The number of customers equals the area of the hexagon, $3 \cdot 46r^2$. Writing a for the overhead costs of each shop, average cost per customer,

$$AC = \frac{a}{3 \cdot 46r^2}.$$

To calculate transport costs we first divide the hexagon into its twelve right-angled triangles. In each, taking the customers living along the base, the nearest lives at distance r and the furthest at

[1] N corresponds to Chamberlin's "ideal adjustment" and to R in Fig. 15 of his *Theory of Monopolistic Competition*, p. 92. The slope of MTC here corresponds to the slope of dd^1 in that diagram.

distance $1 \cdot 15r$. The sum[1] of the distances for the base customers is $0 \cdot 61r^2$, and the total transport cost for the hexagon is twelve times the integral of this, i.e. $2 \cdot 41r^3$. This divided by the number of customers gives average transport cost per customer,

$$\text{ATC} = 0 \cdot 70r.$$

The ideal number of shops is given by the condition that the slopes of AC and ATC must be the same. Differentiating gives

$$\frac{a}{1 \cdot 73r^3} = 0 \cdot 70$$

$$\therefore r = 0 \cdot 93a^{\frac{1}{3}}.$$

Now, in competition a shop will cut its price by one unit so long as the resulting increase of customers reduces AC by more than one unit. Equilibrium therefore results when

$$\frac{a}{1 \cdot 73r^3} = 1$$

$$\therefore r = 0 \cdot 83a^{\frac{1}{3}}.$$

This analysis brings out the relevant points. The number of shops depends on the extent of the economies of scale, the density of population (determining the number of customers per unit of distance), and the inconvenience or cost of distant shopping. The greater the economies of scale, and the less the cost of transport, the fewer shops there will and should be. The denser the population, the larger shops will be, and this is worth noting since many people believe that the decentralisation of urban populations which has occurred since 1920 is one of the principal factors explaining the increase in the numbers engaged in distribution in this country.[2] In any case, given the dispersion of customers, the ideal size of shop is less than the "optimum"; and, given competition, the actual size will be less than the ideal.[3]

[1] I am indebted to Professor R. G. D. Allen for the formula.

[2] E.g. P. Ford, "Changes in the Number of Shops, 1901–1931," *Economic Journal*, June 1936.

[3] The above example assumed that goods are transported as the crow flies. More realistic assumptions do not upset the argument unless immensely complicated routes have to be used. For example, if we assume that main roads run direct from shop to shop, and that side roads are perpendicular to these main roads at intervals of one unit, total transport cost becomes $2 \cdot 98r^3$; the optimum number of shops will be given by the equation $r = 0 \cdot 88a^{\frac{1}{3}}$, and the competitive number remains at $r = 0 \cdot 83a^{\frac{1}{3}}$.

3. Several qualifications are needed before we can derive from this anything like a complete picture.

First, the analysis has so far assumed that there is price competition, and that each shop cuts prices without taking the reaction of its competitors into account. This does not require that the price of every one of the hundreds of commodities it sells should be keenly competitive; it is enough that average gross margins for any class of trade must be adjusted to the level set by competition, and if this is so, the effect on size is the same. But even this is not a complete picture. To begin with, retail prices in certain trades—cigarettes, patent medicines, some groceries, milk, coal, confectionery, books, periodicals, stationery, lamps, cycles, petrol, motors and motor accessories—are maintained by elaborate arrangements between manufacturers, wholesalers and retailers, which impose heavy penalties for price cutting. The assumption that retailers are free to compete in prices, however, holds good in other trades—some groceries, fish, meat, fruit and vegetables, flowers, furniture, most hardware, drapery, footwear, clothes, pottery and others—and to these the analysis applies, subject to further qualifications.

When prices are fixed the number of shops is a direct function of the level at which they are fixed. In terms of Fig. III (which is constructed on the same cost assumptions as Fig. I), equilibrium is given by the point K at which the horizontal price line SP cuts AC. So long as shops are larger than this they will be making profits; new entrants will then be attracted, reducing the share of each in the trade, until abnormal profits vanish. As the price is usually too high under these schemes (for reasons we shall examine later) the number of shops will be excessive. At this point, however, it will pay any one shop to compete by offering better service. If all shops do this, as they must in competition, all make losses unless their number contracts, and in competition it will contract up to the point where a curve showing the effect on sales of increased expenditure on service has the same slope as the new cost curve (including the additional services). In Fig. III we assume that the cost of the extra services is added not to marginal cost but to overheads; and we also assume that to increase the quality of the service at a cost of *x*d. per unit of sales has the same effect in stimulating sales as would reducing the price by *x*d. per unit while keeping the service unchanged. Competitive equilibrium is then given by the intersection of MTC and the fixed price line, to which the number of shops (and AC + S) adjusts itself. Where the extra services take the form of an addition to overhead costs, shops will be larger than they would be if there were competition in price but not in service, but prices will be higher. If they take the form of an addition to marginal costs, shops may be larger or smaller, higher or rising marginal costs making for smaller shops.

Shops may, of course, compete neither in prices nor in service, even though prices are not maintained. If each shopkeeper takes into account the fact that if he cuts prices or offers more service his rivals will follow, shops will be still smaller and more numerous.

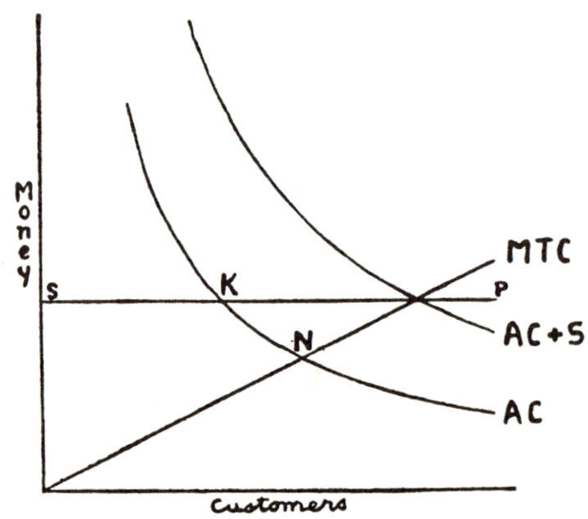

The limit to their smallness will be set by the elasticity of demand in the market as a whole, i.e. by Q in Chamberlin's Fig. 15[1]; in our diagram where elasticity is assumed to be zero it would be one shop for each customer. It is most unlikely in practice that this movement towards the upper limit will get very far. It is certainly unlikely in the United States of America, where aggressive competition is the rule, with chains, super-markets and independents at each other's throats. Competition is not so keen in this country, but competition between the co-operatives, the multiples and the independents is nevertheless keen enough in non-price-maintained trades to keep the size of shops near to N. In the price-maintained trades price competition is ruled out; service competition tends to check the decrease in shop size, but it is not always very strong and, given the fall in wholesale prices

[1] Loc. cit., p. 92.

which had been occurring steadily after 1920, it was possible for more and more redundant shops to establish themselves on an ever-widening gross margin.

4. The second qualification concerns transport costs. The conclusion that in competition there must be too many shops depends on the assumption that customers pay transport costs. If the shop pays transport costs, it will take on an extra customer so long as the price exceeds the cost of transporting to him (marginal selling cost being on our assumptions zero). But since (Fig. I) MTC equals the price (AC + ATC) at the point where AC + ATC is at its minimum, it follows that the point of equilibrium for the shop paying transport costs is the same as the ideal equilibrium, represented by the output OQ. There will be too many shops if customers pay their own transport costs, but the ideal number of shops if there is free delivery.

The reason for this is that free delivery is a form of price discrimination (in this case perfect discrimination), and, if average costs are falling, discrimination usually brings output nearer to the ideal. The discrimination arises because the nearest customers pay a price in excess of AC plus the cost of transporting to them, and the furthest pay the same price which is much below AC plus the cost of transporting to them (indeed the furthest customer contributes nothing towards AC); in a sense the nearer subsidise the further. The same sort of result would be attained by any other form of discrimination, and is not the result of competition in service as such. If all the customers get as much service as they pay for, the result is merely to lift the average cost curve; shops may be larger, but the gap between the ideal and the competitive equilibrium is not diminished. However, there are also forms of service other than delivery which involve discrimination, e.g. credit and subsidised restaurants in department stores. Whenever a service is paid for by some who do not use it, and used by some *who would buy elsewhere but for this service,* the effect is to bring the competitive equilbrium nearer to the ideal equilibrium.

We must also note precisely what transport cost means in this context. MTC is a measure of all the inconvenience associated with buying at a distant shop. It is not the same as what it would cost the shop in money to deliver one's purchases. A customer who shops in the centre of the town may be quite capable of carrying home a pair of shoes without much extra trouble or inconvenience, and if asked to pay an extra sum equal to what delivery would cost the shop, might prefer to carry for himself. When, therefore, one concludes that shops will be larger and of optimum size if they offer free delivery but not otherwise, one concludes too much. If the firm's transport costs exceed the value of the real convenience conferred on the customer, the shop will not reach optimum size even if there is free delivery, and may indeed be smaller than it would be without free delivery if the disparity is great.

5. The third qualification is to remove the assumption of zero elasticity of demand. It will be more profitable for the shopkeeper to lower his price if he can count on selling more to his existing customers as well as on attracting other people's customers, so an elasticity exceeding zero will bring the competitive number of shops nearer to the ideal number, or even below it. There may be no "excess capacity" if elasticity is large enough. Of the many modifications elasticity introduces into the results, this is the important one.

6. Next we must consider the assumption that there cannot be abnormal profits in equilibrium. This rests on two further assumptions. The first is that customers have no irrational preferences for shops, so that if two shops differ in nothing bu their average price levels, customers will always buy from the cheaper. There has been some attempt to explain retailing, using as a large element in the analysis the irrationality, ignorance and inertia of customers.[1] While it is impossible to deny that these factors have some importance, it is impossible to agree to any significant importance in view of the rapid changes constantly taking place in the structure of retailing, as reflected in the relative strengths of independents, multiples, department stores, street markets, and the co-operative societies. Any shopkeeper who used the irrationality, ignorance, or inertia of his customers as major elements in his policy would soon find himself in Carey Street.

The other assumption necessary to keep prices equal to average cost is that continuous variability in the number of customers per shop is possible in each locality. This cannot be taken for granted. In the suburbs a new shop sets up between two other shops, and its impact is borne more heavily by the sales of these shops than it is by the sales of other shops. At any given moment, therefore, with a given number of shops, it may be that if a new shop could

[1] See especially H. Smith: op. cit., Ch. V.

be introduced in such a way as to take trade away equally from all shops (i.e. if all the shops were re-located at shorter intervals and one added), the new shop could remain permanently, but that since it would in fact be limited to sharing in the trade of two or three others, the shop will not be established. Certain consequences flow. First, profits may be abnormal without new shops being established, because there is more than enough for two but not enough for three; the corollary is that shops may be larger and fewer than the true competitive equilibrium. On the other hand, if too many shops come into existence, there is less likelihood of price or service competition, because in a small market sellers are more likely to take account of each other's reactions; and the entry of a new shop results simply in higher prices. There is, however, a check on this. Suburban shops compete not only with each other but also with shops in the large shopping centres, which are more aggressive. This fact makes possible continuous variability; it prevents suburban shopkeepers from exploiting a local monopoly, and keeps down the number of shops.

7. The fifth qualification is now to take full account of the existence of these large shopping centres.

From the analytical point of view, the difference is that we remove the assumptions that the customers are strung out evenly, one in each spot, and that transport costs are involved. For at a shopping centre there are thousands of persons who find themselves there for reasons other than shopping, and who, once there, can shop without counting transport cost. If we remove the assumption of transport costs, and assume large enough numbers of customers, it follows that in a large shopping centre shops should be of "optimum" size, meaning that average cost is at a minimum. The customer in Oxford Street takes real feminine pleasure in shopping; she moves around comparing prices and qualities, consulting her friends, and taking hours (or days) to make up her mind. It would be too much to claim that elasticity of demand is infinite for each shop, especially in the naïve sense that a small shaving of price immediately expands sales; but it is not too much to say that, in trades where the customer shops around, shops with cheap prices will sooner or later bankrupt those which try to sell similar qualities with similar service at a higher price level in the same centre. In the long run, therefore, shops in large shopping centres must approximate to optimum size.

This conclusion at once explains two common phenomena. First that shops in the centre are usually larger than those in the suburbs, and secondly that their prices are in consequence frequently lower[1]; and it reinforces the point that the suburban shop has only a precarious local monopoly. At the same time it raises another question. Since there is usually more than one shop of each kind in a large shopping centre, an "approximate long run infinite elasticity of demand" is consistent only with the assumption that the economies of scale are fairly easily exhausted. Otherwise there would be only one shop of each kind. How true is this?

The evidence is scanty, contradictory, and difficult to assess. It is quite clear that a medium-sized shop has lower costs than a very small one-man shop, if similar factors are similarly remunerated. But, of course, this is not always so. The small man who converts his parlour into a shop where he or his family serve part-time may have very low transfer costs, and be able to carry on indefinitely with low gross margins. To return, however, it is clear that where transfer earnings are similar the medium-sized shop has lower costs than the smallest shops. For example, Colin Clark's analysis[2] of the grocery trade of a number of stores controlled by a large co-operative society revealed the following situation:—

Average turnover £ per week	Costs (including interest but excluding profit) as percentage of turnover
100–200	13·21
200–300	11·51
300–400	11·13
400–500	10·50
500 upwards	10·08

[1] Differences in rent complicate the issue. Higher rents may or may not outweigh larger turnover. For department stores of equal size, rent is decisive in the United States; see E. A. Burnham, "The Department Store and its Community," *Harvard Business Review*, Vol. XVIII, p. 455. It does not seem to be so decisive in England, but the evidence is not so clear; see A. Plant and R. H. Fowler, "Costs of Retail Distribution," *Economica*, May 1939. For some theoretical discussion, see E. H. Chamberlin, loc. cit., Appendix C.

[2] C. Clark, *Conditions of Economic Progress*, p. 334.

A similar picture is suggested by Cadbury Brothers as applying to confectionery shops.[1]

It is in comparing the medium and the large shop that the evidence is inconclusive. The authors of a careful American survey[2] conclude that, apart from the high cost of the one-man business, there is "no convincing evidence of a general tendency for costs to decrease progressively as store size increases," and proceed to quote exceptions. Everything depends on the nature of the trade. The principal economy of large shopkeeping is the economy of having specialist buyers purchasing in large quantities. The more the goods can be standardised the greater is this economy. It is therefore small in the millinery business, but large in the Woolworth type of trade. The classes of shop which most multiply themselves in central shopping centres, those selling women's wear and household goods, are the classes in which standardisation tends to be least, and the advantages of scale small. The shops selling standardised goods are seldom found in great numbers even in the largest shopping centres, because it is more convenient for them to be widely distributed through the suburbs. They secure the economies of large buying through concentrating several shops under one management rather than by having a large turnover per shop; but the number of customers congregating in the centre may be sufficient to support two or three or more in any trade, each of more or less "optimum" size.

The department store fits with difficulty into the pattern of this argument. In a large shopping centre there is usually more than one. Yet the evidence is clear that there are substantial economies of scale, both in the United States[3] and in this country.[4] It is true that the American evidence shows the medium-sized department store having lowest costs, but this is because delivery and publicity expenses are higher for the largest stores, and these expenses are not relevant if we are considering merely competition between two stores in the same centre, with nearly infinite long-run cross elasticities. The large department store should be able to drive all others out of its centre simply by cutting prices. Why, also, does it not drive out the specialist shops?

[1] *Industrial Record*, 1919–39, p. 49.

[2] Twentieth Century Fund, *Does Distribution Cost Too Much?* p. 145.

[3] Cf. E. A. Burnham, "The Influence of Size of Business on Department Store Operating Results," *Harvard Business Review*, Vol. XVI, p. 211.

[4] Cf. A. Plant and R. F. Fowler, loc.

The latter is easier to answer. It must be remembered that even the largest department store is really only a collection of several small or medium-sized shops under one roof. A large department store may be able to buy more cheaply than a small one. But the shoe department of a large department store is not necessarily bigger than an independent shoe shop, and not necessarily able to buy more cheaply. Indeed, department stores are keenly conscious of the competition of the specialist shops. This is one reason why the multiple shop idea has spread over into the department store field, and why some of these multiple department stores have now adopted central buying. But the main strength of the department store is not price competition, but the fact that it offers the opportunity to buy everything under one roof, plus delivery, credit, and various amenities, and on these it concentrates its appeal. It is really doing a different class of trade from the specialist shop, and not strictly comparable.

This also yields the clue to competition between department stores themselves. The price competition is real, and governed also by the need to compete with specialist shops both at the centre and in the suburbs, which may be able to offer lower prices because they offer also less service. But because service is so important, price competition is not decisive. No two department stores have quite the same atmosphere, or give quite the same service, and the larger would not necessarily bankrupt the smaller by cutting its prices 5 per cent. Moreover, even if it could, the struggle would be long and costly. Prudence, and the small number of department stores, demand that while price competition should be real, it should be "based on costs," within the limits of what competition by specialist shops allows. In effect, the department store trade is rather special, and though it has close substitutes, is sufficiently limited for the oligopolistic phenomenon of "excess capacity" to prevail even in the shopping centre.

Moreover, in trying to analyse the existing situation, we must not treat it as if it were in "equilibrium." The department store in the 1930's was going through an awkward phase. When first it appeared, in the second half of the nineteenth century, it was a pioneer of modern methods of retailing, and its wide success was largely due to out-distancing its rivals in this respect. By the 1920's its rivals had caught up with it, and were giving it a stiff fight, and it is doubtful whether it continued to expand relatively to other forms of retail trade. It has been forced to review its

I

policies, to decentralise internal management, to consider central buying with other stores, and to rely more and more on service. As costs of service have risen, the policy of relying on service has itself been brought into question, since some competitors, unhampered by the high costs of free delivery, rest rooms, subsidised cafés, credit, and the rest, have pushed the price feature in their "cash and carry" policy. Most of the department stores in the United States and many in this country were losing money during the nineteen-thirties. It would be unwise to prophesy what policies they will be pursuing in the 'fifties.

8. We have thus two different types of analysis to apply to retailing, one assuming that the customers are dispersed and find a dispersal of shops convenient (with an excessive number[1] of small shops as the result), and the other assuming that the customers are concentrated in shopping centres (with the right number of shops, of optimum size). Both, of course, apply; moreover to some extent they apply to quite different classes of trade. Here the American distinction between "convenience" and "shopping" goods is useful. The former are articles purchased regularly and preferably from the nearest shop. The customer knows from daily experience just what he wants: there is no "shopping around," and the shops tend to be spread evenly over the whole area—beef, fish, cigarettes, groceries, beer, medicines and the like tend to be bought at the nearest outlet. With shopping goods, on the other hand, the customer wishes to compare prices and qualities before she makes up her mind—hats, curtains, dresses, even stockings—and the shops selling these things tend to congregate in shopping centres. The division is not watertight; some convenience goods shops of more or less optimum size are to be found in shopping centres, in competition with the suburban shops; while it is possible to find shops selling shopping goods in isolation in the suburbs, e.g. the ubiquitous draper. Department stores are in both classes of trade.

One further point is needed to complete the picture. So far we have spoken as if shops are to be found either clustered together in a central area or spread over the suburbs in lonely isolation. A little observation shows that nearly all shops are in a centre of some kind. Nevertheless the distinction between the central and the suburban shopping centres remains. The shops which are found together in the suburban shopping area tend to be shops

[1] Unless elasticity of demand is large enough to bridge the gap.

selling different classes of goods. These shops are not in close competition with each other, except in the sense in which all shops are competing for the consumers' incomes, and the fact that these different shops stand together does not invalidate the analysis. The theory of the optimum number of suburban shops becomes instead a theory of the optimum number of suburban shopping centres. Account must, however, be taken of the fact that these centres vary in size. This is due to the fact that the desirable frequency of shops varies in different trades, with the importance of overhead costs, the convenience of nearness, and the percentage of the population consuming the particular commodity. We should expect to find a large number of small centres, and smaller numbers of larger ones. Precisely where each centre is and which centres are large, are determined more by geographical considerations—the layout of streets, the junctions of main roads, the flow of traffic, and so on—than by the differential calculus, but overhead cost, density and convenience, the factors included in our calculations, are plainly not irrelevant. Ranging shopping centres in order of size, from the smallest to the largest, we should find that some suburban centres have sufficient trade to support several shops of one kind, each of optimum size, while in other trades there may be only one shop, of less than optimum size, and in others no shop at all. From the point of view of the trades in the first category this is a central shopping centre, because it is large enough to support more than one shop of optimum size, while from the point of view of the trades in the other categories it is a suburban shopping centre because it is not large enough. As the size of centres increases, so does the number of trades in which shops can be of optimum size, and to which this is a central shopping centre, until we reach the largest centres, with their department stores straining to reach the optimum.

9. We may now return to the end of section 6, where we began to take account of the effect of the existence of central shopping centres on shops in the suburbs. The first effect is a tendency for shops to be both smaller and at greater distances than they would be from each other, because the density of buying population in the suburbs is reduced. On the other hand, suburban shopkeepers, having to face the competition of central shopping areas, are less likely to try to exploit local monopoly positions, and this increase in competitiveness is a factor on the side of lower prices and fewer and larger shops. The extent of price competition, however,

varies. In price-maintained convenience goods trades—and nearly all such trades are price-maintained—the suburban shopkeeper faces only competition in service, which, at a distance, may not be very effective. In such trades it is certain that there will be too many shops. In the shopping goods trades the position is different; the suburban shops are faced with both price and service competition from shops of optimum size at the centre, and are compelled to keep their prices as low as is consistent with the fact that they themselves cannot attain to optimum size. (This is one of the reasons why price maintenance is unlikely to spread over into such trades.)

10. We may conclude by summarising:—

(*a*) Suburban shops should be of less than optimum size; if there is free entry into retailing they will be smaller and more numerous than they should be, unless elasticity of demand is large enough to bridge the gap; and if there is price maintenance they will be still smaller and more numerous, with perhaps too much service.

(*b*) Free delivery and other discriminatory services tend to bring shops nearer the ideal size and number.

(*c*) In central shopping centres shops will be of optimum size, and shops selling shopping goods will tend to cluster together here; department stores are an exception in that they are probably too numerous and too small.

II

COMPETITION IN SERVICE

1. Retailing is not a homogeneous "commodity"; it varies widely in quality, and correspondingly in cost. We must now examine the contention that the effect of competition is an excess of the more expensive forms, as well as the reverse contention, that competition causes the quality of the service to deteriorate.

It is useful to begin by distinguishing the features which make for expense. One is the very existence of service. "Help yourself" shops exist in the United States, and show the lowest margins of all. Then there is the speed with which service is effected—how long the customer has to wait before an assistant attends to him. Speedy service is particularly costly because the flow of customers into the shop is irregular. If the shop tried to keep enough assistants to be able to deal with the largest number of customers ever likely to be in the shop, most of these would be idle for much of the time, sales per assistant low and operating costs high. In retailing as in transport, costs would be much reduced if customers could distribute themselves evenly throughout the day and (though this is not so important) throughout the year. Next comes the quality of the assistants. In some trades the customer relies on the shopkeeper for information on the comparative qualities of the merchandise, and shop assistants have to be specialists trained in its qualities and uses. This means not only a more expensive kind of assistant, but also a smaller average number of customers per assistant than in, for example, the Woolworth type of trade. Another important service is performed when the shop offers the customer a wide choice of styles, colours, sizes or makes from which to suit his requirements. Some shops, especially department stores, add to this the right to return the purchase if on going home the customer changes her mind—American department stores report that one day's sales in eight are returned[1] —and find this a heavy burden. Lifts, escalators, rest rooms, credit, free delivery, information—the list becomes too long for elaboration.

Account must also be taken of forms of retailing which do not involve the customer in going to the shop. Orders by telephone or by mail are convenient if the customer knows just what he wants, and this form of business has low operating costs. Or the shop may go to the customer, in the form of the travelling van or the door-to-door salesman. Here operating costs are usually high.

2. In order to arrive at the conclusion that competition leads to an excess of the more expensive forms of retailing, in substitution for the less expensive, it is necessary to establish one of two propositions—either that customers get what they want, but should not be allowed to get it; or that they get what they do not want, through market imperfection. The first proposition has its adherents; they admit that the customer prefers good service even when there is a real choice open to him of less expensive forms, but they contend that this is a luxury he should not be allowed. In wartime we have all accepted this view in the United Kingdom, in order to release resources for other purposes. In peacetime too, "productive" output would be greater if "distributive" activity were curtailed, and in a planned economy a

[1] Twentieth Century Fund, op. cit., p. 308.

planning authority which attached little value to convenience in shopping relatively to increased outputs of other utilities would undoubtedly take steps to restrict the more expensive forms of retailing. In this country, however, where women exercise the vote, such restrictions are unlikely. To a busy woman—and with the decline of domestic service and the increased entry of women into jobs and professions nearly all women will be busy women—good shopping facilities are essential; if she can get served without waiting, see at once a wide range from which to choose, and obtain delivery, she can get back rapidly to her duties; to reduce such facilities would mean that the public spent more time in shopping, and some of what was gained in distribution costs would be lost in other ways.

It is more important to examine the proposition that some who would prefer less service and lower prices are deprived of it. This depends on market imperfection. In a large shopping centre where all kinds of shops are competing it is highly unlikely. There are shops with much service and high prices, and shops with less service and lower prices, and the customers are free to sort themselves out. In 1931 one of America's leading authorities on retailing[1] wrote:—

> "To judge from what is happening in the department store field and from what is happening in the chain store field, it is a fair generalisation that types of distributive enterprise tend to develop through three stages. They start off very largely on a price basis—as chain stores did, for instance they catch the attention of the consumer by distributing merchandise at low prices because of a low overhead. That is the first stage. The next stage is the 'trading up' of the quality of the merchandise handled. We can see chain stores going through that stage to-day. After they have traded up the quality of the merchandise handled, and some of the price advantage has been lost in the process, distributive enterprises develop into a third stage, characterised by competition in services of all kinds, for instance in allowing customers to return merchandise; by high costs of doing business; by largely competitive advertising; and by an increase in the ratio of the fixed investment to the total investment. Department stores to-day are in that stage."

[1] M. P. McNair, "Trends in Large Scale Retailing," *Harvard Business Review*, Vol. X, p. 39.

This would seem to support the view that the public inevitably prefers better services to low prices, but events have not justified this conclusion. The department stores, having reached the third stage, have found themselves losing so much to cheaper rivals (including the "super-market," which was just making its appearance when the passage was written) that they have greatly extended their "bargain basements," and some of them are beginning to urge on the fraternity that delivery and similar services should be charged for separately, so that the stores can retain some of the custom they have been losing to cheaper rivals. The tendency to higher costs, if it exists, is only like an escalator in the sense that as fast as some move up others come in at the bottom; the better simile would be a cycle, since the fourth stage brings lower costs than the third. The fact that the public is free to choose between the cheaper and the more expensive acts as a check preventing too much service from being offered.

The practice of "price lining" may seem to support the opposite view. If prices tend to stick around certain figures, e.g. the elevenpence three-farthingses, increased efficiency would seem to lead not to lower prices but to better quality at the same price. This, however, is an illusion, since this better quality now sold cheaply was formerly sold at some higher price level. Price lining prevents prices from being continuously variable, but it does not prevent them from falling.

However, we cannot apply the same analysis to shops situated not in central but in local markets. There the element of local monopoly means that the customer has not an effective choice between several shops offering different degrees of service. Here there may well be too much service, especially in price-maintained trades, in the sense that some customers are getting more than they want. In non-price-maintained trades the competitive incentive is not so much to offer service as such, if the shop is able to offer different customers different degrees of service, as to offer types of service which involve price discrimination in favour of marginal customers, and which tend therefore to bring the shop nearer to the ideal size. Is this desirable, or does it mean that there is too much service? There are two sides to the argument. Clearly there is too much service in the sense that the marginal customers are getting more than they pay for: they are being subsidised. On the other hand, since the shop will have more customers, shops will be larger, fewer in number, and less costly. It is the old argument for price discrimination in new form.

If the services offered are real, and performed at minimum cost, we can say that there will not be too much service even in imperfect competition, provided that the imperfection is not due to any significant extent to "irrational" elements. The three services which most merit analysis in this light are information, a range of styles, and delivery.

3. Information is a real service. We are all conscious of the wastes involved in competitive advertising, and tend to dismiss all publicity expenditure as wasteful. That it is not necessarily so has long been emphasised in economic literature.[1] For a market to be perfect all the buyers and all the sellers must know what is available and at what prices. Publicity expenditure which serves this purpose is really useful. Advertising is wasteful only when it is unnecessary because buyers and sellers already know the facts, or when it is false or misleading. Now, while much advertising by manufacturers is wasteful for these reasons, this is not usually the case with retailers' advertisements. Actually, only a very small proportion of retailers think it worth while to advertise, this itself being a tribute to the fact that the retail market is not as imperfect as some writers have suggested. And perusal of the advertisements published by retailers will show that while the element of reputation building is not absent, they tend to concentrate on straightforward information about particular lines which are on offer. It seems therefore legitimate to conclude that in retailing such publicity expenditure as there is performs for the most part a valuable service.

We cannot, however, dismiss manufacturers' advertisements as irrelevant to competition in retailing, for they are not. Since there is competition, every retailer is subject to pressures requiring him to stock as wide a range as his customers are likely to want to choose from, and this is indeed a factor on which manufacturers strongly rely in spending money an advertisements. This, therefore, brings us straight to the second problem, the range of goods retailers carry.

4. If in each commodity demand concentrated on one or two styles, economies of scale could be exploited, and prices would be lower. This is the basic case for the "utility" scheme in wartime

[1] E.g. D. Braithwaite, "The Economic Effects of Advertising," *Economic Journal*, March 1928.

England. The first question is therefore why the market itself does not provide for getting these economies. To some extent it does. If a retailer finds that by concentrating all his efforts on a single style he can buy and sell more cheaply, he has an incentive to do so. The Woolworth type of business, which is one of the most successful forms of retailing, is based on this principle; the multiple shops, the department stores, and many independents also work on this basis to a larger extent than is generally recognised by those who advocate that the "utility" scheme should be made permanent. Broadly speaking, standardisation is the basis of large-scale retailing, and one of the reasons why in so many lines of production the retailer dominates the manufacturer.[1] In small-scale retailing, the retailer is not able to give large orders in standard designs, but relies rather on the wholesaler to do this. The wholesaler is to the small retailer as the centralised buying department is to the multiple shop, and if wholesalers were as efficient as the buyers of large-scale retailing, the whole pattern of retailing would be different. When Mr. Schumacher suggests virtually a state monopoly of wholesaling as the simplest way to control both production and distribution,[2] he certainly puts his finger on the central weakness in the distributive chain (whatever the merits of the particular proposal). More efficient wholesaling would deprive the larger retailers of their principal advantage over the small, and would promote greater standardisation of manufactures.

But, whatever the desire of large retail buyers or wholesalers to standardise, two other forces act as a check. One is the creation of "consumer insistence" by manufacturers' advertisements. The case made for such advertising is varied. (*a*) Some useful commodities, e.g. the typewriter, would never have reached the public as quickly without it. This is undoubtedly true; some advertising performs the useful function of information. But this does not apply to all the £80,000,000 to £100,000,000 a year spent on advertising in this country.[3] (*b*) Advertising frequently leads not to an increase but to a reduction in the number of styles, and to savings in production cost, by persuading the public

[1] Nearly all the important groups of multiple shops in this country are manufacturer chains, in contradistinction to the United States.

[2] E. F. Schumacher, "An Essay on State Control," *Agenda*, February 1944.

[3] This is the estimate made by F. P. Bishop, *The Economics of Advertising*, Ch. III.

to concentrate most of its purchases on one or two well-advertised brands. This also is true. But the opposite is also frequently true; and if from the £100,000,000 we must subtract something for the cases where economies of scale are secured, if we are to have the true cost of advertising, we must also add something for the cases where consumer insistence hinders standardisation. Mr. Bishop also advances two other ingenious arguments. (*c*) Advertising makes people want things they cannot afford; it therefore increases the propensity to consume and consequently increases employment. The argument might be impressive if there were not less costly ways of maintaining employment, but as there are, economists cannot be expected to take the argument seriously. (*d*) The Press is always subsidised; where proprietors cannot get revenue from advertisers they sell themselves to political parties or the Government, and in the long run subsidy by advertisement is far more healthy for the public. This may be true. But there are alternatives. If the Government decided to prohibit advertising in the Press, and if the Press must be subsidised, let the Government undertake to pay a subsidy varying only with circulation; e.g. to pay newspaper proprietors 1d. for each copy sold, on the understanding that there shall be no advertisements. Provided the subsidy were open to all on these terms, the Press would remain independent and free to criticise. It would in fact be much freer than it is to-day, when the political and other views of large advertisers have to be borne in mind.

Some reformers are content to try to control the impact of advertising. There are some who advocate strict legal controls, penalising misrepresentation, as the Federal Trade Commission seeks to do in the United States.[1] Others hope that in this country, as in the United States, independent testing agencies will grow up, private- or State-maintained, to inform the consumer of the true merits of different brands. Or even that the Press will allow manufacturers to speak plainly in their advertisements about the inferiority of their rivals' products.[2] To the present writer none of this seems sufficiently fundamental. What is of value in the case for manufacturers' advertisement is that it supplies information, and that it sometimes concentrates demand on a few styles. But

[1] For a discussion of American attitudes and practices, see M. G. Reid, *Consumers and the Market*, Part VI.

[2] Cf. the discussion by A. Plant, "The Distribution of Proprietary Articles," in *Some Modern Business Problems*, ed. Plant.

both these services could be supplied equally by retailers, at less cost, and more impartially, especially if greater steps, voluntary or compulsory, were taken to promote standardisation, and more so still if something like Chamberlin's advocacy of trade mark infringement proved practicable.[1] It should not be on the manufacturer's strident claims that the public has to rely for information. The retailer, usually a better judge of merchandise than the consumer, is better able to decide which brand is worth buying in large quantities, and pushing. In the view of the present writer, while branding should be retained to facilitate identification, manufacturers should be allowed to advertise only in trade journals for circulation amongst wholesalers and retailers, and not in the ordinary Press. In this country we have already banned advertisement from the wireless, will, it is to be hoped, ban it from the sky, and are always talking about banning it from the hoardings. To ban it from the ordinary Press would not be as revolutionary as it sounds, and would also greatly increase the perfection of the market, and reduce waste.

There remains, however, a further check on retailers which prevents them from carrying as small a range of styles as they might otherwise desire. It is the desire of their customers to be able to choose from as wide a range as possible, and indeed, in some cases, notably women's wear, the desire to have something different from what other people will have. In some cases, in a large shopping centre, this does not matter. If there are enough people who prefer cheapness and standardisation to variety, some retailers will be able to concentrate on mass lines, and to secure for such consumers all the economies of scale. But in other trades it may remain the case that if all customers were compelled to accept the standard brand, costs would be lower than they could be without such compulsion. Should such compulsion be exercised? This is clearly a question for the philosopher rather than for the economist.

5. We come, thirdly, to delivery costs. That the several vans of different shops should be delivering in the same road has long seemed a conspicuous source of waste. The waste, however, such as it is, consists not in the fact of delivery, but in the inefficiency with which delivery is organised. If shopkeepers would use, not their own delivery vans but the services offered by public transport contractors, costs would be reduced, as each contractor could

[1] Op. cit., Appendix E.

deliver on behalf of several different shops. Competition between the shops would not be affected by this any more than competition between manufacturers is affected by common use of the railway system or the post office. That they do not use public transport facilities is due principally to the fact that the convenience of delivering for oneself (plus the slight advertisement value of having one's own vans) outweighs what would be saved. This applies equally to pooled delivery services, such as have been enforced in wartime. Moreover, there is reason to believe that the extent of possible savings is grossly exaggerated. The case most quoted in England is milk delivery. Yet an independent investigator, who made a careful survey in Battersea, concluded[1]:—

> "To limit the number of distributors to a maximum of four in any road would cause such a small increase in the sales of these four as to have an almost negligible effect upon costs. To limit the number to two in this area would increase the sales of the two largest distributors by 66 per cent, but one is not convinced that even to limit it to one distributor would materially reduce the large distributor's costs. With the largest distributor only a small portion of the roundsman's time is taken in covering the actual length of road; most is taken in going from door to door, in bringing the customer to the door and engaging her in conversation. In one respect only does it seem probable that giving a particular area completely to one milkman would materially reduce costs, and that is in preventing people from buying from two or more distributors. In this area 11 per cent of the families bought from two or more distributors; in Oxford, Dr. Murray found nearly 15 per cent dealt with two dairymen. This seems a complete waste, and probably its abolition would reduce distributive costs by 10 per cent, say at least 1d. per gallon.

The principal cause of waste in milk distribution, of course, is the fact that the authorities have maintained the minimum retail price at a level allowing a margin so grossly in excess of the costs of large and efficient distributors that an altogether excessive number of firms is able to exist, and also an excessive amount of service.[2]

[1] H. S. Booker, "A Survey of Milk Distribution," *Economica*, February 1939.

[2] The facts are given in two official papers: *Report by the Food Council to the President of the Board of Trade on Costs and Profits of Retail Milk Distribution in Great Britain*, 1937, and *Report of a Committee appointed to axamine Costs of Milk Distribution*, 1940.

6. Finally we must consider the proposition that competition causes service to deteriorate. The shopkeeper, it is said, pressed by competition, and unable to make both ends meet, is driven to reduce the quality of the product and the service, and to misrepresentation and fraud.

To say that the quality will deteriorate is only another way of saying that the price will rise in competition, and we have already examined the conditions in which this is possible. In a really competitive market a shopkeeper may offer less value for the same money, but this will usually be on his way out. If consumers are unable at the time of making a purchase to distinguish between good and bad quality, a retailer may pass off bad as good, but the consumer will discover the difference on using the article, and retailers who do this will lose goodwill and disappear. It remains possible that there are articles whose quality the consumer cannot distinguish even in the course of use, and which he buys relying solely on the retailer's advice, or on high price as a guarantee of quality. Much is made of this by some writers, quoting quality tests which show low correlation between quality and price. The range of articles to which this applies cannot be very great, and would be smaller still if some teaching on how to use the market were supplied to the consumer through the Press, the wireless, films, women's institutes, guilds, unions, and other media for adult education.

That competition may stimulate fraud cannot be questioned. In some countries the primitive view prevails that every act of sale is a battle of wits, and even the strictest laws prohibiting adulteration or controlling weights and measures or the like cannot entirely outlaw sharp practice. Honesty is the best policy only where shopkeepers are competing in honesty; not where they are competing in dishonesty. Fortunately in this country the competitive forces work in the right direction. Especially is this so where the shopkeeper depends on the regular support of a loyal clientele, and cannot afford to lose their goodwill. It is less so where the customer will buy from any seller infrequently—perhaps only once—as in buying durable goods or buying in the course of a journey. Here the shopkeeper may be tempted to follow too literally the Biblical injunction to take in the stranger. If he does this consistently he will probably sooner or later get a bad name and disappear; but he may get away with it, if done infrequently, or may be replaced merely by someone else who follows the same policy. The best safeguard for the public is to learn to shop around making enquiries before committing oneself to the purchase of expensive durable goods.

7. We may now summarise the conclusions of this section as follows:—

(*a*) In large shopping centres it is unlikely that more service is provided than is wanted; competition between different forms of retailing tends to prevent such waste.

(*b*) In smaller suburban centres some customers may receive some service which they would rather not have; others, through price discrimination, receive more service than they are willing to pay for, but the effect of this is to make shops nearer ideal size.

(*c*) All forms of retailing might have lower costs but for manufacturers' advertisements to the public, and but for the public's desire for variety of styles. How far these should be controlled, however, raises issues independent of the degree of competition in retailing.

(*d*) Service may deteriorate as a result of competition, but this is not likely in this country.

III

UNFAIR COMPETITION

1. In this section we are concerned with arguments that certain forms of competition are unfair and distort the distributive process. The practices in question are (*a*) claiming the status of a retailer without fulfilling all the functions; (*b*) "poaching" in one trade by retailers in another (e.g. grocers selling patent medicines); (*c*) direct sales to the public at "wholesale" prices; (*d*) "special" prices to large traders; (*e*) gift coupons and trading stamps; and (*f*) sales to co-operative societies.

2. We can begin with two points common to all these problems. The first is that the retailer's criterion of what is fair is not the economist's. The retailer characterises as unfair almost anything which upsets his expectations, especially if it does so by diverting trade to a different form of retailing. The economist cannot condemn a practice solely on these grounds.

Secondly, underlying most of these cases is the belief that distortion of the "normal" channels of distribution raises costs. Coupon trading is a good example of this. If chocolate manufacturers give away cameras in redemption of coupons, the retailers of cameras claim that this reduces the sales of cameras through existing outlets, and therefore increases costs. All the forms of "unfair competition" listed above would be attacked on this ground, among others.

For this line of argument to be valid, four propositions must be established. First, that the new form of retailing does diminish the business done by the old. Secondly, that when the business done by the old diminishes, the effect is an increase in its costs, i.e. that the number of shops does not diminish *pari passu*, the remaining shops having the same average turnover as before. Thirdly, that the costs of the new form exceed the marginal costs of the old. And fourthly, that the difference in costs is not justified to the consumer by difference in service or other convenience.

It is not always accepted that the new form of retailing diminishes the business done by the old. For example, some supporters of gift coupons claim that the persons who get cameras through this medium would for the most part not be willing to buy cameras, and that having got the cameras they buy films from photographic dealers and have them developed, so that the trade of the ordinary dealer is not reduced but increased. It is always possible in some cases that the extension of a new cheap form of retailing may so expand demand that even the older and more expensive forms of retailing also benefit (just as publication in the "Penguin" series sometimes increases sales of the expensive edition of a book), but there must also be many cases in which the net effect is that the turnover of the older forms is reduced.

If this is the case, the effect will be different in large shopping centres and in small. The large shopping centre being defined, for any given commodity, as one where the number of customers is large enough to support several shops each of optimum size, the effect will be simply that one or more of these shops is put out of business, the others keeping the same size, costs and prices. In the smaller centres, however, the effect is different. Unless the new form replaces the old form altogether, its effect is to detach some customers lying within the area of each shop. This is a reduction in the density of the buying population, which, as we have already seen, results in smaller shops and higher costs.

When this is the case, some customers are benefiting from the new form of competition at the expense of others who pay higher prices. If it were possible for all customers to transfer to the new form, the public would not be harmed by this. For example, if it could be shown that the effect of the spread of co-operatives was not simply to bankrupt some private traders, but rather to raise the prices paid by non-co-operators, no economist would justify restrictions on co-operatives on this ground, since it is open to all customers to join co-operatives. But the case is different with coupon trading; we cannot advise all persons who want cameras to get them through eating chocolates. Where the cheaper form of distribution is not open to all, the problem is more difficult.

The key to the solution is total costs. If the sum of the costs of the total sales under new and old systems is less than it would cost to distribute the same output through the old system exclusively, the new form is justified. This will be the case so long as the costs (prime plus fixed) of the new form of retailing are less than the marginal costs of the old. But the new form will not be justified even if its average cost (and price) is less than the average cost (and price) of the old if it is not also less than the marginal cost of the old. In these conditions a case can be made for prohibiting the new form of retailing. The problem arises only because some retailers who have falling average costs cannot discriminate in favour of the type of customer to whom the new form of retailing makes its restricted appeal. If they could discriminate they could prevent the new form from establishing itself by quoting prices, based on marginal cost, less than the new form could support. As they cannot discriminate, the new form emerges, and social costs are increased.

To complete the argument, it must be shown that the customers who would patronise the new form would gain only to the extent of the lower price; that there is no special convenience or service attached to the new form, such as would justify higher social costs; in a word, that the two forms of retailing are nearly perfect substitutes. Thus the suburban shopkeeper cannot argue that the cheap shops in the centre should be closed even if he could show that their average costs exceed his marginal costs, for shopping in the suburbs is not an exact substitute for shopping in the centre, and many people who live in the suburbs would find it more convenient to shop in the centre even if prices were the same. Nor, to turn the argument round, can the cheaper forms of retailing apply a similar argument for eliminating the more expensive; the two are not exact substitutes. For the argument to be applicable it must be shown that the price is the only practical difference from the consumer's point of view.

It seems a revolutionary conclusion that costs can sometimes be reduced by eliminating the "cheaper" forms of retailing, but as we shall see, the practical significance of the conclusion is very limited. Let us now take each form of "unfair" competition in turn.

3. A number of retail trade associations in this country have agreed with manufacturers or wholesalers that a person should not receive retailer's discounts on his purchases unless he has or is prepared to have a regular shop, open at the usual hours, carrying certain minimum stocks, and perhaps offering after-sales or other usual services. This "fair trading" policy, as it is called, is found, for example, in the bookselling, photographic and motor car trades.[1] This sort of policy is aimed partly at the small part-time retailer, who keeps a parlour shop, partly at "poaching" in one trade by members of another, and partly at direct sales to the public at wholesale prices. It thus covers the first three cases on our list.

It is most unlikely that this restriction could be justified on the ground that the average costs of those excluded exceed the marginal costs of those that remain. The real costs of the man with the parlour shop are low, because his transfer costs and rent are low. So also are the costs of the "poacher," who enters the extra trade usually because he has already under-utilised premises and staff for his own trade. From the point of view of real costs, one can say broadly that the more "poaching" there is the better, since this gives the average shop in each district a larger total trade and lower costs (the limit to "poaching" is set by the advantages of specialisation). And as for sales direct to the public at wholesale prices, this is the case least likely to fit the argument, since the consumer's cost of retailing to himself is zero (though he may have a heavier transport cost). The "fair trading" policy cannot therefore be justified on the ground that sales through these channels are uneconomic.

Neither is the justification usually attempted on these lines. First, in some trades the retailer says, in effect, "To do my

[1] The fullest survey of the facts about each of the principal retail trades is to be found in a series of articles published in the *Manchester Guardian Commercial Weekly* in the second half of 1938 and the first half of 1939. For books and motor cars the relevant dates are June 24, 1938, and October 28, 1938.

K

business properly I must carry a wide range of models, to offer the public a good choice; it is unfair that I should lose trade to someone who does not do the same." It is not unfair that some shops should stock less wide ranges than others; those customers who wish to be able to consult a wide range are free to do so at the more expensive shops, while others may chose the cheaper. But the argument is more subtle. The retailer with the wide range argues that other retailers benefit from his policy; sales in the other shops are larger because there are shops displaying a wide range; in effect the retailer with the wide range is bearing part of the "information" costs of the whole trade. The argument is unimpressive; no retailer is compelled to act in this philanthropic way. If he really thinks that it is possible to thrive off other people's stock carrying, there is nothing to stop him from doing so. This, however, brings us to the second argument. Manufacturers frequently support the fair trading policy because they think that it is in the interest of the trade as a whole that retailers should carry a wide range of stocks; it has advertising value, and causes total sales to be greater. In discriminating against retailers who do not carry this range they are in effect paying a subsidy to others for advertising. The desirability of this rests therefore on the desirability of advertising, and in particular of advertising simply to divert demand from other commodities to the advertised. This can hardly be justified as "information." The public knows of the existence of the particular class of merchandise, and multiplication of the varieties within the class in order specially to catch its eye deserves no special protection. The third argument is more weighty. It is that in certain trades the retailer should have special qualifications, e.g. that in the photographic trade the public would be badly served by retailers who gave bad advice on the respective merits of cameras, or bad after-sales service. Where the commodity is purchased frequently, the public needs no such certificate of qualification; the buyer soon finds out for himself whether his grocer is to be trusted. But where the service is infrequent, some certificate would be useful; e.g. how is the householder to know whether the radio dealer round the corner can really mend a silent wireless set without at the same time doing irremediable and temporarily concealed damage inside? There is something to be said for requiring retailers in certain durable goods trades to pass some test of competence, particularly in the photographic trade, radios, and garages, as is already done for chemists; or at least for an optional test, enabling the public to distinguish between certified and uncertified. But it is a fundamental principle that such tests must be conducted independently, and not by interested parties, such as manufacturers or a retail trade association.

Lastly, sales to the public at "wholesale" prices are opposed on the ground that it is unfair that the retailer should face such competition from the people who sell to him. This is indeed a common complaint, especially in the drapery, sports goods, cycle, meat, jewellery and outfitting trades,[1] and includes protests against sales to members of clubs at special prices. The saying that "only saps pay retail prices" indicates how common is the practice. A manufacturer (or wholesaler) may adopt it in one of two circumstances. It may be that he is able to distribute to the consumer at a cost less than the margin the retailer claims. If the retailer's margin barely covers the retailer's costs, this means that the manufacturer is able to distribute more cheaply by direct methods of sale, and there is no case for preventing him from doing this. But it may be that the margin exceeds retailers' costs, and that the efficient retailers are prevented from reducing their prices by a resale price maintenance scheme. It would certainly be unfair of manufacturers to undersell retailers who are compelled to maintain prices, but the problem this raises is whether prices should be maintained in this way, and this is reserved for the final part of this paper.

Alternatively, the manufacturer may be discriminating, and earning a higher profit on his sales to retailers than on his sales to the public. This is unlikely to be profitable if it results in sales to the public expanding at the expense of sales to retailers—and if it does not the retailer has no ground for complaint, because the manufacturer is then substituting less for more profitable sales, unless the expansion of direct sales is much greater than the decline of sales through retailers.

A similar problem arises in connection with the allegation that large retailers flourish as a result of obtaining special prices. This problem has arisen much more acutely in the United States than

[1] See the relevant articles in the *Manchester Guardian Commercial Weekly* of August 12, 1938, September 16, 1938, September 23, 1938, November 11, 1938, November 18, 1938, and December 2, 1938. For an American discussion see G. B. Tallman, "When Customers buy at Wholesale," *Harvard Business Review*, Vol. XVII, p. 339.

it has in this country, where the multiple shops are much less aggressively competitive than their American counterparts. The rôle of the chain in the American distributive set-up is played in this country in a different way by the co-operative movement. Multiple, chain and co-operative owe a great part of their success to buying more cheaply than the independent shop. That there are real economies reflected in the lower prices they pay is not open to question; the large retailing organisations relieve the manufacturer of many costs he would incur if selling to small shops, and they perform the wholesaling functions for themselves more cheaply and efficiently than the wholesale firms do for the small independent shop. Nevertheless it is possible that they also get discriminatory prices, based on their great bargaining power. In the United States, where the problem has been widely debated and officially investigated, the evidence is not conclusive.[1] Three reactions may be noted. The first is the "classification" of customers in trade categories. Here, trade associations bring pressure to bear on manufacturers to base their discounts on the trade status of the buyer rather than on quantity bought, so that the price charged for any given quantity will be different according to whether the buyer is a consumer, a retailer, or a wholesaler. This policy is clearly uneconomic from the public point of view, since it hampers the development of efficient large-scale retailing, and tends to ossify the structure of distribution and to preserve intermediaries beyond the extent justified by the services they perform. The second possible reaction is legislation against price discrimination; in the United States the Robinson-Patman Act is intended specially to protect the small shopkeeper against discrimination. The object of such legislation is laudable; some discrimination between consumers can be defended, where average costs are falling, if it brings output nearer the ideal (especially if the discrimination is in favour of the lower income groups), but discrimination between retailers and consumers or between different classes of intermediaries is unfair in itself, as well as likely to cause an uneconomic distortion of the distributive structure. To prevent it by legislation is nevertheless a formidable task. Rather more perhaps may be hoped from the third reaction. This is for retailers to co-operate in buying, so as to secure the full economies of scale. The co-operative retail buying movement has spread very rapidly

[1] For a summary of the discussion, see Twentieth Century Fund, op. cit., p. 83.

in the United States, where it has saved the small shopkeeper, but has made little progress in the United Kingdom, where small retailers prefer the protection of "classification" and price maintenance. Co-operative buying is undoubtedly the most desirable reaction from the public point of view.

4. Retailers object to the distribution of goods through gift coupons and trading stamp schemes because it interferes with their trade. No case can be made out on the basis of real costs. The real costs of handling the goods distributed in this way seem to be rather low, as the work is done on a large scale; on the whole, the customer gets good value for his money. More interesting is the argument that the use of coupons and trading stamps increases market imperfection; customers are tied to particular commodities by coupons, or to particular retailers by trading stamps, and may have their attention diverted from the quality of the goods they are buying, or the prices charged, by the illusion of "getting something for nothing." Some countries have indeed prohibited or restricted coupon trading, usually in order to protect retailers, but the Board of Trade Committee which investigated the practice in 1933[1] concluded that the public suffers no harm, and no new evidence or arguments have since emerged to overthrow this conclusion. Coupon trading, however, is just an adjunct to non-price competition between manufacturers and to manufacturers' advertisements; and the trading stamp is primarily the product of resale price maintenance. If these sources of market imperfection were removed most of this form of trading would disappear.

5. The view that the consumers' co-operative movement is in some sense unfair still seems to persist in some quarters in this country, though recent events suggest that it does not turn many votes! To discuss the argument that the principle of co-operative trading is itself unfair would strain the reader's patience. Only special points deserve mention. One is the suggestion that the co-operative surplus is to some extent due to special prices secured from manufacturers by bargaining power. There is no evidence of this. The exhaustive enquiry published in 1938[2] showed that the surplus arises out of the real economies of co-operative trading, especially lower publicity, rent and interest costs, but above all wholesaling economies. A second point is the insistence of some

[1] *Report of the Committee on Gift Coupons and Trading Stamps*, Cmd. 4385 of 1933.

[2] A. M. Carr-Saunders, P. Sargant Florence, and R. Peers, *Consumers' Co-operation in Great Britain*, esp. Chs. XXII and XXIII.

retail trade associations that where resale prices are maintained it would be unfair to allow co-operatives to pay dividends on purchases of these goods, since the dividend would represent a form of undercutting for which private traders would be penalised. There is some substance in the argument, but its final validity depends on the case for price maintenance, which we shall discuss in the last part of this paper. Finally, it is argued that it is unfair that co-operative dividends are not subject to taxation. The literature on the point is large. The opinion of the present writer is that the co-operative surplus is not comparable with the private trader's profit. That profit contains two elements, remuneration for his labour, and interest on his capital. The comparable items in co-operative trading are the salary paid to managers and the interest paid on shares; the surplus partakes of neither of these elements, but is rather a form of voluntary saving. This view is not, however, accepted universally by economists.[1]

6. We may therefore conclude as to unfair competition that the only valid and significant case is that against price discrimination between classes of buyers, in accordance with trade status; price differentiation should be based rather on the cost of handling quantities.

IV

LIMITATIONS ON COMPETITION

1. To many traders what is unfair is not just certain forms of competition, but the very fact of competition itself, whether it be competition in price, service competition, or the entry of new firms into a trade. Several retail trade associations operate schemes to enforce resale price maintenance, and many would like to imitate the newsagents in enforcing a distance limit.

2. It is not surprising that most retailers of convenience goods, operating as they must on a small scale in local markets, favour price maintenance. It seems to offer them protection from the large shops, of optimum size, in the large centres, who, correspondingly, are on the whole against price maintenance. The protection is illusory. In price maintenance the margin is set normally high enough to cover the costs of most retailers in the trade, and, if competition does not whittle profits away in more costly service,

[1] For discussion, see D. H. Macgreggor, "The Taxation of Co-operative Dividend," *Economic Journal*, March 1933, and C. R. Fay, "Co-operators and the State," ibid., September 1933.

either more retailers are attracted or "poaching" spreads; the number of outlets increases, and turnover per outlet falls; costs per unit of sales rise; pressure is applied for a still higher margin; this attracts still more outlets; and the cycle continues. From the point of view of the retailer, even the highest margin will barely cover his costs, because the number of outlets, and turnover per outlet, will be adjusted to whatever the margin may be. So long, therefore, as there is free entry into a trade, directly or by "poaching," price maintenance is no protection from competition; it is merely a costly and wasteful burden on the public. The drug trade is the stock example of what happens. Before price maintenance was adopted, the number of outlets for patent medicines more or less equalled the number of chemists; to-day, because of the attractive margins, other shops have taken up patent medicines, and outnumber the chemists in this trade by ten to one. Similarly in the tobacco trade there are 23 "poachers" to every one tobacconist, and in the confectionery trade five "poachers" to every "legitimate" confectioner. The chemists have now been driven to bringing organised pressure to bear on manufacturers to restrict the sale of patent medicines to qualified chemists.

Surprise has been expressed that manufacturers should support price maintenance, instead of wishing their goods to be retailed as cheaply as possible. Fear of the repercussions of the "loss leader" has some significance, but only in relation to the more fundamental explanation. The fact is that in many classes of trade sales depend more on there being many outlets than on low prices. This is the reason why the State has for centuries restricted the number of public-houses, and it applies with equal force to confectionery, newspapers, books or cigarettes. Moreover, within any of these classes of trade, it may be of greater advantage to a manufacturer to have his brand available in every shop, than to have it available at a low price. These advertising considerations make manufacturers willing to fix margins high enough to encourage even the least efficient and smallest retailers to stock the brand, and to take the elaborate steps necessary to avoid a differentially low price level or loss leaders in the large central markets which would draw trade from the smaller shops and discourage them from stocking the brand.[1] For shopping goods, which are sold mostly in

[1] In a few cases of price maintenance the manufacturer of a widely advertised brand puts a standard price on the article which allows the retailer only a very small margin. Here the manufacturer is anxious that it be sold as

large shopping centres where sales depend on keen prices rather than on wide stocking, resale prices are never likely to be fixed.

From the public's point of view resale price maintenance is doubly condemned (*a*) because it causes the number of shops and the amount of service to be excessive and prices to be too high; and (*b*) because manufacturers promote it for advertising reasons. And the fact that it does not really in the long run shelter the shopkeeper from competition simply removes any ground for sympathy, and makes the system all the more absurd. It is hardly necessary to consider two arguments which are sometimes advanced; that the public gains from price maintenance because the system tends to enforce a maximum price as well as a minimum, so that the customer cannot be defrauded; or that the public would not have "confidence" in a commodity found selling in different shops at different prices. If it is maximum prices that benefit the public, then fix not minimum but maximum prices; and what happens to public confidence in that wide range of commodities whose retail prices are not fixed?

The case against price maintenance is beyond doubt. It is one of the major sources of waste in distribution, and the public would benefit greatly if it and the boycotts, stop lists, discrimination against co-operative societies, and other paraphernalia by which the system is enforced were made illegal.

3. The licensing of shops, however, raises more difficult problems. We have seen that, even if prices are not maintained, the number of suburban shops may be excessive. A prima facie case for restriction is therefore established.

Any such proposal, however, has to meet a formidable array of objections. First, many people are anxious to maintain an open door in retailing as a refuge for the small man from "wage slavery" into "independence." In many quarters the small trader is regarded as the pillar of society, a view which cannot always survive closer examination of his outlook and prejudices. But, whatever the merits of the small trader, it is certainly not kind to encourage large numbers of small men to enter into retailing. By and large,

cheaply as possible; he hopes that his advertising will compel most retailers to stock it, and knows that more would stock it if the margin were wider, but nevertheless prefers a lower price to wider stocking. His standard price is really a *maximum* price. This is quite a different case from the normal case where it is a *minimum* price that is being enforced. Maintenance of maximum prices is not contrary to the public interest; it is maintenance of minimum prices that causes waste.

the costs of small shopkeeping are high, and the rewards are correspondingly low, frequently much less than wage employment would yield. Neither is it a profession for the unskilled; the ignorance of small retailers is one of the principal reasons for their high rate of bankruptcy. In the United States it has been estimated that half the retail shops opened in any year fail within twelve months, and that the average life of a shop is only five years.[1] Similar information is not available for this country; thanks to price maintenance and a less aggressive atmosphere of competition the mortality rate is probably lower, but it is without doubt very high; to go into retailing is one of the easiest ways of losing the savings of a lifetime. Those who wish to keep retailing open specially to attract the small man seem therefore to be even more dangerous to the small man than they may be to the public.

It is more important to consider whether restricting the number of shops really would benefit the public. At present there is some competition in prices and in service. Restriction of entry might lead merely to an increase in shopkeepers' profits and prices, and to a decline in the quality of the service. The war has taught us how quickly the quality of the service deteriorates in retailing when once the spur of competition is removed, and many members of the public would think that some excess in the number of shops is a small price to pay in order to secure the benefits of competition.

The structure of the distributive trades would also be gravely affected by restriction of entry. For the past century the efficiency of retailing has been improving largely through the expansion of large-scale retailing—co-ops, multiples and department stores—relatively to small-scale retailing. Large-scale retailing is able to operate on margins of anything between 30 per cent and 50 per cent less than those required by small retailers. The small retailer has, indeed, his place in the industry, especially in the sale of shopping goods, where standardisation is not important, and in the sale of convenience goods in small shopping centres, and especially in building up a clientele on the basis of a high quality of personal service. This place would be even larger than it is if the efficiency of small shopkeepers could be improved, e.g. by better training facilities. A woeful ignorance of business principles is one of the chief causes of the wastefulness of small shopkeeping and the high mortality rate. For example, most small shopkeepers

[1] Temporary National Economic Committee, Monograph No. 17, *Problems of Small Businesses*, esp. Ch. II.

try to carry too wide a range of styles, brands, etc., deal with too many wholesalers and manufacturers, and offer too much service, for the limited turnover which they can secure. And the small man would be still more certain of his place if he would turn his eyes from the illusory safety of price maintenance and "classification" to the possibilities of standardisation and co-operative buying, thus challenging the large-scale retailer on his own ground. There is undoubtedly room for small-scale retailing. But what case is there for measures which extend it an artificial protection by preventing the expansion of large-scale retailing, which has been the spearhead of improved efficiency in distribution? The writer is as sensitive as any, and more sensitive than most, to the values of a society in which economic power is widely dispersed through the predominance of small business. But he is highly sensitive, too, to the persistence of poverty, and the need to increase wealth by utilising as far as possible the more productive types of enterprise. To bolster up small-scale retailing beyond its proper place in the distributive structure is to condemn an important part of our economy to waste and inefficiency. It should not be forgotten that one person in seven is engaged in the distributive trades.

More probably, this issue would not arise. For restriction of entry would give the multiples an incentive to buy up more and more small shops—small shopkeeping might not be preserved, but on the contrary might disappear. Nor would the public benefit; the small retailer, protected by his licence, would refuse to sell except for a handsome price, which the multiple organisation would be willing to pay, relying on the licence, and the net effect would be to raise prices against the public. Not only the multiples would play this game, but also the manufacturer. The public-house is a standing example of the incentive the licensing of retail outlets gives to manufacturers to integrate forward and buy up the outlets for monopolistic purposes. Probably the principal result of restricting entry into retailing would be that multiples and manufacturers would buy up the shops, that monopoly would be greatly increased in manufacturing, and that the public would lose more in higher prices and reduced service than it loses from freedom of entry. Though there are too many shops if there is freedom of entry, merely to restrict freedom of entry would probably make the public poorer than before.

4. What causes waste in retailing is not competition but the fact that price competition is not sufficiently effective, especially

in the convenience goods and suburban trades. This is due in the first instance to resale price maintenance, the abolition of which would enable the more efficient retailers to expand and to reduce prices to the consumer, and would reduce the number of shops, releasing resources for other urgent purposes.

But the number of shops might still be too large, and the average shop too small, even if price maintenance were abolished. Fig. I shows the position. In the absence of price competition the average shop will have a size well to the left of N (in terms of Fig. III it will be at K); price competition will increase the size to N; but the ideal size is given by M. Elasticity of demand will bring the competitive size nearer M, but not necessarily right up to it. Theoretically, the simple way to achieve the right number and size of shops is to fix a maximum gross margin QM, whereupon the number of shops will contract, and average size increase to M. But there is nothing simple about this solution in practice. There is in reality no average shop; different gross margins are appropriate in different conditions of population density and different degrees of service. The same margin cannot be fixed for every retailer. Neither is there an average commodity; even within a single class of merchandise different articles need different margins, according to the time it takes to handle them, their size, rate of turnover, and so on. It is true that margins have been elaborately controlled during the war, but no one can pretend that the hit or miss methods used in wartime would be very suitable for permanent peacetime regulation.

It may be suggested that the simplest way out is to fix a maximum margin only for one standard and popular type within each class of merchandise, in the expectation that the margins on all other types will have to correspond. This might work so long as retailers could not escape selling the selected brand. If "utility" production is continued, this can be tried, the Government allowing such low margins that only the appropriate number of shops remains in business. The retailers may be expected to fight the attempt by starting a whispering campaign against the "utility" articles, and persuading consumers to buy only uncontrolled articles. The Government would win so long as it retained power to withhold labour and raw materials from non-"utility" production, but as soon as non-"utility" lines could be freely produced, the limited price control would lose much of its effectiveness.

There is one other theoretical alternative to price fixing, which is equally impracticable, i.e. to give the co-operative societies a monopoly of retailing, or at least a monopoly of retailing convenience goods, since it is in these rather than shopping goods that there is excess capacity. If they had a monopoly of retailing the societies would have no incentive to establish more or less than the right number of shops. The proposal is specially attractive because, whatever their shortcomings in handling shopping goods, the co-operative societies are unquestionably the cheapest distributors of convenience goods in this country, and they would be cheaper still if certain managerial and structural reforms could be effected.[1] But it is politically quite impracticable to establish any such monopoly.

5. There is in fact no practicable solution to the problem of "excess capacity" in retailing, in the sense of reducing the gap between the competitive number and the ideal number of shops. This, however, need not daunt us, for two reasons. First because "excess capacity" exists only where elasticity of demand is insufficient to bridge the gap, on which we have no information. And secondly because, in either case, the actual number is so far in excess of the competitive number that if we could get it down to the competitive level we should have made notable progress. The way to this level is simply to make price maintenance illegal. This is the most urgent reform needed in retailing; its repercussions would revolutionise the distributive structure.

Democrats may rejoice that one result would be a rapid expansion of the consumers' co-operative movement in many trades for which it is specially suited. Here is a movement to which more than half the families in the country belong. Freed from the trammels of price maintenance, and inspired with a sense of its mission, this movement could set prices all along the line at levels which would drive waste out of distribution. It is the pride of the movement that it protected the consumer in the days when adulteration, short weight and fraud were the bugbear of retailing. To protect him from waste would add another page to an already noble history.

[1] For a discussion of needed reforms see Carr-Saunders and others, op. cit., especially Part IV.

[5]

CHAPTER I

FIXED COSTS

This chapter is concerned with the case where similar services are supplied by two different industries, one or both of which has a high ratio of fixed to variable expenses. Gas and electricity and road and rail transport are the outstanding examples, and special reference will be made to them. It has always seemed difficult to fit this type of case into the general rule that price should equal marginal cost because it has never been clear what marginal cost means in such contexts. The first problem is therefore to define the line between marginal and fixed costs.

I

THE ANATOMY OF FIXED COSTS

1. In welfare economics the cost of something is the value to other producers of the resources which are used to produce it; cost is measured by computing what expenses would be saved if production were curtailed and resources released for use elsewhere. This cost differs from cost in the business or accounting sense, which is simply the sum expended on production, because there are expenses which the business man cannot escape by curtailing his output—e.g. the sum invested in specific equipment which is no longer required. The economist's costs are those which can be escaped; fixed costs are those which cannot: escapability is the essence of the distinction. It is not, however, a simple distinction, because some costs are escapable in some senses but not in others, and we must spend a little time on it.

Fixed or inescapable costs fall into four categories:

(*a*) some are inescapable in the short run but not in the long run;
(*b*) some are joint costs, and inescapable only in that sense;
(*c*) some are inescapable for small but not for large changes of output; and
(*d*) some are inescapable in all senses.

2. An entrepreneur makes commitments in relation to the level of output which he expects, and once he has committed himself

to expenses appropriate to that level, he finds that some of his commitments cannot be altered rapidly even if output contracts permanently to a lower level. Some commitments can be escaped at once, but others take time. His commitments are of two classes; commitments under contracts to hire, and commitments by purchase, by investment in construction, or by other methods of capital creation.

Commitments under hiring contracts are the easier class. All such contracts, whether for manual labour, for administrative staff, for machinery, buildings, or for other services, have a time limit. The contract may be escapable at once, because the time limit is short, or because there is provision for discharging it at short notice or because obligations under it (e.g. a lease) can be transferred. The cost immediately escapable may not be as great as that which can be escaped ultimately, when the contract expires, if there is some penalty for immediate discharge, or some loss on transferring the obligations; and the contract may be continued temporarily. But sooner or later the contract expires, and with that comes complete escape.

Investments in assets are more complicated. With these, too, immediate escape is often possible, and its neglect has been one of the commoner errors in economic discussion. The immediately escapable cost is user cost.[1] This may not be as great as that

[1] This is a difficult concept. User cost for any year (or unit of output) can be computed as follows.

(i) The asset can be sold, and the present value of its expected yields in each future year of life, plus its scrap value (also discounted), must exceed the price for which it can be sold. Assume n years of working life; if life is determined by obsolescence, the relevant yields are those of the first n years, but if it is determined by wear and tear, the relevant yields are those of the n most profitable years (after discounting). The corollary is that the yield expected this year must equal at least the difference between the price and the expected yield of the remaining $(n - 1)$ years of working life plus scrap value, if this difference is positive. This is the minimum value of this year's user cost. If the price is not greater than the sum expected in the other $(n - 1)$ years, this minimum user cost is zero.

(ii) This year's yield must also exceed the difference between the price that could be obtained for the asset this year and next year's price if used this year. If this year's expected yield exceeds the sum stipulated in (i) but not this sum, the time pattern of yields in outside uses is different from the time pattern of yields here, and the asset should be used elsewhere this year and returned to use here next year (but this assumes physical wear and tear this year to be the same in either use).

(iii) This year's yield must also exceed the expected yield from any future

which can be escaped when the asset expires and its replacement falls due. Thus hiring contracts and assets are in the same category. Nearly all commitments are immediately escapable, but the cost escapable now may not be as great as that which can be escaped ultimately when the commitment has expired and a new commitment is necessary if production is to continue. Assets differ from hiring contracts only in that a small percentage of assets are of infinite durability, and with these there is only an immediately escapable cost to consider.[1]

The distinction between short-run and long-run cost corresponds to this distinction between immediately and ultimately escapable cost. In practice, however, neither of these distinctions is as simple as is currently implied. Some commitments expire at once, some next week, some next month, some next year, and so on. Escapable cost is not just short-run and long-run, immediate and ultimate. It varies for as far ahead as you care to look. Furthermore, it does not vary continuously with time. If commitments of equal cost significance expired in constant procession, one in each month, and if renewal could then be put on to a month-to-month basis, short-term cost would rise month by month steadily nearer to long-term cost, until all commitments were on a monthly basis. But none of these conditions is fulfilled. The dates at which commitments expire have no regular pattern, and the sums involved vary widely, so that the fluctuations in short-run cost are arbitrary accidents. Then, as each commitment falls due for renewal, say for x years, all those due to expire during those x years have to be considered, since if any of those will not pay and

year which is excluded from use by this year's use. If working life is determined by obsolescence, the value of this is zero. If it is determined by wear and tear, this year must be one of the n most profitable; user cost is the yield of the $(n + 1)$th most profitable year. (This assumes that in its effect on the life of the machine use in any one year is a perfect substitute for use in any other. The problem is more complicated but not insoluble if this is not so.)

This gives us three minimum values for user cost. The relevant one is whichever is the largest. User cost can be zero if obsolescence determines life, if the value in outside uses is small relatively to value here, and if the value in outside uses does not diminish. It cannot be zero if life is determined by wear and tear, for it must then equal at least the yield of the $(n + 1)$th year.

[1] The easier escape from hiring contracts may also be illusory. From the point of view of social cost it is irrelevant whether an asset is hired or purchased; what matters is whether it is specific or not. E.g. if specific labour is dismissed the entrepreneur escapes a private cost, its wage, but if the labour simply becomes unemployed, there is no social saving.

will be discontinued, this may not pay either. The expiry of a single commitment may therefore bring large numbers under review and cause a great jump in immediately escapable cost. And, as each commitment is renewed, short-run cost, which had risen high to include renewal cost, now sinks again to the level of the temporarily inescapable. There is no such quantity as "the marginal cost" of output; there is not even a simple choice between two quantities, short- and long-run cost; there is a large variety of costs to choose from, depending merely on how far ahead you choose to look, and this collection of costs itself varies from day to day, as current commitments alter.

3. Some costs are inescapable only in the sense that they are joint costs. For example, the traffic from A to B may be permanently in excess of the traffic from B to A, and some vehicles will always be returning empty. The marginal cost of using those vehicles is small, and the inescapable cost is heavy. If, however, there were no traffic from A to B, the cost of running from B to A would be easily escapable, and it is inescapable only because it is a joint cost with the cost of running to B. Where there are joint costs neither can be considered escapable or inescapable by itself. Together, the joint cost is escapable; separately, the cost of each part has to be found by difference, by subtracting the yield of the others from the total cost.

Depreciation is one of the most important cases of a joint cost inescapable only in this sense. When an entrepreneur is considering adding extra equipment to his undertaking, he knows that it may yield output in each year of its life, but he is unable to allocate a cost to the output of any one year except by considering the yields of other years. Each year's use, assuming the investment made, has a user cost, but the sum of these user costs may be much less than the cost of the asset, and the difference cannot be allocated to each year, but must be recouped from surpluses. If the industry were expected to be in stationary equilibrium, the amortisation attributable to each year would be easily calculable. Since there is stationary equilibrium, the amount of the surplus in each year is the same, and it must be a sum which, deducting interest on the cost of the equipment, will, when invested yearly at compound interest, yield at the end of the life of the equipment a sum equal to its cost less scrap value. But where conditions are expected to fluctuate, so will the surplus. It may be that the equipment can be kept fully occupied throughout its life, but only by charging different prices at different times, high when demand is strong, and low while it is weak, so that the surplus will sometimes be great and sometimes be small; but again it must be expected that the sum of these surpluses, at the appropriate rate of interest, will equal the cost. It may even be that in some periods no price that would yield any surplus is low enough to keep demand at the level that will occupy the equipment; then the installation of the equipment is justified only if it is expected that the surpluses when demand is strong will be adequate when summed to cover the entire cost. This is only another way of saying that where fluctuations in output are expected, the cost of the equipment, looking ahead before investment is made, is attributable only to periods when it is fully occupied—the entire cost is chargeable to the peaks in proportions depending on what charge keeps the peaks fully occupied.[1]

The net result is that, before any commitment is made, it may be foreseen that there will be successive periods of full and excess capacity. In periods of excess capacity marginal output will give rise to smaller escapable costs than in periods of full capacity,[1] but cost at such periods will be inescapable only in the sense of being a joint cost with other periods.

4. The third category of inescapable commitments consists of those where an expense does not vary with output because it is indivisible. Indivisibility need not be identified with some concrete piece of equipment; it may merely be that a certain expense varies with output, but in smaller proportion. The indivisible element is the difference between the total expense and the product of quantity-of-output times marginal cost, and will itself vary with output if marginal cost is not constant.

Indivisible expenses and fixed costs are frequently taken as synonymous, but they are not. Fixed costs are those which are inescapable, and indivisible costs may be immediately escapable. A railway can decide to run more or fewer carriages, or trains, or to keep open more or fewer stations, or, taking the matter to its

[1] This assumes that life is determined by obsolescence, and that off-peak user cost is zero. If life is determined by obsolescence, off-peak user cost may be zero. If it is determined by wear and tear, off-peak use is at the expense of later peak use, and off-peak use now therefore has the same user cost as peak use now, and there is no difference between peak and off-peak escapable cost. The problems that arise from regular fluctuations in demand are more fully discussed in Chapter II

logical conclusion, to close down altogether. Whatever the indivisible unit, if the expenses attributable to it are escapable, they must be covered if the unit is to be maintained. Confusion on this point has been due to a tacit acceptance of the unit of product as being the unit on which the calculation of economic cost must be based. But there is no greater significance attaching to the passenger in transport than there is to one or other of the indivisible units required for his conveyance, and if the cost of any unit is escapable it must be covered, even though the marginal cost of the product is zero. Marginal cost is not the only real social cost, and indivisible cost is not necessarily fixed.[1]

5. When we say that some costs are inescapable in all senses, we naturally refer to commitments which have already been made, since all costs are escapable *ex-ante*. If in any given situation where commitments have been made we include in escapable costs, long-run escapable and not merely short-run costs, escapable joint costs, and escapable indivisible costs, we are left with two classes of inescapable costs, which constitute the difference between cost to the economist and cost in the accounting sense.

[1] A good deal of the current analysis of monopoly makes nonsense of itself because it fails to recognise this. All costs but marginal costs are said to be relevant only in the long run, whereas indivisible costs are relevant to even the most short-run analysis to the same extent as divisible ones, i.e. to the extent to which they are immediately escapable. Entrepreneurs regard most of their overhead costs as escapable indivisible expenses, and refuse to produce unless they are covered. Economists who think that only marginal costs should count regard this obstinacy with a mixture of surprise, pain and contempt, and are driven to explain it away by calculating "the degree of monopoly power." No fruitful analysis of monopoly can be based on marginal cost only.

In this respect public utility engineers are well ahead of most economists who write on the theory of costs. The latter usually treat costs as being a function of output only. The former divide costs into those which vary with output, demand related standing costs, customer costs, and the residue. The first is generally known as prime cost. The concept of demand related costs is another way of expressing the fact that cost cannot be computed unless we know whether the supply will be taken at the peak or not, and actually the economist's marginal cost can be adapted to take care of this (though it usually is not). Customer costs are indivisible costs varying with the number of customers and not with the amount each takes, e.g. the cost of wiring houses. The residue is the difference between the total and the other three. The simple view of cost as a function of quantity of output only, which elevates marginal cost to the rank of being the only social cost that matters, originates from theories in which all factors of production are assumed to be divisible and non-specific; its transfer to fields where there is a high ratio of fixed costs is untenable.

First, we have included in long-run escapable costs all assets which have to be renewed. That leaves us with assets which do not have to be renewed. There are two classes of these, permanent assets and assets which are not renewed only because demand does not justify renewal. Taking permanent assets first, the analysis depends on whether the amount of these varies with output, i.e. they are divisible (e.g. the amount of land required for rail or road tracks depends on the amount of traffic) or whether they are indivisible (e.g. the legal expenses of floating a company). (*a*) The use of permanent indivisible assets gives rise to no social cost, unless these assets are useful in some other industry; the difference between the price that they would fetch and their original cost is a cost in the accounting but not in the economic sense. (*b*) Whether the use of divisible permanent assets gives rise to social cost, over and above sale value in other uses, depends on whether the undertaking is working to capacity or not. For example, if it is, and an increase in traffic requires the purchase of further land, the cost of land varies with traffic and enters into marginal cost, but if the undertaking is working below capacity, and existing tracks can take further traffic, the cost of land does not enter into marginal cost, and is an accounting but not a social cost (apart from its value in other uses). (*c*) Then there are assets which are not permanent by nature, but which are not being renewed because demand has contracted. E.g. if demand has contracted 25 per cent, the renewable 75 per cent enters into long-run escapable cost, but the other 25 per cent does not, and is an accounting but not a social cost.

The other main source of difference is that accountants are concerned with original cost, but economists with replacement cost. When the latter is below the former, escapable cost is less than original cost. The financial difficulties of this will be referred to in the next section.

II

COST AND PRICE

1. It has now become an axiom that if the price mechanism is accurately to allocate resources, price must equal marginal cost, and recent writers have said even that this rule simplifies the administration of State undertakings since it is virtually the only instruction that need be given to managers to determine output.

We are now in a position to grapple with some of its hidden difficulties.

They are four, corresponding to the categories of fixed cost:

(*a*) the fact that there is a whole range of marginal costs, depending on how far ahead one looks;
(*b*) the fact that marginal cost may fluctuate from one moment to the next;
(*c*) the fact that indivisible escapable costs must be covered; and
(*d*) the fact that the accounting and the economic cost are different.

2. If an industry is working at full capacity the immediately and the ultimately escapable marginal costs coincide. But if there is excess capacity, the immediately escapable may be less than what is ultimately escapable as contracts or assets expire, and looking ahead, there is a whole range of marginal costs from which to choose.

In perfect competition price equals the immediately escapable marginal cost and fluctuates with it. There is one exception. It may be that at a price adequate to cover renewals demand would not be sufficient to occupy all the equipment, but that at a price equal only to immediately escapable cost it would occupy more equipment than is in existence. This is the familiar case where short-run marginal cost rises vertically as full capacity is reached. In this case price will exceed short-run marginal cost, but be less than long-run marginal cost, to an extent depending on elasticity of demand.

The case for basing price in conditions of excess capacity on the immediately escapable cost is that the fullest use is thereby made of existing resources. Suppose, for example, that demand contracts in an industry where the equipment is specific but ultimately renewable. Sooner or later the workable equipment will contract and an equilibrium price be established adequate to cover renewals. But if the price is maintained at that level in the immediate present, while there is excess capacity, some demands which would willingly have paid immediate marginal cost may be excluded at a price equal to long-run marginal cost, and specific equipment is less utilised than it ought to be—a loss of output which continues as long as the equipment lasts, but no longer.

Against this advantage must be set a disadvantage. If the price is fixed at immediate marginal cost so long as the excess capacity lasts, the industry makes a loss not only on the excess capacity, but on all the specific equipment used, including that proportion which is permanently needed, and which must be renewed. There may only, from the long-run point of view, be 10 per cent excess capacity, but the industry will be unable to earn full amortisation quotas even on the 90 per cent which has to be renewed. This transfer of income to the consumer is a gift which he never expected, to which he has no particular right, and which he will receive only temporarily while the excess capacity lasts. The consequences of this are more serious than a mere transfer of income from investor to consumer, for an industry which does not earn its amortisation quotas may have difficulty in renewing the 90 per cent capacity that ought to be renewed, partly because in these days internal reserves are so large a part of the total new investment, partly because, since it has been making losses for some time people will be reluctant to invest in it even though there is a case for a 90 per cent reinvestment, and partly because it is particularly difficult to obtain monies for new investment when an equal or prior claim on all returns must go to existing share and debenture holders who require satisfaction in respect of investments that still have not paid—a difficulty escapable only if a firm is reconstructed every time such circumstances occur.

If price were based not on short-run but on long-run marginal cost, no demands would be served that could not in the long run be maintained, but full amortisation would be earned on all assets which must be renewed, and only to the extent that renewal is needed. Where there are no close substitutes for the product this would probably make little difference to the output of the industry,[1] since demands are not as elastic in the short run as we like to think. Where two similar industries are competing, e.g. road and rail, it will make little difference to their joint output, but the distribution of that output between them may be significantly affected. For example, suppose a long-run trend in favour of road transport at the expense of rail transport. Then if rail charges are based always on long-run cost, road transport will be larger than it would be if rail charges were based on short-run cost, and it will always be larger than it ought strictly to be. But the difference is

[1] Apart from income effects; consumers will not have made a windfall gain from investors, and to the extent to which their expenditure patterns are different, outputs of the industries on which they would spend are affected. There will also be short-run differences in the propensity to consume.

B

only one of time; at any moment the situation will be in long-run (moving) equilibrium instead of still on the move towards it—adjustment is speeded up, but is faster than it should be. It is not obvious that this disadvantage is greater than the disadvantage of having an industry unable to earn amortisation quotas which it will require.

More serious might be the repercussions on the process of eliminating excess capacity. If price equals only immediately escapable cost, the loss of amortisation quotas is a powerful eliminator of redundant firms, though experience shows that the agony may be very long-drawn-out, and that it is not always the right firms that disappear. If price is to be kept at the level of long-run cost the marginal firms are not so easily dislodged, and some scheme for the elimination of the less efficient may have to be applied unless the differences in efficiency are marked. The technical difficulties and the cost of applying such a scheme have to be considered, and may well be decisive in industries where competition on the basis of short-run costs would be fairly rapidly effective. But where we are considering public utilities or State enterprises operated as monopolies, this kind of consideration is hardly relevant, since it is not whole firms that have to be eliminated but parts of a single firm. In such cases the earning of needed amortisation quotas seems the decisive issue.

3. The second difficulty is that where there are fluctuations in demand or supply there will be fluctuations in price. This will be so if price is equal to immediately escapable cost, because that necessarily alters with the passage of time. But it will also be so even in cases where there is no permanent excess capacity, but only periods of temporary excess capacity which are foreseen before the commitment is made, and which are therefore part of the long-run equilibrium situation.

Regular price fluctuations are not much of a problem. It is not always technically possible to arrange for such fluctuations; e.g. in electricity this requires a meter which records the amount consumed in each part of each day of the year, and such meters were not invented until fairly late in the history of the industry. Neither is it always convenient that the price fluctuations should follow changes in demand too closely. Consider, for example, the situation in suburban passenger transport. At the peak hour of the morning the 'bus travels into the city packed; since it has to return to its depot, the marginal cost of taking persons out of the city is negligible, and if price is to be based on marginal cost they should travel practically for nothing. As the peak passes, however, the balance of inward and outward passengers begins to be readjusted; gradually the fare to the city should fall, and the fare from the city rise; and in the evening the fare out should cover nearly all costs, and the fare in be virtually zero. Fares which followed the changes in the balance of traffics too closely would be a nuisance, and most people would prefer a limited number of changes (if any) which only broadly reflected the changing costs. Allowing for these difficulties, regular and foreseeable fluctuations in price are not much of a problem.

Irregular and unforeseeable fluctuations are, however, a nuisance. Such fluctuations are not so great a nuisance in respect of commodities or services where an organised market can be built up, such as cotton or tramp shipping, especially if the organisation can include a futures market, but they are certainly a nuisance in other fields. This is so partly because in an uncertain world one likes to have as many certainties as possible. But it is also partly because, where prices fluctuate the consumer tends to suspect discrimination, and to feel that the price may have risen at the moment he arrives not solely because the impersonal supply and demand factors have changed, but rather because he personally is not as favoured a buyer as someone else. This is one of the reasons why uniform prices have been enforced by the law on railways and taxicabs, and by custom on department stores, hotels, professional men, and in many other fields.

Here again we have to compare the advantage of securing fullest hour-by-hour utilisation of resources with other disadvantages. Foreseeable regular changes in price are fully allowable, but the case for evening out the irregular fluctuations seems to be overwhelming, at least in public utility industries.

4. The third difficulty in equating price to marginal cost is that it leaves uncovered escapable indivisible expenses which ought to be covered if the retention of these resources by the consumers of this commodity is to be justified. Where there are escapable indivisible expenses the rule that price must equal marginal cost is inadequate; the rule should be rather that price must be not less than marginal cost, and there must be enough surplus to cover escapable indivisible expenses. This is obvious enough if the indivisible cost is a "customer cost," incurred for one customer only, e.g. the cost of connecting his house for electricity, which does not

vary with the amount consumed. But it applies equally if the indivisible cost benefits a number of consumers, e.g. the laying of a main for the whole street, or all the consumers. The method of charging which most nearly secures the correct allocation of resources is the two-part tariff, with the variable charge equal to divisible marginal cost, and the fixed charge taking from each consumer the customer cost plus, as contribution to the indivisible expenses, such amount as he can afford to pay. The second nearest approach is price discrimination. Charging the same price to all buyers comes, from this point of view, a poor third.

These methods of charging recover the indivisible cost from consumers' surplus. There may also be a producers' surplus from which it might be recovered. A producers' surplus will exist if marginal cost is rising, and it is important to distinguish different types of surplus. Marginal cost may be rising because applying more of the variable to the indivisible factors yields diminishing returns; or it may be rising because the price of the variable factors rises as more is purchased. In the former case the producers' surplus accrues to the undertaking. As we defined an indivisible cost not as the cost of an indivisible factor, but as the difference between the total expense and the product of quantity-of-output times marginal cost, we have already deducted this surplus in order to arrive at the indivisible cost, and therefore no contribution is available from this type of producers' surplus. If marginal cost rises so fast as to equal or exceed average cost, there will be no indivisible cost in this sense, though there may be indivisible factors. If marginal cost is rising because some variable factor is in inelastic supply, the surplus will be accruing to the undertaking if the variable factor is an asset of which it is purchasing or hiring successive units at rising prices; but it will be accruing to the owners of the factors in the hiring or purchase of which no discrimination is possible. All surpluses accruing to the undertaking are already accounted for. The only producers' surpluses available for consideration are therefore those which accrue to outside owners.[1] Another producers' surplus of this kind may exist even if the factor is not in inelastic supply, if the price that must be paid for it exceeds what it could earn in other industries, e.g. because minimum wages are fixed by trade unions—the railways used to com-

[1] In this case marginal private cost will exceed marginal social cost, which is based on the price of the factors and not on their marginal cost to the undertaking. It is social cost which is relevant.

plain strongly because their wages were more closely regulated than wages in road transport.

Such producers' surpluses, together with what is available from consumers' surplus, ought certainly to be included in the calculation to decide whether the continued incurring of escapable indivisible costs is justified or not. It is unlikely that they can be made available to the undertaking, but whether they are available or not they ought to be included in the calculation, and precision requires that we should say, not that the sum available from consumers' surplus must cover the indivisible cost, but that that sum must cover the indivisible cost less producers' surpluses accruing to outside factors.

The principle underlying the two-part tariff and simple price discrimination is that those who cannot escape must make the largest contribution to indivisible cost, and that those to whom the commodity does not matter much may escape. The man who has to cross Dupuit's bridge to see his dying father is mulcted thoroughly; the man who wishes only to see the scenery on the other side gets off lightly. The public's attitude to price discrimination is not capable of rational exposition. Broadly speaking, it dislikes discrimination, but special cases are tolerated. Discrimination according to income is accepted from doctors, the government or electricity undertakings, and used to be accepted from shopkeepers, but would now probably be resented if tried by the baker or the bus conductor. On the railways it is freely accepted as between commodities, but not as between different parcels of the same commodity. The law allows a lower charge to be made to a man who has canal transport open to him, but the railways may not discriminate for or against a farmer whose land happens to be more fertile than that of his neighbour.

Where there are escapable indivisible expenses to be covered the case for discrimination is clear. It secures an output nearer the optimum, and levies the indivisible cost on those who get the greatest benefit (measured by their consumers' surplus) from retaining the indivisible resource in this line of production. Moreover, it is possible in some cases that the net result may be that everyone pays a lower price for the commodity than he would if there were no discrimination. This is certain if the undertaking is trying to maximise its net revenue and (but not otherwise) if marginal divisible cost is falling. But it is also possible if the undertaking is out merely to cover its costs and could cover them without discrimination, since reducing the price to some persons with elastic demands may increase the surplus over marginal cost which they contribute, and thus allow the price to others also to be reduced. Nevertheless, discrimination between persons as such is always awkward; discrimination is much easier if impersonal categories can be found which more or less arrange themselves in order of elasticity of demand, such as discrimination between types of traffic, between different uses for electric current, or even discrimination according to income. In what follows we shall speak of an industry charging different prices for different services when we mean charging any user on the basis of some impersonal category prices which yield different surpluses over marginal cost. allowing for the fact that the marginal cost may be different, e.g. the difference in the marginal costs of transporting 20 tons of coal and 20 tons of hay.

If the available consumers' surplus is not by itself enough to meet the indivisible cost, but would do so together with the producers' surplus, the undertaking should be maintained. It will, however, run at a loss unless it is allowed to discriminate between its suppliers. A subsidy is then the only way out, if the optimum allocation of resources is to be maintained, but this is not as good a solution as would be some method that collected the producers' surplus, since those who should pay are those who receive the benefit.

When an industry with escapable indivisible expenses is in competition with another offering similar services, the rules for pricing become more precise. In no case should the price of any service be below the marginal cost of performing it. It may exceed marginal cost if the other industry's marginal cost is higher, but in that case it should not be as high as the marginal cost of the other industry, or the other industry may capture trade to which its marginal cost does not entitle it. An industry then performs services only where its divisible marginal cost is the lower, and collects revenue towards its indivisible expenses only to (not more than) the extent that it can perform the service more cheaply than the other industry.

For two industries to exist it must be the case that each industry performs some services at lower divisible marginal cost than the other; from each of its services it will collect towards its indivisible expenses. The amount of revenue which an industry can so collect however, depends on the margins between its divisible marginal costs for each of its services, and what would be the divisible marginal cost of these services to the other industry if it were performing them.

No problem arises if the surplus each receives is adequate to cover escapable indivisible costs. The interesting problems arise if one or both is unable to do so.

If one can cover its escapable indivisible cost but not the other, the one which cannot ought to be closed down (or not started if the commitment is not yet made). There is only one case which seems to throw doubt on this principle. Take the following simplified assumptions. There are two industries, X and Y, both with indivisible costs, and each offers the same services, *a*, *b*, *c* and *d*. X has lower marginal costs for *a* and *b*, and Y lower marginal costs for *c* and *d*. Suppose that there is only one unit of each service, and that the difference between Y's marginal cost and X's marginal cost on *c* and on *d* is so great that Y can earn enough surplus on *c* and *d* to cover all its escapable indivisible costs, and its future is assured. The problem then turns on *a* and *b*. Suppose the cost situation to be as follows, in money units:

	Divisible costs		Indivisible costs	Total
	a	*b*		
X's costs	1	1	2	4
Y's costs	2	3	already covered	5

If the X industry is maintained it should serve *a* and *b* because its marginal costs are lower. As far as competition with Y is concerned, it can extract from *a* and *b* prices of just under 2 and 3 respectively, which would yield a surplus of just under 3 and amply cover its indivisible expenses. But suppose that, quite apart from competition, *b* cannot afford to pay a higher price than 1, while *a*, in the absence of the alternative service offered by Y, would be willing to pay as much as 4. It may be argued that the correct solution is to keep the X industry going, to charge *b* only 1, and to charge *a* 3 but prevent it from transferring to Y, either by legislation or by some arrangement compelling Y to charge more than X. In this way both *a* and *b* will be served by X at a total cost (4) lower than if they were both served by Y (5), and anyway if the X industry were not maintained *b* could not be served at all since it could not afford Y's marginal cost. This is one of the railways' most seductive arguments in the current controversy. The valuable high-rated traffics, it is said, ought to be kept to the railway to contribute towards indivisible expenses to which the low-rated traffics cannot afford to contribute much,[1] and since the railway needs to extract from them more than it would cost to send them by road, some arrangement must be made to prevent road transport from getting them, e.g. compelling road transport to adopt the railway's schedule of charges. It is an attractive fallacy. To return to our example, the argument is really that the service *a*, though it could get itself performed by Y for 2, must pay 3 to X in order that *b* may be carried at a price it can afford, and that this is justifiable because the real value of the service *a* must be at least 3 or it would not be bought at that price. The answer is that in calculating the consumers' surplus on the service *a* performed by X, it is wrong to exclude the possibility of getting the same satisfaction more cheaply from Y; this is as if my consumers' surplus on bread were calculated on the assumption that no potatoes or other foodstuffs were available. Given that the Y industry exists, and offers the service at 2, the maximum consumers' surplus on *a* bought from X is 1, and it would be invalid to charge more just so as to provide resources from which *b* can be served. Alternatively, we can put the argument like this. The Y industry will exist in any case, and can serve *a* at a cost of 2. If therefore the X industry is also maintained, at a total cost of 4, to serve both *a* and *b*, we can say that serving *b* is adding 2 to the total costs that there would be if the X industry were not maintained and *a* were served by Y, and *b* should not be served unless it is willing to pay at least this 2. In no circumstances is it justifiable to make *a* pay more than Y's divisible cost. If anyone considers that *b* is a terribly important service,[2] then by all means subsidise

[1] Actually it is doubtful whether the high-rated traffics do in fact contribute more than the low-rated. Receipts per ton mile (cf. *Annual Railway Returns*, 1938) suggest that they do:

	Coal	Classes 1–6	Classes 7–21
pence per ton mile	1·08	0·96	2·00

But receipts per wagon mile suggest the opposite:

pence per wagon mile	10·51	9·38	5·62

The low-rated traffics have higher marginal costs per wagon mile, but is the difference as great as this?

[2] One of the railway arguments is rather like this. It is important, it says, that the heavy-rated traffics should continue to be carried, and if the other

it sufficiently to make the X industry able to meet its costs—whereupon both *a* and *b* will rightly be served by X—but such a subsidy should come from general taxation; why pick on *a* and compel it to subsidise *b*?

It is also possible that if there is competition between two industries, each with indivisible expenses, neither may be able to pay its way. Consider, on the same assumptions as before, the following cost situation:

	Divisible		Indivisible	Divisible		Indivisible	Total
	a	*b*		*c*	*d*		
X's cost	1	1	4	3	3		12
Y's cost	2	3		1	2	5	13

traffics go by road these traffics will have to pay more to the railway, or if they cannot afford to pay enough to keep the railway going, the railway will have to close and the traffics either not be carried or go by road at enormous cost.

Assume first that the consequence would be that the heavy traffics would pay higher rates by rail, enough to maintain the railway. This, the argument runs, is bad, because it raises the prices of raw materials, and secondly because in altering the ratio of transport costs of raw materials to finished products it gives incentives to alter the location of industry. The first argument seems curious; if an alteration in rates structure lowers costs on finished products and raises them on raw materials, the final price is not necessarily affected; indeed, if we assume that the railway remains but cannot retain the finished products in free competition, then the final price is lowered because total transport cost is lowered. The second is true, but not conclusive; the location pattern has grown up on the basis of a distorted rates structure; if now rates are altered, we may get a different location pattern, but it will be just different, not worse—it may be better since it corresponds more to real costs.

If the consequence would be that heavy traffics could not alone maintain the railway, parts of which then had to be closed, and could not then afford the high cost by rail, they cannot be important traffics in any economic sense. But, as argued above, if they are important, let them be subsidised, but out of the general revenues. This applies equally to the contention that the railway should not be allowed to contract because of its usefulness in war. If we must maintain in peace time railway facilities larger than our peace-time need, the Government should subsidise the railways to the necessary extent. Given a subsidy, competition should then be on the basis of the rule that price must be not less than railway marginal cost but not more than the marginal cost of any available alternative form of transport.

If the consequence would be that the railway would contract and the traffics go by road at high cost, no action is necessary. If they can go by road at high cost they could pay the same price to the railway. If that price would not keep the railway alive, then road transport is actually cheaper and the railway ought not to be maintained.

Neither can pay its way if both industries are established. The X industry will secure *a* and *b*, but the maximum revenue it can get from them is 5, while it needs 6 to keep alive; and Y will secure *c* and *d*, can get only 6, but needs 8. The essence of this situation is that if we take the services for which either of these industries has lower divisible costs, the sum of its divisible and indivisible costs exceeds the divisible costs of the other for those services, so that total costs if there is only one industry must be smaller than if there are two.[1] Consequently, if both industries have indivisible costs and neither can pay when the correct pricing rules are applied, only the one with the lower total costs should be maintained.

The net result may be summed up as follows. Where there are indivisible expenses, price should be not less than marginal cost, but not as much as the marginal cost of competing industries, and the undertaking should not be maintained unless the surplus over divisible costs covers the indivisible expenses. The only exception to this is the case where two industries offer the same services and neither pays if they follow these rules; then only the one with the lower total costs should be retained.

5. The fourth consequence of equating price with escapable cost is that the undertaking's receipts may be greater or less than its expenses. This may happen whenever accounting costs are different from escapable costs, in the circumstances distinguished in Section I, 5.

If price equals marginal cost, a loss will be made on inescapable expenses unless marginal costs rise until they are equal to the average of all costs, escapable and inescapable. If marginal cost exceeds average cost, there will be a profit. This profit is a rent for the use of some scarce resource owned by the undertaking. For example, suppose that the road system can be extended only at rising marginal cost; then if the government based motor taxation on this marginal cost it would probably receive each year a sum well in excess of its expenditure on the roads. The difference is a rental for the use of existing roads, and is a very proper

[1] Take the sum of X's divisible and indivisible costs for *a* and *b* as p, and the sum of Y's divisible and indivisible costs for *c* and *d* as q. Y's divisible costs for *a* and *b* are less than X's divisible and indivisible, say $p - m$, and X's divisible costs for *c* and *d* are less than Y's divisible and indivisible, say $q - n$. Then if there are two industries, total costs are $p + q$. But if there is only one industry total costs are either $p + q - n$ if it is X, or $q + p - m$ if it is Y.

and necessary charge if road transport is not to develop beyond the economic point. In what follows it will be assumed that marginal cost is less than average cost, and that prices based on it cover the escapable but not the inescapable costs. The discussion follows the cost categories of Section I, 5.

If there are inescapable expenses due to the fact that some assets do not have to be renewed, the undertaking will show a loss if price covers only escapable cost.

Take first the indivisible permanent assets, whose value outside the undertaking is less than their original cost. Someone has to bear the difference; why should it be the investors? The expenses were undertaken for the benefit of the consumers, and would not have been undertaken unless it was considered that the consumers were willing to pay enough to justify these resources being specialised to their use. There is no reason why the mere fact that the resources have now been specialised should throw the cost on the investors, or on anyone but those consumers for whose benefit the resources have been put into their present form. Non-renewable and renewable indivisible expenses should, in fact, be treated alike, in that they should be a charge on consumers' surplus, distributed over the consumers in whatever way will least reduce demand; the difference is that renewable indivisible expenses are escapable, and that while in their case the undertaking should be discontinued unless they can be fully used, in the case of non-renewable indivisible expenses the undertaking should go on even if what can be extracted from consumers' surplus is not enough to meet the original cost.

Consider next assets which are permanent but divisible, such as the cost of land for transport tracks. Whether they are escapable or not will depend on whether the industry is working to capacity. If it is working to capacity such expenses enter into marginal cost, and no loss is incurred. If it is working below capacity these expenses are uncovered. Part of the capacity is being used, and part is not, but price being equal to marginal cost, neither part is covered. That part which is in excess is due to mistaken investment on the part of the entrepreneur, and it is right that he should bear the loss. But why should not the consumers pay for that part of the capacity which they use? Resources have had to be specialised to meet their convenience, and the fact of excess capacity should not throw the cost on to the investors. The proper course is to write off the cost of such part as is in excess, but to levy on consumers' surplus, according to what the traffic will bear, to cover as much of the original cost of what is used as can be covered. The difference between divisible renewable and divisible unrenewable assets is that the latter will continue to be used whether the levy on consumers' surplus is adequate to cover the cost or not, whereas the former enter into marginal cost.

Assets which are divisible and renewable, but some of which will not be renewed because of a contraction of demand, have already been dealt with. Price should cover the cost of renewal. The result, however, is that that part of the assets which is not to be renewed will earn no amortisation and will show a loss. The loss is due to mistaken foresight and it is right that the entrepreneur should bear it.

An undertaking may also show a loss or a profit because the cost of replacing its assets rises or falls. If replacement cost rises, escapable cost rises, and price rises above original cost. If replacement cost falls, price falls below original cost. These windfall profits and losses are due to mistaken foresight, and properly remain with the entrepreneur.

6. The net conclusion is that, at least in public utility undertakings and state industries, price should not fluctuate irregularly; should cover not only short-run but also long-run marginal cost; not only long-run marginal cost but also, preferably by way of price discrimination, escapable indivisible cost as well; and not only these, but as much of the cost of non-renewable assets as can be extracted from consumers' surplus by price discrimination (but only to the extent to which such assets are actually used). The only losses the undertaking should bear are losses due to mistaken foresight: where the entrepreneur has failed to estimate correctly the level of output, the amount of consumers' surplus available for unrenewable assets, or a change in replacement cost.

III

THE PRINCIPLES OF CO-ORDINATION

1. The first problem in co-ordination is one of terminology. There is an awful confusion in the voluminous literature on this subject because hardly any writers recognise the logical difference between the framework and the principles of co-ordination. It is possible to co-ordinate two industries by private agreement between the undertakings, by nationalisation, by free competition,

by amalgamation, by legislation dividing the traffic, by licensing, or in other ways. No sound judgment can be passed on any of these schemes until one knows what is its purpose—what principles it will operate to secure the correct division of function between the two industries. The first thing to settle is the principle on which co-ordination should be based; discussion of the framework is subsidiary.

2. The economist's principle is escapable social cost; if two industries can perform the same service, one at a lower social cost than the other, the cheaper should perform it, unless the superior quality of the service offered by the other is worth more than the difference in cost—allowing, e.g. for differences of speed in transport, or in the quality of the space heating done by gas and by electricity.

Some proposals have been based on one or other of two other principles. One is that the revenues of established industries should be protected, so that they can pay interest on invested capital. In so far as this means that an industry must meet all escapable costs, divisible and indivisible, it is included in the economist's principle. But in practice it means more than this, and this is the well-known fallacy. This is the principle that has been applied in the restrictive licensing of road transport in this country.[1] The other principle is that it is better for industries to join together to exploit the market than to fight over it, e.g. that road and rail would do better to have a common rate classification which milked the high-valued traffics, and to share them on some arbitrary principle, than by quarrelling to let such traffics pass at low rates. This principle has seemed from time to time to be the one most likely to be adopted but needs no discussion here.

There is, however, one objection to the escapable cost principle which is very widely held, and which deserves some attention. Some people consider that all the services performed by an industry should be taken as a whole, and that it does not matter if the separate parts pay, so long as the whole pays. According to this, some services should be performed at less than marginal cost, and subsidised from profits made on other services, and an industry which tries to do this may be handicapped if some other

[1] For detailed discussion of its application in decided cases see G. J. Ponsonby, "The New Conditions of Entry into the Road Haulage Business," *Economica*, May 1937; D. N. Chester, *Public Control of Road Passenger Transport*, Ch. XI; and G. Walker, *Road and Rail*, Ch. VII.

industry is allowed to charge only marginal cost for the profitable services which were being relied on for subsidy. There are many points in transport where this kind of policy is urged. For example, it is suggested that some traffics should be carried below marginal cost, or some classes of passengers; that profits should be made where the population is dense and used to provide transport facilities where it is sparse; that there should be flat rates not varying with distance, the short-distance traffic subsidising the very long; or that peak travellers should subsidise the off-peak. There are similar arguments for electricity and gas; e.g. that rates should be uniform throughout the country, with the odd difference that in electricity it is the off-peak consumer who is expected to provide the subsidy.

We have already seen that where there are indivisible elements in cost, not all services should contribute equally to total expenses; each should pay its marginal cost plus what it can afford. The proposals under discussion here are proposals for charging less than marginal cost.

There are three objections. The first is that charging less than marginal cost in different areas distorts the economic factors which influence the distribution of the population. Population growth is stimulated in those regions at the expense of other regions. Part of the result is a gift to landlords and earners of quasi-rents, and to this extent the good intentions of those who make this sort of proposal are simply frustrated; but in so far as their intentions succeed, they distort the location pattern. Now it may be that the location pattern ought to be altered in these ways—broadly speaking that more people ought to be encouraged to live in places now sparsely populated, and vice versa. But it is doubtful whether transport and electricity authorities, acting separately, should be left to decide such matters. They do not necessarily take into account all that is relevant, and they may even pursue contradictory policies—the transport authorities may well be charging specially high rates to a region which is able to afford them only because the electricity authorities are charging specially low ones. The decision that some places are to be made more attractive and others less so is for the town and country planning authorities, and it is for them to say whether the penalties and attractions are to be subsidies to transport and electricity or something else.

The second objection is that if such subsidies are to be paid, it does not follow that they should be levied on other consumers of transport or electricity. It may be convenient to subsidise some users of transport by taxing others, but convenience is not the best principle of taxation.

The third objection is that this "over-all" sort of accounting makes difficult the control of the activities of such undertakings. If a manager is told that every service must cover its marginal cost, accounts can be devised which show whether it does or not, and his efficiency judged accordingly. If he is told only that he must cover all his costs it is more difficult to judge his efficiency, since he may be covering up gross errors in some parts of the undertaking simply by exploiting the consumers in some other part. This, in practice, should prove to be one of the most important principles in the administration of State enterprises—that each part of the enterprise must stand on its own feet. No business man would try to run a department store without separate accounts for each department, and the public's problem of checking the efficiency of different parts of an undertaking is not less important.

Nevertheless, to hold that some services should be subsidised is not necessarily inconsistent with accepting cost as the correct principle for co-ordination, since the decision to subsidise still leaves open the question which of two industries should perform the service. If price is below marginal cost it is unlikely that co-ordination will in practice be based on marginal cost, but there is no theoretical difficulty; all that is required is that the different industries should be equally subsidised so that the difference between their prices should equal the difference between their costs. Cost remains the only principle of co-ordination worthy of serious consideration.

3. Given acceptance of the cost principle, one may decide to put it into effect in more or less rough-and-ready ways. For example, if it is thought that costs are cheaper by rail for all traffics travelling more than 50 miles, or weighing more than 30 lbs. per cubic foot, or requiring less than three changes of wagon if sent by rail, one may issue instructions based on one or more of these principles—in some countries this is the basis of the road-rail legislation. Obviously this is a very distant approach to the cost principle, and most traders in this country would feel that co-ordination here should get beyond such generalisations to more exact consideration of costs for each type of transaction.

4. The nearest approximation to the cost principle is to quote

a price for each separate transaction, based on the cost of each separate transaction, and to use the services of whichever industry is cheaper. These prices may be actual or notional; that is to say, co-ordination may proceed by quoting real prices to the buyer, and letting him choose; or by reserving the choice to the management which then acts on the basis of its own calculations of which would be the cheaper. In practice in this country, for gas and electricity and for road and rail transport, the decision must be left to the buyer. In the case of gas and electricity, no one has ever contemplated leaving it to a fuel overseer to decide which each consumer must use. In the case of transport, some persons have suggested it, but the suggestion is not likely to be accepted. Traders' organisations have always insisted unanimously on freedom of choice between different forms of transport. Some advocates of nationalisation have thought otherwise, but not all; for instance, the Trades Union Congress in its recent report,[1] while paying lip service to managerial decision as an ultimate aim, provides for separate bodies to run road and rail transport, and not, as would otherwise be necessary, for a single manager to operate at each receiving point and decide which form of transport is to be used. Traders value the right to make their own choice because there are so many variables in the quality of transport service, and it is unlikely that any Government will wish to force any other solution on them. Co-ordination must occur through the buyer choosing on the basis of prices which reflect costs.

Exact reflection, we have already seen, has its disadvantages, and they are likely to prove overwhelming. Prices will have to be based on long-run marginal costs rather than short-run; and they must not fluctuate irregularly. Gas and electricity prices already follow these precepts; road transport rates, however, do not and must be brought into line. Most people, including the traders, agree that there should be a codified road rates structure. Admittedly this is not easy to draw up, but it is not more difficult than the codification of railway rates, which has existed for more than fifty years. The main disagreement on this issue has been not whether there should be a code, but on the acceptance of cost as the correct principle for such a code.

We may now consider our two cases in greater detail.

5. The principal practical difficulty in co-ordinating gas and electricity on the cost principle is that presented by the daily peak.

[1] T.U.C., *The Public Operation of Transport*, 1945.

Here the electricity industry is the victim of its history. At its start, electricity was used mainly for lighting, and cheaper rates were offered, correctly based on long-run marginal cost, to stimulate consumption during the day for other purposes. These succeeded so well that in many undertakings the peak has shifted from the evening to the day.[1] Rates have not, however, been properly adjusted to take account of this change. This is partly because rates are sticky, partly because of the technical difficulty which used to exist (now more or less solved) of recording consumption according to the time of day, and partly because of the widespread adoption of the two-part tariff.

The two-part tariff has solid advantages; customer costs, which do not vary with consumption, can be put into the fixed charge, and so can the consumer's contribution to indivisible expenses adjusted to his capacity to pay. Its great disadvantage, however, is that in encouraging customers to use as wide a range of electrical appliances as possible, it does not discriminate between those which come on to the peak and those which do not. The result, according to a recent calculation,[2] is that some of the more expensive forms of consumption barely cover their marginal cost, if that, and make no contribution to indivisible expenses. In the gas industry, which has not so acute a peak problem, as gas can be stored (though distribution costs are effected), the two-part tariff would not have this disadvantage, yet for historical reasons the two-part tariff is much less common here.

The electricity industry has a choice between three solutions. One is to have separate wiring of different types of consumption which occur at different times and are separately recorded. This is done in some cases, e.g. for large commercial water heaters

[1] In some undertakings the position is uncertain and periods during which the peak may occur now cover a large part of the day. Cost allocation becomes a ticklish business when there is a shifting peak. A sub-committee of the Electrical Research Association has studied the problem in a report entitled, *An Improved Method for Allocating to Classes of Consumers the Demand Related Portion of the Standing cost of Electricity Supply*, 1945. The suggested solution is to allocate the full maximum demand charge to all loads whose maximum demand is known to coincide with the station peak, and to allocate to others by a formula taking both their maximum demands and their consumption during the potential peak period into account, on the theory that a load with a high load factor is likely to affect the peak more than a load with a low load factor.

[2] Report by the Fuel and Power Advisory Council, *Domestic Fuel Policy*, Cmd. 6762, 1946.

C

charged only at night; but it would be too expensive to apply to the domestic consumer. The second alternative is to have meters which record peak and off-peak consumption separately. These are unpopular in the industry partly because of their cost (which would probably fall if they were demanded in large numbers), partly because of a sort of conservatism which accepts charging different prices for different uses but resists the idea of a price difference based on time, and partly because they might have to be complicated to meet the needs of undertakings whose peaks are imminently liable to shift in incidence. The third possibility, and the easiest to bring into effect, would be to vary the fixed charge according to the appliances used by the consumer, so that a man who used a fire would pay more than a man who used only lamps, and a man who had an electric cooker still more, the difference depending on the extent to which the appliance is likely to increase the size of the peak. The difficulty in applying this is the difficulty of checking the number of appliances the consumer is using and detecting secret appliances, but this is not so difficult as it sounds since it is possible to guess roughly from the consumption shown by the meter whether the consumer is likely to have more appliances than he admits to or not; this makes detection much easier than the Postmaster General's problem of detecting those who forget to buy a wireless licence.

6. In transport the principal problem in basing price on cost is the cost of the tracks.

If the cost of the tracks used by road and rail were independent of the traffic each carried, the solution would be simple; their costs would not be part of marginal cost, and should not enter into prices in such a way as to divert traffic from one to the other. The solution advocated by Brigadier-General Sir Osborne Mance[1] is of this kind; he proposes that the Government take over financial responsibility for railway tracks and roads, leaving road and rail to compete on the basis of other costs. The validity of this solution depends on the assumption that total track costs would not be affected if as a result some traffics were diverted from one system to the other. Now this is a question of fact to be determined by the Government. General Mance first made this proposal for East Africa, where it is clearly arguable that the Government would have to maintain both a railway and a road net the sizes of which would not be much affected by any likely traffic changes in the

[1] H. O. Mance, *The Road and Rail Transport Problem*, 1940.

near future. In this country the best reasons for considering that the position may be similar are the argument that the size of the road system is determined mainly by the number of private cars travelling on bank holidays, and that the number of commercial vehicles, which are more closely competitive with the railways, has little effect on road costs; and the military case for maintaining larger road and rail networks than are required in peace time. If these arguments add up to the conclusion that expenditure on road and rail tracks is largely independent of competition between road and rail, then it ought certainly not to be taken into account in that competition.

This decision has to be made by those who know the relevant facts, in this case the Government. In countries where it is decided that track expenditure depends on whether traffic goes by road or by rail, such expenditure is part of the marginal costs of traffic, and should be reflected in prices.[1] This is where non-renewable expenditure presents difficulty. To extend their facilities, both road and rail have to purchase land and put it into suitable form for tracks. This expense is a part of marginal cost, so long as the system is not working below capacity. A great battle has raged over the issue whether road transport should pay enough to cover the interest on all past investment of this kind. The railways are expected to pay such interest, if they can, and claim that it is unfair that road transport should get a "legacy from the past" which they cannot share. Their contention would be the nonsense which economists have usually asserted it to be if there were excess capacity in roads as there is in railways. But there is not. Every extension of the road system involves heavy expenditure on land and conversion, and the charge made to road transport should be at a rate which covers this. If it is at such a rate we can be pretty sure that it will be adequate to pay interest on the entire network of roads, assuming constant marginal cost, and much more than this if we assume that extending the road network takes place at rising marginal cost. Some economists have argued that road transport ought to pay only a sum equal to the annual

[1] Most of the proposals for "putting road and rail on an equal basis in respect of track costs" violate this principle. Such are: (*a*) that the Government should meet the cost of all tracks out of taxation; (*b*) that the Government should own all tracks and charge vehicles, whether road or rail, *the same* ton-mile rate for use of the tracks; (*c*) that road transport should pay in taxes a total sum equal to the cost of railway tracks. Equality of charge is economic only if there is equality of cost.

expenditure on the roads, but this is not so. Given constant marginal cost, road transport ought to pay on existing roads not only their maintenance but also interest, and given rising marginal cost it should pay also a rent. The railways have reached what is probably a true conclusion via an invalid argument.

Let us suppose, however, that it is not the case that there are rising marginal costs in extending the road net, and that to charge marginal cost would leave an indivisible cost uncovered. The indivisible expenditure is divided into the escapable (renewable) and the inescapable (which is not shown in current road finance, but for which items appear in railway accounts). Each system must cover its escapable indivisible expenditure separately, out of consumers' surplus. Since the traffics in which each system is superior will be different, those goods which make a high contribution to the indivisible costs of the railway will make none to road costs and vice versa. Each system will have a rates structure, but these structures will not be similar, as is so often proposed, but opposites. The high-rated traffics of road transport will be the low-rated traffics of the railway, and vice versa.

Assuming that the Government owns the road (or the railway track) but not the vehicle, how should it charge the users of the track? That part of the cost of the road which varies with use should enter into marginal cost. This happens automatically if it is levied as a tax on petrol (or coal) or some other index or record of vehicle miles run.[1] To some extent, however, cost varies with the number of vehicles rather than the miles they run, because the roads have to be wide and numerous enough to take the maximum number of vehicles wanting to run, and on bank holidays they are nearly all out; to this extent the tax should be on the vehicle, irrespective of mileage. Theoretically one should separate out these two sources of variation in costs, as the electric undertakings separate out standing from running costs, and set the fixed and variable taxes accordingly; but in practice exact division is probably not very important.

The escapable indivisible part of the track cost is more difficult. This must not enter into marginal cost, and should therefore definitely not be recovered by a tax on fuel or on the vehicle. The correct solution is that when rates are being fixed a sum should

[1] There are crucial problems here in deciding which classes of vehicle do most damage; see Ministry of Transport (Salter), *Report of the Conference on Road and Rail Transport*, 1932.

be added to all rates that can bear it, in so far as they can; carriers (including persons carrying on their own account) should then make regular declarations of what they have carried, and pay the appropriate tolls—just as cinemas collect and pay over entertainment duty. (This filling of a large gap in our statistics of transport would in any case be very valuable.) There would doubtless be some attempts to defraud, but if the ultimate penalty were loss of licence, evasion would probably not be very great. In any case, the problem arises only to the extent to which transport remains in private ownership. In a nationalised transport system the appropriate tolls would be added to prices and the rest would be mere book work. (It should be remembered that we are assuming that marginal cost of the track is less than average cost: if it is not none of this arises as the indivisible expenses are covered simply by charging marginal cost.)

There remain the inescapable costs to which the owners of the track are entitled in so far as they can get them from the users. Strictly, each system should be treated separately, the railway getting what it can from its traffics, and road authorities the same. General Mance, who believes that more or less all railway and road track expenses are inescapable, has suggested that they should be pooled, so that in effect goods going by rail might contribute towards the maintenance of roads, and vice versa. If railway traffics cannot yield from their consumers' surplus enough to cover inescapable expenses, the loss has to be borne somewhere. At present the shareholders bear it; and if the Government owned the tracks and found itself in a similar position, the Government would bear it for railways as it does for roads (no interest charge is recorded on past investments in roads). If the Government has to bear a loss, it will levy taxes on the community. There is no obvious reason why it should levy specially on traffic going by one system to meet losses on another; this might or might not prove the most convenient source of revenue, but convenience is only one of the canons of taxation.

One of the difficult problems is the difference between different tracks. Not only are some roads less expensive to build than others per mile, but the density of traffic varies from one to another, and if rates were the same some would make profits and others losses. The railway companies get over this by charging exceptional rates on routes with high traffic density, and the co-existence side by side of two competing systems, road and rail, applying different principles, must have caused some uneconomic diversion of traffic in the past. A nationalised road transport industry could be brought into line with railway practice, its ton-mile rates varying with traffic densities on the routes to be used. But the problem is soluble even if road transport is not nationalised, on lines already suggested. If road rates are codified, the rate including a toll to be paid over to the Government at regular intervals, the amount of the toll can be adjusted to traffic density, traffics passing between some places paying lower tolls than others. A road rates code would in any case have to take account of density, back loads, and the other matters which distinguish one route from another, so this would not be a new principle. However, a Government seeking to avoid complications might decide that the simplest thing was to have a uniform rate throughout the country. If it did, co-ordination of road and rail would be upset unless the railways were put on the same basis. From the point of view of co-ordination it does not matter much which basis is adopted; what matters is that road and rail tracks should both be paid for on the same principles.

It will be obvious that the co-ordination of road and rail on the basis of cost is no simple matter. All the work of determining in actual figures what part of track costs varies with traffic, and what part is indivisible but escapable, remains to be done, also the task of allocating these costs properly to traffics on the basis of what they will bear, taking into account the limits set to each system's charge by the marginal cost of the other. The calculations involved may lead some to conclude that it would be too costly to try to co-ordinate on the basis of cost, but once it is recognised that at best only broad approximations will be possible, the work can be kept within reasonable limits, especially as it is the initial allocations that are difficult, and the year-to-year changes are small. Only the Government possesses the information on which to base the allocations; all that outsiders can do is to set out what seem to be the logical categories.

IV

THE FRAMEWORK OF CO-ORDINATION

1. The principle that co-ordination should be based on cost is independent of the framework adopted to secure co-ordination. In this country four methods have been considered, (1) free price competition, (2) restrictive licensing, (3) private agreement, and (4) amalgamation, including nationalisation.

2. The first problem which free competition presents is co-ordination in the building of road and rail tracks. We have seen, in Section II, 4 that, given two industries with indivisibilities, price competition between them can secure proper co-ordination. If, however, the facilities are not given, or questions of extending them arise, competition between indivisible elements does not work smoothly. If, for example, a railway company is contemplating laying a new track, whether this should be done or not will depend to some extent on whether the road authorities propose to build parallel and/or feeder roads. Such uncertainties hold up development; they have, for instance, been one of the obstacles to the electrification of the railways. If the sums of money involved were small, and development could proceed a little at a time, the competitive process would adjust the facilities provided by competing industries. But where the sums are so large and indivisible, under-development through uncertainty on the one hand, or over-development through ignorance of rival proposals on the other, can best be avoided by consultation. The network of railway tracks and of roads should be planned as a whole, following the principle elucidated in Section II, 4, that both should be provided, in competition with each other, where with price discrimination both would pay, but that only one should be provided if only one by itself would pay.

Now the present situation in this country is particularly anomalous because, not only are road authorities separate from the railway track authorities, but roads are provided in competition with railway tracks without the authorities having to consider whether these roads earn their cost or not. Road and rail track building should clearly be done at least in consultation; and would probably be done best if there were a single authority, i.e. if the Government nationalised the railway tracks and planned road and rail tracks together. Nationalisation of railway vehicles and operation does not, of course, follow from the nationalisation of the tracks, and it has often been proposed that the one should be done without the other. In what follows we shall assume that road and rail tracks are commonly owned by the Government, which charges rail and road vehicle operators for their use. What we shall discuss is the co-ordination of the service provided by such operators, in terms of the choice between free competition, licensing, and amalgamation, including nationalisation.

3. Free price competition could secure a very precise co-

ordination, based on hour-to-hour changes in cost. To achieve it, road and rail would have to be placed on an equal footing; the railways relieved of their obligations to carry and given freedom to vary their rates at will, and road transport freed from restrictive licensing. This is generally admitted. What has not been generally accepted, although the railways have always pressed the point strongly, is that it would involve a revolution in the treatment of road costs, both in deciding what was to be levied, and in deciding how it was to be levied, and to the extent to which there may be escapable indivisible elements in road costs it would require road rates to be put on to a what-the-traffic-would-bear basis. In the light of all this, no one can pretend that the competition between road and rail in pre-war years was either fair or based on cost, or that the resulting traffic diversions were not to some extent uneconomic in the social sense. However, given the necessary adjustments, free price competition based on cost could certainly achieve a proper co-ordination.

The disadvantages we have already seen. Since rates would be based not on long-run but on short-run marginal cost, the railways, which suffer from excess capacity, would have difficulty in earning amortisation quotas on that part of their investment which requires renewal, though perhaps this would not be so great a problem if the tracks were disintegrated, since the excess capacity lies there rather than in railway operation. In any case, rates would fluctuate freely from hour to hour, and there would be opportunities for personal discrimination. There are not many persons who feel that the advantage of full hour-to-hour utilisation of resources is great enough to outweigh these disadvantages.

A more limited competition would be possible if both road and rail had their rates fixed by a tribunal on the basis of long-run escapable cost, ironing out fluctuations. It would then be necessary to prevent departures from these rates, and to impose common carrier obligations on both. Charging less than the minimum would be difficult to detect, but could be controlled by making the ultimate penalty forfeiture of licence; no great difficulty seems to be expected in enforcing the minimum road rates now widely proposed.

4. Restrictive licensing does not make any clear contribution towards co-ordination on the basis of cost. For it to be helpful, one must be able to assume that the cost situation demands that there should be fewer road vehicles, and to hope that those which are

licensed will concentrate on the traffics where their marginal costs really are lower than the marginal costs of rail transport. The latter effect will be attained only if road and rail rates correctly reflect the respective costs, and if it is possible for them to do this there is no need for restrictive licensing. In practice there is no pretence in this country that the licensing of road vehicles is based on cost; the avowed object of the Commissioners is to protect the revenues of existing undertakings.

Restrictive licensing of public contractors but not of traders carrying on their own account, and of public passenger vehicles but not of private cars, is obviously uneconomic. It has led to a great expansion of private transport at the expense of public transport, though the latter is more economic. All road transport should be restricted or none. Moreover, if the number of vehicles is restricted below the profitable number, those who get licences are given a semi-monopolistic position which at once reflects itself in the licence acquiring a money value. Why should this gift be presented to operators? If licences are to be restricted they should be sold. But exactly the same results would be achieved by increasing the level of road taxation. The basic problem in coordination is to make road taxation reflect road costs, and if this is done restrictive licensing is unnecessary.

5. Road and rail interests could by private agreement create and maintain rate structures which were based on cost principles. Agreement has been reached on having a road rates structure, but there is no evidence that it is to be based on cost. The interest of the railways is to protect their revenues, and the joint interest of road and rail is to adopt a common classification which enables both to milk the most profitable traffics, sharing the proceeds on some agreed basis. As we have seen, road and rail rates structures should be opposites, in the sense that the goods profitable to the one should be unprofitable to the other; no other structure achieves co-ordination on a cost basis.

6. Some amalgamation has taken place through railway purchase of road undertakings, but the process is likely to be completed by the nationalisation of road and rail transport which has now been announced.

It is not proposed, and is not likely, that road and rail will be fused in the sense that at each point of contact with the public one man will be responsible for both. Separate organisations will be maintained, fusing only at the top. The choice between road and rail will therefore be left to the public. There may be crude attempts to confine it by regulations requiring some traffics to go by rail, e.g. long-distance or heavy traffics, but no such crude approximation to cost is either necessary or a necessary part of nationalisation. There is no reason why the nationalised undertakings should not fix their prices to reflect costs and just let the public make its own choice.

The danger of a nationalised service is its inheritance. It is partly that the Government inherits twenty years of legislation hostile to road transport and a "Whitehall climate" that demands the protection of railway revenues. It is still more the fact that the Government is almost certain to have to pay for the railways more than the railways will be able to earn unless they are bolstered up by restricting road transport. A Government under an obligation to make its railway accounts balance would probably be foolish enough to restrict other forms of transport. This must have wide repercussions. If publicly owned road transport is restricted, either in quantity or by charging prices exceeding costs, the citizens will operate vehicles on their own account under "C" licence, and we shall see continued that uneconomic expansion of traders' transport at the expense of public transport which the licensing system produced before the war. This will threaten the nationalised system, reducing its traffic and profits, and sooner or later the Government will find itself wanting to place restrictions on the right of traders to carry for themselves.

The way out of this is to begin by writing off boldly the excess of the amount which has to be paid to the railway shareholders, so that the nationalised service may start without that burden of over-capitalisation which the L.P.T.B. has to carry. Put on to the books of the new undertaking no more than it can be expected to meet, on its own merits. That would leave the Government free to deal with road transport on its own merits. Most of the apparent case for nationalisation of road transport would vanish. The case for nationalising the railways is presumably that there are notable economies of scale, and that such large concentrations of economic power should be under full public control (though these economies are associated with the tracks rather than with vehicle operation; if the tracks are nationalised there may even be a case for more regional disintegration of vehicle operation, whether this also is nationalised or not). No such argument applies to road transport, and nationalising road transport may merely impart a bureaucratic inefficiency to an industry that might remain more flexible if left to operate on a small scale. The best case for nationalising road transport is that if the railways are nationalised at too high a price, they can be made to pay only by restricting road transport. This best case is a bad one anyway; and would disappear if the water in the price to be paid for the railways were written off immediately.

[6]

Depreciation

Depreciation and Obsolescence as Factors in Costing*

W. ARTHUR LEWIS
Professor of Political Economy, Princeton University

I The Meaning of Depreciation

THE value of an asset usually changes with time. In some cases the asset becomes more valuable as time passes. For example, wine matures with time. Favoured sites in a rapidly growing city become more valuable as population grows. The assets used to produce a new commodity become more valuable as the commodity becomes more popular. And most assets increase in monetary value in an inflationary situation, though the "real" value of some, corrected for changes in the general price level, may actually be falling.

Inflation apart, most physical assets decline in value after a time, even though there may be passages in their life when they are appreciating in value. In some cases the decline in value can be prevented by continually reinvesting in the asset, to replace what is lost. For example, the farmer maintains the value of his land by investing fertilisers, and by spending money on soil practices which conserve fertility. Buildings and bridges can be kept going for a very long time in the same way. Even some machinery can be kept going; one can still find in some factories steam boilers which were first installed eighty years ago. But most man-made assets eventually give out altogether.

Depreciation measures the amount by which the value of an asset falls through time. This depends partly on how well the asset is maintained—whether the buildings are painted regularly, whether leaks in the boiler are fixed at once, whether broken parts are immediately replaced, and so on. The cost of maintenance and repair is not usually included in depreciation. The cost of keeping the asset "in a good state of repair" is usually calculated separately, and treated as an operating expense on the same footing as wages and raw materials. Depreciation therefore measures the extent to which the value of the asset has deteriorated although it is being kept in a good state of repair. What constitutes a good state of repair is a matter for the judgement of the management, or, if the management wishes to sell the asset, it is a matter for the consensus of the second-hand market.

There are half-a-dozen reasons why an asset may deteriorate in value even though it is well maintained. First, portions of the asset may be consumed in process of use; for example, rubber tyres are worn away. Secondly, the physical yield of the asset may decline; for example the

210

physical output of most radio valves declines with use. Thirdly the asset may become more costly to operate, either because it uses more labour or materials per unit of output, or because it breaks down more often and maintenance costs rise. Fourthly, a new machine may be invented which is cheaper than the existing machine ever was, whether because it is cheaper to build and instal, or because it requires a smaller input of labour or materials per unit of output. And fifthly, the asset may lose value because new products come on the market which the buyers prefer.

We can group these reasons so as to distinguish between depreciation and obsolescence. Obsolescence is that loss in value which is due to the competition of new inventions. It corresponds therefore to the fourth and fifth reasons listed above. Depreciation is all that other loss in value which would occur even if the asset did not have to compete with new inventions.

Depreciation itself may further be analysed according to whether it occurs only in so far as the asset is used, or whether the asset falls in value whether it is used or not. This distinction is important to economic analysis because economic analysis is concerned with the effect of decisions to produce. If the asset will deteriorate in value equally whether it is used ot not, the deterioration in value does not enter into the decision whether to use or not, except in so far as it affects the prior decision whether to retain the asset or to dispose of it.

In what follows we shall make no use of the distinction between depreciation and obsolescence. We shall use the term "depreciation" to cover all deterioration in the value of an asset which is maintained in good repair, whether this deterioration is due to the emergence of competing assets or products or not. The distinction we shall be using is between deterioration which is due to use and deterioration which is independent of use.

II The Purpose of Measuring Depreciation

All the problems of measuring depreciation which this chapter discusses arise out of the fact that "the value of an asset" is not a unique quantity. An asset has different values for different purposes, so we get different amounts of depreciation according to the purpose of our measurement. In practice, depreciation is measured for four different purposes, which may well yield answers:

(a) In order to compute tax liability.
(b) In order to decide for how much to buy or sell the asset in the second-hand market.
(c) In order to decide what part of the gross profit to distribute to the owners of the business.
(d) In order to decide how much to charge the consumers of the product.

(a) *Tax liability*

Within the framework of legislation, the income tax authorities make their own rules for the calculation of depreciation. These rules are based more or less upon current business practice, but they do not coincide with business practice.

(b) *Valuation of assets*
The second occasion for measuring depreciation is when the asset is valued for purchase or sale in the second-hand market. The difference between the original cost of the asset and its present value measures the amount of depreciation which has occurred.

In estimating present value the original cost of the asset is irrelevant. What the asset is worth now depends on its earning power in the future, irrespective of what price may have been paid for it in the past, or of how much it may have earned in the past. In formal terms its present value is the sum of expected future benefits (including final scrap value) discounted at the appropriate rate of interest. This is a subjective rather than an objective quantity, since it depends upon guessing what the future benefits may be, and on choosing a rate of interest appropriate to this type of investment.

There are several obstacles in the way of giving quantitative expression to this concept of value.

First the future life of the asset is not predictable, even if one assumes that potential yield in each year is known. This is because the asset may cease to exist for unpredictable physical reasons, no less than for economic reasons. If one buys one hundred of a particular type of asset, and subjects each item to roughly the same use, it is improbable that all hundred will give out at the same time. Some will break down immediately, some will last almost indefinitely, and the life span of the rest will be distributed, with a marked bunching around one particular length of life. In other words, the life table of a hundred machines somewhat resembles the life table of a hundred men. Engineers try to meet this situation by calculating mortality tables for each important class of asset. Thus, the best one can do in valuing an asset is to assume that it will have an average life, in the sense determined by such a table, while recognising that actual life may be greater or less.

Secondly, there is not one potential pattern of yield, but several. If the asset is used heavily at the beginning, operating costs may be higher and yield may be lower in later years than if the asset is used less intensively at the start. Length of physical or of economic life may also be affected. Hence the problem is not simply to discount back future benefits, but also to pick that pattern of use which yields the highest discounted value. The problem raises no theoretical difficulty, but in practice it depends on making an enormous number of inter-related guesses.

Thirdly, much of the guessing about future yields is so uncertain as hardly to be worth while. One way out is to assume that future yields will be the same as current or as past yields. Another way out is to assume that yields in later years will be so small as not to be worth taking into account. Either way the calculation is hazardous.

Fourthly and most fundamentally, for a great many assets the concept of the net yield of the particular asset is meaningless, because this asset collaborates with so many other assets in producing the final product that it is not feasible to isolate even its marginal contribution. What is the marginal contribution of the office chairs, or of the parking lot for staff cars, or of the boiler which raises steam for the works? One can think of the assets as a whole yielding a stream of future benefits which can be estimated, but for many individual assets is it useless to ask what the future stream of benefits will be.

Given these objections, the most practicable way to value some assets is not to estimate their future yields but to compare them with the cost of replacing them new. If an asset would not be worth replacing if it were suddenly destroyed, this escape is barred. But if the asset would be worth replacing, then its present value is equal to the cost of replacing it minus some allowance for expired service, minus also some allowance for the superior efficiency of the replacement (more product, or more attractive product, or lower operating costs). Here too some guesswork is involved, but it is not so formidable as is the guessing of the stream of future yields.

Whichever method of valuation one uses, a wide margin may exist between the value of an asset to its owner and the value to the most favourable prospective purchaser. We shall call the value to the owner "the inside value", and the price which the asset would fetch second-hand "the scrap value". The inside value depends upon the use the owner is making of the asset, and on the discount rate he uses. The prospective buyer may take a very different view of the future, or may work with a different discount rate. He may also not have such good opportunities open to him for using the asset profitably, so that the use to which he would put it may be quite different. Even if his calculations were exactly the same as those of the owner, he would still have to take into account the cost of removing the asset and installing it in a new place, plus any commissions payable to the brokers in the second-hand market.

The theory of asset replacement is treated in another chapter. All we need to note at this point is the fact that when the purpose of valuation is to decide whether to scrap the asset or to keep it, the relevant calculations have to be made not in terms of the sum originally paid for the asset, but in terms of present costs and future yields.

In this context, as in any other, depreciation measures the extent to which the value of an asset has deteriorated in the course of a year (or other time period). If we seek to quantify it, however, we get two different answers, one showing the deterioration in scrap value, and the other showing the deterioration in inside value to the owner.

(c) *Calculating net profit*

The third purpose of calculating depreciation is to prevent the asset's owner from consuming his capital; i.e., to ensure that he will have in a depreciation fund at the end of the asset's life a sum equal to the amount originally paid for the asset. The law imposes this requirement upon most public companies ("dividends must not be paid out of capital") though not on all. And in any case "good business practice" requires the owners of a business to set aside from their gross profits what is required to maintain their capital intact, before deciding what part of the profits may be currently consumed.

But what is meant by maintaining capital intact? This concept has no unique meaning.

(1) In current accounting practice the meaning is usually to maintain

constant the original money value of the investment; and this is also most often the meaning sanctioned by law. This means that there should be deducted from gross profits during the life of the asset sums which will amount at the end of the asset's life to its original cost. We leave for later discussion the question how these sums should be spread over the asset's life, noting for the moment only that, when dealing with fixed assets (as distinct from liquid assets) current practice takes no account of year to year changes either in the scrap value or in the owner's inside value. For the moment we confine ourselves to discussing how much depreciation should be set aside in total over the whole life of the asset.

(2) Suppose that the price of the particular asset is unchanged, and that the general price level is unchanged, but that a new model of the asset is invented which costs the same but yields a much greater output. Then when the asset is replaced by the new model, the owner's capital is unchanged in general purchasing power, and in relation to other people's capital. But the real productive capacity of his firm is increased, and therefore in terms of real output his real capital is increased. Here we meet the distinction between maintaining real capital intact in terms of general purchasing power, and maintaining real capital constant in terms of the real productive capacity of a particular firm. This distinction becomes important and troublesome when the asset's price moves in different proportions from the general price level.

(3) If the price of the asset changes proportionately with changes in the general price level, the problem is as simple as in the case where all prices are unchanged. The competitive price of the product rises, and so does gross profit. Hence if depreciation is charged at replacement cost enough can be saved in the fund to replace the asset without bringing fresh finance into the business; while at the same time real consumption can be maintained nearly intact (intact if the price rise occurs immediately after the asset has been bought; but if it occurs later in the life of the asset, heavy additions need to be made to the depreciation fund in later years to make up for the deficiency in earlier years, unless the fund has been invested in assets whose value has risen correspondingly, *e.g.*, in equities, in real estate or in inventories). The distinction between maintaining intact the individual's command over goods in general and maintaining intact the capital in terms of real output capacity does not arise.

(4) Now suppose that at the end of the asset's life the cost of replacing it has risen, though the general level of prices remains the same as when the investment was first made. If the depreciation fund contains only the original money cost, the sum saved thereby will not be sufficient to replace the asset. Should the amount set aside for depreciation therefore rise as the cost of replacing the asset rises, in order to maintain *real* capital intact? In a competitive market the price of the product will have risen, because the cost of maintaining or expanding output has risen, and owners of assets purchased at the old price will have been earning higher gross profits out of which they could set aside larger amounts for depreciation, while maintaining consumption nearly intact. On the other hand, since the average level of prices is assumed to be constant, the relative position of the owners of these assets vis-a-vis other members of the community remains

unchanged in real terms if depreciation is set aside equal only to original cost. The extra profit is a windfall gain, which can be consumed while maintaining real capital (in the sense of command over goods and services in general) intact.

Conversely, one may assume that the money cost of replacing the particular asset falls, while the general price level remains unchanged. Owners will then in competitive conditions earn lower gross profits, and be able to replace the asset with smaller sums of money, while maintaining consumption more or less. If they do this, however, their capital will fall relatively to other people's, and they will not be maintaining it in terms of command over goods and services in general.

Here we see the conflict between depreciation for the purpose of price formation in competitive conditions and depreciation for the purpose of maintaining intact the real spending power of owners. From the moment the asset's price changes, the asset-cost which will enter into competitive pricing is the cost of replacing the asset; but the asset-cost which is relevant to maintaining the individual's capital intact is the original cost of the old asset, adjusted only for changes in the general price level. There is the same conflict between price formation in competitive conditions and price fixing in monopolistic or other conditions where pricing is based on what is considered fair; *i.e.* on recompensing producers in accordance with their past expenditure; in competition the product's price will be based on new asset cost, whereas in "fair" pricing the product's price will be based on old asset cost.

This distinction between depreciation to maintain general command over goods and services intact, and depreciation to maintain productive capacity of the firm intact, is important whenever the price of the asset moves differently from the general price level. Some writers claim to be able to prove that in these cases it is more "scientific" to base depreciation upon the asset price than upon the general price level; but this is not so. Their claim is based upon a confusion between depreciation for price determination and depreciation for maintaining capital intact.

If the firm wishes to maximise its profits, it should relate the price of its product to marginal cost. Then, insofar as the price of the asset is reflected in marginal cost, marginal cost will rise as the asset's price rises, even if the general price level is constant. It can also be shown, on the general assumptions of welfare economics, that the price of the product should rise as the replacement cost of the asset rises.

However, this does not throw light upon depreciation for maintaining capital intact. Given the price rise, the asset's owner will make a windfall profit, which he may legitimately consume if he so desires; it cannot be proved that he ought to save it by writing it off as depreciation. Conversely, if the asset's price falls, he should lower his prices, and will make a windfall loss. If he decides to reduce depreciation accordingly he will be able to maintain his consumption intact temporarily and his productive capacity intact permanently, but he will end up a poorer man in comparison with other citizens, since his capital will not be maintained intact in terms of general purchasing power; and his consumption will therefore also in due course fall. Very few of the accountants who recommend writing up depreciation when the asset's price rises, would also recommend writing it down when the asset's price falls relatively to the general price level; indeed, in the case of public companies, the law would not allow them to do so, since this would be "paying dividends out of capital".

The conclusion seems to be that the asset price is relevant to price determination, but it is the general price level which is relevant to maintaining capital intact, in the usual meaning of this phrase. Thus, when one speaks of maintaining capital intact it must be clear whether one means

(i) in terms of money or in real terms, so that the original money investment is multiplied by an index number of prices; and

(ii) if in real terms, whether one means to maintain the owner's capital intact in terms of real output capacity of the particular asset, or in terms of general command over goods and services. If the former, the relevant price index is the price index of the particular asset; if the latter, it is an index of the general purchasing power of money.

(d) *Price policy*

A firm cannot always make its own price. If it has to accept the market price, or to follow a lead given by some other firm, it does not need to measure depreciation for the purpose of setting prices, though it will need some measure of depreciation for other purposes, such as for taxation, or as a guide to dividend policy, or as an element in deciding how much to produce. A firm can set its own price only if its market is less than perfectly competitive, and if, given market imperfection, it has some freedom of manoeuvre vis-a-vis rival firms.

In a competitive market, price is set by marginal cost, which is the difference made to total cost by producing one unit of output more or less (though the concept of a "unit" of output raises difficulties to which we shall revert later). Given the market price, each firm finds it profitable to produce the quantity whose marginal cost equals price; and given the demand, the market process determines a price such that the marginal firm finds it just worth while to remain in the particular line of business.

Now the element of depreciation which enters into marginal cost is "user cost", which may be defined briefly for the present as the difference made to the value of the firm's assets by the decision to produce one unit of output more or less. If the firm has surplus capacity, (*i.e.* spares, excess, or idle capacity) and if the value of assets does not vary with use, user cost may be (but is not necessarily) zero. Whereas, if the firm is working at full capacity, the expansion of output requires the installation of extra capacity, and so user cost may be very high. In neither case is user cost a function of the original cost of the assets already installed, unless it happens in the full capacity case that the cost per unit of output of installing new assets is the same as the cost per unit of output of existing assets.

In a non-competitive market, price is not tied in the same way to marginal cost, and so the depreciation concept used in price determination is not necessarily user cost. Usually marginal cost sets a lower limit to price, but even this is not necessarily so. Sometimes a firm will sell below marginal cost, temporarily, as for example in order to retain important customers during an economic blizzard, or permanently, in order to promote the sale of some other product which yields a more than compensating profit, or, as in the case of some public utilities, because law or custom requires that certain unremunerative services be maintained. More usually the firm will charge something more than marginal cost, according to the quantities it thinks it can sell at different prices. In many cases, if market conditions permit, the firm will set prices at what it considers to be a "fair" level, fair both to itself and to its customers.

The concept of a "fair" price plays a considerable part in price determination in practice. It is applied to all public utilities regulated by law or by public commission. It is used also by many other firms, whether on moral grounds, or whether because they are afraid to attract hostile comment or public investigation or regulation if they charge more, or whether because they are afraid that if they charge more than is fair, new competition will be stimulated.

Almost invariably the depreciation concept which is used in determining a "fair" price is not user cost, but depreciation for the purpose of maintaining capital intact, using one of the several meanings of this term. This depreciation is therefore measured with reference to the past cost of assets already installed (usually not even corrected by a price index), and bears no relation to user cost, which is measured with reference to the future. The two concepts may by accident coincide. But they will certainly coincide only in the special case where there is no surplus capacity, and the price of assets is unchanged, and output is directly proportional to input (that is, there are no economies or diseconomies of scale). Given all three of these conditions, or some accidentally appropriate combination, depreciation for calculating marginal cost and depreciation for determining a "fair" price will coincide; but otherwise, and more usually, the concepts yield different results.

Many economists have argued that user cost, as calculated for marginal cost, is the only legitimate concept to use for price determination, but the argument cannot be sustained without exceeding the confines of economic analysis. It rests on the proposition that the national output is maximised if the output of each commodity is such as would obtain if every commodity were sold at a price equal to its marginal cost; provided that at the same time the consumers of each commodity derive from it, in total, satisfactions which they value more highly than its total escapable cost. This proposition is valid, given the usual restrictive assumptions of welfare economics. On the other hand, maximising the national output is not the only objective of social policy. Many people also consider that social policy should be fair, and if a policy which would maximise the national output would also be unfair, economics cannot prove that output maximisation is more important than the fairness.

It is not even possible to deduce from the conditions for output maximisation that price should equal marginal cost. There are two conditions, not one; a marginal condition and a total condition. There is no more reason to translate the marginal condition into "price must equal marginal cost" than there is to translate the total condition into "total revenue must equal total escapable cost". The very act of translation into price terms moves us on to a different plane, where we have to think in terms of what is a practicable method of pricing, and have also to remember that the act of levying a price serves not only to determine outputs, but also to redistribute incomes from one set of persons to another. If we nevertheless perform this illegitimate act of translation, a better rendering would seem to be "marginal price must equal marginal cost *and* the total paid must equal total escapable cost". Thus in those cases where, because of an indivisible item of cost, average cost exceeds marginal cost, the right policy would be not to charge marginal cost, but to use some such system as the two-part tariff, the block quantity discount tariff, or some other form of price discrimination, with the object both of having a marginal price equal to marginal cost and also of raising in total a sum equal to total cost.

This discussion, however, has taken us beyond the limits of our present subject matter. This chapter is not concerned with determining what the relation between price and cost ought to be, or even with establishing what the relation is currently in the real world. Our assignment is simply to define depreciation for the purpose of calculating cost. The definition has yielded two different concepts: depreciation as measured for cost where cost relates to past expenditure, and depreciation as measured for user cost. The two succeeding sections examine these concepts in greater detail.

III Depreciation as Capital Maintenance

In this section we are concerned with the depreciation concept which springs from the desire to maintain capital intact. When we considered this concept in the preceding section we confined ourselves to discussing what sum should be raised in total over the whole life of an asset; now we address ourselves to the question how this sum should be spread over the life from one year to another. In this context life must be interpreted in accordance with average expectations, such as are yielded by the engineer's asset mortality tables.

The most common practice in the United States of America has been to charge a constant sum each year as depreciation. Usually this sum is the total required divided by the number of years over which it is to be levied. Thus, if an asset is expected to have a life of ten years, and a scrap value at the end of the tenth year of £100, and if the total sum required to be maintained is £1,500 ,then £1,400 must be raised in depreciation over ten years, and therefore £140 will be written off each year. This is known as the "straight line" method of depreciation.

Since the sums which are written off each year can be invested inside or outside the business, they are capable of earning interest. If this interest is credited to the depreciation fund, the total sum available at the end of ten years will be more than £1,400. Thus, if compound interest is credited at 5 per cent annum, the total sum will be not £1,400 but £1,761. Accordingly it has been argued that the correct sum to raise annually is that sum which reinvested annually at compound interest will aggregate to the required total. This is known as the "sinking fund" method. In this case the annual write-off would be £111·3, which invested annually at compound interest will be worth £1,400 at the end of ten years. Obviously the validity of the argument depends upon whether the depreciation quotas actually are reinvested profitably, or are invested at a loss (*e.g.* a capital loss), or are held in liquid form. It also depends on whether one thinks it matters whether interest earned on depreciation quotas goes into the depreciation fund or into general revenue. As we shall see in the next section, if we assume perfect competition, full capacity and static conditions, the depreciation which enters into price will have to take account of the compound interest element. But depreciation for price determination and depreciation for maintaining capital intact are two different concepts. If the sole purpose of writing depreciation off in the books is to maintain capital intact, and not to determine prices or to value assets for scrapping, it does not seem to matter much into what fund one pays the interest earned on depreciation quotas.

It is convenient to approach the question how depreciation should be spread over the life of an asset from one year to another by considering possible disadvantages of writing-off the same amount in each year. These may be listed as follows:

(a) The fact that the price of the asset may change during its lifetime.
(b) The fact that the earning power of the asset fluctuates.
(c) The fact that the value of the asset does not decline by a constant amount each year.
(d) The fact that depreciation measured in this way may mislead those who determine the firm's price and output policy.

(a) *Price changes*

We have seen that if capital is to be maintained in a real sense, and not just in terms of money, accumulated depreciation must equal the original cost of the asset multiplied by the appropriate price index number—what is appropriate depending upon whether what we are maintaining intact is the firm's productive power or the value of the shareholders' capital in general purchasing power. It follows that writing off a constant sum each year is not consistent with maintaining real capital if prices change.

If one determines that total depreciation must equal original cost multiplied by an index number, the write-off from year to year may assume a queer pattern. For example, if the price index number halves when the depreciation fund already contains two-thirds of the original cost, depreciation in the remaining years is negative. Or, if the price index number doubles when three quarters of its life has already expired, the sum to be levied as depreciation in the remaining quarter of life becomes enormous. If the depreciation fund has been invested in assets which have also appreciated in value, the extra depreciation can be met simply by bringing the capital appreciation into the books; but in other cases it has to be written off against profits. Of course, if the price of the asset doubles, gross profit will probably also sharply increase, so that it is possible both to keep net profit constant and also to levy more as depreciation; but in extreme cases it may be impossible to make up the whole deficit without sharply reducing net profits in the last years of life, or even showing a net loss. This is one reason why accountants and income tax authorities are reluctant to give up basing depreciation on original money cost only, and shift to index number calculations only in periods of sharp and persistent inflation. Needless to say, this results in evading one set of problems at the cost of being entangled in another—the fact that the depreciation fund is not serving to maintain real capital intact.

(b) *Fluctuations in earnings*

Insofar as the purpose of measuring depreciation is to withhold from dividend distribution over the whole life of an asset a sum equal to its cost, there is no particular reason to withhold the same sum in each year; the only guide is convenience. If one were trying to measure by how much the assets had declined in value during the year, there might be a unique answer, but this is not the purpose of those who write off a constant sum in each year, and the sum they write off is not based on measuring the decline in asset values, whether conceived as scrap or as inside values. Again, if one were measuring user cost for price determination the answer might be unique, but this is neither the purpose of the constant write-off, nor the solution it yields. One is therefore left with no guide but convenience.

Now, if the firm's profit fluctuates sharply, it may be most convenient to write off very large sums during profitable years, and very small sums during lean years. This introduces greater stability into dividend distributions, and into consumption. Indeed, from the national point of view, it would help to mitigate cyclical fluctuations if firms would distribute rather less during booms and rather more during recessions. This would come about automatically if the rule of thumb for calculating depreciation were to relate the annual sum to the gross profit ratio. (If replacement policy followed the same principle the effect on the economy would be destabilising; but we are here discussing not replacement but depreciation.)

Many accountants would be unhappy if the depreciation write-off fluctuated with earnings, since this might open the door to abuses by business managements. So long as the accountant has a rule of thumb, the amount written off in depreciation is not open to managerial manipulation; whereas, if a discretionary element enters, the result may be that the errors are in the direction of writing off too little. On the other hand, there are already some discretionary elements, under various guises. Directors do have special write-offs at convenient moments, and they do create special reserves from time to time. Accountants continue to base their calculations on original cost, while directors take account of inflation by creating special funds, not on a constant annual basis, but as is convenient from time to time, having regard to profit fluctuations from year to year.

Indeed, nowadays when in most prosperous businesses dividends are but a small proportion of gross profits, and are kept more or less stable irrespective of annual fluctuations in profits, it does not matter much whether dividends are kept stable by putting a fluctuating amount into the dividend reserve fund, or by putting a fluctuating amount into the depreciation fund. The point has significance only in those other firms which live from hand to mouth, and in these firms it may well be the best practical policy for those concerned to pretend that it would be scientifically incorrect to reduce depreciation quotas in years of low profits. Otherwise it becomes harder to ensure that dividends are not paid out of capital.

(c) *Asset valuation*
If a constant amount if written off in each year the value of the asset as shown in the books will bear no relationship to its real value. The value of most assets deteriorates very sharply in the early years of life, and more slowly thereafter. The main reason for this is that the early years are the most productive, and the most trouble-free. Hence net yield is highest in the first four or five years, and may then fall rapidly. In addition, the scrap value of an asset falls as soon as it is bought and installed, since, even if it is sold immediately in perfect condition, the cost of selling it and of dismantling any fixtures in which it has been embodied, has to be subtracted from the price which it could fetch if it were in the maker's warehouse.

Therefore, still sticking to rule of thumb methods, if one wanted the book value of an asset to be a truer reflection of its real value (whether its scrap or its inside value) the "diminishing balance" method of depreciation, which is widely used in the United Kingdom, would be superior both to the straight-line method, which has been general in the U.S.A., and also to the sinking-fund method, which is the favourite of the mathematically inclined. The diminishing balance method writes off each year not a constant amount but a constant proportion of the amount still standing in the books. For example, if one wants to write an asset down to 5 per cent of its value in 12 years (*i.e.* allowing 5 per cent for ultimate scrap value), one should write off 22·1 per cent of the amount on the books at the end of each year (ignoring interest on the depreciation fund). Thus by the end of three years (the first 25 per cent of its life) the asset has been written down by 53 per cent of its value; and at the end of six years (the first half of its life) it has been written down by 77 per cent. This is much more realistic than it would be to value the asset at three-quarters of its original price when it was three years old.

It may be objected that nobody expects the balance sheet value of a fixed asset to be its true value; neither its scrap value nor its inside value is relevant since the asset is not normally for sale. If any question of selling it arises, a special investigation can be made for the purpose of valuation. Indeed, to emphasise that depreciation in this context is not linked to the value of the assets, some writers refer to the writing off as "amortisation',' a term which more properly applies to the provision made for repaying a loan.

The same answer can be made to the comment that if the asset appears in the books at a false valuation, the owner will be misled in deciding whether or not to replace it by a new asset; delaying replacement if book value is too high, and replacing too soon if book value is too low. It is often alleged that some businessmen base their replacement decisions on the book value of their assets, so that accelerated depreciation encourages early replacement, while straight-line depreciation causes assets to be replaced less frequently. As we saw in the preceding section, replacement policy should be based upon the discounted future revenue of the asset, which we have been calling its "inside value", so decisions made on any other basis are erroneous. But since replacement happens only once in an asset's lifetime, a special investigation can be made for the purpose when necessary.

The argument that the books need not show the real value of the assets (in the sense of discounted future yield) is founded upon the proposition that the sole purpose of writing off depreciation annually is to keep funds within the business. Even on this basis, however, the constant annual write-off can be criticised. In the first place, if the assets lose half their value within the first quarter of their life, but only a quarter of their value is retained within the business, then capital has not been maintained intact. The gap will be closed in the later years of life by retaining funds in excess of real depreciation. This leads to the second criticism, which is that it may be dangerous to fix for depreciation a time-pattern which differs from the yield pattern of the asset. If the asset is going to yield disproportionately in its earlier years, it is unsafe to distribute dividends disproportionately in earlier years, relying on cutting dividends in later years even more than is necessary because of high depreciation levies which have been postponed. It seems both safer and more convenient to write down substantially when profits are substantial, and to leave little to be written off in later years when profits are low. Such a policy has also the advantage, shared by the policy of allowing depreciation to fluctuate with fluctuations in yields, that it makes more stable the sum shown as net profit in each year, and so helps to stabilise personal consumption and saving.

Some businessmen are disposed to go even further: to write off the asset not over the whole course of its life, but completely within four or five years, or even in extreme cases completely within the first year. The main argument for this is caution. Since what an asset will yield after five years from now is even less predictable than what it will earn in the next five years, it is thought prudent to provide for the possibility that it may be completely out-moded in five years. At the same time, the early write-off forces the owner to restrain his consumption until he has got his money back, after which it is safe to enjoy his profits to the full. Depreciation could not be calculated on this basis for determining prices in a market where the firm had several rivals, since the business would then go mainly to the firms which had already written down their assets and no firm would get business in the first year of its assets' life. But the purpose of accelerated depreciation is to influence not price policy but dividend policy. Quite different calculations are made for determining prices.

The difference which the method of depreciation makes to the amount written off annually is much greater in the case of a single asset than it is when all the assets of the firm are considered together, some of which are nearer the end of their life than others. There is a limiting case where the method makes no difference to aggregate depreciation. This is the case where (i) the stock of capital is constant, with asset prices unchanged, and (ii) the average age of the assets is constant because all assets are of the same type, and one is scrapped and replaced every year. On these assumptions, the total sum levied in depreciation in each year is the same whether one uses the straight line method, or the diminishing balance method, or whether one writes off each asset completely in the first year. This limiting case, however, must be very rare, if it is ever found, and the slightest relaxation of the assumptions will alter the result. For example, if gross investment is assumed not to be constant, but to be growing by a constant percentage each year, then the stock of capital ceases to be constant, and grows in each year. Methods involving an earlier write-off then bring in more depreciation in each year than does the straight line method. Adoption of these methods then also affects the financial position of the firm. For example, on these assumptions less income tax is payable so long as the business continues to grow, provided that the tax authorities permit use of the diminishing balance or other accelerated methods than if they insist on the straight line method. Also the business saves more, and needs less external money to finance its expansion.

In most firms the stock of capital is constant most of the time, since expansion takes place in spurts and not at a regular rate each year. The average age, however, is not constant, since a lot of equipment is installed together at one time, and average age increases every year until it is replaced. In these circumstances the earlier write-off methods make a substantial difference to the time-pattern of aggregate depreciation. The firm also accumulates funds which it will not need for some time, since most of the cost of plant is written off long before it falls due for replacement. These funds can safely be used for expanding the business.

The proposition that more is saved with accelerated depreciation so long as the business is expanding but not otherwise is easily illustrated by an arithmetical example. Take a new business just coming into existence, and assume that it invests £100 a year gross. Assume that the assets are identical, that they have a life of four years, and that their price is constant. Then the stock of capital will increase every year for four years, after which it will be constant, the gross investment of subsequent years serving merely to replace the asset scrapped in each year. If the firm uses the straight line method, depreciation in successive years will be

25 50 75 100 100 100 . . .

and the new money brought into the business will be

100 75 50 25 0 0 . . .

But if the firm writes each asset off completely in its first year, depreciation will be

100 100 100 100 100 100 . . .

and the new money brought into the business will be

100 0 0 0 0 0 . . .

Once the stock of capital becomes constant, in the fifth year and after, the two methods yield the same results, but in the earlier period, while the stock of capital is still growing, the results are substantially different. The second method raises 400 in depreciation in the first four years, and keeps new money down to 100; whereas the straight line method raises only 250 in depreciation in the same period, and involves raising 250 in new money. Of course, if the owner puts up all the money, his total income, saving and consumption over the first four years will be the same by either method; the difference is significant only where it is not necessarily the original owners who put up new money when it is required.

Since limiting cases are seldom relevant, it is for most firms significant to decide whether to write off a constant amount each year, or whether to accelerate depreciation. If the firm's assets grow less productive with age, balance sheet values will be significantly greater than real values in the earlier years if it writes off the same amount each year. Also, if it is expanding, accelerated depreciation will contribute more funds in each year than straight-line depreciation. To write off each asset completely in the first year is an extreme decision, which goes to the other extreme of depressing balance sheet values significantly below real values, and which also results in substantial saving if the business is expanding. However, where to draw the line between a constant and an immediate write-off is a matter for business decision; it is not a question to which there is a "scientific" answer.

(d) *Price determination*

The final objection to calculating depreciation by writing off the same amount each year is that a pricing policy based on this method of depreciation might lead to undesirable loss of business if competition is keen. In a competitive market the element of depreciation which enters into prices is user cost, which may fluctuate widely from one year to the next, in accordance with the extent of surplus capacity. Indeed this objection holds not only against the straight line method, but also against any other method of depreciation which is not based on assessing user cost whenever a pricing decision has to be made. Apart from the fact that these are rule of thumb methods, whereas the assessment of user cost requires assessment of the particular conditions of the moment, there is the even more fundamental obstacle that, whereas the purpose of these methods is the maintenance of capital intact, actual market conditions may be such that appropriate pricing is not consistent with maintaining capital intact. Strictly, depreciation for maintaining capital intact measures the difference in the value of an asset from one moment to another, whereas user cost measures only that part of the difference which is due to use. Even in the full capacity case, depreciation for pricing is based on the cost of replacing the asset, whereas depreciation for maintaining capital intact should presumably be based on the original cost of the asset, adjusted for changes in the general price level.

These objections are met by asserting that the purpose of writing off depreciation in the accounts is not to determine price policy, any more than it is to determine replacement policy, or to show the scrap value of the assets. The purpose is simply to retain within the business enough funds to replace the owners' capital when the asset's life expires. All these other objectives are valid objectives, but they call for special calculations as required.

The truth is that each purpose for which depreciation is measured requires a different concept. Nothing but confusion would flow from deciding that one of these concepts is more "scientific" than all the others, and from trying to make it serve all purposes.

(e) *Conclusion*

The conclusions of this section may be stated briefly as follows:

(1) Depreciation for the purpose of maintaining capital intact is different

from other depreciation concepts, and calculations made for this purpose are not necessarily appropriate for other purposes.

(2) If capital maintenance is defined in real rather than in money terms, changes in prices may call for considerable variation in the amounts written off from year to year.

(3) If profits fluctuate, it is more convenient for the shareholder to write off depreciation in years of high profits rather than to write off a constant amount in each year, but this point is not significant in firms which maintain a dividend stabilisation reserve or its equivalent.

(4) If the yield of the assets declines rapidly in the early years, it is more appropriate to write off most of the depreciation in the early years than to spread depreciation evenly over the life of the assets. But the significance of this point depends not only on the time pattern of yields, but also on whether the stock of capital and its average age are constant, on the degree of caution in managerial estimates of future yields, and on the extent to which depreciation is used as a source of saving for expanding the firm.

IV Depreciation as User Cost

In this section cost means differential cost: the difference which is made to total cost by changes in the level of output. This is the cost concept which is relevant in those situations where price is determined not by charging what is "fair", but by calculating the minimum which could be charged without out-of-pocket expense, and by adding something (which may be zero or negative) to this minimum.

For this purpose the test which must be applied to an item of expenditure is whether it is "escapable", *i.e.*, whether it varies with changes in output. If an item of expense cannot be escaped by reducing output, it does not enter into the calculation of user cost.

We have avoided the term "marginal" cost, and used the term "escapable", because the term marginal relates to a change of output by one unit only. But the concept of a unit is ambiguous wherever there are indivisible items of expenditure. For example, a railway company may calculate the cost of carrying one more passenger, or of adding one more carriage to the train, or of running one more train, or of working one more station. What is escapable at one of these levels of decisions may be inescapable at a different level, but at each level all that is escapable is relevant. The term "marginal" is therefore not appropriately indentified with the cost concept we need, unless it is defined in such a way that the term "unit of output" is an elastic concept, stretched to suit the relevant level of decision. This ties in with the comment made earlier to the effect that it is erroneous to say that price should equal marginal cost; for, if what is involved is a comparison between the consumer's valuation of the product and the escapable cost of production, the term "marginal" is misleading unless it is stretched to include changes in the scale of output at the relevant level of decision.

The concept of escapability has not only a quantity dimension, but also a time dimension. Costs which are inescapable today may yet be escapable next week. For example, at any time a firm is committed by its contracts. It may be hiring resources (buildings, staff, machinery, etc.) at a level surplus to its current requirements. If the firm is calculating the escapable cost of making an addition to output, it must know not only the size of the addition (whether it is within the capacity already on hand) but also for how long this addition will last. If the addition will be completed within the lifetime of existing contracts, and if the firm has no other use for the surplus capacity, then the cost of these contracts is not escapable, and does not enter into the calculation of differential costs. But if contracts would expire while the additional output is still wanted, the cost of renewing these contracts will then have become escapable, and will be a part of differential cost. The same applies to the fixed assets of the firm. Decisions which will be fully executed within the lifetime of all existing assets are not in the same category as decisions of longer term, which embrace periods during which the question of replacing some assets will arise.

We must also remember that assets fall due for replacement at different times. Expiry of an asset may put the firm into the position that it is at full capacity with respect to that type of asset, while it has surplus capacity in others. Assets which fall due for replacement have to be considered in terms of full capacity user cost. What is more, some of these assets bring complicated decisions in their train. Asset A may expire in year n, and assets B and C may be due to expire in years $(n + 4)$ and $(n + 6)$ respectively. A may be an expensive asset with a long life, such that there is no point in replacing A in year n unless one has already decided to replace B and C when their turn comes. Hence the expiry of A in year n may make year n the year of decision for B and C also. In this year of decision all relevant assets will be reviewed, and unless the group as a whole is expected to pay (*e.g.*, unless it may pay to renew B in year $(n + 4)$ and C in year $(n + 6)$), A will not now be renewed.

Thus, in calculating user cost one must distinguish between commitments which have already been made, and commitments which have not yet been entered into; and even within the category of existing commitments, one must distinguish between those which expire within the relevant period, and those which do not. The analysis which follows is accordingly separated in accordance with this distinction. We consider first the case where the firm is already committed to assets, with surplus capacity; and then the case where, because it is working at full capacity, the analysis of the cost of expanding output can be made without reference to existing commitments.

(a) *Surplus capacity cost*

In this part of the analysis we assume that the firm has surplus capacity, such that it can produce additional output without any additional investment. The problem is to define user cost, meaning the difference made to asset values by the decision to increase output.

First, we must be certain that surplus capacity exists in all the relevant senses. The quantity dimension must be right. That is to say, the additional output under consideration must not be so large that if it were taken on there would no longer be surplus capacity. New business of this magnitude, even though it merely eliminated surplus capacity without requiring new investment, would put the firm into the full capacity category. To take on such an order would prevent the firm from taking on some other order which might come along, so calculations would have to be made in terms of the potential yield from orders which this one eliminates; thus we would no longer be assuming surplus capacity.

Also in the quantity dimension one must remember the existence of indivisibilities. There may be surplus capacity for some types of assets but not for others; surplus capacity in railway tracks, for example, but not surplus engines or carriages. Then we get a mixture of two user costs; one for the assets which would have to be installed, or which would now be fully occupied, and another for those which would continue to have surplus capacity even if this order were accepted.

Then there is the time dimension. We must be certain that the order fits wholly into a period of surplus capacity, since an order which overlaps a period of full capacity imposes a need for additional investment, and must be treated accordingly. Any replacements which fall due during the relevant period, and any later replacements which these in turn may bring in their train, must be treated as full capacity items.

If we are certain that surplus capacity will exist for all the relevant time, the problem becomes simple. We have to isolate what difference is made to the cost or value of the assets by taking on additional business.

First it may be that some of the assets the firm is using have merely been hired, on contracts which permit the firm to return them during the period under consideration. Thus the cost, or some part of the cost, of these assets is escapable if the firm chooses not to produce, and must be included in user cost. On the other hand, though the firm may have the right to return the assets, it may find it more convenient or more profitable to keep them, in the interest of expected future output. Then their current rental belongs not to the user cost of this period but to the user cost of the periods for which they are being kept.

Similarly, the firm is in a position to scrap its surplus assets instead of using them. The decision whether to use them therefore involves both the question whether to keep them, and also the question whether to use them or to keep them unused. The first question involves measuring what Professor David Solomons has called "the retainer cost"[1], while the second involves measuring "wear and tear".

The retainer cost is the cost of holding the assets unused. This is the interest on the sum the assets would fetch if they were sold, plus any deterioration in their value during the period for which they are held. For the purpose of measuring this deterioration, the value of the assets at the beginning of the period is their scrap value, but the value at the end of the period depends on whether the assets will be sold at the end of the period (in which case it is the scrap value), or will continue to be held by the firm (in which case it is the inside value).

Let us first assume that the asset will be sold at the end of the period. Writing S for scrap value, r for the relevant rate of interest, the subscripts 0 and 1 for the beginning and end of the period, and the subscripts u and n to indicate whether the asset is used or not used during the period, the *retainer cost* is:

Depreciation

$$(S_0 - S_{n1}) + rS_0 \qquad (1a)$$

and *wear and tear* is

$$S_{n1} - S_{u1} \qquad (2a)$$

User cost is the sum of these two, namely

$$(S_0 - S_{n1} + r\ S_0) + (S_{n1} - S_{u1}) \qquad (3a)$$

In deciding whether to use the asset or not, the firm has to consider both the retainer cost and the wear and tear. However, retainer cost is relevant only if it is positive. For if the asset will rise in value by more than the interest cost, it will be held whether it is used or not, and the amount by which it will rise in value is not relevant in determining whether to use it or not. It is only if the asset will fall in value, or will rise in value by less than the interest cost, that the question arises whether the asset should be held; and it is only in this case that retainer cost enters into the cost of using the asset. In this case, *user cost* reduces to

$$S_0 - S_{u1} + r\ S_0 \qquad (4a)$$

So much for the case where the asset will be sold at the end of the period. If it will not be sold, we have to substitute inside value at the end of the period, V_1, for scrap value at the end of the period, S_1. *Retainer cost* is then

$$(S_0 - V_{n1}) + r\ S_0 \qquad (1b)$$

Wear and tear is

$$V_{n1} - V_{u1} \qquad (2b)$$

and *user cost* is the sum of the two

$$(S_0 - V_{n1} + r\ S_0) + (V_{n1} - V_{u1}) \qquad (3b)$$

Here again the first term is not relevant unless it is positive, in which case *user cost* reduces to

$$S_0 - V_1 + r\ S_0 \qquad (4b)$$

It is a matter of the choice of words whether to define user cost so that it includes retainer cost, or is confined to wear and tear only. Retainer cost, if positive, is part of the cost of use; it enters into marginal cost, and is relevant to profit maximisation. It differs from Marshall's supplementary cost, which is the sum required to maintain capital intact. Retainer cost was neglected by Lord Keynes in his definition of user cost in *The General Theory of Employment, Interest and Money*, because he assumed that the assets are retained whether they are used or not; *i.e.*, he assumed that retainer cost is zero or negative. (Keynes' chief interest was in the economy considered as a whole). However, since retainer cost may be positive, and since retention is necessary to use, it seems better to define user cost to include retainer cost as well as wear and tear. Moreover, as we shall see, this formulation makes it easier to tie together the analysis of the cost of using surplus capacity and the analysis of the cost of using assets at full capacity.

If the first term of equations 3a or 3b is zero or negative, and is therefore irrelevant, the equation becomes equivalent to saying that user cost is equal to the value of wear and tear caused by use. This second term may be positive or negative. It is negative if use helps to maintain value. It is positive only in those cases where economic life is shortened by use, and is not determined by obsolescence or by physical deterioration due to the elements. In these circumstances the cost of present use is that some future use of the asset is thereby eliminated, and the value of this cost is the discounted present value of the gross profit which will thus be lost (if it can be calculated). Thus, we may assume the asset to be still capable of yielding m years of output, its actual life n years being greater than m if there are some intervals during which production is unprofitable. The owner chooses the m most profitable years, and the user cost is the discounted present value of the profit which could be earned in the marginally profitable year which is just included or just excluded from the list. (From the standpoint of years which are included it is the $(m + 1)$ the most profitable year, which is the year that they displace; whereas from the standpoint of the excluded years, it is the mth most profitable year, which has displaced them. For convenience we shall refer to the marginally most profitable year as the mth). This mth year may be any year 1, 2, . . ., n in the sequence of n years.

The position of the mth year in the sequence does not affect decisions. After this year has passed, calculations continue to be based on the fact that each remaining output-year of the asset's capacity has already been booked for some output at least as valuable as the mth, if not also more valuable. Wear and tear now becomes equal to the least valuable output which still remains. But if expectations of yield remain unchanged, this makes no difference to what is included or excluded.

The preceding paragraphs have calculated user cost in terms of output years, but this is easily translated into terms of the cost of marginal output. If the asset is capable of producing m units of output through its life, the owner chooses the m most profitable (when allowance is made for periods of asset idleness, the actual life of the asset, n years, exceeds the equivalent period which it would take to produce m units of output without interruption). Marginal wear and tear is then the discounted present value of the marginally included mth unit of output. In every year the asset will be used intensively up to the point where the discounted yield on the marginal unit of output equals the discounted value of the mth unit of output.

The case where fluctuations in output are expected is especially interesting, since these involve periods of surplus capacity lying between periods of full capacity. It is necessary to be certain that additional work taken on in periods of temporary surplus capacity will not spread over into periods of full capacity. An order for continuous supply "until further notice" must be treated as an order requiring additional assets of its own if it will extend over periods of full capacity.

If additional output is demanded which is limited to a period of surplus capacity, with retainer cost zero or negative, user cost is zero if the asset's life does not depend on use, and is wear and tear (*i.e.* discounted value of use in the displaced $(m + 1)$th period) if life depends upon use. Many kinds of business have regular fluctuations in output, due to the coincidence of regular fluctuations in demand with the impossibility or the high cost of storing the product or service; and in many such businesses the user cost of assets in the surplus periods is zero or nearly zero. Examples are transportation, electricity, hotels, places of entertainment, and so on. Such businesses usually recognise that user cost in slack periods is zero or rather small, and they adjust their prices so that virtually the whole cost of their assets is raised in periods of full capacity. One well known exception is the British electricity supply industry, which has traditionally charged the same price at all times, and which is only slowly and in marginal traffic experimenting with charging lower prices for off-peak supplies.

(b) *Full capacity cost*

We now assume that the firm is operating at full capacity, and is calculating the cost of taking on new business. This involves installing additional capacity. How is the cost of this capacity to be allocated between different outputs or different years?

At this stage we need hardly reiterate that the cost of existing capacity throws no light on the problem. It cannot be assumed that the cost of additional output will be proportionately the same as the cost of existing output. Neither is the answer to be found by adding the cost of the addition to existing cost, and dividing the whole by the new level of output. The additional output must be costed separately.

Given the cost of the new asset and its potential capacity over the whole of its lifetime, an average cost per unit of capacity could be calculated. Better still, if the asset is expected to be worked below capacity for part of the time, total cost could be divided by expected total output instead of by full capacity output. But these averages would be irrelevant. Suppose that the yield of the asset is expected to fluctuate, in accordance with fluctuations in demand, which will show up as fluctuations in price or in output. If we arrived at user cost simply by averaging total cost we should find some periods in which yield would not cover user cost so defined, and in which production should therefore not take place. But this result would be incorrect, since cost arbitrarily determined in this way does not really tell us what difference, if any, production makes to costs in that or any subsequent period.

There are only two cases where user cost may be deduced directly from the original cost of the asset, and neither of these occurs frequently.

The first is the case where the asset will yield the same amount in each year. User cost may then be interpreted as the minimum sum which the annual yield must be if the investment is to be worth while. This sum is given by the formula.

$$S_0 \cdot \frac{r(1 + r)^m}{(1 + r)^m - 1} \tag{5}$$

where S_0 is the original cost of the asset, and m the number of years of useful life.

In the other case we have to assume that the inside value of the asset and its scrap value (or purchase price) are always the same, presumably because the market is perfect in every sense. Then, applying the formula derived in the preceding section, the user cost of the first year reduces to the formula already given

$$S_0(1 + r) - S_{u1} \quad (4a)$$

which is the interest on the purchase price plus the decline in the market value of the asset during the year. Each succeeding year has a corresponding cost. When these are summed, the total equals the original cost of the asset, plus interest on the sum outstanding in each year. The result is possible, however, only because we have assumed that scrap value is at all times the measure of cost; we then get the same sort of answer that we would get if we assumed the firm to be hiring the asset instead of buying it.

In the normal case scrap value is not the same as inside value, and yield is not constant from year to year. User cost cannot then be computed with reference to original cost.

An asset must be thought of as yielding a series of different services through its life, the difference consisting in the timing. Once installed, it yields a number of services in unalterable proportions, each service being the capacity to produce at a particular time. These capacities are a "joint product," and the appropriate analysis is that of joint supply in fixed proportions.

The solution to the joint supply case with fixed proportions is that the total cost cannot be allocated between the products other than by the market process. Mere averaging will not do. The products taken together must yield the total cost, but some will yield a larger portion and others a smaller portion or nothing, in accordance with what the market will bear. At some times during its life the asset will have a high yield, while at other times it will have a low yield. The firm must get what it can at different times, subject only to the condition that the asset should not be installed unless the firm expects to earn its total cost over the lifetime of the asset.

Let us take a concrete example. The firm is already working at full capacity. It makes a new contact, and is asked to quote for a new order. An additional asset would have to be installed, and we assume that the life of the asset is known, and is not determined by wear and tear. If the order is for a quantity equal to full capacity of the asset throughout its life, the answer is simple: cost per unit is total cost divided by total quantity, if interest is excluded when calculating cost, or is in accordance with the formula (5) given on page 230, which includes interest in cost. More probably the order is for a short period only, leaving open the question whether it will be renewed, and if it is renewed, whether demand will be steady or fluctuating. The firm has then to make its best guess as to what other business will be available to supplement this order at times when it is not keeping the asset fully occupied; and to replace the order altogether if it should not be repeated, or if it should be repeated with intervals of less than full capacity. In this way the firm makes its best guess as to the projected time pattern of use of the asset. As already mentioned in Section II, this guessing has many complications—isolating the yield of the particular asset, choosing the best time pattern of use, and so on—but some such guessing cannot be avoided when deciding whether an asset is worth buying or not. If the firm regards the future as very uncertain, once the original order is completed, it will want to recoup the major part of the asset's cost from this first order, even though this order may be completed very early in the life of the asset. Alternatively it may think that prospects will grow better with time. It may be anxious to take on this order as a gateway to better things; to a connection with a prized and long desired customer, or to a foothold in what is considered to be an expanding market. Then it will deliberately add very little for depreciation to the prices of earlier outputs, in the expectation of a fuller harvest later. (How much it will retain from profits in each year as depreciation, if it wishes to maintain the value of its capital intact, is a separate question, to which, as we have already seen in Section III of this chapter, it may decide to give a different answer).

It should be noted that the analysis applies whenever some fluctuation in the asset's yield is foreseen, even though the asset is expected to work at full capacity throughout its life. Yield may vary at full capacity because the price of ouput varies, or because of variations in operating costs. Thus yield may be expected to decline progressively throughout the asset's life, or it may be expected to fluctuate. The case where surplus capacity is expected at some periods is merely the limiting case in which expected yield is zero.

These results can be tested against the formulae for user cost which were given above in discussing the surplus capacity case. In terms of these formulae, the cost of purchasing an additional asset is identified with S_0, since this is the sum that can be saved by not purchasing.

Let us calculate user cost in the first year. If the asset will be sold at the end of the first year the problem of allocating costs between years does not arise. If the asset will not be sold, the relevant formula is again

$$(S_0 + rS_0 - V_{n1}) + (V_{n1} - V_{u1}) \qquad (3b)$$

If the inside value of the asset substantially exceeds its original cost, V_{n1} may exceed S_0 by more than the interest cost. Then the first term (the retainer cost) will be negative, and only the second term will count. In the limiting case $S_0 = V_0$, since, if the inside value exceeds the cost of buying and installing the asset, investment will be pushed to the point where these two are marginally equal. In this case user cost reduces to

$$rV_0 + (V_0 - V_{u1}) \qquad (5b)$$

where the second term is the depreciation in the inside value of the asset during the year. Since the value of the asset is the sum of the discounted yields in each year, the main element in this depreciation is the yield of the first year (the rest is due to the fact that the yield of subsequent years is discounted back one year less in V_{u1} than in V_0). We deduce, therefore, that the main element in the user cost of the first year is the yield of that year, provided that originally the asset is not marginally profitable. If we can further identify S_1 with V_{u1}, we will get a series of user costs which when added together will just exhaust the total cost, each year being represented by its expected yield. However, if the inside value and the scrap value ever diverge, summation no longer gives this simple result.

Normally retainer cost is zero or negative, at least after the first year, and user cost consists only of wear and tear. This is zero if life is determined by obsolescence or by mere passage of time, in which case the cost of the asset has again to be allocated in accordance with yields. If life is determined by wear and tear, user cost will be the discounted yield of the marginally excluded $(m + 1)^{th}$ year. In the limiting case where yields are the same in each year user cost can be determined by the formula already given,

$$\frac{r(1 + r)^m}{(1 + r)^m - 1} \qquad (5)$$

related either to S_0, if the investment is marginally profitable, or to V_0, if V_0 exceeds S_0. The limiting case, however, is unusual. Where yields vary from one year to the next, the marginally excluded yield will be below the average of the included yields, and will bear no fixed relationship to S_0 or to V_0. There is a minimum below which the yield must not fall if the asset is to be used, but if we wish to allocate the full cost of the asset between the years, we are still thrown back on the proposition that each year must yield what it can above user cost, so that the sum of the discounted yields is not less than original cost.

(c) *Conclusion*

User cost is an unsatisfactory concept in practice because it turns upon estimates of the future yield of an asset in each period of its life. Accordingly, except in simple cases where user cost is zero or negative, the estimates are highly speculative and subjective, and are of the sort which change easily between breakfast and lunch. These uncertainties are inherent in the problem. Moreover, they separate this calculation in degree but not in kind from other business calculations, since most business decisions have in the last analysis to be based upon guesses about the future. The main practical result of this uncertainty is that in estimating user cost, business men tend to attach small value to distant yields, and tend to require an asset to pay for itself in a very short time. Some firms in the United States of America are reported not to embark upon new investment inless they expect the investment to pay for itself within four years of coming into full production. No doubt there is wide variation in this respect between individuals, between industries, and between countries; but in view of the uncertainties we need not be surprised that most business men tend to take only rather roughly a concept to which economists have tried to bring so much precision.

NOTES

* I am indebted to Professors Robert Eisner, A. D. Scott, and David Solomons for helpful comments on the manuscript.

[1] See "Economic and Accounting Concepts of Cost and Value", M. Backer (editor) *Modern Accounting Theory*. Englewood Cliffs, N.J.: Prentice Hall, 1966, p. 135.

PART TWO

WORLD TRADE

[7]

World Production, Prices and Trade, 1870-1960

The level of international trade depends upon the level of world production, and on prices ; and, since prices depend on production, the level of international trade is thus a direct function of world output. The purpose of this article is to unravel these relationships, and to express them quantitatively. It will emerge that, apart from the effects of war, if we have certain index numbers of production, we can deduce from them the index numbers of prices and of international trade.

The process of unravelling has to be done in stages. First we examine the statistics of world trade in manufactured commodities, and show how these can be derived from statistics of the quantity of primary products entering into world trade, and of the terms of trade. Then we relate the quantity of primary products to world production of manufactures. And finally we relate the terms of trade to world production of manufactures, on the one hand, and of primary products on the other. Thus eventually we are able to deduce trade and prices from statistics of production.

I. World Trade in Manufactures.

For statistics of world trade as a whole, we are dependent upon magnificent work done by the League of Nations. In *Industrialisation and Foreign Trade* series were published extending from 1876 to 1938, and showing separately the trade in manufactures and the trade in primary products. These figures were published as quinquennial averages. Subsequently they have been revised, and a new series exists of annual figures, extending from 1881. These figures have not yet been published, but they have been made available to me by the courtesy of Dr. F. Hilgerdt, now of the United Nations Secretariat, who has been responsible for their compilation. It is these annual figures that have been used in this article for the analysis of international trade.

TABLE I

WORLD PRODUCTION AND TRADE

	Production			Trade		
	Manufactures		Food	Manufactures Ratio, %	Primary Products	
	A	B			Value	Quantum
	1	2	3	4	5	6
1870	19·8	23·8	—	—	—	—
1871	21·5	25·9	—	—	—	—
1872	23·6	27·9	—	—	—	—
1873	23·5	28·0	—	—	—	—
1874	23·5	28·2	—	—	—	—
1875	22·8	27·4	—	—	—	—
1876	23·6	28·7	—	—	—	—
1877	24·2	29·1	—	—	—	—
1878	24·7	29·3	—	—	—	—
1879	25·1	28·8	—	—	—	—
1880	27·4	30·4	—	—	—	—
1881	28·8	31·5	—	35·6	36·4	36·2
1882	30·8	34·1	—	36·6	37·5	37·1
1883	31·9	35·4	—	36·5	37·8	38·7
1884	31·0	34·7	—	37·7	36·0	39·0
1885	30·7	35·0	—	37·9	33·9	39·2
1886	32·6	34·8	—	38·2	33·4	41·1
1887	34·9	37·7	—	38·1	34·3	42·5
1888	36·8	40·2	—	39·2	36·2	43·4
1889	39·8	43·8	—	37·4	40·0	46·8
1890	41·9	45·2	—	37·0	41·6	48·4
1891	42·3	45·4	—	34·7	43·1	50·0
1892	42·8	44·5	—	34·3	40·7	49·5
1893	41·2	44·8	—	35·3	39·9	49·1
1894	42·5	47·6	—	35·2	39·6	52·7
1895	46·7	50·3	—	35·6	40·4	56·4
1896	47·7	53·8	—	37·1	42·3	57·9
1897	50·0	55·9	—	36·0	44·8	61·0
1898	54·5	59·7	—	33·9	47·5	64·7
1899	58·5	63·3	—	35·2	50·4	65·6
1900	58·7	63·1	—	34·4	53·9	62·5
1901	60·9	62·5	—	34·8	53·9	65·6
1902	65·9	66·3	—	35·1	55·6	68·8
1903	67·3	67·6	—	34·9	59·5	72·0
1904	67·5	70·4	—	35·6	61·2	73·9
1905	74·7	74·7	—	36·6	65·2	78·4
1906	78·1	76·8	—	36·1	71·4	80·4
1907	80·6	80·1	—	36·1	75·1	80·4
1908	73·5	77·5	—	38·9	69·0	77·7
1909	81·0	81·7	—	36·3	76·4	85·7

TABLE I—*continued*

WORLD PRODUCTION AND TRADE

	Production			Trade		
	Manufactures		Food	Manu-factures Ratio, %	Primary Products	
	A	B			Value	Quantum
	1	2	3	4	5	6
1910	86·4	87·4	—	35·0	84·7	87·0
1911	87·8	91·6	—	35·7	88·2	92·6
1912	95·4	96·6	—	36·0	97·5	99·7
1913	100·0	100·0	100	37·0	100·0	100·0
1921	85·5	77·7	96	41·5	104·5	79·7
1922	104·8	92·2	104	41·1	112·5	92·1
1923	109·9	90·9	108	39·6	122·1	85·5
1924	116·3	106·2	107	38·0	40·0	99·0
1925	125·4	111·9	113	35·9	165·0	110·8
1926	129·9	114·3	112	36·8	155·0	109·0
1927	138·9	128·4	117	36·8	163·0	120·1
1928	144·4	133·3	122	38·3	164·7	124·8
1929	154·8	139·3	121	38·7	167·0	132·3
1930	135·5	127·9	121	38·8	136·1	130·1
1931	116·7	113·8	123	39·2	95·6	122·3
1932	100·0	103·9	125	36·5	67·3	114·8
1933	112·9	113·7	127	37·0	59·5	111·9
1934	125·3	127·4	126	37·6	56·4	110·2
1935	139·8	139·4	124	37·0	58·4	117·3
1936	157·4	149·5	128	36·5	63·7	121·6
1937	172·6	164·6	131	36·7	78·3	133·6
1938	154·5	161·4	133	40·1	63·8	118·6
1950	250·3	200·9	139	36·4	184·0	147·9

Series 1. *World Production of Manufactures, including the U.S.A., but excluding the U.S.S.R.*

Series 2. *World Production of Manufactures, excluding both the U.S.A. and the U.S.S.R.*

Series 3. *World Production of Food, excluding the U.S.S.R.*

Series 4. *Ratio of the value of Manufactures imported by all countries, to the value of all imports.*

Series 5. *The value of Primary Products entering into international trade.*

Series 6. *The quantity of Primary Products entering into international trade.*

All Series are index numbers, with 1913 as base, except Series 4. For notes on sources, etc., see Statistical Appendix.

If we look at the statistics of world trade in manufactures, the most striking fact which emerges is that, in terms of money value, the trade in manufactures is more or less a constant proportion of world trade. This can be seen by running one's eye down series 4 in Table I. The proportion was 35·6% in 1881, and 36·4% in 1950. The average of the figures appearing in series 4 is 36·9%.

The relative constancy of this proportion over seventy years is a baffling phenomenon. Some people would expect to find the trade in manufactures an increasing proportion of world trade over the years, because world production of manufactures increases more rapidly than world production of primary products. Other people, on the other hand, expect the opposite; they would have expected the spread of industrialisation through the world to diminish the share of manufactures in world trade. Neither school has been right.

There is a plausible explanation for the constancy of the share of manufactures. World trade consists, to a large extent, of the exchange of manufactures against primary products. Industrial countries import the larger part of the primary produce entering into international trade, and non-industrial countries import the larger part of the manufactures. According to a League of Nations calculation,[1] the twelve leading manufacturing nations took 74% of the primary products entering into international trade in 1935, but only 35% of the manufactures. In so far as world trade consists of an exchange of manufactures for primary products, the proportions cannot change; an increased purchase of primary products will be associated with increased sale of manufactures in the same proportion, and *vice versa*.

However, world trade is not exclusively an exchange of manufactures against primary products. If it were, the share of each would be 50%, whereas in fact the share of primary products is more than one and a half times as great as the share of manufactures. Some primary products are exchanged against each other; some manufactures are also exchanged

[1]Quoted in *Industrialisation and Foreign Trade*, p. 19.

against each other ; and there is an exchange of both against invisible services.[1]

There is therefore no *prima facie* reason why manufactures should be a constant proportion of world trade. Neither is the proportion constant from year to year. There are variations which cannot be explained. The annual variations do not fit the trade cycle, and cannot be reduced substantially by lagging (*e.g.* on the theory that this year's purchase of manufactures derives from last year's sales of primary products). Using moving averages gives less variation than does using annual figures, but there still remain differences of the average proportion from one decade to another which cannot be explained. It is not a matter of price, since the average proportion does not correlate with the price, being low in the 1890's, when manufactures are dear, and high in the 1930's when manufactures are again dear. Neither does it correlate with tariff levels. There is a fairly good correlation, before 1913, with the level of foreign investment, the share of manufactures being highest when foreign investment is highest ; but the relation breaks down altogether after 1913. Further analysis may reveal the secret, and explain what determines the share of manufactures in world trade. All that we can say at present is that over seventy years the annual proportion has seldom moved more than two points away from 37%.

Thus, if we treat the share of manufactures in world trade as constant, we do some violence to the facts, but not much violence. It is convenient to treat it as constant, and to see what follows.

Let us use the following symbols :

M_T, an index number of the volume of trade in manufactures ;
M_P, an index number of the price of manufactures in money ;
C_T, an index number of the volume of trade in primary products ;
C_P, an index number of the price of primary products in money.

[1]A. O. Hirschmann attempts to measure these exchanges in "The Commodity Structure of World Trade," *Quarterly Journal of Economics*, 1943.

Then, when we say that the share of manufactures is constant, we say that

$$M_T \times M_P = C_T \times C_P$$

the left-hand side of the equation yielding an index number of the money value of manufactures entering into international trade, and the right hand side yielding an index of the money value of primary products entering into international trade.

We are interested in the determinants of the volume of trade in manufactures, so we shall keep M_T only on the left-hand side, with the result :

$$M_T = C_T \times (C_P \div M_P)$$

$C_P \div M_P$ is the terms of trade between primary products and manufactures. The result is therefore equivalent to saying that, if we know the quantity of primary products being bought, and the price being paid for them (relatively to the price of manufactures), we can derive the quantity of manufactures.

Our next tasks are therefore to find the determinants of the quantity of primary products entering into trade, and of the terms of trade between manufactures and primary products.

II. The Quantum of Trade in Primary Products.

The fact that the leading industrial countries take three-quarters of the primary products entering into international trade, suggests that there should be some relationship between the wealth of these countries, and the quantity of this trade. For the wealth of these countries the simplest index to use is the index of world production of manufactures, which again we owe to Dr. Hilgerdt's splendid work for the League of Nations.

The index of world production of manufactures published in *Industrialisation and Foreign Trade* cannot be used for this purpose as it stands. In the first place, the U.S.S.R. must be excluded. There are two reasons for this. The first is that the League's index incorporates the official manufacturing index of the U.S.S.R. This index shows an enormous increase of production in the nineteen thirties, which is known to have been exaggerated by misuse of price statistics. However, even if a more correct U.S.S.R. series were available, it would still be necessary to exclude the U.S.S.R. This is because the U.S.S.R. developed in the twenties and thirties as a self-sufficient economy, doing less international trade than Tsarist Russia. The growth of manufacturing in the U.S.S.R. is not therefore reflected in trade statistics, and before we make comparisons involving international trade we must first exclude the U.S.S.R. from the world index of manufacturing.

Similar reasoning, it turns out, applies to the U.S.A. For if we plot, year by year, quantity of primary products traded (corrected for price changes) against world manufacturing production, (excluding the U.S.S.R. but including the U.S.A.), on logarithmic scales, the result is almost a straight line from 1881 to 1913. But the figures for the nineteen twenties, though they also lie on a straight line, do not lie on the same straight line as those for 1881 to 1913. The line of the nineteen twenties lies to the right, indicating that there has been an increase of manufacturing production during the war without a corresponding increase of imports. Whereas, if one uses for manufacturing a series which excludes both the U.S.A. and the U.S.S.R., the result from 1881 to 1929 is a single straight line.[1]

Table I gives both manufacturing series, series 1 including the U.S.A., and series 2, excluding the U.S.A. Both exclude the U.S.S.R. In Chart I, series 2 is plotted against series 6, on logarithmic scales. The result, from 1881 to 1929, is a straight line with the formula

$$\log C_T = 0{\cdot}1238 + 0{\cdot}8702 \log M_N$$

where C_T is the index number of quantum of trade in primary products, and M_N the index number of world production of manufactures (excluding both the U.S.A. and the U.S.S.R.), both index numbers from the base 1913 = 10·00.

It is not hard to see why a better result is obtained when the U.S.A. is excluded. For the U.S.A. economy is a largely

[1]It is anomalous to plot trade figures which include U.S.A. trade against output figures which exclude U.S.A. output, but this cannot be helped since we do not have separate annual trade figures for the U.S.A. and the rest of the world since 1881, on a comparable basis. The anomaly is not great because U.S.A. imports of primary products were only about ten per cent. of the world total in 1913.

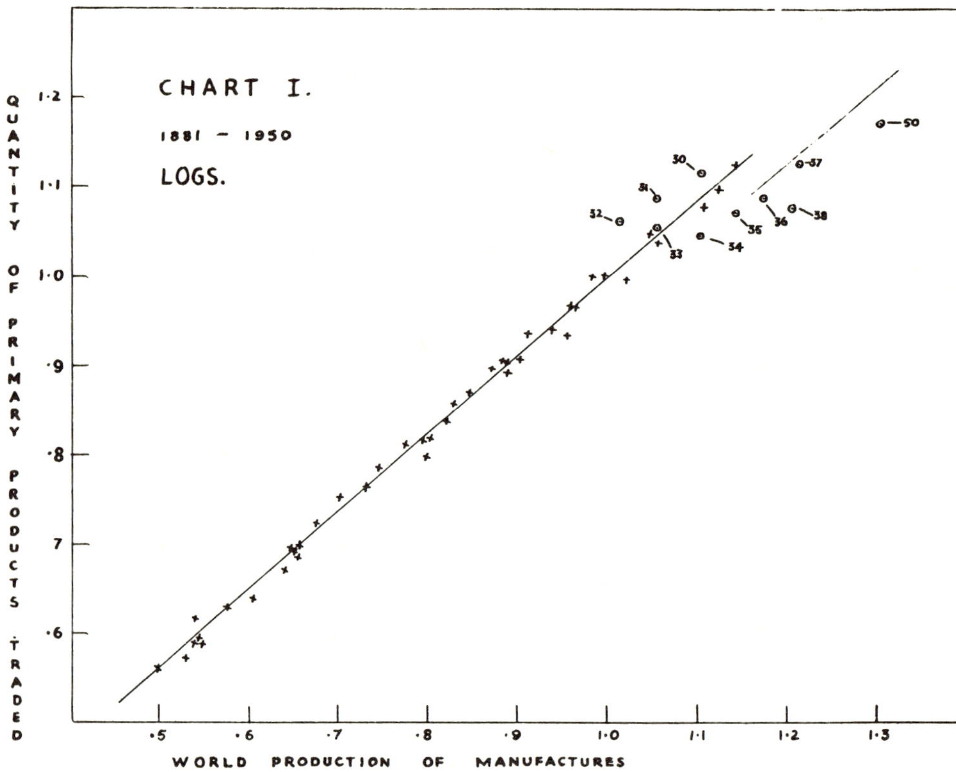

self-sufficient economy. In the period 1881 to 1913, the U.S.A. and other countries expand pretty constantly, and the fact that they expand at different rates does not prevent our relationship from coming out as a straight line ; it merely helps to determine the coefficient of M_N. When we come to the war, however, the U.S.A. expands while the other countries do not. A straight line relationship is resumed after the war, but the relative growth of the self-sufficient U.S.A. prevents the two straight lines from being the same. When we plot instead an index which excludes the U.S.A., we get the same straight line right up to 1929, and this indicates that the war had very little effect on the propensity to import of the major countries.[1]

The straight line which we have found shows that, for small changes, a 1% increase in world manufacturing is associated with an 0·87% increase in world trade in primary products.

Does not the price of primary products, *i.e.* the terms of trade, affect the relationship? The answer is in the negative. If we use the formula

$$\log C_T = a + b \log M_N - c \log P_C$$

where P_C stands for the terms of trade,
the elasticity of demand over the period 1881 to 1929 as a whole comes out at —0·02, which is hardly significant. On the other hand, if we use the same formula over short periods of a few years, we get quite high elasticities. The explanation is that there is a good correlation with deviations of the price from a moving average, but not with the average price itself. This is therefore, a spurious correlation.

The truth is that if we take C_T as dependent on M_N only, then actual C_T lies below the straight line in booms and above the straight line in slumps. This can be seen in the following way. If we use the results of our previous regression analysis, where the coefficient of M_N is 0·8702, and calculate from it what C_T should be in each year, we can divide actual C_T by calculated C_T, to show the divergence. We do this in the following series, running from boom year to boom year.

[1]Actually, if the war had had no effect whatever on the relationship between trade and output, the points for the Nineteen-twenties should lie not on the line extending from 1881 to 1913, but a little above it. This is because the disproportionate increase in U.S.A. output should be reflected in disproportionately larger trade. However, the difference is small, because U.S.A. trade is small. The meagre data available suggest that the coefficient of M_N for the U.S.A. only was about 0·8, and for the rest of the world about 0·85. From this we may calculate roughly that world trade in primary products in the 'twenties was about one per cent. lower than it ought to have been, having regard to levels of manufacturing output. This deficiency is well within the range of errors in the data. If there was a real deficiency, it is to be attributed to increased self-sufficiency promoted by the war, and not to tariffs, which were no higher in the 'twenties than in 1913 (cf. my *Economic Survey*, 1919-1939, p. 151).

PERCENTAGE DIVERGENCE BETWEEN ACTUAL AND CALCULATED C_T

1882	—3·9	1890	—2·1	1900	—5·4	1907	—1·0
83	—3·1	91	0·7	01	0·0	08	—1·6
84	—0·6	92	1·6	02	—0·2	09	3·6
85	—1·0	93	0·0	03	2·6	10	—0·8
86	4·4	94	1·9	04	1·7	11	1·3
87	0·7	95	4·0	05	2·5	12	4·2
88	—2·8	96	0·7	06	2·6	13	1·4
89	—2·6	97	2·6	07	—1·0		
1890	—2·1	98	2·7				
		99	—0·9				
		1900	—5·4				

The minuses, it will be seen, appear at the top and bottom of each column, the boom years, while the pluses are in the middle.

What this signifies is that, while it is true that trade falls in the slump and rises in the boom, the year by year fluctuation of trade is not as great as the year by year fluctuation of production of manufactures. Stocks of primary products are accumulated by importing countries during the slump, and are used up during the boom. Also, food consumption fluctuates less than does manufacturing output.[1]

(It is also noticeable that actual imports exceed expected imports for almost the whole of the 1890's. This is consistent with the fact that the 1890's were rather a depressed decade. But there may also be another explanation. When we were examining the ratio of the trade in manufactures to total trade, we were puzzled by the ratio for manufactures being rather low in the 1890's. Now, by quite a different route, we find the trade in primary products rather high in the same decade. The explanation of both these phenomena may be errors in the data. The process by which the League of Nations has split world trade into the categories of manufactures and primary products is rather rough, and it is just possible that too little has been assigned to the one and too much to the other in the 'nineties).

So far, we have noted only the existence of a straight line relationship from 1881 to 1929. Reference to Chart I will show what happened in the great slump of the 1930's. At

[1]No doubt most of the cyclical fluctuation can be explained without reference to price. Nevertheless there ought to be a significant price elasticity, both in the short run and in the long, because primary products include food, the demand for which is significantly sensitive to price changes.

first, trade fell less than production of manufactures, as we usually expect of slumps ; the points move left of the line. Then, in 1933 and 1934, manufacturing revives, without any revival of trade. After 1934 something like a straight line relation may have been in course of re-establishment, with something like the old slope, but the movement is now well to the right of the old straight line. The industrial countries have become more self-sufficient, as a consequence of the slump.

It would, however, be wrong to assume that if we drew a line running more or less through the points for 1935, 1936 and 1937, with a slope of 0·87, we should be on a new path which took account of all the effects of the slump. Such a line would *over-estimate* the degree of self-sufficiency induced by the slump up to that time. For, one reason why trade was so low in those years was that the slump was worst of all in the United States, and so U.S. imports of primary products were abnormally low. Our manufacturing index does not include the U.S.A., but our index of trade does include the U.S.A.

We can see that this is important if we plot the trade figures against not the index which excludes the U.S.A., but the index which includes the U.S.A. Then the figures for 1921 to 1929 lie on a straight line, but the points after 1930 are all further to the left, in relation to their straight line than are the corresponding points in Chart I. Also, the point for 1938 lies on a line with the points for 1936 and 1937, instead of lying well below them as it does in Chart I. In fact the deficiency of trade shown in 1938 is only about 10%, as compared with the 21% that appears in Chart I. This deficit of 10% is a truer measure of the amount of self-sufficiency promoted by the slump in the industrial world as a whole up to 1938.

In Chart I we have put in a straight line running parallel to the original straight line, but 10% below it. If there was no further increase in self-sufficiency after 1938, the point for 1950 should lie on or about this straight line. But, as Chart I shows, it lies a further 9% below the lower line.

This further deficit in 1950 cannot as yet be interpreted. Some part of it may be due to measures taken to promote self-sufficiency in the thirties which had not fully fructified in 1938.

Some part of it may be due to the war—though, as we have seen, the first world war did not affect our straight line. Some part may be due to changes in the structure of manufacturing production, from industries which use much imported raw material to industries which are more labour intensive. And some part is due to the shortage of primary products since the war, which has caused some industrial countries to import less food and raw materials than they would have liked to do. We shall not know how much is due to this third cause until the shortage comes to an end. And not until then shall we know, as well, whether the incremental relationship of 0·87 has survived both the slump of the 'thirties and the second world war.

III. The Price of Raw Materials.

The third step in our analysis is to measure the determinants of the terms of trade. We take this in two stages ; first to determine the price of raw materials, in terms of manufactures, and then to determine the price of food.

Hereinafter, whenever we use the word "price" we mean price in terms of manufactures : the "real" or "terms of trade" price. The relevant series are series 11 and 12 in Table II.

For demand we use world production of manufactures, excluding the U.S.S.R. (series 1). There could be no better theoretical index of demand. In practice, indices of industrial production are usually compiled partly by measuring the output of product and partly by measuring the input of raw materials. An index based wholly upon the latter would be an exact index of the consumption of raw materials, whereas an index based wholly upon the former should grow faster than the consumption of raw materials, because of increasing economy in raw material use. Our series probably under-estimates raw material economy.

For supply we had intended to use an annual index of world production of raw materials since 1870, devised by the late Carl Snyder. These figures have never been published, but two articles describing the series, and reproducing it in graphical form, were published by Mr. Snyder in the *Revue de l'Institut Internationale de Statistique* in 1934. Mr. Snyder gave

TABLE II

PRICES (IN GOLD) AND TERMS OF TRADE

	Prices (in gold)				Terms of Trade		
	Raw Materials	Food	Primary Products	Manu-factures	Raw Materials	Food	Primary Products
	7	8	9	10	11	12	13
1870	116	121	118·0	106	109·4	114·1	111·3
1871	104	126	112·8	110	94·9	115·1	103·0
1872	118	131	123·2	117	100·9	112·0	105·2
1873	121	131	127·0	119	101·7	110·1	106·7
1874	113	130	119·8	114	99·5	114·5	105·5
1875	107	126	114·6	111	96·4	113·4	103·2
1876	101	122	109·4	106	95·3	115·1	103·2
1877	97	131	110·6	105	92·8	125·4	105·9
1878	91	119	102·2	100	91·5	119·6	102·8
1879	86	113	96·8	97	88·7	116·5	99·8
1880	92	117	102·0	102	90·2	114·7	100·0
1881	89	118	100·6	99	89·9	119·3	101·6
1882	89	119	101·0	98	91·2	122·0	103·6
1883	87	114	97·8	97	90·2	118·2	100·5
1884	84	105	92·4	95	88·9	111·1	97·8
1885	79	98	86·4	90	87·7	109·0	96·0
1886	74	92	81·2	88	84·6	105·2	92·6
1887	74	91	80·8	86	86·1	106·5	94·5
1888	77	93	83·4	87	88·6	106·9	95·9
1889	79	95	85·4	88	90·3	108·6	97·6
1890	82	92	86·0	90	91·1	102·2	95·6
1891	79	97	86·2	90	87·8	107·8	95·5
1892	75	93	82·2	88	85·3	105·6	93·4
1893	74	92	81·2	85	87·0	108·3	95·5
1894	70	83	75·2	81	86·4	102·5	92·8
1895	66	80	71·6	80	82·5	100·0	89·5
1896	69	79	73·0	81	85·2	97·6	90·1
1897	69	80	73·4	80	86·8	100·6	92·3
1898	67	83	73·4	79	85·4	105·7	93·5
1899	74	81	76·8	81	91·4	100·0	94·8
1900	89	82	86·2	88	101·1	93·2	98·0
1901	81	84	82·2	86	94·8	98·2	96·1
1902	78	85	80·8	84	92·8	101·2	96·1
1903	81	85	82·6	86	94·2	98·9	96·0
1904	82	84	82·8	88	93·2	95·5	94·1
1905	81	87	83·2	90	90·5	97·2	92·9
1906	90	87	88·8	92	98·4	95·1	97·1
1907	95	91	93·4	95	100·0	95·8	98·3
1908	86	93	88·8	95	90·4	97·9	93·5
1909	85	96	89·2	94	90·4	102·1	95·0

TABLE II—*continued*

PRICES (IN GOLD) AND TERMS OF TRADE

	Prices (in gold)				Terms of Trade		
	Raw Materials	Food	Primary Products	Manu-factures	Raw Materials	Food	Primary Products
	7	8	9	10	11	12	13
1910	97	98	97·4	102	95·6	96·6	96·0
1911	94	97	95·2	97	96·9	100·0	98·2
1912	95	102	97·8	98	97·4	104·7	100·3
1913	100	100	100·0	100	100·0	100·0	100·0
1921	120	148	131·2	186	64·5	79·6	70·5
1922	119	127	122·2	161	73·9	78·9	75·9
1923	133	156	142·2	157	84·7	99·4	90·6
1924	133	154	141·4	153	86·9	100·7	92·4
1925	149	149	149·0	159	93·7	93·7	93·7
1926	141	144	142·2	156	90·4	92·3	91·2
1927	129	146	135·8	146	88·3	100·0	93·0
1928	124	144	132·0	148	83·8	97·3	89·2
1929	121	134	126·2	142	85·2	94·4	88·9
1930	99	113	104·6	133	74·2	84·7	78·6
1931	71	89	78·2	111	64·1	80·4	70·5
1932	53	67	58·6	90	58·8	74·3	65·1
1933	48	61	53·2	80	59·8	76·0	66·5
1934	48	56	51·2	71	67·6	78·9	72·1
1935	47	54	49·8	68	69·0	79·2	73·2
1936	50	56	52·4	68	73·4	82·2	77·1
1937	57	61	58·6	72	78·7	84·2	81·4
1938	51	58	53·8	72	71·1	80·9	74·7
1950	126	122	124·4	122	103·4	100·1	102·0

Series 7. Price of Raw Materials.
Series 8. Price of Food.
Series 9. Price of Primary Products (i.e. Food and Raw Materials together).
Series 10. Price of Manufactured Commodities.
Series 11. Series 7 divided by Series 10.
Series 12. Series 8 divided by Series 10.
Series 13. Series 9 divided by Series 10.

All Series are index numbers, with 1913 as base. For notes on sources, etc., see Statistical Appendix. For purposes of division, the original figures from which Series 10 has been derived, were used to one place of decimals.

a copy of the original figures to Mr. E. H. Stern, who in turn has very kindly made them available to me.

Unfortunately the Snyder series cannot be used for our purpose. In the first place, it rises more steeply than the manufacturing index, thereby suggesting that, with the passage of the years, the world used raw materials not more but less economically. If we accept the Snyder series, the world manufacturing index is too high in the 1870's ; while, if we accept the latter, the former is too low.

This difficulty is not fundamental, since we could escape it by starting our series in 1880 instead of 1870. A more fundamental difficulty is that the Snyder series and the manufacturing series follow each other very closely through boom and slump, and through secular depression and recovery. This is not only because the manufacturing index is partly compiled from raw material statistics. It is also because, raw materials being produced largely on a commercial basis, their output adjusts rapidly to demand. If the adjustment were complete, the two series would show exactly proportionate movements, and the difference between them would not in any way correlate with the price. In practice, the adjustment is not complete. Raw material production falls less in the slump, and rises less in the boom. But the adjustment is sufficiently large, both as between boom and slump, and as between one decade and another, to make it impossible to obtain a useful correlation with the price.

Here one would be stumped but for noticing a curious phenomenon. This is that, if one treats raw material production as having increased by a constant proportion from one year to the next, the result yields an excellent correlation with the price. The effect of doing this is to say that the price of raw materials depends not on demand and *actual* output, but on demand and *potential* output, which is obviously true ; if demand falls and output falls correspondingly, price will nevertheless fall because there is excess capacity. The boldness lies in assuming that potential output increases in constant ratio through boom and slump. The only defence for this assumption is that it works !

What we have done is to correlate five year moving averages (because our main interest is secular rather than cyclical) of demand and price, with a series which assumes a constant annual increase of potential output. We do this separately for the years before 1913, and for 1921 onwards, because we cannot assume that the war had no effect on the increase of potential output. The averages are geometric, since all the work has to be done in logarithms.

The result of this procedure is that what we get is not a demand function but a supply function. This function assumes that whatever supply is needed will be made available, and shows how the price varies as actual supply rises or falls relatively to "normal" supply.[1]

Because of doubt as to the validity of the manufacturing index in the eighteen seventies, we have used only figures for the years 1881 to 1913. This yields the result

$$\log P_{RM} = 0{\cdot}6806 + 0{\cdot}8622 \log M_Q - 0{\cdot}0131R$$

where P_{RM} is the index number of the price of raw materials (1913 = 10·00), M_Q is the index of manufacturing production (including the U.S.A.) and R is the number of years since 1871.

And, correlating from 1921 to 1938 yields the result

$$\log P_{RM} = 0{\cdot}0396 + 0{\cdot}8561 \log M_Q - 0{\cdot}0142N$$

where N is the number of years since 1922.

The coefficient of M_Q is the reciprocal of the elasticity of supply. Our first ground for confidence is that we get practically the same result for pre-war as for post-war years, namely an elasticity of supply of 1·16 or 1·17.

The coefficients of R and N show by how much the price would fall each year if manufacturing output were unchanged. Here also the results are very close, namely 3·1% per annum before the war, and 3·3% per annum thereafter. This coefficient is composed of three elements, namely of the annual increase in potential raw material production, of the annual fall in raw material consumption per unit of output, and of the

[1]If both demand and supply were elastic with respect to price we should need two equations. But we are assuming in effect that the demand for raw materials is absolutely inelastic. The resulting supply elasticity is a short run elasticity only. Long run supply is assumed (or rather "found") to increase at a constant rate, irrespective of price, after about 1880.

elasticity of supply. The higher post-war coefficient may be due mainly to the second of these elements, since the fact that post-war manufacturing indices are based more upon Censuses of Production and less upon statistics of raw material consumption would show up in our formula as an increase in the rate of economising the use of raw materials.

The second, and even more important ground for confidence, is that these formulae give an unexpectedly good fit ; unexpected because, though the work has been done with five year moving averages, which damp the cyclical and emphasise the secular movement, the formulae give a good fit when applied to the annual data. The fit is good both for the cyclical and for the secular movement. This can be seen in Chart II.

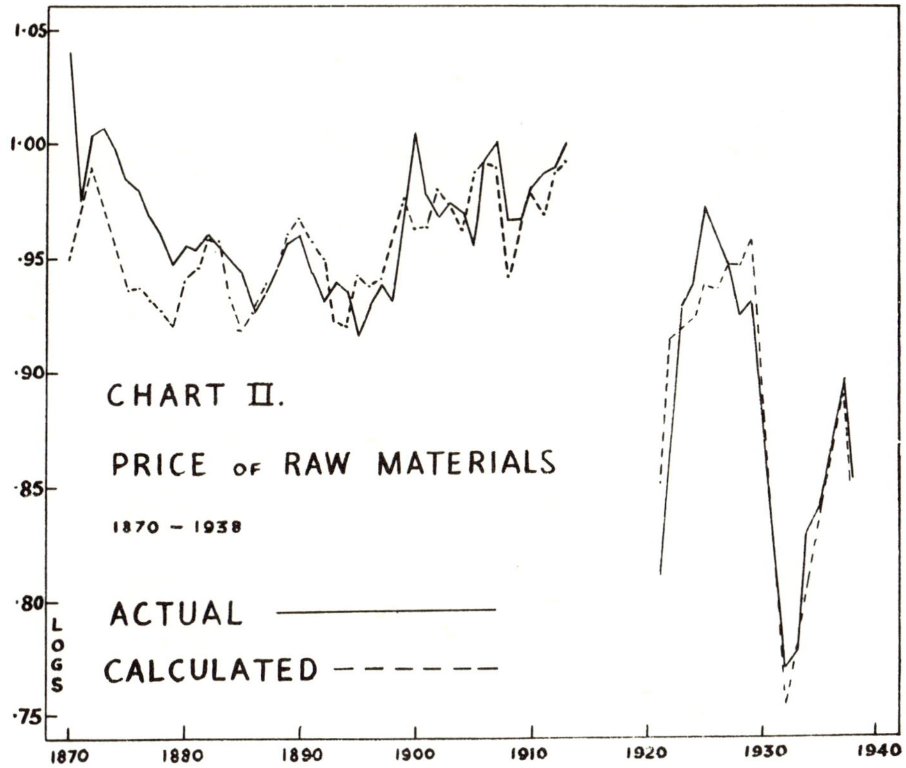

The differences revealed by Chart II are as interesting as the agreements. First, the points of inflexion are not exactly the same. They are the same from 1907 onwards, but before that, in about half the cases, the turning points of the actual price lag one year behind the turning points of the calculated price. This is because in the earlier years international trade in manufactures was dominated by textiles, whose price was very volatile. The price of iron and steel also fluctuated much more widely in the Nineteenth century than it did in the Twentieth. The prices of these manufactures turned just about as swiftly as the price of raw materials, and though the raw material price would within two years have moved in greater proportion, it was touch and go which would move more within the first twelve months. This lag has now disappeared.

There is also a significant difference between the actual price and the calculated price from 1873 to 1879. The price did not fall as much in those years as it should have fallen if world manufacturing output stagnated in this period as much as the index says that it did. The index is not very reliable for the seventies ; it is based on data for four countries only, and the data are highly speculative. And it is also possible that potential raw material output was not growing as rapidly before 1880 as it did thereafter.

IV. The Price of Food.

In the case of food, the supply fluctuates very little through boom and slump. We assume that food is produced, and sold for whatever price it will fetch. What our formula is then assumed to yield is a demand function. Doubtless the supply in any year depends on prices in previous years, but, so long as it does not depend on the price in the same year, this does not invalidate our equation.

A Snyder series exists, giving world production of food year by year since 1870. Unfortunately this series also is incompatible with the world manufacturing index. When put together, they yield an elasticity of demand which never falls below —1·5, and which is sometimes even positive, according to the period one takes, and according to whether or not one deflates the series by an index of population growth. The trouble is that, according to the Snyder series, world food production grew at an average annual rate of 2·4% in the three decades before the first world war. This rate is not consistent with the growth of real income, as measured by the manufacturing index, in the sense that if food production grew as fast as this, the price of food should have fallen even faster than it did.

Of course, it is also arguable that the world manufacturing index is not a good index of the demand for food. It is, however, a better index than one might first think. It reflects the growth of population and the growth of wealth, and it concentrates on the movement of income of the industrialised world, which is also the part of the world with the greatest food production (more than four-fifths of the world total),[1] and the part which determines prices. An index of real income would be still better, but none exists.

For the period before 1913 we have no alternative to Snyder's index of food production, which we have had to abandon with great reluctance. But for the inter-war years we have a series devised by the League of Nations (series 3 in Table I), which yields the following result, when five year moving averages are correlated :

$$\log P_F = 1{\cdot}9000 + 0{\cdot}5821 \log M_Q - 1{\cdot}4908 \log F$$

where P_F is an index of the price of food, M_Q an index of the production of manufactures (including the U.S.A.), and F an index of food production (1913 = 10.00).

This formula inspires confidence, for several reasons.

In the first place, the coefficients are about what we would expect. The elasticity of demand is the reciprocal of the coefficient of F ; that is to say it works out at —0·67. Mr. J. N. R. Stone, in the *Journal of the Royal Statistical Society*, 1945, and Mr. J. Tobin in the same journal, 1950, find elasticities of demand for food in the United States ranging between —0·5 and —0·6. Food is more of a luxury to the

[1]As measured by League of Nations, *World Production and Prices* 1938/39, p. 93. If meat and milk are excluded, the share of Asia and Africa in world food production is about 40 per cent.

world as a whole than it is to the U.S.A., where the income elasticity of demand for food is lower. Hence our finding of an elasticity of —0·67 for the world as a whole seems very reasonable.

The coefficient of M_Q is slightly more complex. In industrial countries a 1% increase in manufacturing is usually associated with about a 0·5% increase in real income as a whole. Estimates of the income elasticity of demand for food vary widely, but the Allen and Bowley studies put it at around 0·8 for working-class families in Europe, whose incomes are above the average for the world as a whole. If we take it at 0·8, then a 1% increase in M_Q would increase the demand for food by 0·5 × 0·8 = 0·4%. And if the elasticity of demand is 0·67, this would raise the price by 0·4 × 1·4908, *i.e.* by 0·6%. The coefficient we actually get, 0·5821, is therefore very close to the coefficient we should expect.

The second ground for confidence is that the formula gives a good fit, even when it is applied to the annual data, as is done in Chart III.

The most exciting feature of the fit is the extremities. Neither 1913 nor 1950 was included, in deriving the formula, and it is therefore most satisfying to find that, despite the intervention of two wars, the formula still holds.

The actual price for 1913 is 100. The calculated price is 98. This difference of 2% is well within the range of error in the data. It could be fully accounted for if the League's food index is slightly more than 1% too low, or if the linking of post-war manufacturing or prices is out by a corresponding amount.

The calculated price for 1950 is 102·3. The actual price shown in Table II is 100·1. This again is well within the range of error. Moreover, as is explained in the Statistical Appendix, the price of food entering into world trade was rather less than the price of food as a whole, since the biggest buyer of food in international trade, the U.K., was getting some of her supplies in 1950 at prices below current world prices. The calculated price can therefore be regarded as an excellent fit.

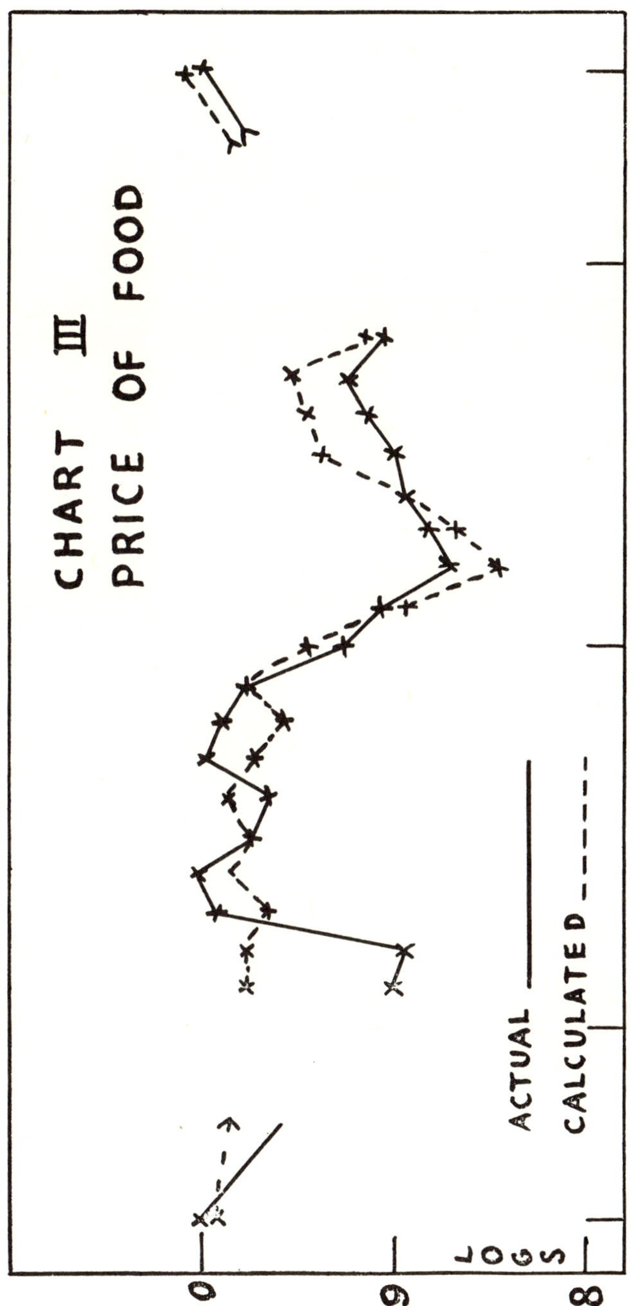
CHART III
PRICE OF FOOD
ACTUAL
CALCULATED
LOGS
1.0
.9
.8
1913
1920
1930
1940
1950

We have every reason for confidence in a formula which not merely conforms to expectations based on other data, but which also gives the right prices over the span of two world wars.

V. The Great Depression, 1873-1894.

Our major task is now completed. Given production indices, we can derive from them the level of trade in primary products, the terms of trade, and thence the level of trade in manufactures. In a moment we shall use these formulae for bold speculations about the future. But first, let us make some random remarks relating to the course of production and prices in the past.

Chart II brings out clearly the "Kondratieff" movement, both in raw material prices and in manufacturing production, from 1870 to the first world war.

The price of food is not shown in this chart. Its movement is not the same as that of raw materials. For one thing, the real price of raw materials was about the same in 1872 as in 1913, while the price of food shows a very large fall. And, for another, the two prices do not move together. The price of raw materials started to fall in 1873, and reached its lowest point in 1895, following in its course almost exactly the same path as industrial production. But the price of food rose in the seventies ; did not begin its dramatic decline until 1882 ; and did not check its fall until 1900. This has bearing upon the belief that the prices of all primary products move in sympathy with each other. This is not the case. As we have seen, the demand is the same in both cases, but the conditions of supply are quite different, the supply of food being much more inflexible not only secularly (the annual increase in raw material supply is nearly twice as great), but also cyclically.

The "calculated" series in Chart II is almost equivalent to the index of manufacturing production, after a secular trend increasing by 3·6% per annum has been removed.

It shows the Kondratieff downswing in production quite clearly, in that each of the slumps, up to a turning point in 1894, is very severe ; so that, even though the annual rate of growth of production from peak year to peak year is almost constant from 1882 to 1907, the average production from year to year grows more slowly before 1894 than it does thereafter.

Chart II also shows that the upswing did not carry through from 1907 to 1913. The slump of 1908 was very severe, and the 1913 peak was rather low. If a fifty year cycle exists, it does not follow any simple pattern.

The same remark must be made about the twenty year cycle, to which Professor Brinley Thomas has drawn attention.[1] There is evidence that the boom which culminated in 1890 was more powerful than the boom which preceded in it 1882-83. One might speak of an eighteen year cycle, with peaks in 1872, 1890 and 1907, super-imposed upon a deep Kondratieff swing. The obstacle to this is the peak of 1899, which ought to be rather low, if it is to fit into an eighteen year cycle, but which, on the contrary, is very vigorous, however one measures it.

It seems premature to talk of long cycles. Certainly some booms are vigorous while others are mild, and some slumps are mild while others are severe. But there is no clear pattern in the order of the mild and the severe. *Ad hoc* investigation is still the most fruitful approach to this problem.

VI. The Inter-War Years.

We can make more progress in analysing what happened after 1913.

First of all, we can measure the cost of the war, in terms of its effect in lowering world production.

If we measure from the peak year 1890 to the peak year 1913, industrial production increased at a cumulative rate of 3·9% per annum. If it had increased at this rate from 1913 to the peak year 1929, the index would have stood at 182·3, instead of at 154·8. Hence the war cost four-and-a-half years of growth of industrial production.

The loss of potential raw material output can be measured by applying our pre-war formula to the post-war data, since both pre-war and post-war formulae show nearly the same rate of growth of output. The average price ruling in 1925-29 is

[1] "Migration and the Rhythm of Economic Growth," *The Manchester School,* September, 1951.

compatible with manufacturing production only if 1927 is year 54¾ since 1871. Since it is year 56, the loss of growth of raw material potential was 1¼ years.

The rate of growth of food production can also be derived from our formula. The average price and average demand ruling in 1888-92 are compatible only with a food production index of 66·7, and a rate of growth to 1913 of 1·8% per annum. Snyder's index is 58·3, and his rate of growth 2·4% per annum, probably because he gives too much weight to production in the Western world, and too little to the stable production of the rest. However, if we use our rate of growth, average production in 1925-29 should have been 128·2. If we take Snyder's rate of growth, it should have been 138·9. The actual figure was 116·9, which represents 5·2 years loss of growth at our rate, and 7·3 years loss at Snyder's rate. (The loss is so high at Snyder's rate that it confirms our opinion that his index very much over-estimates the pre-war rate of growth of food production).

This analysis shows that food production suffered more than any other activity from the effects of the war. The price of food was nevertheless lower in the twenties than it was in 1913. The explanation of this paradox is that the pre-war rate of growth was so high that it was causing the price of food to fall almost continuously. The war checked production relatively to demand, but not enough to prevent a further fall in the price.

The consequence of the lost years of growth of manufacturing production was that the terms of trade, which had been moving in favour of primary producers from 1895 to 1913, turned against them in the 'twenties. Stocks accumulated. The League of Nations index of stocks of primary products [1] shows end of year stocks accumulating steadily from its commencement in 1925 :

1925	1926	1927	1928	1929
76	82	86	90	100

Hence, when the boom broke in 1929, what might have been a slump of ordinary dimensions turned into a catastrophic fall of

[1] *World Production and Prices*, 1937/38, p. 121.

commodity prices, with all the serious deflationary effects which any violent fall of prices must be expected to bring in its train.

It is now possible also to understand what happened to international trade in the nineteen twenties. Trade was low in the sense that the rate of growth of the volume of trade from 1913 to 1929 was below the pre-war rate. But in any other sense the volume of trade was normal. As we can see from Chart I, the pre-war relation between trade in primary products and manufacturing production was well maintained; there may have been a slight deficit of trade of about 1%. And the volume of trade in manufactures was even higher than we should have expected it to be, having regard to the level of manufacturing output and to terms of trade unfavourable to primary producers; the share of manufactures in total trade was greater than before the war. Suggestions were being made in the twenties that trade in manufacturing had been reduced by the industrialisation of new countries. These suggestions can now be seen to be wholly without foundation.

In the 'thirties, trade in manufactures maintained its normal relation to trade in primary products, having regard to the terms of trade. But after 1933 the volume of trade in primary products shrank relatively to manufacturing production. This cannot be attributed to the industrialisation of new countries, since the industrialisation of these countries did not proceed any more rapidly after 1933 than it had done before. It is to be attributed rather to the measures taken by industrial countries to promote domestic revival without a corresponding increase of imports. The import of primary produce was too low, but, having regard to the level of these imports, and to the low prices paid for primary products, the trade in manufactures was as large as it ought to have been.[1]

VII. 1950.

If the first world war caused the terms of trade to move against primary products, why has the second world war moved the terms of trade in their favour?

[1]This section supersedes the analysis of this problem given in my *Economic Survey*, 1919-1939, pp. 149-156. The argument is the same, but the statistical analysis is carried further.

Part of the answer is that this war had a relatively more devastating effect upon primary production, especially in the countries occupied by Japan. Thus, using the techniques of the last section, we may calculate that the second world war cost, in loss of years growth of production, 3·1 years for manufacturing, 12·3 years for raw materials, and 9·5 years for food (using our rate, not Snyder's).[1]

That manufacturing lost only three years of growth is due to the fact that, whereas the war checked production in every other country, its effect in the United States was to put an end to a slump which had lasted for ten years, and which had shown no sign of coming to an end. Thus, while production in the world excluding the U.S.S.R. and the U.S.A. increased only by 22%, between 1937 and 1950, production in the U.S.A. increased by 77%.

To say that raw materials production lost 12·3 years of growth is equivalent to saying that actual production in 1950 was no greater than *potential* production in 1938. But the real reason for this is not the war but the virtual cessation of foreign investment in the primary producing countries ever since 1929.

Between 1911 and 1913, the average annual capital export of Britain, France, Germany and the United States, to the rest of the world was $1,400 million. This dropped, between 1924 and 1928, to $860 million, worth, at 1911-13 prices not more than $550 million. (There was much foreign investment in the twenties, but the lion's share went to Germany, instead of to raw material producing countries). Then, after the great slump, foreign investment ceased altogether ; Britain and the United States, on the contrary, withdrew substantial sums from the rest of the world.

[1]The task of analysing the course of events since 1945 is made much more difficult by the fact that the United Nations has not resumed publication of two invaluable annual surveys which the League of Nations used to publish, *viz* : *World Production and Prices* and the *Review of World Trade*. In consequence, there are no longer series for world trade in primary and in manufactured commodities, for world prices, or for raw material production. This is a sad deficiency.

Actual production of raw materials, which needs to grow by about 40% in a decade, was only 16% higher [1] in 1937 than in 1929. And world food production per head of the population, which grows 8% in a decade, was no higher at the end of the 'thirties than it was at the beginning.

To the cessation of foreign investment we must add the effects of the war on agricultural production, which were particularly severe in the Far East. The natural result was an acute shortage both of food and of raw materials in 1950, and very favourable prices for primary products.

As we have already seen, the volume of primary products entering into international trade in 1950 was perhaps as much as 9% below what it should have been, in relation to world manufacturing production. The shortage of primary products probably accounts for most of this.

The volume of manufactures in world trade, on the other hand, was "normal," in the sense that it was what we would expect it to be, knowing how much primary produce was being sold, and the price it was fetching. The deficit in the volume of primary products was more than compensated by the rise in price, with the consequence that the volume of trade in manufactures was 36% higher in 1950 than it was in 1937.

VIII. 1960.

Given the level of production, we can use our formulae to derive prices and the level of international trade. It may help to draw the whole argument together if we guess at production levels for 1960, and then work the exercise.

Naturally, this is not a prediction for 1960. We have no means of knowing how rapidly production will grow in the course of the fifties. And we cannot be certain that our formulae will still apply in 1960, even where they give a good fit over many past decades. This is an exercise, and not a prediction.

To start the exercise, we have to guess at the levels of world manufacturing production and world food production in

[1]An index number of actual production of raw materials, from 1920 to 1938, will be found in League of Nations, *World Production and Prices*, 1938/39.

1960. No guess can be made for an actual year, since much depends on where the year fits into the trade cycle. When we speak of 1960, therefore, we mean the average of the five years 1958 to 1962. Similarly, our year of departure, 1950, has to be assumed to be an "average" year.

No guess can be made, also, if there is a major war. The exercise assumes that no major war occurs in the Nineteen fifties.

World manufacturing production, including the U.S.A., increased by 3·9% per annum from 1890 to 1913. If we manage slumps better in the fifties than we did in the past, it may increase perhaps by 5% per annum. It is quite possible that there will not be enough raw materials even for the lower of these rates, but we shall assume that the necessary foreign investments will be made. We shall work with both 3·9% and 5% per annum. Corresponding increases for world manufacturing production, excluding the U.S.A., are 3·3% and 4·2%.

According to our formula, the pre-1913 rate of growth of food production cannot have exceeded 1·8% per annum, though Snyder's index puts it as high as 2·4% per annum. The prospects for food production in the nineteen fifties are not bright. There is little foreign investment taking place in agricultural countries ; political conditions are insecure ; there is no longer a stream of international migrants settling on virgin soils ; and most countries seem intent on fostering industry rather than agriculture. All these adverse circumstances may be changed as food prices rise, and make agricultural production very profitable relatively to other activities. High prices are bound sooner or later to stimulate supply. But this effect may not be fully felt within the next ten years. We work therefore with two assumptions ; that food production may increase by 2% per annum, and that it may increase only by 1·3% per annum.

We now apply our formulae to these assumptions.

First, if the incremental relationship between manufacturing production and volume of trade in primary products is still 0·87, then trade will increase by 35% on the lower assumption, or by 43% on the higher assumption. Now, as we have seen, there was a shortage of primary products in 1950. If primary production increases sufficiently to make this good, trade will be correspondingly larger in 1960. But, in what follows, we ignore this possibility.

There is another very important possibility which we ignore. So far, all our production figures have excluded the U.S.S.R. This is because the U.S.S.R. is almost self-sufficient. This, however, may not continue. All available evidence suggests that the U.S.S.R. is increasing production of manufactures at an enormous rate, while failing to make corresponding headway in agriculture. The effect of this, sooner or later, must be to drive the U.S.S.R. into the world markets for primary products, and to cause a large expansion of the trade in these products, and a big increase in their prices. Much the same is happening in the other countries under Soviet influence, with ultimately the same result. Whether this will be effective by 1960 cannot be foretold, and we ignore the possibility in subsequent calculations.

We calculate next the price of raw materials, using the formula for 1921-1938. It is rash to assume that this formula still holds. The annual increase in potential output of raw materials has probably dropped, because of the drying up of foreign investment. The elasticity of supply may be smaller upwards than downwards. And raw material economy may be greater because of high prices. To use the 1921-1938 formula is to assume that any such changes cancel each other out, and this is obviously rash. The result, nevertheless, is that raw material prices are the same in 1960 as in 1950, on the lower assumption, and are 10% higher on the higher assumption. Both these figures are probably seriously under-estimated.

If manufacturing production is assumed to grow only by 3·9% per annum, while food production grows by as much as 2% per annum, then the price of food will fall 8% by 1960. At the other limit, if manufacturing grows by 5%, and food only by 1·3%, then the price of food will rise by 10%. The other alternatives lie within this range.

These food and raw material prices combine to give terms of trade for primary products as a whole with a lower limit of a fall of 3% and an upper limit of a rise of 10%.

We can now calculate the level of trade in manufactures. For this we assume that the share of manufactures in world trade will be about the same in 1960 as it was in 1950. This is the most confident of all our assumptions so far. Then, applying the upper and lower limits of the volume of trade in primary products, and of the price of primary products, we conclude that the volume of trade in manufactures will increase by between 31% and 57%.

These results may be tabulated as follows : –

INDEX NUMBERS IN 1960, BASE 1950 = 100

	Lower assumptions	Higher assumptions
Manufacturing Production	147	163
Food Production	114	122
Price of Raw Materials	100	110
Price of Food	92	110
Trade in Primary Products	135	143
Trade in Manufactures	131	157

Finally, it may be noted that our calculation of price comes out at a much lower level than that made by Mr. Colin Clark in *The Economics of* 1960. Mr. Clark takes account of the affects of the further industrialisation of the Soviet countries, and his result should therefore be higher than our figure, which makes no allowance for these developments. Nevertheless, the difference is substantial. He predicts that in 1960 the price of primary products will be 90% above the average level of 1924-1935. Whereas our calculation lies between 22% and 39% above 1924/1935. No doubt there will be as many guesses about the level of 1960 as there are guessers.

W. Arthur Lewis

University of Manchester.

STATISTICAL APPENDIX.

Production of Manufactures.

A World index for 1870-1938 is given in League of Nations, *Industrialisation and Foreign Trade,* Annex A, with the figures for individual countries, from which it has been derived. The weights assigned to the U.S.A. and the U.S.S.R. were 42·5% and 4% respectively, and these weights were used for making the series given in Table I. These weights apply to the average of the years 1925-1929, and the series shown in Table I have to be calculated from the League's index with 1925-1929 = 100, and not from the index with 1913 = 100.

The World index incorporates Hoffman's index of industrial production in the U.K. The downward bias of this index is such that, when comparison is made with the Censuses of Production of 1907 and 1924, Hoffman's index is seen to under-estimate the increase of post-war production by at least 20%. Accordingly, 20% has been added to the post-war U.K. figures used in the World index, thus increasing this index by rather less than 2%.

The figures for 1950 are derived from United Nations, *Monthly Bulletin of Statistics.*

Production of Food.

This is based principally on two League of Nations' indices. *The Memorandum on Production and Trade,* 1923 *to* 1928/29, contains an index of food production for 1913 and from 1923 to 1928, while *World Production and Prices* 1938/39, contains an index from 1925 to 1938. The latter index includes vegetable oils and tea, coffee and cocoa, which the former does not, but the *Memorandum* gives the information necessary for devising an index which includes these commodities. Both publications also include information on the U.S.S.R. share of production, which is excluded from the index shown in Table I. The coverage of the latter index remains more complete than that of the earlier (it includes also milk, fruit and fish, for which earlier information is not available), so the two series have been linked at their earliest common year, which is 1925. Neither of these series includes 1921 and 1922, which have been taken from a third League of Nations index, also published in the same number of *World Production and Prices,* which is comparable with the other index in that volume, except that it excludes livestock products.

The figure for 1950 is calculated from Food and Agriculture Organisation, *The State of Food and Agriculture : Review and Outlook,* 1951, which gives an index of "food crops" on page 5, and gives other information about livestock, fruit and beverages on pages 51 to 67.

International Trade.

Quinquennial averages from 1876 to 1938 are published in *Industrialisation and Foreign Trade.* These figures have been revised, and a new annual exists, which has not yet been published, but which has been made available to me by the courtesy of Dr. F. Hilgerdt, of the Economic Division of the United Nations.

The definitions of primary products and of manufactures are as in *Industrialisation and Foreign Trade*, Annex B.

The figures are in U.S. gold dollars of 1913 parity, which differ from U.S. dollars after the devaluation in 1933.

The revised sum of imports and exports of primary products in 1913 is 24,970 million dollars, and the revised sum of imports and exports of manufactures is 15,140 million dollars in 1913.

The figures for 1950 are estimated in a roundabout way, since the United Nations statistics do not distinguish between manufactures and primary products, as the League of Nations used to do.

The value of manufactures exported is calculated for 1937 and 1950 by Dr. H. Tyszynski, in his article "World Trade in Manufactured Commodities, 1899-1950," *Manchester School*, September 1951. This calculation shows an increase of 309% in sterling value, which translates into an increase of 132% in dollar value. The United Nations *Monthly Bulletin of Statistics* shows that the dollar value of all trade increased in the same period by 134%. The change in the ratio of manufactures to total trade can thus be calculated. Also, applying weights of 3 for primary products and 2 for manufactures, it follows that the value of trade in primary products increased in this period by 135%.

PRICES.

The prices used in this study are not the same as those used in *Industrialisation and Foreign Trade*. In the first place, the League's study used the Sauerbeck index for the prices of primary products. Here, however, raw material and food prices are used separately, and the price of primary products in general is found by weighting according to relative importance in world trade. The series for prices of manufactures is also different. The main difference, however is in the prices chosen for the 1920's. *Industrialisation and Foreign Trade* uses British prices up to 1929. British prices, however, were out of line with world prices in the 1920's, the price of manufactures in particular, being too high. One consequence of this is that *Industrialisation and Foreign Trade's* estimate of the volume of world trade in the 1920's comes out at too low a level, as can be seen when it is compared with the estimate made by the League of Nations' statistical division, and published in the *Review of World Trade* for 1938. These latter estimates are much more reliable, since they are based on the individual trade returns of many countries.

The reliability of the series shown in Table II can be tested in the following manner. If we use weights of 9, 6 and 10 for raw materials, food and manufactures respectively (based on the above *Review of World*

Trade, p. 61), we can calculate an index of prices of all goods entering into international trade, which compares with the Review's estimate, and with the series used in *Industrialisation and Foreign Trade* as follows :

	1913	1924	1925	1926	1927	1928	1929
Our series	100	146	153	148	140	138	133
Review's estimate . .	100	146	151	141	139	138	133
I. & F. T. series . .	100	157	165	157	150	148	142

This good correspondence is due to using U.S. and U.K. prices, instead of U.K. prices only.

Prices for 1950 have been reached in a roundabout way, since no single country's prices are any longer representative of world trade.

The starting point is the United Nations *Monthly Bulletin of Statistics*, which shows the average price of all goods in international trade increasing from 1938 to 1950 by 107%. This is accepted, since the U.N. calculations are based on trade statistics of many countries.

In the same period, the dollar price of U.K. exports of manufactures rose 57%, and the price of U.S. exports of manufactures rose 76% (*International Financial Statistics*). The price of all exports from Europe (U.N. *Monthly Bulletin*) rose 75%. Not all of Europe's exports are manufactures, and the prices of primary products have risen by more than the prices of manufactures. Hence it is assumed that the average price of all manufactures entering into world trade has increased by 70%.

Using the same weights as before, it follows that the prices of primary products have risen by 132%.

The dollar price of raw materials imported into the U.K. rose by 156% between 1938 and 1950. In 1950 the U.K. was no longer getting any significant amount of raw materials on bulk contracts at prices below world prices. The corresponding U.S. increase was 136%. The two countries import rather different commodities. If we split the difference, the raw materials price is taken as having increased by 146%.

Applying the same weights as before, it follows that the price of food increased by 111%. It certainly increased, for the world as a whole, by more than the increase in the U.K. import price, which was 90% (food was still bought in 1950 on bulk contracts below world prices). The B.L.S. index of the wholesale price of food in the U.S. increased by 126%. The figure of 111% for world trade as a whole is therefore probably very near the mark, and this nearness itself confirms the other prices we are using for 1950.

As with the statistics of international trade, these prices are all expressed in U.S. gold dollars of 1913 parity.

Raw Materials. From 1870 to 1913 we use the composite price of raw materials imported into or exported from the U.K., which is given by Werner Schlote in *Entwicklung und Strukturwandlungen des englischen Aussenhandels*. From 1913 to 1929 the series in Table II is the unweighted arithmetic average of imports into the U.K., as given by Schlote, and of imports into the U.S.A. of crude materials and of semi-manufactures, as given in the *Statistical Abstract of the United States*. From 1929 to 1938, the figures in the *Review of World Trade for* 1938 are used.

Food. From 1870 to 1913 the series is Schlote's index of the price of food imported into the U.K. From 1913 to 1929 we use the unweighted arithmetic average of food imports into the U.K., and of imports into the U.S.A. of crude foodstuffs and of manufactured foodstuffs. From 1929 to 1938, the figures in the *Review of World Trade for* 1938 are used.

Manufactures. From 1870 to 1913 the series is the unweighted arithmetic average of the price of imports into the U.K. and exports from the U.K., given by Schlote. *Industrialisation and Foreign Trade* uses a weighted index, which gives much more importance to exports than to imports. The import and export series coincide at the beginning and at the end of the period, but not in the middle, the prices of British manufactures falling during the Great Depression much more than the prices of manufactures of other countries. Since the British share of world trade was much less than half, it is arguable that more weight should be given to the import than to the export series ; on the other hand the composition of U.K. exports of manufactures is more representative of world trade than is the composition of U.K. imports. From 1913 to 1929 we use the unweighted arithmetic average of imports into and exports from the U.K. and the U.S.A. The two import series are very close together, and lie between the two export series, which are far apart. From 1929 to 1938, the figures in the *Review of World Trade* are used.

[8]

TRADE DRIVES

by W. Arthur Lewis

Professor of Political Economy, University of Manchester

I.

IF this country's standard of living is to rise at a reasonable rate over the coming years, our exports must increase on the average by at least 3 per cent. per annum. " I see no reason ", Mr. Butler said at Blackpool, " why in the next quarter of a century, if we run our policy properly and soundly, we should not double our standard of living in this country ". This is an ambitious target. No other nation in the world has so far succeeded in doubling its standard of living in twenty-five years, except perhaps Japan. It would mean raising industrial production in this country by about 5 per cent. per annum, and increasing our imports and exports by about 4 per cent. per annum. An export target of 3 per cent. per annum corresponds to raising our standard of living by about 2 per cent. per annum, which is the American rate. We may not quite manage this, but it is not an unreasonable objective.

To some people it seems impossible that British exports should increase by 3 per cent. per annum. They argue first, that the demand for manufactures in world trade will not increase fast enough for this, and secondly, that whatever may happen to the total demand, the British share of this trade is bound to diminish.

1

The first of these arguments is easily rejected; to examine the second is the main objective of this article.

As I have shown elsewhere,[1] the share of manufactures in world trade has not been diminished by industrialisation; it has remained constant at about 37 per cent. ever since the eighteen-seventies. In normal times (i.e. excluding Great Wars and the Great Depression of the thirties) it increases on the average by over 3 per cent. per annum. It would be strange if this were not so. The industrial countries buy more food and raw materials as they expand, and the agricultural countries are thus enabled in the same proportion to buy more manufactures. World trade in manufactures would cease to expand only if the industrial countries ceased to expand, or if the production of food and of raw materials ceased to expand. It is always possible that the world will give too little attention to producing food and raw materials, and too much to industrialisation, but this has not yet happened. After the dislocation created by the Second World War, primary production has now recovered. Production of food and of raw materials is increasing as fast as ever before, and all the signs are that world trade in manufactures will grow as rapidly in the next decade or so as it has done in the past.

If world trade in manufactures increases by 3 per cent. per annum, and British trade also by 3 per cent. per annum, then the British share of trade will be held

1 " World Production, Prices and Trade, 1870-1960 ", *The Manchester School of Economic and Social Studies*, May 1952.

constant. Our target can therefore be expressed in the terms that we must hold our proportionate share of world trade in manufactures constant in the coming decades.

To do this would be to reverse a trend of very long standing. Ever since the 1870's Britain's share of world trade in manufactures has been falling. This can be seen in the following table:

Percentage share of World Exports of Manufactures[2]

	1883	1913	1929	1937	1953
U.K.	39·8	27·3	21·7	20·8	19·8
Germany ..	19·4	24·2	19·3	20·8	12·3[3]
U.S.A. ..	5·5	11·6	19·0	18·2	25·5[4]
Japan	0·2	2·2	3·6	6·7	3·4
Others ..	35·1	34·7	36·4	33·5	39·0
Total ..	100	100	100	100	100

This Table shows that Britain's share of trade has fallen sharply in every decade. Even after what we regard as the magnificent post-war spurt, our share of world trade is less than it was in 1937. The trade

2 The figures for 1913, 1929 and 1937 are based upon H. Tyszynski, "World Trade in Manufactured Commodities, 1899-1950", *The Manchester School*, September 1951, with the difference that allowance is made for exports from Holland, Czechoslovakia and Austria (or Austria-Hungary).

3 Western Germany.

4 Excluding military aid.

lost by Germany and by Japan has gone chiefly to the United States, to France, to Switzerland and to Belgium, whose shares are much above the pre-war level. What chance is there of reversing this trend, to the extent of keeping our share of trade constant at around 20 per cent. for the next two or three decades ?

II.

I have approached this question by asking its opposite, namely: how did other countries succeed in increasing their share of world trade ? This is a fascinating subject, with which I propose to linger for the remainder of this article.

The world has seen four big trade drives in the last century and a half. First, there was the British drive, from 1820 to 1860. During those decades the physical volume of our exports of manufactures increased by 5·6 per cent. per annum. Then the cotton famine administered a check in the sixties, and in the seventies our rate of growth fell to 2·0 per cent. per annum, compared with 3·3 per cent. per annum for the world as a whole. The second trade drive was that of the Germans, starting in the seventies, and followed closely by the Americans, starting in the eighties. Then as now, there was enormous talk about German competition, and only the barest whispers about American competition, but then, as now, the Americans were capturing trade faster than the Germans; as the figures show, the Americans captured 6·1 per cent. of world trade between 1883 and 1913, while the Germans captured 4·8 per cent. And fourthly we have the

Japanese drive, which was moderate up to 1929, and then captured 3·1 per cent. of world trade in the course of eight years during which world trade was contracting.

In trying to understand trade drives, as in most other things, we must distinguish the " how " and the " why ". What means these countries used to capture trade is one question; why they set out to capture trade is another. As we shall see the first of these questions is relatively easy to answer, and we shall deal with it in this section. In the next section we shall try to discover why these trade drives were launched, and shall find how hard it is to reach satisfactory conclusions.

All these four trade drives have the same common features. They were achieved by (a) keen prices, (b) a flood of salesmen, (c) large-scale organisation of selling, (d) attention to customer detail, and (e) liberal credit. Each of these factors deserves some attention.

Let us begin with prices. Keen prices were a factor in each of the four trade drives, though not necessarily the decisive factor. Take the period before the First World War. Between 1883 and 1912 German prices of manufactured exports fell by 26 per cent. more than British prices, and this contributed to Germany's capturing 5 and Britain's losing 13 per cent. of world trade, but it was not the only factor. The contemporary literature of the eighties and nineties, while recognising the fall of German prices, asserts that British prices were nevertheless still quite competitive with German prices, and attributes the German success to more aggressive sales technique. Similarly, the prices of Japanese exports fell much more sharply than those of her competitors in the 1930's; but if the Japanese had confined themselves to cutting their prices and waiting for trade, they would have made little impact on the world's markets.

Much attention is usually given to the circumstances which make it possible for manufacturers to offer low prices. It may be alleged that the government is subsidising exports, or that goods are being dumped (i.e. sold at lower prices abroad than at home), or that the foreign exchange rate is being manipulated, or simply that wages are too low. Government subsidies to exports played no significant part in any of our four cases. Dumping and low wages were much discussed in the German case, and exchange manipulation and low wages in the Japanese case. In truth, all low prices boil down in the last analysis to low wages, in the sense that at the existing level of productivity prices would be higher if wages were higher. Wages cannot usefully be considered except in relation to productivity; and if when wages and productivity are taken together the result is low prices, this in turn has to be considered in relation to a country's trading as a whole, since, if costs of production were the same in all countries, there would be no trade. A country's prices are too low only if the result is that it is exporting more than it is importing. On this test it makes sense to say, in 1954, that U.S. wages and prices are too low, but it does not make sense for the

British to say that Japanese or Indian wages are too low, any more than it makes sense for the Americans to say that British wages are too low.

The second feature common to all trade drives is the flooding of the world's markets with salesmen. The British led the way in the first half of the nineteenth century, a major part of their success being due to the establishment of British trading houses in the four corners of the earth. The Germans followed in the last quarter of the nineteenth century, and the flood of Japanese salesmen in the 1930's is of recent memory.

There was, however, one important difference between the British method and the policies pursued in later drives. The British established wholesale trading houses, not tied to the manufacturers at home, whereas the three other countries, while relying to some extent on merchant houses, also to a greater extent than the British sent out salesmen who were direct representatives of manufacturing firms. This difference can be decisive. For one thing, these British merchant houses are not committed to selling British goods. When the German trade drive began, the Germans gained a good deal by selling to British wholesaling houses, either in Britain or in the overseas markets; and in the same way the great British trading houses in Asia or in Africa are quick to buy Japanese goods, if only because they lose trade to their non-British competitors if they do not. So, while the German or American or Japanese salesman in foreign markets is there to sell goods made in his home country, the British trader or salesman in foreign markets is under no such obligation. If manufacturers want to sell abroad, they must send out their own people, and not rely exclusively on merchant houses. This difference may have also some importance as the simpler consumer goods disappear from international trade, and as machinery and capital goods grow in importance. Selling and servicing such goods requires specialised knowledge, and demands perhaps a greater tie to the particular manufacturer than the trading house normally likes—with its policy of being free always to buy in the cheapest market. The great trading houses deny that they handle this type of trade less efficiently than do direct manufacturer representatives, but it is probably not without significance that an increasing proportion of manufacturers seeks direct representation.

This brings us to the third feature—the large-scale organisation of selling. It is not possible for every manufacturer to have a salesman in every market. The merchant house embodies the economies of large-scale organisation because it sells the goods of several hundred manufacturers. But if the merchant house is not appropriate to the trade drive, because of its desire not to be tied, the sending out of representatives is possible only if manufacturers will club together to do their export trade co-operatively. This was the line pursued by Germany in the eighties, and again by Japan in the thirties. This was also the most important arena of government intervention in both cases. Both the German and the Japanese governments urged their manufacturers to form export associations, and in both cases small sums were paid out of the public purse to cover the administrative expenses of such associations.

The U.S. government paid no such subsidies, but it went at least so far as to amend the Sherman Act to exempt such associations from the anti-trust operations.

Attempts to promote export associations of this kind have met with little success in this country, partly because of the dominance of merchant houses, partly because the philosophical traditions of British business men, up to and after the First World War, favoured competition rather than association, and partly because the atmosphere of a trade drive has not existed since 1870. How important a role such associations should play we cannot tell until Britain actually launches herself upon a new drive for exports.

The fourth feature of a trade drive is willingness to please the customer in every way. If he wishes, he can have his catalogues in Arabic, his measurements in centimetres, and his quotations c.i.f. He can order standard designs, or submit his own specifications. He can have immediate delivery from stock. He can buy large quantities, or small quantities. Such things one takes for granted as the small change of selling techniques, but they recur again and again in explanations of British loss of markets to others, whether one is reading the literature of 1884 or of 1954. Particularly important in these days is the provision of after-sales service, including spare part depots and repair facilities, for machinery. This writer can testify from his own experience that many business buyers in Asia and in Africa believe that they get better after-sales service for American or for German machinery than they do for British; but whether their belief is justified he is in no position to say.

Lastly, there is the offer of liberal credit. This is a new feature in the literature of trade drives; not much was written on the subject before the 1930's. All the same, the provision of credit played an important part in the expansion of British trade in the nineteenth century. Railways, harbours, and capital works of many kinds were sponsored by British capitalists, who organised the finance, and gave the work to British factories. Recent negotiations to build steel plants in India are in the same tradition. Nowadays the overseas countries are interested in building factories, power stations, irrigation works, and capital works of all kinds, and the country which is forward in organising the finance for such undertakings is the one most likely to get these contracts.

III.

It is easy to see what a country must do if it wishes to keep or to increase its share of world trade in manufactures. It is much harder to understand how it comes to embark upon a trade drive.

It is harder to understand because it is not "a country" that embarks upon a trade drive, but individual business men. Governments had nothing to do with initiating the British trade drive after 1820, or the American drive after 1880, and very little to do with the German drive after 1870, or the Japanese drive after 1930. In all these cases it was individual business men who decided that foreign trade was very important, and who thereupon flooded the market with salesmen, printed catalogues in Spanish, slashed their prices, and did all those other things which capture foreign trade. What came over British business men in the

1820's, or German business men in the 1870's, or Americans in the 1880's, to make them act in this way ?

Various theories float around, but none of them is wholly convincing. For example, the most popular theory of our day is that if British exports are not increasing rapidly this is because the income tax rate is so high. The income tax rate may be too high, but since the decline of the British share of world trade began in the 1870's, income tax can hardly explain the phenomenon. The same goes for the explanation in terms of inflation at home. The evils of our own day are to be deplored, but they cannot be used to explain a phenomenon of eighty years' standing.

Another theory is that the British success in the first half of the nineteenth century was accidental—something that happened while the other countries were sleeping—and that it was only natural that in due course they would claim their rights. In particular stress is placed upon geography; it is observed that Germany carved out the continent of Europe as her chief market, that the United States now dominates the Latin American and Canadian markets, that Japan was taking over the Asian markets, and that Britain's greatest successes have been in the British Empire. No doubt geographical propinquity is important in explaining trade, but it does not explain why the Asian market should go to Japan, rather than to India (much richer in resources), or the European market to Germany rather than to Britain or to France. Neither does it explain why one nation is " awake " when others are " sleeping "; this explanation is merely a restatement of the problem.

Another explanation turns on the size of the home market. We are sometimes told that the United States has a large home market, and that exporting therefore comes easily to her. It would be more plausible to argue that it is the country which has a small home market which is driven to export. Thus, both Belgium and Switzerland have succeeded in holding their share of world trade in manufactures over the past seventy years, despite the smallness of their home markets; or perhaps because the smallness of their home markets forced them to expand their exports rapidly if their production was to expand.

Another model attributes trade drives to successful innovation. The British in 1820 had discovered the secret of successful mass production of textiles and of steel; they had therefore a cost advantage which laid the world's markets at their feet. By 1880 they had lost this advantage, and the discovery of new technical processes for exploiting phosphoric iron ores gave an advantage to Germany, and to the United States. At the same time the United States was pioneering in mass producing machines, with standardised parts, and this gave her an additional advantage. But there are obstacles to accepting this interpretation. In the 1890's German iron and steel was no better or cheaper than British; there was no real lead. Again, machinery was only 21 per cent. of U.S. exports of manufactures in 1913, and the U.S. held only 22 per cent. of world exports of machinery, compared with Britain's 26 per cent. and Germany's 38 per cent. Also, Japan had no lead in anything in 1930. Leadership in innovation fits the British expansion from 1820 to

1860, but it cannot explain the German, the U.S., or the Japanese drives.

These three trade drives are probably best explained simply as a by-product of domestic investment drives. When a nation begins to expand rapidly, its imports of food and raw materials expand rapidly. This is a deflationary factor, absorbing purchasing power generated in producing manufactures. Manufacturers are therefore forced to look outside the country for export markets to counterbalance the drain of purchasing power through imports. At the same time, the imports give to foreigners the money with which to buy manufactures, and so imports provide the market for exports, as well as exerting pressure in that direction. In this model deflation in the home market forces manufacturers to seek export markets, but this happens only because they are presumed to have an irresistible urge to invest; in the absence of this urge, the increase of imports would reduce investment instead of increasing exports. The decisive factor is this irresistible urge to invest, of which the export drive is merely a by-product. Germany, the U.S.A. and Japan seem to have been seized by such urges, and this is probably the best explanation of their export drives. Why they were seized by these urges is an even larger question, which we cannot pursue here.

We are left then with two possible cases: an urge to invest may start an export drive, as in the German case, or a strong world demand for one's exports may stimulate home investment, as in the British case. An export drive may be the cause of rapid economic growth, or merely its by-product.

13

If home investment is sluggish, can anything be done to force manufacturers into the export market ? Merely to let in more imports would probably discourage investment rather than stimulate sluggish investors. Some countries have tried other tricks—fixing export quotas for each industry, and tying raw material allocations to these quotas (possible only in a controlled economy); relieving earnings in export trade from some taxation; manipulating foreign exchange rates in such a way as to give exporters a profit on the exchange; and so on. If private investment is pouring forth vigorously such manoeuvres are unnecessary, since the investment drive will create the export drive; but if both investment and exports are sluggish, a country may be driven to inject stimuli of these kinds.

IV.

The British case remains a puzzle. British capitalists invested heavily in manufacturing industry up to the 1870's, and then the spring broke. Industrial production, which had been increasing by nearly 4 per cent. per annum, dropped to a rate of growth of 1·8 per cent. per annum, up to 1913. Exports of manufactures dropped from a rate of growth of 5·6 to 2·0 per cent. per annum. Why this happened we do not know. It may be that the rise of Germany and of the U.S.A. deprived Britain of markets, and so discouraged home investment. This, however, is hard to accept. The rise of a new country need not deprive an old country of its trade. The new country's demand for imports puts extra purchasing power into the market, and, provided the supply of primary products responds, the new trade does not in any way eat into the old. Correspondingly there is nothing reprehensible about a trade drive, or harmful to others, provided that the expanding country is willing to expand its imports as rapidly as its exports, and provided that supplies of food and raw materials are expanding.

A more plausible explanation is that Britain found it more profitable after 1870 to provide services for the world, than to provide manufactures, so that British capital was diverted to a great expansion of shipping, of insurance, and of foreign investment. These provided the earnings needed to pay for imports; and so the rate of growth of exports, and of industrial production, declined.

Whatever the reason may have been, for seventy years, till 1939, British capitalists invested a smaller part of the national income in manufacturing than did the capitalists of other industrial nations; wherefore British industrial production grew more slowly than that of other nations, and Britain's share of world trade dropped in every decade. Then from 1946 there was a great surge of investment and of exports; our hearts rose, but the surge was checked in 1950.

Few would doubt that we need an average annual increase of industrial production of 3 to 4 per cent., and of exports of 3 per cent. We need what for us in these days amounts to a trade drive: to hold our share of world exports constant. But how do we get it started ?

[9]

INTERNATIONAL ECONOMICS

INTERNATIONAL COMPETITION IN MANUFACTURES

By W. Arthur Lewis
University of Manchester, England

I

These reflections are stimulated by the current problems of two countries: Great Britain and India. Both countries are short of arable land, relatively to population. Hence, as their national incomes rise, whether because of population growth or because of growing productivity, both need to import more food and raw materials. Both desire more rapid rates of growth than they have experienced in recent decades. In Britain there is general talk of an increase of 3 per cent per annum per capita, which is more than twice as great as the rate achieved in the forty years before the first World War, which rate was in turn higher than that of the next three decades. If a 3 per cent per capita rate is achieved, it may be expected to be accompanied by rapidly growing exports of manufactures. Similarly, India's plans are bound to run into difficulties for the same reason unless India's exports of manufactures grow rapidly to pay for imports of food and raw materials. In fact, I have suggested in a recent article (in *Capital,* Bombay, December, 1954) that current Indian aspirations will involve India's capturing an extra 6 per cent of world trade in manufactures during the next twenty-five years.

The British and Indian need for rapidly growing exports of manufactures has sent me to the records seeking to discover how a country captures a significantly larger share of world trade in manufactures in a short time. This quest has begun with a statistical exercise—the compilation of a table showing annual exports of manufactures by the leading countries of the world since 1880, covering an estimated 96 per cent of world trade in manufactures at the starting point. Publication of this table is reserved for a later occasion. All that need be said at present is that comparability has been achieved by relying on the very detailed reclassification of trade returns for the years 1899, 1913, 1929, 1937, and 1950 which the late Dr. Tyszynski published in *Manchester School* in September, 1951. For the moment we will concentrate on a few countries in selected boom years, beginning with 1883. The results are shown in the accompanying table.

PERCENTAGE SHARES OF WORLD TRADE IN MANUFACTURES

	1883	1890	1899	1913	1929	1937	1954
U.S.A.	3.4	3.9	9.8	11.0	18.2	17.3	25.8
U.K.	37.1	35.8	28.4	25.4	20.4	19.1	15.8
Germany	17.2	17.2	19.5	23.0	18.4	19.7	11.6*
France	14.6	14.5	12.6	10.6	9.4	5.2	7.1
Belgium	4.8	5.1	4.9	4.3	4.9	5.2	4.8
Canada	0.1	0.1	0.3	0.6	2.9	4.2	4.8
Japan	0.1	0.3	1.3	2.1	3.4	6.4	3.7
Others	22.7	23.1	23.2	23.0	22.4	22.9	26.4

* Western Germany.

In recent history, four countries have captured substantial shares of world trade in manufactures over short periods. The first was Britain, starting at the end of the Napoleonic Wars and continuing until about 1860, during which period the volume of her exports of manufactures increased by 5.6 per cent per annum. The second country was Germany, capturing about 6 per cent of world trade between 1890 and 1913. Thirdly, the United States, which even more spectacularly captured 6 per cent between 1890 and 1899—not to mention the even larger gains resulting from two world wars. Finally, there is Japan, whose capture of 3 per cent of world trade in manufactures between 1929 and 1937 attracts special attention mainly because it occurred over a period during which the total volume of world trade contracted.

II

In trying to understand these successes we have as usual to distinguish between the "how" and the "why." "How" is easy to answer. Every successful drive for trade in manufactures contains five elements: keen prices, a flood of salesmen, large-scale organization of selling, attention to customers' wishes, and liberal credit. Econometricians usually put all the emphasis on the first element, prices, because this is the easiest to measure. Businessmen, however, usually attribute much greater importance to sales effort, and it is clear enough that success or failure in selling is not always attributable to prices.

I have investigated the "how" question elsewhere (*District Bank Review,* December, 1954), and lack of space compels me to push on to the "why." What makes a country decide to use the appropriate selling techniques at a certain stage in its history, so that suddenly its manufacturers launch a drive which captures 5 per cent or so of world trade in a decade or two? Or, to turn the question around, how can one account for the persistent decline of Britain and of France?

III

We can begin by brushing away three British excuses. Today nearly every British businessman blames high taxes for the inadequacy of British exports. "What incentives have we," he asks, "to launch on such risky business?" One cannot prove that this factor is not important today; but it was certainly not important between 1883 and 1913, when Britain lost 12 per cent of world trade. Moreover, though it is often alleged that British businessmen have less incentives than Americans, the fact is that the proportion of profits paid in taxation (adding income and corporation taxes) is higher in the United States than in Britain. One cannot prove that the taxation excuse is not valid, but one must be forgiven for treating it with skepticism.

A second excuse popular in Britain today is inflation, which keeps in the home market goods which should be exported. Here again we have an argument which cannot explain the long decline of six decades before the second World War. As to its current validity, one notes that the French have had more inflation than most since 1945 but have increased their share of world trade in manufactures for the first time in many decades. Insofar as inflation is associated with accelerated capital formation, as in France, it bears fruit in accelerated growth, which makes possible both greater home consumption and also larger exports. It is beyond dispute that inflation may reduce exports, but in the historical perspective of so many decades it seems desirable to seek also for more fundamental causes.

One must take more seriously the argument that there was no British failure in the export sphere before the first World War. After all, through the last four decades before the war there was a mounting surplus on the balance of payments, due to invisible earnings growing very rapidly. It is therefore arguable that Britain exported as much as she needed to, and may even have exported too much, in the sense that some of the exported capital was lost. On the other hand, the reason why a slow growth of exports sufficed was that there was a slow growth of imports, which in turn was due to a slow growth of production and of national income. As Mr. Coppock has shown (*Manchester School*, January, 1956) there was a climacteric in the British economy in the 1870's, after which the rate of growth was much below the rate of the first three-quarters of the century. Since exports of manufactures were about one-third of industrial production, it is even arguable that the slow growth of production was due to the slow growth of exports. If production had grown more rapidly, imports would have grown more rapidly, and balance-of-payments difficulties would have arisen unless exports had grown more rapidly. So we need say no more for the present than that production, imports and exports, grew rather slowly, both in comparison with the second and third quarters of the nineteenth century and also in comparison with contemporary growth rates in Germany and in the United States.

IV

Now let us examine the reasons offered for German and American success in exporting manufactures, concentrating on the period 1890 to 1913.

The main feature of this period is the rapid growth of steel production and the expansion of iron and steel and machinery exports relative to textile exports. Thus if one takes the exports of Britain, France, Germany, and the United States as given in the British compilation of 1909 (*Statistics of British and Foreign Trade and Industry,* Cmd. 4954), between 1890 and 1907, the combined exports of iron and steel manufactures and machinery increased by 126 per cent in value, while the combined exports of cotton and woolen yarns and manufactures increased only by 47 per cent. The British kept up with the textile trade, their exports increasing by 40 per cent as compared with 47 per cent; but they were left behind in iron and steel and machinery, increasing their exports by 79 per cent as compared with 126 per cent. They also failed to keep up in steel production, increasing from 3.6 to 6.5 million tons, as compared with Germany's 2.2 to 11.9 million tons and the U.S.A.'s 4.3 to 23.4 million tons. This is the principal feature of the period. What accounts for it? We shall consider briefly five possible explanations.

First, natural resources. This is an obvious explanation of the enormous American expansion, but it does not easily explain why Germany went ahead so much more rapidly than Britain. It is true that the Gilchrist-Thomas process enabled Germany to exploit the phosphoric ores of Lorraine, but this removed a disadvantage rather than conferred an advantage. The ores were poor, and because of high transport cost they were not very attractive to the Ruhr. In terms of iron content, the Ruhr in 1901 was getting 53 per cent of its ore from Spain and Sweden, and only 15 per cent from Lorraine (N. J. G. Pounds, *The Ruhr,* page 112). Besides, Britain also had large supplies of cheap phosphoric ores. There is no reason to suppose that Germany had the advantage over Britain in ore supplies.

Secondly, geographical location. Germany's success was based on capturing the markets of Europe. Between 1890 and 1913, her exports (including food and raw materials) increased by 344 million pounds. Seventy-five per cent of this increase was to Europe. In the same period, only 34 per cent of Britain's increase was to Europe, 90 million pounds as against Germany's 259 million. But this cannot be attributed entirely to geography. It is easy to see why Germany monopolized the markets of Russia or of Austria-Hungary. But by 1913 she was also selling more than Britain to Italy, to Norway, to Sweden, and indeed to every other European country except Spain, where she was running neck and neck. Germany was also selling more to the United States. Britain had virtually abandoned to Germany those markets which were absorbing ever increasing quantities of steel and of machinery to concentrate on those agricultural markets where consumer goods and railway equipment were still in great demand.

The United States, also, it should be noted, did not depend primarily on geographical location. Much of the big increase in the U.S. share of world trade between 1890 and 1899 was due to iron and steel manufactures (including machinery), the export of which increased from 29 million to 122 million dollars. There was a substantial increase to Canada, whose share in these exports rose from 10 to 18 per cent, but the share of other American countries slumped from 41 to 20 per cent, and much the biggest absolute rise was in the share of Europe, from 24 to 39 per cent. Up-and-coming nations sell all around the world, not just to their next-door neighbors.

Thirdly, technological leadership. Britain had acquired her commanding position through her innovations in textiles and in iron manufacture. As David Hume had pointed out in his essay "Of Money" in 1752, this kind of advantage must be temporary: "Manufactures gradually shift their places, leaving those countries and provinces which they have already enriched, and flying to others, whither they are allured by the cheapness of provisions and labour."[1] Hume's arguments explain why Britain has lost the cotton export trade to Japan and to India, but in 1913 this had not yet happened; Britain was still supreme in textiles. Her failure was rather a failure to achieve technological leadership in the new trades, especially in steel, in machinery, and, less important, in chemicals. Wages were a little higher in Britain than in Germany, but this seems to have been of minor importance. The failure in chemicals is usually explained by saying that the British did not have sufficient respect for scientific training as compared with the Germans. The pioneering in electrical engineering was done in the United States, partly because the vested interest of the municipalities in gas obstructed the spread of electric lighting in Britain. (J. H. Dunning, *Manchester School,* September, 1956.) Various other explanations are offered of American pioneering in other kinds of machinery, of which perhaps the most important is the relatively high ratio of unskilled to skilled labor. But all of these explanations leave one doubtful. For it is not

[1] See the excellent discussion by J. M. Low in the *Manchester School,* September, 1952.

necessary to be a pioneer in order to have a large export trade. It is sufficient to be a quick imitator. Britain would have done well enough if she had merely imitated German and American innovations. Japan, Belgium, and Switzerland owe more of their success as exporters of manufactures to imitation than they do to innovation.

We have spoken of failure to pioneer, but there was not complete failure to imitate. Britain did pass over to steel production, reaching 8 million tons in 1913, as compared with Germany's 19 million tons; and she was exporting 38 million pounds of industrial and electrical equipment in 1913, compared with Germany's 57 million pounds. There was an undoubted failure to sell machinery to Europe, but since she was doing well in selling metal products in other continents—as well as the limited demand of those other continents permitted—it is not so clear whether the emphasis should be on failure to sell machinery or on failure to sell to Europe; in other words, whether it was the nature of the product or the nature of the market that was the limiting factor. Perhaps there were elements of both.

Both elements can be explained to some extent, fourthly, by the doctrine of momentum. According to this doctrine, Britain equipped herself in the first half of the nineteenth century to sell cotton and railway materials, and she thus got into a rut which unfitted her to sell steel and machinery at the end of the century. There are several aspects to this, some emphasizing the nature of the product and others the nature of the sales effort required.

1. First, the willingness to invest. Investors are like sheep. It was proved at the beginning of the nineteenth century that Britain could sell cotton; so money was poured into this trade. As more cotton was produced, markets were forced open all over the world, by a stream of salesmen. Profits were reinvested in cotton. This could go on so long as there were new or expanding markets for cotton to conquer. But once it slowed down, the funds no longer going into cotton would not necessarily go into creating or expanding some other industry. They might just as easily go into foreign bonds. The same may be suggested, though with less plausibility, of the slow transfer from iron to steel. Long after steel had far surpassed iron, Britain remained the world's largest exporter of pig iron.

2. Secondly, the export organization created in the first half of the century—the merchant house—was not so appropriate for selling steel or machinery. It flourished selling consumer goods in agricultural countries; but the rich and expanding European market for industrial equipment escaped it.

3. The same is probably true of the financing of foreign trade; machinery requires something intermediate between the three-months

bill and the twenty-year bonds in which Britain excelled. Germany's intermediate credit terms were more to the point.

4. The attitude towards science in industry may be attributed to the same cause. The professional scientist played little part in the eighteenth-century innovations in textiles and iron manufacture, on which British success was based. Consequently there was little respect for him in British industry, and exaggerated respect for the self-made man. This became a disadvantage in a later era when science was contributing to innovation.

5. The conservatism of British steel producers was a byword at the end of the nineteenth century. They lagged in copying German and American innovations in fuel consumption, in chemical control of processes, and in mechanization; and above all, although Britain had large reserves of phosphoric ores, they left it to Germany to develop cheap basic Bessemer steel, which soon came pouring into the British market, while they clung to expensive acid open-hearth steel. It is sometimes argued that newcomers have an advantage over originators because they install the latest equipment, while the originators are stuck with old-fashioned plant which it does not pay to scrap. However, considering that British steel output doubled between 1890 and 1913, there was plenty of opportunity to adopt new methods. This conservatism was attributed at the time to the industry being in the hands of old family firms with aging directors; it was probably due at least in part to the self-satisfaction which tends to follow successful pioneering.

6. The slow growth of the engineering industries was probably even more important than the slow growth of the steel industry, since the latter was presumably due to the former. By 1913, home consumption of steel per capita had reached 405 pounds in Germany but only 330 pounds in Britain. This in turn was due to low domestic capital formation, not compensated by capital export; not compensated because, whereas capital export to the agricultural countries provided a market for railway equipment and for textiles, home investment (or for that matter, capital export to Europe, which was mainly left to Germany and to France) would have stimulated the engineering industries producing new types of industrial, electrical, or public utility equipment, and these were the industries where leadership passed to Germany and to the United States. The low level of capital formation at home was sometimes attributed to abundance of skilled labor, but this argument is rather doubtful. It may apply when capital is substituted for skill; but much capital was substituted for mere brawn, some economized materials, and some incorporated new techniques not available in existing skills. Besides, capital was at least as cheap in Britain as in Germany or the United States, if not cheaper. Conservatism was at least a part of the answer.

7. Some contemporaries found their explanation in financial institutions. Cotton and iron had largely been self-financing, so the London capital market had concentrated on gilt-edged securities and on foreign investment, to the exclusion of domestic industry. Steel and engineering needed greater funds if they were to adopt the large-scale production methods favored by Germany and by the U.S.A. But whereas in those countries industry could borrow from banks and other institutions, in Britain momentum kept the capital market to its accustomed tracks, with the effect that ever increasing sums were invested overseas. It is clear that the capital market was to some extent imprisoned in its own habits—it went on investing overseas in the eighties though the terms of trade were moving against agriculture, and again in the twenties, though the real surplus was small (Britain was borrowing short to lend long). But it is not as clear that British industrialists could not have raised more funds for home investment if they had tried.

8. Cotton and iron factories were small, and so Britain acquired a firm belief in individualism and in atomistic competition. Steel, machinery, and chemicals, on the other hand, are notable for large enterprises, mergers, and monopolistic behavior. Insofar as these industries need a monopolistic atmosphere in which to survive, the British climate was unfavorable.

9. British superiority in the first half of the century convinced industrialists of the virtues of free trade. Consequently, when new industries began at the end of the century in which they held no superiority, Germany and the U.S.A. poured manufactures into the British market and made it difficult for comparable British firms to reach the scale of production needed to become viable. Between 1883 and 1913, Britain increased the volume of her import of manufactures faster than anything else: food imports by 2.0 per cent per annum, raw materials by 1.8 per cent per annum, but manufactures by 3.4 per cent per annum. On the other hand, since Britain's net imports of metallic goods (excluding nonferrous metals) in 1913 were only 36 million pounds, as compared with net exports of metallic goods of 127 million pounds, it is not so obvious that the absence of a tariff was decisive. If imports depressed prices as much as the argument requires, would they not also have been larger in relation to total output?

There is no space to discuss each of these aspects of the doctrine of momentum in detail. Not all would bear closer investigation; but its general plausibility seems beyond dispute.

Thus we come to the last of the explanations of a successful export drive, which is the impact upon imports and exports of rapid industrial growth. As industry grows rapidly, so does domestic income and so, therefore, does the demand for food and for raw materials. In short-of-land countries, such as Britain, Germany, and Japan, this forces a rapid increase in imports of food and raw materials. Now an increase in imports is deflationary; so manufacturers can keep going only by expanding their exports of manufactures, and this they are able to do because the country's imports provide foreign countries with the necessary purchasing power. Manufacturers will only behave in this way, however, if they have an irresistible urge to invest, coupled with the will and the techniques required for selling exports of manufactures. If the urge to invest is weak or if selling techniques are poor, the deflationary pressure of imports simply checks the investment drive and slows down industrialization to the pace which the rate of growth of exports is able to support. This seems to have been the basic difference between Germany and Japan, on the one hand, and Britain, on the other. The Germans had the irresistible urge to invest in steel, machinery, chemicals, and such in the last decades of the nineteenth century, and broke into export markets, using whatever techniques were necessary. The British, by momentum and tradition, were otherwise occupied. In earlier decades they had had an irresistible urge to invest in cotton and in iron, which had carried them breaking into world markets with the necessary techniques. The rate of expansion which this permitted slowed down after 1860, but rather than invest at home at the old rate in the newer industries, they slowed down home investment to the pace of cotton and iron and put their money instead into foreign investment in agricultural countries, where it financed sales of cotton and railway materials without adding to Britain's productive capacity.

But what would have happened if Britain had invested more at home and less abroad? The impact effect would have been smaller exports. However, let us assume that production and imports would have grown faster and that manufacturers would have been driven into a faster rate of growth of exports. How would this have affected the terms of trade? They would probably have worsened, but we cannot be sure by how much. British capital exports would have been a smaller proportion of income, but since income would be growing more rapidly, the absolute deficiency would constantly diminish. Moreover, British savings might have been higher, giving greater scope for home and foreign investment simultaneously; the adverse terms of trade after 1900 seem to have been accompanied by wider profit margins and larger savings. Again, the deficiency in British capital exports might have been made good by other nations, attracted into the field by improving terms for primary products. If we assume that British exports would have grown faster, possibly German exports may in consequence have grown less rapidly. This might have checked German home investment and made Germany a larger exporter of capital. In other words, if the British urge to invest had been more irresistible than the German, it might have been the Germans who turned to capital export instead of to home investment. In any event, the terms of trade would have had to worsen quite sharply to offset all the benefits of greater home production. The capital-output ratio at home was only 3½ to 1, compared with returns of 20 to 1 from foreign investment; and even if one doubts that the marginal capital-income ratio was constant at this level, there is little reason to doubt that—apart from the terms of trade—investment at home would have raised real income faster than investment abroad. One cannot prove that the gain would not all have been offset by adverse terms of trade, but one may remain very doubtful that it would.

V

As in all scientific enquiry, seeking causes of economic growth is like peeling an onion; as each skin is removed, a new one is revealed. Our explanation of export drives has left us with the not very attractive concepts of "momentum" and "an irresistible urge to invest." If Britain and India are to have the successes they desire in the next two decades, these are the forces by which they must be driven. But how does a nation work itself up into this frame of mind? Why did Germany suddenly go this way in the last quarter of the nineteenth century? Here we pass from international economics into the sphere of philosophical speculation; so I gladly leave the subject to another occasion.

[10]

ASPECTS OF TROPICAL TRADE

I

Agricultural Products

The engine of growth in the temperate world has been industrial production. The demands of industry, and the incomes generated thereby, have constituted an ever-expanding market for other sectors of the economy. When industry has faltered, every other sector has been depressed, and when industry has gone ahead, all other sectors have been more prosperous.

In the tropics the engine of growth until recent years has been exports, directed largely to the temperate countries, and responding largely to the impulses generated by temperate industrial production. My purpose in this essay is to see how both the volume of tropical trade and the terms of trade have reacted to industrial growth.

This has involved a lot of new statistical work, which is described in an Appendix to the paper. Let me just indicate briefly in one paragraph the nature of the material. I have chosen seven years when world production and trade were at cyclical peaks, namely, 1883, 1899, 1913, 1929, 1937, 1955 and 1965. For industrial production I have used the O.E.C.D. index of the O.E.C.D. countries since 1901 (including the U.S.A, and Canada but not Japan), and have joined this to the League of Nations index for the earlier years. Trade from 1929 onwards is easy to compile because the data have been published in convenient form by the United Nations Statistical Office, but for earlier years I have had to go back to trade returns, a task of no mean difficulty, since in 1883 I have separate data for 74 tropical countries. For prices I have compiled an annual index for agricultural products exported by tropical countries, a new annual index for manufactures, and an index for minerals exported by tropical countires. Finally let me define tropical countries. These are roughly the countries lying between 30° N and 30° S. Among the countries excluded are Chile, Uruguay, Argentina, the Union of South Africa, all of North Africa and the Middle East (except Egypt), China and Hong Kong. Thus we include Bolivia and Paraguay, Egypt and Southern Rhodesia, Indochina and the islands of Oceania.

The Volume of Trade

For me the most surprising outcome of this exercise has been to discover how rapidly tropical trade was growing in the period before the first world war. According to my figures, between 1883 and 1913 the quantum of tropical trade grew by 3.6 per cent per annum. Table 1 shows some comparative growth rates. The rate for tropical trade is slightly higher than the rate one would get by adding together industrial production in the four leading countries, the U.S.A., Britain, Germany and France, which would be 3.2 per cent, though not quite as high as the League of Nations (excessive) estimate for the world as a whole, unless one converts to a per capita basis, to take account of the slower growth of tropical populations in this period.

Between 1913 and 1950 the tropics passed through a long depression, associated with world wars and adverse terms of trade. The rate of growth of tropical trade fell to 2.2 per cent per annum between 1913 and 1955. However, since 1955 the volume of tropical trade has again grown very rapidly, namely, by 4.5 per cent. Indeed it has grown as rapidly as industrial production in the O.E.C.D. countries (excluding Japan).

Let me pause here to explain my surprise at finding the engine of growth beating so powerfully in the tropics before the first world war. Growing up in the academic world of the 1930's, I absorbed the conventional view that while economic growth was relatively easy to achieve in the temperate world it was rather difficult in the tropical world because the tropical peoples had the wrong kinds of social institutions; or were not sufficiently materialistic; or disliked hard work; or simply because the tropics were too hot. This remained the conventional view right up to the end of the 1950's; but in the early sixties this position was clearly no longer tenable. Since the second world war industrial production has been growing more

TABLE 1. *Growth rates 1883–1913*

Industry	p.a.
U.S.A.	4.8
Germany	4.2
World	4.0
O.E.C.D.	3.7
Tropical trade	3.6
U.K.	2.0
France	1.8

rapidly in the tropics than it has ever grown in the temperate countries of Western Europe or North America; and in a number of tropical countries the growth rate even of agriculture has been such that gross domestic product has been growing by more than 5 per cent per annum. Many people have not yet noticed that since the war gross domestic product is growing as fast in the underdeveloped countries as a whole as in the developed, namely, by about 4 $^{1}/_{2}$ per cent per annum. We still have a flood of books and articles explaining why, because of wrong institutions or wrong ideas or too much heat, it is impossible for the underdeveloped countries to do what they are actually doing; but there is always a lag between events and our understanding of them.

It is this fact that the impossible is now happening that caused me to go back to the period before 1913 to see whether it is really true that the tropics were stagnant while the temperate countries were going ahead so rapidly. As soon as one looks at the facts there is no doubt as to the answer. The tropics were transformed during the period 1880 to 1913; built themselves railways, ports, towns, water supplies, schools, hospitals and other such amenities which were almost completely absent in 1850. Why then was it possible for people to be thinking in 1940 or 1950 that economic growth would not be possible in the tropics on the same scale as in the temperate zones, until deep spiritual and social transformations had occurred? I offer four reasons.

The first reason is that in the 1880's trade was a smaller proportion of tropical economies than manufacturing was of temperate economies. So even if the two engines had beaten at the same pace (as they did on the per capita basis) the manufacturing engine may have had greater effect on the temperate economies than the trade engine on the tropical economies. This does not necessarily follow; it is all a matter of the extent of internal linkages. But given the large proportion of tropical peoples still living in subsistence isolation at that time, it seems plausible that the "multiplier" effect of tropical trade was smaller than that of temperate manufacturing.

The second reason is that productivity was much lower in the tropics in 1880 than in the temperate world, especially agricultural productivity, in the sense that food output per man was much higher in Europe than in Africa or in Asia. If two quantities are growing at the same rate but one is larger than the other, it is easy to miss the fact that the smaller is growing just as fast.

The third reason was our preoccupation with India. Members of my

TABLE 2. *Index no. of exports, 1913, in current dollars*
1883=100

Ecuador 439, Brazil 373, Mexico 352, Colombia 334, Central America 298, Peru 297, Cuba 236, Haiti 155, Venezuela 146, Other West Indies 97[a]

West Africa 517, Central and East Africa 343, Egypt 257, Mauritius 56[a]

Thailand 538, Ceylon 523, Indo-China 426, Indonesia 311, Burma 297,[b] India 221, Phillipines 212

Pacific Islands 343

Price of manufactures, 92

[a] Collapse of sugar prices after 1883. [b] Excludes rice exports to India.
2% p.a.=181, 3% p.a.=242, 4% p.a.=324, 5% p.a.=432.
Source: See Statistical appendix.

seminar at Princeton University have just completed a series of studies of the development of individual tropical countries from 1880 to 1913, on a comparative basis. One of their conclusions is that the growth of world trade at this time set off powerful impulses in every tropical country which had already a stable and modern type of government, with the sole exceptions of India and the sugar colonies.

Table 2 shows the effect on the trade of the principal countries and regions. The failure of the sugar colonies stands out; it would take them all of 70 years to recover from the collapse of sugar prices after 1883. Next come the countries with unstable governments like Haiti and Venezuela, or medieval governments, like Ethiopia or Mozambique. The Phillipines and Cuba almost fall into this category, since they languished under Spanish rule until 1898. Apart from the sugar colonies the only country which breaches our rule is India.

The reason for this is simple. At that time tropical farmers gave priority to producing food; they were not yet sufficiently confident of the market economy to switch from growing food to exclusive reliance on commercial crops. In this they conformed to the model described by Adam Smith, rather than to that of the classical economists. Adam Smith had said that trade enriches a country by enabling a country to use resources that would otherwise be idle. The classical economists asserted that Smith was wrong; trade benefitted a country by enabling it to switch its resources from one use to another.[1] Insofar as concerns the tropical farmers, Adam Smith turns

[1] The arguments have been reviewed by Hla Myint in "The Classical Theory of International Trade and the Underdeveloped Countries", *Economic Journal,* June 1958.

out to have been right. Nowadays they will switch from foodstuffs to more profitable crops, but at the end of the nineteenth century, when they were only just learning to produce for distant world markets, this was a risk that few were prepared to take. The expansion of commercial crops was not at the expense of production, and could therefore occur only where it was possible to bring additional idle land into cultivation.

The zest with which this was done was remarkable. In 1870 Lower Burma was mainly swampland. As the world demand for rice expanded, Burmese moved down from the higher lands of Upper Burma into the swamps, and by 1913 the exports of Lower Burma had risen from half a million tons of rice to over three million. In much the same way the farmers of the Gold Coast created the largest cocoa industry in the world between 1880 and 1913, without even waiting for a proper transportation network. The response did not depend on race, religion, or culture. Table 2 shows rapid growth in all tropical areas, whether the participants were Catholic, Buddhist, Pagan, white, black, or yellow; aggressive, as the Colombians are said to be, happy-go-lucky like the Brazilians, or "mystical" like the Burmese. Wherever fresh lands existed that could be profitably used, the people responded abundantly.

India did not so abundantly exploit the opportunities created by the expansion of world trade because it had little additional fertile land to cultivate; it was already heavily populated, its soils exhausted, and its yields notoriously low. There was still a lot of marginal land which population pressure would duly force into cultivation, but even this was limited, since, as the Census Commissioner of 1951 indicated, an index of the area cultivated per head would fall from 100 in 1891 and 1911 to 77 in 1951. In these circumstances, to raise agricultural productivity would require heavy expenditure on irrigation. The British began to extend the irrigation network in this period, but not with the same vigour as they pushed the railways. In consequence, while the agricultural exports of the tropics excluding India increased between 1883 and 1913 at an average rate of 3.0 per cent per annum, India's agricultural exports increased only by 1.4 per cent per annum, and, according to Dr. Blyn,[2] non-food production (since she consumed much of her own cotton and jute) only by 1.9 per cent per annum. In other words the average Indian farmer failed to get himself a cash crop, as the Japanese farmer got silk, or the Brazilian coffee, the Ghanaian cocoa, or the Burmese rice, and his country remained locked in the poverty

[2] George Blyn, *Agricultural Trends in India, 1891–1947*. Philadelphia, 1967.

of a subsistence agriculture. But India is not typical, even of the rest of Southern Asia, as Table 2 shows.

Our fourth reason for being to sure in the 1950's that the tropics could not develop was what had happened to them in the inter-war period. The terms of trade moved against tropical agriculture in the 20's and 30's. By 1937 tropical development had almost come to a standstill; the average growth rate of the volume of trade sank between 1929 and 1937 to 1.6 per cent per annum, and the purchasing power of exports over manufactures had actually fallen. In a word, the tropics were prosperous up to 1913; but this was followed by 37 years of depression, in which a new generation grew up for whom it was easy to believe that tropical development had never occurred and was impossible.

Agricultural Products

The link between the engines of growth in the temperate world and in the tropics is the demand of the former for the agricultural products of the latter. The tropics also produce and export minerals and manufactures, but these do not display the same simple relationship to temperate industrial production as is displayed by agricultural exports.

This relationship is shown in Fig. 1. Both axes are logarithmic. The x axis is for temperate industrial production, the y axis for the volume of tropical agricultural exports in the same year. A straight line connecting 1899 and 1913 falls almost exactly on 1883, but is about 19 per cent above 1965.

The figures for 1929 and 1937 lie to the left of this line. This is easy to understand. The rate of growth of tropical output was affected very little by the war, whereas the combination of war and postwar recession cost about five years' normal growth of industrial production. The terms of trade held up in the early part of the 1920's but by 1929 were already down to 89 on a 1913 base. The situation worsened still more in the thirties; 1937 is still further from the line, and the terms of trade have dropped to 74.

This adverse experience brought tropical development nearly to a standstill, with the result that 1955 is on the other side of the line.

One should not attach too much significance to a line connecting 1899 with 1913, even though it also covers 1883. However, for what it is worth it does suggest some structural change. It was always the case that the demand for tropical agricultural products grew less rapidly than industrial production; the slope of the line is 0.84. The factors explaining this are

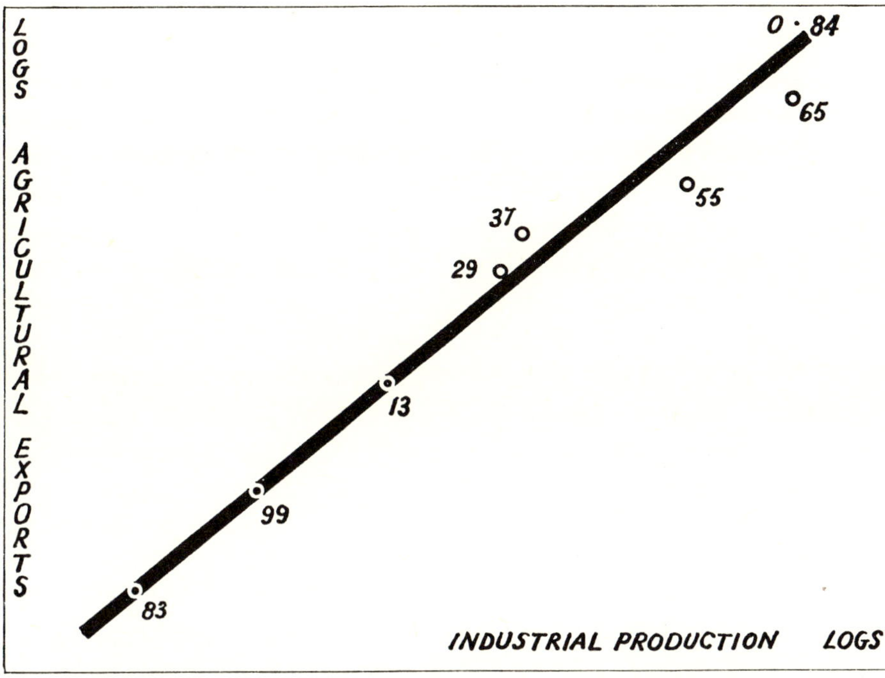

Fig. 1.

well known—development of synthetics, low income elasticity of demand for beverages, etc.—but these forces have been at work from the beginning. Indigo, opium and cinchona, important in 1883, had already almost disappeared by 1913; and coffee had already reached temporary saturation by 1900. The slope from 1955 to 1965 is again 0.84, so if the diagram represents a demand relationship, what we have had is a once-and-for-all downward shift, indicating that factors which were always present were somewhat accelerated during the second world war. Strictly, all that the diagram tells us is what has happened to supplies; tropical export supplies have not kept up. The fact that the terms of trade were adverse to the tropics in 1965 suggests that the trouble is a deficiency of demand rather than of supply; but this is somewhat counteracted by the fact that tropical agricultural trade was not rising as fast as world trade in agricultural products. Bringing the terms of trade into the picture suggest that the 19 per cent gap, if not just a statistical error, is due both to deficiency of demand for some commodities (e.g., beverages, rubber) and to deficiency of supply of others (notably cereals).

If we stick with the demand relationship, these figures yield the conclusion that over the long pull, the agricultural engine of growth has driven the tropics only about 84 per cent as fast as the industrial engine has driven the temperate world. However, agriculture is not the whole picture. Trade in minerals and manufactures has grown much faster, rising from about 23 per cent of total trade in 1913 to 39 per cent in 1965. A line for total trade against industrial production would have a slope of 1.00 for 1899 to 1913, of 1.20 from 1913 to 1937, and again of 1.00 from 1955 to 1965. The deficit in the volume of tropical trade, as against temperate industrial production, occurs entirely between 1937 and 1955, that is to say as a result of the second world war. I shall not be saying anything about minerals in these two lectures, but will talk about manufactures next time.

Let us come back to the behaviour of the trade in agricultural products since 1955. The average rate of growth of volume was 3.8 per cent, but since the terms of trade deteriorated by 21 per cent over the decade, the purchasing power of tropical agricultural exports, which is what really matters, increased only by 1.3 per cent per annum between 1955 and 1965. This is a very weak engine indeed. Those tropical countries which depended on agricultural exports alone would be in a very bad way.

The reason for this agricultural failure is well known. It is that the products which the tropics are trying to sell are no longer those which the world needs urgently. Between 1955 and 1965 world trade in agricultural products grew by 54 per cent, while tropical trade in agricultural products grew only by 44 per cent. There was a booming demand for cereals, livestock products, feeding stuffs and fruit, while the tropics were pushing tea, cocoa, coffee, sugar and rubber, for which the demand is sluggish.

All this can be seen in Table 3, which gives a succinct picture of the current crisis of tropical agriculture. The agricultural exports of North America and Western Europe have boomed, since these are the continents exporting foodstuffs; their prices have also been well maintained. The tropical continents are lagging in volume, and even so their prices fell sharply, as they sought to push upon the world what the world did not want. This table, combined with the fact that exports of tropical manufactures increased by 149 per cent, also shows that the old division of the world, into the agricultural exporting tropics and the manufactures exporting temperate countries has already broken down.

One would think that the resolution of the crisis must lie in curtailing supplies of the no longer booming commodities, and switching instead to

TABLE 3. *Exports of agricultural products,*[a] *1965*
1955=100

	Volume	Price	Value
North America	180	109	195
W. Europe	154	108	170
WORLD	155	97	151
Africa	144	89	128
Latin America	142	89	127
Far East	130	93	122

[a] Including forestry and fisheries. Source: F.A.O., *The State of Food and Agriculture.*

greater food production; but just at this time a new supplier, tropical Africa is forging ahead in the world market for just these agricultural commodities which are already in surplus supply.

Africa is a newcomer to world trade. In 1913 Sub-Saharan Africa's exports were only 6.2 per cent of tropical trade. By 1937 they were 13.3, by 1955 18.2, and by 1965 21.4 per cent of tropical trade. Sub-Saharan Africa is doing better in world trade than the rest of the underdeveloped world. This, too, is seldom recognised. We hear a lot about the relative stagnation of those parts of Africa which are on the fringes of the desert. Not many people know that some of the fastest growing countries in the world are in what is called "black Africa" (to distinguish the centre from both North and South).

African exports of commercial crops are growing rapidly because this is where Africa's comparative advantage lies, as compared with Latin America and the cultivation of food. African productivity in tree crops such as cocoa or coffee is not significantly different from Latin American productivity. But productivity in arable crops, and especially in domestic food, is lower in Africa than in, say, Brazil. This is partly due to the African farmer cultivating smaller acreages per head with inferior tools. But there is also a difference in yields per acre, due to superior technical practices. Thus the yield of maize averages only about 6 cwt. per acre in West Africa,[3] as against 11 cwt. in Brazil.[4] It follows that a price of commercial crops in terms of food which may repel the Brazilian farmer, may nevertheless attract the African farmer because of his lower opportunity costs. And since Africa

[3] B. F. Johnston, *The Staple Food Economies of Western Tropical Agricultue,* p. 126. Stanford, 1958.

[4] W. H. Nicholls and R. M. Pavia, *Ninety-Nine Fazendas,* Chapter IV. (Mimeographed.) Vanderbilt University, 1967.

is only now being opened up with metalled roads and trucks, we can expect a very rapid spread of commercial agriculture to continue for some time even at what Asian and Latin American farmers think of as very low prices.

This of course puts still greater pressure on Asia and Latin America to move over into greater production of foodstuffs. There is no question about the volume of demand, for in addition to temperate demand there is tropical demand itself. Africa and Asia are now net importers of cereals, and the large deficit of tropical Latin America is not much smaller than Argentina's surplus. The tropics as a whole has a large net deficit of food which is a drain on its balance of payments.

It has often been suggested that the tropical countries could and should eliminate this deficit by greater production and exchange. Most tropical countries are now trying to become more self-sufficient in food, and doubtless as the new technologies are developed, and the new extension services begin to pay off, several countries will achieve self-sufficiency. Exchange between tropical countries is a different matter. For example, at present India's food deficit is financed by soft loans from the United States. With greater production Latin America could sell India more cereals in exchange for steel. What then happens to American aid to India? It would have to be untied from cereals, and made available to purchase other commodities. If it were merely to disappear the volume of commodities available to India would be reduced. The model is further complicated if the United States uses tied loans to finance both cereals to India and steel to Latin America; this produces the maximum distortion of tropical trade. In order to facilitate greater exchanges of this kind, the underdeveloped countries have asked for one modification of current aid tying practices, namely that they be allowed to use any aid to buy from any other underdeveloped country. So India could not use U.S. aid to buy from France or Germany, but could use it to buy from Brazil or Malaya. It seems hopeless to ask that aid be untied altogether, but the development of inter-tropical trade, whether in agricultural products or in machinery, is bound to be handicapped if this more limited concession is not granted.

To return specifically to food, the principal factor keeping down Asian and Latin American production of food, relatively to commercial crops, has been the relationship of prices. For while the price of wheat,[5] on a 1913

[5] This is the imported price of wheat, c.i.f. London, in dollars.

base, averaged 193 over the ten years 1956/65, the average price of tropical agricultural exports over this period stood at 217. Despite the adverse terms of trade of tropical exports in terms of manufactures (averaging 89 on the same basis), the tropical farmers stay with these crops because their prices are still favourable relatively to food prices.

The Terms of Trade: Theory

This brings me to the last topic I wish to treat today, namely, what determines the terms of trade for tropical exports. I wish first to examine the theory of the matter, and then to show how the relevant statistics support my theory.

Why does a man growing cocoa earn one tenth of the wage of a man making steel ingots? I was taught that the answer depended on the relative marginal utilities of cocoa and steel, but this has never made any sense to me. My alternative answer can be put in a nutshell. Each of these men has the alternative of growing food. Their relative incomes are therefore determined by their relative productivities in growing food; and the relative prices of steel and cocoa are determined by these relative incomes and by productivities in steel and cocoa. Demand is important in the short run, but the long term determinants are the conditions of supply.

Let me now elaborate this in a formal model. The analysis depends on two pillars:

(*a*) The chief product of tropical countries is food. Their standard of living is therefore determined in the first instance by their output of food per head.

(*b*) The commercial crops which tropical countries export (tea, coffee, etc.) are a small part of their agricultural output; for example, in Nigeria exports are 14 per cent of agricultural output. In the nineteenth century the number of acres and now also the number of persons suitable for commercial production greatly exceed the requirements of the current level of output. There is thus an infinitely elastic supply of commercial products at prices fixed by the relative outputs per head of food and of commercial products.

Some further simplifications are needed to start the model off:

(*c*) Food is homogeneous. Wheat, rice, yams, etc., can all be translated into units of equivalent nutritional value which will always exchange at the same price, because food can be traded between all countries. The possibility that prices may diverge robs the model of precision but makes little difference to the reality of its conclusions.

(*d*) manufactured goods are also homogeneous;

(*e*) tropical commercial products (hereinafter called commercials) are also homogeneous.

(*f*) output per head of manufactures and of food is the same in all temperate countries.

(*g*) output per head of food and of commercials is the same in all tropical countries.

(*h*) there are no transport costs.

These assumptions allow us to start with a model in which initially there are only two countries, say, Germany and Brazil, and three products, say, steel, food and coffee. Let us assume outputs per head as follows, per standard unit of time:

	Steel	Food	Coffee
In Germany	3	3	—
In Brazil	—	1	1

Since food is homogeneous, whether produced in Germany or in Brazil, the model gives us both the factoral and the commodity terms of trade. The commodity terms (found by reading hortizontally) are

$$1 \text{ steel} = 1 \text{ food} = 1 \text{ coffee.}$$

The factoral terms are determined by relative productivities in food; so initially, if we call output per head "the wage,"

$$1 \text{ German wage} = 3 \text{ Brazilian wages.}$$

The comparative cost model with two countries and three goods is over a hundred years old, but it is normally assumed that one country will produce two of the goods, and the other country one of the goods. This makes the terms of trade indeterminate within wide limits. The core of my proposition is that both countries are producing food, and this ties the terms of trade rigidly.

Now let us study the effects of changes in productivity. An increase in the productivity of coffee cannot benefit Brazil, since the supply is infinitely elastic. If productivity doubles, the price will halve, and all the benefit will accrue to Germany. This is well illustrated by what has happened to the prices of sugar and rubber, the only two tropical crops in which productivity has increased spectacularly over the last hundred years, mainly through biological improvement. If we divide index numbers of their prices by our index of the prices of all tropical commercials we get the following results

	1880/4	1910/3	1925/9	1960/4
Sugar	100	61	44	54
Rubber	100	163	44	19

Competition forces prices down as technology improves.

For the same reasons, increases in steel productivity benefit "Brazil". So, if food productivity were constant in both countries, the terms of trade would depend on the relative rates of growth of productivity in "steel" and in "coffee".

Although sugar and rubber are the only two cases of large increases in tropical productivity, the same effect is achieved if a new country comes into the market with lower costs of producing commercials relatively to food. We have already seen that Africa's entry into world markets fits this pattern. We represent this case formally by assuming that a new tropical country (call it Guinea) is added to the model, giving us three countries and three goods. If Guinea has the same relative productivities as Brazil in food and coffe (say in absolute terms 1 : 1 or 0.5 : 0.5 or 2.2.) then the commodity terms of trade are unaltered. But if it produces coffee more cheaply than Brazil in relative terms (the absolutes don't matter), then it will drive down the price and drive Brazil out of the market. Thus assume the new situation to be

	Steel	Food	Coffee
Germany	3	3	
Brazil		1	1
Guinea		0.6	0.9

The commodity terms of trade now become

$$1 \text{ steel} = 1 \text{ food} = 1.5 \text{ coffee}$$

and coffee production becomes unprofitable in Brazil, despite the fact that productivity is higher there than in Guinea.

Let us now return to the two-country model and assume that productivity remains constant in Brazil in both food and coffee. This is more or less the situation which has prevailed in tropical agriculture over the last hundred years, with some exceptions.

The factoral terms of trade will now depend simply on what happens to German productivity in food. Historically there has been an ever-widening gap in food productivity per person as between the tropics and the temperate world, and this is the main reason for the ever-widening gap between temperate and tropical standards of living.

Moreover, an increase in German food productivity not only widens the factoral gap; it also changes the commodity terms of trade unfavourably to the tropics. For example, if German food productivity doubles while all other productivities remain the same, the terms of trade become

1 steel = 2 food = 2 coffee

and the price of steel has doubled in terms of coffee.

Given our assumption that productivities are constant in Brazil, the commodity terms of trade will depend on changes in German productivity. If German steel and German food productivity increase at the same rates, the terms of trade between coffee and steel will be constant. If German productivity rises faster in steel than in food, the price of steel will fall in terms of coffee.

Historically, then, what mainly determines the price of coffee is the price of food; and what determines the terms of trade of coffee in terms of steel is the terms of trade between food and steel in the temperate world. One has to make a double step; not to compare coffee dircetly with steel; but first to compare the price of coffee with that of food, which depends on what is happening in the tropical world; and then compare the price of food with that of steel, which depends on what is happening in the temperate world. Without making this double step centering on food, one cannot hope to understand the terms of trade for tropical crops.

What then has happened to the terms of trade for food against steel in the temperate world? It is difficult to generalize, since there is no clear trend. Industrial productivity alters fairly constantly from decade to decade, while agricultural productivity alters in long spurts. The relative price of food probably depends more than anything else on changes in American output. According to Kendrick,[6] manhour productivity rose faster in manufacturing (146 per cent) than in agriculture (34 per cent) between 1890 and 1929, but rose faster in agriculture (166 per cent) than in manufacturing (87 per cent) between 1929 and 1957. For the whole period 1890–1957 we get average growth rates of 2.3 per cent per annum in manufacturing and 1.9 per cent

[6] J. W. Kendrick, *Productivity Trends in the U.S.A.*, N.B.E.R., 1961.

per annum in agriculture, which would have moved the terms of trade against manufactures if changes in productivity per head were the only element in relative prices.

There are, moreover, divergencies from relative productivity which our model does not take into account. These we may list briefly as follows:

(i) Other factors than labour are used to raise productivity per head. Insofar as one sector has been absorbing more man-made factors than the other, that sector's price per head will not fall as much as relative productivities may indicate.

(ii) Agriculture uses a scarce factor, land. Insofar as any particular product comes up against a relative shortage of specially suitable land, the price of that product will rise faster than productivity would indicate. This element has probably not been significant in the temperate world since the transport revolutions of the mid-nineteenth century opened up new lands and reduced agricultural prices. In the tropics, taken as a whole, limitation of natural resources affects mineral rather than commercial crop production.

(iii) Prices may diverge from relative productivities temporarily. There are marked cyclical changes in the terms of trade associated with cyclical swings in industrial production. Besides, supply takes some time to adjust to changes in demand, so we must not expect the long-term supply price to prevail in every year.

(iv) Prices will diverge from those postulated, if the price of food to the German farmer moves differently from the price to the Brazilian farmer, e.g., because of tariffs or local subsidies. The side which raises its food price relatively to the other's will improve the terms of trade for its product. What matters in our equations is not the world trade price, but the price received by the producer (this applies to steel and coffee as well as to food).

Finally, we must note the decisive limitation on the usefulness of this model which comes into play if the terms of trade between steel and coffee diverge too widely in either direction. This limitation is that there is some price at which Germany will produce "coffee" (synthetic rubber, detergents, etc.), and some price at which Brazil will produce steel. We have been able to ignore this possibility by assuming that initially the comparative cost margins are so wide that the terms of trade must be within the limits set by this possibility. This was roughly true up to about 1929, but as we shall see in a moment has ceased to be true

To take account of this possibility we rewrite the original conditions as

	Steel	Food	Coffee
In Germany	3	3	1
In Brazil	0.5	1	1

We can then state the situation as follows.

(1) As far as steel/coffee relative productivities are concerned, if taken alone, 1 coffee may buy anything from 0.5 steel to 3 steel.

(2) But the possibility of trading food fixes the terms of trade at 1 coffee = 1 steel.

(3) If German food productivity starts to rise while all other productivities are constant, Brazil will start to make its own steel as German food productivity passes 6. Suppose for example that German food productivity becomes 9. Then if Brazil continues to buy steel from Germany the price will be 1 coffee = 0.3 steel, but Brazil can make for herself 0.5 steel as against 1 coffee, so she will cease to buy steel from Germany. In other words a relative rise in food productivity in the temperate world forces the tropical countries to industrialize. Kendrick's figures show this relative rise since 1929, which helps to explain the currently adverse terms of trade for tropical products.

(4) If Brazilian food productivity starts to rise, while all other productivities are constant, Germany will start to make synthetic coffee as Brazilian food productivity passes 3.

Thus the terms of trade are tied rigidly by productivities only for so long as it pays both countries to produce both food and one other commodity. As soon as productivites move outside these limits, the terms of trade cease to be tied rigidly.

The Terms of Trade: Statistics

So much for the theory; now to our statistical test. My argument is that the prices of tropical products are tied to the price of food, and not to the price of manufactures. If the argument is right, the terms of trade of tropicals in terms of food will show constancy, in the sense that departures in either direction will be reversed, unless the relative tropical productivities have changed.

Our statistical materials are described in the Statistical Appendix to this paper. Briefly they are

(1) An index of the prices of tropical agricultural commodities from 1871 to 1965.

(2) An index of the price in London of wheat imported from America, which we use as the world price of food. (Since the tropical countries for most of this period imported flour rather than wheat, the price of flour would be more appropriate. However there is very little difference between these two indexes except in the years immediately after the second world war, when the flour index is kept down by food subsidies and becomes unrepresentative.)

(3) An index of the price of manufactures exported by the leading exporters.

We have divided the index of tropical prices first by the wheat index and then by the index of the price of manufactures. The results are shown in our graph in five-year moving averages. The average of 1899/1913 is taken as 100. In what follows this will be called the prewar price.

The upper curve shows the price of tropicals in terms of wheat. It rises in the seventies, and then more or less stabilises until the first world war, much as our theory would expect it to do. The bulge in the nineties is due to a sharp fall in the price of wheat in 1893/5, which the moving average then spreads over the whole decade. If we take the average for the 1890's without 1893/5, the result is only 3 per cent above the prewar average. After the war the curve is back on line up to the middle twenties. This says that my theory has held over a period of 40 years, from the 80's to the 20's. Tropical commercial prices *are* tied to the price of food

To continue, the curve shows that the price of tropicals fell below the price of food (speaking relatively) in the second half of the twenties, and fell even more drastically during the thirties. The explanation in the twenties was that the war had dislocated the industrial countries more than the tropical countries; in the thirties the great depression pushed tropical prices down more than the price of wheat.

The result of this was to check the expansion of tropical commercial production. The second world war did this to an even greater extent, while food production had to be maintained. As a consequence, the early fifties found the prices of tropical commercials, relatively to food, some 60 per cent above the prewar level. The consequence is as we would expect. The output of tropical commercials has been expanding rapidly (especially rapidly in Africa) and their prices have been tumbling down. Their price in 1965 was down to 12 per cent above the prewar tropicals/wheat ratio. Since then it has continued to fall sharply.

Can we expect it to fall some more, or has it now reached its "natural" level, given the infinite elasticity of supply? There are two conflicting factors. On the one hand, productivity has risen more in commercials than in food, so we should expect the price of commercials to continue to fall until it is significantly below the prewar ratio. On the other hand, export taxes and Marketing Boards reduce the price of the tropical producer significantly below the export price, and this force tends in the opposite direction, by checking the growth of supplies.

We do not know enough to say what the equilibrium ratio now is, but our theory that supply will keep the price of commercials moving pretty closely to that of wheat seems very well borne out by the historical data.

The nub of our analysis is that to understand the terms of trade between tropicals and manufactures one must break the problem into two parts (*a*) the tropicals/wheat ratio, and (*b*) the wheat/manufactures ratio. The first is determined by events in the tropical countries, whereas the second is determined by events in the temperate countries.

The lower curve on our graph shows the price of tropicals in terms of manufactures. Differences between this curve and the upper curve are due to changes in the relative prices of wheat and manufactures; a widening of the distance between the two curves indicates a relative fall in the price of wheat. The two curves behave in roughly the same way, except in three periods.

(*a*) The price of wheat was rather high in the 1870's. It fell in the first half of the 80's. Thereafter wheat, tropicals and manufactures moved at roughly the same levels until the first world war.

(*b*) The price of wheat fell more than the price of manufactures in the 1930's. So the price of tropical commercials, already depressed in terms of wheat, was even more depressed in terms of manufactures.

(*c*) The price of wheat did not rise as much as the price of manufactures after the second world war. We have already seen the reason for this: in the U.S.A. agricultural productivity has risen by twice as much as manufacturing productivity. So tropical prices, which were 60 per cent above the prewar level relatively to wheat in the first half of the 50's, were only 25 per cent above relatively to the price of manufactures. Wheat and manufactures then stayed more or less constant in terms of each other, but rising supply brought tropical prices down in terms of wheat, and therefore of manufactures. In 1965 they were already 11 per cent below the prewar level in terms of manufactures.

Fundamentally, therefore, the reason for the currently unfavourable terms

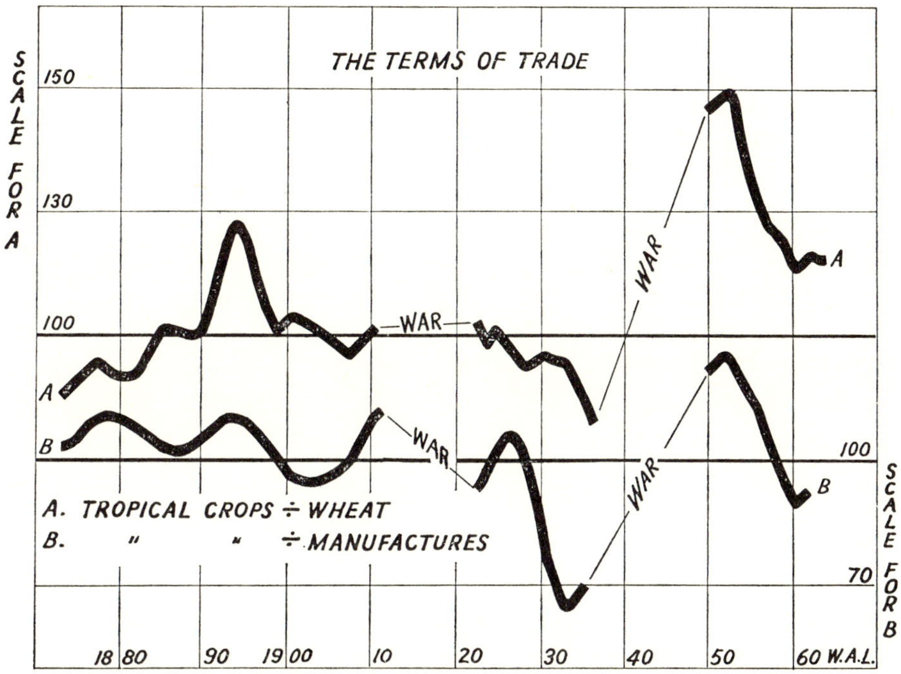

Fig. 2.

of trade which the tropical countries were experiencing is the fact that, compared with the situation before the first world war, the price of wheat has risen less than the price of manufactures. And the fundamental reasons for that are the tremendous revolution in agricultural productivity in the United States (biological, chemical and mechanical), coupled with the relative immobility of farm populations, which keeps supply ahead of demand.

In this situation, what are the tropical countries to do? One obvious answer we now know to be wrong. An obvious answer would be to increase their productivity in commercial crops; but this could not benefit them; it would simply drive down commercial prices to the same extent. This is an important conclusion. For the last eighty years the tropical countries have put practically all their agricultural research and extension funds and effort into trying to raise the productivity of export crops like cocoa, tea, or rubber, and virtually no effort into food productivity. From their point of view, this effort was wholly misdirected.

Four alternatives are open:

First, they may unite to try to raise the price of commercials relatively to food, through international commodity agreements. This they have been trying off and on for the last forty years, without much success, mainly because too many producers are involved, with essentially different interests. Nowadays commodity agreements tend to be an international conspiracy against Africa, since it is the expansion of her output which tends to cause much of the trouble.

Secondly, they may unite to raise their domestic food prices relatively to the world price of wheat—e.g., by the simple device of imposing tariffs on imported cereals. This is not really a practical proposition since it would raise the domestic cost of living, and would be seen by the urban community as a check on industrialisation.

Thirdly, they may devote greater resources to research and extension designed to raise domestic food productivity. This would solve many problems since it simultaneously would improve the terms of trade of commercial exports relatively to imported manufactures, would raise the average standard of living, would narrow the factoral gap, and would reduce the drain of foreign exchange for buying food. The tropical farmer's problem is that despite low prices, relatively to manufactures, food production is still attractive to temperate farmers because of the enormous increase in temperate productivity in recent years. These relatively low food prices trap the tropical farmer in producing non-food commodities even at depressed prices unless he also can raise his food productivity.

Would this, in practice, move the terms of trade against food, and so also against commercial crops? I have been assuming explicitly that an increase in tropical production of maize will not reduce the price of maize relatively to wheat, or the price of wheat (thus displaced from tropical markets) relatively to manufactures. Such assumptions clearly do not hold in the short run. In the long run it is legitimate to regard the various cereals as close substitutes for each other—if only because they are all fed to livestock. Whether an increase in tropical production affects the terms of trade of wheat against manufactures in the long run depends on whether it leads to an even faster contraction of American farming. With tropical populations about to increase by 3 per cent per annum for a decade or two, and urban populations growing by 5 per cent per annum it seems unlikely that we shall run into surpluses of cereals, however effective the tropics may be in raising their productivity. And if the terms of trade for cerealds hold, any general increase in tropical cereals productivity will raise the prices of other tropical crops.

The solution does not depend on accepting the old view that the comparative advantage of the temperate world is in manufactures and of the tropical world in agriculture, which no longer commands solid support. Harsh climatic conditions make the maintenance of soil fertility much more difficult in the tropical than in the temperate world, whereas there is no fundamental reason why the tropical peoples should not learn to be as efficient in manufacturing as the temperate peoples, and they have all the basic raw materials and fuels required for this purpose. It is not inconceivable that the long run economic division of world trade is between temperate agriculture and tropical manufacturing.

This brings me to the fourth possible solution of the current agricultural crisis, which is to transfer more resources out of agriculture into industrial production. This is automatically stimulated by the movement of the terms of trade in favour of manufactures, but it would in any case be inevitable.

For the tropical countries are no longer content to let their rate of growth be dependent on how much tropical agricultural produce the temperate countries are willing to take. As we have seen, the engine of growth through tropical agricultural exports beats only about 80 per cent as fast as the engine of industrial growth in the temperate world. This is not good enough for the tropics, who want to grow at least as fast as the temperate world, if not faster, to make up leeway. Even if the terms of trade had not moved against the tropics between 1955 and 1965, a volume growth rate of 3.8 per cent per annum, which was as much as temperate demand could support, is not large enough for countries who want their gross domestic products to grow by 5 or 6 per cent per year. Faster growth requires accelerated imports and therefore accelerated exports. The period where agricultural exports could be the principal engine of growth has come to an end. Like all developing countries, the tropics must diversify their economies, and this is the subject of my second lecture.

II

Manufactures

In my first lecture I pointed out that the engine of growth was pounding nearly as powerfully in the tropical countries in their prosperous period before 1913 as in the temperate countries. Why then was their industrialization so long delayed?

The popular answer to this question is that the countries which industrialize first have an advantage over latecomers, which enables them to keep the latecomers out. In its most alarming form this answer even postulates that it is of the nature of things that rich areas will grow ever richer at the expense of poor areas which grow ever poorer.

The answer to this was given a long time ago by David Hume.[7] While there are advantages to being first (especially experience, and scale of operations) there are also disadvantages, including that costs rise relatively to the costs of less developed areas, and drive into those areas any industry for which the first area does not have very special advantages. Hume was interested primarily in the gold flows which result from unbalanced trade. Later experience enables us to add many other costs; congestion; overspecialisation; neglect of or hostility to new industries; commitment to old technology; and so on. In fact the literature which sets out the disadvantages of being first is now as large as that which talks of backwash effects, and at least in England, is more persuasive. Lancashire virtually destroyed India's cotton spinning industry in the first half of the nineteenth century, but already by the end of that century Indian yarn exports, based on cheap labour, were eating heavily into British trade in third markets. This does not mean that there are no advantages in being first; it means only that there are advantages for some trades and disadvantages for others.

There are three reasons why industrialization was delayed until after 1913, and therefore in most cases until after 1950, since in the tropics the Great War was followed by 35 years of depression.

The first reason is that before 1913 agricultural production was profitable. We are apt to forget that migrants left industrial Britain and Germany to

[7] In "Of the Balance of Trade" and "Of the Jealousy of Trade", *Political Discourses*, 1752.

find much higher standards of living in the agricultural plains of Australia or Argentina or North America. It is obviously more profitable to industrialize than to export coffee in 1965, but this was not necessarily so before 1913.

The second reason was that the tropics were behind Western Europe in infrastructure in 1880. They used the proceeds of exports to build themselves roads, schools, ports, water supplies and so on. They were particularly handicapped in not having a large and experienced middle class, either commercial or professional. For them 1880 to 1913 was a period of preparation for industrialization, much like earlier periods in Europe.

The third reason was the commercial policy of the European empires. Industrialization made its beginnings in Latin America; for example by 1913 Brazil was producing over three-quarters of its domestic consumption of cotton textiles,[8] and was inhibited from going into iron and steel mainly by deficiency in coal. The situation was different in Asia and Africa, which were almost wholly partitioned into European colonies. India, for example, started off well in cotton manufacture, but the India Office in London continually pressured the Indian Government to keep the import duties low, and when in 1894 import duties were raised to 5 per cent, insisted on imposing a countervailing excise duty of 5 per cent on Indian production of cotton yarn, followed in 1896 by an equivalent excise duty on cotton cloth. Similarly the Indian Government's desire to foster a local iron and steel industry, to supply the large demands of the railways and other public works, was completely frustrated by orders from London, until the very end of the nineteenth century.[9]

The result of this long delay in starting industrialization is that when the tropical countries did start, they had a relatively large and easy market in import substitution. This is why their rate of growth of industrial production is so much higher than anything achieved in Western Europe, averaging around 7 per cent, with some figures for large scale industry as high as 15 per cent per annum.

Import Substitution

These high growth rates of manufacturing have frequently occasioned some disappointment.

---

[8] Calculated from Stanley Stein, *The Brazilian Cotton Manufacture*, Cambrigde, Mass. 1957.

[9] The full story is told in S. K. Sen, *Studies in Industrial Policy and Development of India*, 1858–1914. Calcutta, 1964.

In the first place, employment has not grown as rapidly as output. This is normal, since productivity should increase year by year. But the gap has been wider than was expected.

Industrial productivity now grows faster than it used to in the early decades of industrialization anyway. Between 1880 and 1913 industrial productivity grew by less than 2 per cent per annum in both Germany and the United States, and only by about 1 per cent per annum in Britain and France; whereas since the second world war productivity has been growing by nearly 3 per cent even in Britain, which is now the slowest of these four. The explanations are familiar. An industrial revolution powered by electricity has much wider scope than one based directly on steam; two wars and a great depression created a backlong of potential innovation; organized research and development pay dividends; so does scientific management.

Beyond this it is now recognized that the rate of growth of productivity is itself a function of the rate of growth of employment. The workers added to the labour force work in factories equipped with the latest technology. Their output therefore exceeds the average of the existing stock of workers. And it is simple arithmetic that where the marginal exceeds the average, the increase in the average is a function of the increase in the stock.[10] So the faster employment grows, the faster productivity grows; or, in terms of output, productivity will rise faster when output is growing by 10 per cent per annum than when output is growing by 5 per cent per annum. This phenomenon must be expected to operate with some force in those tropical countries which, say in 1950, had some manufacturing industry (perhaps

[10] Let $X = 1.0 = E$ be the value of output and the number of persons employed respectively at the initial point. Let the marginal product of a man (along with other resources) be constant but greater than the average product (because technology is improving and some of it is embodied in new capital). We write in any unit of time:

$$\Delta X = x, \quad \Delta E = e$$

$$x = ke, \quad k > 1.$$

$$\text{Productivity} = y = \frac{1+x}{1+e} = \frac{1+ke}{1+e}$$

The rate of growth of productivity

$$\frac{dy}{de} = \frac{k-1}{(1+e)^2}$$

The rate of growth of productivity is a positive function of the rate of growth of employment; the faster employment grows, the higher productivity will be.

10 per cent of the population) established before the war, and operating with fairly low efficiency. Indeed, it is not surprising that in some of these cases high growth rates of output have been accompanied temporarily by declines in industrial employment (e.g., Ceylon, Kenya).

Several tropical countries have been disconcerted by the low increases in industrial employment that have come from heavy capital investment in manufacturing. Rapid increases in urban unemployment are now a phenomenon throughout the tropics, so measures to increase employment are thought to be as important as measures to increase industrial output. The reasons for these increases in unemployment have often been examined. They include the disruptive effects of modernity on the countryside—whether primary schools, radio, cinema or other communications media; the growing disparity between government expenditures in the towns and in the countryside; the widening gap between farm incomes, often deliberately kept down by government policies, and urban wages, deliberately raised every year by trade union action. This last cause, high urban wages, is of special interest to us because it is further argued that it promotes excessively high capital intensity in industrialization.

Economists work with the notion that the appropriate degree of capital intensity is to be found by using shadow prices for wages and foreign exchange, reflecting the real scarcity or abundance of these factors. They also believe that use of shadow prices would show that much of the current industrialization in the tropics is over capitalized. There are limits to this analysis. It works where a machine is used to do what human labour could do equally well—especially moving things around in factories, or on construction sites, or in mines. But some machines substitute for skill rather than for power; they bring precision or standardisation to the product; or they cut down on wastage of materials or on the cost of supervision; or they may even, as in electrolytic processes, make a product that human labour by itself cannot make. Much industrial machinery falls into this category. Shadow pricing would reduce the number of conveyor belts, fork-lift trucks, bulldozers and cranes, but would probably have little effect on the choice of machines for the actual manufacturing processes. Besides, the feasibility of shadow pricing is much in doubt. If the machines do the job for half the money cost of labour, they are going to be used even if the shadow price of labour is thought to be near zero.

The actual experience of tropical countries cannot easily be established statistically. *The U.N. Statistical Year Book* shows a lower growth rate of productivity in "less Industrialized" than in "industrialized" countries. Its figure for the less industrialized is just under 3 per cent, but its basis is very shaky, since data are available for relatively few countries, and most of these run out well above 3 per cent (e.g., India 4, Pakistan 8, Kenya 10). Given the capital/labour ratios of these countries it is clear that some of them would do better to use less capital-intensive technologies, especially in the movement of goods rather than in their processing, and get themselves more employment at the expense of lower productivity.

Recent industrialization is also disappointing because so little of the proceeds remain at home. Take Nigeria as an example. According to the Industrial Census of 1963, only 31 per cent of value added was paid as wages and salaries, and the breakdown of that 31 per cent was 22 per cent to Nigerians and 9 per cent to expatriates. If one calculates the net value added remaining to Nigerians, including profits taxes, it cannot be much more than 30 per cent of gross value added, or, say, 20 per cent of the price of the product. Since many commodities are produced in Nigeria using imported raw materials, imported machinery and imported supervisors, only because tariff protection is much in excess of 20 per cent, it is safe to conclude that some industries cost Nigeria more foreign exchange than they save.

The low share of wages and salaries in value added is a common phenomenon in underdeveloped countries. From the United Nations' survey called the *Growth of World Industry* one can calculate this percentage for several countries. The results are shown in Table 4.

Part of the reason why the share of capital is higher in low wage than in high-wage countries is that machines cost more in the low-wage countries; have to be imported from the high-wage countries; are not so well maintained; and have shorter lives. But judging by the willingness of private foreign capital to build factories in these countries we may also deduce that part of the reason is that profits are higher in the low-wage than in the high-wage countries, over a fairly wide range of industries—whether because of tariffs, or because of comparative costs we do not know.

One respect in which these countries are handicapped is that the part of value added which belongs to depreciation automatically goes abroad for replacement of machinery. But this is just one aspect of the general proposition that a given level of saving generates less new employment in an underdeveloped than in a developed country. The employment generated by the use of the capital goods may be the same, but whereas the developed

TABLE 4. *Wages and salaries as percentage of value added in manufacturing, circa 1963*

Denmark	59	Venezuela	38[a]	Brazil	26
Sweden	57	Japan	37	Nigeria	25
U.K.	53	Jamaica	33	Phillipines	24
Norway	51	Colombia	32	Ivory Coast	24
U.S.A.	49	Peru	29	Iran	22
Israel	46	Ghana	26		

[a] 1953.

country makes its own capital goods, the underdeveloped country's savings give employment to the machine makers of foreign countries. In the neo-classical model it doesn't matter where savings are spent, since extra imports automatically give rise to extra exports. But in the real world the level of employment in the non-subsistence part of the economy does depend on the propensity to import. If the tropics could produce a wider range of manufactures, this same propensity to invest would generate a higher level of industrial employment. This is of some importance in explaining why, though net investment is as high a proportion of national income in the tropics as it is in the temperate countries (thanks to foreign aid), the effects of all this investment on employment seem so disappointingly small.

The remedy is of course not less industrialization but more. For it is only greater industrialization that will eliminate the difficulties; will provide a pool of trained supervisors who eliminate expatriates; will make markets big enough to justify local production of machinery; will raise the productive skills of workers; and will increase domestic savings, so that profits no longer go abroad.

Unfortunately, import substitution by itself cannot for long support a 10 per cent growth rate of industrial production. If national income is growing by 5 per cent per annum, the use of manufactures grows only by 7 or at most 8 per cent, so production at 10 per cent is bound to catch up with demand sooner or later. Several tropical countries have already reached the point where they have eliminated imports of all the more obvious kinds of light manufactures, and can no longer grow at 10 per cent unless they move massively into heavy industry, or alternatively move massively into exporting light manufactures.

Some evidence bearing on this subject is presented in Table 5. The idea underlying this analysis is that in countries which do not manufacture base metals (S.I.T.C. 67 and 68, iron and steel, copper, etc.), the import of base

TABLE 5. *Ratio of certain imports to imports of base metals*[a]

	Metal small wares[b]	Textiles[c]	Other light mfrs[d]	Chemicals (Non-Ag)[e]	Value of metals $m.
Oceania	1.32	1.40	5.06	1.37	7
West Africa	.89	2.38	2.71	1.14	157
East Africa[f]	.81	2.12	2.98	1.41	104
Caribbean[g]	.81	1.37	3.59	1.90	112
Asia[h]	.51	1.47	1.54	1.01	333
Latin America[i]	.44	.64	1.35	1.36	238
U.A.R.	.31	.65	2.17	1.58	56
Pakistan	.26	.15	.50	.61	143
Finland	.30	.55	.27	.89	159
Norway	.28	.61	.45	.87	181
New Zealand	.27	.85	.34	.76	128
Denmark	.26	.71	.78	.74	265
Average of 4	.28	.68	.46	.82	

[a] S.I.T.C. 67 and 68. [b] S.I.T.C. 69. [c] S.I.T.C. 65. [d] S.I.T.C. 6 plus 8 minus 65, 67, 68, 69. [e] S.I.T.C. 5 minus 561.
[f] Includes Sudan, Rhodesia, Mauritius, Madagascar.
[g] Excludes Cuba; includes Central America.
[h] Excludes India, Pakistan.
[i] Cuba, Colombia, Ecuador, Peru, Venezuela.

metals is a fair index of industrial sophistication. Their capacity to produce light manufactures for themselves ought to be roughly in proportion to their imports of base metals; their consumption of light manufactures should be in about the same proportion; and so their imports of light manufactures should also be in about the same proportion. Light manufactures are defined for this purpose as

(1) S.I.T.C. 69, metal products, which does not include machinery, but includes such metal wares as agricultural implements and cutlery. To avoid confusion we shall call these "metal smallwares".

(2) S.I.T.C. 65, textiles,

(3) S.I.T.C. 8, miscellaneous manufactures,

(4) S.I.T.C. 6 excluding 65, 67, 68 and 69; and

(5) S.I.T.C. 5 Chemicals, excluding fertilisers.

Fertilisers are excluded because they mostly involve considerable economies of scale. Some other chemicals should also be excluded, but this is done effectively by the test we use, as we shall see in a moment.

The upper part of Table 5 shows for 1965 the ratio of the imports of light manufactures in various categories to imports of base metals, for those tropical countries (aggregated by region) which do not smelt significant quantities of base metals for their own use[11] and whose imports are reported in sufficient detail in the U.N. *Yearbook of International Trade Statistics.*

For comparison, we have also taken four developed countries which smelt insignificant quantities of base metals. Their ratios are given at the bottom of the table, and are averaged without weighting. These averages are later used as indicating what import ratios sophisticated areas might be expected to have.

The first column of the table shows the extent to which regions import metal smallwares, or make smallwares for themselves from imported metals. This turns out to be an excellent index of industrial sophistication. Countries tend to begin industrialization using fibres, wood and such soft raw materials; moving into metal manufactures is equivalent to passing from high school into university; the next step, the manufacture of machinery, being equivalent to graduation with a Ph. D. We have ordered regions in the table in accordance with this index.

Two aspects of the results suggest that our test is appropriate; one is the similarity of our results for our four widely dispersed developed countries; and the other is the similar ordering of the columns for the less developed. Of course, I say "suggest" rather than "prove".

If now we use our average for the four developed countries, it suggests that Pakistan has already reached the limits of import substitution of light manufactures, that the U.A.R. is at about this limit in metal smallwares and in textiles, and that Latin America has reached this limit in textiles. Naturally the grouping hides individual cases, which are not always close to their regional averages.

It is not to be expected that every small country will produce all of the light manufactures it consumes, but it could be expected that the tropics taken together could eliminate imports of light manufactures from the rest of the world. If we use the average ratios for our four developed non-smelting countries to indicate what imports might be expected for the tropical countries in Table 5, taken as a whole, we get the results shown in Table 6.

The conclusion appears to be that these countries have over $3 billion of excess imports of light manufactures, which is 55 per cent of their actual imports of light manufactures. The conclusion must be modified to take account of the fact that some of the countries are so small that they

---

[11] We thus exclude India, Brazil and Mexico.

TABLE 6. *Imports of light manufactures,*[a] *1965* ($m.)

	Actual imports	Expected imports	Surplus imports
Metal smallwares (69)	652	322	330
Textiles (65)	1456	781	674
Other (8+other 6)	2195	529	1666
Chemicals (5 excl. 561)	1385	942	442
	5687	2574	3113

[a] Applies only to the countries in Table 5; i.e., excludes India, Brazil, Mexico.

will inevitably have a higher ratio of imports even of light manufactures than our four developed countries. Whatever the true degree of excess may be in this sense, if we consider these countries together as a single market, the whole actual import of $5.7 billion (minus perhaps some chemicals) constitutes a demand which could be supplied internally within the tropics, by countries producing either for themselves or for export to other tropical countries.

I repeat that the argument is not that each tropical country become nearly self-sufficient in light manufactures, but that through regional specialization they could considerably reduce their bill for these manufactures which now come from the developed industrial countries, except to the extent of about $1 billion of light manufactures which they now export to each other. To save $4 billion in this way would make a considerable difference to the balance of payments between the tropical and the temperate world.

This analysis covers all manufactures except machinery and transport equipment (S.I.T.C. 7). The tropical countries (including those excluded from Table 5) imported in 1965 machinery and transport equipment valued at over $7 billion. This is the fastest growing item in their imports. There is no doubt that their imports and exports cannot come into equilibrium until they produce more machinery for themselves.

It is not necessary for me to argue before this learned body that the tropics are not preordained by divine purpose always to import machinery from the temperate world. The proposition that they must concentrate on light rather than heavy manufactures has no validity. If heavy manufacture is identified with the smelting of metalliferous ores—whether iron or copper of bauxite–the appropriate location is determined by the locations of ores

TABLE 7. *Value added in machinery as % of manufacturing*

Ghana	2.3	Kenya	10.4	Denmark	28.8
Peru	3.8	India	18.1	U.S.A.	29.6
Malaya	6.0	Brazil	19.6	Japan	30.5
Colombia	6.9	Finland	21.3	U.K.	34.0
Mexico	9.0	New Zealand	21.3	Sweden	35.5
Phillipines	9.8	Norway	22.0		

and fuels, and not by a country's average daily temperature. If the distinction turns on the amount of capital required per person employed, this factor tends to be grossly exaggerated. Capital is a very mobile factor, and the differences in capital costs from one location to another are not always the decisive element. In the more sophisticated industrial products, skills and the size of the market are frequently much more important. Both these are functions of time, as well as of other elements; for with the passage of time both skills and the size of the market grow. This is why the manufacture of machinery, so highly dependent on skills and market size, is the last stage of industrialization; moving into it is as we have said like graduating with the Ph. D. There is no fundamental reason why the tropics should not produce its quota of Ph. D's.

The share of machinery in industrial output increases as the economy becomes more sophisticated. This is seen in Table 7, which is calculated from the U.N. publication, *The Growth of World Industry 1953–65,* and is based on Censuses of Manufacturing taken around the year 1963. Machinery is here defined as items 36, 37 and 38 of the International Standard Industrial Classification. The ratios are value added in machinery to value added in manufacturing.

If we take as our standard the average of the ratios achieved by Finland, New Zealand and Norway (21.5 per cent) the only two tropical countries near this standard are Brazil and India. It is not to be expected that every tropical country will reach this standard. What we should expect instead is that in each region two or three of the larger countries will become exporters of machinery to their neighbours, and will thus approach a ratio of about 30 per cent (say, Brazil, Mexico, Nigeria, U.A.R., Kenya, Pakistan, India, Singapore and Indonesia). Most of these still have a very long way to go. Some are held up by looking in the wrong direction—by putting the emphasis on producing metals (especially steel plants) instead of emphasising the manufacture of machinery using imported metals. Steel can be imported cheaply, and making it offers little employment relatively to the capital involved. The real payoff in employment, especially for skilled artisans, is in making machinery rather than in making steel.

Exports of Manufactures

Our analysis of import substitution has thus led naturally to the subject of exports of manufactures, since the main way now left of cutting imports from the developed countries is for tropical countries to export more to each other. Beyond this, of course, it is also possible to export to the temperate world.

World trade in manufactures has been booming. Whereas between 1883 and 1913 the volume of this trade grew only by 3.5 per cent per annum, and between 1924 and 1937 only by 1.9 per cent per annum, the quantum of world trade in manufactures grew between 1955 and 1965 by 8 per cent per annum.

It is easy to show that much of the recent high growth rate results merely from the low inter-war rate. During the great depression world trade in manufactures was depressed much below its normal level by unemployment, tariffs, import quotas and exchange restrictions. These restrictions were largely cleared away in the 1950's and 60's, so naturally the trade in manufactures has bounced back.

In Fig. 3 the index of industrial production of the O.E.C.D. countries is on the horizontal axis. The vertical axis gives imports of manufactures into the O.E.C.D. countries from each other in constant 1955 prices.[12] Both axes are logarithmic. Between 1899 and 1913 imports of manufactures and industrial production grew at virtually the same rate; the straight line connecting these two dates has a slope of 0.99. Imports were depressed in 1929 because Europe, which has a higher import propensity than the U.S.A., had been set back by the war, and was still in a state of relative depression, with high unemployment rates. This situation worsened in the thirties, with a great blossoming of tariffs, quotas and exchanges restrictions. The chart brings out the results of the great liberation of trade since 1955, as well as full unemployment. By 1965 imports were only 4 per cent below the line established between 1899 and 1913. If we were to add imports from Japan and from the tropics, which grew so much faster after 1955 than before, the

[12] For sources, see Statistical appendix.

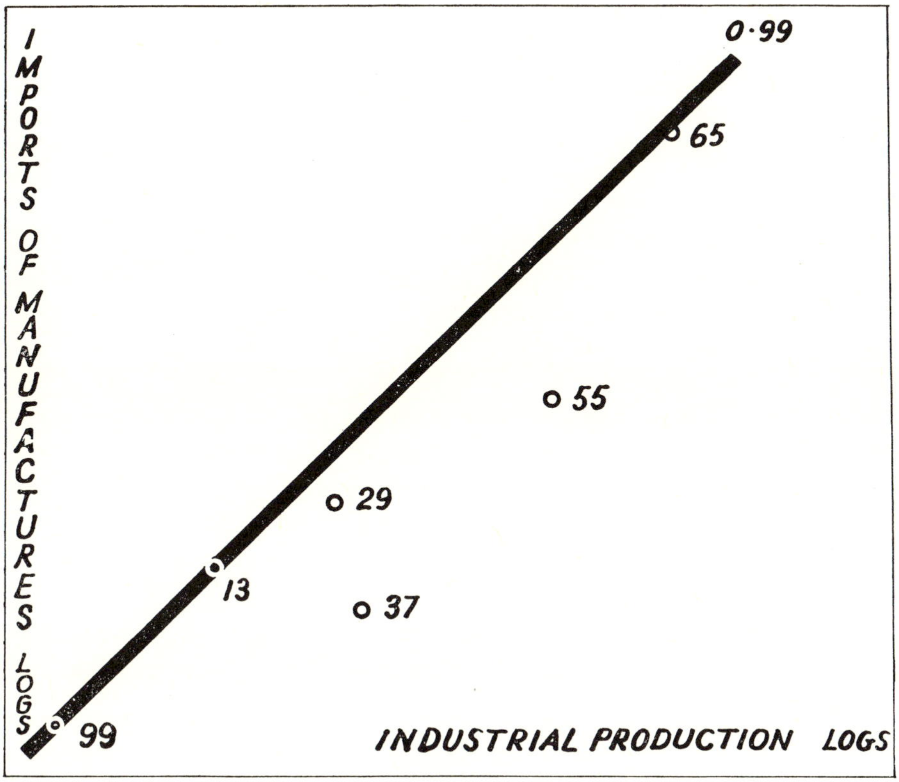

Fig. 3.

total would probably be on the left of the appropriate line. This is what one would expect, since trade is now much freer than it has ever been before.

The chart suggests two points. First, that the very high growth rate of world trade in manufactures since the war is only a temporary phenomenon; sooner or later a more "normal" rate of growth, in the historical sense, should re-establish itself. Secondly, the chart suggests that this normal rate of growth may be in a one to one relationship with industrial production. The popular belief that it is normal for imports of manufactures to grow less rapidly than industrial production may be wrong.

Rapid growth of exports has occurred not only in the O.E.C.D. countries, but in the tropics as well; the growth of the world market presented an opportunity which the tropics did not fail to seize. Tropical exports of manufactures (excluding metals) rose from about $0.85 billion in 1955 to $2.39 billion in 1966. If we adopt the U.N. price index number of 113 for

TABLE 8. *Tropical exports of manufactures,*[a] *1965* ($m.)

Textiles (65)	814
Chemicals (5)	281
Machinery (7)	155
Clothing (841)	95
Leather (61)	90
Wood manufactures (63)	65
Miscellaneous (rest of 6 and 8)[a]	765
Total	2265

[a] Excluding non-ferrous metals (S.I.T.C. 68).

all manufactured exports (1965 on 1955), it follows that the quantum of manufactured exports from the tropics rose in this period at an average annual rate of 9 per cent. The distribution of these exports between commodities is seen in Table 8.

O.E.C.D. countries imported $22.7 billion of light manufactures in 1965, and exported $26.8 billion. This is the sum of S.I.T.C. sections 6 and 8, minus metals (67, 68). The comparable export from the tropics in that year was only $1.8 billion dollars or only about 8 per cent of O.E.C.D. imports, yet the O.E.C.D. countries took extra special pains to keep these tropical exports out, by means of quotas and a new international textile agreement. The core of their case for these exclusions was that it is embarrassing for the tropical countries to be coming into world trade via light manufactures, when the share of light manufactures in world trade has been shrinking sharply for quite some time. For example, the sum of S.I.T.C. sections 6 and 8 (excluding 67, iron and steel) in the manufactured exports of O.E.C.D. countries, including Japan, shrank from 40 per cent in 1955 to 35 per cent in 1965. But this proposition is somewhat beside the point, since, though the relative share of light manufactures fell, the absolute amount increased very considerably. Even the O.E.C.D. import of textiles (65) increased by $2 billion over these ten years. O.E.C.D. imports of all light manufactures rose between 1959 and 1965 by $11.3 billion dollars; i.e., they doubled. The tropical countries contributed not more than $ 1 billion to this increase. Indeed, at a time when the O.E.C.D. countries were rapidly dismantling their trade barriers against each other, they were equally feverishly creating new barriers to keep out light manufactures from the tropics, thus fulfilling the Biblical saying that "to him that hath shall be given, while from him that hath not shall be taken away even that which he hath".

This is the context in which the tropical countries are now protesting vigorously at one international conference after another against those measures which discriminate against their exports of manufactures. In particular, against the textile agreement, against the great number of quotas which still operate against other commodities, against the almost universal system of levying differential duties on tropical products, higher on processed than on unprocessed materials, and against the fact that tariff rates on manufactures of the kind sold by the tropics are much higher than rates on manufactures of the kind the industrial countries buy from each other. This kind of protest will continue and grow, since the tropical countries also need a share of the expanding world trade in manufactures, but it will no doubt be some time before the world's conscience is brought to grips with this issue.

Although the trade in light manufactures has increased very substantially, the developed countries' point that trade grows much faster in machinery should not be entirely overlooked, especially if the rate of growth of trade in manufactures decelerates as some normal ratio of trade to production returns in the O.E.C.D. countries. If all the tropical countries were to concentrate on producing light manufactures for themselves and for sale to other countries, there would be sharp tensions in international trade. The moral is that tropical countries must move towards producing machinery as fast as the size of their markets and the accumulation of skills permit. For some time only two or three will be in a position to export significant quantities of machinery; but another dozen or so, reaching the limits of their own markets for light manufactures, should break through into producing some of their own machines, instead of being driven relentlessly towards ever increasing exports of light manufactures to a world increasingly reluctant to import light manufactures. It would be ironical if the tropics should try to solve its trade problems by moving out of forcing tea and coffee on to reluctant temperate buyers, into forcing cotton fabrics and footwear on reluctant temperate buyers. A faster move into producing machinery is clearly in line with the trend of world demand.[13]

Apart from protesting against the restrictions on tropical trade, these countries have also recently united in asking that the developed countries

[13] Since tropical exporters of machinery will not be able to afford to export capital, they will depend on their customers being able to raise untied long- and medium-term finance in the industrial countries.

accord tariff preferences to manufactures from underdeveloped countries over manufactures from developed countries. This proposal has indeed already been accepted by the leading manufacturing countries, though we are still far from setting a date at which it may take effect. Given the large amount of light manufactures now imported by the O.E.C.D. countries—some twelve times the export from the tropics in 1965—such a concession should prove most valuable to at least a dozen tropical countries if it comes into effect.

Besides competing in the O.E.C.D. markets, the tropics can also compete in their own markets. In 1965 they imported manufactures, excluding metals, valued at $14.1 billion dollars; to wit $2.3 billion of chemicals, $4.7 billion of light manufactures and $7.2 billion of machinery and transport equipment. At least $12.5 billion of this came from outside the region. It follows that the tropics do not have to depend on competing with O.E.C.D. countries in O.E.C.D. markets. They can just as well compete with O.E.C.D. in their own tropical markets.

This point sometimes comes as a surprise to policy-makers in the tropics. We have got so accustomed to the idea that the tropics trades with the temperate world that we tend to assume that the chief way to expand tropical trade is to sell more to the temperate countries. Actually, as Germany industrialized in the second half of the nineteenth century, she did not concentrate primarily on breaking into the British and French markets, though she did this too. She looked rather to the countries around her in Eastern and Central Europe, who were even more impoverished than she, and made big gains there. Similarly Japan's trade drive in the 1930's was directed not at the industrial nations but at Asia and Africa and Latin America. This is where the rising new exporters should surely be looking, rather than to European and North American markets, since it is surely easier to beat your competitors in third markets than it is to beat them at home, once you have established the machinery for making customer contacts.

The continuous discussion of the possibility of creating new customs unions or common markets in Africa and Asia and Latin America indicates that many people have seen the light, though the paucity of actual results also indicates how difficult the problems is. The basic difficulty centers in the fact that only a handful of tropical countries are currently in a position to benefit from expanded opportunities for exporting manufactures. Twelve of these accounted for 85 per cent of the trade.[14] The problem stands out clearly if one asks the following question: Since among themselves the tropical countries now import over $14 billion of manufactures, why do they have to wait for preferences for their exports in O.E.C.D. markets? Why do they not just accord preferences to each other in their own markets, in line with the already agreed principle that discrimination against developed countries is acceptable? The answer is because this would benefit the leading twelve at the expense of the remaining seventy, who might now have to pay higher prices to these twelve than they would have had to pay to O.E.C.D. countries. The problem differs only in scale when one shifts from global tropical preferences to more limited regional preferences, customs unions or free trade areas. In each region one or two countries stand out as the ones most likely to benefit at the expense of their regional partners, who are therefore not anxious to rush in without some clearer indication of what the balance sheet of profits and losses is likely to be.

To make progress in regional integration one has to begin by recognizing that every country in the region wants to have some industries of its own, which it is going to protect against all comers. The situation therefore requires bargaining, rather than blanket prescriptions. The basis for bargaining is the distinction between those industries which can survive on a small scale, and those which need a large market. At a pinch the former can even be excluded altogether from the free trade agreement, while agreement may be reached to parcel out the latter between the partners; or if one or two more developed partners will get the large scale industries members can at least agree to compensate the less developed members in other ways—such as paying somewhat higher prices for their food and raw material exports; or removing restriction on their nationals immigrating in search of work; or locating in them other regional institutions such as colleges, research stations, or other inter-governmental organizations which do not have to be in the more developed centres. Unless the bargain is negotiated in some such detail the strains between the more developed and the less developed partners in the free trade areas are bound to become unbearable, in these early

[14] The leading exporters of manufactures (5–8 minus 67 and 68) in 1965 were as follows (figures in $m.): India 799, Singapore 295, Pakistan 190, Mexico 170, Brazil 124, U.A.R. 123, Rhodesia 116, Philippines 66, Malaya 64, Colombia 34, El Salvador 32, Trinidad 28. Kenya is also a substantial exporter if her trade with Uganda and Tanzania is counted as foreign trade (56).

stages of development, where so much importance attaches in people's minds to the infant industries argument. This is the clear lesson of the two most successful free trade agreements in the tropics—the East African Customs Union and the Central American Common Market.

Preferences and customs unions are not as important to the more industrialized tropical countries as is sometimes thought, since much of this discussion assumes that tropical manufactures cannot be sold without protection. If this were so, exports would not be expanding by 9 per cent per annum, and the O.E.C.D. countries would not be so busy putting up barriers to keep tropical manufactures out.

For the leading tropical countries, the real problems of continued success are more probably related to the structure of export organizations and to the financing of foreign trade. Food and raw materials are sold easily on international commodity exchanges, but manufactures have to be sold by sellers and buyers seeking each other out. How does a manufacturer in Caracas find himself a market in Bogota or Lima or Port-of-Spain? Is he to maintain his own corps of salesmen? Or to assist in establishing a wholesale exporting business in Venezuela? Or to put himself into the hands of commission agents in Colombia? There is a large literature on modes of organising export drives into which we need not now enter, but which emphasises that price and quality are not all that is required for success. There is also the problem of financing export sales, which has caused every large industrial exporting country to create special agencies and funds for this purpose. Tropical exporters, launching a trade drive in manufactures, will have to tread much the same organisational path as their predecessors have trodden.

They will also have to become just as concerned about the movement of money wage levels as all other industrial countries have now become. The *United Nations Statistical Year Book* gives data on money wages in manufacturing for a number of countries, and I have extracted those which interest us more particularly. The ratio of money wages in 1964 based on 1957 runs as follows:

U.S.A.	126	Singapore	121	Trinidad	180
U.K.	146	U.A.R.	122	Jamaica	189
Sweden	162	Philippines	123	Mexico	197
Japan	172	India	124	Peru	198
Denmark	174	Kenya	148	Colombia	339
France	174	Ceylon	149		
W. Germany	174	Pakistan	152		

Weighting the industrial countries by their exports of manufactures in 1965 gives an average increase of 55 per cent over the whole period. The Asian and African countries on the list did better than this; their weighted average is only 27 per cent; though it must be remembered that the U.N. estimates that industrial productivity was also rising less rapidly in these countries than in the industrial world. The countries which have had the greatest wage inflations, as we would expect, are those of the Caribbean and Latin America. This is particularly important to Brazil (for which we do not have the data) because Brazil could easily become a major supplier of engineering products to the rest of the world if she could only bring order into her financial system. Latin America could neglect the disadvantages of high inflation rates when her exports were chiefly agricultural; as industry grows in importance one may guess that those who need stability to meet international competition, namely the industrial classes (both workers and capitalists) will acquire more political power.

Let me sum up these two lectures by trying to bring out problems which remain for solution. I would start from the proposition that temperate demand for the traditional tropical agricultural products will grow by less than 4 per cent a year, while the target for tropical income is going to be 6 per cent per year. This creates a trade gap, which can be closed only in the following ways:

(1) by a continuous increase in foreign aid, such that tropical imports from the temperate countries may grow by 6 per cent per year;

(2) by tropical countries exporting manufactures to temperate countries at a rapidly increasing rate; or

(3) by tropical countries becoming more self-sufficient, i.e. meeting each other's needs for foodstuffs and for manufactures.

Since foreign aid cannot increase forever, and since also the temperate countries are not particularly hospitable towards manufactures from the tropics, we reach sooner or later the third alernative—much greater trade in food and manufactures between the tropical countries themselves. I have pointed out that such trade is currently hampered by the tying of foreign aid, but this is a marginal adjustment which might fairly soon be made.

The current outlook is good. The weak spots are an excessive rate of growth of traditional agricultural exports; and a tendency towards over-specialization in light manufactures. The first weakness will be eliminated as greater effort goes into food production, and the second as the larger tropical countries, led by Brazil and India, shift more of their industrial resources into making and exporting machinery. The tropics have all the basic requirements for vigorous growth; plenty of cultivable land, except for India, Java and Egypt, but enough elsewhere to feed these three until the new population policies begin to take effect; a surplus of practically all the basic raw materials and of fuel; and a demonstrated willingness to respond to economic opportunities. The period 1913 to 1950 was a terrible interruption of incipient development. If we can keep the world economy moving along, and reduce the barriers to tropical trade the rate of tropical change will continue to confound our pessimists.

Statistical Appendix

1. Tropical Exports

Table 9 is a condensation of a much larger table which includes all the statistical reporting units in the tropics, except a few very small islands. The data for 1937, 1955 and 1965 are given on a comparable basis in various numbers of the United Nations *Yearbook of International Trade Statistics*. The League of Nations *Review of World Trade* gives data for 1913 and 1929 for most countries but not all. For 1900 the most useful source is the U.S. *Government's Commercial Relations of the U.S.* Britain, Germany and France published complete data for their colonies in their annual statistical abstracts. The most useful other general source is the U.S. *Statistical Abstract of Foreign Countries,* published in 1909. Most missing data can be obtained from the published British or American consular reports, but a few gaps have had to be filled by interpolation.

In the table gold and silver are included for all producing countries which had export surpluses of these metals.

The columns may not add to the totals shown because of rounding.

2. Prices

1. Table 10 contains an index of the prices of tropical agricultural products, c.i.f. London, but converted to U.S. dollar equivalents, except for the years 1871–78, which are based on sterling. The commodities and weights used are as follows:

	Weight	
	1913	1953
Cocoa	3	6
Coffee	15	28
Cotton	16	14
Hides	9	3
Jute	7	4
Palm oil	10	9
Rice	11	7
Rubber	10	9
Sugar	11	12
Tea	6	6
Timber	2	3
	100	100

TABLE 9. *Exports* ($m.)

	1883	1899	1913	1929	1937	1955	1965
Africa							
Belgian Congo[a]	2	7	12	41	74	454	343
British Central	1	2	4	39	122	502	1,033
British East[b]	7	9	14	59	87	325	517
British West	13	17	69	156	192	674	1,259
Egypt	61	76	157	253	200	397	605
French Equatorial[c]	1	3	10	13	21	172	335
French West[d]	4	13	25	49	54	326	591
Portuguese	7	15	21	34	32	175	328
Other[e]	30	19	49	109	105	452	699
America, North							
Br. West Indies[f]	45	41	42	82	93	371	842
Central America	15	22	44	97	76	406	766
Fr. West Indies	13	10	12	19	23	61	81
Mexico	37	71	130	285	247	670	1,146
Netherlands W. I.	2	2	5	127	152	829	661
Other[g]	78	65	187	312	213	745	845
America, South							
Bolivia	8	12	37	51	35	98	107
Brazil	85	162	316	462	350	1,423	1,596
Colombia[h]	12	19	40	129	108	616	617
Ecuador	4	8	16	17	13	88	178
Paraguay	1	2	6	13	9	35	57
Peru	15	16	45	117	94	269	669
Venezuela	20	15	29	149	193	1,874	2,786
Asia							
Ceylon	14	33	73	139	124	407	409
India[i]	342	357	802	1190	921	1,917	2,442
Indo-China	16	27	67	106	106	110	142
Indonesia[j]	80	101	249	582	548	940	725
Malaya[k]	74	107	200	547	559	1,647	2,301
Philippines	24	15	51	163	153	413	768
Thailand	8	15	43	94	76	332	627
Pacific Islands	5	8	18	32	34	153	260
	1020	1274	2769	5462	5011	16,882	23,735

[a] Includes Ruanda.
[b] Includes Tanganyika throughout.
[c] Includes Cameroons throughout.
[d] Includes Togo throughout.
[e] Includes Comoro, Eritrea, Ethiopia, Liberia, Madagascar, Mauritius, Reunion, Seychelles, Somalia, Sudan.
[f] Includes Bahamas, Guyana, British Honduras.
[g] Includes Cuba, Dominican Rep., Haiti.
[h] Includes Panama throughout.
[i] Includes Burma, French India, Pakistan, Portuguese India.
[j] Includes Dutch New Guinea, Timor.
[k] Includes Brunei, Sabah, Sarawak, Singapore.

TABLE 10. *Prices* (*$ except 1871–78*)

	Tropical crops 1	Wheat 2	Manu- factures 3	Crops ÷ Wheat 4	Crops ÷ Manufrs. 5
1871	120.5	153.8	124.2	78.3	97.0
72	127.8	161.5	132.6	79.1	96.4
73	127.1	173.8	134.9	73.1	94.2
74	126.1	156.9	128.7	80.4	98.0
75	120.2	132.3	125.8	90.9	95.5
76	116.5	132.3	120.2	88.1	96.9
77	123.1	150.7	113.9	81.7	108.1
78	116.8	132.3	112.8	88.3	103.5
79	112.5	132.3	110.0	85.0	102.3
1880	116.2	140.0	115.6	83.0	100.5
81	110.5	143.0	109.9	77.3	100.5
82	109.9	133.8	110.8	82.1	99.2
83	109.2	123.0	108.8	88.8	100.4
84	99.7	100.0	105.7	99.7	94.3
85	93.0	95.4	99.4	97.5	93.6
86	87.2	95.4	95.0	91.4	91.8
87	88.0	94.8	94.5	92.8	93.1
88	89.2	101.5	96.3	87.9	92.6
89	93.8	96.9	96.6	96.8	97.1
1890	94.9	96.9	98.7	97.9	96.1
91	95.3	109.2	96.3	87.3	99.0
92	93.5	90.7	90.9	103.1	102.9
93	94.4	76.9	89.0	122.8	106.1
94	88.3	64.6	84.7	136.7	104.3
95	84.8	70.7	85.6	119.9	99.1
96	87.9	80.0	88.5	109.9	99.3
97	85.3	95.4	85.5	89.4	99.8
98	82.7	101.5	85.0	81.5	97.3
99	81.2	83.0	89.8	97.8	90.4
1900	84.7	86.1	96.4	98.4	87.9
01	82.4	83.0	93.5	99.3	88.1
02	76.1	83.0	90.6	91.7	84.0
03	79.9	84.6	92.1	94.4	86.8
04	83.9	92.3	92.8	90.9	90.4
05	83.9	93.8	93.1	89.4	90.1
06	85.5	89.2	95.3	95.8	89.7
07	89.6	98.4	99.7	91.1	89.9
08	86.1	103.0	96.6	83.6	89.1
09	88.3	113.8	93.3	77.6	94.6
1910	102.5	100.0	94.9	102.5	108.0
11	99.5	96.9	95.8	102.7	103.9
12	103.5	104.6	97.4	98.9	106.3
13	100.0	100.0	100.0	100.0	100.0
1920	220.6	190.8	212.3	115.6	103.9
21	103.0	161.1	177.0	63.9	58.2
22	117.5	132.8	149.3	88.5	78.7
23	133.0	121.9	143.5	109.1	92.7
24	140.5	134.2	140.1	104.7	100.3
25	149.0	169.0	146.8	88.2	101.5
26	136.1	161.5	142.0	84.3	95.8
27	129.3	159.9	134.2	80.9	96.3
28	130.8	140.0	134.0	93.4	97.6
29	118.7	140.0	133.0	84.8	89.2

Table 10. (Continued.)

	Tropical Crops 1	Wheat 2	Manu-factures 3	Crops ÷ Wheat 4	Crops ÷ Manufrs. 5
1930	82.5	101.5	124.9	81.3	66.1
31	61.6	64.6	103.9	95.3	59.3
32	46.5	54.3	84.4	85.6	55.1
33	51.5	59.7	93.2	86.3	55.3
34	69.9	79.8	111.4	87.6	62.7
1935	67.1	86.1	107.5	77.9	62.4
36	72.2	96.9	107.8	74.5	67.0
37	84.6	136.9	114.8	61.8	73.7
38	64.7	107.7	113.5	60.1	57.0
1948	216.4	166.5	233.9	130.0	92.5
49	218.2	185.4	219.0	117.7	99.6
1950	242.1	169.5	194.5	142.8	124.5
51	313.7	167.2	231.4	187.6	135.6
52	256.9	171.6	236.3	149.7	108.7
53	230.0	176.9	226.5	130.0	101.5
54	252.7	196.3	224.0	128.7	112.8
55	233.8	200.7	224.0	116.7	104.4
56	257.7	206.0	233.9	125.1	110.2
57	232.7	192.8	241.3	120.7	96.4
58	208.8	185.7	238.8	112.4	87.4
59	196.3	184.8	236.3	106.2	83.1
1960	203.5	184.8	241.3	110.1	84.3
61	192.7	187.5	243.7	102.8	79.1
62	186.9	191.0	243.7	97.8	76.7
63	236.4	192.8	246.2	122.6	96.0
64	243.5	202.5	248.7	120.2	97.9
65	209.3	202.5	253.6	103.4	82.5

The 1913 weights are used from 1871 to 1929; the 1953 weights from 1929 to 1965. The weights are based on data in P. Lamartine Yates, *Forty Years of Foreign Trade,* London, 1959. The weights reflect only the volume of tropical trade in these commodities, not total trade; the price of palm oil is used to represent all vegetable oils.

The prices from 1871 to 1913 are those published by the Board of Trade. They are conveniently located in the *Eighteenth Abstract of Labour Statistics* (1926). From 1913 most of the prices are those of the Sauerbeck-Statist index, published annually in the *Journal of the Royal Statistical Society.*

2. The wheat price is the c.i.f. price of wheat imported into England, also converted into dollars, and also from the Sauerbeck-Statist series.

3. The United Nations indexes of the world price of exported manufactures, from 1948 onwards, have been linked to the League of Nations

TABLE 11. *Volume of total trade* ($m.)

	Gross total[a]	Oil import[a]	Net total[a]	Price index	Quantity (1913 prices)
1883	1,020		1,020	106.0	962
1899	1,274		1,274	82.2	1,550
1913	2,769		2,769	100.0	2,769
1929	5,462	75	5,387	119.2	4,519
1937	5,011	119	4,892	95.2	5,138
1955	16,882	706	16,176	240.5	6,725
1965	23,735	676	23,059	220.9	10,438

[a] At current prices.

index from 1929 onwards. Prices from 1880 to 1929 are based on British, German and U.S. indices of the export prices of manufactures, weighted by the values of 1913. The British index is from W. Schlote, *British Overseas Trade,* Oxford, 1952. The German index is from W. Hoffmann, *Das Wachstum der Deutschen Wirtschaft,* Berlin, 1965. The American index is from R. G. Lipsey, *Price and Quantity Trends in the Foreign Trade of the United States,* Princeton, 1963. There are no U.S. or German indices for 1871 to 1880; a simple average of British import and export indexes is used. The year 1913 is linked to 1929 on the basis of A. Maizels, *Industrial Growth and World Trade,* Cambridge, 1963.

3. *The Volume of Trade*

1. Trade in current prices is inflated by the export of oil from Venezuela for refining in Aruba; it has therefore been reduced in Table 11 by deducting the imports of oil into Aruba.

TABLE 12. *Volume of agricultural trade* ($m.)

	Total trade[a]	Minerals inc. gold[a]	Manufactures[a]	Agricultural[a]	Price index	Quantity (1913 prices)
1883	1,020	50	40	930	109.2	852
1899	1,274	109	100	1,065	81.2	1311
1913	2,769	365	274	2,130	100.0	2130
1929	5,387	1031	407	3,949	118.7	3327
1937	4,892	1285	291	3,316	84.6	3919
1955	16,176	4475	850	10,851	233.8	4641
1965	23,059	6711	2265	14,083	209.3	6728

[a] At current prices.

TABLE 13. *"O.E.C.D" production and trade*

	Industrial production	"Imports of manufactures"[a] ($m.)
1883	34	
1899	56	4,979
1913	100	8,494
1929	152	10,618
1937	168	7,265
1955	322	15,435
1965	499	40,131

[a] At 1955 prices.

The price index used for total trade in Table 11 is composed of the index of tropical agricultural prices, the index of the price of manufactures and a special index of the prices of minerals and metals imported from the tropics.

2. The trade in agricultural products is found by subtracting the trade in minerals and manufactures from total trade. Minerals includes non-ferrous metals and gold.

The figures for 1913 are based on Yates, *op. cit.* Those for 1929 to 1965 are based on the trade year books of the League of Nations and the United Nations. Coverage is almost complete for 1965; rather more doubtful for 1955, and more doubtful still for the earlier years. Figures for 1883 and 1899 involve some guessing; fortunately in 1883 tropical export of minerals and manufactures was still very small in relation to agricultural exports.

4. "O.E.C.D."

1. One uses inverted commas to emphasize that not all O.E.C.D. countries are included.

2. The earliest edition of O.E.C.D.'s *Industrial Production: Historical Statistics* gives a composite index for the European members of O.E.C.D. from 1901 on, plus data for the U.S.A. and Canada. I have added the U.S.A. and Canada, supplementing the Canadian data from the League of Nations's *Industrialization and Foreign Trade.* Later issues include the U.S.A., Canada and Japan from 1957 onwards; I have deleted Japan.

The resulting index has the same rate of growth as the League of Nations world index over 1913 or 1929. I have therefore linked the two at 1901 to obtain 1899. The League figure for 1883 is, however, suspiciously low, giving a growth rate of 3.95 per cent per annum to 1913, as against the figure I get for Britain, France, Germany and the U.S.A. combined, of 3.25 per cent using the latest revisions. Some European countries grew faster than these four combined, but their weight was not big enough to make so much difference. I have assumed that O.E.C.D. members not in my index accounted in 1899 for 10 per cent of O.E.C.D. output, and were growing at 5.0 per cent p.a. This, combined with my index, makes the O.E.C.D. growth rate between 1883 and 1899 about 3.3 per cent p.a. and gives for 1883 an index of 34.

3. "Imports" of manufactures are really exports of manufactures from member countries to each other. The data are given by Maizels in 1955 prices from 1899 to 1955. I have obtained 1965 from the O.E.C.D.'s *Commodity Trade: Exports*. Not all O.E.C.D. countries are included, but the only "large" importer excluded from this table is Japan.

Imports from non-member countries are not included. These, together with imports from Japan, were more significant in 1965 than in earlier years.

[11]

The Slowing Down of the Engine of Growth

By W. ARTHUR LEWIS*

Let me begin by stating my problem. For the past hundred years the rate of growth of output in the developing world has depended on the rate of growth of output in the developed world. When the developed grow fast, the developing grow fast, and when the developed slow down, the developing slow down. Is this linkage inevitable? More specifically, the world has just gone through two decades of unprecedented growth, with world trade growing twice as fast as ever before, at about 8 percent per annum in real terms, compared with 0.9 percent between 1913 and 1939, and less than 4 percent per annum between 1873 and 1913. During these prosperous decades, the less developed countries (*LDC*s) have demonstrated their capacity to increase their total output at 6 percent per annum, and have indeed adopted 6 percent as the minimum average target for *LDC*s as a whole. But what is to happen if the more developed countries (*MDC*s) return to their former growth rates, and raise their trade at only 4 percent per annum: is it inevitable that the growth of the *LDC*s will also fall significantly below their target? My purpose is not to predict what is going to happen, but to explore existing relationships and how they may change.

The extraordinary growth rates of the two decades before 1973 surprised everybody. We knew that the world economy experiences long swings in activity; that world trade, for example, grew faster between 1830 and 1873 than it grew between 1873 and 1913, that is to say, between 4 and 5 percent before 1873, compared with between 3 and 4 percent after 1873. But a jump to 8 percent was inconceivable.

Some people were even more surprised by the performance of the *LDC*s. In 1950 these people were sceptical of the capacity of *LDC*s to grow rapidly because of inappropriate attitudes, institutions, or climates. The sun was thought to be too hot for hard work, or the people too spendthrift, the government too corrupt, the fertility rate too high, the religion too other worldly, and so on. This kind of analysis has now almost completely gone from the literature. In discussions at the end of the 1940's, noting that the *U.S.* national income per head had grown at about 2 percent a year over long periods, and noting that *LDC* populations were growing at about 1 percent, economists in United Nations circles were boldly discussing the possibility that the *LDC* growth rate might be 3 percent. The United Nations at the end of the 1950's fixed 5 percent as the target for the 1960's, meaning by "target" something that was unattainable but inspirational. Then to everybody's surprise UN figures showed 5 percent being averaged already by the middle 1960's. So the target was raised to 6 percent for the 1970's, but the figures showed 6 percent already in the early 1970's, and the UN was just getting ready to fix 7 percent for the 1980's when the recession started in 1974. I do not vouch for the accuracy of any of these performance figures, but I think *LDC*s have demonstrated beyond doubt their capacity to use physical and human resources productively.

The fast pace of world trade also played havoc with development theory. The collapse of international trade in the 1930's had seemed irreversible, so much so that Keynes had even declared that we didn't need much of it anyway. So in the 1940's and 1950's we created a whole set of theories which make sense if world trade is stagnant—balanced growth, regional integration, the two-gap model, structural inflation—but which have little relevance in a world where trade is

*Princeton University. This article is a revised version of the lecture W. A. Lewis delivered in Stockholm, Sweden, December, 1979, when he received the Nobel Prize in Economic Science.

growing at 8 percent per annum. Also many countries, basing their policies on the same assumption, oriented inwards mainly towards import substitution. The fact that world trade was growing rapidly was not universally recognized until the second half of the 1960's. Then nearly every country discovered the virtues of exporting. Now we are in danger of being caught out again. Since 1973 the growth rate of world trade has halved, and nobody knows whether this is temporary or permanent. But most of our economic writing continues to assume implicitly that a return to 8 percent is only just around the corner.

I

Let me come back to the relationship between *MDC*s and *LDC*s. The principal link through which the former control the growth rate of the latter is trade. As *MDC*s grow faster, the rate of growth of their imports accelerates and *LDC*s export more. We can measure this link. The growth rate of world trade in primary products over the period 1873 to 1913 was 0.87 times the growth rate of industrial production in the developed countries; and just about the same relationship, about 0.87, also ruled in the two decades to 1973.[1] World trade in primary products is a wider concept than exports from developing countries, but the two are sufficiently closely related for it to serve as a proxy. We need no elaborate statistical proof that trade depends on prosperity in the industrial countries. More interesting is the evidence that the relationship was quantitatively the same over a hundred years, so that the two-thirds increase in the rate of growth of exports of primary products from *LDC*s was no more or less than could be predicted from the increased rate of growth of *MDC* production.

Most interesting is that the coefficient is less than one, viz. 0.87. This means that if the engines of growth were industrial production in *MDC*s and exports of primary products in *LDC*s, then the *MDC* engine was beating slightly faster than the *LDC* engine. The effects of equal beating would not necessarily be exactly the same. And there are side effects that strengthen the connection. When the beat is faster the terms of trade are expected to be more favorable to the *LDC*s (though that did not happen this time). The domestic market prospers, so *LDC* industrialization for the domestic market is speeded; this happened. The *MDC*s relax their barriers to imports of manufactures, so this trade accelerates as well. Foreign capital flows into minerals, manufactures, and infrastructure. And foreign countries take more migrants, so that the homeward flow of remittances to *LDC*s is larger in prosperous times.

Putting it all together, including the fact that industrial production grew faster in *LDC*s than in *MDC*s, it is not surprising that the rate of growth of gross domestic product was just about the same in *LDC*s and in *MDC*s over the quarter of a century ending in 1973, namely about 5 percent per annum. Since *LDC* population was growing faster than *MDC* population, there is a big gap in the growth rates of output per head, about 4 percent in *MDC*s, against 2.5 percent in *LDC*s. The performance of *LDC*s was remarkable in absolute terms, but the gap between *MDC*s and *LDC*s in income per head continued to widen rapidly.

Now we come to our dilemma. The objective of most people who are concerned with these matters is to narrow the per capita gap between *MDC*s and *LDC*s. But how is one to do this if they are linked to equal growth of total output? One might perhaps conceive a lower rate of growth of *MDC*s. Many *MDC* voices are calling for this—the environmentalists, the persons who fear exhaustion of exhaustible resources, the advocates of greater grace and leisure in our lives, and others. But if the *MDC* growth rate falls, the *LDC* growth rate will fall too, and *LDC*s will get the worst of it, since the terms of trade will move against them. Given the link, it is in the interest of *LDC*s that the *MDC*s should grow as rapidly as they can.

[1]For data, see my *Growth and Fluctuations 1870–1913*, pp. 175–76.

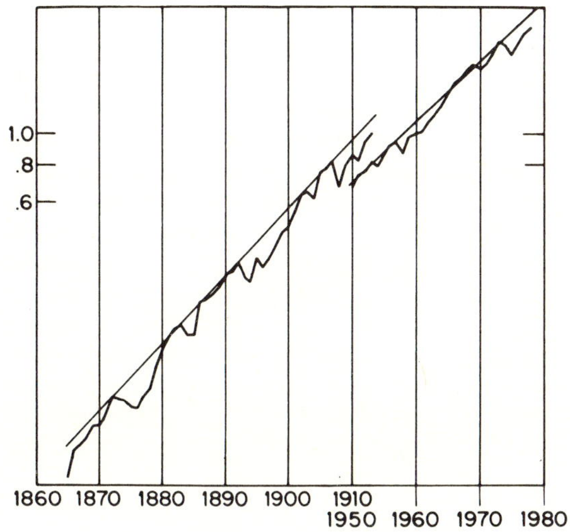

FIGURE 1. U.S. INDUSTRIAL PRODUCTION, 1865-1913 AND 1950-78

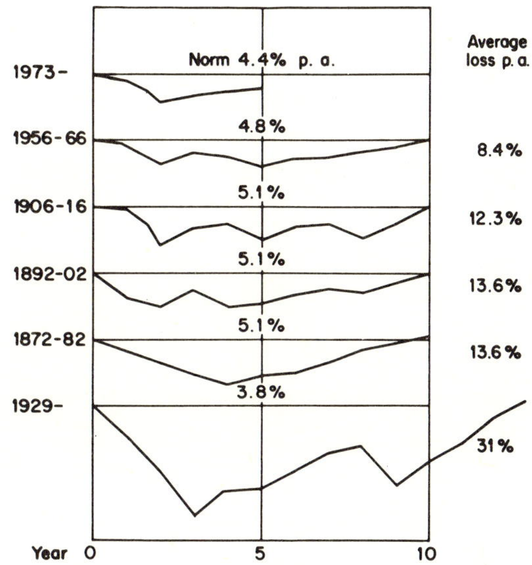

FIGURE 2. U.S. GREAT DEPRESSIONS: DEVIATION OF ACTUAL FROM "CAPACITY" INDUSTRIAL PRODUCTION

Three questions come to mind. First, what is likely to happen to the speed of *MDC* growth? Secondly, can *LDC*s maintain fast growth even in face of a decline of *MDC* growth? And thirdly, is it desirable that *LDC* development depend on rapid growth of exports to *MDC*s? My main purpose in this paper is to consider the second question, but I shall also briefly explore the first. The third question, on the desirability of *LDC/MDC* trade, may be left to another occasion.

II

Many people now assert that the world economy has made one of those major turns that it makes from time to time, as it did in 1873 when world trade settled into a growth rate only about two-thirds of that of the preceding half-century. However, part of the evidence they adduce is merely evidence of cyclical and not secular decline—high unemployment rates, low profits,[2] low investment ratios, low savings, and a slower growth rate of productivity are the familiar elements of cyclical downswing, and throw no light-term trends.

Over the past century, the United States has experienced a series of Great Depressions, each of which took ten years to complete itself, except for that of 1929, which took twelve years. The starting points of these depressions were 1873, 1893, 1907, 1929, 1957, and 1974. Figure 1 shows *U.S.* industrial production on a semilogarithmic scale, where the straight lines indicate the rate of growth along the peaks, and the potential output at that rate.[3] The difference

[2]Evidence of a decline in the profits ratio, often cited, is hard to interpret. In the United States, industrial production runs along a ceiling when the ratio of manufacturers' profits to sales is around 5 percent (after tax). The ratio averaged 4.8 over 1951–56 and 5.1 over 1966–69, which were also years of full employment (less than 4 percent unemployed). The basis of the series changes between 1973 and 1974; on the new basis, the ceiling would be about 6 percent. That the profit ratio averaged 5.4 in 1976 and 5.3 in 1977 merely indicates, along with elevated unemployment, the continuance of cyclical deficiency in those years. Series from the *Economic Report of the President*.

[3]From 1923, the index is that of the Federal Reserve Board. Prior to 1913, the index is that of Edwin Frickey, as amended by the National Bureau of Economic Research statisticians. For references, see my *Growth and Fluctuations 1890-1913*, pp. 272-73. Construction is excluded. The charts are semilogarithmic. The slope of the straight line from 1872 to 1906 indicates growth at 5.1 percent per annum; that from 1951 to 1973

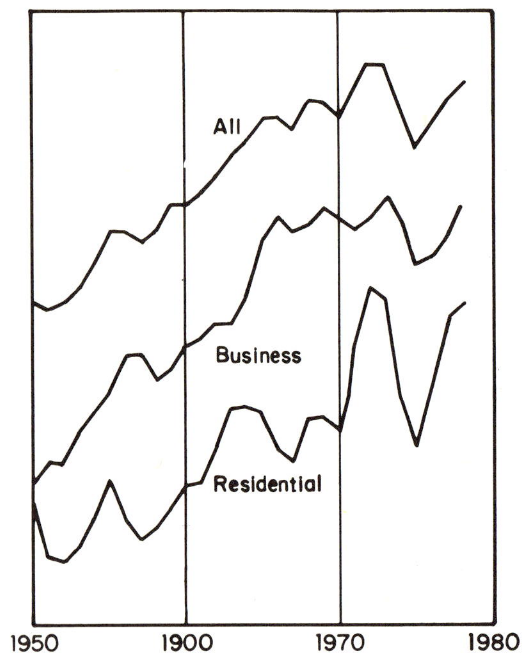

FIGURE 3. U.S. CONSTRUCTION

between actual and potential output is shown in Figure 2 for each of these Great Depressions separately.[4] The depression at the top of the figure is the one we are now experiencing. It seems to conform to pattern. For example, as is well known, these Great Depressions are associated with similar long fluctuations in construction activity. Figure 3 shows that this association is unchanged, despite Moses Abramovitz's optimistic prediction to the contrary; deep depressions in both business and residential construction are at the heart of our current depression.[5] Again, suggestions that the *U.S* economy was overheated at the end of 1978 (year 5) seem implausible—they confuse lack of capacity due to many years of low construction in face of rising population, with lack of capacity due to high demand. Shortage of capacity after years of depression is what triggers a new investment boom. If the past repeats itself, a spurt of activity in the early 1980's (growth at 6 to 7 percent per annum) should bring *U.S.* industrial production back on to its prosperity line by 1983. This does not rule out the possibility of a minor fluctuation in the interim. There is, of course, no basis for predicting that the past will repeat itself, but equally there is no basis for predicting that this depression will go on forever.[6]

If then we reject all evidence that can be explained by six years of depression, we are left with a number of arguments that are being advanced to suggest that the prosperity of 1950–73 was special and not repeatable. I shall merely list them, because to pursue each of them would take us too far off course. Here are the leading six:

1. The fast growth of Europe after World War II was due to catching up on a backlog of innovations whose feasibility and profitability the United States had demonstrated by 1950, but whose utilization had been delayed in Europe by two world wars and the Great Depression—telephones, automobiles, refrigerators, television, aeroplanes, and so on. This backlog, it is claimed, is now exhausted.

2. There is no new innovation of Schumpeterian magnitude to take its place. This proposition could be established only by hindsight; expenditure on research and development by private industry may have declined, but this may only be a cyclical event.

3. Western Europe's reserves of surplus labor in agriculture, petty retailing, and

indicates growth at 4.4 percent per annum. In Figure 1, the position of the lower curve in relation to the upper reflects that industrial output in 1956 was 20 percent less than it would have been if it had grown at 4.4 percent per annum since 1913. The interwar curve is omitted. Its familiar shape would show output rising at 3.8 percent per annum before 1929, then plunging into the Great Depression.

[4]The depression of 1929 is of such a different magnitude from the rest that it has been taken out of its sequence, and put at the bottom of the figure.

[5]Expenditure on structures at 1972 prices; Tables B2 and B7 of the *Economic Report of the President*. It can be seen in Figure 2 that the two postwar depressions are notably less deep than the pre-1913 depressions.

[6]The National Bureau of Economic Research has trained us to think of the Kitchin as the reference cycle (forty months), so any depression that extends beyond eighteen months feels like the end of the world. Our economic journalists have even lower horizons, since they seldom get beyond comparing this year with last. We cannot understand what is happening without at least a ten-year perspective.

elsewhere, which facilitated rapid expansion of industry and other high-level occupations is now exhausted, and immigration of cheap labor from Southern Europe will not be resumed.

4. We shall run into a shortage of minerals; of copper, tin, bauxite, and others, because transnational companies and *LDC* governments cannot agree on terms for new investment; and of oil because of OPEC's conservation policies. This imbalance is one of the two primary sources of inflation. The other primary source is the spiralling of prices as organized groups bargain for an annual increase in income of at least 5 percent (plus last year's increase in prices) in an economy where productivity rises by 3 percent per annum or less. Attempts to control inflation through controlling the money supply touch neither of these primary sources, unless pushed to the level of 15 percent unemployment, which is not politically feasible. Whether the monetary authorities opt for stagflation or for massive unemployment, the rate of growth is slowed.

5. The preference of consumers in rich countries for services rather than manufactured commodities will result in relative decline of the industrial population. Among the effects of this may be a decline in the rate of growth of imports of primary production.

6. High levels of taxation may diminish initiative, enterprise, and the rate of growth.

I list these propositions neither to support them nor to controvert them, but only to remind us that the world economy has had long periods of prosperity (like 1850 to 1873) and long periods of relative stagnation (say 1913 to 1950) so that there is nothing strange in the idea that the next two or three decades may turn out to be difficult. But there is also nothing strange in the idea that they may turn out to be rather prosperous.

III

In what follows I shall assume that industrial production in *MDC*s grows more slowly than it was growing before 1973, and that the imports of these countries grow only at 4 percent a year, over the next twenty years. This is not a prediction; it is merely the assumption whose consequences we are seeking to analyze.

I shall also assume that *LDC*s want their *GDP* to grow at 6 percent per annum, and that this requires their imports to grow at 6 percent. This linkage follows from the further assumption that the individual *LDC* will not become more self-sufficient, perhaps because it is too small; though *LDC*s as a group will have to be more self-sufficient. No importance attaches to whether the figure for imports is the same as the figure for the growth of gross domestic product; all that matters is that the growth rate of exports from *LDC*s is assumed to be significantly higher than the rate of growth of imports of *LDC* commodities into *MDC*s. The *LDC*s will continue to pay for some of their imports out of proceeds of transfers, including foreign aid and private foreign investment, but we shall assume that this still leaves *LDC*s needing, say, a 6 percent growth rate for exports, while *MDC*s are assumed to increase their imports from *LDC*s only at 4 percent a year. The problem is how to reconcile these two growth rates.

There could theoretically be a simple way, namely for *LDC*s to have an ever increasing share of *MDC* imports, but we have closed this door. The main link between *MDC* and *LDC* economies has been the *MDC* demand for *LDC* primary commodities. This has been a link in terms of physical volume, not much affected by prices. The *LDC*s could not sell significantly more primary produce by reducing prices; on the contrary, they would earn substantially less purchasing power as the terms of trade deteriorated. The *LDC*s could earn more by reducing the volume or by joining together in raising prices. The direct effect of these actions would be to reduce output, but this could be offset by investing the extra earnings judiciously. However none of this seems to be in the cards; so we shall assume that our problem cannot be solved by accelerated or decelerated production of primary commodities normally exported to *MDC*s.

What about manufactures? These are now nearly 40 percent of the exports of the non-OPEC *LDC*s, and are still their fastest growing export. Could the whole problem be solved simply by increasing the growth rate of manufactured exports to *MDC*s, in substitution for primary products? I shall assume that this cannot be done, since if it can be done my paper ends abruptly. Also I do not think that it can be done. The *MDC*s are willing to let in manufactured exports when they are prosperous, since they then have many growing industries that can take in people displaced by imports. Our assumption that the *MDC* growth rate is low rules out this possibility. It would indeed be more appropriate to assume that *MDC*s will take less manufactures from *LDC*s rather than more.

Our basic assumptions therefore are that *LDC*s need to have their exports grow at 6 percent a year, but *MDC*s will increase their imports from *LDC*s only at 4 percent a year. What is to happen to the growth of *LDC* output?

Let me concede at once that from the standpoint of the individual *LDC* it matters not at all what the *MDC* growth rate may be. Given resources and flexibility, it can always sell more to *MDC*s. However, it thereby displaces some other *LDC*'s trade. What one can do cannot be done by all.

At the level of arithmetic this problem now has only one solution. If total sales from *LDC*s increase at 6 percent, while sales to *MDC*s increase at 4 percent, sales to the rest of the world (given weights of seven to three) must increase initially at about 11 percent per annum. Ignoring the socialist countries, which could help by buying much more from *LDC*s but won't, the *LDC*s can solve the problem only by accelerating sharply their trade with each other.

Inter-*LDC* trade is still rather small—about 19 percent of the exports of non-OPEC *LDC*s.[7] The percentage did not change significantly over the two decades to 1973 despite all the effort that was put into creating and servicing regional trade institutions. Can this trade take up the slack left by *MDC*s as *MDC*s slow down?

The answer is in the affirmative. Currently the *LDC*s depend on the *MDC*s for food, fertilizers, cement, steel, and machinery. Taken as a group, *LDC*s could quickly end their dependence for the first four, and gradually throw off their dependence for machinery. They also import a considerable quantity of light manufactures for which they are not in any sense dependent (some $31 billion in 1977, compared with $47 billion of engineering products). They could quickly rid themselves of these, and more gradually throw off their dependence for machinery.

The *LDC*s are capable of feeding themselves now, if they adopt appropriate agrarian policies and, as our eleven new international tropical agricultural research institutes give us better varieties and improved technology, output should more than keep up with population. The problem is to get through the period while the birth rate remains obstinately high to the less-frightening times when the birth rate will have dropped below twenty per thousand. It may be a near thing, but we should make it.

As for fertilizers, cement, and steel, these are made by applying standard technology to raw materials that are widely available outside the *MDC*s. Machinery is more bothersome because important parts of this trade involve economies of scale, continually improving technology, and patented or secret knowledge. However, several *LDC*s are moving into this field, and already machinery is 15 percent or more of the output of manufactures in at least eight *LDC*s (India, Brazil, Singapore, Chile, Korea, Argentina, Mexico, and Israel).[8] The *LDC* exports of engineering products are also growing rapidly, and contrary to popular belief, already exceed *LDC* exports of textiles and clothing in value. There is no reason why *LDC*s as a group should not become nearly self-sufficient in standard types of equipment.

If all this scope exists for inter-*LDC* trade, why have the regional customs unions not been more successful? Note three reasons.

First, a region is not a homogenous area. Some countries are much more

[7]Trade data in this and the next two paragraphs are from GATT, *International Trade 1977–78*.

[8]Share of machinery in manufactures calculated from United Nations, *Yearbook of Industrial Statistics 1976*.

advanced than others in industrial competitiveness, to an almost inconceivable extent. These advanced countries attract more new industries than the less advanced, who feel exploited by the customs union. The union then survives only if costly measures are taken to placate the less advanced, and these measures are difficult to negotiate.

Secondly, the usefulness of the union is maximized in sharing out industries with substantial economies of scale, extending over the whole regional market. Each country is anxious to keep for itself all those industries that can attain the economies of scale within the national market. Destruction of any of these industries by competition from another member of the union causes a political uproar. The union is therefore safest when it does not require internal free trade in all commodities, but instead concentrates on those few "integration" industries as they are called which need the whole regional market. Even this more modest task is hard to negotiate if each member country is to have its fair share of integration industries.

The third reason why the customs unions have not done better is that their basic assumption—that a country should trade most with its next-door neighbors—is no longer true in these days of very low transport costs. For reasons of climate, soil, and history, the next-door neighbor is probably in the same business, and not a potential customer or supplier. He is equally poor, and therefore offers an equally limited market. The *LDC*s developing new industrial products are drawn to large rich *LDC* markets rather than to those of their neighbors. Frankly, in the 1950's and 1960's, aggressive developers did not much need the support of customs unions; these offer more to their members when world trade is stagnant than when it is booming.

It follows, therefore, that in the situation we are analyzing, where world trade decelerates, customs unions would be more highly prized and would be made more effective, especially in regard to large-scale industries with region-wide economies of scale. But even so, the leading commodities that *LDC*s would now have to produce to a greater extent for each other cannot be shared out between next door neighbors on a political basis. Food, fertilizers, cement, steel, and fuel pick their locations more in terms of raw material availability, and machinery will come in the first instance from those *LDC*s that already have a substantial industrial base. This new *LDC* trade would be worldwide, just as European and *U.S.* trade are worldwide.

IV

I am therefore arguing that it is physically feasible for *LDC*s to maintain a high rate of growth even if *MDC*s decide otherwise for themselves. How does physical feasibility translate into an effective economic framework?

One way would be to follow the customs union route, with *LDC*s giving preferential treatment to imports from other *LDC*s. The nucleus of this exists already in the Protocol Relating to Trade Negotiations among Developing Countries which came into force in 1973, with the blessing of GATT, and which provides for negotiated preferential arrangements among sixteen of the bigger and more advanced *LDC*s. The philosophy of such an arrangement is in line with the spirit of Bretton Woods, which recognized the rights of countries to impose restrictions on other countries which were tending persistently to run balance-of-payments surpluses, as would be the situation if the *LDC*s were growing faster than the *MDC*s. One may doubt however whether such different countries will get very far along the route of preferential concessions. If they are to prefer each other's goods, this will have to be because they are competitive in price with those of *MDC*s.

In the economist's model this competitiveness would come about automatically. The *LDC*s would run a balance-of-payments deficit because of the *MDC* slowdown, yet persist in their own rapid growth instead of slowing down themselves. Adjustment comes in the old gold standard version through an outflow of gold that reduces their price levels; or in the modern versions by devaluation, which has the same effect. The real world is more complicated. Inflation is universal, but aggressive sellers of manufactures have to keep their prices down; so this set of *LDC*s would need special emphasis on inflation controls. Devaluation cannot be avoided when prices cease to be competitive, but is palliative rather than curative in situations when it triggers further increases in domestic costs that reinstate the differential that it was meant to eliminate. The *LDC*s have the same problem as the *MDC*s: the domestic price level can no longer be controlled merely by twirling general controls such as the rate of interest, or the supply of money, or the rate of exchange for the currency. They too now experience the cost-push element in price determination, for which the only remedy is some sort of incomes policy. We expect more from the economic system than our grandparents did in the nineteenth century, by way of full employment and faster growth, and should not be surprised that the economic system requires more from us, by way of supporting institutions.

These new aggressive *LDC*s, exporting machinery to each other, may also have problems in financing their trade. Nearly every *LDC* has a separate currency. We are envisioning Nigeria selling cereals to India for rupees, with which it buys machinery from Brazil. Some kind of clearing agreement may become necessary; otherwise *LDC* traders will tend to do business with each other in one or more *MDC* currencies, and will be constrained by the relative scarcity of such currencies. Perhaps the International Monetary Fund would straighten this out. A more serious problem will be to finance the export of capital goods from one *LDC* to another, since the seller is expected to help finance the buyer. It is not likely that the *LDC* exporters can do this on their own. We must assume that they will be allowed to raise untied loans in the *MDC* financial markets, perhaps using the regional development banks as intermediaries to a greater extent than is now the case.

But the real problem is not whether *LDC*s can become competitive and hold their own in each other's markets. Problems of pricing and foreign exchange can work themselves out in the world market. The real problem is whether *LDC*s will persist in rapid growth despite the slowdown of the *MDC*s. If the economy is still dependent, the balance-of-payments weakness will pull it down; but if it has attained self-sustaining growth, the weakness in the foreign exchanges merely launches a drive to export to other *LDC*s, and the weakness in the balance of payments is then only transitional.

If a sufficient number of *LDC*s reach self-sustaining growth, we are into a new world. For this will mean that instead of trade determining the rate of growth of *LDC* production, it will be the growth of *LDC* production that determines *LDC* trade, and internal forces that will determine the rate of growth of production. Not many countries are ready to make this switch. India is an obvious possibility, along with some of the other subscribers to the Protocol of 1973. It is not possible for all *LDC*s to make this switch and neither is it necessary, for if leading *LDC*s grow fast and import heavily, they will substitute to some extent for the former rapid growth of *MDC*s. For those who use the language of center and periphery, this means that a number of countries leave the periphery and join the center. Or if they are specially linked to each other by preferential trade and currency arrangements, one may even speak of the creation of a new center consisting of former peripheral nations that have built a new engine of growth together.

The shadow on this picture is what happens to those *LDC*s whose best option has been to export raw materials to *MDC*s. Our exercise starts from the assumption that the growth rate of *MDC* demand is reduced, so these face surpluses and unfavorable terms of trade. We have provided an escape for *LDC*s that can turn to exporting food or manufactures, but we have not assumed that the new core *LDC*s will substitute for the *MDC*s by drinking more coffee or tea, or using more rubber and jute. This solution therefore involves some hardships for the less adaptable *LDC*s, constrained by climate or by the small size of their markets. A framework for helping them exists already in the IMF's compensatory financing, and in the EEC's STABEX support; but these are meant for temporary fluctuations. Bigger and more persistent support would be required.

Transnational corporations would probably play some part in the establishment of this new inter-*LDC* trading network. The cadre of domestic entrepreneurs is adequate in the more advanced industrial *LDC*s to manage most of the range of light consumer goods and light engineering products. One of our main concerns, however, is to diminish reliance on *MDC*s for heavy machinery and such, and this extends into fields where experience is limited. Since we are assuming that the market will send out price signals favoring production in *LDC*s, whether because of tariffs or of currency adjustments, transnational corporations will be eager to preserve their markets by establishing subsidiaries behind the protective barrier. Hostility to such corporations is universal and their influence is diminishing in most sectors, especially in mining, public utilities, distribution, and finance; but not in manufacturing, where judging by advertisements in the *New York Times* and the financial press, *LDC* governments are only too anxious to invite the participation of transnational corporations. There are plenty of restrictions—on the hiring of expatriate staff, on percentages of equity owned by foreigners, on borrowing in the local market, on technology, and so on. Also, in many cases joint ownership with local capitalists or with government agencies is prescribed. A government anxious to promote industrialization and a corporation anxious to preserve or extend its market find common ground.

The awkward part of the exercise is to sustain the momentum of 6 percent growth through the transition from dependence on *MDC* trade to dependence on *LDC* markets. During this transition the leading industrial *LDC*s must establish their footholds in each others' markets, as well as those of other *LDC*s; also the agrarian changes must occur which both feed the urban population and present a growing market for its goods and services. It is possible that some of the leading *LDC*s can take this in their stride, just as German industrialists launched their trade drive in the 1880's, followed by the United States after 1895, by Japan in the 1930's, and more recently by Brazil. They do not have to begin with machinery, since *LDC*s still import so much light manufactures from *MDC*s. They can start here and move more gradually into machinery.

At the other extreme, it is also possible that there is simply not yet enough entrepreneurial steam in the leading *LDC*s to make this transition without a supporting framework. I have already mentioned the main international elements of such a framework, namely preferential tariff and currency arrangements. The domestic element consists of the maintenance of home demand in the face of stagnant world trade in primary products, so that the economy can continue to go forward instead of collapsing. Much of the responsibility for maintaining momentum then falls on the government, given its large share of the cash economy, and also the extent to which it regulates or supports the private sector. It has to carry the responsibility for a large investment program (private and public) in human and physical capital. This responsibility could not be carried without external aid. The *MDC*s would have to be in a mood to say: we will not give you more trade; here for a while is more aid instead.

The recession that started in 1974 has now lasted long enough for *LDC*s to consider the possibility that *MDC*s intend to maintain rates of *GNP* growth which will allow world trade to expand only at around 4 percent a year. This would be a major blow to *LDC* growth aspirations, unless new steps were taken to support rising participation of *LDC*s in *LDC* trade. I have been trying to analyze what these steps might be. They ought to figure prominently in current North-South negotiations, but in fact they do not, since these negotiations tacitly assume that high *MDC* growth rates will soon be resumed. Perhaps this assumption will turn out to be correct; economics does not foretell the future. For the least, *LDC*s should be discussing among themselves in what directions they would wish to go, prior to negotiations with the *MDC*s.

Of course, the problems tackled in this paper would not arise at all if *MDC*s were willing to allow *LDC*s a greater share of *MDC* markets. This would be the logical evolution of a situation where *LDC*s grow faster than *MDC*s; trade with *LDC*s should become an ever-increasing portion of *MDC* trade. We live in a strange world. Through the 1960's and 1970's, *MDC*s have been dismantling their barriers to each other's trade while increasing their barriers to *LDC* trade. Since imports of manufactures from developing countries are only 2 percent of the consumption of manufactures in OECD countries, this indicates exceptional sensitivity to minor change. Lack of sensitivity, on the other hand, characterizes the failure of developed countries to recognize that dependence is mutual, in that the non-OPEC *LDC*s take 20 percent of OECD exports, and could therefore by their prosperity help a little to sustain OECD prosperity. It can hardly be an OECD interest to force the *LDC*s into discriminating against OECD sources.

Nor would these problems arise if the *MDC*s would return to the attack on mass poverty within their own borders which they launched so successfully in the 1950's and 1960's, and have now abandoned; since what we all really need is that world trade recapture its growth rate of 8 percent a year. But that is a different story.

REFERENCES

M. Abramovitz, "The Passing of the Kuznets Cycle," *Economica*, Nov. 1968, *35*, 349–67.

W. Arthur Lewis, *Growth and Fluctuations 1870–1913*, London; Boston 1978.

GATT, *International Trade 1977–78*, Geneva 1978.

United Nations, *Yearbook of Industrial Statistics 1976*, Vol. 1, New York 1978.

UNCTAD, *Handbook of International Trade and Development Statistics, Supplement 1977*, New York 1978.

U.S. Council of Economic Advisers, *Economic Report of the President*, Washington, various years.

[12]

1 The Rate of Growth of World Trade, 1830–1973

Arthur Lewis (USA)

I

Why did world trade grow so rapidly after the Second World War, up at least to the recession commencing in 1974? The growth rate from say 1953 to 1973 averaged 8.0 per cent per year.[1] The period immediately preceding the war was disastrous; 1913 to 1939 averaged only 0.9 per cent per year. But even in the so-called golden age of capitalism, say 1873 to 1913, the rate of growth of world trade averaged only 3.3 per cent per year.

The jump to 8 per cent per year caught us by surprise. Economists had adjusted themselves to the idea that international trade could no longer serve as an 'engine of growth', to use a phrase of Dennis Robertson's. A whole subset of development themes was invented to cope with a world where trade was stagnant—balanced growth, import substitution, structural inflation, the two-gap model, regional integration—all these are vital if world trade is growing at 1 per cent per year, but are trivial for countries with some flexibility, if it is growing at 8 per cent. It took some time to realise that world trade was growing at unprecedented speed; now we are in danger of assuming that it will always grow at this speed, and if it does not, we may again take some time to catch up.

This paper originated in the desire to discover whether this fast postwar speed was indeed unprecedented, by pushing our data of world trade further back into the nineteenth century; and if there were earlier periods of fast growth, whether we could identify their causes and make useful comparisons with our own experiences. The paper has turned out differently from its original plan. It was to have been a long analytical exercise accompanied by a brief statistical appendix. Instead, preparing the statistical appendixes has taken all the time available; they have become almost a separate paper.

The trouble is that hard data (customs returns based on current values) get scarcer as one pushes backwards, to the extent that it does not seem worthwhile to attempt a guess for all countries before 1850. Already in that year about half of our total of world trade is based on estimates of varying quality, compared with 20 per cent in 1872. Hitherto all quantitative discussion of world trade before 1870 has derived from a small table in Mulhall's *Dictionary of Statistics*, which contains figures for the sum of imports and exports at 20-year intervals starting in 1830. Simultaneously with testing his results, I offer an annual series.

II

The sum of the exports of the USA, UK, France and Germany[2] grew at 4.8 per cent per annum (constant prices) between 1830 and 1860, comparing with 3.4 per cent per annum between 1883 and 1913. The UK was in the lead, averaging 5.6 per cent to 1860, followed by the US and France, each with 5.0 per cent; Germany had not yet got into its stride.

The rest of the world may already have been growing at the rate it achieved between 1853 and 1872, which was 4.0 per cent per annum. If so, then the growth rate for world trade as a whole from 1830 to 1860 was 4.4 per cent per annum. This rate is not approached again until the period 1899 to 1913, which averaged 3.8 per cent.

Figure 1 obscures the earlier turning point, because the Civil War cut US exports (of which cotton had been the largest item) most severely.[3] If one excludes the USA, the turning-point is then clearly at 1872. World trade as a whole apart from the USA grows at 4.3 per cent from 1853 to 1872, at 2.7 from 1872 to 1899 and at 4.1 per cent from 1899 to 1913.

Exports of manufactures and of primary products grew at roughly the same fast rates between 1853 and 1872 and more slowly between 1872 and 1899. But after 1899 exports of manufactures grew rapidly, while exports of primary products maintained their previous pace. This absence of a Kondratiev upturn in primary products is also borne out by the League of Nations figures in *Industrialisation and Foreign Trade*.[4] Changes in the relative rates of growth of exports of manufactures and of primary products before 1914 are explored in Appendix IV.

III

In order to arrive at causes, we use a model in which the main driving

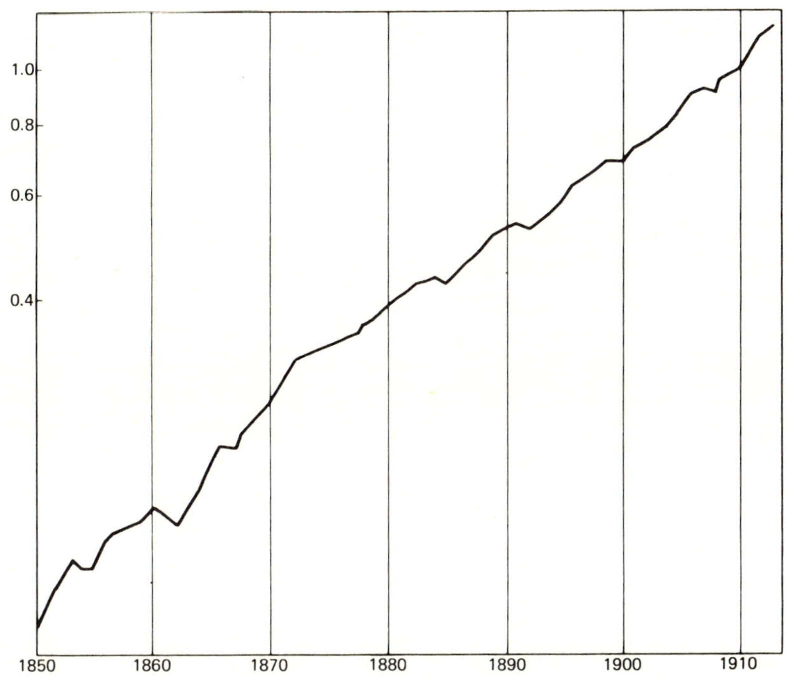

Fig. 1 World exports at 1913 prices, 1850–1913

force is the rate of growth of manufacturing in the leading industrial countries. Their growth causes them to import more, and they pay for their imports with exports. This model is part of the family that sees the development of 'peripheral' countries as a response to the industrialisation of the 'core' countries. However, the model is only a device for arranging our data; it does not yield any results on its own.

We are going to translate world trade into a function of industrial production (I) in the core countries. World trade equals the imports of core countries plus the imports of peripheral countries. The imports of peripheral countries divide into imports from core countries and imports from each other (h). Imports into peripheral from core countries are in payment for imports into core from peripheral countries—subject to capital transfers (k) and to service earnings (s); subject also, if we are comparing different dates, to changes in the terms of trade. One final element is to divide imported goods into manufactures (m) and primary products (c). Putting all this together, and taking m and c to be propensities, we get that the volume of world trade

$$Q = (m_0 + c_0)I + p(m_1 + c_1)I + k - ps + h$$

where m_0 and c_0 are propensities for total imports into core countries while m_1 and c_1 are for their imports from the periphery only.[5]

Our task is then to compare the behaviour of each of these elements during our subperiods.

We begin with I, industrial production. World trade will grow faster in one period than another if the growth rate of core industrial production accelerates, even if the propensities are constant. What happened to core industrial production?

Its growth rate was higher than ever between 1953 and 1973, and this certainly contributed to the rapid growth of world trade. Other factors helped, to which we shall return.

What about the comparison between 1830 to 1860 and 1872 to 1899? The growth rate of core countries was almost certainly reduced in the last quarter of the nineteenth century. Hoffmann's index[6] shows this for Britain, and my revision[7] of his index confirms his results, though reaching back only as far as 1854. Crouzet gets the same result for France.[8] Hoffmann's figures for Germany[9] are very doubtful, but do not show retardation. Germany may even have been growing faster in the last quarter than over 1830 to 1860. The USA was not a core country in our sense in the nineteenth century, but in comparison with the 1850s it too shows no retardation, if one is not trapped by the wide swings of its Kuznets cycle.[10]

British and French retardation should make a difference of about 0.3 points to the growth rate of industry. Bairoch[11] indeed gets 2.6 for all Europe between 1830 and 1860, and 2.2 between 1872 and 1900. The golden age of capitalism was really a silver age. This deceleration goes some way towards explaining why the growth rates for world trade over these same periods were say 4.2 and 3.0, but it does not go all the way.

What happened to industrial production after 1899 is still controversial. Bairoch finds acceleration for Europe as a whole, and this accords with Schumpeter's Kondratiev thesis. My study for the aggregate of the USA, Britain, France and Germany shows however a constant rate of growth from 1872 to 1913, allowing for periods of severe Kuznets depression.[12] This accords with the steady growth rate of world trade in primary products shown above. Peripheral Europe was industrialising more rapidly after about 1890 (Russia, Austria, Italy and others), but these countries were still exporters of primary products, and their industrialisation would not have added greatly to imports of primary products. Even if the world was industrialising more rapidly this would not be inconsistent with the steady growth rate of the core and of world trade.

IV

Next we come to the propensity to import primary products. This is the big difference between 1830 to 1860 and subsequent periods. The contrast is especially marked with 1953 to 1973, since the driving force in the latter period is an increased propensity to import manufactures.

The driving force of 1830 to 1860 was the propensity to import raw materials, not food or manufactures. Imports of manufactures into the core countries were rather small. Food and raw materials rose from 93 per cent of French imports in 1830 to 97 per cent in 1860. According to Bondi's calculations, between 1828 and 1864 German imports of primary products rose from 79 to 89 per cent of imports.[13] In the British case imports of manufactures rose as fast as imports of primaries, but the contribution of British imports of manufactures to the rate of growth of world trade was negligible, since in 1860 manufactures were only 7 per cent of British imports.

The driving force was raw materials, not food. The elasticity of French imports of raw materials with respect to industrial production was about 2 for 1830 to 1860, and about 1.4 for 1872 to 1899. The British raw material elasticity fell from about 1.5 to about 0.84. Food imports became important only after 1870, when American wheat flooded European markets. The dynamic force was cotton, which was on the fast-growing segment of its logistic curve in the first half of the nineteenth century. UK domestic consumption of cotton[14] rose by 4.0 per cent per annum between 1828–32 and 1856–60, but only by 1.6 per cent per annum between 1880–84 and 1905–09. Neither was this phenomenon confined to Britain. According to Sundbärg[15] cotton consumption in the rest of the world rose by 6.0 per cent per annum between 1826–30 and 1856–60, but by 3.3 per cent per annum between the latter date and 1896–1900.

The other side of this coin is the foreign trade of the USA, where in 1860 manufactures were 60 per cent of imports but only 11 per cent of exports. US imports of manufactures and of primary products were both growing at over 6 per cent per annum. Exports were growing at 5 per cent per annum, the difference being accounted for mainly by improving terms of trade and to a minor extent by capital import. Our model treats US foreign trade as a dependent variable rather than a prime mover over this period, since we assume that the USA grew cotton because the UK was willing to buy it, and would not have grown it but for the pull of demand.

The fact that the driving force was in raw materials discounts the proposition that world trade decelerated after 1872 because of the return to high tariff barriers, after the liberalising trends of the preceding half-century. These new tariffs were on food and manufactures, but not on raw materials; and the decline in the growth rate of raw material imports was particularly marked in the UK (1830–60 3.5 per cent[16] per annum, 1872–99 1.8 per cent per annum) which had no tariffs. Tariffs are relevant to the elasticities of food and manufactures, but not of raw materials.

Apart from the logistic principle, there is another reason why the propensity to import raw materials should vary with stages of industrialisation. In the early stages a country may be self-sufficient in a wide range of raw materials, which it then outgrows. For example, Japan had all the coal it needed until the First World War. Britain used to be self-sufficient in iron ore, copper and tin. These are minerals, but a country's demand may also outgrow its supply of agricultural requirements, either due to geographical factors, or comparative costs. We could then get the kinds of growth paths shown in Figure 2, where industrial production grows at a constant rate (the diagram is semi-logarithmic); import of raw materials begins later, and then rises asymptotically; and finally reduces its elasticity. The final stage is due to economy in the use of raw materials, and to the constant rise of value added in manufacturing relative to raw materials used. It is not easy to

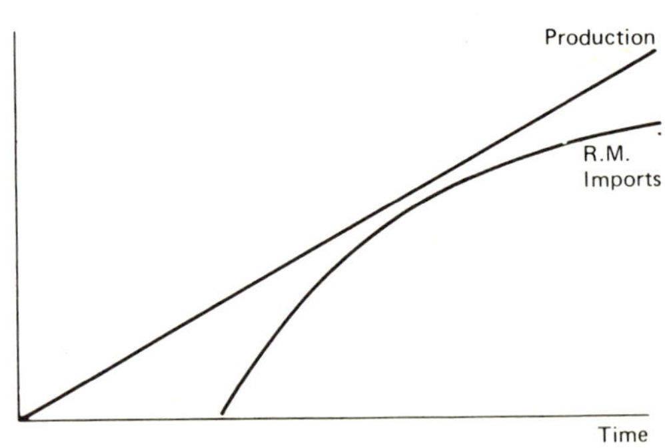

Fig. 2

quantify these trends but they are generally recognised, and give reason to expect that our *c* will fall as our *I* rises over time.[17]

The rate of growth of raw material imports slowed down after 1860; cotton did not resume its dominance over the growth of world trade. Despite the emergence of wheat, trade in primary products settled down to a steady rate of growth a little smaller than that of industrial production. To quote an earlier study:

> World manufacturing seems to have grown at about 3.6 per cent per annum between 1883 and 1913, and world trade in primary products at about 3.1 per cent per annum, giving an elasticity of about 0.86. Between 1950–52 and 1969–71 world manufacturing grew at 5.9 per cent per annum and world trade in primary products at 5.1 per cent per annum, yielding an elasticity of 0.87. So here is one coefficient which has remained constant over nearly a century.[18]

The rate of growth of world trade in primary products was unexpectedly and unprecedentedly high after the Second World War. This was the effect of rapid industrialisation on an unchanged propensity to import.[19]

V

The driving force of world trade after the Second World War was the imports of manufactures by the core countries. The demand thus generated was not confined to the core countries themselves, but spread over to the LDCs as well. Table 1 shows aspects of this. In current prices world trade in manufactures multiplied by 10.5 between 1953 and 1973, compared with 2.2 for world trade in beverages and sugar. The share of manufactures in world trade, which had been more or less constant (in current prices) since the last quarter of the nineteenth century, suddenly rose from 46 to 61 per cent. Strangely, with the exception of fuel, manufactures are the only grôup in which the LDCs maintained their share of world trade, growing as fast as the industriial countries. Manufactures thus rose to 21 per cent of LDC exports, or more than the exports of beverages, sugar and agricultural raw materials added together. Already manufactures constitute more than 20 per cent of the exports of some 20 LDCs, and there are more than 50 LDCs whose exports of manufactures exceed $25 million.

What accounts for this reversal? The share of imports of manufac-

TABLE 1
WORLD TRADE 1953–73

	Total 1973 $ billion	*Multiple 1973/1953*	*LDC shares 1953*	*1973*
Beverages and sugar	10.6	2.2	0.88	0.82
Agricultural raw materials	34.7	3.5	0.39	0.28
Food	75.4	6.6	0.35	0.19
Minerals and metals	32.4	6.6	0.50	0.29
Fuel	65.0	8.7	0.61	0.69
Manufactures	346.7	10.5	0.067	0.069
Total	564.8	7.9	0.30	0.20

tures in the industrial countries' consumption of manufactures had fallen steadily over several decades. According to Maizels's figures the ratio for Western Europe fell from 20 per cent in 1899 to 19 per cent in 1913 and less than 10 per cent in 1937.[20] That the ratio of imports to production would fall with industrialisation acquired the status of a law. That the 1937 ratio was abnormally low could be seen from the fact that it implied a negative elasticity. So it was no surprise when the ratio rose to 11 per cent in 1955. Even the return to the 1899 level by 1965 was surprising only for the speed with which it occurred. The explosion however continued; by 1973 the ratio of imports to consumption of manufactures in Western Europe was about 30 per cent. Tariffs are much lower than in 1899 or 1913, so a higher ratio is appropriate. But will the ratio continue to rise? It cannot rise indefinitely, since this would ultimately mean that European countries consumed only what they imported, and exported all that they produced—an outcome inconsistent with the fact that a significant part of industrial production is tied locationally to the domestic consumer market. Ultimately therefore this ratio must stabilise or fall. If it stabilises, imports will rise no faster than production, and the growth rate of trade in manufactures will drop back from the 11 per cent per annum level of 1953–73 to more like 5 per cent per annum. How soon this will happen we cannot of course predict. As far as we can tell, the ratio could continue to rise beyond say 40 or 50 per cent before altering direction.

It is tempting to connect changes in this ratio primarily with changes in tariff levels, but the direction of initial causality is not established (that tariffs reduce imports is not disputed). World trade in manufactures[21] rose at 4.1 per cent per annum between 1853 and 1872, at 3.1 per cent per annum between 1872 and 1899 and at 4.3 per cent between 1899 and 1913. The fast pace of 1899 to 1913 is irrelevant to the argument; it was connected with capital export and the terms of trade. But the slowdown after 1872 is at the core of the argument. This preceded the raising of tariff levels; tariffs were raised because trade was slack, and not the other way round. The propensity *m* is not a constant, but a variable which moves in the same direction as the rate of growth of industrial production. A fast pace of production increases imports of primary products and exports of manufactures (via the primary producers' increased purchasing power). Bottlenecks in manufacturing increase and order books lengthen, so imports of manufactures increase, beyond what would occur if production were growing less rapidly. Economies of scale are more fully exploited, good trade also weakens the protectionist forces, and tariff barriers are reduced. When industry slackens all this is reversed, and imports of manufactures decline faster than production.

Thus the explosive growth rate of world trade in manufactures after the Second World War was a natural product of the faster pace of industrialisation. Industrial production of OECD countries was rising at about 3.3 per cent per annum in the last quarter of the nineteenth century, with world trade in manufactures rising at about 3 per cent, giving an elasticity of about 0.9. The elasticity for 1953–73 is about 2.0. About half the growth rate of imports (about 5 per cent per annum) could be explained by a constant propensity; some part results from the greater import propensity of rapidly expanding markets, and the rest is due to other causes.

VI

The most important of these other causes in the nineteenth century was changes in the terms of trade. This played a major role in the trade explosion of 1830–60. Thus over this period UK imports grew at 4.1 per cent per annum, and UK exports at 5.6 per cent per annum, the change in the terms of trade adding 1.5 percentage points to the growth rate of British exports (capital exports were still small).

The terms of trade of Western Europe continued to deteriorate until the beginning of the 1880s, when they turned around and improved for nearly two decades. The fact that they were improving is one of the reasons why world trade in manufactures grew so slowly over the two decades that British historians call 'the Great Depression'. After 1895 the terms of trade again deteriorated, adding half a percentage point per year to the growth rate of European exports.[22]

These are the direct income effects. It is also possible that *p* is related both to *c* and to the rate of growth of *I*. A change in the terms of trade making primary products cheaper might increase the volume of imports, either via the price elasticity of demand, or via driving domestic producers out of business. The price elasticity of demand for food and raw materials is low enough within the revelant price ranges to be ignored. But competition with domestic producers is very real, as with the entry of US wheat into European markets. One can only assume that the value of *c* would have fallen even more after 1880 but for the terms of trade (the competition of US wheat).

The effect of the terms of trade on the rate of growth of industry is more controversial. The argument is that the reduced purchasing power of the farmers restricts the market for industry. The theoretical answer is that the purchasing power of the farmers falls only to the extent that the purchasing power of the industrial sector increases. I have examined the problem elsewhere, especially in relation to France, and remain sceptical.[23]

These changes in the terms of trade derive from changes in the relative growth rates of industrial and agricultural production.[24] The decisive change can be either industrial or agricultural. After 1872 the growth rate of industrial production slowed, but at the same time the opening up of the Middle West flooded Europe with agricultural products, and the terms of trade moved sharply in favour of industry. The growth rate of industry does not seem to have changed between 1872 and 1913, but the US agricultural frontier closed after 1890, and the terms of trade reversed themselves in favour of agriculture. Between 1913 and 1939 the deficiency was in industrial demand, so the terms of trade again reversed themselves, this time to favour industry. The period 1953–73 is interesting because it is the first in which we have rapid industrialisation with the terms of trade moving against agriculture. Agricultural potential increased enormously after the Second World War, partly because of a worldwide green revolution (hybrids, pesticides, fertilisèrs—still predominantly a temperate phenomenon), and partly because of the opening up of Asia, Africa and Latin America by roads and trucks. The increased rate of industrialisation was therefore more than matched by the increase in agricultural potential, and the terms of trade moved against agriculture. Therefore the terms of trade do not help in explaining the fast growth of world trade after 1953 (as they do for after 1830 or after 1899). On the contrary, exports would have grown even faster but for the change in the terms of trade.

The period 1953–73 is also anomalous in another sense. In the past industrial and agricultural prices have moved in the same directions (both upwards or downwards), the changes in the terms of trade resulting from faster movement of one group or the other. But in this period industrial prices were moving upwards although agricultural prices were moving downwards. This was due primarily to a change in the magnitude of money wage rate changes in the industrial countries. At the end of the nineteenth century industrial wage rates changed typically by 1 to 1½ per cent per annum, just about keeping pace with the change in productivity. Now the forces which kept money wage changes close to changes in productivity have ceased to operate, and the gap grows wider in each decade. The economic system has mutated, and market economies may now expect ever-rising prices no matter what happens to the terms of trade.

VII

Capital export rose steadily over the thirty years before the First World War, subject to wide fluctuations. We do not know whether it was larger in 1873 than in 1883; it probably was. In 1883 it was equivalent to 4.7 per cent of world exports[25]; in 1890 to 7.9 per cent, in 1899 to 8.3 per cent and in 1913 to 9.1 per cent. Appendix IV shows that capital export accounts for about one-third of the increased growth rate of exports of manufactures after 1899.

When we turn to 1953–73 the orders of magnitude are much lower than in 1913. The amount of capital exported in 1973 is not known precisely. The transfer of resources to developing countries in that year[26] was equal to about 4.7 per cent of world exports; the unknown element is the extent of transfers between developed countries. For that year only seven members of OECD reported a net inflow of long-term capital, amounting to another 1.8 per cent of world exports.[27] Clearly capital export is relatively smaller now than it was before the First World War. However, for its contribution to the rate of growth from 1953–73 we must compare 1973 with 1953 and not with 1913. The situation in 1953 is not known precisely. We may guess that capital export made a significant but not large contribution to the rate of growth of exports between 1953–73.

VIII

Exports of services have probably diminished relatively to exports of goods, making it necessary for the core countries to export more goods in payment for their imports.

The cost of transport seems not to have risen as much as the cost of goods. This is reflected in the difference between the value of world exports f.c.b. and of world imports c.i.f. which used to be 8 per cent, and has been running only at about 4 per cent. However most of this change occurred before the 1950s, and some of it may be due to the larger proportion of manufactures in world trade, since the difference was always wider in primary products.

Apart from this, developing countries now provide more services for themselves, own relatively more ships, run their own insurance business, and do more domestic banking. They have also built up a tourist industry, of some \$8 to \$10 billion a year. (One may also mention here the remittances of migrant workers, which are almost as large as the tourist expenditures.)

These trends require the core countries to export more commodities in payment for their imports.

IX

We come finally to the trade of the peripheral countries with each other. This has always been small. We have a count showing that in 1883 the four leading countries UK, USA, France and Germany imported from the tropical countries and East Asia goods valued at \$1,086 million c.i.f., or say \$978 million f.o.b.[28]. Exports from these countries totalled \$1,235 million in that year, so 21 per cent went other than to the leading four. We would probably exaggerate if we put their exports to each other at 10 per cent, which would make them less than 2 per cent of world trade.

In 1953 exports of LDCs to each other were 25 per cent of their trade; by 1973 this was down to 20 per cent, despite two decades of efforts at regional integration. These figures were equivalent to about 7 per cent of world trade in 1953 and 4 per cent in 1973. They are so small that changes in them make no significant contribution to understanding changes in the rate of growth of world trade. Presumably if the leading countries slow down, larger and more successful efforts will be made to effect regional integration; a period of booming world trade is not propitious for efforts in this direction.

X

We can now answer the question with which we began: what caused the explosion of world trade? The basic underlying cause was the faster pace of growth in the industrial countries, but there were other positive and negative elements. The terms of trade were a negative factor; trade between developing countries was too small to have much effect; the propensity to import raw materials and food was neutral; capital export was neutral or insignificant; and the relative decline of service income was positive if not large. The biggest factor, the propensity to import manufactures, would have been raised by faster industrial growth even if tariff levels had remained unchanged, but it was also bolstered by declining tariffs.

We seek to understand the past in order to chart the future. Can this fast pace be resumed after we get out of the current recession? This becomes two separate questions: can industry resume its fast pace, and can the propensity to import manufactures continue to increase.

I cannot answer first question easily. People who think that fast growth has ended advance one or other of five reasons.

(1) The mature industrial countries (excluding the USA) have exhausted their reservoirs of low-paid labour and, without immigration, can no longer grow fast through internal transfers or expansion of labour participation.

(2) Fast growth in Europe was due to catching up on a backlog of innovations which had been accumulating since 1900, and whose economic feasibility the USA had already demonstrated.

(3) There are no great innovations in sight, of Schumpeterian quality.

(4) Consumer demand has shifted at the margin from manufactures to services, whose crawling productivity will keep down the rate of growth.

(5) The ratio of profits to national income has been declining for some time in leading industrial countries.

I cite these beliefs neither to endorse them nor to controvert them, but I note that every major downturn (1847, 1872, 1893, 1907, 1929, 1974) has brought forth predictions that the market economy will never again grow so rapidly, and that these predictions have always been wrong. This does not imply that such a prediction will *always* be wrong.

The second question is easier. Currently Western European countries import about a third of the manufactures that they consume. This proportion can continue to rise, but not indefinitely, and when it stops rising the rate of growth of their imports of manufactures will drop to or below the 5 per cent per annum rate which now appears to be their maximum 'natural' rate of industrial growth. Whether that date is set for the 1980s or the 1990s I do not know.

ENDNOTES

1. I have chosen 1953 because we have a detailed breakdown for that year in Paul Lamartine Yates's, *Fifty Years of Foreign Trade* (London: Allen & Unwin, 1959).
2. Germany is a difficult case. There are no customs values before 1872, and those from 1872 to 1879 have to be rejected (see Appendix I).
3. Actual exports fell less than recorded exports because of cotton exports from the South evading the Federal records.
4. See Chart 7.1 and accompanying text in my book, *Growth and Fluctuations* 1870–1913 (London: Allen & Unwin 1958).
5. If we use m_2 snd c_2 for imports of core countries from each other, this reduces to

$$\{(m_2 + c_2) + (1 + p)(m_1 + c_1)\}I + k - ps + h.$$

A further elaboration would recognise that the terms of trade for commodities and for services may diverge. In this paper we do not investigate the differences between the various compartments of m and c.

6. Walter G. Hoffmann, *British Industry* 1700–1950 (Oxford: Blackwell, 1955).
7. Op. cit., Appendix I.
8. Francois Crouzet, 'Un Indice annual de l'Industrie Francaise', *Annales, Economies, Société, Civilisations* (1970)
9. Walter G. Hoffmann, *Das Wachstum Der deutschen Wirtschaft seit der Mitte des* 19. *Jahrhunderts* (Berlin: Springer-Verlag, 1965).
10. Gallman's figures for manufacturing yield a growth rate of 6.0 per cent between 1874 and 1894, which are comparable dates. This is slightly higher than his rate for 1849 to 1859, but below his rate for 1839 to 1849 (9.9 per cent). Lebergott's data also show the labour force in manufacturing growing faster from 1870 to 1900 (at just under 3 per cent) than from 1850 to 1860; and it also shows explosive growth during the 1840s. Robert E. Gallman, 'Commodity Output 1839–1899', in Conference on Research in Income and Wealth, *Trends in The American Economy in the Nineteenth Century*, Studies in Income and Wealth, Vol. 24 (Princeton, 1960). Also Stanley Lebergott, *Manpower in Economic Growth* (New York: McGraw-Hill, 1964).

11. Paul Bairoch, *Commerce Extérieur et développement économique de l'Europe au XIXe siècle* (Paris: Mouton, 1976).
12. The result depends very much on what figures one uses for German production in the 1870s. Hoffman used the customs returns to get raw material usage, but the customs returns were defective, and the methods then used were abandoned in 1879. This problem is discussed in Appendix I, in the context of deriving a series for German exports. Its relevance to industrial production is discussed in Appendix II of *Growth and Fluctuations*, op. cit. If one uses more realistic figures for German production, then core industrial production grows at a constant secular rate from 1872 to 1913.
13. Gerhard Bondi, *Deutschlands Aussenhandel 1815–1870* (Berlin: Akadamie-Verlag, 1958) page 146.
14. This is the sum of net imports of cotton plus changes in stocks minus exports of yarn and cloth. Calculated from data in Robert Robson, *The Cotton Industry in Britain* (London: Macmillan, 1957). Robson incorporates the earlier work of Ellison.
15. Gustav Sundbarg, *Aperçus Statistiques Internationaux* (New York: Gordon & Breach, 1968). Our figure is mill absorption of cotton minus UK domestic consumption as defined above.
16. Actually 1829–31 to 1859–61 and 1871–73 to 1898–1900.
17. On economy in the use of raw materials see C. T. Saunders, 'The Consumption of Raw Materials in the UK, 1851–1950', *Journal of Royal Statistical Society*, cxv, Part III (1952).
18. W. A. Lewis, op. cit., page 175. Appendix IV yields a higher growth rate for primary products between 1883 and 1913, 3.36 in fact.
19. Incidentally, those who believe that the outburst of imperialism in the last quarter of the nineteenth century was mainly due to a search for raw materials must take into account that the propensity to import raw materials was lower in the second half of the nineteenth century than in the first half, but of course politics lags behind economic events.
20. Calculated from Alfred Maizels, *Industrial Growth and World Trade* (Cambridge: Cambridge University Press, 1969). But the ratio of trade in manufactures to industrial production grew over this period. See Appendix IV for further discussion of the situation before 1914.
21. Source: Appendix IV.
22. These terms of trade are calculated from data in Appendix IV.
23. *Growth and Fluctuations, 1890–1913*, op. cit., pp. 44 to 50.
24. If we were working with a model in which the dynamic force was the growth of primary production in the peripheral countries, this is the point where we would start: by studying changes in the relative growth rates of production of industry and agriculture and the effects of these changes on the terms of trade. We would arrange our data differently, but would end up considering the same phenomena—the propensities to import, price elasticty, capital export, etc. Choice of models depends to some extent on how wide a range of influence one attributes to changes in the terms of trade.
25. Relying on Arthur I. Bloomfield, *Patterns of Fluctuations in International Investment Before 1914* (Princeton Studies in International Finance No. 21, 1968). This is the sum of outflows from the UK, France and Germany,

minus inflow into the USA.

26. As reported by the Development Assistance Committee of OECD: *Development Cooperation* (annual).
27. Derived by aggregating item 77b d in the country pages of IMF's monthly *International Financial Statistics*. The definitions may not be watertight, since nearly half of this capital flow went to Germany, which reported borrowing \$4.6 billion in 1972 and \$4.5 billion in 1973.
28. W. A. Lewis, op. cit., pp. 167–8.

Note: The appendixes to this essay have been omitted in this volume.

PART THREE

DUAL ECONOMIES

[13]

Economic Development with Unlimited Supplies of Labour

1. This essay is written in the classical tradition, making the classical assumption, and asking the classical question. The classics, from Smith to Marx, all assumed, or argued, that an unlimited supply of labour was available at subsistence wages. They then enquired how production grows through time. They found the answer in capital accumulation, which they explained in terms of their analysis of the distribution of income. Classical systems thus determined simultaneously income distribution and income growth, with the relative prices of commodities as a minor bye-product.

Interest in prices and in income distribution survived into the neo-classical era, but labour ceased to be unlimited in supply, and the formal model of economic analysis was no longer expected to explain the expansion of the system through time. These changes of assumption and of interest served well enough in the European parts of the world, where labour was indeed limited in supply, and where for the next half century it looked as if economic expansion could indeed be assumed to be automatic. On the other hand over the greater part of Asia labour is unlimited in supply, and economic expansion certainly cannot be taken for granted. Asia's problems, however, attracted very few economists during the neo-classical era (even the Asian economists themselves absorbed the assumptions and preoccupations of European economics) and hardly any progress has been made for nearly a century with the kind of economics which would throw light upon the problems of countries with surplus populations.

When Keynes's *General Theory* appeared, it was thought at first that this was the book which would illuminate the problems of countries with surplus labour, since it assumed an unlimited supply of labour at the current price, and also, in its final pages, made a few remarks on secular economic expansion. Further reflection, however, revealed that Keynes's book assumed not only that labour is unlimited in supply, but also, and more fundamentally, that land and capital are unlimited in supply—more fundamentally both in the short run sense that once the monetary tap is turned the real limit to expansion is not physical resources but the limited supply of labour, and also in the long run sense that secular expansion is embarrassed not by a shortage but by a superfluity of saving. Given the Keynesian remedies the neo-classical system comes into its own again. Hence, from the point of view of countries with surplus labour, Keynesianism is only a footnote to neo-classicism—albeit a long, important and fascinating footnote. The student of such economies has therefore to work right back to the classical economists before he finds an analytical framework into which he can relevantly fit his problems.

The purpose of this essay is thus to see what can be made of the classical framework in solving problems of distribution, accumulation, and growth, first in a closed and then in an open economy. It is not primarily an essay in the history of economic doctrine, and will not therefore spend time on individual writers, enquiring what they meant, or assessing its validity or truth. Our purpose is rather to bring their framework up-to-date, in the light of modern knowledge, and to see how far it then helps us to understand the contemporary problems of large areas of the earth.

I. THE CLOSED ECONOMY.

2. We have to begin by elaborating the assumption of an unlimited supply of labour, and by establishing that it is a useful assumption. We are not arguing, let it be repeated, that this assumption should be made for all areas of the world. It is obviously not true of the United Kingdom, or of North West Europe. It is not true either of some of the countries usually now lumped together as under-developed ; for example there is an acute shortage of male labour in some parts of Africa and of Latin America. On the other hand it is obviously the relevant assumption for the economies of Egypt, of India, or of Jamaica. Our present task is not to supersede

neo-classical economics, but merely to elaborate a different framework for those countries which the neo-classical (and Keynesian) assumptions do not fit.

In the first place, an unlimited supply of labour may be said to exist in those countries where population is so large relatively to capital and natural resources, that there are large sectors of the economy where the marginal productivity of labour is negligible, zero, or even negative. Several writers have drawn attention to the existence of such "disguised" unemployment in the agricultural sector, demonstrating in each case that the family holding is so small that if some members of the family obtained other employment the remaining members could cultivate the holding just as well (of course they would have to work harder : the argument includes the proposition that they would be willing to work harder in these circumstances). The phenomenon is not, however, by any means confined to the countryside. Another large sector to which it applies is the whole range of casual jobs—the workers on the docks, the young men who rush forward asking to carry your bag as you appear, the jobbing gardener, and the like. These occupations usually have a multiple of the number they need, each of them earning very small sums from occasional employment ; frequently their number could be halved without reducing output in this sector. Petty retail trading is also exactly of this type ; it is enormously expanded in over-populated economies ; each trader makes only a few sales ; markets are crowded with stalls, and if the number of stalls were greatly reduced the consumers would be no whit worse off—they might even be better off, since retail margins might fall. Twenty years ago one could not write these sentences without having to stop and explain why in these circumstances, the casual labourers do not bid their earnings down to zero, or why the farmers' product is not similarly all eaten up in rent, but these propositions present no terrors to contemporary economists.

A little more explanation has to be given of those cases where the workers are not self-employed, but are working for wages, since it is harder to believe that employers will pay wages exceeding marginal productivity. The most important of these sectors is domestic service, which is usually even more inflated in over-populated countries than is petty trading (in Barbados 16 per cent. of the population is in domestic service). The reason is that in over-populated countries the code of ethical behaviour so shapes itself that it becomes good form for each person to offer as much employment as he can. The line between employees and dependents is very thinly drawn. Social prestige requires people to have servants, and the grand seigneur may have to keep a whole army of retainers who are really little more than a burden upon his purse. This is found not only in domestic service, but in every sector of employment. Most businesses in under-developed countries employ a large number of "messengers," whose contribution is almost negligible ; you see them sitting outside office doors, or hanging around in the courtyard. And even in the severest slump the agricultural or commercial employer is expected to keep his labour force somehow or other—it would be immoral to turn them out, for how would they eat, in countries where the only form of unemployment assistance is the charity of relatives? So it comes about that even in the sectors where people are working for wages, and above all the domestic sector, marginal productivity may be negligible or even zero.

Whether marginal productivity is zero or negligible is not, however, of fundamental importance to our analysis. The price of labour, in these economies, is a wage at the subsistence level (we define this later). The supply of labour is therefore "unlimited" so long as the supply of labour at this price exceeds the demand. In this situation, new industries can be created, or old industries expanded without limit at the existing wage ; or, to put it more exactly, shortage of labour is no limit to the creation of new sources of employment. If we cease to ask whether the marginal productivity of labour is negligible and ask instead only the question from what sectors would additional labour be available if new industries were created offering employment at subsistence wages, the answer becomes even more comprehensive. For we have then not only the farmers, the casuals, the petty traders and the retainers (domestic and commercial), but we have also three other classes from which to choose.

First of all, there are the wives and daughters of the household. The employment of women outside the household depends upon a great number of factors, religious and conventional, and is certainly not exclusively a matter of employment opportunities. There are, however, a number of countries where the current limit is for practical purposes only employment opportunities. This is true, for example, even inside the United Kingdom. The proportion of women gainfully employed in the U.K. varies enormously from one region to another according to employment opportunities for women. For example, in 1939 whereas there were 52 women gainfully employed for every 100 men in Lancashire, there were only 15 women gainfully employed for every 100 men in South Wales. Similarly in the Gold Coast, although there is an acute shortage of male labour, any industry which offered good employment to women would be besieged with applications. The transfer of women's work from the household to commercial employment is one of the most notable features of economic development. It is not by any means all gain, but the gain is substantial because most of the things which women otherwise do in the household can in fact be done much better or more cheaply outside, thanks to the large scale economies of specialisation, and also to the use of capital (grinding grain, fetching water from the river, making cloth, making clothes, cooking the midday meal, teaching children, nursing the sick, etc.). One of the surest ways of increasing the national income is therefore to create new sources of employment for women outside the home.

The second source of labour for expanding industries is the increase in the poulation resulting from the excess of births over deaths. This source is important in any dynamic analysis of how capital accumulation can occur, and employment can increase, without any increase in real wages. It was therefore a cornerstone of Ricardo's system. Strictly speaking, population increase is not relevant either to the classical analysis, or to the analysis which follows in this article, unless it can be shown that the increase of population is caused by economic development and would not otherwise be so large. The proof of this proposition was supplied to the classical economists by the Malthusian law of population. There is already an enormous literature of the genus : "What Malthus *Really* Meant," into which we need not enter. Modern population theory has advanced a little by analysing separately the effects of economic development upon the birth rate, and its effects on the death rate. Of the former, we know little. There is no evidence that the birth rate ever rises with economic development. In Western Europe it has fallen during the last eighty years. We are not quite sure why ; we suspect that it was for reasons associated with development, and we hope that the same thing may happen in the rest of the world as development spreads. Of the death rate we are more certain. It comes down with development from around 40 to around 12 per thousand ; in the first stage because better communications and trade eliminate death from local famines ; in the second stage because better public health facilities banish the great epidemic diseases of plague, smallpox, cholera, malaria, yellow fever (and eventually tuberculosis) ; and in the third stage because widespread facilities for treating the sick snatch from the jaws of death many who would otherwise perish in infancy or in their prime. Because the effect of development on the death rate is so swift and certain, while its effect on the birth rate is unsure and retarded, we can say for certain that the immediate effect of economic development is to cause the population to grow ; after some decades it begins to grow (we hope) less rapidly. Hence in any society where the death rate is around 40 per thousand, the effect of economic development will be to generate an increase in the supply of labour.

Marx offered a third source of labour to add to the reserve army, namely the unemployment generated by increasing efficiency. Ricardo had admitted that the creation of machinery could reduce employment. Marx seized upon the argument, and in effect generalised it, for into the pit of unemployment he threw not only those displaced by machinery, but also the self-employed and petty capitalists who could not compete with larger capitalists of increasing size, enjoying the benefits of the economies of scale. Nowadays we reject this argument on empirical grounds. It is clear that the effect of capital accumulation in the past has been to reduce the size of the reserve army, and not to increase it, so we have lost interest in arguments about what is "theoretically" possible.

When we take account of all the sources we have now listed—the farmers, the casuals, the petty traders, the retainers (domestic and commercial), women in the household, and population growth—it is clear enough that there can be in an over-populated economy an enormous expansion of new industries or new employment opportunities without any shortage of unskilled labour becoming apparent in the labour market. From the point of view of the effect of economic development on wages, the supply of labour is practically unlimited.

This applies only to unskilled labour. There may at any time be a shortage of skilled workers of any grade—ranging from masons, electricians or welders to engineers, biologists or administrators. Skilled labour may be the bottleneck in expansion, just like capital or land. Skilled labour, however, is only what Marshall might have called a "quasi-bottleneck," if he had not had so nice a sense of elegant language. For it is only a very temporary bottleneck, in the sense that if the capital is available for development, the capitalists or their government will soon provide the facilities for training more skilled people. The real bottlenecks to expansion are therefore capital and natural resources, and we can proceed on the assumption that so long as these are available the necessary skills will be provided as well, though perhaps with some time lag.

3. If unlimited labour is available, while capital is scarce, we know from the Law of Variable Proportions that the capital should not be spread thinly over all the labour. Only so much labour should be used with capital as will reduce the marginal productivity of labour to zero. In practice, however, labour is not available at a zero wage.

Capital will therefore be applied only up to the point where the marginal productivity of labour equals the current wage. This is illustrated in Figure I. The horizontal axis measures the quantity of labour, and the vertical axis its marginal product. There is a fixed amount of capital. *OW* is the current wage. If the marginal product of labour were zero outside the capitalist sector, *OR* ought to be employed. But it will pay to employ only *OM* in the capitalist sector. *WNP* is the capitalists' surplus. *OWPM* goes in wages to workers in the capitalist sector, while workers outside this sector (*i.e.* beyond *M*) earn what they can in the subsistence sector of the economy.

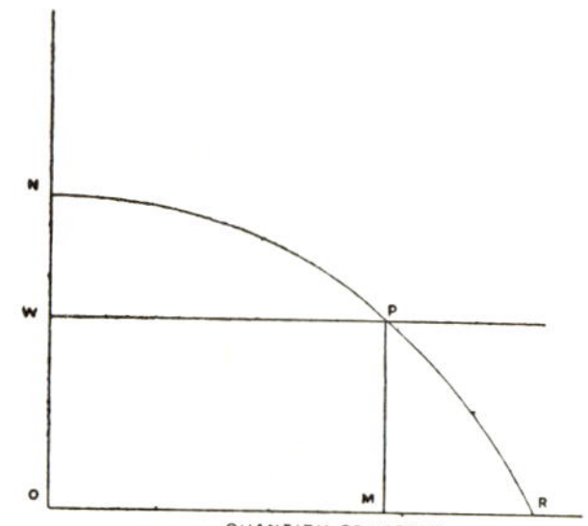

FIGURE I

The analysis requires further elaboration. In the first place, after what we have said earlier on about some employers in these economies keeping retainers, it may seem strange to be arguing now that labour will be employed up to the point where the wage equals the marginal productivity. Nevertheless, this is probably the right assumption to make when we are set upon analysing the expansion of the capitalist sector of the economy. For the type of capitalist who brings about economic expansion is not the same as the type of employer who treats his employees like retainers. He is more commercially minded, and more conscious of efficiency, cost and profitability. Hence, if our interest is in an expanding capitalist sector, the assumption of profit maximisation is probably a fair approximation to the truth.

Next, we note the use of the terms "capitalist" sector and "subsistence" sector. The capitalist sector is that part of the economy which uses reproducible capital, and pays capitalists for the use thereof. (This coincides with Smith's definition of the productive workers, who are those who work with capital and whose product can therefore be sold at a price above their wages). We can think, if we like, of capitalists hiring out their capital to peasants ; in which case, there being by definition an unlimited number of peasants, only some will get capital, and these will have to pay for its use a price which leaves them only subsistence earnings. More usually, however, the use of capital is controlled by capitalists, who hire the services of labour. The classical analysis was therefore conducted on the assumption that capital was used for hiring people. It does not make any difference to the argument, and for convenience we will follow this usage. The subsistence sector is by difference all that part of the economy which is not using reproducible capital. Output per head is lower in this sector than in the capitalist sector, because it is not fructified by capital (this is why it was called "unproductive" ; the distinction between productive and unproductive had nothing to do with whether the work yielded utility, as some neo-classicists have scornfully but erroneously asserted). As more capital becomes available more workers can be drawn into the capitalist from the subsistence sector, and their output per head rises as they move from the one sector to the other.

Thirdly we take account of the fact that the capitalist sector, like the subsistence sector, can also be subdivided. What we have is not one island of expanding capitalist employment, surrounded by a vast sea of subsistence workers, but rather a number of such tiny islands. This is very typical of countries in their early stages of development. We find a few industries highly capitalised, such as mining or electric power, side by side with the most primitive techniques ; a few high class shops, surrounded by masses of old style traders ; a few highly capitalised plantations, surrounded by a sea of peasants. But we find the same contrasts also outside their economic life. There are one or two modern towns, with the finest architecture, water supplies, communications and the like, into which people drift from other towns and villages which might almost belong to another planet. There is the same contrast even between people ; between the few highly westernised, trousered, natives, educated in western universities, speaking western languages, and glorying in Beethoven, Mill, Marx or Einstein, and the great mass of their countrymen who live in quite other worlds.

Capital and new ideas are not thinly diffused throughout the economy ; they are highly concentrated at a number of points, from which they spread outwards.

Though the capitalised sector can be subdivided into islands, it remains a single sector because of the effect of competition in tending to equalise the earnings on capital. The competitive principle does not demand that the same amount of capital per person be employed on each "island," or that average profit per unit of capital be the same, but only that the marginal profit be the same. Thus, even if marginal profits were the same all round, islands which yield diminishing returns may be more profitable than others, the earliest capitalists having cornered the vantage points. But in any case marginal profits are not the same all round. In backward economies knowledge is one of the scarcest goods. Capitalists have experience of certain types of investment, say of trading or plantation agriculture, and not of other types, say of manufacturing, and they stick to what they know. So the economy is frequently lopsided in the sense that there is excessive investment in some parts and under-investment in others. Also, financial institutions are more highly developed for some purposes than for others—capital can be got cheaply for trade, but not for house building or for peasant agriculture, for instance. Even in a very highly developed economy the tendency for capital to flow evenly through the economy is very weak ; in a backward economy it hardly exists. Inevitably what one gets are very heavily developed patches of the economy, surrounded by economic darkness.

Next we must say something about the wage level. The wage which the expanding capitalist sector has to pay is determined by what people can earn outside that sector. The classical economists used to think of the wage as being determined by what is required for subsistence consumption, and this may be the right solution in some cases. However, in economies where the majority of the people are peasant farmers, working on their own land, we have a more objective index, for the minimum at which labour can be had is now set by the average product of the farmer ; men will not leave the family farm to seek employment if the wage is worth less than they would be able to consume if they remained at home. This objective standard, alas, disappears again if the farmers have to pay rent, for their net earnings will then depend upon the amount of rent they have to pay, and in overpopulated countries the rent will probably be adjusted so as to leave them just enough for a conventional level of subsistence. It is not, however, of great importance to the argument whether earnings in the subsistence sector are determined objectively by the level of peasant productivity, or subjectively in terms of a conventional standard of living. Whatever the mechanism, the result is an unlimited supply of labour for which this is the minimum level of earnings.

The fact that the wage level in the capitalist sector depends upon earnings in the subsistence sector is sometimes of immense political importance, since its effect is that capitalists have a direct interest in holding down the productivity of the subsistence workers. Thus, the owners of plantations have no interest in seeing knowledge of new techniques or new seeds conveyed to the peasants, and if they are influential in the government, they will not be found using their influence to expand the facilities for agricultural extension. They will not support proposals for land settlement, and are often instead to be found engaged in turning the peasants off their lands. (Cf. Marx on "Primary Accumulation"). This is one of the worst features of imperialism, for instance. The imperialists invest capital and hire workers; it is to their advantage to keep wages low, and even in those cases where they do not actually go out of their way to impoverish the subsistence economy, they will at least very seldom be found doing anything to make it more productive. In actual fact the record of every imperial power in Africa in modern times is one of impoverishing the subsistence economy, either by taking away the people's land, or by demanding forced labour in the capitalist sector, or by imposing taxes to drive people to work for capitalist employers. Compared with what they have spent on providing facilities for European agriculture or mining, their expenditure on the improvement of African agriculture has been negligible. The failure of imperialism to raise living standards is not wholly to be attributed to self interest, but there are many places where it can be traced directly to the effects of having imperial capital invested in agriculture or in mining.

Earnings in the subsistence sector set a floor to wages in the capitalist sector, but in practice wages have to be higher than this, and there is usually a gap of 30 per cent. or more between capitalist wages and subsistence earnings. This gap may be explained in several ways. Part of the difference is illusory, because of the higher cost of living in the capitalist sector. This may be due to the capitalist sector being concentrated in congested towns, so that rents and transport costs are higher. All the same, there is also usually a substantial difference in real wages. This may be required because of the psychological cost of transferring from the easy going way of life of the subsistence sector to the more regimented and urbanised environment of the capitalist sector. Or it may be a recognition of the fact that even the unskilled worker is of more use to the capitalist sector after he has been there for some time than is the raw recruit from the country. Or it may itself represent a difference in conventional standards, workers in the capitalist sector acquiring tastes and a social prestige which have conventionally to be recognised by higher real wages. That this last may be the explanation is suggested by cases where the capitalist workers organise themselves into trade unions and strive to protect or increase their differential. But the differential exists even where there are no unions.

The effect of this gap is shown diagrammatically in Figure II, which is drawn on the same basis as Figure I. *OS* now represents subsistence earnings, and *OW* the capitalist wage (real not money). To borrow an analogy from the sea, the frontier of competition between capitalist and subsistence labour now appears not as a beach but as a cliff.

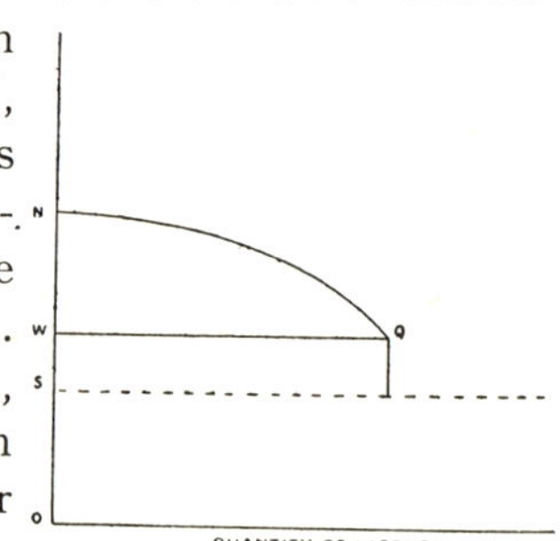

FIGURE II.

This phenomenon of a gap between the earnings of competing suppliers is found even in the most advanced economies. Much of the difference between the earnings of different classes of the population (grades of skill, of education, of responsibility or of prestige) can be described only in these terms. Neither is the phenomenon confined to labour. We know of course that two firms in a competitive market need not have the same average profits if one has some superiority to the other ; we reflect this difference in rents, and ask only that marginal rates of profit should be the same. We know also that marginal rates will not be the same if ignorance prevails—this point we have mentioned earlier. What is often puzzling in a competitive industry is to find a difference in marginal profits, or marginal costs, without ignorance, and yet without the more efficient firm driving its rivals out of business. It is as if the more efficient says : "I could compete with you, but I won't," which is also what subsistence labour says when it does not transfer to capitalist employment unless real wages are substantially higher. The more efficient firm, instead of competing wherever its real costs are marginally less than its rivals, establishes for itself superior standards of remuneration. It pays its workers more and lavishes welfare services, scholarships and pensions upon them. It demands a higher rate on its marginal investments ; where its competitors would be satisfied with 10%, it demands 20%, to keep up its average record. It goes in for prestige expenditure, contributing to hospitals, universities, flood relief and such. Its highest executives spend their time sitting on public committees, and have to have deputies to do their work. When all this is taken into account it is not at all surprising to find a competitive equilibrium in which high cost firms survive easily side by side with firms of much greater efficiency.

4. So far we have merely been setting the stage. Now the play begins. For we can now begin to trace the process of economic expansion.

The key to the process is the use which is made of the capitalist surplus. In so far as this is reinvested in creating new capital, the capitalist sector expands, taking more people into capitalist employment out of the subsistence sector. The surplus is then larger still, capital formation is still greater, and so the process continues until the labour surplus disappears.

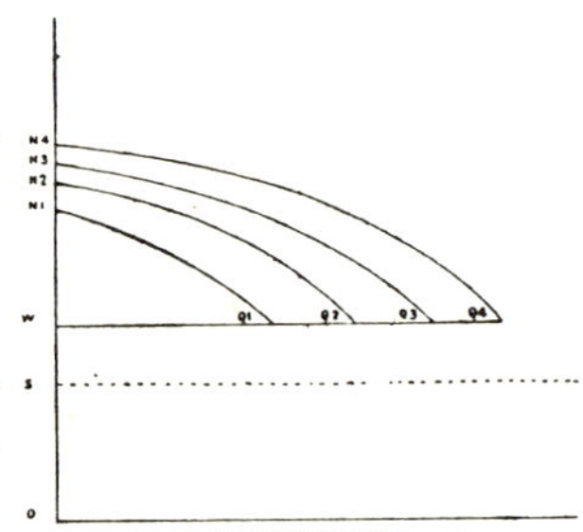

QUANTITY OF LABOUR
FIGURE III

OS is as before average subsistence earnings, and *OW* the capitalist wage. WN_1Q_1 represents the surplus in the initial stage. Since some of this is reinvested, the amount of fixed capital increases. Hence the schedule of the marginal productivity of labour is now raised throughout, to the level of N_2Q_2. Both the surplus and capitalist employment are now larger. Further reinvestment raises the schedule of the marginal productivity of labour to N_3Q_3. And the process continues so long as there is surplus labour.

Various comments are needed in elaboration. First, as to the relationship between capital, technical progress, and productivity. In theory it should be possible to distinguish between the growth of capital and the growth of technical knowledge, but in practice it is neither possible nor necessary for this analysis. As a matter of statistical analysis, differentiating the effects of capital and of knowledge in any industry is straightforward if the product is homogeneous through time, if the physical inputs are also unchanged (in kind) and if the relative prices of the inputs have remained constant. But when we try to do it for any industry in practice we usually find that the product has changed, the inputs have changed and relative prices have changed, so that we get any number of indices of technical progress from the same data, according to the assumptions and the type of index number which we use. In any case, for the purpose of this analysis it is unnecessary to distinguish between capital formation and the growth of knowledge within the capitalist sector. Growth of technical knowledge outside the capitalist sector would be fundamentally important, since it would raise the level of wages, and so reduce the capitalist surplus. But inside the capitalist sector knowledge and capital work in the same direction, to raise the surplus and to increase employment. They also work together. The application of new technical knowledge usually requires new investment, and whether the new knowledge is capital-saving (and thus equivalent to an increase in capital) or labour-saving (and thus equivalent to an increase in the marginal productivity of labour) makes no difference to our diagram. Capital and technical knowledge also work together in the sense that in economies where techniques are stagnant savings are not so readily applied to increasing productive capital ; in such economies it is more usual to use savings for building pyramids, churches, and other such durable consumer goods. Accordingly, in this analysis the growth of productive capital and the growth of technical knowledge are treated as a single phenomenon (just as we earlier decided that we could treat the growth of the supply of skilled labour and the growth of capital as a single phenomenon in long run analysis).

Next we must consider more closely the capitalist surplus. Malthus wanted to know what the capitalists would do with this ever-growing surplus ; surely this would be an embarrassing glut of commodities ? Ricardo replied that there would be no glut ; what the capitalists did not consume themselves, they would use for paying the wages of workers to create more fixed capital (this is a free interpretation, since the classical economists associated the expansion of employment with an increase of circulating rather than of fixed capital). This new fixed capital would then in the next stage make possible the employment of more people in the capitalist sector. Malthus persisted ; why should the capitalists produce more capital to produce a larger surplus which could only be used for producing still more capital and so *ad infinitum* ? To this Marx supplied one answer : capitalists have a passion for accumulating capital. Ricardo supplied another : if they don't want to accumulate, they will consume instead of saving ; provided there is no propensity to hoard, there will be no glut. Employment in the next stage will not be as big as it would have been if they had created more fixed capital and so brought more workers into the capitalist sector, but so long as there is no hoarding it makes no difference to the current level of employment whether capitalists decide to consume or to save. Malthus then raised another question; suppose that the capitalists do save and invest without hoarding, surely the fact that capital is growing more rapidly than consumption must so lower the rate of profit on capital that there comes a point when they decide that it is not worth while to invest? This, Ricardo replied, is impossible; since the supply of labour is unlimited, you can always find employment for any amount of capital. This is absolutely correct, for his model; in the neo-classical model capital grows faster than labour, and so one has to ask whether the rate of profit will not fall, but in the classical model the unlimited supply of labour means that the capital/labour ratio, and therefore the rate of surplus, can be held constant for any quantity of capital (*i.e.*, unlimited "widening" is possible). The only fly in the ointment is that there may develop a shortage of natural resources, so that though the capitalists get any amount of labour at a constant wage, they have to pay ever rising rents to landlords. This was what worried Ricardo; it was important to him to distinguish that part of the surplus which goes to landlords from that part which goes to capitalists, since he believed that economic development inevitably increases the relative scarcity of land. We are not so certain of this as he was. Certainly development increases the rent of urban sites fantastically, but its effect on rural rents depends on the rate of technical progress in agriculture, which Malthus and Ricardo both gravely under-estimated. If we assume technical progress in agriculture, no hoarding, and unlimited labour at a constant wage, the rate of profit on capital cannot fall. On the contrary it must increase, since all the benefit of technical progress in the capitalist sector accrues to the capitalists.

Marx's interest in the surplus was ethical as well as scientific. He regarded it as robbery of the workers. His descendants are less certain of this. The surplus, after all, is only partly consumed; the other part is used for capital formation. As for the part which is consumed, some of it is a genuine payment for service rendered—for managerial or entrepreneurial services, as well as for the services of public administrators, whether these are paid salaries out of taxes, or whether they live off their rents or *rentes* while performing unpaid public duties as magistrates, lord-lieutenants, or the like. Even in the U.S.S.R. all these functionaries are paid out of the surplus, and handsomely paid too. It is arguable that these services are over-paid; this is why we have progressive taxation, and it is also one of the more dubious arguments for nationalisation (more dubious because the functionaries of public corporations have to be paid the market rate if the economy is only partially nationalised). But it is not arguable that all this part of the surplus (*i.e.* the part consumed) morally belongs to the workers, in any sense. As for the part which is used for capital formation, the experience of the U.S.S.R. is that this is increased, and not reduced, by transforming the ownership of capital. Expropriation deprives the capitalists of control over this part of the surplus, and of the right to consume this part at some later date, but it does nothing whatever to transfer this part of the surplus to the workers. Marx's emotional approach was a natural reaction to the classical writers, who sometimes in unguarded moments wrote as if the capitalist surplus and its increase were all that counted in the national income (c.f. Ricardo, who called it "the net revenue" of production). All this, however, is by the way; for our present interest is not in ethical questions, but in how the model works.

5. The central problem in the theory of economic development is to understand the process by which a community which was previously saving and investing 4 or 5 per cent. of its national income or less, converts itself into an economy where voluntary saving is running at about 12 to 15 per cent. of national income or more. This is the central problem because the central fact of economic development is rapid capital accumulation (including knowledge and skills with capital). We cannot explain any "industrial" revolution (as the economic historians pretend to do) until we can explain why saving increased relatively to national income.

It is possible that the explanation is simply that some psychological change occurs which causes people to be more thrifty. This, however is not a plausible explanation. We are interested not in the people in general, but only say in the 10 per cent. of them with the largest incomes, who in countries with surplus labour receive up to 40 per cent. of the national income (nearer 30 per cent. in more developed countries). The remaining 90 per cent. of the people never manage to save a significant fraction of their incomes. The important question is why does the top 10 per cent. save more ? The reason may be because they decide to consume less, but this reason does not square with the facts. There is no evidence of a fall in personal consumption by the top 10 per cent. at a time when industrial revolutions are occurring. It is also possible that, though they do not save any more, the top 10 per cent. spend less of their income on durable consumer goods (tombs, country houses, temples) and more on productive capital. Certainly, if one compares different civilisations this is a striking difference in the disposition of income. Civilisations in which there is a rapid growth of technical knowledge or expansion of other opportunities present more profitable outlets for investment than do technologically stagnant civilisations, and tempt capital into productive channels rather than into the building of monuments. But if one takes a country only over the course of the hundred years during which it undergoes a revolution in the rate of capital formation, there is no noticeable change in this regard. Certainly, judging by the novels, the top 10 per cent. in England were not spending noticeably less on durable consumer goods in 1800 than they were in 1700.

Much the most plausible explanation is that people save more because they have more to save. This is not to say merely that the national income per head is larger, since there is no clear evidence that the proportion of the national income saved increases with national income per head—at any rate our fragmentary evidence for the United Kingdom and for the United States suggests that this is not so. The explanation is much more likely to be that saving increases relatively to the national income because the incomes of the savers increase relatively to the national income. The central fact of economic development is that the distribution of incomes is altered in favour of the saving class.

Practically all saving is done by people who receive profits or rents. Workers' savings are very small. The middle-classes save a little, but in practically every community the savings of the middle-classes out of their salaries are of little consequence for productive investment. Most members of the middle-class are engaged in the perpetual struggle to keep up with the Jones's; if they manage to save enough to buy the house in which they live, they are doing well. They may save to educate their children, or to subsist in their old age, but this saving is virtually offset by the savings being used up for the same purposes. Insurance is the middle-class's favourite form of saving in modern societies, yet in the U.K., where the habit is extremely well developed, the annual net increase in insurance funds from all classes, rich, middle, and poor is less than 1½ per cent. of the national income. It is doubtful if the wage and salary classes ever anywhere save as much as 3 per cent. of the national income, net (possible exception: Japan). If we are interested in savings, we must concentrate attention upon profits and rents.

For our purpose it does not matter whether profits are distributed or undistributed; the major source of savings is profits, and if we find that savings are increasing as a proportion of the national income, we may take it for granted that this is because the share of profits in the national income is increasing. (As a refinement, for highly taxed communities, we should say profits net of taxes upon profits, whether personal income or corporate taxes). Our problem then becomes what are the circumstances in which the share of profits in the national income increases?

The modified classical model which we are using here has the virtue of answering the question. In the beginning, the national income consists almost entirely of subsistence income. Abstracting from population growth and assuming that the marginal product of labour is zero, this subsistence income remains constant throughout the expansion, since by definition labour can be yielded up to the expanding capitalist sector without reducing subsistence output. The process therefore increases the capitalist surplus and the income of capitalist employees, taken together, as a proportion of the national income. It is possible to imagine conditions in which the surplus nevertheless does not increase relatively to national income. This requires that capitalist employment should expand relatively much faster than the surplus, so that within the capitalist sector gross margins or profit plus rent are falling sharply relatively to wages. We know that this does not happen. Even if gross margins were constant, profits in our model would be increasing relatively to national income. But gross margins are not likely to be constant in our model, which assumes that practically the whole benefit of capital accumulation and of technical progress goes into the surplus ; because real wages are constant, all that the workers get out of the expansion is that more of them are employed at a wage above the subsistence earnings. The model says, in effect, that if unlimited supplies of labour are available at a constant real wage, and if any part of profits is reinvested in productive capacity, profits will grow continuously relatively to the national income, and capital formation will also grow relatively to the national income.

The model also covers the case of a technical revolution. Some historians have suggested that the capital for the British Industrial Revolution came out of profits made possible by a spate of inventions occurring together. This is extremely hard to fit into the neo-classical model, since it involves the assumption that these inventions raised the marginal productivity of capital more than they raised the marginal productivity of labour, a proposition which it is hard to establish in any economy where labour is scarce. (If we do not make this assumption, other incomes rise just as fast as profits, and investment does not increase relatively to national income). On the other hand the suggestion fits beautifully into the modified classical model, since in this model practically the whole benefit of inventions goes into the surplus, and becomes available for further capital accumulation.

This model also helps us to face squarely the nature of the economic problem of backward countries. If we ask "why do they save so little, the truthful answer is not "because they are so poor," as we might be tempted to conclude from the path-breaking and praiseworthy correlations of Mr. Colin Clark. The truthful answer is "because their capitalist sector is so small" (remembering that "capitalist" here does not mean private capitalist, but would apply equally to state capitalist). If they had a larger capitalist sector, profits would be a greater part of their national income, and saving and investment would also be relatively larger. (The state capitalist can accumulate capital even faster than the private capitalist, since he can use for the purpose not only the profits of the capitalist sector, but also what he can force or tax out of the subsistence sector).

Another point which we must note is that though the increase of the capitalist sector involves an increase in the inequality of incomes, as between capitalists and the rest, mere inequality of income is not enough to ensure a high level of saving. In point of fact the inequality of income is *greater* in over-populated under-developed countries than it is in advanced industrial nations, for the simple reason that agricultural rents are so high in the former. Eighteenth century British economists took it for granted that the landlord class is given to prodigal consumption rather than to productive investment, and this is certainly true of landlords in under-developed countries. Hence, given two countries of equal incomes, in which distribution is more unequal in one than in the other, savings may be greater where distribution is more equal if profits are higher relatively to rents. It is the inequality which goes with profits that favours capital formation, and not the inequality which goes with rents. Correspondingly, it is very hard to argue that these countries cannot afford to save more, when 40 per cent. or so of the national income is going to the top 10 per cent., and so much of rent incomes is squandered.

Behind this analysis also lies the sociological problem of the emergence of a capitalist class, that is to say of a group of men who think in terms of investing capital productively. The dominant classes in backward economies—landlords, traders moneylenders, priests, soldiers, princes—do not normally think in these terms. What causes a society to grow a capitalist class is a very difficult question, to which probably, there is no general answer. Most countries seem to begin by importing their capitalists from abroad ; and in these days many (*e.g.* U.S.S.R., India) are growing a class of state capitalists who, for political reasons of one sort or another, are determined to create capital rapidly on public account. As for indigenous private capitalists, their emergence is probably bound up with the emergence of new opportunities, especially something that widens the market, associated with some new technique which greatly increases the productivity of labour if labour and capital are used together. Once a capitalist sector has emerged, it is only a matter of time before it becomes sizeable. If very little technical progress is occurring, the surplus will grow only slowly. But if for one reason or another the opportunities for using capital productivity increase rapidly, the surplus will also grow rapidly, and the capitalist class with it.

6. In our model so far capital is created only out of profits earned. In the real world, however, capitalists also create capital as a result of a net increase in the supply of money—especially bank credit. We have now also to take account of this.

In the neo-classical model capital can be created only by withdrawing resources from producing consumer goods. In our model, however, there is surplus labour, and if (as we shall assume) its marginal productivity is zero, and if, also, capital can be created by labour without withdrawing scarce land and capital from other uses, then capital can be created without reducing the output of consumer goods. This second proviso is important, since if we need capital or land to make capital the results in our model are the same as the results in the neo-classical model, despite the fact that there is surplus labour. However, in practice the proviso is often fulfilled. Food cannot be grown without land, but roads, viaducts, irrigation channels and buildings can be created by human labour with hardly any capital to speak of—witness the Pyramids, or the marvellous railway tunnels built in the mid-nineteenth century almost with bare hands. Even in modern industrial countries constructional activity, which lends itself to hand labour, is as much as 50 or 60 per cent. of gross fixed investment, so it is not difficult to think of labour creating capital without using any but the simplest tools. The classical economists were not wrong in thinking of lack of circulating capital as being a more serious obstacle to expansion in their world than lack of fixed capital. In the analysis which follows in this section we assume that surplus labour cannot be used to make consumer goods without using up more land or capital, but can be used to make capital goods without using any scarce factors.

If a community is short of capital, and has idle resources which can be set to creating capital, it seems very desirable on the face of the matter that this should be done, even if it means creating extra money to finance the extra employment. There is no loss of other output while the new capital is being made, and when it comes into use it will raise output and employment in just the same way as would capital financed not by credit creation but out of profits. The difference between profit-financed and credit-financed capital is not in the ultimate effects on output, but in the immediate effects on prices and on the distribution of income.

Before we come to the effects on prices, however, we should pause a moment to notice what happens to the output of consumer goods in this model and the others while credit-financed capital is being created, but before it begins to be used. In the neo-classical model an increase in capital formation has to be accompanied by a corresponding fall in the output of consumer goods, since scarce resources can do one or the other. In the Keynesian model an increase in capital formation also increases the output of consumer goods, and if the multiplier exceeds 2, the output of consumer goods increases even more than capital formation. In our model capital formation goes up, but the output of consumer goods is not immediately affected. This is one of those crucial cases where it is important to be certain that one is using the right model when it comes to giving advice on economic policy.

In our model, if surplus labour is put to capital formation and paid out of new money, prices rise, because the stream of money purchases is swollen while the output of consumer goods is for the time being constant. What is happening is that the fixed amount of consumer goods is being redistributed, towards the workers newly employed, away from the rest of the community (this is where the lack of circulating capital comes into the picture). This process is not "forced saving" in the useful sense of that term. In the neo-classical model the output of consumer goods is reduced, forcing the community as a whole to save. In our model, however, consumer goods output is not at any time reduced ; there is a forced redistribution of consumption, but not forced saving. And, of course, as soon as the capital goods begin to yield output, consumption begins to rise.

This inflationary process does not go on forever ; it comes to an end when voluntary savings increase to a level where they are equal to the inflated level of investment. Since savings are a function of profits, this means that the inflation continues until profits increase so much relatively to the national income that capitalists can now finance the higher rate of investment out of their profits without any further recourse to monetary expansion. Essentially equilibrium is secured by raising the ratio of profits to the national income. The equilibrator need not however be profits ; it might equally be government receipts, if there is a structure of taxes such that the ratio of government receipts to the national income rises automatically as the national income rises. This seems to be just about what happened in the U.S.S.R. In the crucial years when the economy was being transformed from a 5 per cent. to a (probably) 20 per cent. net saver, there was a tremendous inflation of prices (apparently prices rose about 700 per cent. in a decade), but the inflationary profits largely went to the government in the form of turnover tax, and by the end of the decade a new equilibrium was in sight.

It is not, however, always a simple matter to raise profits relatively to national income simply by turning on the monetary tap. The simplest and most extreme model of an inflation would be to assume that when the capitalists finance capital formation by creating credit, the money all comes back to them in the very next round in the form of an increase in their profits. In such a model profits, voluntary savings and capital formation can be raised to any desired level in a very short time, with only a small increase in prices. Something like this may well apply in the U.S.S.R. In real terms, however, this implies that there has been a fall in the share of the national income received by other people, including a fall in their real consumption, since they have had to release consumer goods for the previously unemployed who are now engaged in capital formation. It may be the farmers who are worse off, this showing itself in the prices of manufactures rising relatively to farm prices. Or it may be the workers in the capitalist sector who are worse off, because farm prices and the prices of manufactures rise faster than their wages. Or the blow may be falling upon salaried workers, pensioners, landlords or creditors. Now in the real world none of these classes will take this lying down. In the U.S.S.R., where the intention was that the capital formation should be at the expense of the farmers, it led in the end to organised violence on both sides. In our model it is hard to get away with it at the expense of the workers, since the wage in the capitalist sector must stand at a certain minimum level above subsistence earnings if labour is to be available. Generally, what happens as prices rise is that new contracts have to be made to take account of rising price levels. Some classes get caught, but only temporarily.

Now, if one pursued this argument logically, it would lead to the conclusion that equilibrium could never be reached—at any rate, so long as the banking system is content to supply all "legitimate" demands for money. If none of the other classes can be soaked, it seems impossible for profits to rise relatively to the national income for more than a temporary space, and it therefore seems impossible to reach an equilibrium level of savings equal to the new level of investment. The inflation, once begun goes on forever. This, however, is not possible for another reason, namely the fact that the real national income is not fixed, but rising, as a result of the capital formation. Therefore all that is required is that capitalists' real incomes rise faster than other people's. Beyond the first year or two, when the additional consumer goods begin to appear, it is not necessary for any class to reduce its consumption. By the time the process of recontracting has begun, output has also begun to rise, and it is therefore possible to reach a *modus vivendi*.

We can give an exact description of this equilibrium in our modified classical model. In this model the average subsistence real income is given, and so also therefore is the real wage in the capitalist sector. It is not possible, by inflation or otherwise, to reach a new equilibrium in which the capitalist surplus has increased at the expense of either of these. If, therefore, the capitalists begin to finance capital formation out of credit, they lower the real incomes of the others only temporarily. Wages would then be chasing prices continuously but for the fact that, since output is growing all the time, profits are growing all the time. Hence the part of the investment which is financed out of credit is diminishing all the time, until equilibrium is reached. For example, suppose that an investment of £100 a year yields £20 a year profit, of which £10 a year is saved. Then, if capitalists invest an extra £100 a year, all of which in the first year is financed out of credit, by the eleventh year profits will be £200 a year greater, savings will be £100 a year greater and there will be no further monetary pressure on prices. All that will remain from the episode is that there will be £1,000 more useful productive capital at work than there would have if the credit creation had not taken place.

Thus we have two simple models marking the extreme cases. In the first, all the credit created comes back to the capitalists at once as profits (or to the state capitalist as taxes). Equilibrium is then reached easily, with the capitalists gaining at the expense of all others. In the other model the capitalists can only gain temporarily; equilibrium then takes much longer to reach, but it is reached eventually. In the first case we need only an expansion of money income ; but in the second case it is the expansion of real income which eventually brings the capitalists the required proportion of the national income.

The fact that capital formation increases real output must also be borne in mind in the analysis of the effects of credit creation upon prices. The inflations which loom most in our minds are those which occur in war-time, when resources are being withdrawn from producing consumer goods. If the supply of money is increasing while the output of goods is falling, anything can happen to prices. Inflation for the purpose of capital formation, however, is a very different kettle of fish. For it results in increasing consumer goods output, and this results in falling prices if the quantity of money is held constant.

Perhaps it may be as well to illustrate a simple case. Suppose that £100 is invested every year, in the first instance by creating credit, and that each investment yields £30 a year in its second year and after. Suppose that it costs nothing to reap the yield ; the price of £30 charged for the product being pure rent derived from its scarcity (investment in an irrigation works is a nearly perfect illustration). Then, if we use the Keynesian formula for a demand inflation, and assume the multiplier to be 2, money income will rise to an equilibrium level of + £200 a year. Output, however, will begin to increase by + £30 a year from the second year onward. By the eighth year output will have increased by + £210, while money income will have increased only by slightly less than + £200. Thereafter prices will be below the initial level, and will fall continuously. The alleged precision of this analysis is of course subject to all the usual objections against applying multiplier analysis to inflationary conditions, namely the instability of the propensity to consume, the effect of secondary investment, and the dangers of cost inflation. But though the precision is spurious, the result is nevertheless real. Inflation for purposes of capital formation is self-destructive. Prices begin to rise, but are sooner or later overtaken by rising output, and may, in the last state end up lower than they were at the beginning.

We may now sum up this section. Capital formation is financed not only out of profits but also out of an expansion of credit. This speeds up the growth of capital, and the growth of real income. It also results in some redistribution of the national income, either temporarily or permanently, according to the assumptions one makes—in the model we are using, the redistribution is only temporary. It also prevents prices from falling, as they otherwise would (if money is constant and output rising), and it may drive prices up substantially if (as in our model) the distribution of income cannot be altered permanently by monetary measures, since prices will then continue to rise until real output has risen enough to effect the required redistribution. Thereafter prices fall further, since inflation raises prices while capital is being created, but the increased output which then results brings them down again.

One point remains. We have seen that if new money is used to finance capital formation the rise of prices eventually peters out, as savings grow into equilibrium with investment ; and reverses itself, as the output of consumer goods begins to pour out. The new equilibrium, however, may take a long time to reach, and if also the flow of new money is substantial the resulting rise of prices may strike fear into the hearts of the public. People do not panic if prices rise for two or three years ; but after that they may begin to lose confidence in money, and it may become necessary to call a drastic halt. This is the most important practical limitation on the extent to which capital formation can be financed in this way. This is why the banking authorities have always tended to alternate short periods of easy credit with sharp periods of restriction. Bank credit moves three steps up and one step down instead of moving up continuously. This also brings us to the threshold of the trade cycle. If capital were financed exclusively out of profits, and if there were also no hoarding, capital formation would proceed steadily. It is mainly the existence of an elastic credit system which makes the trade cycle an integral part of the mechanism of economic development in an unplanned economy. It is not necessary, however, for us to enter into analysis of the cycle since in this respect the model we are using does not yield results different from those of other models.

7. We have said very little so far about the activities of government, since our basic model uses only capitalists, their employees, and subsistence producers. Governments affect the process of capital accumulation in many ways, however, and not least by the inflations into which they run. Many governments in backward countries are also currently anxious to use surplus man-power for capital formation, and as there is a great deal that can be done with labour and a few tools (roads, irrigation, river walls, schools and so on), it is useful to say something on the subject. We shall therefore in this section analyse the effect of inflation-financed government formation of capital, and thereby also give ourselves the chance to recapitulate the analysis of the previous section.

The results, it will be remembered, lie within two extremes. At one extreme all the money spent by the government comes back to it in taxes, and this is accepted by all classes. In this case, prices rise very little. At the other extreme, all classes refuse to accept a redistribution between themselves and the government. In this case prices tend to rise continuously, except that rising output (as a result of the capital formed) sooner or later catches up with prices and brings them down again. Rising output will also increase the government's "normal" share of the national income, and all monetary pressure will cease when the "normal" share has risen to the level of the inflated share which it was trying to get.

These results give us the questions we must ask. (1). What part of marginal income returns automatically to the government? (2). What effect does inflation have upon the various classes? And (3). What effect has government capital formation upon output?

(One other point must be remembered. In all this analysis so far we have assumed a closed economy. In an open economy inflation plays havoc with the balance of payments. We have therefore to assume that the government has strict control over foreign transactions. This assumption holds for some backward economies ; others would get into an awful mess if they launched upon inflationary finance).

It is not possible that all the money spent by the government should come back to it in the first round, since this would presume that the government took 100 per cent. of marginal income. If the government takes any part of marginal income, some of the money will come back to it ; but even the Keynesian multiplier will not bring it all back unless taxation is the only leakage (*i.e.* there is no saving). The larger the government's share of marginal incomes, the more it will get back, the quicker it will get it, and the smaller will be the effect on prices.

Since the second world war a number of governments of modern industrial states seem to be taking around 40 to 50 per cent. of marginal incomes in taxation, and this is one of the major reasons why their price levels have not risen more, despite heavy pressure on resources for capital formation, defence, etc. In backward countries, however, governments take only a very small part of marginal incomes. The best placed governments from this point of view are those in countries where output is concentrated in a few large units (mines, plantations) and therefore easily taxed, or where foreign trade is a large part of the national income, and is thus easily reached by import and export duties. One of the worst off is India, with a large part of its output produced by subsistence producers and small scale units, hard to reach, and with less than ten per cent. of national income passing in foreign trade. In many cases, marginal taxation is less than average taxation, for when money incomes rise, the government continues to charge the same prices for railway travel or for stamps, and hesitates to raise land taxes on the peasants, with the result that money incomes rise faster than government receipts. No government should consider deficit financing without assuring itself that a large part of increases in money income will automatically come back to itself. By contrast, the U.S.S.R., with its very high rate of turnover tax, automatically mops up surplus funds injected into the system, before they are able to generate much demand inflation *via* the multiplier process.

The next question is the effect of inflation upon the distribution of income. The surplus money raises prices, some more than others. The government will probably try to prevent prices from rising, but will succeed better with some than with others. It is easy to apply price control to large scale enterprises, but very hard to prevent the farmers from raising food prices, or the petty traders from making big margins. From the point of view of capital formation, the best thing that can happen is for the surplus money to roll into the pockets of people who will reinvest it productively. The merchant classes would probably use it mainly for speculation in those commodities that are getting scarce. The middle-classes would mainly buy big American cars with it, or go on trips to Europe, wangling the foreign exchange somehow. The peasants ought to use it to improve their farms, but probably most would use it only to pay off debt, or to buy more land. There is really only one class that is pretty certain to reinvest its profits productively, and that is the class of industrialists. The effects of an inflation on secondary capital formation therefore depend first on how large the industrial class is, and secondly on whether the benefit goes largely to this class. In countries which have only a small industrial class, inflation leads mainly to speculation in commodities and in land, and to the hoarding of foreign exchange. But in any country which has a substantial industrialist class, with the passion this class has for ruling over bigger and better factories, even the most frightening inflations (*e.g.* Germany from 1919) leave behind a substantial increase in capital formation. (Have we hit here upon some deep psychological instinct which drives the industrialist to use his wealth more creatively than others? Probably not. It is just that his job is of the kind where passion for success results in capital formation. The peasant farmer wants to have more land, not more capital on his land (unless he is a modern capitalist farmer) so his passion is dissipated merely in changes in the price and distribution of land. The merchant wants to have a wider margin, or a quicker turnover, neither of which increases fixed capital. The banker wants more deposits. Only the industralist's passion drives towards using profits to create a bigger empire of bricks and steel). It follows that it is in industrial communities that inflations are most helpful to capital formation ; whereas in countries where the industrial class is negligible there is nothing to show for the inflation when it is over, except the original investment which started it off. We should also note that many governments do not like the fact that inflation enables industrialists to earn the extra profits with which they create fixed capital, since this results in an increase of private fortunes. They therefore do all they can to prevent the inflation from increasing the profits of industrialists. More especially, they clamp down on industrial prices, which are also from the administrative point of view the easiest prices to control. Since it is the industrialist class which saves most, the result is to exacerbate the inflation. It would be much sounder to pursue policies which would result in the profits of industrialists rising more rapidly than other incomes, and then to tax these profits away, either immediately, or at death.

Inflation continues to be generated so long as the community is not willing to hold an amount equal to the increased investment expenditure. It is not therefore enough that savings should increase to this extent, for if these savings are used for additional investment the initial gap still remains. The gap is closed only if the savings are hoarded, or used to buy government bonds, so that the government can now finance its investments by borrowing, instead of by creating new money. Hence in practice, if the government wishes the inflation to be ended without reducing its investment, it must find means of bringing into its coffers as much in taxes or in loans as it is spending. If it is failing to do this, the inflation will continue ; it is then better that it should continue because capitalists are spending their profits on further capital formation than because other classes are chasing a limited output of consumer goods; but if it is desired to end inflation as soon as possible, all classes should be encouraged to invest in government bonds rather than to spend in other ways.

Finally we come to the relation between capital and output. If the intention is to finance capital formation by creating credit, the best objects for such a policy are those which yield a large income quickly. To finance school building by creating credit is asking for trouble. On the other hand, there are a lot of agricultural programmes (water supplies, fertilisers, seed farms, extension) where quick and substantial results may be expected from modest expenditure. If there are idle resources available for capital formation it is foolish not to use them simply because of technical or political difficulties in raising taxes. But it would be equally foolish to use them on programmes which take a long time to give a small result, when there are others which could give a large result quickly.

We may sum up as follows. If labour is abundant and physical resources scarce, the primary effect on output is exactly the same whether the government creates capital out of taxation or out of credit creation : the output of consumer goods is unchanged, but is redistributed. Hence credit creation must be seen primarily as an alternative to taxation, which is worth the troubles it brings only if trying to raise taxes would bring even more troubles. Credit creation has however one further lead upon taxation in that if it also redistributes income towards the industrial class (if there is an industrial class), it will speed up capital formation out of profits. If it is impossible to increase taxation, and the alternative is between creating capital out of credit, and not creating it at all, the choice one has then to make is between stable prices or rising output. There is no simple formula for making this choice. In some communities any further inflation of prices would ruin their fragile social or political equilibrium ; in others this equilibrium will be destroyed if there is not a sharp increase in output in the near future ; and in still others the equilibrium will be ruined either way.

8. We may now resume our analysis. We have seen that if unlimited labour is available at a constant real wage, the capitalist surplus will rise continuously, and annual investment will be a rising proportion of the national income. Needless to say, this cannot go on forever.

The process must stop when capital accumulation has caught up with population, so that there is no longer surplus labour. But it may stop before that. It may stop of course for any number of reasons which are outside our system of analysis, ranging from earthquake or bubonic plague to social revolution. But it may also stop for the economic reason that, although there is a labour surplus, real wages may nevertheless rise so high as to reduce capitalists' profits to the level at which profits are all consumed and there is no net investment.

This may happen for one of four reasons. First, if capital accumulation is proceeding faster than population growth, and is therefore reducing absolutely the number of people in the subsistence sector, the average product per man in that sector rises automatically, not because production alters, but because there are fewer mouths to share the product. After a while the change actually becomes noticeable, and the capitalist wage begins to be forced up. Secondly, the increase in the size of the capitalist sector relatively to the subsistence sector may turn the terms of trade against the capitalist sector (if they are producing different things) and so force the capitalists to pay workers a higher percentage of their product, in order to keep their real income constant. Thirdly, the subsistence sector may also become more productive in the technical sense. For example, it may begin to imitate the techniques of the capitalist sector ; the peasants may get hold of some of the new seeds, or hear about the new fertilisers or rotations. They may also benefit directly from some of the capitalist investments, *e.g.*, in irrigation works, in transport facilities, or in electricity. Anything which raises the productivity of the subsistence sector (average per person) will raise real wages in the capitalist sector, and will therefore reduce the capitalist surplus and the rate of capital accumulation, unless it at the same time more than correspondingly moves the terms of trade against the subsistence sector. Alternatively, even if the productivity of the capitalist sector is unchanged, the workers in the capitalist sector may imitate the capitalist way of life, and may thus need more to live on. The subsistence level is only a conventional idea, and conventions change. The effect of this would be to widen the gap between earnings in the subsistence sector, and wages in the capitalist sector. This is hard to do, if labour is abundant, but it may be achieved by a combination of trade union pressure and capitalist conscience. If it is achieved, it will reduce the capitalist surplus, and also the rate of capital accumulation.

The most interesting of these possibilities is that the terms of trade may move against the capitalist sector. This assumes that the capitalist and subsistence sectors are producing different things. In practice this is a question of the relationship between industry and agriculture. If the capitalists are investing in plantation agriculture side by side with their investment in industry, we can think of the capitalist sector as self-contained. The expansion of this sector does not then generate any demand for anything produced in the subsistence sector, and there are therefore no terms of trade to upset the picture we have drawn. To bring the terms of trade in, the simplest assumption to make is that the subsistence sector consists of peasants producing food, while the capitalist sector produces everything else.

Now if the capitalist sector produces no food, its expansion increases the demand for food, raises the price of food in terms of capitalist products, and so reduces profits. This is one of the senses in which industrialisation is dependent upon agricultural improvement ; it is not profitable to produce a growing volume of manufactures unless agricultural production is growing simultaneously. This is also why industrial and agrarian revolutions always go together, and why economies in which agriculture is stagnant do not show industrial development. Hence, if we postulate that the capitalist sector is not producing food, we must either postulate that the subsistence sector is increasing its output, or else conclude that the expansion of the capitalist sector will be brought to an end through adverse terms of trade eating into profits. (Ricardo's problem of increasing rents is first cousin to this conclusion ; he worried about rents increasing *inside* the capitalist sector, whereas we are dealing with rents *outside* the sector).

On the other hand, if we assume that the subsistence sector is producing more food, while we escape the Scylla of adverse terms of trade we may be caught by the Charybdis of real wages rising because the subsistence sector is more productive. We escape both Scylla and Charybdis if rising productivity in the subsistence sector is more than offset by improving terms of trade. However, if the subsistence sector is producing food, the elasticity of demand for which is less than unity, increases in productivity will be more than offset by reductions in price. A rise in the productivity of the subsistence sector hurts the capitalist sector if there is no trade between the two, or if the demand of the capitalist sector for the subsistence sector's product is elastic. On the assumptions we have made, a rise in food productivity benefits the capitalist sector. Nevertheless, when we take rising demand into account, it is not at all unlikely that the price of food will not fall as fast as productivity increases, and this will force the capitalists to pay out a larger part of their product as wages.

If there is no hope of prices falling as fast as productivity increases (because demand is increasing), the capitalists' next best move is to prevent the farmer from getting all his extra production. In Japan this was achieved by raising rents against the farmers, and by taxing them more heavily, so that a large part of the rapid increase in productivity which occurred (between 1880 and 1910 it doubled) was taken away from the farmers and used for capital formation ; at the same time the holding down of the farmers' income itself held down wages, to the advantage of profits in the capitalist sector. Much the same happened in the U.S.S.R., where farm incomes per head were held down, in spite of farm mechanisation and the considerable release of labour to the towns ; this was done jointly by raising the prices of manufactures relatively to farm products, and also by levying heavy taxes upon the collective farms.

This also defines for us the case in which it is true to say that it is agriculture which finances industrialisation. If the capitalist sector is self-contained, its expansion is in no way dependent upon the peasants. The surplus is wholly "at the expense" of the workers in the capitalist sector. But if the capitalist sector depends upon the peasants for food, it is essential to get the peasants to produce more, while if at the same time they can be prevented from enjoying the full fruit of their extra production, wages can be reduced relatively to the capitalist surplus. By contrast a state which is ruled by peasants may be happy and prosperous, but it is not likely to show such a rapid accumulation of capital. (*E.g.*, will China and the U.S.S.R. diverge in this respect ?).

We conclude, therefore, that the expansion of the capitalist sector may be stopped because the price of subsistence goods rises, or because the price is not falling as fast as subsistence productivity per head is rising, or because capitalist workers raise their standard of what they need for subsistence. Any of these would raise wages relatively to the surplus. If none of these processes is enough to stop capital accumulation, the capitalist sector will continue to expand until there is no surplus labour left. This can happen even if population is growing. For example, if it takes 3 per cent. of annual income invested to employ 1 per cent. more people, an annual net investment of 12 per cent. can cope with as much as a 4 per cent. increase in population. But population in Western Europe at the relevant times grew only by 1 per cent. or so per annum (which is also the present rate of growth in India), and rates of growth exceeding 2½ per cent. per annum are even now rather rare. We cannot say that capital will always grow faster than labour (it obviously has not done so in Asia), but we can say that if conditions are favourable for the capitalist surplus to grow more rapidly than population, there must come a day when capital accumulation has caught up with labour supply. Ricardo and Malthus did not provide for this in their models, because they over-estimated the rate of growth of population. Marx did not provide for it either, because he had persuaded himself that capital accumulation increases unemployment instead of reducing it, (he has a curious model in which the short run effect of accumulation is to reduce unemployment, raise wages and thus provoke a crisis, while the long run effect is to increase the reserve army of unemployed). Of the classical economists only Adam Smith saw clearly that capital accumulation would eventually create a shortage of labour, and raise wages above the subsistence level.

When the labour surplus disappears our model of the closed economy no longer holds. Wages are no longer tied to a subsistence level. Adam Smith thought they would then depend upon the degree of monopoly (a doctrine which was re-presented in the 1930's as one of the novelties of modern economic analysis). The neo-classicists invented the doctrine of marginal productivity. The problem is not yet solved to anyone's satisfaction, except in static models which take no account of capital accumulation and of technical progress. It is, however, outside the terms of reference of this essay and we will not pursue it here.

Our task is not, however, finished. In the classical world all countries have surplus labour. In the neo-classical world labour is scarce in all countries. In the real world, however, countries which achieve labour scarcity continue to be surrounded by others which have abundant labour. Instead of concentrating on one country, and examining the expansion of its capitalist sector, we now have to see this country as part of the expanding capitalist sector of the world economy as a whole, and to enquire how the distribution of income inside the country and its rate of capital accumulation, are affected by the fact that there is abundant labour available elsewhere at a subsistence wage.

II. THE OPEN ECONOMY.

9. When capital accumulation catches up with the labour supply, wages begin to rise above the subsistence level, and the capitalist surplus is adversely affected. However, if there is still surplus labour in other countries, the capitalists can avoid this in one of two ways, by encouraging immigration or by exporting their capital to countries where there is still abundant labour at a subsistence wage. We must examine each of these in turn.

10. Let us first clear out of the way the effects of the immigration of skilled workers, since our main concern is with

an abundant immigration of unskilled workers released by the subsistence sectors of other countries. It is theoretically possible that the immigration of skilled workers may reduce the demand for the services of native unskilled workers, but this is most unlikely. More probably it will make possible new investments and industries which were not possible before, and will thus increase the demand for all kinds of labour, relatively to its supply.

We must also get out of the way relatively small immigrations. If 100,000 Puerto Ricans emigrate to the United States every year, the effect on U.S. wages is negligible. U.S. wages are not pulled down to the Puerto Rican level; it is Puerto Rican wages which are then pulled up to the U.S. level.

Mass immigration is quite a different kettle of fish. If there were free immigration from India and China to the U.S.A., the wage level of the U.S.A. would certainly be pulled down towards the Indian and Chinese levels. In fact in a competitive model the U.S. wage could exceed the Asian wage only by an amount covering migration costs plus the "cliff" to which we have already referred. The result is the same whether one assumes increasing or diminishing returns to labour. Wages are constant at subsistence level plus. All the benefit of increasing returns goes into the capitalist surplus.

This is one of the reasons why, in every country where the wage level is relatively high, the trade unions are bitterly hostile to immigration, except of people in special categories, and take steps to have it restricted. The result is that real wages are higher than they would otherwise be, while profits, capital resources, and total output are smaller than they would otherwise be.

11. The export of capital is therefore a much easier way out for the capitalists, since trade unions are quick to restrict immigration, but much slower in bringing the export of capital under control.

The effect of exporting capital is to reduce the creation of fixed capital at home, and therefore to reduce the demand for labour. Labour will still be required to create the capital (*e.g.* to make machines for export), but domestic labour will no longer be required to work with the capital, as it would also be if the capital were invested at home.

This, however, is only one side of the picture, for the capital may be used in foreign countries in ways which raise the standard of living of the capital exporting country (and so offset wholly or partly the first effect), or in ways which lower it (thus aggravating the first effect). The result depends on the type of competition which there is between the capital exporting and the capital importing countries.

12. Let us assume, to begin with, that there is no competition, and even no trade. Both countries are self-sufficient. Wages however are rising in country *A*, while labour is abundant in country *B*. *A's* capitalists therefore invest their capital in *B*. Trade returns show first the export surplus from *A*, representing the transfer of capital, and later the import surplus representing the return home of dividends. There is no effect on the workers in *A* other than that their wages cease to rise, as they would have if the capital were invested instead at home. If *A's* resources and *B's* resources are exactly the same, wages cannot rise in *A* until capital accumulation in *B* has wiped out *B's* labour surplus.

Now in the real world the resources of two countries are not exactly alike, and it cannot be taken for granted that it will be more profitable to invest in *B* if profits are falling in *A* (which also cannot be taken for granted). The profitability of investing in a country depends upon its natural resources, upon its human material, and upon the amount of capital already invested there.

The most productive investments are those which are made to open up rich, easily accessible natural resources, such as fertile soil, ores, coal or oil. This is the principal reason why most of the capital exported in the last hundred years went to the Americas and to Australasia rather than to India or to China, where the known resources were already being used. In the well developed parts of the world (in the resource sense) the main opportunity for productive investment lies in improving techniques—these countries are well (even over-) developed in the resource sense, but under-developed in their techniques. It is profitable to use capital to introduce new techniques, but this is not as profitable as using capital to make available both new techniques and also new resources. This also explains why the United Kingdom rapidly became a capital exporting country (the limits of its natural resources were soon reached), whereas the United States is very late in reaching this stage, since its natural resources are so extensive that capital investment at home is still very profitable even though wages are very high.

Productivity depends also on the human material. Even though the genetic composition of peoples may be much the same, as far as potential productivity may be concerned, their cultural inheritance is very different. Differences in literacy, forms of government, attitudes to work, and social relations generally may make a big difference to productivity. Capitalists naturally find it more profitable and safer to invest in countries where the atmosphere is capitalist than they do in widely different cultures.

But this is not all. For the productivity of investment in *B* depends not only upon *B's* natural resources and its human institutions, but also upon the efficiency of all other industries whose services the new investment would require to use. This depends partly upon how highly capitalised these other industries are. The productivity of one investment depends upon other investments having been made before. Hence it may be more profitable to invest capital in countries which already have a lot of capital than to invest it in a new country. If this were always so, no capital would be exported, and the gap between wages in the surplus (labour) and non-surplus countries would not diminish but would widen. In practice capital export is small, and the gap does widen, and we cannot at all exclude the possibility that there is a natural tendency for capital to flow towards the capitalised, and to shun the un-capitalised.

If we could assume that there is a natural tendency for the rate of profit to fall in a closed economy, we could say that however low the rate may be in other countries, the rate in the closed economy must ultimately fall towards the level elsewhere, after which capital export must begin. Practically all the best known economists of every school, in every century, have affirmed that such a tendency exists, though their reasons have varied widely. The most notable exception is Marshall, who gave the right answer, which is that increasing capital per head tends to lower the yield of capital, while increasing technical knowledge tends to raise it. Thus, said Marshall, the yield fell from 10 per cent. in the Middle Ages to 3 per cent. in the middle of the eighteenth century—a long period of slow technical growth—after which the decline was arrested by the great increase in opportunities for using capital. This being so, the natural tendency for the yield of capital to fall is nothing but a popular myth. The yield may fall or it may not ; we cannot foretell.

We get a different answer, however, if we turn from the rate of profit on capital in general to the rate in particular lines of investment. In any particular line the possibilities of further expansion are soon exhausted, or at any rate greatly reduced. All industries develop on a logistic pattern, growing fairly slowly at first, then rapidly, and later on growing again quite slowly. Hence the investors in any particular line sooner or later come to a point where there is not much more scope for investment in that line at home. It is open to them to put their accumulating profits into quite different industries. But there is also the temptation to stick to the field in which they have specialised knowledge, and to use their profits to take the industry into new countries.

What brings about the exportation of capital is not inevitably falling home profits, or rising wages at home, but simply the fact that foreign countries having different resources unutilised in different degrees there are some profitable opportunities for investment abroad. This is not even dependent on capital accumulation having caught up with surplus labour at home; for even if there is still surplus labour at home, available at subsistence wages, investment opportunities abroad may be more profitable. Many capitalists residing in surplus labour countries invest their capital in England or the United States.

We must therefore beware of saying that a country will begin to export capital as soon as capital accumulation at home catches up with labour supply. All the same, countries do export capital, and we can say that if labour is scarce in those countries, the effect is to reduce the demand for labour in those countries and thus to prevent wages from rising as much as they otherwise would.

13. Let us now assume that the two countries do not compete, but trade with each other. There are two variants of this case. One where the two countries produce only one good, but a different good in each. Here wage levels are not determined in relation to each other. In the second case, each country produces two or more goods, one of which is common to both, and is the good produced in the subsistence sector.

Suppose that in the first case country *A* produces wheat, and country *B* produces peanuts. Relative prices are determined solely by supply and demand. Assume that a capitalist sector develops in *A*, applying new techniques to wheat production. At first it may get unlimited labour at an average wage in wheat related to average subsistence wheat production. In due course, however, the surplus is eliminated and wheat wages start to rise. If the capitalist techniques which fructified wheat production are equally applicable to peanuts, it will pay to export capital to *B*, where unlimited labour is available at a wage related to average subsistence output of peanuts.

As in the case discussed before, wages in *A* will be held down by the profitability of investing capital in *B*. A new element, however enters into consideration, because of the effects of investment on the terms of trade. When capital is being invested in *A*, and raising the output of wheat, the price of peanuts will rise relatively. Hence the capitalist workers in *A* as well as subsistence workers in *A* will be worse off in terms of peanuts, though earning the same real wage in wheat. And the workers in *B* will be better off in terms of wheat, while earning the same in peanuts. When capital is invested in *B* the opposite happens : the terms of trade are moved against the *B* workers in favour of the *A* workers.

The moral is that capital export may benefit the workers on balance if it is applied to increasing the supply of things they import. For example, in the Britain of 1850 exclusive investment at home in the cotton industry, while tending to raise wages, might also still more have depressed the terms of trade against the cotton industry.

When we pass to the second case, the result is the same, except that the terms of trade are now determinate. Assume that both countries produce food, but do not trade in it. Country *A* also produces steel, and country *B* also produces rubber. If *B* can release unlimited supplies of labour from subsistence food production, wages in *B* will equal average (not marginal) product in food (abstracting from the difference between subsistence and capitalist wages). In *A* also the wage cannot fall below productivity in the food industry. We may simplify by assuming in the first instance that labour is the sole factor of production and that one day's labour

in *A* produces 3 food or 3 steel
in *B* ,, 1 food or 1 rubber.

Earnings in *A* will then be three times earnings in *B* (the difference in food productivity). And the rate of exchange will be 1 food = 1 steel = 1 rubber. Suppose now that productivity increases in *B's* rubber industry only, so that one day's labour produces instead 3 rubber. This is excellent for the workers in *A*, since 1 steel will now buy 3 rubber. But it will do the workers in *B* no good whatsoever (except in so far as they purchase rubber), since their wage will continue to be 1 food. If on the other hand the subsistence economy became more productive, wages would rise correspondingly. Suppose that 1 day's labour in *B* now produced 3 food or 1 rubber, wages would be as high in *B* as in *A*, and the price of rubber would now be 1 rubber = 3 steel. Workers in *A* are benefitted if productivity in *B* increases in what they buy, and are worse off if productivity in *B* increases in *B's* subsistence sector.

Workers in *B* are benefitted only if productivity increases in their subsistence sector ; all other increases in productivity are lost in the terms of trade.

We have here the key to the question why tropical produce is so cheap. Take for example the case of sugar. This is an industry in which productivity is extremely high by any biological standard. It is also an industry in which output per acre has about trebled over the course of the last 75 years, a rate of growth of productivity which is unparalled by any other major industry in the world—certainly not by the wheat industry. Nevertheless workers in the sugar industry continue to walk barefooted and to live in shacks, while workers in wheat enjoy among the highest living standards in the world. The reason is that wages in the sugar industry are related to the fact that the subsistence sectors of tropical economies are able to release however many workers the sugar industry may want, at wages which are low, because tropical food production per head is low. However vastly productive the sugar industry may become, the benefit accrues chiefly to industrial purchasers in the form of lower prices for sugar. (The capitalists who invest in sugar do not come into the argument because their earnings are determined not by productivity in sugar but by the general rate of profit on capital ; this is why our leaving capital out of this and subsequent analysis of the effects of changing productivity upon wages and the terms of trade simplifies the analysis without significantly affecting its results). To raise the price of sugar, you must increase the productivity of the tropical subsistence food economies. Now the contribution of the temperate world to the tropical world, whether in capital or in knowledge, has in the main been confined to the commercial crops for export, where the benefit mainly accrues to the temperate world in lower prices. The prices of tropical commercial crops will always permit only subsistence wages until, for a change, capital and knowledge are put at the disposal of the subsistence producers to increase the productivity of tropical food production for home consumption.

The analysis applies to all tropical commercial products of which an unlimited supply can be produced because unlimited natural resources exist, in relation to demand—*e.g.*, land of suitable quality. It does not apply where natural resources of a particular kind are scarce. For example, the lands suitable for cultivating sugar or peanuts are very extensive. But mineral bearing lands, or lands with just the right suitability for cocoa, are relatively scarce. Hence the price of a mineral, or of cocoa, may rise to any level consistent with demand. If the lands are owned by capitalists, employing workers, this will make little difference to their wages. But if these scarce lands are owned by peasants, the peasants may of course become rich. In general the peasants have got little out of their mineral bearing lands, especially when these have been expropriated by imperial governments (or declared to be Crown property) and sold to foreign capitalists for a song. Cocoa is the only case (a doubtful one) where it seems that a world scarcity of suitable land may now permanently bring to the peasants earnings higher than they could obtain from subsistence food production.

This is not to say that the tropical countries gain *nothing* from having foreign capital invested in commercial production for export. They gain an additional source of employment, and of taxation. The accumulation of fixed capital in their midst also brings nearer the day when the demand for labour will catch up with the supply (though even this will not raise wages in any one tropical country until they start to rise in all, since capital would otherwise merely transfer itself to the countries where there is still a surplus). What they do not gain is rising real wages ; the whole benefit of increasing productivity in the commercial sector goes to the foreign consumer, at least in the early stages. In the latest stages they may also gain if their peasants imitate the capitalist techniques, so that subsistence productivity rises ; or if the continual increase in the output of commercial crops moves the terms of trade in favour of subsistence food production ; either of these changes would react upon real wages (see section 8), but would do so effectively only when the changes have extended throughout the tropical world.

14. In the next case we assume that the two countries can produce the same things, and trade with each other. *A* is the country where labour is scarce, *B* the country where unlimited labour is available in the subsistence (food) sector. Using the classical framework for the Law of Comparative Costs we write that one day's labour

in *A* produces 3 food or 3 cotton manufactures
in *B* ,, 2 ,, or 1 ,, ,,

This, of course, gives the wrong answer to the question "who should specialise in which," since we have written the average instead of the marginal products. We can assume that these coincide in *A*, and also in cotton manufacture in *B*. Then we should write, in marginal terms,

in *A* produces 3 food or 3 cotton manufactures
in *B* ,, 0 ,, or 1 ,, ,,

B should specialise in cotton manufacture and import food. In practice, however, wages will be 2 food in *B* and between 3 food and 6 food in *A*, at which levels it will be "cheaper" for *B* to export food and import cotton.

This divergence between the actual and what it ought to be is the most serious difference which the existence of surplus labour makes to the neo-classical theory of international trade. It has caught out many economists, who have wrongly advised under-developed countries on the basis of current money costs, instead of lifting the veil to see what lies beneath. It has also caught out many countries, which have allowed (or been forced to allow) their industries to be destroyed by cheap foreign imports, with the sole effect of increasing the size of the labour surplus, when the national income would have been increased if the domestic industries had instead been protected against imports. The fault is not that of the Law of Comparative Costs, which remains valid if written in real marginal terms, but of those who have forgotten that money costs are entirely misleading in economies where there is surplus labour at the ruling wage.

Of course if labour is a free good but the two industries use some scarce resource, such as land or capital, the comparison has to be made not in terms of labour cost but in terms of the scarce resource. Thus, even though labour is unemployed, it may be more economic to use capital to increase the production of food than to use it in creating new manufacturing industries. Adam Smith was as usual on the ball ; this was the substance of his argument that a tariff could not raise the national income even if it increased employment, since it would simply be diverting capital from more to less productive uses. (The Keynesian model doesn't help, since it assumes unlimited capital as well as unemployment). All the same, there may be cases where it is more economic to use capital to create new industries, rather than to fructify old ones, and where this is nevertheless not the most profitable thing to do, in the financial sense, because labour has to be paid a wage when its marginal productivity is really zero. Moreover, many manufacturing activities do not in fact use any other scarce resource but labour. The handicraft and cottage industries especially, which may provide employment for up to ten per cent. of the people in backward countries, use no capital resources to speak of. Yet these are the very first industries to be destroyed by cheap imports of manufactures (*e.g.* the havoc wrought to the Indian cotton industry in the first half of the nineteenth century).

The Law of Comparative Costs, rightly applied, enables us to predict the pattern of international trade. We can say that those countries which have inadequate agricultural resources in relation to their populations (*e.g.* India, Japan, Egypt, Great Britain, Jamaica) must live by importing agricultural products and exporting manufactures ; metal manufactures if they have the coal and ores (India, Great Britain) and light manufactures if they have not (Japan, Egypt, Jamaica). Correspondingly countries which are rich in agricultural land (U.S.A., Argentina), should be net exporters of agricultural products at relatively good terms of trade. Currently this pattern is distorted by the divergence between money and real costs. But if world population continues to grow at its current rate, this pattern must emerge in due course, unless there are revolutionary developments in agricultural science.

Let us, however continue to examine this case, assuming that no distortion is taking place. As before *A* is developed while *B* has surplus labour in food. Suppose that one day's labour

in *A* produces 5 food or 5 cotton manufactures
in *B* ,, 1 ,, or 3 ,, ,, (average)

B ought to specialise in cotton, and will actually do so. Wages and prices are determinate. The wage in *B* will be 1 food, the price of cotton will be 1 cotton equals $\frac{1}{3}$ food, the wage in *A* will be 5 food, and *A* will get all the benefit of the exchange. Suppose now that productivity increases in *B's* cotton industry. *B's* wage is unchanged, and the whole benefit accrues to *A*. But if productivity increases in *B's* food industry (the average rising say from 1 to 2) *B's* wage will rise (from 1 food to 2 food). *A's* wage will still be 5 food, but cotton will now be dearer (1 cotton equals $\frac{2}{3}$ food), to the advantage of *B* and disadvantage of *A*. (*B's* wage is determinate because there is unlimited labour available at a subsistence wage ; and all the benefit of the exchange goes to *A* because *B* is producing both commodities).

15. It is time to say a word about the effect of increasing the subsistence productivity in countries with surplus labour. The analysis is the same as we made for the closed economy (section 8), except that we must now think of the world as a whole as the closed economy. We must also think of the commercial sector of these economies as being a part of the world capitalist sector.

Then, if the world capitalist sector is not dependent on the peasants for food, even to feed its plantation and mining labourers in the surplus countries, an increase in the productivity of the peasants must raise wages against the capitalists. To have this effect, however, productivity must rise in all these countries, otherwise the capitalists will simply transfer from those countries where subsistence productivity has risen to those where it has not.

If, on the other hand, we assume that the capitalists need the peasants' food, and that the demand for food is inelastic, then increased productivity reduces the price of food even more, and so reduces the share of capitalist workers in the capitalist product. This again assumes that the changes are world-wide ; if one country raises its productivity, the price of food will not fall ; wages will rise in that country, and capitalists will move elsewhere. However, even if the price of food falls, the peasants eat most of their output, and will still be better off. For example, suppose a peasant produces 100 food, eats 80 food, and sells 20 food for 20 manufactures. Suppose now that his productivity increases to 200, reducing the price of food by more than half, say to 0·4. The peasant can now have 30 manufactures, costing 75 food, and still eat 125 food instead of 80. The standard of living in the surplus countries is thus raised nearer to that of the advanced countries, but the terms of trade move against both the food and the commercial products of the surplus countries (would move in favour of the commercial products if the elasticity of demand for food were 1·0 or more).

In practice, food production in tropical countries with surplus labour is only a small part of world food production (Asia and Africa together produce less than 20 per cent. of the world's food). Hence increases in food productivity in the tropics could not reduce the price of food *pari passu*. Real wages would therefore rise, and the terms of trade would move in favour of tropical commercial products. This would hurt labour in the industrial countries in so far as it was buying such products, and benefit it in so far as tropical countries were competing in industrial production.

16. This brings us finally to the case where the two countries *A* and *B* produce competing goods to sell in third markets. This need not detain us long. If capital is exported in ways which raise subsistence productivity in the capital importing country, the workers in the capital exporting country will benefit, since the wages of their rivals will be raised. If, however, it is exported to increase productivity in the exporting sector of the capital importing country, the workers in the capital exporting country will be doubly hit, first by the reduced

capital accumulation at home, and then again by the fall in their rivals' prices.

17. We may conclude as follows. Capital export tends to reduce wages in capital exporting countries. This is wholly or partly offset if the capital is applied to cheapening the things which the workers import, or to raising wage costs in countries which compete in third markets (by raising productivity in their subsistence sectors). The reduction in wages is however aggravated if the capital is invested in ways which raise the cost of imports (by increasing productivity in subsistence sectors), or which increase the productivity of competing exports. We have also seen that capital importing countries with surplus labour do not gain an increase in real wages from having foreign capital invested in them, unless this capital results in increased productivity in the commodities they produce for their own consumption.

III. SUMMARY.

18. We may summarise this article as follows :

1. In many economies an unlimited supply of labour is available at a subsistence wage. This was the classical model. The neo-classical model (including the Keynesian) when applied to such economies gives erroneous results.

2. The main sources from which workers come as economic development proceeds are subsistence agriculture, casual labour, petty trade, domestic service, wives and daughters in the household, and the increase of population. In most but not all of these sectors, if the country is over-populated relatively to its natural resources, the marginal productivity of labour is negligible, zero, or even negative.

3. The subsistence wage at which this surplus labour is available for employment may be determined by a conventional view of the minimum required for subsistence ; or it may be equal to the average product per man in subsistence agriculture, plus a margin.

4. In such an economy employment expands in a capitalist sector as capital formation occurs.

5. Capital formation and technical progress result not in raising wages, but in raising the share of profits in the national income.

6. The reason why savings are low in an undeveloped economy relatively to national income is not that the people are poor, but that capitalist profits are low relatively to national income. As the capitalist sector expands, profits grow relatively, and an increasing proportion of national income is re-invested.

7. Capital is formed not only out of profits but also out of credit creation. The real cost of capital created by inflation is zero in this model, and this capital is just as useful as what is created in more respectable fashion (*i.e.* out of profits).

8. Inflation for the purpose of getting hold of resources for war may be cumulative ; but inflation for the purpose of creating productive capital is self-destructive. Prices rise as the capital is created, and fall again as its output reaches the market.

9. The capitalist sector cannot expand in these ways indefinitely, since capital accumulation can proceed faster than population can grow. When the surplus is exhausted, wages begin to rise above the subsistence level.

10. The country is still, however, surrounded by other countries which have surplus labour. Accordingly as soon as its wages begin to rise, mass immigration and the export of capital operate to check the rise.

11. Mass immigration of unskilled labour might even raise output per head, but its effect would be to keep wages in all countries near the subsistence level of the poorest countries.

12. The export of capital reduces capital formation at home, and so keeps wages down. This is offset if the capital export cheapens the things which workers import, or raises wage costs in competing countries. But it is aggravated if the capital export raises the cost of imports or reduces costs in competing countries.

13. The importation of foreign capital does not raise real wages in countries which have surplus labour, unless the capital results in increased productivity in the commodities which they produce for their own consumption.

14. The main reason why tropical *commercial* produce is so cheap, in terms of the standard of living it affords, is the inefficiency of tropical *food* production per man. Practically all the benefit of increasing efficiency in export industries goes to the foreign consumer ; whereas raising efficiency in subsistence food production would automatically make commercial produce dearer.

15. The Law of Comparative Costs is just as valid in countries with surplus labour as it is in others. But whereas in the latter it is a valid foundation of arguments for free trade, in the former it is an equally valid foundation of arguments for protection.

W. Arthur Lewis

Manchester.

[14]

Unlimited Labour: Further Notes

In an article published in this journal four years ago[1] I showed how the classical assumption, that labour is available to the capitalist sector of an economy in perfectly elastic supply, leads to different conclusions from the neo-classical assumption that the supply of labour is inelastic, and illumines several problems of economic growth which modern economics cannot solve. The following notes set out in more detail the classical position on a number of these matters, and also make some further deductions from the classical model. I return to this subject because of its practical importance. More than half the world's population (mainly in Asia and in Eastern Europe) lives in conditions which correspond to the classical and not to the neo-classical assumptions. These peoples have more to learn from the classical analysis than from anything which has been published since 1870, so it is very desirable to study classical writings and translate their findings into modern language.[2] Besides, it is time that the classical writers had a square deal. For the past fifty years economists have been judging them from the standpoint of neo-classical analysis, giving them marks for intelligent anticipations of the neo-classical theory of value (as if they were primarily value theorists, and as if the neo-classical assumptions applied in their day), and dismissing everything else, especially the theory of development in which they were chiefly interested.[3] Hence studying the classics in the context to which they belong is overdue as much in terms of justice as of utility.

Since the principal elements of the classical model of development were set out in the article to which I have referred, I begin here with the briefest recapitulation. The model can be translated into modern terms by applying the Law of Diminishing Returns in its modern version. In Figure I the quantity of

[1]"Economic Development with Unlimited Supplies of Labour," *The Manchester School*, May, 1954.

[2]Classical political economy is as widely taught and studied in Japan as is neo-classical economics. Southern Asia, however, is still under the sway of the neo-classical system.

[3]The latest example of this distorted treatment is J. A. Schumpeter's *History of Economic Analysis*.

1

FIG. I.

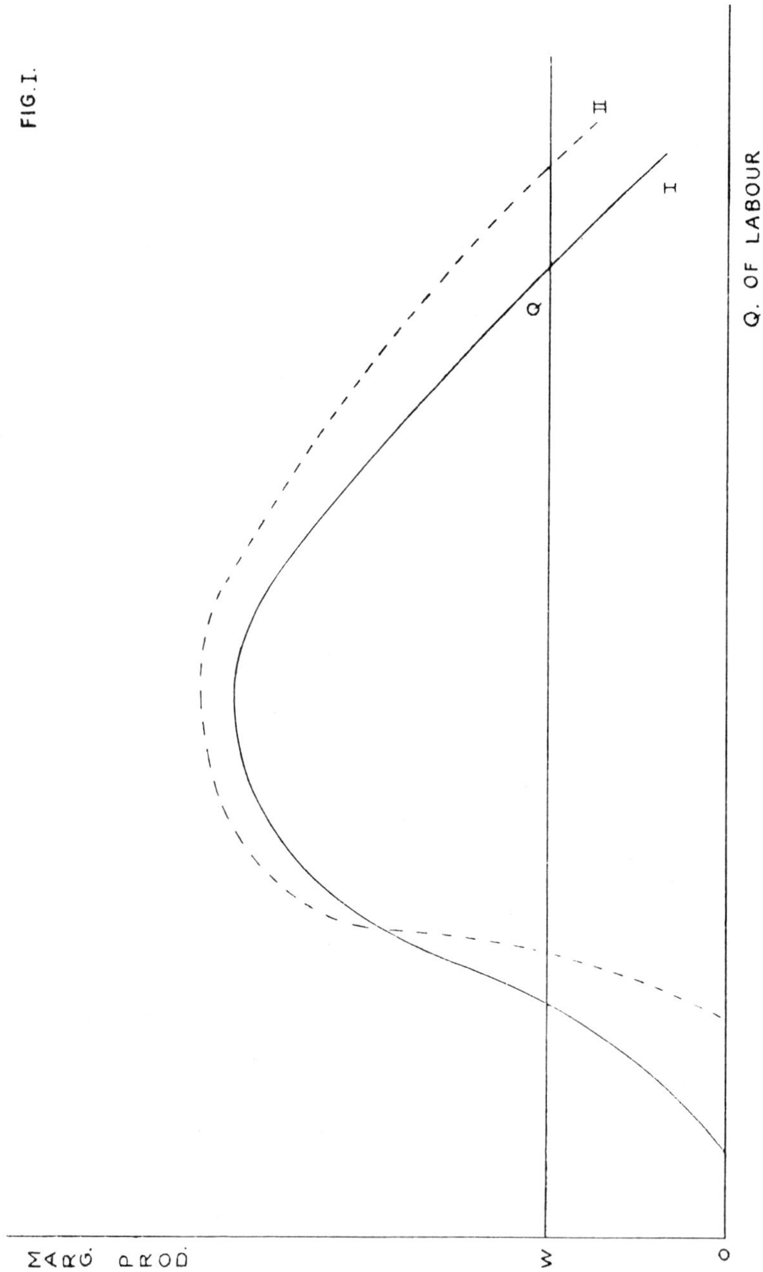

labour is measured on the horizontal axis ; the marginal productivity of labour on the vertical axis. The curve *I* shows the marginal product of labour with a given quantity of capital. If the wage is *OW*, employment will be *WQ*, provided that the surplus over wages is positive (the area under curve *I* up to *Q*, minus the rectangle *OQ*). The fact that there is not enough capital to provide employment for everybody is a vital distinction between this model and neo-classical analysis.

The system is dynamic. Since some saving occurs, capital will increase. So the marginal productivity curve will move outward, taking say the position *II*, and employment will increase continuously.

My earlier article discussed in some detail the sources from which labour flows toward capitalist employment. The classical economists put population growth first, but there are many other sources, which may be listed as peasant agriculture, cottage industry, casual labour, petty trade, domestic service, and wives and daughters entering the labour market.[1] Population growth, it should be noted, includes immigration, which has been an important source of expansion in several countries.[2] Apart from population growth, the classical economists relied on a transfer of labour from "productive" to "unproductive" employment, and it is useful to begin by probing this distinction.

[1]Most countries in the early stages of economic development have not one economy but two—a high wage economy (mines, plantations, factories, large-scale transport, etc.) and a low earnings economy (family farms, handicraft workers, domestic servants, petty traders, casual labourers, etc.). As development occurs, labour transfers from the low earnings to the high wage economy. It is of little consequence whether persons moving out of the low earnings economy have been in "disguised unemployment," or whether their marginal product has been zero, negative, or merely small. All that the analysis requires is that the supply willing to move at the current wage rate should greatly exceed the demand.

[2]The model can be used for regional analysis, where one part of a country (such as a town or province) is expanding relatively to the rest. Since output is determined by technical factors only and not by competitive valuation, the analysis cannot be applied to the firm, or to any other sector of an economy to which capital is also assumed to be in perfectly elastic supply. In the same way if the value of the region's output is determined by extra-regional competition, the analysis has to be modified to take account of this. See Part II of my earlier article (*loc. cit.*).

I. Productive and Unproductive Labour.

As Adam Smith set out the distinction, there are two elements to productive labour. First, its output consists of wage goods, and excludes services.[1] Secondly, productive labour produces a surplus over wages, and has therefore a larger average product than unproductive labour. The distinction was made and used only for the purpose of analysing capital accumulation.[2] Wage goods were produced by a roundabout process, involving time, so the number of productive labourers could not be expanded without saving.[3] Given saving, some labour could be transferred from service trades to producing more wage goods. This increase in the output of wage goods would enable the society to carry a larger population. The increase in the surplus, resulting from the increase in the number of productive workers, would also make possible still more saving. So there could be yet more expansion, in a continuing chain.

We must explore both the importance attached to wage goods, and also the notion of the surplus.

(*a*) *The Importance of Wage Goods.*

The classical economists approached the analysis of accumulation *via* the consumption of wage goods. They divided the consumers into three classes : (1) capitalists and landlords, (2) producers of services and luxuries, and

[1]Strictly, Smith's distinction is between commodities and services. But our modern distinction between wage goods and other output seems really to be what he was striving after, and fits his analysis best.

[2]Neo-classical economists have attacked the distinction from the standpoint of value theory, but since it was not intended for that context, the attack is irrelevant.

[3]We have difficulty in following the classical analysis of capital formation because they concentrated on the need to finance the period between ploughing and harvesting, which to us seems a relatively simple problem. We can understand them better by presuming this period to be lengthened from months to several years, whereupon reminiscences of Bohm-Bawerk make us feel more at home. Another difficulty is that, whereas the classics wrote in terms of consumer goods being produced by capitalistic processes, we now most often distinguish a sector producing consumer goods, and a sector producing capital goods. This way of thinking originated with Marx, who, following Ricardo's insight into the problem presented by machinery, devoted much attention to distinguishing sharply between fixed and circulating capital.

(3) producers of wage goods. In the wider sense the consumption of the producers of non-wage goods was part of the consumption of capitalists and landlords, since they regarded class (2) as being maintained by class (1) for its amusement, etc. out of the surplus extracted from class (3). Thus, when they spoke of the capitalists saving they sometimes meant reducing their personal consumption of wage goods, but more often they meant merely having fewer servants, and so reducing the numbers maintained in class (2).

For our purposes it is convenient to add another class, namely persons engaged in making capital goods. We then get four classes of consumers of wage goods

(1) capitalists and landlords
(2) producers of services and luxuries
(3) producers of capital goods
(4) producers of wage goods.

The first three classes are maintained out of the surplus produced by the fourth above its own consumption.

The problem is to increase the number in class (3), the producers of capital goods. This can be done in one of two ways. Either, consumption by one of the other three classes must fall. Or else the output of wage goods must increase, and the increase in class (3) be financed out of this increase in wage goods output.

These are relatively trivial propositions, yet they have been neglected recently by policy makers. The classical approach to capital formation via the consumption of wage goods does have the merit of reducing the problem to its simplest terms.

The temptation to neglect the first proposition—that if the output of wage goods is given, capital formation cannot be increased without reducing somebody's consumption—is very strong in those over-populated countries where there is surplus labour on the family farms (in the sense that if some labour left the farm to work on investment projects the output of farm products would not be reduced significantly). The transfer can indeed be achieved without disturbing consumption if the farmers are going to work on Community Development projects without pay ; any person can make more capital goods for himself without consuming more wage goods, if he so desires.

But when surplus workers have to be paid to work on investment projects, the demand for wage goods is increased, partly because the workers will not accept the work unless they are paid more than they would get if they stayed on the farm, and partly because the family left at home consumes more per head.

Accordingly, even when there is surplus labour, employing more people on investment projects means cutting consumption somewhere, if the output of wage goods is fixed. The employer (call him for convenience the government, since in these cases it is most often the government) has to find a fund of "saving" from somewhere to finance the additional capital formation.

First, let us note that if the fund is found by taxing capitalists or landlords it will probably result not in reducing their personal consumption of wage goods, but in reducing their employment of other workers, whether workers in class (2) services and luxuries, or workers in class (3) engaged in capital formation. In either case greater employment by the government is offset by equally smaller employment by capitalists and landlords. Ultimately, however, employment increases in the former case, since the increase in the amount of fixed capital in existence will permit larger employment and a greater national income.

Secondly, let us ask how large the fund of saving needs to be. This depends partly on the extent to which consumption on the family farm falls as members move off the farm. Suppose that to employ a man requires 100 units of wage goods, and that his leaving the farm releases 30 units. Then, if the government can get hold of the 30 so released, it need find only 70 elsewhere. If it actually finds 100 elsewhere, then the total employment resulting is increased to the equivalent of

$$100 + 30 + 9 + 2{\cdot}7 + 0{\cdot}81 + \ldots = 142{\cdot}9$$

This is the concept which Vakil and Brahmanand have called "the consumption multiplier."[1] The concept has theoretical validity, but one may doubt its practical utility. Since it is

[1]C. N. Vakil and P. R. Brahmanand, *Planning for an Expanding Economy*, Bombay, 1956. The authors have written a thoughtful treatise, which essentially seeks to rehabilitate much of the classical system for application to countries with surplus labour. The concept referred to here, however, was originated by Nurkse (*op. cit.*), who decided that it was not worth naming.

unlikely that the government could get hold of the 30 units presumed to be released, the authors are right to formulate the proposition in terms of a multiplier rather than in terms of a reduction in the sum the government must find elsewhere. On the other hand, the assumption that 30 units will be released, and be used by the farm family in ways which increase off-farm employment, seems equally unlikely. For, in practice the departure of one member of the family does not in these circumstances of extreme poverty reduce the consumption of wage goods on the farm. Not only do the others consume what he has left behind, but they usually also expect him to send something back out of his wage, so that they may consume marginally even more than he was consuming before.[1]

So much for capital formation, given the output of wage goods. The other proposition—that if it is difficult to decrease the consumption of any class, an increase in capital formation requires an increase in wage goods output—has also been neglected. Thus, economists in the U.S.S.R., China, Eastern Europe, India and elsewhere have debated the question : "Should we concentrate on producing capital goods first and consumer goods second, or should the order be reversed ?" Our scheme enables us to answer this question at once. We can only put capital goods first in so far as somebody's consumption can be reduced. Beyond this point, capital formation can be increased only be increasing simultaneously the output of wage goods. Hence in a poor country, where it is difficult to reduce consumption, the necessary condition for increasing capital formation is to increase the output of wage goods so as to provide an extra surplus which can be impounded for capital formation.[2] Is it not odd that it is the Marxist policy

[1]However the multiplier does not in any case fall below unity, since remittances reduce the worker's own consumption.

[2]Vakil and Brahmanand (*loc. cit.*) use this point for a wholesale condemnation of the trend of Indian planning. Their strictures seem greatly exaggerated. The Indian planners have shown their awareness of the point by their great stress on raising agricultural productivity, and by their plans to increase the output of cottage industries. Whether the supply of consumer goods will meet the demand is doubtful, but if it does not, the reason will be the over-optimism of the planners, rather than their failure to recognize the case for expanding the output of wage-goods. The authors also advance an argument for producing the required wage-goods with machines, instead of with surplus labour, but this is a separate issue, which we take up in the part of this paper which deals with technological unemployment.

makers, presumably bred in the classical tradition, who have most often neglected this proposition?

(*b*) *The Superior Productivity of the Capitalist Sector*

The second element of the distinction between productive and unproductive labour is that the former produces a surplus, so that a transfer of workers from the latter to the former raises the national income, increases the total surplus over wages, and so makes possible further expansion. Adam Smith tied this to the distinction between wage goods and other output, but the tie is not important. Thus Malthus explained that, from the angle of the surplus, whether the workers make commodities is unimportant; and he thought that the terminology could be improved:

> "If we do not confine wealth to tangible and material objects, we might call all labour productive, but productive in different degrees; and the only change that would be required in Adam Smith's work, on account of this mode of considering the subject, would be, the substitution of the terms more productive and less productive, for those of productive and unproductive.
>
> All labour, for instance, might be stated to be productive of value to the amount of the value paid for it, and in proportion to the degree in which the produce of the different kinds of labour, when sold at the price of free competition, exceeds in value the price of the labour employed upon them.[1]"

Here the distinction turns upon the surplus which a labourer produces above his own wages. This surplus is profit and rent; it accrues to capitalists and landlords because the labourer works with means of production which do not belong to him, to produce a commodity (or service) which is sold for a profit. This in turn gives us the definition of the capitalist sector of an economy, as used in this model: the capitalist sector is that sector of the economy where labour is employed for wages for profit-making purposes. Labour employed for wages with no intention of resale (e.g., domestic servants in the home, as distinct from the services of office cleaners) is excluded, as is all labour which is not employed for wages, whether such labour works with capital or not (e.g., peasant agriculture). So the non-capitalist sector includes both some employees and also the self-employed.

[1]T. R. Malthus, *Principles of Political Economy*, page 38.

The average product of a worker in the capitalist sector exceeds that of a worker outside this sector because it reproduces wages *plus a surplus*. This idea is found in all the classical writers. The surplus exists because the labourer in this sector is working with capital ; or if the self-employed sector is also using capital, the surplus exists because the capitalist sector uses even more capital per head.[1] Productivity must be higher in the capitalist sector because the employment will not be offered unless there is a surplus over wages, and will not be accepted unless wages are at least as high as the average product of the self-employed sector, which is what the worker could otherwise earn.[2]

Thus, this aspect of the distinction between productive and unproductive workers can be restated as follows, in modern language : In the early stages of economic development there is not enough capital to provide employment for everybody in the capitalist sector. Even if marginal products were the same,[3] the average product of labour would still be higher in the capitalist sector than outside. Capital accumulation makes it possible to increase the ratio of workers inside the capitalist sector to workers outside, and so raises national income.

In this model the dynamic force is capitalist accumulation, resulting in the expansion of capitalist employment. This is not the only possible theoretical model of growth. One could have a model in which the dynamic force was located in the self-employed sector. For example, growth could be due to the expansion of peasant agriculture. Peasant agriculture may

[1]If some of the self-employed hire capital, paying interest on it, they are really within the capitalist sector. See my earlier article, *loc. cit.*, pp. 146-7.

[2]Servants in the home may also be using capital, e.g., vacuum cleaners, but the psychic surplus which their employment yields to their employers (and which alone justifies their employment) does not count in this context, since it is not saleable and usable to provide employment for somebody else, as is the surplus which accrues to a cleaning agency which hires out the services of cleaners. The national income statisticians also ignore psychic surpluses.

[3]In perfect competition the marginal product of workers inside and outside the capitalist sector would be the same. In my earlier article (*loc. cit.*), I have explained why this is not so in practice. Because a difference exists, a transfer of workers into the capitalist sector would increase the national income even if there were no increase of capital.

become more productive for various reasons. New crops, improved seeds, new markets, roads, water supplies, etc. make peasants richer. So, in an economy which had abundant land but few capitalists, peasant agriculture might be expanding more rapidly than capitalist employment. In practice this is not very likely. If the peasants are growing rich they will demand increasing supplies of non-agricultural goods and services of the kind which are most efficiently produced on a capitalist basis, whether as aids to their production (e.g., transport facilities), or else for personal consumption. Hence the very prosperity of peasant agriculture will cause the capitalist sector to expand.[1] Historically, capitalist employment has everywhere expanded relatively to peasant agriculture in developing economies, and this relative expansion, as we have seen, must itself be raising the national income, since if the capitalist sector is expanding, productivity must be higher inside the capitalist sector than outside it.

Accordingly, however productive and dynamic the self-employed sector of the economy may be, the expansion of the capitalist sector relatively to the rest of the economy is an important part of the process of economic growth. The fact that this model concentrates on analysing capitalist expansion should not be taken as implying lack of interest in how peasants can be enriched.[2]

II. Technological Unemployment.

So long as unlimited labour is available at a constant wage, capital accumulation must increase employment, since it cannot pay to use capital as a substitute for labour. This follows from the Law of Diminishing Returns : extra capital

[1]It will not, however, be expanding at constant real wages unless the commodity terms of trade are moving in its favour. See below. Part III, section (*c*). The argument above shows that peasant prosperity expands capitalist employment to supply the home market; but it may at the same time cause capitalist employment for other purposes (e.g., for export) to decline. Though unlikely, it is theoretically possible for the net result to be a decline in capitalist employment.

[2]This would hardly be worth saying if one reviewer of my book *The Theory of Economic Growth* had not implied the opposite, in spite of the fact that large sections of the book are concerned with how to enrich the peasants !

FIG. II

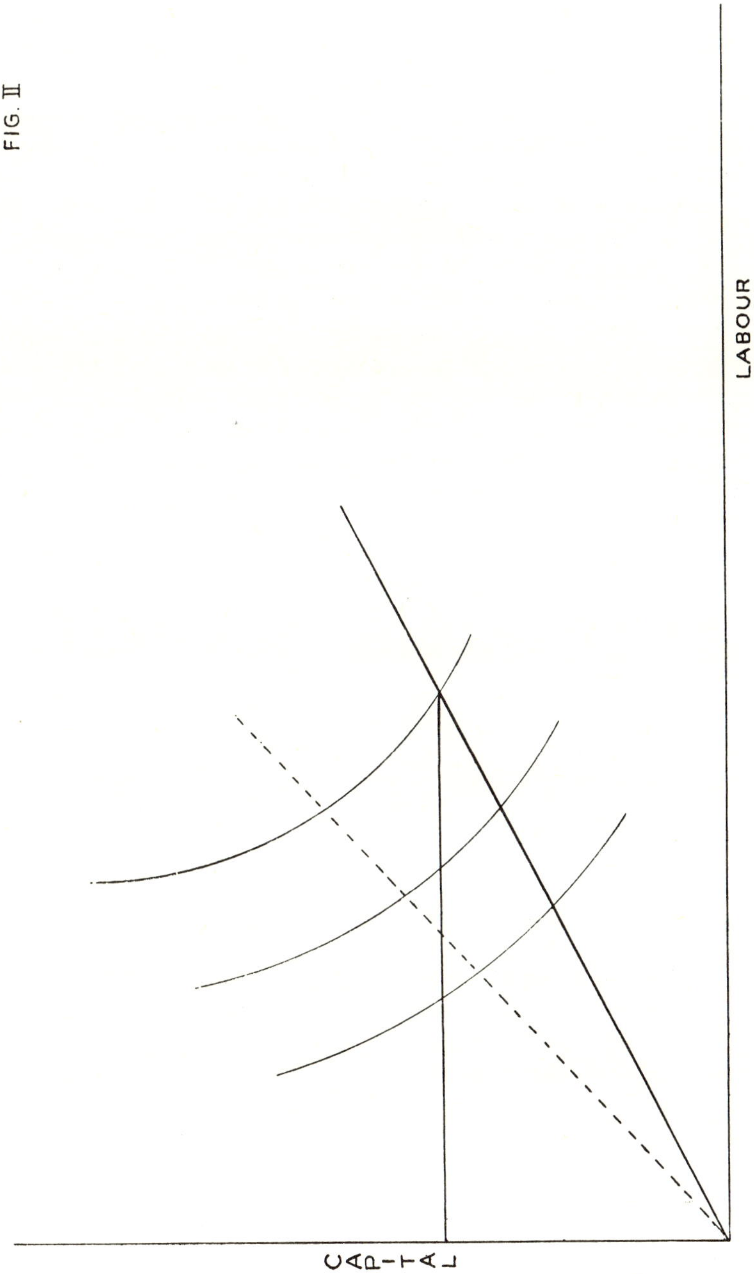

must yield more when combined with extra labour than if it were merely added to existing capital with the same labour.

Technological change, on the other hand, may increase, reduce or leave unchanged the demand for labour with a given quantity of capital. The neo-classical and the classical formulations of this proposition are not quite the same. In the neo-classical formulation we hold *relative* wages constant, and, assuming that the isoquants fulfil the conditions of constant returns to scale, we can read off along a straight "Engel" line how much employment corresponds to how much capital. Technological change alters the isoquants, and thus gives us a new Engel line, which may run to the right or the left of the old one. If it coincides with the old one the innovation is said to be neutral as between labour and capital. If it runs to the left, the innovation is biassed in favour of capital, and full employment is maintained only by lowering relative wages : absolute wages may, however, still have increased, since the innovation may have increased the national income.

In the classical system, on the other hand, it is the absolute level of wages that is held constant. The innovation must reduce the wage rate relatively to the return on capital, since it will not be adopted unless it increases the return on capital. Thus it must increase the absolute surplus over wages, but it may increase or reduce employment or leave it unchanged ; and even national income as a whole, may be increased, reduced or left unchanged.

Ricardo stated this correctly,[1] and though he was berated by McCulloch [2] for making this concession to the enemies of capitalism, he stuck to his guns. J. S. Mill agreed with him.[3]

The same problem can be formulated in another way : should capital be used where it is marginally most profitable, or where the capital-output ratio is marginally lowest ? This problem does not arise in the neo-classical model ; since the quantity of labour is fixed in that model, we maximise output by maximising the return on capital. But in a system where the

[1] *Principles of Political Economy and Taxation*, Chapter XXXI, "On Machinery."

[2] *Letters of Ricardo to Malthus*, Bonar edition, p. 184.

[3] *Principles of Political Economy*, Vol. I, Book I, Chapter VI.

FIG. III

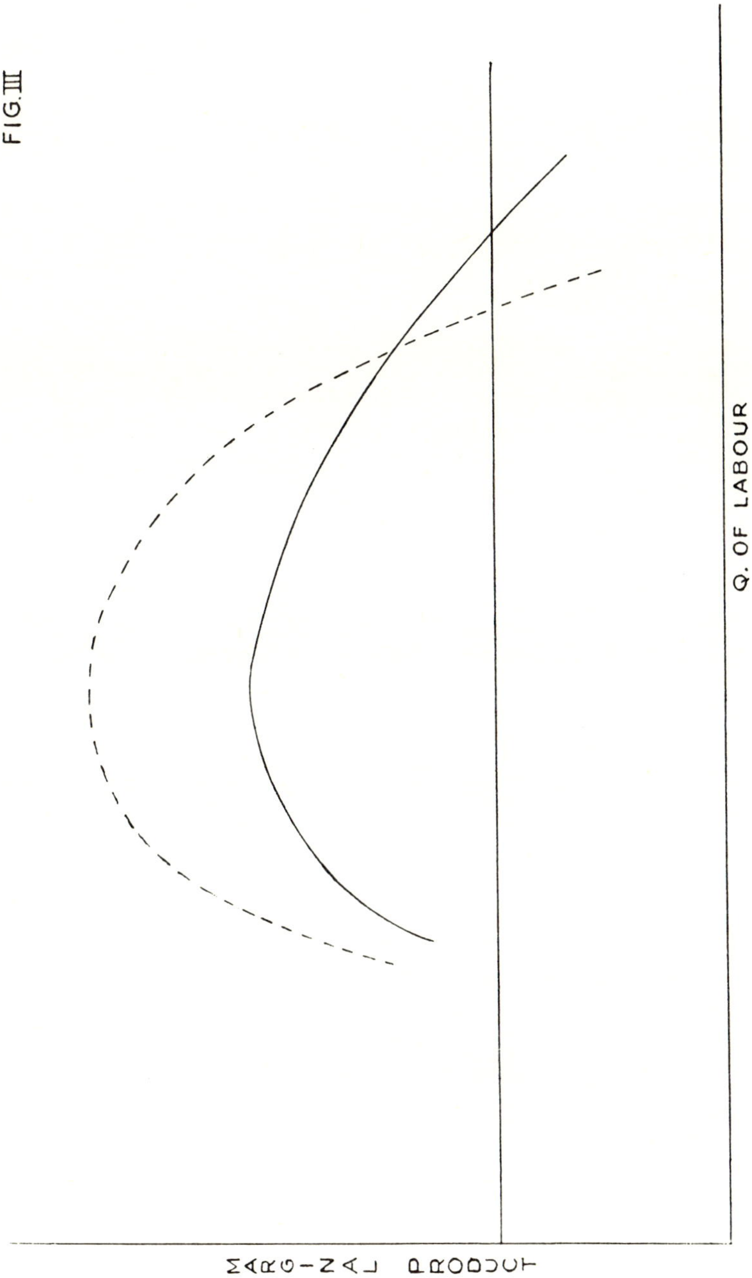

quantity of employment is variable, the most profitable uses of capital need not be those which maximise output or employment. Adam Smith was troubled by this difference—as many recent writers have been—and he devoted Chapter V of Book II to the subject. Malthus also touched on it, in the passage already quoted. Ricardo answered that what matters is not to maximise output but to maximise the surplus over wages.[1]

This was the same answer which he and Mill gave on the subject of technological unemployment. They argued that technological change must in the long run be favourable to employment, even though it might temporarily reduce employment. This was because the innovation must increase absolutely the surplus over wages, or it would not be adopted. Since the surplus increased, capital accumulation would proceed more rapidly, and so employment must increase more rapidly.

We have thus two forces operating in different directions : capital accumulation, which must increase employment, and technological change, which may sometimes reduce employment. One cannot say *a priori* which must win out. Using hindsight we can see that Ricardo was right : even though some technological change reduces employment, the combination of capital accumulation and of the kind of technological change which increases employment, has brought about an immense increase in the demand for labour. This is the classical answer to those who want to restrict innovation in order to protect employment.

The validity of this answer, however, depends upon several conditions. First, it depends upon the assumption that it is more important to maximise output and employment in the long run than in the short run. This in turn depends partly on how rapidly capital is accumulating, since this determines how short the short run is. One is more likely to accept the objective of maximising the surplus if capitalists are using most of the surplus for capital accumulation than if they are using it mostly for consumption.

Secondly, the argument depends on the assumption that the rate of accumulation depends primarily upon the level of

[1]*Op. cit.*, Chapter XXVI. Also *Notes on Malthus*, Sraffa edition, pages 18-22.

profits. This is true enough in a pure capitalist system, but it may not be true in a directed economy. For example, in an increasing number of countries, saving is financed to some extent out of taxes, levied upon all classes of the economy. If saving is a function not of profit but of national income, then the rate of accumulation is maximised by maximising not profit but national income, and innovations which reduce the national income (or fail to increase it) while increasing profits should be resisted.

Given that accumulation is a function of profit, the application of the Ricardian argument depends thirdly upon the assumption that the market for capital is perfect. Otherwise it has first to be demonstrated that capital could not be used more profitably in some alternative way than in exploiting the innovation which involves technological unemployment. In a perfect market economy, where capital flows always towards the most profitable uses, this may be taken for granted, but conditions may be different in the real world.

Thus, in India, much capital formation is done by the government, at low interest rates. The real return on irrigation works, steel plants, railways and roads is not measured by the interest yielded by government bonds, or by the profits earned at the prices fixed by the government. Indian planners believe the real social return on capital used in such purposes exceeds the real social return on capital invested in new cotton mills ; since, given that there is surplus labour in the cottage industry, capital investment in cotton yields no more cotton goods than would otherwise be available—it merely reduces employment. The return to private shareholders is nevertheless higher in cotton than in lending to the government. If the planners are right, the national income is increased by prohibiting further investment in cotton at present, and by channeling savings into more productive uses, until the catching up of demand with supply from existing cottage sources, raises the real productivity of new investment in cotton beyond marginal productivity in other sectors.

The only difference which the accumulation argument makes to this reasoning is to substitute maximisation of the surplus over consumption for maximisation of national income.

Instead of saying that the Indian planners are right if the real social marginal productivity of capital is greater elsewhere than in cotton, one must say that they are right if capital creates a greater surplus elsewhere than it does in cotton. Conversely, if one wishes to prove them wrong, one must show that investment in cotton would lead to a greater increase in savings than would investment in irrigation, steel, or other alternative uses of capital. This their critics have not even tried to do.[1]

III. The Rate of Profit.

(*a*) *The Connection between Profit and Accumulation.*

The expansion of the capitalist sector does not depend upon whether saving is done out of profits or out of other incomes. Whether saving is done out of wages, salaries, rents, or the incomes of the self-employed, so long as saving is channeled into investment in the capitalist sector, that sector will expand.

The assumption that most saving comes out of profit is relevant only in the context of explaining why the ratio of saving to national income increases in the first stage of economic development. For this explanation to work one need not assume that all saving comes out of profit ; it is necessary only that the marginal propensity to save should be higher out of profits than out of other incomes. Then it will follow that, as the capitalist sector expands, and profits rise relatively to national income, the ratio of savings to national income will rise.

[1]Vakil and Brahmanand (*loc. cit.*) found a fierce criticism of India's protection of cottage weaving upon the argument that factory production gives rise to a greater surplus of savings than does cottage production. But they never mention that the imperfection of the capital market makes it possible that capital could be more profitably used (in the real sense) in other sectors, giving rise to a larger savings potential and a greater increase in savings than would accrue from profits in capitalist cotton production.

It is useful to have this explanation of the rise in the savings ratio which accompanies economic growth.[1] As argued in my earlier article, the rival explanations do not carry conviction : saving does not rise automatically with income per head ; it is not a function of inequality as such, which is also not necessarily greater in rich than in poor countries ; and class by class, there is no evidence of increasing thriftiness during the relevant periods. The proposition that the marginal propensity to save is higher out of profits than out of other incomes is the best explanation we have of why the savings ratio rises in the first stage of economic development.

Moreover, the model explains not only why the savings ratio rises in the first stage of development, but also why it ceases to rise in the second stage, and this adds to its merit.

The classical economists did not all assert that profit is the source of saving. They agreed that a high rate of profit acts as an incentive to saving, but this is a different matter. They also agreed that saving comes mainly out of the surplus over wages, i.e., in their system, out of rents and profits. Malthus asserted that saving is done out of profit, while landlords use their income rather for consumption.[2] In this he was preceded by David Hume [3] and by William Spence [4] and was followed

[1]U.S. statistics do not show a significant increase in the savings ratio in the forty years before the first World War. This may be due to imperfections of the statistics, but it may also have other explanations. One is that since the country was being peopled with immigrants, who are notoriously thrift-minded, the propensity to save out of non-profit incomes may have been higher than elsewhere ; the farmers in particular seem to have been very thrifty (farmers employing labour count as capitalists in the Ricardian system). Another is that in a country developed with immigrant labour the non-capitalist sector may be very small from the start ; there is then little room for expansion of the capitalist sector relatively to the economy as a whole, so profits rise relatively to national income only if the profit margin is rising in the capitalist sector (see below, section (*b*)). A third possible explanation is that wages were rising rapidly, so profits did not rise as much relatively to national income as they would have done if wages had been constant. Wages were rising partly because productivity was increasing in the sources whence labour was being recruited (from Europe and also from domestic agriculture) (see below, section (*c*)). There was also an inflow of foreign capital, helping to raise wages.

[2]*Op. cit.*, pp. 465-6.

[3]*Essays, Moral, Political and Literary*, Vol. I, Part II, Essay IV, "Of Interest."

[4]*Britain Independent of Commerce*, 1808, quoted in Maurice Dobb, *Political Economy and Capitalism*, p. 51.

by Marx.[1] Smith, Ricardo, and J. S. Mill, however, are silent on this issue. Ricardo probably accepted the Malthusian version. At any rate, he had so many opportunities to dispute it, and he disputed so much else, that one may reasonably conclude from his silence that he was willing to accept it.

(*b*) *The First Stage of Development.*

So long as unlimited labour is available at a fixed real wage, the share of profits in the national income will increase. There are two reasons for this. First the share of profits in the capitalist sector may increase. And secondly the capitalist sector will expand relatively to national income.

Let us note first that in this system the rate of profit on capital cannot fall. As Ricardo pointed out,[2] however big the increase in capital may be, it can always be matched by a proportionate increase in the employment of labour. With given technology and unlimited labour at constant wages, no "deepening" of capital takes place ; only "widening." So the rate of profit on capital is constant. This was the point Ricardo continually reiterated to Malthus : the rate of profit could fall only if wages were rising. Ricardo thought that diminishing returns to land would raise wages, but we shall come to this in section (*c*).

Assuming away diminishing returns to land, the rate of profit on capital cannot fall. On the contrary, it must rise, because all the benefit of technological progress accrues to capital, the wage rate being constant. Thus, the rate of profit rises all the time, while the wage rate is constant. What happens to the relative share of profits depends partly on what technological progress does to the demand for labour. Relative shares in the capitalist sector will be constant if technological change increases the demand for labour in exactly the same proportion as it raises the rate of profit ; but the relative share of profits will rise if technological progress reduces the demand for labour, or leaves it unchanged, or increases it insufficiently. Though technological change must raise the profit rate relatively to

[1] *Capital*, Vol. I, Chapter XXIV, Section 3, "Separation of Surplus Valı into Capital and Revenue."

[2] *Principles of Political Economy and Taxation*, Sraffa editioı Chapter XXI, p. 289.

the wage rate, we cannot say *a priori* whether it will raise the share of profits in the capitalist sector, and therefore the ratio of saving. But, from what we know of innovations, it is not improbable that on balance the share of profits in the capitalist sector will rise.

Whatever the effect of innovations may be, the share of profits must rise relatively to national income for another reason, namely, the expansion of the capitalist sector relatively to the rest. This may not always be important. It will not be important if there is not much non-capitalist sector to begin with. Thus, if the capitalist sector expands by bringing immigrants into an empty country, capitalist sector and national economy virtually coincide. If the immigrants are available at a constant wage, the profit ratio may grow because of technological change, but not because the capitalist sector expands relatively to the national economy. Even if the non-capitalist sector is large, the capitalist sector will not expand relatively to the whole if the non-capitalist sector is growing as rapidly. This is unlikely, for reasons given when we discussed the superior productivity in the capitalist sector.

Thus, so long as labour is available at a constant wage, profits will grow relatively to national income, unless innovations are on balance highly favourable to the demand for labour; the savings ratio will grow, and the rate of growth of national income will accelerate.

(*c*) *The Turning Point.*

This acceleration must continue so long as the share of profits in the national income is increasing. Anything which raises wages relatively to profits will check the speed at which the rate of profit on capital is increasing; it may stabilise the share of profits (and so the rate of growth of the economy), or it may even cause the share of profits to fall. (As before, what happens to relative shares depends on what happens to employment as well as on what happens to rates of wages and profits).

Profits may be checked for one of three classes of reasons: (*i*) Wages may rise, or profits fall, for exogenous reasons not due to the expansion of the capitalist sector itself. (*ii*) The terms of trade may turn against the capitalist sector because of its expansion. Either (*i*) or (*ii*) may end the expansion of the capitalist sector even though there is still surplus labour available at the ruling wage. If not, expansion must eventually result in (*iii*) the supply of labour becoming inelastic, because capital accumulation has caught up with the labour supply.

(*i*) *Exogenous factors.* In this category we include checks which do not themselves result from the expansion of the capitalist sector. There are several possibilities, including natural disasters such as epidemics or earthquakes. We consider just three economic examples.

First, real wages may rise even though the labour supply is abundant. In the classical system the normal level of wages is the subsistence level at which the working class exactly reproduces its numbers. In Asia or Africa the wage floor is set by the productivity of small scale agriculture : men will not accept wage employment unless it yields at least as much as they would consume if they remained on the farm. In practice it must yield even more, perhaps as much as 50 per cent. more ; and thus the floor is set to wages. On the other hand, while the existence of excess supply makes it possible for capitalists to hold the wage at this level, they do not necessarily keep it there. For one thing, they may have moralistic notions which limit the rate of profit on capital ; e.g., they may think that a profit margin of say 25 per cent. is adequate, and they may therefore deliberately raise wages as productivity increases. Or they may react in the same way towards trade union pressure, or even to ward off the growth of unions. Thus, large industrial corporations in Japan pay wages twice as high as small industrial employers pay. If this is how capitalists normally behave, there will be an ever-widening gap between the wages they pay, and the subsistence wage at which unlimited labour is still available. This is consistent with Marx's proposition that the rate of exploitation or surplus value is constant,[1] which amounts to saying that the wage rate

[1]*Capital*, Book III, Chapter XIII "The Theory of the Law" (of the falling tendency of the rate of profit). There are "Counteracting Causes" in Chapter XIV, but the availability of labour at a constant wage rate, which is so important to the rest of his system, and which is inconsistent with Chapter XIII, is not mentioned here.

rises as rapidly as productivity ; elsewhere he says the opposite —wages are constant at the subsistence level—but he may have been unintentionally right. If so, rising wages are not an exogenous but an endogenous check. However, if we assume that wages rise proportionately with productivity, this does not stop capitalist expansion. It makes profits a constant proportion of income in the capitalist sector. Profits will still be a rising proportion of national income if there is a non-capitalist sector which is not expanding so rapidly. If there is no non-capitalist sector (e.g., a country developed by immigration for capitalist employment) profits and saving are a constant proportion of national income throughout, and the rate of capitalist expansion does not accelerate.[1]

Alternatively, wages may rise exogenously because the source from which labour is recruited is experiencing increasing productivity. Thus, if labour is being recruited from abroad, through immigration, from countries where wages are rising, wages will have to rise at home, too, or the rate of expansion will be checked. Malaya did not have to pay rising wages to Indians or to Chinese for this reason, but North America may have had to pay rising wages to European immigrants. Similarly, if labour is being recruited from peasant agriculture, where productivity is rising, it may be necessary to pay higher wages. This depends partly on whether the capitalist sector and the peasant sector trade with each other. If they do not trade, rising productivity in the peasant sector will certainly

[1]The evidence as to the behaviour of wages during the British industrial revolution is conflicting. Even contemporary writers disagreed. Professor T. S. Ashton suggests that we should think in terms of two groups of workers : those who benefited from the expansion of factory employment, and those who did not ("masses of unskilled or poorly skilled workers—seasonally employed agricultural workers and handloom weavers in particular"). There is no doubt that the former group increased in numbers relatively to the latter. Since the wage rate was higher in the capitalist sector than outside, this transfer of workers into the capitalist sector would automatically raise the "average" standard of life of the workers in the economy as a whole, even if the real wage in the capitalist sector remained constant. See "The Standard of Life of the Workers in England, 1790-1830" in *Capitalism and the Historians*, ed. F. A. Hayek. The question whether real wages *in the capitalist sector* rose during the first half of the nineteenth century remains unsettled. What with Irish immigration and a falling death rate, capital seems not to have caught up with labour supply until the second half of the century.

force up wages in the capitalist sector. If they trade, however, rising productivity may to some extent be offset by deteriorating terms of trade, even to the point where wages, considered not in terms of wage goods in general, but in terms of the commodities produced in the capitalist sector, may actually be reduced because the terms of trade are moving in favour of the capitalist sector.

A rise in real wages stops the profit rate from growing as rapidly as it otherwise would, but it does not necessarily bring expansion to an end. It will not even stop the acceleration of growth, if productivity is rising faster than wages. There may have been cases, in the real world, where the capitalist sector of a country ceased to expand because of an exogenous rise in wages, but one cannot think of many such cases. On the other hand, this is happening all the time in the expansion of towns or regions within a country, where the expansion of employment in one place, relatively to the rest of the economy, is brought to an end because developments elsewhere raise wages and drain away labour.

(*ii*) *The Terms of Trade.* Profits may be checked because the expansion of the capitalist sector moves the terms of trade against it. In these cases real wages remain constant, in terms of purchasing power over wage goods in general, but profits fall because a larger amount of the capitalist product has to be surrendered to and by the workers in order to purchase the constant quantity of wage goods.

The classical economists all predicted this fate for capitalism, because they believed that diminishing returns in agriculture would move the terms of trade in favour of landlords. Adam Smith had stated the opposite. In his system there is more than adequate technological improvement in agriculture, and rents diminish constantly relatively to national income.[1] So far Smith has proved right and the Ricardians wrong in all countries where agriculture is on a capitalist basis.

The position is quite different, however, in countries where agriculture is on a peasant basis. We know that productivity can increase sharply in peasant agriculture if research is being

[1] *The Wealth of Nations*, Modern Library edition, Book II, Chapter III, page 318.

done into peasant problems, and if an agricultural extension system, an agricultural credit system, roads, water supplies and so on are provided on an adequate basis. We also know, however, that peasant agriculture has a tendency to stagnate in the absence of such measures, and also that such measures have been adopted in relatively few countries. If the capitalist sector trades with the peasant sector (e.g., depends on it for food or for raw materials and therefore for markets), its continued expansion would be menaced if the peasant sector were stagnant, since this would move the terms of trade against the capitalist sector. In practice, failure of peasant agriculture to increase its productivity has probably been the chief reason holding down the expansion of the industrial sector in most of the under-developed countries of the world.

If domestic agriculture fails to expand, capitalist industry can nevertheless continue its expansion if it can substitute foreign trade. The expansion of industry then leads to ever-increasing imports of food and raw materials, matched by exports of manufactures. This, however, depends on the skill of the industrialists in opening up foreign markets. If they are inefficient competitors in foreign trade, the terms of trade will turn against them ; the expansion of home industry has then to be slowed down to the rate which the expansion of foreign trade is able to carry.[1]

An adverse movement of the terms is due to "unbalanced growth" of the various sectors of the economy. This may occur at any stage of economic development, at the beginning, in the middle, or after a century of rapid progress. It is probably the main reason why only a few countries have made substantial progress.

(*iii*) *Exhaustion of the Surplus.* It is possible for the capitalist sector to cease expanding long before the labour surplus is exhausted. Wages may be rising for exogenous reasons faster than productivity, so that expansion is checked even though at any time there is an excess supply of labour at the market rate. Similarly, profits may fall relatively to wages, through adverse terms of trade, although there is a perfectly

[1]For further discussion of this phenomenon, see my article "International Competition in Manufactures," *American Economic Review*, May, 1957.

elastic labour supply at a wage rate constant in terms of its purchasing power over wage goods. The system may, however, escape either of these fates. In that case, the capitalist sector will expand until capital accumulation catches up with the labour supply, whereupon we reach a new stage of economic development.

If the capitalist sector expands fast enough, it must sooner or later embrace the whole economy ; and wages will start to rise long before this happens.[1] Adam Smith recognized that capital could catch up with labour supply, and raise wages in the process.[2] Malthus, Ricardo and the other classical economists denied this, because they thought that population growth must keep up with accumulation. In this they were wrong. Medical knowledge was not in their day adequate to reduce death rates below 20 per 1,000 in Europe (North America seems to have been healthier) so the population could not increase faster than 2 per cent. per annum. Even to-day increases exceeding 3 per cent. per annum are most exceptional. Since capital can increase by more than 3 per cent. per annum, there is no difficulty in exhausting the labour surplus in due course.

Marx rejected the Malthusian population theory, but still thought that there would always be a surplus. He recognized that capital could catch up with the labour supply, since accumulation, as distinct from technological change, always increases employment if wages are constant. He argued, however, that once the limit of labour supply was reached, accumulation would raise wages, this would promote the "deepening" of capital, and so wages would fall back to their previous subsistence level.[3] This is an error in the same class as "if the demand increases the price will rise ; this will reduce the demand, and so the price will return to its previous level." Deepening and a rise in wages are not substitutes for each other ; deepening occurs only to the extent that wages rise. One can

[1]As people transfer from the non-capitalist to the capitalist sector, pressure is relieved, real consumption per head increases, and this shows itself sooner or later in a rise in the supply price of labour, even though there is still a labour surplus.

[2]*Op. cit.*, Book I, Chapter VIII, pp. 68-70.

[3]*Capital*, Vol. I, Chapter XXV.

make better sense of Marx by ignoring this error, and resting his case instead upon adverse technological inventions. Then, as soon as capital catches up with labour, and starts to raise wages, capitalists turn to the kind of innovation which reduces the demand for labour. No matter how fast capital may accumulate, the argument must continue, capitalists are always able to find enough technological innovations of the adverse kind to offset capital accumulation and also those innovations which increase the demand for labour. Now such a statement is a statement of fact. Marx gave no reason why it should be so. Yet practically the whole of his system rests on this assertion about the nature of technological progress—for it is this that keeps wages at the subsistence level, this that (in his under-consumption moods) produces the disproportion between saving and consumption, this that produces the ever-increasing reserve army of unemployed, this that increases the misery of the working-class, and so this that ultimately brings revolution and communism. Seldom has so much depended upon so little.

Where Marx was right was in making the point that for a while the capitalist sector creates surplus labour by invading sectors to which it is superior, especially by putting the handicraft workers out of business, and also by reducing the labour requirement in agriculture, if it is permitted to reorganize agriculture on a capitalist basis. A corollary of this is that, from the point of view of capitalist expansion, even a pre-capitalist economy with abundant land is capable of developing a labour surplus. For example in most of Africa and Latin America labour is more or less fully employed, since there is no shortage of cultivable land. However, a labour surplus could be created by the expansion of capitalist production at the expense of pre-capitalist forms of handwork, in manufacturing, in agriculture and elsewhere. But this substitution cannot continue forever. Sooner or later the pre-capitalist forms are all destroyed, and the labour surplus is exhausted.

Once capital catches up with labour, the supply of labour becomes inelastic. The countries which have surplus labour have never reached this stage. Their capitalist sectors have begun to expand at one period or another, but their expansion has hitherto always been checked by an unbalanced development, with labour still in excess-supply.

(*d*) *The Second Stage of Development.*

When capital catches up with labour supply, an economy enters upon the second stage of development. Classical economics ceases to apply ; we are in the world of neo-classical economics, where all the factors of production are scarce, in the sense that their supply is inelastic. Wages are no longer constant as accumulation proceeds ; the benefits of improved technology do not all accrue to profits ; and the profit margin does not necessarily increase all the time.[1]

Adam Smith seems to be the only economist to have recognized that there are these two different stages of economic development, with two different sets of results. Marx recognized that capital must sooner or later catch up with labour supply, but he evaded the issue.[2] The neo-classical economists in their turn have ignored the existence of the first stage ; have erroneously applied second-stage analysis to first-stage problems ; and have rudely brushed aside the classical writers as if their model were a mere evasion of reality. Failure to grasp the distinction between the two stages of development is the main reason why the historians of economic thought have made so little sense of the classical writers.

Once the second stage is reached, what happens to the profit ratio, savings, etc. ? Classical economics does not deal with this problem. Neo-classical writers have put forward

[1]Some pre-capitalist economies, where land is abundant (e.g., in Africa) have a formal similarity to second stage capitalist economies, in the sense that they have no labour surplus. Nevertheless, since a capitalist sector could expand within these economies at constant wages, by destroying their small scale manufacturing and agricultural sectors, and so producing a labour surplus, these economies are more properly regarded as being in a stage which precedes the first stage of capitalist expansion than as being in the second stage. In other words, Adam Smith and Karl Marx throw more light on how these economies will develop than does Walras or Pigou.

[2]Lenin recognized that there is more than one stage of capitalism, but he gave the wrong reason for this. Following Marx, he did not see that real wages must rise, and he attributed the phenomena of the second stage (capital export, etc.) to the concentration of capital in monopolies. Also he had no warrant for suggesting that there are only two stages. V. I. Lenin, *Imperialism, the Last Stage of Capitalism.*

many theories of distribution (marginal productivity, perfectly elastic supply of capital, the degree of monopoly, Keynesian equilibrium between investment and saving via the profit ratio, etc.) but their very profusion shows how unsatisfactory they all are.

Whichever neo-classical theory may win the day, it seems that one of the facts it will have to explain is why the ratio of profits to national income becomes relatively stable (apart from cyclical variations) in the second stage. The classical model cannot explain this, but if one accepts the stability, the classical model can throw light on the level at which the ratio stabilises. For, since the ratio rises during the first stage and then stabilises, the task of explaining where it stabilises really belongs to the first stage, and so to the classical model.

This line of explanation traces back to the proposition that during the first stage technological innovation raises the rate of profit on capital, but not the wage rate. Wherefore, unless innovations are on balance very favourable to employment (raising employment as much as they raise the profit rate) the profit margin will increase all the time. We may represent the situation schematically by supposing that technology has been raising productivity steadily since some such arbitrary date as 1800 A.D., and has raised profits faster than employment. Then, in every country in the first stage of development, the potential profit margin would rise from 1800 to such date as it entered its second stage of development. It follows that profit margins will be lowest in countries which reach their second stage earliest, and will be highest in countries where the second stage is longest delayed. It follows also that the countries which begin to develop latest will stabilise with higher savings ratios and higher rates of growth than those which reach their second stage earliest. The conclusion is subject to many modifications. (1) The effect of innovations on employment is not the same in every country. (2) The capitalist sectors of different countries do not use the same technology at the same time. (3) Subsistence wages are not the same in different countries, and are increasing at different rates ; profit margins should be much higher in countries where the peasants' productivity is low, such as Central Africa, than where it is high, such as Japan.

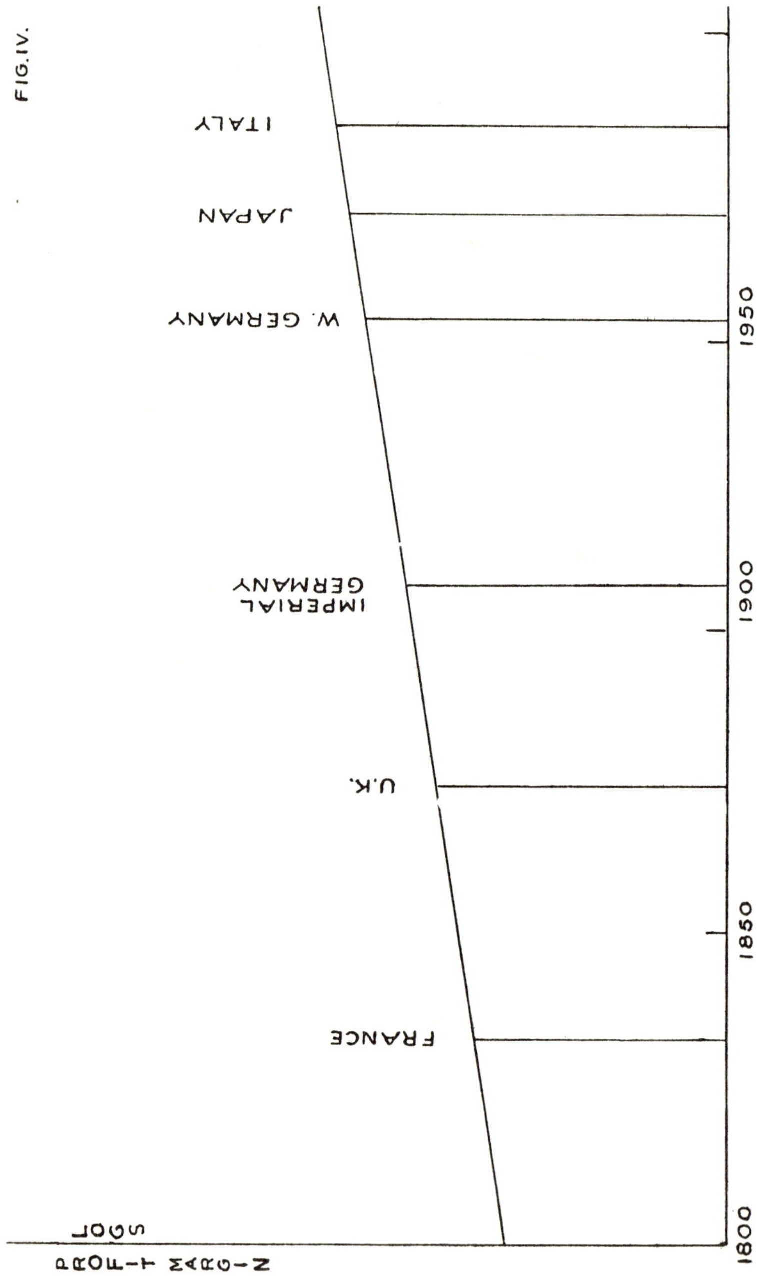
FIG.IV.
ITALY
JAPAN
W. GERMANY
IMPERIAL GERMANY
U.K.
FRANCE
1800
1850
1900
1950

(4) The margin between actual wages and the subsistence level is not the same everywhere. And (5) the international migration of capital tends to prevent differences in the rate of profit from being as wide as they would otherwise be. Nevertheless, there is a little evidence supporting the order which is indicated in the accompanying diagram. France seems to have reached her second stage earliest in Western Europe, because of her slow population growth and comparatively stagnant agriculture. Western Germany entered upon a new first stage after the second world war, because of refugee immigration ; she has recently re-entered the second stage. Of the advanced capitalist countries, profit margins seem to be highest in Western Germany, in Japan (which now expects to reach its turning point in about ten years, because of the sharp fall in its birth rate) and in Italy, where the labour surplus is still substantial.

IV. Ricardian Socialism.

Analysis is not the same as prescription. This model shows that employment expands as the share of national income accruing to private profits increases. It does not follow that those who make this analysis advocate increasing the share of private profits in the national income.

Both Adam Smith and Ricardo refuted this charge specifically. In Adam Smith's model the rate of wages rises continuously, and both the rate of profits and also the share of rent in the national income fall. He welcomed this state of affairs :

> "Is this improvement in the circumstances of the lower ranks of the people to be regarded as an advantage or as an inconveniency to the society ? The answer seems at first sight abundantly plain. Servants, labourers and workmen of different kinds, make up the far greater part of every great political society. But what improves the circumstances of the greater part can never be regarded as an inconveniency to the whole. No society can surely be flourishing and happy, of which the far greater part of the members are poor and miserable. It is but equity, besides, that they who feed, clothe and lodge the whole body of the people, should have such a share of the produce of their own labour as to be themselves tolerably fed, clothed and lodged." [1]

[1] *Op. cit.*, page 78. See also pp. 87 and 92-5.

Even Ricardo wanted wages to rise at the expense of both profits and rents. What prevented this, in his model, was that population increases if the wage rate rises above the natural rate. However,

> "It is not to be understood that the natural price of labour, estimated even in food and necessaries, is absolutely fixed and constant. It varies at different times in the same country, and very materially differs in different countries. It essentially depends on the habits and customs of the people . . . The friends of humanity cannot but wish that in all countries the labouring classes should have a taste for comforts and enjoyments, and that they should be stimulated by all legal means in their exertions to procure them. There cannot be a better security against a super-abundant population.[1] "

With these words Ricardo opened the door to the socialists, for these words implied that rent and profit were an arbitrary levy, the size of which was determined wholly by the attitude of the working classes toward reproduction, as reflected in the natural price below which they would not maintain the labour force. The argument was thus shifted from the analytical to the ethical plane. What right had land and capital to share in the produce of labour ? As Thomas Hodgskin put it :

> "The landlord and the capitalist produce nothing. Capital is the product of labour, and profit is nothing but a portion of that produce, uncharitably exacted for permitting the labourer to consume a part of what he has himself produced.[2] "

Marx despised these Ricardian socialists. He called them "utopians" because they shifted from the analytical to the ethical plane. He preferred his own "scientific" demonstration that the socialist revolution was inevitable. But apart from the failure of his "science," in the last analysis it is on the ethical plane that social problems have to be solved.

The capitalist has found defenders along two lines. First, the marginal productivity theory of distribution denies that the whole produce is due to labour, and claims to be able to show precisely how much is contributed respectively by labour, by land, and by capital "at the margin." This returns the question to the analytical plane, without answering the ethical question. Even if one can calculate the marginal productivity

[1] *Principles*, pp. 96,. 100.

[2] Quoted in Esther Lowenthal, *The Ricardian Socialists.*

of land, it does not follow that a particular group of citizens, entitled landowners, should receive a sum equal to marginal product times quantity. The marginal productivity theory shows how much *land* puts in *at the margin,* and how much *landowners* are able to extract *in total,* in a purely competitive society ; but it does not tell us how much landowners *should* get, if anything.

The second line of defence proceeds along Benthamite lines by demonstrating that it is necessary to the good of society as a whole, including the workers, that capitalists should receive a large share of the product—both to encourage enterprise, and also as a source of saving. This implies that neither enterprise nor saving is possible without private profit. The answers to this are well known. The school of co-operators advances co-operative enterprise and saving as one alternative; the socialists advance public enterprise and public saving as another alternative. The answers to these answers are also well known. Thus the purpose of this postscript is fulfilled : to warn the reader that he should not try to deduce directly from this model of economic expansion any prescription relating to the social institutions which economic development requires.

W. Arthur Lewis

University of Manchester.

APPENDIX

I take this opportunity to draw attention to two errors in the earlier article, which have been pointed out by Professor Harry Johnson.

1. On page 174 it is implied that if the elasticity of demand for food were unity, increased productivity in the subsistence sector would be exactly offset by an adverse price movement. This neglects the fact that, since the subsistence workers consume some of their own product, their income elasticity of demand for it has to be taken into account as well as the buyers' price elasticity. My formulation would have been correct only if the subsistence workers sold all they produce. However, the main points of the paragraph are unaffected, namely that the capitalist sector benefits if the change in the terms of trade more than offsets the increase in productivity, and secondly that this is what happens in practice.

2. On pages 182-3 it is assumed that "both countries produce food but do not trade in it," as well as that each produces a second product. It is then concluded that the relative prices of these second products are determinate. However, these relative prices are determinate only because it is assumed that one unit of food in country *A* must equal one unit of food in country *B*, and it is only the possibility of trade in food which ensures this equality. My assumption therefore is not that they do not trade in food, but that whether they do or not, equilibrium is maintained by the possibility of trade. But, given that this is the assumption, case two on pages 182-3 is really only a special example of case three on page 185.

[15]

Topic 2: Employment Policy in an Underdeveloped Area

EMPLOYMENT POLICY IN AN UNDERDEVELOPED AREA

By

W. A. Lewis

I

Most countries in the early stages of economic development have not one economy, but two. They have a high wage economy and a low earnings economy. Broadly speaking, in the high wage economy we find people employed by plantations, factories, mines, large-scale transportation and so forth. And in the low earnings economy we find people in family farms, handicrafts, domestic servants, petty traders, casual labour and so on.

The relative proportions of the population engaged in these two different economies depends upon the amount of capital offering employment in the high wage economy, and upon the level of wages in that economy. Given the amount of physical resources, and the state of the arts, we may conceive, in the usual neo-classical terms, of the volume of employment being determined by people being taken on in the high-wage economy up to the point where the marginal productivity of labour equals the wage. All the rest of the labour force then fares as best it can in the low earnings economy.

The best measure of overpopulation is to be found in the low earnings sector, because when the high wage sector has taken what it wants at the given levels of wages, of capital, and of technology, the rest of the people have to squeeze themselves in as best they can. In countries where agriculture is on the basis of family farms we find the surplus population on the farms. In overpopulated countries where there are not family farms, such as Barbados, you find the surplus population in domestic service, in petty trading, casual labour, and other such occupations. It is irrelevant to the analysis whether the marginal productivity of labour in this sector is negative, zero, or merely small. So long as it is lower than the wage that is paid in the high wage sector, there will be a surplus in the labour market; that is to say, that at the going wage in the high wage sector capitalists can always get more labour if they so desire. This is a typical feature of economies in the first stages of economic development.

In most of these economies the level of wages is determined by the productivity of the family farmers. They have one acre, one and a half acres, two acres, or three acres, and given their techniques, the amounts of capital, and the amounts of land that they have at their disposal, their productivity sets

42

the minimum. The actual wage in the high wage sector is always significantly above the earnings in the low earning sector, seldom less than fifty per cent more. In Japan I was told this April that the large factories are paying wages that are twice as high as are paid by the small factories. The gap widens all the time. It widens partly because in these days trade unions are effective in the high wage sector, and push the wage up all the time; and partly because even in the absence of trade unions it is a habit of capitalists to pass on to the workers in their firms some part of the benefit of high technology and of high capital intensity. So wages tend to rise in the high wage sector as productivity rises in that sector, and the gap between the high wage of that sector and the earnings in the rest of the economy tends to widen. Mr. Thorne commented yesterday that he had found evidence of this in Jamaica.

One should note that overpopulation does not necessarily show itself in unemployment. The high wage sector having taken such labour as it requires, the rest of the people have to squeeze themselves into the other sector. If one gets unemployment it is partly because provision is made for the unemployed. If there is no provision for the unemployed people cannot afford to be unemployed, and somehow or other they will have to find some kind of means of subsistence in the rest of the economy.

The development of unemployment in the underdeveloped countries is a comparatively recent phenomenon. There have always been beggars in the towns, but within recent years there has been in all the underdeveloped countries an enormous drift of workers from the countryside into a few large commercial capitals – the phenomenon that was mentioned this morning. An enormous growth has taken place in towns like Calcutta, Djarkarta, or Kingston, all over the world, in which the population is increasing at enormous rates – much faster than the employment possibilities of these towns, and much faster than new houses can be built. Slum areas are growing, and we have all the usual phenomena – juvenile delinquency, crime, political agitation, and so on.

This drift has several causes. It is due partly to relief – in the underdeveloped world we are now kinder to the unemployed than we used to be fifty or one hundred years ago; more provision is made for the unemployed in these towns. It is due partly to the fact that such development as is taking place in these towns itself provides better opportunities for casual employment so that these towns are developing a great number of hangers-on, who work for one day a week, or two days a week, carry your bag, and so on. It is due partly to the awakening in the countryside. Education is spreading into the countryside, and the modern world is reaching the countryside in all sorts of ways. People in the countryside are becoming dissatisfied, seeking adventure, drifting into these vast towns of which they hear. And it is also due partly to the growing wage gap itself, which by raising the level of those who have employment in the towns, attracts more and more people to come into these towns.

It is very difficult to know how to cope with this increase in urban unemployment. The normal way to cope with unemployment is to provide work, but this is no solution in this case. On the contrary it merely aggravates the problem, because the more work you provide in the towns the more people will drift into the towns, and there is no certainty that you can win the race. So long as there exists a large pool of people in the low earnings sector of the economy, then the more work the towns offer, the bigger is likely to be the drift into the towns. No one ought to say that he knows how to cure unemployment in this situation, or that he has a means of providing sufficient employment rapidly for all those who are unemployed in the towns. He may have a hundred thousand unemployed in the town and provide employment for a hundred and twenty thousand, and at the end of that process still have two hundred thousand unemployed because still more have been attracted by his success.

Though this is a relatively new phenomenon in the underdeveloped countries, it is not a phenomenon without precedents. For example, this drift gave very much trouble and much cause for thought in the second and the third British industrial revolutions; the second in the reign of Queen Elizabeth the First, when substantial industrialization took place under the benevolent dictatorship of Lord Burleigh; and the third, and the more familiar one, in the second half of the eighteenth century. In both these periods we read of great migrations from the countryside, agrarian revolutions occurring at the same time; we read of great increases in vagabondage, as it was called in those days, and we find government on both occasions trying to cope with the problem by using the crudest means, namely, to send people back. That, in a sense, is the simplest way of dealing with this problem; to prevent people from coming to the towns, and if they come to the towns to send them back or lock them up. This method is used, even today in the Union of South Africa for the purpose of preventing the African population from drifting into the towns. Less drastically, one might simply refuse to recognize the existence of unemployment by providing no relief for it; thus trying to discourage people from coming into the towns by making it as unpleasant as possible for them to be there. But even this is not wholly successful, because the drift is not entirely due to relief measures, and is to be found even in those towns where there are no relief measures. So long as there is some possibility of casual employment at a relatively high wage there will be people taking the risk.

In talking about this problem this morning we said that to prevent the growth of these towns one should concentrate on development elsewhere; development in other towns and, of course, development in rural areas. I doubt whether development in rural areas would be adequate to stop this drift. Development in rural areas is limited by the shortage of natural resources which we have by definition in overpopulated countries. Combined with the rapid growth of population this makes it pretty certain that however much you do to develop the rural areas you will still have a surplus which will be drifting into the towns. Personally, therefore, I regard this part of the problem as insoluble. I think it is inevitable that we shall have a considerable amount of unemployment in the towns at this stage of economic development, however rapidly we may be providing jobs. Therefore, if we wish to measure our achievements in development, we must measure them not by the fall of unemployment, but by the increase in employment. The success that we have in creating employment is what is relevant rather than our failure in reducing unemployment. For we are not likely to do very much to reduce unemployment in a short period of a decade or so. Let us then turn from unemployment to discussing the level of employment in the general context of economic development.

II

Economic development proceeds in two ways. First productivity is raised all round, in both the high wage and the low earnings sectors of the economy. And secondly the high wage part of the economy is expanded relatively to the low earnings part, thus reducing the surplus in domestic service, family farming, and so forth. Both these are important processes. I would be more happy speaking about the first since it is the easier problem. We know what needs to be done to raise the general level of productivity in all the various sectors of the economy; my instructions, however, are to speak about the second — about the expansion of employment in the high wage sector of the economy so that some of the surplus is drained off and the high wage sector expands. So my remarks this afternoon are confined entirely to this problem.

The level of employment in the high wage sector of the economy depends upon three things. It depends first upon the physical resources of that sector; secondly on the technology used in that sector; and thirdly on the wage level. What I have to say will be set in the framework of analyzing each of these three influences. They are somewhat dissimilar in that whereas an increase in resources always raises the level of employment in this sector, an improvement in technology may increase employment or it may reduce employment. Similarly a rise in wages may increase employment or reduce employment.

Take first the increase in resources. An increase in the amount of resources must increase the level of employment in this sector, given the wage rate, and the technology in use. This follows from the law of diminishing returns. If you are given more capital it must pay you better to use the more capital with more labour, than to use the more capital with the same quantity of labour. Hence, contrary to what has sometimes been suggested, capital accumulation must increase the level of employment, unless it is accompanied by adverse changes in technology or in wages, of the kinds to which we shall refer later.

Now one must not make the mistake of equating "physical resources" with capital. The distinction between man-made resources and natural resources is fundamental in this context. An increase in population can be matched by an increase in man-made resources. One can conceive of trebling the population and trebling the amount of capital, and if it were only a matter of man-made capital the discussion we had this morning about whether overpopulation is possible would be unnecessary. Since capital can increase faster than population, overpopulation in this morning's sense would be impossible. But capital is not a perfect substitute for natural resources, such as land, water and minerals, and therefore a shortage of natural resources can be an obstacle to enonomic development. This is the basic answer to this morning's question. A country is beginning to be overpopulated when the substitution of capital for natural resources is becoming more and more expensive.

Are the West Indian territories overpopulated already in this sense? There seems to me no doubt that the islands, with the exception of Trinidad, are overpopulated in this sense, one of the simplest indications being the fact that in the last fifty years the population has increased enormously without any comparable increase in the area of land under cultivation. There is doubtless room for increasing the natural resources by some expenditure of capital, making more land by drainage and soil conservation, water preservation, and so on; but as we saw on Sunday in our tour of the Yallahs Valley this is a very expensive operation and the extent to which it becomes necessary is itself the index of overpopulation.

If one turns from the islands to the mainland territories the picture is somewhat different. It is improper to include British Honduras. The people of British Honduras have made it clear to us in no uncertain terms that they do not propose to let us in. British Honduras is not available to the West Indies for development. Unless we propose to invade British Honduras, make war, conquer the territory and colonize it, the size of British Honduras is irrelevant to any discussion on the prospects of the West Indian Federation. British Guiana has told us to keep out, but it is whispered that there is a possibility that it may come into the Federation, and therefore there may be some point in considering its prospects. I find it very hard to assess the agricultural possibilities of British Guiana. It is very clear that the coastal areas, although very fertile, are also extremely difficult to maintain because of the high cost of the drainage system. It is also clear that as one moves from the coastal areas much of the immediate hinterland is barren. Much money is now being spent on opening up land for cultivation, but there is already a large surplus population in British Guiana, growing rapidly, which has prior claims. So, whatever the ultimate prospects may be fifty years from now, for immediate practical purposes we must conclude that the land area available to the inhabitants of the West Indies Federation is the area of the islands. We must therefore conclude that the West Indies Fëderation is an overpopulated area where shortage of natural resources is an obstacle to economic development.

Now the classical economists, in particular Ricardo, made much of this fact that the shortage of natural resources is an obstacle to economic development, when they were writing about the development of a closed economic system. They foresaw economic stagnation for the world as a whole arising out of this obstacle. But when they were writing about an open economy they came to quite a different conclusion. Taking not the world as a whole but any particular part of it, they rescued it by bringing in the law of comparative costs. Even if a country is short of natural resources it can nevertheless make a good living by importing the products of natural resources and exporting the products of labour and capital. This is whence we derive the proposition that any overpopulated country in which development is taking place — we notice the qualification, in which development is taking place — will have to import more and more food and raw materials and to export manufactures in exchange. This proposition is well exemplified by history, ancient and modern. In ancient history by the development of ancient Greece; in modern history by the development of Britain, Germany, Japan and India, (whose exports are already more than half manufactures). If our analysis of the West Indian territories is correct the same must happen in due course in the West Indies.

Now this proposition, although it has the full backing not only of economic theory and of economic history, ancient and modern, is for some reason always resisted in the West Indies. We have had a series of official reports which have denied it. They have said in effect: "The West Indies is obviously agricultural. Land is obviously its main resource; obviously the most important thing to do is to develop the land, and any talk about industrial development for export market is silly". This is complete nonsense. This kind of statement can be made of any country at the appropriate stage of its development. You could have said of England in 1800: "England is obviously agricultural, most of its people are engaged in agriculture. Land is its main resource. Obviously England should concentrate on agriculture and any talk of industrial development for export markets is silly". One could have said that of Germany in 1850, or of the United States as late as 1900. It is obviously nonsensical. What is important in this context is not where the country now is, but what its future must be, having regard to the limits of its natural resources and to the principle of comparative cost.

The persistence of this attitude is hard to understand. In 1949 I was asked by the Caribbean Commission to write a report on this subject. In the light of this analysis I turned to consider what possible markets there might be for light manufactures exported from the West Indies. I said that the countries in a similar position to the West Indies, especially Latin America, were likely to develop the same kind of manufactures as the West Indies, so that it was useless to look for major markets there. One should look for markets rather to the countries which were well endowed with industrial resources, particularly with heavy industry; these would find it profitable to concentrate on manufacturing heavy industries, and would be able to import light manufactures. I gave Britain as an example. At once several people said that I was talking through my hat, as Britain being a highly developed industrial country, would not import manufactures. Well within the next three or four years Britain developed an enormous importation of textiles from India and Hong Kong, revealing a market which if the West Indies had gone into it would have provided a very substantial level of employment here for us. What was the difference between India and Hong Kong on the one hand, and the West Indies on the other? . . . I suggest to you among other phenomena a lack of initiative, a lack of imagination, a lack of willingness to take the risks of developing an export trade in manufactures. This willingness to take risks is not evenly spread throughout the world, but we shall have to develop it here if we are to make a living from our meagre resources.

Now I hope you will not misunderstand me. I have never anywhere suggested that industrialization is the one and only solution for West Indian problems. The West Indies, or any other country, has to make the best use of every resource that it has; of land, of water, of mountain scenery, of climate, and of skill; every conceivable resource that we have must be exploited to the full. All I have said on this subject is that when we have exploited everything that we can exploit to the full we will find . . . that the net result will be that we have developed ourselves as importers of food and raw materials and as exporters of manufactures. Why this proposition is still regarded in the West Indies as revolutionary beats me.

III

These remarks on industrialization have diverted me from my theme. I have said that the level of employment in the high wage sector of economy depends upon three things: upon the resources used in that sector, upon its technology, and upon the level of wages. I have said that an increase of resources must lead to an increase in employment, subject to an appropriate deployment of international trade. I come now to technology.

Instinctively we all stress the importance of technology and of education in economic development. Nevertheless it is a very old story that an improvement in technology may actually reduce employment and indeed in the extreme case may even reduce the national income. The theoretical argument dates back to the last chapter of Ricardo's *Principles*. Ricardo wrestled with the problem. He admitted that in the short run the new technology might reduce the national income, but he argued that it could not do so in the long run. He believed that the level of saving and investment depends not on the size of national income but on the amount of profits. So the higher the level of profits the higher the level of saving; and therefore the higher the rate of capital accumulation. Now, said Ricardo, what is important in the long run is the increase in the level of employment, and this is dependent upon the rate of capital accumulation. A new technology will not be adopted unless it raises profits, and in raising profits it raises the rate of saving and the rate of capital accumulation. It therefore raises the rate at which employment grows. The absolute level of income and of employment may be reduced by the new technology, but since the rate of growth is increased, employment must in the long run be greater than it would have been without the new technology.

If one accepts the Ricardian postulate that the level of saving is a function of the level of profits rather than of national income, then the most important thing to do in economic development is to maximize profits – don't mind about employment in the short run, and don't even mind the national income. The most important thing to do is to maximize profits and the rate of capital accumulation, and so ultimately the level of employment and the national income. The Ricardian postulate I should think valid of pure capitalist economies. But it does not have to be valid; economies do not have to be conducted on the basis that the level of saving is primarily a function of the level of profits. I shall argue later that the West Indian economy should not be conducted on that basis, and it will follow from this argument that I do not accept the Ricardian conclusion.

My approach to this problem follows a different line. One can establish theoretically as Ricardo did, that some kinds of technological progress are harmful to the level of income and of employment even though they increase profits. Not all kinds; much technological progress increases the level of employment, and much is neutral. However, some types have adverse effects. Yet in practice I would be very reluctant to interfere with technological progress because one can never be certain what technological progess is going to do. It always opens up new opportunities the ultimate results of which cannot be foreseen. For example, when the British started to build cotton factories it was undoubtedly arguable that as the hand loom weavers could produce what was wanted, the increase in profits was not matched by an increase in output; all one got at first was more profits and less employment. Nevertheless it turned out that the introduction of the factory system was the important thing and not the production of cotton. What was important was that the cotton factories pioneered in a new technique of organizing human labour on a large scale, which spread all through the world, and applied ultimately to nearly every kind of production. So that one can never be certain that technological progress will be adverse, because one cannot foresee its ultimate effects.

This problem has not arisen to any great extent in the West Indies, mainly because the amount of small scale production for the home market has not been large. In some islands measures have been taken to restrain the development of large scale factories in the extraction of oil from copra, in the interest of small scale production. Much the same argument is used in retail trading. For example, in parts of West Africa there has been a clamour to restrain improvements in the technology of retail trade, in order to protect the interests of small traders; this issue being tied up in West Africa also with racial considerations, the innovators being largely Syrians and the small traders Africans. The most important case in the West Indies is the sugar industry. Barbados is probably the best example of this. The island is undoubtedly overpopulated, with a vast surplus of labour. It obviously does not make economic sense for the Barbadians to use their limited foreign exchange reserves to import machinery to do forms of work on sugar plantations which could just as well be done by human labour. And yet at the current level of wages it pays the sugar producers to do so. Their case is that since they produce for a competitive market they cannot neglect innovations which are introduced elsewhere.

One could answer this case by subsidizing labour, i.e., by subsidizing employment. Thus one would lower the cost of labour relatively to the cost of imported machinery and thereby make it more profitable for the Barbadian planters to use labour rather than to use machinery. This however, brings me to the third factor, the wage level which determines the level of employment in the high wage sector, and I would like to turn to exploring this.

IV

Just as in the case of technological improvements the result may run either way, so in the case of wages an increase in wages may either reduce or increase the level of employment. We are all accustomed to thinking that an increase in wages must necessarily reduce employment, but of course there has been much evidence to the contrary.

There are two exceptional cases. There is the case where the increase in wages improves the physical or the psychological condition of the labourer, and therefore makes it possible for him to do correspondingly more work. This phenomenon is frequently found in the early stages of capitalism before capitalists have learnt their business. It is obviously not in the interest of an employer to pay a man such low wages that he is not able to do his work properly. In most modern economies capitalists have learned to enquire very carefully how many calories are being consumed by their workers, how much protein, and how happy they are at their work. I should imagine that in the West Indies, sugar employers, bauxite employers and oil employers are very well up on these matters, so that this exception does not apply in their case, though I can well imagine that there are many other parts of the West Indian economy where it would apply.

The second exception is where the increase in wages squeezes profits, wakes the employer up, and forces him to adopt new managerial techniques. This phenomenon too belongs to the early stages of capitalism and is not very likely in the more advanced sectors of the West Indian economy, though very likely indeed over a considerable range.

Apart from these two exceptions, if one lowered the level of wages — real wages — one would have more employment. There would be less substitution of capital for labour; and there would also be an incentive to adopt technologies which are more appropriate to a low wage level. In an open economy where some capital comes in and some goes out, it might lead to a very large increase in the level of employment, since a fall in wages might make employment so profitable that there was a very large influx of capital from abroad. Similarly a rise in wages may lead to a very large efflux of capital because of the fall in the rate of profit. Most observers of the West Indian scene have concluded that real wages are too high in the West Indies in the sense that if wages were lower the national income in the West Indies would be larger, and the volume of employment would also be larger. I see no reason to dispute this judgment. The evidence for it is the slow growth of employment in the high wage sector of the economy, and the continuance of a large pool in the low earnings sector. However, where do we go from here?

There is no prospect of reducing the level of money wages; consequently if one wished to proceed by reducing the level of real wages, one would have to investigate the routes for lowering real wages without lowering money wages. This is essentially a matter of raising the cost of living without raising money wages correspondingly. It can be done in various ways. Firstly, one could raise import duties; this raises the cost of living, and stimulates the production of import substitutes, thus increasing employment. Or, if the imports continue to come in, use the proceeds of the taxation to subsidize the production of exports; raise employment in that way. Secondly there is the possibility of devaluation, which is the simplest way to achieve at the same time both a cut in imports and an increase in exports. Devaluation is the orthodox remedy for the high wage situation, the remedy which has been adopted at one time or another by every single advanced country in the world – the United States, France, Germany, Britain – any country that you may care to name except Switzerland. Yet whenever this matter is suggested in the West Indies hands are raised in horror – this is a form of wickedness which we would never contemplate! Bearing this horror in mind I hasten to remind you that I am not advocating devaluation, I am merely engaged in exploring various ways that there are of reducing the level of real wages without reducing money wages. The third of these is to increase employment by subsidizing employers, presumably levying the taxes on the employees, which would reduce their real standards of living and at the same time increase the profits of employers. One method of doing this, which is now universal in the West Indies, is pioneer tax relief. Pioneer tax relief is a form of subsidy to employers. The loss of revenue presumably has to be made up by taxing the rest of the population.

All these methods have the same purpose of lowering the level of real wages, increasing the level of profits, and increasing employment and the national income. They are therefore all subject to the same objections. Firstly they are subject to the objection that with the fall in real wages there is an increase in profit. This is indeed the whole point of the exercise: to make it more profitable for employers to employ more people. One should note that it is an increase in the rate of profit, and not necessarily an increase in the share of profits in the national income since the latter depends on what happens to the level of employment. If a small increase in the rate of profit could bring about a large increase in the level of employment the share of wages in the national income would actually be increased and there would be also a very much larger national income. If you don't like this, then you must think in terms not of a capitalist economy but of a socialist economy, because this is how capitalist economies work. They depend for their dynamic on private profits. If you want to run a system on this basis you must have a high rate of profit. Not that a socialist economy can afford a much higher wage level; here too profits are needed in order to pay for public services through taxation, and in order to finance capital formation. The main difference is that the profits are on public rather than on private account.

The second objection to all these methods of trying to reduce real wages is that they may be ineffective. If when the cost of living rises, workers merely demand and get correspondingly higher money wages, the exercise is pointless. Now something like this tends to happen, but it is clear that it need not and does not usually go all the way. Many countries have devalued, and though there has been some increase in money wages, the increase has not been large enough completely to offset the devaluation.

The third objection is at the administrative level, and it runs much as follows. The economic system is full of imperfections, and there is therefore always the strong temptation to take administrative action to remedy its defects. However, administrative action is itself worse than the defects which it seeks to remedy, because the moment a government begins to "interfere" with the economic system it opens the way to forms of corruption, lobbying and administrative inefficiency which are worse than the defects which you are trying to deal with. This objection is clearly valid in a number of countries; and clearly untrue in a number of other countries. Whether it is true or untrue of the British West Indian Federation you will be able to answer better than I.

V

Now I have reached the end of my analysis. I can sum it up as follows. The level of employment and of national income can be increased in three ways. By spending more upon technology, by operating upon wages, and by increasing the quantity of physical resources. Under the heading of technology we must obviously encourage all those innovations which are favourable to employment and to output as a whole. We could also discourage those which are certain to reduce employment or output, but I have suggested that we would be wiser not to restrict technological improvement. So the net result under this heading is an enormous programme of expenditure, on research, education, and the improvement of the human material.

Under wages, we could reduce real wages not by forcing down money wages but by raising the cost of living through one of the various ways that

I mentioned. The purpose of this would be to raise profits and so employment and income, at the expense of reducing the standards of living of those who work. How far this is politically practicable I am not competent to judge. Perhaps I should reiterate that this is not the only way to increase the level of employment; this is one of three ways, and if you judge that it is politically impracticable to do anything whatsoever about the level of wages then it follows not that you must have a low level of employment, but that you must be prepared to do all the more to improve technology and to provide capital resources. For, whatever the level of wages may be, the level of employment and output will always be larger if labour is more productive.

Our third remedy is more capital. Very fortunately it has been left to Mr. Prest and to Sir Donald MacDougall to tell us in detail where this is to come from, but I wish to forestall them by saying my piece on this subject, because I wish to say very firmly that in my judgment the West Indies can supply all the capital that is required if it is prepared to do so.

Let us first ask what is the required order of magnitude. We need for development purposes something like an extra five or six per cent of national income in order to add something like two per cent per annum to our present rate of growth. Five or six per cent of the national income per annum is the price. It is a very low price even if you were to assume that we achieved it all at once by having an immediate reduction in consumption. For if by taking six per cent off now, we could raise consumption by two per cent per annum, we should have caught up again in three years. Three years of investing six per cent more of the national income would bring us back to where we would otherwise have been, and give us a faster rate of increase of the national income than we had before. Now to do it all at once would be heroic. Well, the national income per head is actually increasing. So all that we need to do is to stop consumption per head increasing so rapidly for a while, and within say ten years we could have increased the amount of resources available for development purposes by five or six per cent of national income painlessly, in the sense of without having caused consumption to stop growing.

How would we get hold of this six per cent? By taxation. It cannot be done simply by making propaganda urging people to save. It could be done by increasing the level of taxation and using the proceeds for capital formation and for the improvement of the human material. That is to say, for spending in the public sector on research, education, public health and so forth, and for spending in the public and private sectors on capital formation; in the public sector on land reclamation, electricity, water supplies, and so on; and by lending capital to the private sector, through the agricultural credit institutions, and through industrial banks and residential building agencies.

This opinion that the West Indies can raise all the capital it needs from its own resources is bound to shock many people, because West Indians like to feel that ours is a poor community. But the fact of the matter is that at least half of the people in the world are poorer than we are. The standard of living in the West Indies is higher than the standard of living in India, or China, in most of the countries of Asia, and in most of the countries of Africa. The West Indies is not a poor community; it is in the upper bracket of world income. It is capable of producing the extra five or six per cent of resources which is required for this job, just as Ceylon and Ghana are finding the money they need for development by taxing themselves. It is not necessary for us to send our statesmen around the world begging for help. If help is given to us let us accept it, but let us not sit down and say nothing can be done until the rest of the world out of its goodness of heart is willing to grant us charity.

And now I have done altogether. The task of the economist *qua* economist in analyzing the problems of economic development is very simple. There is no secret formula for economic development. Economists do not know anything more about this than is known to the man in the street. Development means building for the future by restraining ourselves in the present. Very simple analytically, difficult politically. But when one says that though some policy is the right thing to do it is difficult to achieve politically, one is saying only that in a democratic community it is the duty of all of us who think we understand these matters to take part in educating our fellow citizens. In a democratic community the right thing can always be done if the makers of public opinion understand that it is the right thing. This is the challenge which now faces the West Indies. Our statesmen have to use all their courage, all their imagination, and all their powers of persuasion to make our people understand that this is a job which has to be done, and which can be done. There are still people in the world who doubt whether we shall rise to this occasion. It is for us to prove them wrong.

[16]

Unemployment in developing countries

W. ARTHUR LEWIS

My subject is urban unemployment, which is growing rapidly in many under-developed countries. Economists have written at length on rural unemployment, but urban unemployment is new to our literature. There have always been unemployed in the towns, but it has been assumed that this was due to lack of development, and would diminish with development. Now we can see that this is not so. The under-developed countries have been doing quite well over the past fifteen years. Their growth rate averages more than 4 per cent per annum, whereas a dozen years ago most people expected no more than 3 per cent. Unemployment seems to be growing most rapidly in the countries which are developing most rapidly, and at first glance looks like a by-product of development itself.

Apart from lack of development, it used to be fashionable to attribute unemployment to population pressure, but this also is now clearly untenable. In a well-organized social system everybody finds some source of income, however large the population may be. In the countryside agriculture is organized on the basis of family farming. As population grows the family holding gets smaller and smaller, but everyone is attached to some farming unit, from which he derives an income. In the towns the social code demands that all who can afford it keep as many domestic servants as possible, and the relationship involves the so-called masters and mistresses in wide responsibilities for the servants and their families, far beyond anything in the normal capitalist contract of employment. Then there are vast hordes in retail trade, and very large numbers living by casual and part-time employment in various sectors, especially building and transportation. Retail margins are high, and so is the hourly rate for casual work. If retailers or casual workers were kept busy all day every day their incomes would be enormously higher than those of the farmers. But the great excess of people in these trades keeps the average income not much above the rural earnings. So a state of equilibrium is established

---

Sir Arthur Lewis is Professor of Public and International Affairs at Princeton University. He was a member of the U.N. Group of Experts on under-developed countries and a consultant to the Economic Commission for Asia and the Far East. He is the author of *The Theory of Economic Growth* and *Politics in West Africa* (London, Allen and Unwin, 1955 and 1965 respectively) and other works. This article is the text of the sixteenth Stevenson Memorial Lecture delivered at Chatham House on 18 October 1966.

between town and country such that there is just enough casual unemployment in the towns and disguised unemployment on the farms to keep the percentage of population living in towns constant.

India is still in this condition of balance between town and country. In nearly every other country in the under-developed world, the urban proportion grew swiftly between 1950 and 1960, but the Indian census reports no significant change in urbanization during that decade. Relative wage rates and the relative amounts of casual unemployment and disguised unemployment seem to have remained in equilibrium. But in many other countries this state of equilibrium has come to an end. People have been pouring out of the countryside into the towns, and as employment opportunities have not risen so rapidly in the towns, the proportion of unemployment has been rising. What we have to try to understand is both why the exodus from the countryside has stepped up and also why the towns, despite high investment rates, have not been able to provide enough employment for the newcomers. I shall take each of these aspects in turn.

Flow of population to the towns

The supply of people offering themselves for wage employment in the towns has increased for three main reasons. First, the gap between urban wages and rural earnings has widened enormously. Secondly, in many countries, mainly African, rapid acceleration of schooling in the countryside has speeded up the drift of young people to the towns. Thirdly, development and welfare expenditures have been concentrated disproportionately on towns, thus making the towns relatively more attractive. Let me say a word about each of these.

We are used to the idea that unskilled wages are higher in the towns than in the countryside, and usually expect a margin of 50 per cent above the rural income to compensate for the higher cost and inconvenience of urban life. This gap has widened sharply in recent years. Cases are now not uncommon where the minimum wage paid, say to government employees, is two or three times the farmer's income. The biggest anomalies are found in the countries with rich mines. For example, the lowest wage on the bauxite mines in Jamaica is about five times the normal earnings of, say, a jobbing gardener. The high wages established by a few firms in profitable new industries, or by politicians newly arrived in office on a wave of civil service unrest, tend to pull up wages throughout the rest of the economy. For one thing, the trade unions in each sector strive to get their wages up to the highest that other industries are paying. And in any case people are unwilling to work for low wages in traditional occupations when their cousins are getting high wages in new industries. The general effect is that urban wages have been rising sharply while the farmers' real earnings have remained constant. This disturbance of the traditional equilibrium sends more people into the towns and mining areas, looking for work and counting that even one or two days' work a week will be worth having. In countries like Jamaica or Nigeria it is now quite common for heavy unemployment in the towns to co-exist with a shortage of labour in the countryside.

Most students of development economics are familiar with the model of the dual economy in which a modern capitalist sector expands relatively to a traditional subsistence sector at a real wage which remains constant over a long initial period. There seems to be historical justification for this model in nineteenth-century Europe, though the historians are still arguing about the British standard of living in the first half of the nineteenth century. And the model seems also to fit the case of Japan. It also works not too badly even for contemporary India or Egypt. But clearly in much of the developing world today the wage level of the expanding sector has cut itself loose from the standard of living of the great mass of the people in the traditional sector. Why this has happened cannot be explained by traditional economic theory. Clearly marginal productivity has nothing to do with it. For even if the wage is assumed to be equal to marginal product in the modern sector, it is not marginal product that determines the wage but the wage that determines the level of employment and its marginal product. The real explanation must lie in the emergence of new political and social factors which determine urban wages without reference to demand and supply.

Whatever the cause may be, the effect of the widening gap between urban and rural earnings is an unprecedented outflow of people from the countryside, faster than they can be absorbed by the towns. No doubt, there is some equilibrium level of urban unemployment which corresponds to each ratio of urban to rural incomes, subject to some maximum unemployment level at which the chance of getting even one day's work a week becomes so small that it is better to go back to the countryside. But we do not yet know how far this process can go.

The second reason I have advanced for the outflow from the countryside is accelerated schooling. This phenomenon is confined to Africa. The emphasis is not on the word 'schooling' but on the word 'accelerated'. Some people say that it is schooling that causes the migration, but this is unlikely, since literacy and rural life are not incompatible. Others say that anything which enables country folk to find out what happens in towns will cause migration, since life in the towns is attractive, while life in the villages is dull. This also seems unlikely, since if the average villager is offered the same real income in town or village he stays in the village. People born and bred in the towns dislike village life; but people born and bred in the villages have an equal dislike for urban life.

The rapid acceleration of African school numbers has produced a disequilibrium between expectation and reality. Ten years ago less than 20 per cent of African children were in school. Now the figure probably exceeds a half, and in some parts of West Africa is up to 80 per cent. When only 20 per cent were in school, all who completed school could find well-paid jobs waiting for them in the towns, paying several times a farmer's income. Hence, the rural school was identified in the minds of parents and children as a route to a well-paid urban career. This is no longer possible when more than half the children complete the curriculum. Indeed, the superior jobs available to a primary school leaver are even more restricted now since a further 10 per cent of children are going through the secondary schools and driving the primary school leaver lower down in the hierarchy.

This is a transitional phenomenon. It cannot take more than a decade for rural children to learn that the towns cannot now offer them employment. Then the great majority will remain in the countryside and make the best of the opportunities available there. But in the meantime many African towns are clogged with school leavers, turning into juvenile delinquents because they cannot find the types of job they expect—or any job at all.

The third factor promoting the exodus has been excessive concentration of development expenditures on the towns—whether the investment in productive enterprises such as factories or the investment in infrastructure, including water supplies or medical services. When the first draft of Ghana's second Development Plan was completed, I pointed out to Nkrumah that he was planning to spend 50 per cent of the money in Accra, which has only 5 per cent of the population. 'Why not?', he asked me. 'When you think of England, you think of London; when you think of France you think of Paris; when you think of Russia, you think of Moscow.' 'No, sir', I said. 'When I think of England, I do not think of London because I live in Manchester, and this is also why I know that capital cities exploit the rest of the country.'

This over-concentration on the cities has many causes. One of these is the kind of identification of national pride with civic monuments, to which Nkrumah was referring. Another cause is political. The most ambitious politicians gravitate to the cities and above all to the capital; city voices, therefore, have most say in deciding where money is to be spent. A third element is a fallacious identification between industrialization and urban size, which leads people to want to concentrate all their factories in one or two very large cities. As a matter of fact, most investigations of the economics of city size show that the economies of scale are exhausted well before one reaches a city size of 300,000. It would be quite economic to develop a large number of small country towns, each with some factories, electric power, secondary schools, a hospital, and such other amenities as attract population. People are more likely to remain on the farms when the nearest town is only thirty miles away on a good road than when everything one wants is concentrated in one or two distant centres.

The welfare expenditures follow the same pattern as the development expenditures. Here the politician faces a difficult problem. As unemployment rises in the cities, the case for relief payments becomes overwhelming. But if one pays to the urban unemployed a subsistence subvention, one will attract even more people from the countryside. Strong-minded politicians have usually done the opposite. It has been quite common in history to pay relief only to persons who were born in the town. It has also been common to restrict entry into the town, and the right to live there, to persons who produce evidence that they have employment there. Five years ago the Nigerian Government rounded up all the 'beggars' in Lagos and sent them back to their native villages, from which, of course, they duly returned. The twentieth century is hostile to such measures because they interfere with individual freedom, but the twentieth century solution of paying outdoor relief must aggravate the problem when it is confined to the urban poor.

I have been enumerating the reasons for the increased outflow from the farms, citing wages, schooling, and unbalanced development and welfare expenditures. Earlier I had rejected population growth, pointing out that, when the social system is in equilibrium, surplus population does not flood into the towns but remains in the countryside. But, of course, when the equilibrium breaks down, and the excessive flow begins, then the greater the population pressure the larger the potential overflow. The rapid rate of population growth since the end of the war has, therefore, compounded all the other causes.

Lack of employment in towns

Now let me turn to the other side of the question. Why do the towns provide additional employment for so few people? As we have seen, output has been growing rapidly, by more than 4 per cent a year; manufacturing by 7 to 8 per cent a year. The ratio of investment in new capital has also been high. Yet net employment has expanded slowly. There are some spectacular cases. In his book on Puerto Rico, Professor Lloyd Reynolds reports that, despite enormous investment and a striking increase in output, the number of persons employed was no greater in 1960 than in 1950.[1] In nearby Jamaica during the 1950s output grew by 8 per cent a year and net investment averaged 18 per cent; 11 per cent of the labour force migrated, but unemployment was as great in 1960 as in 1950. The extreme case is reported by Messrs Ndegwa and Norbye,[2] who say

[1] *Wages, productivity, and industrialisation* (Yale Economic Growth Centre publication, 1965).

[2] Philip Ndegwa and O. D. K. Norbye, *Rural Development*, paper for a Conference on Education, Employment, and Rural Development, Nairobi, September 1966 (mimeographed).

that in Kenya between 1954 and 1964, while private real output increased by 4 per cent per annum, excluding subsistence, the corresponding employment *declined* by 1 per cent per annum. In the nineteenth century 15 per cent per annum gross investment would increase non-agricultural employment much more than it does in today's developing countries.

Two factors contribute to the small employment generated by current investment. One is that much of this investment is wasteful, in the sense that cost factors are deliberately ignored. Another is that, as a result of price distortions, investment is more capital-intensive than it should be.

The excessive role of the prestige element in public investment is well known; but private investors also are enabled to ignore cost factors insofar as their investments are heavily protected. Waste shows up in the large scale on which things are done, resulting in under-utilization of capital—factories built in anticipation of demand, super-highways carrying only a few cars per hour, vast airports and terminal buildings—all these are common sights. A third aspect of waste is the tendency to build everything lavishly. This is particularly true of government building. The countries which had their industrial revolutions in the nineteenth century used capital very sparingly; it therefore went a long way and provided much employment and output. In contrast, under-developed countries today waste capital in a big way; thus it is not surprising that at the end of heavy investment programmes the amount of new employment created turns out to be much smaller than had been expected. We are always being told that these countries are short of capital, yet under-utilized capital and wasted capital are among their most obvious characteristics.

This waste of capital for prestige reasons is also a problem which can be solved only at the political level, since it is due to the peculiar value system of the current crop of politicians. There are signs that this situation is altering as the politicians who led the independence movements are displaced by a new set. The leadership of an independence movement requires an aggressive, flamboyant personality, with more than a touch of paranoia. Such men are seldom capable of laying sound political and economic foundations after independence has been achieved, for this requires the conciliatory arts of peace rather than the blustering arts of war. It also calls for government by men who gather facts and think rather than by men who follow mainly their emotions, instincts, and hunches. No wonder then that Africans have done well in every sphere over the past ten years save that of politics. We can think with pride of the achievements of our scholars, farmers, entrepreneurs, novelists, boxers, athletes, or any other group you care to name; only the antics of our politicians have made us hang our heads in shame. The set of politicians who came to power at independence are now discredited in most of their countries, from which they are rapidly disappearing. As the new schools and universities pour out their products, we can hope for a better sense of values.

Waste due to the distortions of the price system is analytically more difficult. Three of these distortions all point in the same direction. The rates at which governments borrow are low, relatively to the real shortage of capital. Foreign-exchange rates are too high in those countries (not all) which are experiencing balance-of-payments difficulties. And urban wages exceed the marginal product of labour in agriculture. Each of these promotes a greater substitution of machinery for labour than is justified by real factor scarcities. Investment is too capital-intensive and so employs too little labour.

Many people have remarked on the high capital-intensity of the investments taking place in factories, mines, and construction. But the effect of high wages is also felt in other spheres which normally employ far more people than the factories. One of these is domestic service. The housewife may keep a couple of servants at a pound a week each, but when wages go up to three pounds she instals instead a cooker, refrigerator, vacuum cleaner, and washing machine. Similarly at low wages the average commercial establishment is swimming with clerks and messengers. As wages rise, offices are mechanized and retailing converts to self-service. Since the expansion of services normally absorbs more people than the expansion of manufacturing, the fact that the service industries are now tending to throw out surplus workers instead of taking more in is probably just as important an explanation of growing unemployment as is the high capital-intensity of the new factories.

Many people find it hard to see how one can reduce the income of a country by introducing a more productive technology. To clarify this, let us first consider how an innovation in a particular industry may affect employment in that industry. One can distinguish three cases:

(*a*) The labour cost per unit of output is not reduced. For example, the innovation may make it possible to produce a new product; to use natural resources previously unexploited; to reduce wastage of raw materials; to standardize the product or produce more uniform quality; to reduce the need for supervisory staff by making processes more automatic; or to eliminate scarce skills. If the innovation does not reduce the labour cost per unit it will increase employment, so we need not worry.

(*b*) Labour per unit of output is reduced, but the demand for the product is elastic enough to prevent employment from falling. The most important cases falling under this head are export industries which can survive only if they can keep their money costs in line with world prices. The argument for an innovation may then be not that it will increase employment, but that employment would fall even more if the innovation were not introduced.

(*c*) Labour per unit of output falls, and the demand is not sufficiently elastic to prevent employment from falling.

The controversy centres on this third case. Everybody favours innovations of the previous two types, because they increase output without reducing employment. In this third case, one has to consider both employment in the industry which uses a new machine and also the employment generated in making the machine. Net employment declines only if the decline in the machine-using industry exceeds the increase in the machine-making industry. If an increase in imports automatically ensures an equivalent increase in exports, investment will create employment whether machines are made at home or bought from abroad. But if the equilibrating mechanism works imperfectly, then the greater the dependence on foreign machines, the smaller will be the net employment created by investing in new technology.

The question one has to ask is whether the cost of the innovation is less than the value of the labour saved. The money cost of the innovation must be less than the money cost of the labour saved, otherwise the entrepreneur will not invest in the innovation, but money costs and real costs may not be the same. Let us take two cases:

(*a*) Labour could produce in other industries as much as it earns in this one. Hence the money cost of labour is equal to its real cost. If the money cost of capital is also its real cost (interest and foreign-exchange rates are right) then the innovation should be adopted. This is the neo-classical full employment equilibrium, where all prices are just right.

(*b*) The wage in this industry exceeds the marginal product of labour elsewhere to such an extent that the cost of the innovation exceeds the value of the labour which it displaces. This is common in underdeveloped countries both because wages are too high and also because the real cost of capital is masked by incorrect interest and foreign-exchange rates.

In this comparison between the cost of the innovation and the value of the labour displaced each side deserves equal emphasis. One set of economists has focussed on the value of the labour displaced, urging us to use shadow prices instead of actual prices to determine whether an investment should be made or permitted. Another set focusses on the cost of the innovation, urging that most research effort be put into changes which will increase output at little cost. In agriculture one looks to biological change—better seeds, pesticides, new rotations—rather than to labour-saving machinery. In small-scale industry one emphasizes management—better accounting, control of inventory, better marketing, and so on. Mr Schumacher[3] emphasizes 'intermediate' technology, which presumably means inexpensive rather than expensive equipment, per unit of labour saved. Both sides of the argument are right. On the one

[3] Mr Schumacher is a director of the Intermediate Technology Development Group Ltd, set up in London in 1966.

hand, we need more research into changes which will increase output tremendously at little cost, whether biological, managerial, or mechanical changes. And on the other hand, we need administrative measures which will discourage entrepreneurs from making capital-intensive investments which are profitable to them, but which because of a distorted price mechanism involve a net loss to the economy.

It is not in practice difficult to recognize what kind of innovation is beneficial and what kind merely creates unemployment. The big waste of capital in under-developed countries has tended to be not in the mechanical processes for transforming raw materials into manufactured products, since these new processes have usually also improved the product and reduced the wastage of raw materials. The wastage has come mainly in substituting capital for labour in moving things about; in the handling of materials inside the factory; in packaging; in moving earth; in mining; and in building and construction. The bulldozer, the conveyor belt, and the crane usually achieve nothing that labour could not do equally well. They spend scarce foreign exchange solely in order to produce unemployment.

I hope I have made the point that an innovation is not to be condemned merely because it reduces employment. A developing society needs to have both employment-creating and employment-destroying innovations. In a full-employment economy, inventions which create employment, causing some industries to grow, could not be exploited unless in other sectors other innovations were destroying employment, to make a transfer of labour possible. In broad sectoral terms, new inventions in manufacturing industry and in large-scale communications absorb labour, while new inventions in agriculture, retail distribution, small-scale transport, and domestic service release labour. Statisticians then find that while part of the increase in national income is due to an all-round increase in productivity, an important part is due merely to workers transferring out of the less productive contracting sectors into the more productive expanding sectors.

The mechanism for keeping these two sets of innovations—the employment-creating and the employment-destroying—in step with each other is not very good. Fifty years ago economists believed that these things happened automatically. If unemployment emerged, wages were too high; they would fall and, by altering the ratio of labour to other factors, would restore full employment. It is still open to argument whether advanced economies work in this fashion. In any case, in under-developed countries, where the subsistence level sets a minimum to real wages, there is no mechanism to ensure full employment.

An earlier economist, Karl Marx, believed that in the capitalist system employment-destroying innovations would always be excessive relatively to employment-creating innovations, and he therefore predicted an ever-growing army of unemployed. He was wrong in Europe. In the second half of the nineteenth century these two types just about balanced each other. There were not enough employment-creating innovations to create a shortage of labour, but there were always enough to prevent a secular growth of unemployment.

Since the second World War the employment-creating innovations have been on top in Europe. European economies have had a persistent shortage of labour, draining workers out of agriculture, retailing, old-fashioned forms of transport, and domestic service rather faster than these sectors have been able to modernize, so that throughout Western Europe the less productive sectors have been kept manned only by immigration. The experience has been notably different in North America, where there is no shortage of unskilled labour, and where for a decade the rate of unemployment has seldom fallen below 5 per cent.

The problem is also very different in under-developed countries precisely because they lag so far behind technologically. In every one of their sectors the opportunities for saving labour are immense, and this tends to be done not by building up their own engineering industries but mainly by importing machines from abroad. Their distorted price structures favour undue capital-intensity, and even if they did not, there is no automatic mechanism to ensure them the right mix of employment-creating and employment-destroying innovations. Marx was wrong about developing societies in the nineteenth century, but it does not follow that he will prove wrong about developing societies in the twentieth century. The governments of such societies need positive programmes to keep capital-intensity under control.

Let me sum up. Urban unemployment is increasing both because people are leaving the countryside too fast and also because employment in the towns is too capital-intensive. Each side of this has several causes, so there is no single measure which can restore equilibrium. The various possibilities follow from the analysis—wage control and a wider distribution of development and welfare expenditures to check the yawning gap between urban and rural incomes; and greater respect for costs, both real and money costs, to make capital yield more employment. At present not much progress is possible along such lines because people are only just beginning to recognize that development can create more unemployment than it absorbs, and until this sinks in they will continue to expect the problem to solve itself.

[17]

Reprinted from:
INTERNATIONAL ECONOMICS AND DEVELOPMENT

Academic Press, Inc., New York and London

REFLECTIONS ON UNLIMITED LABOR

W. ARTHUR LEWIS
Princeton University, Princeton, New Jersey

This paper seeks to clarify and expand two articles which I published on this subject ten and fourteen years ago, respectively [25, 26]. Clarification seems necessary since the large literature to which they have given rise is somewhat confusing.

I. Some Misconceptions

The purpose of the model was to provide a mechanism explaining the rapid growth of the proportion of domestic savings in the national income in the early stages of an economy whose growth is due to the expansion of capitalist forms of production. The chief historical example on which the model was based was that of Great Britain where, as we may deduce from the later figures of Deane and Cole, net saving seems to have risen from about 5 per cent before 1780 to 7 per cent in the early 1800s, to 12 per cent around 1870, at which level it stabilized [8, pp. 265–267]. A similar rise is shown for the United States by Gallman [13, p. 11], starting around the 1840s with gross domestic saving at 14 per cent, and continuing up to 28 per cent in the 1890s, where the figure stabilizes. Similar changes can be found since the second world war for many less-developed countries such as India or Jamaica.

The explanation of capitalist sector growth provided by the model turned on the higher than average propensity to save from profit income, and on the rise of the share of profits in the national income in the initial spurt of economic development. Some such model was needed at the time of writing, since the dynamic models then in use usually assumed constant savings and profits ratios. Even today our economic journals still publish many articles on savings functions which do not distinguish between profits and other incomes; a notable exception, specially valuable for bringing in less-developed countries, is the article by Houthakker [18].

Given the purpose of the model, the division of the economy into two sectors had to turn on profits. The two sectors are a capitalist and a noncapitalist sector, where "capitalist" is defined in the classical sense as a man who hires labor and resells its output for a profit. So a domestic servant is in the capitalist sector when working in a hotel but not when working in a private home.

This distinction was vital for my purpose. Other writers, with different purposes, have made different divisions. A now popular division is between industry and agriculture, but capitalist production cannot be identified with manufacturing, as anyone familiar with a plantation economy must know. The model is intended to work equally well whether the capitalists are agriculturists or industrialists or anything else, and indeed in its first version (as we shall see in a moment) the model presupposes that the capitalist sector is self-sufficient and contains every kind of economic activity.

This explanation may serve to refute the charge that the model identifies economic growth with industrialization. A further misconception is that it necessarily identifies economic growth with capitalist production. The anti-socialist aspect of this attack is easily beaten off. Since a capitalist is one who hires labor for profit, it makes no difference to the model whether the capitalists are private or public; the model gives a pretty good explanation of the sharp rise in the share of savings in the U.S.S.R. between, say, 1929 and 1939. The accusation that the model disparages peasant production is on a different plane. The model does not deny that peasants can grow rich by producing more, or more valuable output; it does not argue that capitalist production is more valuable; it is not normative. This author is delighted that there are economies where the productivity of peasants increases steadily and that some portion of that increase goes into capital formation. This does not render it useless or dangerous to study models of economies where, in the initial stages, the dynamism of growth is located in capitalist expansion.

In the model, the noncapitalist sector serves for a time as a reservoir from which the capitalist sector draws labor. The original paper makes clear that this labor does not all come from agriculture—a fact which has escaped the attention of many subsequent writers. The paper mentions *inter alia* domestic service and the self-employed (especially in handicrafts and petty retailing). It also points out that the labor force itself expands through the increased participation of women, as well as by natural increase and by immigration. The last of these sources, immigration, played a substantial role in economic development during the nineteenth century (e.g., U.S.A., Brazil, Malaya, Australia) and, according to Kindleberger [23], is an important explanation of why some European economies have grown faster than others since the second world war.

The existence of such a reservoir is important to the model, since it explains why the capitalist labor force can for a time grow faster than the 3 per cent per annum limit which natural increase would now impose on the less-developed countries, or the 1.5 per cent population limit on Western Europe in the nineteenth century. This is important in explaining why profits can grow much faster than national income. But it receives added significance in these days, since we have observed that in one part of the capitalist sector, namely manufacturing industry, the rate of growth of productivity per head is a positive function of the rate of growth of employment. For this means that productivity can grow faster if there is a labor reservoir than if there is not.

In the model, the capitalist sector is said to have unlimited access to a labor supply, thanks to the existence of this reservoir. The use of the word "unlimited" has caused confusion. It means that if capitalists offer additional employment at the existing wage, there will be far more candidates than they require: the supply curve of labor is infinitely elastic at the ruling wage. One condition for this is that the ruling wage in the capitalist sector exceeds the earnings in the noncapitalist sector of those who are willing to transfer themselves. The other condition is that any tendency which the transfer may set in motion for earnings per head to rise in the noncapitalist sector must initially be offset by the effect of increases in the labor force (natural increase, immigration, or greater female participation). This is discussed more fully later in this paper. The model does not attempt to derive the conventional wage: as in the classical system, this depends not only on productivity but also on social attitudes. The model simply postulates as facts that in the initial stage the supply of labor at the given wage exceeds the demand, and that this condition will continue for some time despite the expansion of the capitalist sector. This postulate is inconsistent neither with history nor with reason.

Since all that the model needs is the fact that supply exceeds demand at the current wage it was not necessary to say anything about the productivity of marginal units of labor in the reservoir, beyond noting that it must be less than the wage offered by capitalists. As the original article said: "Whether marginal productivity is zero or negligible is not however of fundamental importance to our analysis" (p. 142). It was probably a mistake to mention marginal productivity at all, since this has merely led to an irrelevant and intemperate controversy.

This debate has been further confused by the fact that I did not mean by "marginal product is zero" what most of the subsequent writers have meant.

I meant (and said so explicitly) the marginal product of a man, whereas they mean the marginal product of a manhour. For example, in many countries the market stalls (or the handicraft industries) are crowded with people who are not as fully occupied as they would wish to be. If ten per cent of these people were removed, the amount traded would be the same, since those who remained would do more trade. This is the sense in which the marginal product of men in that industry is zero. It is a significant sense, and its significance is not diminished by pointing out that the fact that others have to do more work to keep the total product constant proves that the marginal product of manhours is positive. That an intelligent man like Professor Wellisz [34] believes that my model stands or falls by whether marginal productivity per manhour is zero testifies only to the obscurity of my writing.

Why did I bring in zero marginal productivity (per person)? For two reasons, neither of which is fundamental to the model. Since all the model requires is that the supply of labor exceed the demand, zero marginal productivity was not a necessary condition. My first reason for introducing it was that I was concerned with the relative rates of growth of output in the capitalist and noncapitalist sectors, since this affected the share of profits and thus of savings in national income. Relative rates of growth would depend partly on how the output of the noncapitalist sector would be affected by the loss of labor, so I mentioned zero marginal product as a limiting case. This is clearly a peripheral reference.

The second reason is not even a part of the model. I was concerned, as many others have been, with the possibility that underemployed labor might be put to productive capital formation. This again raises the question by how much the output of the noncapitalist sector would thereby be reduced, and zero is again the limiting case. But it makes no difference whether the loss of noncapitalist output is zero or positive, so long as it is less than the value added by the labor in the sector to which it is transferred.

Egypt is an excellent case, because it illustrates both the kind of labor market which the model fits, and also the misconceptions even of some distinguished writers on this subject. Here is a passage from Hansen and Marzouk [15, p. 16–17] which specifically rejects the model, while actually describing a situation which exactly fits it! After noting the "remarkable" stability of prices in the 1950s, the authors continue:

> A basic condition for the price stability is to be found in the labour market. Although the supply of labour is certainly not infinitely elastic in the Arthur Lewis sense (absolute surplus labour in agriculture probably never did exist in Egypt), there is no doubt that the supply has increased so rapidly during the postwar years that the increasing demand has never led to a real shortage, at least in the major categories of labour. Construction is probably the only sector where labour shortage and wage drift has been a real problem. And Government money wage rates have, if anything, been falling for the post-war period as a whole.

Elsewhere they state specifically, referring to agricultural labor, that "during the fifties the wage rate remained unchanged" (p. 78).

The authors' confusion, in using an infinitely elastic labor supply to explain why the price level and money wages remained constant, while at the same time denying that the labor supply was infinitely elastic, derives from their erroneous identification of infinite elasticity with a zero manhour marginal product of labor in agriculture. Elsewhere in their analysis they supply adequate explanations for the elastic labor supply:

(a) Population was growing by about 3 per cent per annum (p. 23);

(b) In spite of this, the agricultural labor force remained constant. There was terrific migration to other occupations, whose potential labor force must thus have been growing by about 6 or 7 per cent per annum (p. 61);

(c) There was considerable underemployment in the service industries, such that between 1952 and 1962 the numbers in commerce increased only by 49 per cent, whereas the volume of goods handled increased by 65 per cent (p. 320). The government service was notoriously overstaffed;

(d) The proportion of women in the labor force was only 10 per cent (p. 37).

These are typical phenomena of an infinitely elastic supply situation.

Though zero marginal productivity (whether per person or per manhour) makes no difference to my model, there is so much confused writing about marginal productivity in the agriculture of overpopulated countries that I will complete this section with a few remarks on this subject.

First as to manhour productivity, it is quite certain that if farmers were willing to work longer hours they would produce more. Agricultural extension officers show the farmers many ways of increasing output per acre (e.g., transplanting instead of broadcasting seed, or weeding their plots more frequently) which the farmers often reject because they involve more work. Moreover most of these require work not at the peak season (usually but not always the harvesting), but in earlier slack seasons when the farmers are undoubtedly underemployed. They do not work because the extra work would not in their view be adequately compensated by the extra output. So here is an example of a situation where the marginal product of persons is zero (in my sense that output would be the same with fewer people) while the marginal product of manhours is positive in the sense that more work would raise output.

So far I am assuming that the time of the farmers is not fully occupied. The proposition that, if one member of the family migrates, the others will do his work has also been attacked (e.g. [2]). The argument runs as follows: The departure of, say, the fifth working member of a family gives each of the others in effect one fourth more land to cultivate. Assuming constant returns to scale, if each works one fourth more hours on one fourth more land he will get one fourth more product, leaving total output the same as it was before the fifth member left. But the marginal value of output is diminishing in terms of leisure, so if a person was originally in equilibrium he will not work one fourth longer to get only one fourth more output.

One can reply to this in two ways. One can accept the approach through the valuation of leisure, but reject the valuation given to leisure. In particular there is no basis for the assumption that the supply curve of work is upward sloping (in terms of output) throughout the relevant range. A person is trained by his parents or his society that he should work for at least so many hours per day, and until this point is reached he may give no thought to leisure. Indeed, if he can get, say, only 6 hours at his regular job, he may gladly work an extra three hours at half price in some other situation, partly for the money, and partly for self-respect. If in addition he has a fixed idea of what his time is worth, the best representation of his supply curve of work is a horizontal straight line which turns upward sharply when he passes what he considers to be the right number of hours per day.

Figure 1 expresses this situation. Curve I shows the marginal yield of work to the individual worker when the family has five working members on its two acres. Agricultural extension agents want the worker to go beyond the point where this curve cuts the labor supply curve, but he refuses to do so, even though he has much idle time. Curve II shows the situation when the family is reduced to four working members. The farmer now works one fourth more time on one fourth more land with the same marginal product. Without empirical data one cannot assert that the supply curve of labor is horizontal in these circumstances, but this assumption is as reasonable and more likely than the assumption that the supply curve is rising throughout the day.

The other answer is to reject this type of analysis for people in these situations. A farm family with 2 acres wishes to cultivate the farm in accordance with the standards of its community. It will do what needs to be done whether there are 4 or 5 working members of the family. The mistress of the house likes it to be clean. If the opening of a nearby factory reduces the number of her servants from 5 to 4, she will still keep up the standards of her class, even if this means that she and her children must now do a little more for them-

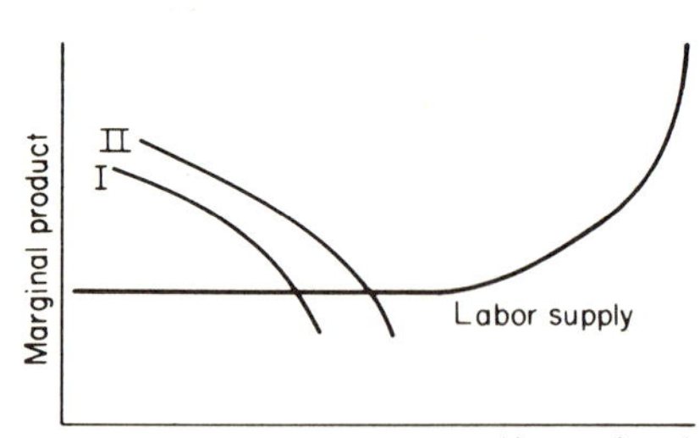

Fig. 1.

selves. Marginal analysis applies to the means by which individuals attain their goals. It is not correct to assume that the goals will be altered just because they become marginally more costly or more easy to attain. Keeping the farm cultivated is amenable to marginal analysis if it is a means, but not if it is a goal.

Let us however move away from these cases, in which the existence of leisure is implicitly accepted, and pass to the attack on underemployment itself. Nobody denies that in the overpopulated countries handicraft workers, petty traders, dock workers, domestic servants, and casual workers have a lot of spare time on their hands, and that most of them (except the domestic servants) would be glad to exchange extra work for extra income at the current rate. Neither does anybody deny that there is much seasonal unemployment in agriculture. The dispute is confined to the situation on small family farms at the peak of the agricultural season, in some parts of Asia and the Middle East.

The argument turns mostly on the labor situation at the time of harvesting, which for most crops (but not, e.g., for manioc) makes the peak demand for labor. The reason for this peak is usually that once the harvest is ready it must be reaped as quickly as possible if it is not to spoil by remaining on the stalk, or to be spoiled by a change in the weather. For this reason, no practicable number of people is too large at this time, since the more hands, the faster the harvesting is completed. It may nevertheless be possible to take off the same harvest with fewer hands if each person works more hours per day, or if the harvesting is spread over a few more days: there is no fixed ratio of number of persons to tons of crop. Harvests vary enormously from one year to another, but somehow or other even the largest harvest gets reaped—although not always the complete 100 per cent. Hansen and Marzouk [15] note that the labor force in Egyptian agriculture was the same in 1960 as in 1950, but was reaping a 25 per cent larger harvest at the later date without any significant increase in machinery. But they fail to deduce the corollary that the farmers could probably have taken off the 1950 harvest with a labor force smaller by (say) 10 per cent. In spite of all they say about labor shortage, one may surmise that if the harvest is 10 per cent larger five years from now, the present labor force will manage to take it off somehow or other.

Even if there were a fixed ratio of men to tons in harvesting, one cannot justify keeping men idle for eleven months so that they may harvest for the twelfth. In the days before harvesting machinery, the standard European solution was for these men to work at nonagricultural occupations during eleven months of the year, and go into the fields for the twelfth. Where this practice is followed, a peak demand for labor at harvest time is quite consistent with transferring men from agriculture into other occupations during the rest of the year.

I do not believe that the productivity of a manhour is zero in agriculture, domestic service, petty retailing, handicrafts, or any other part of the noncapitalist reservoir. Nevertheless, I have seen nothing in the now vast literature of underemployment to alter my belief that in India or Egypt one could mobilize a group equal to, say, ten per cent of the unskilled noncapitalist labor force without significantly reducing the output of the noncapitalist sectors from which they were withdrawn. (One might not be able to use this group effectively without drawing skilled labor, supervisors, food, raw materials, or capital equipment from the other sectors, but that is a different story.) Professor Schultz's doubtful statistics [32] about India's influenza epidemic in 1918–1919 do not meet the conditions specified, because the labor must come *only* from the small family farms and other underemployed pockets; besides at the time of which he speaks India's population was smaller by 200 million than it is today. Professor Paglin [1, 30] confuses total input with labor input. His figures actually show (though he did not spot this) that the marginal productivity of labor on small farms is zero or negative, but only because bullocks, which are also underemployed on small farms, are treated as a continuously variable input. Most of the other articles relate to the marginal productivity of manhours, or embrace the naive idea that there is a fixed ratio of men to tons harvested, and are therefore not germane.

What our colleagues want to emphasize is that even in very overpopulated countries like India or Java, agricultural output could be increased by additional inputs of labor, if the farmers could be persuaded to spend more time on transplanting, weeding, fertilizing, etc. I agree with this completely, and have always favored heavy expenditure on agricultural extension, But this position is not inconsistent with recognizing that, as things now stand in such countries, labor squads could be recruited for useful works off the farms without significantly reducing agricultural output, since those who were left behind would manage to do what needs to be done.

However, this is all an irrelevant digression, since the model in no way depends on the marginal product in agriculture, whether per person or per manhour. All we need is a situation where the supply of labor exceeds the demand, in the capitalist sector—a situation which may exist either because the capitalist wage significantly exceeds noncapitalist earnings, or because the labor force is increasing (natural increase, immigration, or female participation). We do not even need to know why supply exceeds demand; it is enough for our purposes that it does.

II. The Model's Turning Points

It is important to realize that this model comes in three different versions.

In the first version we have (i) a closed economy and (ii) no trade between the two sectors. The capitalist sector is completely self-contained, except that it imports labor. The first turning point then comes only when the labor supply ceases to be infinitely elastic and the wage starts rising through pressure from the noncapitalist sector. One can vary this model slightly to take in whole countries developed by immigration, such as Malaya or the U.S.A.; or to consider the effects of immigration on growth in Western Europe during the 1950s.

In the second version (i) we have a closed economy, but (ii) the capitalist sector depends on trade with the noncapitalist sector, e.g., for food or raw materials. Now we have an additional turning point, since the capitalist sector may be choked by adverse terms of trade, even if the labor reservoir is still teeming with people.

The third model is a variant of the second. Here we have (i) an open economy whose capitalist sector (ii) trades either with the labor reservoir or with the outside world. Here the capitalist sector can escape the stagnation of the noncapitalist sector by importing from the ouside world, but the resulting import surplus may slow growth or produce structural inflation.

A. Model One

It is useful to begin with a model in which the capitalist sector is self-contained, since this enables us to focus attention upon the labor supply, without considering the terms of trade. Besides there are many economies where the capitalist sector gets labor from the noncapitalist, but neither food nor raw materials.

In this version the supply of labor exceeds the demand at the current wage. One would expect this wage to hold constant for some time as the capitalist sector expands. There are two turning points. The first occurs when the check to the growth of the noncapitalist sector raises average earnings there to the point that the capitalist wage is forced upwards. The second turning point comes when the marginal product is the same in the capitalist and noncapitalist sectors, so that we have reached the neoclassical one-sector economy.[1]

The first turning point comes when the changes in the noncapitalist sector begin to react on the wage. We must distinguish between exogenous and endogenous changes. The supply price of labor may rise because something happens to make people richer in the noncapitalist sector, e.g., the farmers may begin to grow a profitable crop for export; or may learn to use fertilizers. Favorable exogenous changes may be expected to raise wages; we must look out for them in any attempts at historical verification, but we cannot take

[1] The second turning point is exactly the same as in Fei and Ranis [10, pp. 201–5]. The definition of the first turning point is also the same, but the mechanism for reaching it is different, since Fei and Ranis are working with Model II, in which the capitalist sector depends on the noncapitalist for agricultural products.

them into the model. (In the same way, as we shall see in a moment, the wage rate may rise exogenously for reasons which have nothing to do with the noncapitalist sector; e.g., because the government enacts minimum wage legislation.) The model incorporates only those endogenous changes in wages which result directly from the transfer of labor from the noncapitalist sector.

This transfer automatically causes consumption per head to be higher than it would otherwise be in the noncapitalist sector. If the people transferred are farmers, farm output will fall by less than their consumption, since land is assumed to be scarce (their consumption equaled average product, which exceeded marginal product). If the people transferred were in petty retailing or handicrafts, those who remain will get more trade.

Several writers (e.g., [7, 14]) have assumed that this increase in noncapitalist consumption per head must immediately force up the capitalist wage, but there are two reasons why this is not so. The first of these is that in my model, as distinct from those used by these and other writers, there is a substantial gap between the capitalist wage and noncapitalist consumption per head, and this gap is not fixed rigidly. If one transfers 5 per cent of the labor force from the noncapitalist sector one is increasing very substantially (perhaps doubling) the capitalist labor force, but the difference this makes to consumption per head in the noncapitalist sector is small and need not be enough to force up the capitalist wage. That wage is determined conventionally, and we know that conventional money wages hold stable even when prices move a few points in one direction or the other.

This is one factor which distinguishes my model from those of some other writers who, desiring to find some reasonable basis for the conventional wage, tie it rigidly to agricultural productivity. This tie seems especially appropriate if one further assumes, as they tend to do, that the reservoir consists exclusively of agriculturists, which of course is not the case. Their rigid assumptions yield precise numbers for wages and earnings, and one can calculate precisely how these numbers alter as labor transfers from one sector to the other. But what is gained in precision is lost in realism.

The second reason why the conventional wage does not necessarily rise as labor is transferred is that in my model the labor force in the noncapitalist sector is still growing in the first stage (though not proportionately as fast as in the capitalist sector). At this stage, therefore, the transfer does not raise consumption per head in the noncapitalist sector in the absolute sense; it merely prevents consumption from falling by as much as it otherwise would. The increase in the labor force may be due to population increase, to greater participation of women, or to migration.[2] We should also remember Marx's

[2] Clapham [6, pp. 168–169] remarks that as French peasants migrated to the towns at the end of the nineteenth century, Belgians, Spaniards, Poles, and Italians immigrated into French farming in their place.

point that capitalism creates its own labor force; competition from factories may put the handicraft workers out of business; increasing use of domestic appliances may throw the domestic servants onto the labor market.[3] In sum, there are forces at work tending to reduce consumption per head in the non-capitalist sector. These would not necessarily have reduced the capitalist wage, since, as we have just said, the gap between the capitalist wage and noncapitalist consumption is flexible, and the conventional wage may hold constant despite a few percentage points of rise or fall in noncapitalist consumption per head.

Thus, bearing all these factors in mind and, in particular, the population factor, there is no reason to expect the capitalist wage to rise endogenously as soon as the capitalist sector begins to grow. It may rise immediately, or an increase may be long delayed: this is a matter for historical research in each case.

Ultimately the capitalist wage must rise, since a successful transformation implies that the capitalist sector has grown rapidly enough to overtake population growth and reach the second turning point.

Critics of the model make enormous play with the question of how long it takes to reach the first turning point, i.e., the question whether there really is a period during which the wage is constant. But this question is of no consequence. The decisive turning point is not the first but the second, for it is here that we pass the boundary into the neoclassical system. The model would have achieved all that it set out to do even if it could be shown (and it cannot) that historically there never has been a case where the real wage did not begin to grow as soon as the capitalist sector began to expand.

The point becomes even clearer when we investigate what is meant by "the real wage." Everyone recognizes that we are talking about unskilled labor, so this is not the problem; skilled wages will certainly rise as skills increase. We are also talking about capitalist wages and not the wages of domestic servants —this is part of our definition. The problem is not in defining the wage, but in defining "real."

"Real" wage has many meanings. The most common is the money wage rate w divided by the cost of living c:

(1) w/c denotes cost of living wage.

However, since we are also interested in the relationship between the income of the capitalist worker and the income of the noncapitalist worker a, by which it is ultimately affected, we must also consider the relationship

(2) w/a denotes factoral wage.

[3] There is much less resistance today than there was in 1954 to the idea of an unlimited supply of labor being available to the capitalist sector, since swelling urban unemployment has emerged as the biggest problem of the seventies, *as a result of the modernization process itself.*

Ultimately, however, what interests us is profit, which depends *inter alia* on the ratio of wages to prices. A crude index of this is given by dividing the wage index by an index of the price p received by capitalists:

(3) w/p denotes wage/price ratio.

This is not a good index of profits, because profits also depend on productivity, i.e., on real output Q divided by the quantity of labor L. Also the price of the product includes the cost of raw materials, which should be deducted to get the value added price of the product v. Profit then depends on the ratio of wages to value added:

(4) wL/vQ denotes product-wage.

If the system does not import raw materials, as in this first version of the model, the product-wage becomes

$$wL/pQ.$$

Given this wide variety of types of real wage, what do we mean when we talk about the real wage being constant, for the purpose of this model? The answer derives from what we are seeking. Our interest is in the share of profits in the national income, which is determined by two factors: the share of the capitalist sector as a whole in the national income, and the share of profits in the capitalist sector (which is unity minus the product wage) The share of the capitalist sector in national income will grow so long as the product-wage is favorable to growth. We can therefore concentrate our attention in the first instance on the product-wage.

We can now formulate more precisely what we are after. The model postulates that the product-wage will fall (the profit ratio rise) during an initial period because capitalists will not have to share with their workers the fruit of technological advance (Q/L). During this initial period the wage-price ratio (w/p) is assumed to be constant, but sooner or later the rise in noncapitalist consumption per head (a) forces up w. This is the first turning point. From here on both w/p and Q/L are rising. Sooner or later w/p will be rising faster than Q/L, which means that the profit ratio will have begun to fall. We enter the neoclassical system at the second turning point, where the marginal product of labor is the same throughout the system. We also believe that at this point the product-wage wL/pQ stabilizes, although we have no theoretical explanation why this should happen. It is sufficient for our purposes that sooner or later we expect the product-wage to start rising, as we move from the first turning point towards the second.

Thus to test the historical validity of the model, the questions to ask for any particular country are (i) was w/p initially constant, and (ii) did wL/pQ ultimately rise?

As to the first question, the data are not easy to find, since even in those cases where we can put together some kind of money wage index it is very hard to make an index of the price of domestic capitalist output (which has, in an open economy, to be not p but v). In a closed economy with a self-contained capitalist sector, if we can assume that the prices of capital goods and consumer goods all move together, we can write

$$p = v = c,$$

and ask ourselves the simpler question—whether the real cost of living wage remained constant initially. This is also difficult to answer, but it is easier to find data for w/c than for w/v. However, even if we get an answer for w/c we have to remember that in the real world p, v, and c are not equal to each other, and that therefore the answer we get for the cost-of-living wage is not conclusive for w/p.

When the first article was being written, the historical wages data uppermost in my mind were those for the cost of living wage in Great Britain in the first half of the nineteenth century, and the U.S.S.R. in the 1930s. Historians still dispute what happened to the real wage rate in the first half of the nineteenth century [16, 17], but it seems a good bet that the rate of increase was slight. Deane and Cole's version [8] of Wood's data on money wage rates shows a rise in Great Britain from 70 in 1790 to 100 in 1840. Phelps Brown and Hopkins's index [4] of the price of consumables rises in that period from 68 to 100, indicating a slight *decline* in the real wage rate over those 50 years. Indeed the Phelps Brown–Hopkins index of the real wage rate of building craftsmen shows it only 4 per cent higher in 1840–1844 than it had been ninety years earlier in 1750–1754. One can get different results with different figures, but it is safest to conclude that the cost-of-living wage did not rise substantially in Great Britain during the first fifty years of the industrial revolution. (This is not inconsistent with the standard of living rising through a fall in underemployment or movement from worse into better paid jobs; wages per head can rise even if wage rates are constant.)

The British case is not necessarily typical. The wage–price ratio (w/p) will remain constant only if noncapitalist earnings a are not rising, or if the capitalists are not sharing productivity gains with their workers. Both conditions may have been met in Britain 150 years ago, but there are plenty of other cases. Thus, in the U.S.A. productivity on family farms was rising sharply in the middle of the nineteenth century, through the adoption of machinery, so industrial wages could not have been held constant. Similarly, in Japan farm productivity was rising at the end of the century. Okhawa's cost of living data [29] starting only in 1893, show real wages rising by 17 per cent in the 18 years from 1893/95 to 1911/13. They did not rise as fast as industrial productivity; he puts the productivity increase in secondary industry at 38 per cent, which is rather low for our purpose, since it includes handicrafts. Thus the capitalists conceded part of the increase in productivity to the workers, but they did not concede it proportionately. According to Okhawa the terms of trade between primary and secondary sectors altered little in this period, so profits in the industrial sector must have risen relatively to wages.

Study of the Japanese materials brings out another important phenomenon, which is also found elsewhere, namely, a widening gap between industrial and agricultural wages. The data given in Minami [28] show the real agricultural wage constant in the two decades before the first world war, when the industrial wage was rising, and agricultural productivity rising even faster. How do agricultural wages remain constant while farmers' incomes are rising? The answer is already in our model. The agricultural wage initially exceeds the marginal product of labor. It is established conventionally for the landless (or insufficiently landed) class. Farmers employ laborers for tasks whose productivity exceeds the wage; less productive tasks they do at other times with their own family labor. The agricultural wage of landless laborers is not tied to the farmers' incomes, and may stay constant or rise very slowly for a long time, even though farm income is rising.

In sum, we are now talking about three different kinds of earnings:

(1) the wages of landless laborers,
(2) the earnings of small farmers,
(3) the earnings of unskilled industrial workers.

The crucial test of whether labor is in surplus supply in the countryside will be what happens to the wages of landless agricultural laborers. If, as in Japan, or allegedly in Egypt, these remain constant while the other two are rising, we can be quite sure that a labor surplus exists. What interests our model, however, is the wage that the capitalists have to pay, and there is no doubt that this may rise even in the face of a labor surplus in the countryside.

When we turn to the less-developed countries of our own times and ask what is happening to the industrial wage, the answer, from a very large number, if not from all, is that the cost of living wage w/c is rising, even in situations where there is open mass urban unemployment, not to speak of underemployment. Why is this happening?

In some countries rising a is clearly a contributing factor. The small farmers' output of food per head is more or less constant, but their output of coffee, cocoa, peanuts, rubber, cotton, etc., has been rising swiftly, and in some countries, especially in Africa, the increase in output per head has been greater than the decline in the price received by the farmers. In those countries one would expect the capitalist wage to be forced up.

However, the evidence, even from such favorably placed countries, is that in most places the gap between w and a has widened; wages have risen much faster than farmers' incomes. This means that the capitalists are sharing productivity gains with the workers to a greater extent than one would expect if the abundance of the labor supply were the only element to be considered. Why they are doing this is not clear,[4] though explanations have been offered [12, 27, 31].

It seems therefore that what we should expect in overpopulated countries is that the real agricultural wage will remain constant, if the laborers are landless. What happens to the urban wage will depend partly on what is happening to a (the farmers' income) and partly on the extent to which the capitalists share technological gains with their workers. The industrial wage may well be rising faster than industrial prices, but this will not cut into profit unless it is also rising faster than industrial productivity. If we assume that the capitalists share technological gains equally, the product-wage will remain constant. It makes little difference to the model whether one assumes w/p constant or wL/pQ constant. The system expands faster on the first assumption than on the second, but it is still capable of rapid expansion until wages start rising faster than productivity.

Whether the product-wage stays constant or falls somewhat in the initial stages of development, it must ultimately rise when the combination of rising a and diminution of the labor reservoir combine to push up w/p faster than labor productivity. We cannot document this historically, since we do not have profit–wage data for the first three quarters of the nineteenth century for the countries which are now developed, but contemporary cross-country data throw light on the situation.

The United Nations' "The Growth of World Industry 1953–1965" [33] summarizes data from censuses of manufactures taken between 1961 and 1963 (with the exception of Venezuela, which are from 1953). Comparable data for the percentage share of wages and salaries in value added can be computed for several countries, e.g.,

Denmark	59	Venezuela	38	Ghana	26
Sweden	57	Japan	37	Brazil	26
U.K.	53	Jamaica	33	Nigeria	25
Norway	51	Colombia	32	Philippines	24
U.S.A.	49	Peru	29	Ivory Coast	24
Israel	46			Iran	22

The difference between the highly industrialized and the least industrialized countries is striking. Some part of the difference is due to heavier depreciation

[4] That they will pay a w higher than a to get higher productivity through higher consumption of food, etc., is clear enough. But this does not explain why the gap between w and a should *widen* continually for unskilled labor.

cost in the least industrialized countries (imported capital costs relatively more, and the life of equipment is relatively shorter), but removing this element would still leave net profits much lower relative to wages in the most-developed countries.

The cross-country data do not, like the historical data, support the notion that the real wage or even the product-wage is constant initially (most of the countries shown here are not overpopulated). They show very high initial profits, and, since the capitalist sector is growing very rapidly (the modal rate of growth of large scale manufacturing in Asian and African countries is about 10 per cent per year), they are consistent with a rapid increase in the share of profits in the national income as a whole, in the countries at the bottom of the list. The generalization which the cross-country data would support for our own times (as distinct from the 19th century) is that the share of profits in national income grows rapidly at the start because both the profit margin and the rate of growth of the capitalist sector (relative to the whole) are high, and that the share of profits declines and eventually stabilizes at a lower level, because both the profit margin and the relative growth rate of the capitalist sector are reduced. For evidence that initially the profit margin increases before beginning to decline and ultimately stabilizing (second turning point), we have to look at historical data from countries known to have had large labor reservoirs (England and Japan).

The cross-country data support the proposition that the profit margin ultimately stabilizes. More appropriate evidence can be derived from the U.S. Censuses of Manufactures. From these one can calculate the following ratios of wages and salaries to value added:

1899	48.6%
1909	50.3%
1929	46.7%
1963	48.6%

Recognizing that 1909 was a relatively depressed and 1929 a relatively prosperous year, one may surmise that changes in the later stages of development are very small in comparison with those which occur in the middle years.

Let us return for a moment to the widening of the gap between w and a which results from capitalists sharing the gains of technology in spite of the abundance of labor. Whatever their reason for doing this, the consequences for unemployment and underemployment are serious. The ratio of w to a is one of the factors determining how many people flock into the capitalist sector looking for work. Apart from full-time jobs this sector offers much casual employment (at the docks, in building, etc.), so everybody who looks for work stands some statistical chance of getting casual employment—

whether for 5, 10, or 20 days per month. Others can become self-employed, in retailing or handicrafts, doing some business, though not much. The higher the wage, the greater the inflow, and the less work for each person, though presumably to each level of w/a there corresponds some degree of underemployment which would be enough to stop further migration. As the ratio of w to a has risen since 1950, there has been a massive exit from the countryside into unemployment and underemployment in the towns. This is now one of the major problems of underdeveloped countries.

Here we tie into another problem, namely, what is the appropriate capital intensity for economies where the wage rate in the capitalist sector exceeds the marginal product outside that sector. This has been investigated by a long line of writers, summarized by Chenery [5], and the debate continues [9, 11, 24]. But the issue is largely political, and our model throws no light on it.

In sum, the model seems to survive the tests of its relevance if one sticks to what is crucial in it, namely, first, the abundance of labor at the current wage, which facilitates the rapid growth of capitalist output and profits; and second, the notion that in due course wages will rise faster than profits until some upper leveling-off is reached. If the model is not destroyed by showing that the marginal product of manhours in agriculture is not zero, neither is it rendered useless by showing that the real (cost of living) wage is not necessarily constant.

B. Model Two

In this version our two sectors produce different commodities and therefore trade with each other. Thus the capitalist sector faces the additional hazard that it may be checked by adverse terms of trade, arising out of the pressure of its own demands, long before any shortage of labor begins to be felt.

This is the version which has been worked out in great detail by Fei and Ranis working with models in which each of the variables is or can be precisely determined. Jorgensen and others also prefer to work with this model. It is a good model for studying the economic history of countries before about 1870, when railways, steamships, and the Suez Canal began the great explosion of world trade. Until then transport costs were so high that countries had virtually to be self-sufficient in basic necessities. But since then the terms of trade are determined by international rather than national forces. If the capitalists were hindered by failure of the noncapitalist sector to produce what was wanted, the capitalists would simply import from other countries whatever they might need (including food for their workers and raw materials for their machines).

This is true for the great majority of countries now underdeveloped, and mainly dependent on foreign trade. It is still not true, however, of huge economies like those of the U.S.S.R. or India, which have been developing with their price levels largely isolated from those of the world market. It is still possible for such economies to grind to a standstill through overemphasis on industry and underemphasis on agriculture, showing up in shortages of food, raw materials, and foreign exchange—contemporary Indian experience illustrates only too vividly the continued relevance of this model. Let us, therefore, pursue it.

For the moment (until we reach model three), we assume a closed economy without international trade. We simplify by assuming that just two commodities are produced, and our interest is in the terms of trade between them. Thus our specifications are altered. The division between the two sectors now turns on commodities rather than on capitalists; it makes no difference to us whether there are capitalists in the slow-growing sector, provided we specify that their profits are not reinvested in the fast-growing sector. What we still need is a substantial initial difference between real wages in the two sectors, so that labor supply is not initially a problem to the fast-growing sector. Following the conventions, we will now divide the economy into an industrial and an agricultural sector, with industry paying significantly higher wages than agriculture.

Thus stated, the problem is an exercise in the study of unbalanced growth in a closed economy. It is normally approached by specifying the conditions under which balance (which here means constant terms of trade) would be maintained. But this balance carries no normative implications. The industrial sector may grow quite rapidly for some time, even if the terms of trade are moving against it. And since industry has no intrinsic merit over agriculture, economic policy does not require that the terms of trade be moved in favor of industry. The only economists who wish to impoverish the peasants are those who have set the creation of a modern industrial state as their target for its own sake.

Since what we are studying is the behavior of the terms of trade between two sectors, ready answers are already available in the corpus of international trade theory; such an answer was given by Johnson [19]. We define the variables as follows:

- e price elasticity of demand,
- z income elasticity of demand,
- r rate of growth of output,
- p price of agricultural products relatively to manufactures,
- a subscript denoting the agricultural sector,
- m subscript denoting the industrial sector.

Then, after various manipulations detailed by Johnson (p. 141), we get the annual change in the terms of trade:

$$\frac{dp}{dt} \times \frac{1}{p} = \frac{z_a r_m - z_m r_a}{e_a + e_m - 1}.$$

From this, it follows that the terms of trade will be constant if

$$z_a r_m = z_m r_a ,$$

i.e., if

$$z_m / z_a = r_m / r_a .$$

This equality means that the terms of trade will be constant if the relative growth rates of industry and agriculture are the same as the relative income elasticities. For example, if the income elasticity of demand for manufactures is twice that for agricultural products, then the output of manufactures must grow twice as fast as the output of agricultural products if the terms of trade are to remain constant.

This neat answer reminds us that the terms of trade may move in either direction. If agricultural productivity is rising very fast, the terms of trade will move in favor of industry, which can then pay a lower product-wage and expand faster. (Since labor is available, expansion does not depend on consumption; more capital can be used to hire proportionately more workers [25].) But if agricultural productivity rises too slowly, rapid growth of manufacturing will be checked by a constantly rising product-wage. Several writers (e.g., [3]) have explored the case of "immiserizing growth," which is an extreme form of this proposition.

It should be noted that nothing in the analysis requires the terms of trade to be constant; movement checks or helps the rate of expansion of the industrial sector, by checking or spurring the rate of growth of profits, but since industry and industrial workers are not more valuable than agriculture or farmers, the analysis has no emotional content. Also, even if the terms of trade are rising, industrial expansion will not necessarily cease. Productivity is rising in the industrial sector, so if real wages (w/c) are constant, the profit margin will not fall unless the terms of trade rise faster than industrial productivity. Real wages cannot be constant if agricultural productivity is rising significantly, since this would be moving the factoral terms of trade against industry. So what will happen to profits in any particular case will depend on a race between agricultural productivity, industrial productivity, real wages (which may rise on their own for exogenous reasons), and the commodity terms of trade. If one makes precise assumptions about these magnitudes one can get precise answers, as Fei and Ranis have done. We will not dwell on this model, since it has nothing to add to their work.

C. Model Three

As mentioned, in most of the world since 1870 the terms of trade are determined increasingly, not by the relative growths of the two sectors of the same economy, but by the world market in which it is possible to buy and sell.

In model three, a rapidly growing industrial sector faced by a too slow agricultural sector is forced to import and to pay for its imports by exporting.

However, in order to export more it may have to lower its prices, thus squeezing its profits. Its real wages, in terms of agricultural products, are fixed by definition. If we take as given the propensity to import and the inflexibility of the agricultural sector, we can see that the possible rate of growth of such an economy is determined by its propensity to export.

Alternatively the country may devalue its currency. This raises (in domestic currency) the price of food and raw materials, and therefore by definition raises money wages. This is the well-known case of "structural inflation," in which a spiral of rising wages and prices is set off.

The open economy may run into trouble even if the agricultural sector is not stagnant. As the economy develops, the product-wage rises. This change in the distribution of income will alter the propensity to import—favorably if the economy specializes in consumer goods, but unfavorably if it specializes in producing capital goods.

This gives us a different aspect of "balanced growth." A country must plan its development in such a way as to be sure that its exports will keep pace with needed imports. If it fails to do this, the rate of growth of output will be constrained by the rate of growth of export earnings. All this is now familiar ground [27, pp. 38–55].

Finally, the behavior of capitalists as profit margins diminish relatively to wages cannot be predicted. The original article drew attention to the temptation to export capital, but Kindleberger [23] has pointed out that dynamic capitalists may react rather by speeding up labor-saving innovations. We are still in the dark as to why entrepreneurs act more creatively in some countries than in others, or at one period rather than another in the history of the same country.

REFERENCES

[1] Bennett, R. L., Surplus Agricultural Labour and Development: Comment, *Amer. Econ. Rev.* (March 1967).

[2] Berry, R. A., and Soligo, R., Rural-Urban Migration, Agricultural Output, and the Supply Price of Labour in a Labour-Surplus Economy, *Oxford Econ. Papers* (July 1968).

[3] Bhagwati, J., International Trade and Economic Expansion, *Amer. Econ. Rev.* (December 1958).

[4] Brown, E. H. Phelps, and Hopkins, S. V., Seven Centuries of the Prices of Consumables, Compared with Builders' Wage Rates, *Economica* (November 1956).

[5] Chenery, H. B., Comparative Advantage and Development Policy, *Amer. Econ. Rev.* (March 1961).

[6] Clapham, J. H., "The Economic Development of France and Germany 1815–1914." Cambridge Univ. Press, London and New York, 1951.

[7] Cumper, G. E., Lewis's Two-Sector Model of Development and the Theory of Wages, *Social Econ. Stud.* (March 1963).

[8] Deane, P., and Cole, W. A., "British Economic Growth 1688–1959." Cambridge Univ. Press, London and New York, 1964.

[9] Dixit, A. K., Optimal Development in the Labour Surplus Economy, *Rev. Econ. Stud.* (January 1968).

[10] Fei, J. C., and Ranis, G., "The Development of the Labour Surplus Economy." Irwin, Homewood, Illinois, 1964.

[11] Fei, J. C., and Ranis, G., Innovation, Capital Accumulation and Economic Development, *Amer. Econ. Rev.* (June 1963).

[12] Frank, C. R., Jr., Urban Unemployment and Economic Growth in Africa, *Oxford Econ. Papers* (July 1968).

[13] Gallman, R. E., Gross National Product in the United States 1834–1909, *in* "Studies in Income and Wealth," Vol. 30, New York, 1966.

[14] Hagen, E. E., "The Economics of Development." Irwin, Homewood, Illinois, 1968.

[15] Hansen, B., and Marzouk, G. A., "Development and Economic Policy in the U.A.R." London, 1965.

[16] Hartwell, R. M., The Rising Standard of Living in England, 1800–1850, *Econ. Hist. Rev.* (April 1961). Also rejoinder to Hobsbawm in *Econ. Hist. Rev.* (August 1963).

[17] Hobsbawm, E. J., The Standard of Living During the Industrial Revolution, *Econ. Hist. Rev.* (August 1963).

[18] Houthakker, H. S., On Some Determinants of Saving in Developed and Underdeveloped Countries, *in* "Problems in Economic Development" (E. A. G. Robinson, ed.). London, 1965.

[19] Johnson, H. G., "International Trade and Economic Growth." London, 1958.

[20] Jorgenson, D. W., The Development of a Dual Economy, *Econ. J.* (June 1961).

[21] Jorgenson, D. W., Testing Alternative Theories of the Development of a Dual Economy, *in* "The Theory and Design of Economic Development" (I. Adelman and E. Thorbecke, eds.) Johns Hopkins Press, Baltimore, 1966.

[22] Jorgenson, D. W., Surplus Agricultural Labour and a Dual Economy, *Oxford Econ. Papers* (November 1967).

[23] Kindleberger, C. P., "Europe's Postwar Growth." Cambridge, Massachusetts, 1967.

[24] Lefeber, L., Planning in a Surplus Labor Economy, *Amer. Econ. Rev.* (June 1968).

[25] Lewis, W. A., Economic Development with Unlimited Supplies of Labor, *Manchester School* (May 1954).

[26] Lewis, W. A., Unlimited Labor: Further Notes, *Manchester School* (January 1958).

[27] Lewis, W. A., "Development Planning." Harper, London and New York, 1966.

[28] Minami, R., The Turning Point in the Japanese Economy, *Quart. J. Econ.* (August 1968).

[29] Okhawa, K., "The Growth Rate of the Japanese Economy since 1878." Tokyo, 1957.

[30] Paglin, M., Surplus Agricultural Labour and Development, *Amer. Econ. Rev.* (September 1965).

[31] Reynolds, L. G., Wages and Employment in a Labour Surplus Economy, *Amer. Econ. Rev.* (January 1965).
[32] Schultz, T. W., "Transforming Traditional Agriculture." New Haven, Connecticut, 1964.
[33] United Nations, "The Growth of World Industry 1953–1965." New York, 1967.
[34] Wellisz, S., Dual Economies, Disguised Unemployment and the Unlimited Supply of Labor, *Economica* (February 1968).

[18]

3 Development and Distribution

W. ARTHUR LEWIS

Surprise that the poor are still poor after two decades of rapid growth has become a constant refrain, but development theorists have always maintained that growth is an inegalitarian process. This was so in the classical models of Smith, Ricardo and Marx. Theorists since the Second World War approached the subject differently, via the behaviour of different sectors of the economy, but reached the same conclusion. If anything surprises, it must be the surprise.

The purpose of this note is to sketch a framework for considering the relationship between growth and distribution.

Our starting point is that growth takes place in enclaves, surrounded by traditional activities. The first section will list the effects of a development enclave on traditional activities. The second section will examine the evolution of distribution within a developing enclave. The third section will analyse the effects on growth of some policies of redistribution.

I EFFECTS OF THE DEVELOPMENT ENCLAVES

Development must be inegalitarian because it does not start in every part of an economy at the same time. Somebody develops a mine, and employs a thousand people. Or farmers in one province start planting cocoa, which will grow only in 10 per cent of the country. Or the Green Revolution arrives, to benefit those farmers who have plenty of rain or access to irrigation, while offering nothing to the other 50 per cent in drier regions.

There may be one such an enclave in an economy, or several; but at the start development enclaves include only a small minority of the population. Since most of the people in LDCs are food farmers the productivity of this majority could have risen only if there had been major changes in food farming. This has only recently begun.

The growth of an enclave has effects on the rest of the economy, which are both good and bad. They need only be listed.

The growth of an enclave may help to enrich the traditional sectors in one or more of the following ways.

1. It buys commodities and services from the traditional sector.

26

2. It provides work for people coming into the enclave from traditional sectors.

3. Some of these people send remittances back home.

4. It sells commodities and services to the traditional sector more cheaply than they can be obtained elsewhere.

5. It establishes for its own purposes infrastructure (railways, ports, electric power, water supplies, roads, hospitals, etc.) which is then used by people in the traditional sector at less than average cost.

6. It is taxed, and some part of its taxes provides services used by people in the traditional sectors (schools, courts, agricultural extension, public health, etc.).

7. It serves as an example of the productivity of new techniques, institutions, and methods of organisation. This example helps to modernise the traditional sector.

In a developed society, these benefits would spread swiftly and surely, but this may not happen in a traditional society. Take the first of these advantages: the fact that the enclave imports food, raw materials, intermediate products, machinery and services. The effect of these purchases on traditional sectors depends on its marginal propensity to import from them. If one assumes that all savings are reinvested and the proceeds of all taxes are spent, then imports are the only leakage, and the import multiplier is the reciprocal of the marginal propensity to import. If the traditional sectors could supply all the import requirements of the enclave, the multiplier would be infinite, and the development enclave would expand rapidly to take in the whole economy. But if the traditional sector could supply none of the import requirements, the multiplier would be unity, and the enclave would not expand at all. Note that we are not here asserting that a low propensity to import must also benefit developed economies; we are referring only to an initial stage where productivity is raised by expanding the enclave relatively to traditional output.

Failure of traditional sectors to respond swiftly or significantly to economic opportunities (price changes, increases in demand or supply) shows up in our models as low elasticities of demand and supply. This essentially structuralist element distinguishes development theory from both the Walrasian and the Keynesian systems: to some extent in analysis – because postulated changes have different results – but even more in policy recommendations.

This failure of response is also one reason why development widens inequality: incomes rise in the enclave, while all around in the traditional sectors incomes may remain the same. The differences can be astonishingly wide: the average income in the cocoa region may be five times as high as the average income of surrounding provinces – a degree of difference which could not persist very long in a developed country, where labour would be flowing rapidly to the richer region and capital flowing rapidly to the poorer.

These tremendous regional differences are not what people mean when they speak of the failure of the benefits of development to 'trickle down', because they are then usually thinking of the distribution of income by deciles or quintiles within the enclave itself. What happens to this distribution is a controversial question to which we shall come in a moment. But in practice, the inegalitarianism of the development process derives not so much from failure to trickle down vertically as from the failure of horizontal spread from the enclaves to the traditional sectors.

Indeed, incomes in the traditional sector may not even remain the same; they may be reduced in consequence of the development of the enclaves. This may happen for one or more of the following reasons.

1. The development enclave may be predatory on the traditional sectors. It may, for example, as so often in Latin America and Africa, drive people off their lands, reduce them to serfdom, or put taxes on them to force them to work for wages. It may, as Stalin did to the Russian farmers, seize their food to feed the towns; or, as Latin American élites do, turn the terms of trade against the countryside through import substitution policies.

2. Products of the enclaves may compete with and destroy traditional trades. The instinct of economists is to assert that every trade destroyed is replaced by a new one. Ricardo made this claim in early arguments, with regard to the effects of machinery, but later dropped it, and invented instead the 'trickle down'. Essentially his point was that machinery could destroy employment, but would raise profits and therefore saving, and therefore create new employment; which is true – but the employment created may be less than that destroyed, unless a high propensity to save out of profits is combined with a low capital/labour ratio. Marx made the point a cornerstone of his analysis. He thought mainly of the destruction of handicraft industries, but we have seen many more examples: office machinery destroys clerical jobs; household equipment destroys domestic service; railways destroy porterage; the Green Revolution impoverishes those farmers who cannot use its inputs for lack of water. Marx's claim that capitalism creates its own labour force may be even more true today, when all these accumulated inventions descend upon traditional sectors at once, than it was in the nineteenth century when destructive change was relatively slower.

3. The wage level of the enclave may be so high that it destroys employment in other sectors, by raising the offer price of labour above its marginal productivity in those sectors. For example agriculture is disappearing from the British Caribbean and from Venezuela because neither the wage-earners nor the peasants can

get from it the remuneration which the much higher earnings of their cousins in mining have taught them to expect. So one highly profitable industry may destroy in other sectors more employment than it provides in its own.

4. The development of the enclave may result in geographical polarisation. The enclave attracts to itself much of the best brains and enterprise and capital; thus draining the traditional sectors of their dynamic potential. Since it is not feasible for a country to develop with an equal distribution of the population over each square mile, it is highly desirable to have a number of these 'growth poles'. But market and political forces do not produce the optimum number of growth poles. What we tend to get is excessive concentration in a handful of towns, plus increasing depression in many regions.

5. The modern enclaves introduce public health and sanitation, which tends also to penetrate into the traditional areas. The death rate therefore falls sharply, and population growth accelerates. This can be accommodated by traditional societies which still have plenty of land, as in parts of Africa and Latin America. Elsewhere, population growth reduces income per head outside the enclaves.

6. The development of an enclave stimulates excessive migration from the countryside. Explanations of this abound, including the effects of schooling, the differential concentration of public services in the towns, population growth, and the widening gap between urban wages and rural earnings. Currently the most popular explanation focuses on the relationship between rural and urban earnings. However, the phenomenon was just as pronounced in the nineteenth century, when as many as a million people might leave Europe in one year to seek their fortunes in the new world. Excessive migration damages the enclave itself, by increasing its unemployment rate and its rate of slum formation. Whether it damages or benefits the rural areas will largely depend on whether they are overpopulated.

This is a formidable list of adverse possibilities. Whether in any particular country the developing enclave does more to enrich or to impoverish the traditional sectors probably depends most on whether the government coerces or helps the traditional sectors, and on the nature of the enclaves. In the absence of coercion the peoples in the traditional sectors will almost certainly respond creatively to the new challenges of the modernisation in their midst. This will take some time, since learning is involved, but as Adam Smith said, it is human nature to 'barter and truck', and the human spirit is irrepressible unless it is shackled. The nature of the enclave also counts. If foreigners open up a mine, they will not care much whether their supplies are purchased locally or abroad; whereas, if peasant farmers are planting some new profitable crop, they will automatically buy more from the rural workshops and village industries. It is frequently necessary to coerce industrial or mining or plantation enclaves to get them to buy more of their requirements locally, to share their infrastructure with the public, and to train local staff.

Beyond this, the traditional sectors benefit from the tax revenues which the government derives from the enclaves. Those who believe that the poor have not benefited from the development of the last two decades forget what they have gained from the public services: the number of children in school has multiplied by four; smallpox has been banished from this planet, and malaria is no longer found in territories inhabited by 80 per cent of the LDC population; the infant mortality rate has fallen by two-thirds; innumerable villages now have a water supply, a paved road and regular motor transport; and so on. An index of mass welfare, which took in not just the output of wage-goods but also such things as the number of hospital beds per thousand, or the percentage of population living within half a mile of a public water tap, would show that the poor have gained much more from development than it is now fashionable to believe.

But the main point, of course, is that the masses, being farmers, cannot improve their productivity without a new crop, new seeds, or higher prices.

II INSIDE THE ENCLAVE

Now we come to distribution inside the enclave itself. We shall start with the functional distribution into wages and salaries, rents and profits, since changes in distribution in terms of other categories (e.g. size, race) usually derive from changes in relations between the factors of production, or their ownership pattern.

How growth affects distribution depends on the pattern of growth. We shall begin with what is common to all growth patterns, and then analyse the results of differing patterns.

Wages and Salaries.

Take first unskilled labour. If the country is sparsely populated, as were Latin America and Africa in the eighteenth and nineteenth centuries, the development enclave may have difficulty in recruiting labour, and may resort to various forms of coercion and indenture.

The proposition that in the early days an enclave will find all the labour it wants at a constant real wage belongs only to societies where labour is relatively abundant, and where therefore the labour force of the enclave is small in relation to the total labour force. In most LDCs today, with rapid population growth, and mounting urban unemployment, the classical assumption of an unlimited labour supply at a constant wage should undoubtedly obtain. (This is the wage of the *new* recruit; not his increased wage after months of acquiring skills.)

In fact, however, the situation varies widely. It seems to be established, after much controversy, that the real unskilled wage in Britain was not significantly higher in 1830 than in 1780, but our current experience is very mixed. Real wages in manufacturing have risen only slightly in India or Pakistan, while they have risen rapidly in Jamaica or Nigeria. There is no difficulty in understanding why urban wages rise rapidly in those cases where farmers' incomes have also been rising rapidly, whether because of rising productivity in cereals (e.g. Thailand) or because of favourable terms of trade for agricultural exports (e.g. Uganda). What puzzles us is a rapid increase in urban wages in situations where agricultural incomes are more or less constant. We cite trade unions, government-sponsored minimum wages, the vulnerability of foreign employers. Perhaps our theory of wages is wrong. On the strength of nineteenth-century experience, when a business was owned and managed by a family, we take it for granted that an employer will not pay a wage one cent higher than he has to. But in these days the managing director sees himself as leader of a team, with responsibilities to his workmates just as great as his responsibilities to customers or shareholders. If the business does well it is natural for him to share the proceeds with the workers, even though this pushes their wages way above the free market level. And, of course, if enough good employers behave in this way, the expectations of the unemployed are raised; their supply price rises, and therefore the free market price itself also rises with the productivity of the best firms.

We need a lot more facts about wages and labour markets in LDCs. Meanwhile we should note that in so far as wages have risen in the enclaves *pari passu* with productivity, the inegalitarianism of the development process has been due not to failure of vertical trickle down, but to failure of horizontal pushing outwards of the borders of the enclave.

Whatever may happen to unskilled wages, development always brings a huge upward differentiation of the labour force, into skilled workers, supervisors, lower middle, middle middle and professional classes. This expansion of the middle is how development reduces inequality, right from its beginning, and is the chief reason why more developed countries are less unequal than less developed countries. It is a principal source of satisfaction to those at the bottom; the labourer himself may not have benefited from development, but his son has become a mechanic, and his daughter is a teacher.

This process of upgrading seems to go on forever, long after the country has joined the ranks of MDCs. Development increases the supply of middle skills, while creating acute shortages of unskilled labour, and especially labour for menial jobs. This is met in the first instance by bringing people into the enclave out of the traditional sector: raiding domestic service, handicrafts, petty trading, petty transportation, agriculture and so on. Then the household is raided; first the servants and then the wives are recruited into modern employments. Simultaneously, these jobs are mechanised to cope with increasing labour scarcities. At some point (early in West Africa, late in Western Europe) the door is opened to immigrants from other, less developed countries. The effect of all this is to prevent the bottom wage level from rising as fast as it otherwise would.

Moving still further up the hierarchy, we have the emergence of the professional and managerial classes. Some of these are sons of the nobility, but most have moved upward in income and status. In Europe more than half the university students have middle-class backgrounds; this is not so in LDCs.

Modernisation depends on the creation of this modernising élite; this, and the creation of a savings capacity, are the two keys to economic development, and must therefore have priority in any modernising scheme. Unfortunately this is an expensive group; relatively more expensive in the LDCs of this century than in the LDCs of the nineteenth century. There are two reasons for this. First, ever since the sixteenth century Western Europe has concentrated on producing university and secondary graduates in such numbers that 'clerks' have always been cheap; universal primary education was their lowest priority. Today's LDCs, however, with the exception of India, Egypt, and two or three others, neglected higher education until recently. They therefore had to import such people from abroad, and established traditional pay and status for these jobs far out of line with average income per head. The second reason is that this group is very highly mobile internationally. Racial and national prejudices having diminished, LDC nationals with high qualifications can find jobs almost anywhere. This limits the ability of their native countries to hold their salaries down to levels comparable with those of other groups who cannot enter a brisk international market.

Rent.
The rising share of rent with economic development troubled practically all economists from the time of Adam Smith to Henry George. Their fears were not realised in the sphere of agricultural rents. In the nineteenth century this was because the effective supply of land was increased by opening up the American continents, Australasia and elsewhere. In the twentieth century technology has brought a new check to agricultural rents, namely the chemical and biological revolutions which are doubling and trebling yields per acre. This revolution is

only just beginning in LDCs. What its outcome will be over the next fifty years, combined with rising populations, is anybody's guess.

Meanwhile concern has shifted from agricultural to urban rents. Perhaps those who profit most from development are the persons who own the lands on which the rapidly growing towns are sited. This is unearned income in its purest form. Left-of-centre politicians have grumbled about it for years, but without making significant headway.

Profits.

Development raises the share of profits in the national income because development enclaves, which have a high profit ratio, expand relatively to traditional sectors, where what we call profit on capital is much lower (though the share of income which is on a residual rather than a contractual basis may be even larger).

There is some evidence that the share of profits inside the enclave is higher in LDCs than in MDCs; at any rate, in large-scale manufacturing. Whether the relative share of profits rises still further or falls will depend, as we have already noted, on whether labour income rises as fast as productivity. There is evidence that countries now developed have gone through a phase in which the relative shares of wages and profits remained constant over decades; and still later evidence of a tendency for the profit share to decline in the most advanced countries. But our inquiry is confined to the LDC stage of development.

Patterns of Growth.

We said at the beginning that distribution will depend on the pattern of growth. The three main ingredients are: the original distribution of property, economic structure (i.e. large v. small-scale organisation, which is also related to technology), and dependence on foreign resources. Thus at one pole one may find an enclave like deep mining, financed and manned by foreigners, with a high capital/labour ratio and no domestic linkages; whereas at the other end one could find a peasant economy growing rich from exporting cocoa, rubber, cotton or rice, and investing in its own skills and industrial enterprises. The following attempts to separate out the various elements which link these patterns to income distribution.

1. The economy may be organised into many very small firms, or a few very large firms, or some intermediate conbination. This structural difference affects distribution not only through greater or smaller dispersion of material assets, but also because the opportunities for monopolistic organisation, whether by employers or by employees, are somewhat greater in the large scale pattern.

2. The economy may come to specialise more in types of trades using highly capital-intensive technology, or it may not. This depends partly on natural resources and other determinants of

location. For example, alluvial ore mining is much less capital-intensive than deep underground mining. Excessive capital intensity may also be a response to prices (foreign exchange rate, interest rate, wages) which do not accurately reflect relative scarcities; attempts to alter this by use of shadow prices usually also involve a change in distribution (e.g. wage subsidies). Changes in technology may affect the scale of operations; for example small farmers can adopt hybrid seeds and fertilisers just like large farmers, but some mechanical innovations favour the larger enterprises. Capital intensity also bears directly on the relative shares of labour and capital in output; on the numbers employed, and therefore the relative size of the enclave; and on the willingness of capitalists to resist wage demands, which is weaker when wages are a small part of total cost. Also some technologies rely more heavily than others on imported equipment.

3. Distribution is affected by the extent to which the country relies on imports – whether of food, raw materials, consumer goods or other manufactures. Depending on its resources and skills, a country may be better or worse off for greater or smaller participation in foreign trade: how this will affect distribution is a different question. The traditional neo-classical answer is of course that trade raises the earnings of abundant factors relatively to the earnings of scarce factors. Concern for the balance of payments leads towards directing domestic demand and exports towards commodities or services which use the more abundant factors, and the effect on distribution will depend on whether such trades use more or less of the resources commanded by the poor.

4. Distribution is further affected by the degree to which the country is dependent on foreign countries for capital or skills, including entrepreneurship. The profits of domestic capital may or may not be lower than those of imported capital, but they are more likely to be spent on domestic goods and services; and are also more likely to be reinvested domestically. Domestic skills are almost always cheaper than imported skills, given equal training; yet some coercion of foreign enterprises may be required. As for entrepreneurship, an economy has not matured until it has ceased to depend on foreigners for initiative and for efficient management; this is one of the conditions for switching the engine of growth from external to internal sources of energy.

5. The original distribution of income will depend on the original distribution of property, and through tastes, scale of operations, choice of technology and other elements already mentioned, will further determine the path of future distribution, both of income and of new assets. It is usually predicted that the concentration of assets will increase, because those who have large assets manage them better, save more, have greater ability to withstand cyclical or

other mishaps, exert more coercive power, and even perhaps have better luck. The argument is powerful, and this does seem to be what happens to the ownership of land in densely populated countries. But with respect to the ownership of industrial assets the evidence is inconclusive. With respect to skills, the evidence is of widening rather than narrowing, mainly because public education opens the doors of opportunity. But there are cases of restricted competition. One case which has attracted much attention is where a particular ethnic group (e.g. allegedly Ibos in Northern Nigeria, or Indians in Burma, or Protestants in Ulster) displays more than proportionate initiative, and helps to preserve its success by favouring its own members in employment, credit and trade.

6. Finally, the speed of growth will itself affect distribution. Growth feeds on itself. Allegedly one reason for the high ratio of household savings in Japan is that growth of consumption cannot keep up with the pace of income growth. Or, in manufacturing, by Verdoorn's law, productivity increases *pari passu* with the rate of growth. Hence rapid growth alters the relative quantities of the factors of production, and the derived demands, and therefore the distribution of income.

One cannot always foresee the pattern which growth will take, since this is influenced by changes in world demand and supply; yet many of the elements in distribution are susceptible to public control. These include: the original distribution of property, the extent of investment in education and skill formation, the degree of support for small-scale enterprise (both industrial and agricultural), the development or use of appropriate technology, the use of local rather than imported materials, the use of local skills, the extent of foreign entrepreneurship, the ratio of domestic savings to national income; and so on. Nowadays most LDC governments are trying to influence the distribution of income through one or more of these elements. Currently the major emphasis is on reducing the share of foreigners in gross domestic product, which is seen (sometimes correctly and sometimes not) as a brake on the rate of growth, no less than as a source of inequality. Very few governments concern themselves with the share of the poor in net national product, though failure to develop the human potential in the lower half of the social scale is often a greater brake on the rate of growth and a more relevant source of inequality.

When we take all these factors into account, can we arrive at clear predictions of what will happen to distribution inside the enclave as development proceeds? All schools of economics have tried their hand at this, but their favourite forecast – the falling rate of profit – has not yet come to pass. We hazard only the following three propositions:

1. The share of profits relatively to wages will rise in the early stages of development.

2. The owners of the land on which towns are sited will reap a harvest.

3. Income of people in the middle range (say the tenth to the sixtieth percentiles) will rise faster than total national income.

The first of these three forecasts is the least secure, since it presumes that capitalists are not coerced into paying more than the free market wage, and do not choose to pay more than they have to.[1]

III REDISTRIBUTION AND GROWTH

We will now reverse our question. We have been asking how growth affects distribution. Now we will ask how distribution affects growth.

The simplest way to proceed is to analyse the case where the government redistributes income either by expropriating the rich or by taxing them. We confine the term 'expropriation' to cases where the government acquires private assets at prices which lower the owner's net worth. If the government nationalises and pays market value there is no change in distribution except in so far as extensive nationalisation may itself either increase or reduce the market value of private assets. We also omit from the analysis the fact that if taxes enter into marginal costs they may have marginal effects on resource allocation which may themselves affect income distribution; this is the regular route of the economics of public finance.

This is not the only way to redistribute income. The government could instead act directly on the pattern of growth in ways that affect distribution, but if we were to follow this line, we would mainly be repeating what we have just said in Section II. We shall in any case be drawn into this topic again, since the kind of redistribution we are analysing may itself affect the pattern of growth.

Perhaps before proceeding we should enter one further caveat. We are not asking the question whether a government would be allowed to engage in redistribution; or, since many governments have done this in the past, what set of circumstances makes this possible. We are assuming that the government can have a progressive tax structure, and are asking only how this would affect the rate of growth.

Attention focuses on two points: the effect of redistribution on the efficiency of asset management, and its effect on savings and investment.

The effect of expropriation on asset management depends on who manages the assets after expropriation. The government may itself keep and manage the assets; or, as sometimes in nationalising the mines, it may keep the assets but enter into management contracts with private enterprise; or, as in some land reform, it may transfer ownership of the assets to private persons, to manage on their own behalf individually or collectively.

There is no intrinsic reason why a government taking over a going concern should not be able to manage it as efficiently as private interests, but governments differ very widely in this respect. In general LDC governments have two levels of managerial efficiency; this is something which comes as part of the process of modernisation. So in general, and with noble exceptions, LDC enterprises are poorly managed; equipment is poorly maintained; they are overstaffed with boondogglers; and top management is selected on particularistic rather than universalistic principles. Very many LDC political leaders realise this themselves, and this is why they prefer joint ventures or management contracts to direct operation by public officials.

Land reform is of two kinds. In one case the land has been farmed by peasants paying rents, and the reform transfers legal ownership from the landlords to the peasants without affecting the scale of farm operations. This is generally expected to raise the level of farming. Since the farmers no longer have to share the proceeds of their efforts with landlords, it is expected that they will invest more time and purchased inputs in their farms, and so raise yields per acre. Most of the evidence bears this out, though not quite all.

In the other case the landowners themselves operate large-scale farming with wage labour. What happens to efficiency then depends on what the governemnt does with the land after expropriation. It may keep it as a state farm, or hand it to farmers to operate collectively, or break it up into small family farms. The first two of these options, state farms and collectives, are usually associated with low efficiency. The efficiency of the third depends on the level of technology involved (small farmers can handle some kinds of high level technology more easily than others) and upon the package of agricultural services established as a framework for small farmers.

Turn next to the effects of redistribution, whether by expropriation or by taxation, on savings and investment.

Note first that the two are not the same. Redistribution may reduce investment without reducing domestic saving. For example, expropriation of foreign enterprises presumably discourages new foreign investment, and wise governments therefore do not embark upon this road until they are satisfied that their economies have reached a stage where they can dispense with new foreign investment. Again, expropriation of domestic assets may lead to a flight of domestic savings, with accompanying balance of payments troubles.

However, the main analytical interest is in saving, and the most useful approach to saving is a functional analysis, distinguishing between the savings of landlords and the savings of capitalists.

It is part of the classical tradition that landowners save very little; wherefore expropriating or taxing them reduces saving very little. It hurts handicraft workers and those who supply services to the landowners; but this is presumably offset by improvement of the situations of those persons to whom expenditure is deflected. Indeed, as noted above, saving may increase, if additional peasant saving is large enough. The proposition is a three-quarters truth. At the very time that the classical economists were formulating it, British landowners were investing in opening up coalmines, and in improving marginal lands. Similarly, some Indian landowners have invested in improving their lands, and their disappearance has sometimes been felt in lowered yields. By and large, however, the proposition may stand.

Suppose that a tax on landowners reduces their consumption. The government may save and invest the proceeds, in which case the rate of growth will accelerate. Or the government may spend the money on providing social services for the poor – medical care, education, subsidised housing and so on. Or it may actually make cash payments to the poor – old age pensions, unemployment assistance, family allowances, etc.

A transfer of consumption from the rich to the poor obviously improves distribution, but it may also actually increase output. The traditional case is where increased consumption raises the productivity of the poor, through better nutrition, or health or education. On top of this, in the Keynesian analysis, if the rich have a higher propensity to import than the poor, the import multiplier is increased by the transfer, and total output increases. Our Latin-American colleagues emphasise this proposition. However, if the rich landowners respond to taxes not by importing fewer cars and refrigerators but by cutting their expenditures on retainers and domestic handicrafts, there is no change in the multiplier. The third case derives from differences in the relative labour intensity of goods consumed by the rich and by the poor. It used to be said that the Industrial Revolution proceeded faster in England than in France because the French rich purchased artistic handicrafts (tapestries, say) not amenable to mechanisation, while the English rich bought factory goods. Now we are sometimes told that in LDCs the rich buy capital-intensive goods while the poor buy labour-intensive goods – cloth, shoes, food – so that a transfer of income would increase employment. If the capital equipment comes from abroad, this is just another version of a change in the import multiplier. The proposition has independent validity if the equipment is made within the country, but having regard once more to the large share of services in the consumption of the rich, one may wonder whether their consumption of domestic goods is at the margin significantly more capital-intensive than the consumption of the poor.

So much for landowners; people do not worry very much about potential ill effects of redistributing assets or income from them. The main anxiety centres on the effect of taxes on incomes derived from profits; especially the effect on savings. This is because the marginal propensity to save is higher out of profit incomes than out of other incomes. The best data on proportions of income saved come from Japan,[(2)] for the year 1961.

Percentage of Income Saved

Corporations	41.5
Unincorporated business	18.4
Wages and salaries	14.4
Farmers	13.6

Similar data exist for the United States[(3)] and for some LDCs.[(4)]

The first source of anxiety is therefore for what happens to savings when enterprises are transferred to public ownership and operation. There is no problem if the enterprises continue to be as profitable, and continue to save; but if their profits evaporate, or are raided for assistance to the current budget, instead of being reinvested, then the community's propensity to save is reduced. This has been a major problem in Britain, where public enterprises either just break even or run at a loss, with the consequence that every increase in nationalisation in that country reduces the propensity to save. This is not an inevitable characteristic of public enterprises; the high savings propensity of Communist countries is fed principally by the high profits of their public enterprises, plus high excise taxes, which in their context comes to the same thing. Until LDCs learn to make substantial profits from public enterprises, mainly for reinvestment, further nationalisation will reduce savings.

Taxes upon capitalists must also reduce capitalist savings, except in so far as they can be passed on. (If passed on there is no redistribution, and our problem does not arise.) The net effect of such taxes on saving therefore depends on what the government does with the money.

If the government gives priority to development, it must give priority to public saving. One difference between LDCs today and European economies in 1800 is that the former lack a *rentier* class, i.e. a class of savers who hold bonds and equities in portfolio. Europe built up this class, first to hold government bonds in the first half of the eighteenth century, then to hold turnpike and canal stock in the second half of the eighteenth century, then moving on to railway stocks and foreign bonds in the nineteenth century, and finally coming to industrial equities. Our LDCs do not have this *rentier* class. They have rich landowners, who spend on services, and rich capitalists, who invest in their own businesses, but they have few portfolio investors, and this is one reason why they have so much trouble financing their public utilities and depend so much on foreign capital for this sector of capital formation. It is not necessary to create a *rentier* class for this purpose.

Public saving can do the same job, and from the socialist standpoint a better job.

Another important case is where a principal source of wealth is an exhausting natural resource, like a mineral or a forest needing regeneration, or a tree crop threatened with diminishing demand in foreign markets, like rubber or coffee. It is then desirable to use much of the current proceeds from this asset to create new assets which will replace it. This might happen automatically if the asset was managed by domestic capitalists; but if it is managed by foreign capitalists they are more likely to reinvest their capital at home; and if it is managed by small farmers, their horizon may be too low. Public saving and investment may be the only solution.

Let us now classify how the government may redistribute money raised at the expense of private saving, and how growth may be affected.

1. It may spend the money to raise the consumption of the poor, in ways already listed, whether through expanding the social services or by making cash payments to the poor. This may raise the productivity of the poor enough to counter the adverse effect on growth of reduced saving. If not, one has to trade off reduced inequality against higher growth. For example, Cuba is alleged to have one of the slowest rates in the world, combined with the least relative inequality in the world. A net assessment of this performance, for comparison with say Brazil, must depend on personal taste; there is no scientific formula for this trade-off.

2. The government may not spend on consumption; it may save the money and invest it in various ways.

2a. It may invest it inside the enclave in the same sectors in which the private savers would have invested it – infrastructure, housing, factories and so on, whether owning these assets itself, or functioning as an investment banker. In this case it has substituted publicly-owned for privately-owned new assets, as the principles of socialism require.

2b. It may use the money to change distribution by changing the enclave's pattern of growth. For example, it may concentrate on financing and otherwise aiding small business, or develop less capital-intensive technologies, or open up new natural resources which displace foreign imports, or stimulate domestic entrepreneurship, or pursue any of the other policies implicit in what we have said about how different patterns of growth influence distribution. These changes of direction may accelerate or decelerate the growth rate; some do the one and some do the other. If such a change of direction decelerates growth, while improving distribution, an additional element will enter into the trade-off, if the thing that the government is doing is thought to have merit on its own. For example, a government may wish to make a particular investment (say opening up some expensive natural resource) both because it is expected to improve distribution (e.g. belongs to some particularly impoverished tribe) and also because this meets some other national objective (pride in not depending on foreign sources; preparation for defence). In such a case the trade-off is between growth on the one side with both distribution and the merits of the chosen pattern on the other side.

2c. Finally the government may invest outside the enclave money which the private capitalists would have invested inside the enclave. This is strongly defensible on distributional grounds, but it may also be a more economic investment. For example, we have seen that there is excessive geographical polarisation, which the government can usefully counter by supporting new growth poles. Again, private capitalists overinvest in towns and underinvest in agriculture and rural areas; government investing can make up this deficiency. Moreover an increase of agricultural productivity raises the demand for manufactured goods, so investment in agriculture may permit faster growth of industry.

To conclude, much of the discussion of distribution and growth assumes that these two must be at the expense of each other, but this is not so. In deciding to make the rich less rich, the government has at least a theoretical choice between using the proceeds to increase consumption, and using the proceeds to bring about a different pattern of investment and of ownership. The USSR used its revolution to increase its growth rate rather than immediate consumption; whereas Cuba used its revolution to increase immediate consumption rather than the growth rate. The government has three choices, not two.

(i) Leave distribution and growth unchanged.

(ii) Redistribute from the rich and maintain (or increase) the growth rate.

(iii) Redistribute from the rich and increase consumption. A reduction in inequality does not necessarily imply a fall in the rate of growth.

NOTES

1. Perhaps one should add here how misleading it is to judge what is happening to distribution by looking at Gini coefficients for the whole economy. Since the enclaves earn more per head and grow faster than the traditional sectors, Gini inequality is bound to increase in the early stages, until the traditional sectors themselves take off. It is even theoretically possible for equality to be increasing inside the enclaves and inside the traditional sectors, and yet for the overall average to show decreasing equality. To understand what is happening we need also to look at separate indexes for the enclaves and for the rest of the economy.

2. Ohkawa, K. and Rosovsky, H. *Japanese Economic Growth*, Stanford, 1973, pages 168–9.
3. Burmeister, E. and Taubman, P. 'Labour and Non-Labour Income Saving Propensities,' *Canadian Journal of Economics*, January 1969.
4. Snyder, Donald 'Econometric Studies of Household Saving Behavior in Developing Countries,' *Journal of Development Studies*, January 1974.

[19]

THE DUAL ECONOMY REVISITED

by W. ARTHUR LEWIS
Princeton University

I welcome the Editor's invitation to contribute to this anniversary symposium. My thoughts on the subject have wandered not in the direction of new theoretical concepts, but rather towards a set of reflections on the usefulness of the dual economy model. Like most other models this one has illuminated both more and less than was intended; more in the extent to which it is used by some writers to explain recent developments in mature industrial countries (notably Kindleberger, 1967; Cornwall, 1977), and less in the speed with which real wages have risen in some labour-rich developing societies, in defiance not only of the model but also of previous historical experience. These reflections are therefore mainly factual.

The dual economy model comes in a wide range of specifications, since each writer is free to make his own assumptions. The version that I am using here has three characteristics. First, there are two sectors, hereinafter called "modern" and "traditional", such that the modern sector grows by recruiting labour from the traditional. Secondly, unskilled labour is paid more in the modern sector than in the traditional sector for the same quantity and quality of work. And thirdly, unskilled labour is initially abundant[1] in the sense that at the current wage much more labour is offered to the modern sector than that sector wishes to hire.

The model focusses on explaining the distribution of income inside the modern sector, and therefore the rate of growth of the modern sector, but it has many other ramifications.

This essay will not concern itself with the mechanics of the model; or with comparisons between this and the numerous other versions of two-sector models. It will concentrate on three general topics:

1. The effects of the modern and traditional sectors on each other.
2. The sources of labour abundance.
3. The maintenance of differentials in the labour market.

[1]The phrase "surplus labour" is not used in this essay since it causes emotional distress. As always, the idea intended to be conveyed is that of an infinitely elastic supply of labour to the modern sector at the current wage.

I Effects of the Modern and Traditional Sectors on Each Other

A number of writers have expressed surprise and disillusionment that the rapid expansion of modern sectors that has occurred in LDCs over the past two decades has not "trickled down" to bring equal prosperity to the traditional sectors.

Actually, there is no reason to expect the traditional always to benefit from expansion of the modern. There are forces working for benefit and forces working for loss; the net result will vary from case to case.

Expansion of the modern sector may benefit the traditional in four ways, each of which has its loss counterpart: through provision of employment, through sharing physical facilities, through modernisation of ideas and institutions, and through trade.

The first medium is employment. The modern sector employs persons who move over from the traditional sector. They earn more in the modern sector, have better opportunities for their children, and rise at least a notch in social status. The Gini coefficient may actually show a rise in inequality, since the share of national output accruing to the bottom 50 per cent may fall;[2] but most people would favour an upward movement that makes some poor people earn more without making anybody else worse off.[3] A good deal of the "benefit" of development takes the form of creating a middle class, widely defined as the occupational categories lying between the landed gentry and the unskilled urban proletariat. If this is a benefit, it should be taken into account when assessing the progress of development.

These are part of the gains to the modern sector from its own expansion. The traditional sector shares in that some of its people move into the modern sector with its opportunities, earn money and send remittances home. The extent of the gain depends a great deal on how much population pressure the traditional sector is feeling. At one extreme the country is underpopulated, and the modern sector

[2]The effect of transferring one man from the bottom half of the distribution to the top half is to increase the total income of the bottom half by the difference between his earnings and those of the median (who now moves into the bottom half) and also to increase the total income of the top half by the difference between his new earnings and those of the median. Whether this move increases or reduces the relative share of the bottom half of the distribution will depend on the actual magnitudes.

[3]This is a guess, and the exceptions are numerous. But it appears that "most people" favour lotteries, where those who gain do so without effort and wholly at the expense of other people.

is getting labour only by exercising force of some kind;[4] while at the other extreme population is increasing at 3 per cent per annum in an already overcrowded countryside. Where population is scarce the expansion of the modern sector is frequently predatory—not only in that labour is taken by force, but also in that the relative shortage of adult males in their prime disrupts the village economy and village life in general. At the other extreme, where population is dense, expansion of the modern sector throws a life line to the traditional sector. In this case people will pour out of the traditional sector faster than the modern sector can absorb them, and unemployment will increase no matter how rapidly modern sector employment may increase.

To continue with the effects of expansion of the modern sector, we have summarised the second set as "the sharing of physical facilities". The modern sector builds for itself infrastructure (railways, roads, ports, hospitals, water supplies, electricity, etc.) which is used also by the traditional sector, on payment of marginal cost or less. The modern sector is also taxed to pay for schools, public health services, etc., and the traditional sector normally (though not inevitably) gets more of these services than it pays for. To tax its developed sectors and subsidise its under-developed sectors is one of the most powerful ways that a government can use to ensure that the benefits of development trickle down. Statisticians measuring changes in the distribution of income try to assess these non-cash benefits when dealing with developed countries, but tend to overlook their importance when dealing with LDCs.

The third set of effects of the expansion of the modern sector is the modernisation of ideas and institutions in the traditional sector. New technologies raise output; girls are allowed to attend school; land tenure systems are revised; farmers are introduced to co-operative agricultural institutions and so on. Alas the new ideas are not always appropriate—so we get inappropriate technology; or even if appropriate, ideas need to be introduced more gradually in line with other changes—so we get an outpouring of university graduates into an economy which cannot as yet absorb them. That social change entails inappropriate as well as appropriate changes seems to be inevitable.

The last set of effects of the expansion of the modern sector has to do with trade between the two sectors. There may be no such trade. Theoretically the modern sector could be self-contained, with its own

[4]Slavery, indentured labour, prohibiting the small farmers from growing profitable cash crops on their own (e.g., coffee in Kenya), levying taxes payable only in cash, where cash can be had only through working for wages, etc.

factories, mines and farms. Or, more likely, it may export part of its product to the outside world in return for needed imports. This latter type of enclave development has been very common; for example, Asian plantation economies exported (say) rubber, and imported rice and cloth for their workers. It is one reason why there was so much scope for import substitution in the third quarter of our century.

If the modern sector depends on the traditional for part of its needs (e.g., food, raw materials), its continued expansion will depend on similar expansion of the commodities in the traditional sector. Otherwise the terms of trade will move against it. However, the effects on the modern sector of rising productivity in the traditional sector move in opposite directions. The product-wage rises in the modern sector as traditional productivity rises, but this is countered by improved terms of trade, and the net effect on the product-wage may be in either direction.[5]

Benefits are not confined to changes in the terms of trade; changes in the volume of trade are also important. Thus in India industrial production rises in years of good harvests and falls in years of bad harvests; because industrial production depends partly on the availability of raw materials and partly on the farmers' income (marketable surplus). The condition for this is a highly elastic supply of industrial goods, due to existence of idle productive capacity, whether in factories or in the handicrafts sector. With a low elasticity of supply for industry a good harvest would ruin the farmers and might (through unemployment) ruin some industrial workers too.

Now in small countries it is unlikely that expansion of the modern sector will be choked off by an adverse movement in the terms of trade since it can buy and sell on the world market at constant terms of trade. Hence this possibility is important only for closed or very large economies. The other side of this coin is that the traditional sector's terms of trade are not improved by the expansion of the modern sector, a proposition of some importance when used to illuminate the world economy as a whole, and the factoral terms of trade between MDCs and LDCs. Insofar as the commodities that LDCs export are a small part of their agricultural output, these commodities are available at constant prices in terms of foodstuffs. (For further analysis see my Wicksell Lectures, 1969, *Aspects of Tropical Trade 1883-1965*. Also my *The Evolution of the International Economic Order*, 1978.)

[5]There is an important *caveat*. An improvement of the terms of trade reduces the modern sector's exports, and it may take part of its "benefits" in enforced "leisure" (unemployment). In economies with instantaneous adjustments we leave it to Say's Law to take care of such possibilities, but in the real world short- and long-run effects have to be distinguished.

The traditional sector may also be damaged by buying imports from the modern sector (or from abroad). Textbooks on international trade theory are concerned with all the assumptions one has to make for it to be true that such trade must benefit both parties.[6] Since this set of assumptions does not always hold in LDCs, especially in their traditional sectors, an influx of imports may damage the economy even if paid for by exports.

Most of the literature of international trade theory assumes that the distribution of productive resources remains unchanged as between countries, and only goods flow; whereas the development process is much affected by the migration of capital, entrepreneurship, skills, unskilled labour and technology, over a long period of time —and this yields very different results. The dynamic aspect of the effect of modern upon traditional sectors is most easily understood in the light of growth pole theory. Essentially, when an industrial centre begins to grow there are economies of scale and economies of propinquity which make it attractive to more and more newcomers.[7] It grows by underselling and destroying its rivals. It therefore attracts unto itself the skills, capital and entrepreneurship of other areas, which tend to wind down correspondingly.

This polarisation of growth is a commonplace of economic history. It is now working powerfully in LDCs, where a small number of towns is growing at 5 to 10 per cent per annum, at the expense of the rest of the economy. There are many other examples of destructive effects. The Italian North sucked the skills and capital and entrepreneurship out of the Italian South. Northeast Brazil and Northwest England are other victims. Economic historians of India mark the period 1830-1860 as one where the economy retrograded, in response to a flood of imports from the U.K. growth pole. This is also an element in the dependency theory promoted in Latin America, where economic development in powerful centres pushes down the least developed countries instead of pulling them up.

What determines whether a region will be depressed or stimulated by developments elsewhere? The first answer must be its own natural resources. If these are abundant and easily developed, the region is

[6]All prices, including wages, must correspond to real social costs; no economies of scale; relative productivities are not altered by a time factor, such as learning; exchange rates or relative price levels are such that trade will balance at full employment levels. Non-economists, for whom market demand is not sacrosanct, would add that terms of trade would not be affected if tastes were altered so as to be more appropriate to the country's natural resources and skills.

[7]We owe the term *pôle de croissance* to Perroux (1955) but the essentials of the argument are in Young (1928).

likely to respond to a growing demand. If poorly endowed with natural resources, like Japan or Switzerland, a region depends for its development on enterprise and skill. The crucial question will therefore be whether such enterprise and skill as it possesses is drained off to the growth pole or comes into efflorescence at home. What creates such efflorescence is hard to pinpoint. An important element is popular and official support. Enterprise does not flourish in resource poor countries where it is not acceptable ideologically, or cannot rely on government support.

In any case, we have looked only at the initial phase of growth pole theory. The pole does not grow forever; if it did, the whole of the world's population would by now be living in the county of Lancashire, where the industrial revolution began. After a while the economies of scale are exhausted, and give place to the diseconomies of congestion. The economy ossifies; its institutions and ideas have become specialised and relevant only to the two or three industries in which it has had special advantages, and it is now shunned by new industries which find elsewhere lower rents, lower wages, space and greater welcome. While growth pole theorists stress the power and destructiveness of established centres, economic historians tend to be impressed rather with the disadvantages of having been first.

We must not overplay the growth pole theme in development economics, and to argue that the fact that some countries are developed prevents the development of any others would be to overplay it. The rapid growth of British cotton exports after 1830 seems to have had this destructive effect on a number of textile industries, especially in Latin America and in Asia, but this seems to have run its course by about 1880, after which British trade moved on to the defensive. By 1880 national income per head had begun to move upwards in most LDCs, and the stagnation of 1914-1945 was not peculiar to LDCs. Some LDCs have gone ahead rapidly. By 1970 the number of countries where less than 50 per cent of the labour force remained in agriculture had reached 60; and in 1979 it is not the LDCs that refuse to import manufactures from the MDCs, but the MDCs who are scared of LDC manufactures and are raising barriers to keep them out.

Just so we must not overplay the likelihood that the expansion of the modern sector will damage the traditional sector within the same country. It may do so, but we have also seen half a dozen reasons why benefits may exceed losses. Each case must be looked at separately.

The moral for policy makers is of course not to rely on "trickle down" to benefit the traditional sector, but to attack the problems of that sector directly. The great majority of economists writing on this subject since 1940 have advocated strong measures to raise agricultural output, including land reform, agricultural extension, irrigation, cheap credit, etc.; and have indeed (rightly or wrongly) bolstered their case by arguing that this would also stimulate industrialisation by providing a wider market. Nowadays a bogus history of economic thought floats around in which the economists of the fifties were rooting for industry to the neglect of agriculture, but this was not so. The economics of the 1950s was obsessed by balanced growth, arguing that development of industry alone would be constrained by the farmers' poverty, and that development of agriculture alone would turn the terms of trade against agriculture and bankrupt the farmers. As it happened most Governments neglected agriculture for reasons of their own, but this was in spite of and not in accordance with economists' advice.[8]

Nowadays the real difficulty in the way of agricultural transformation is not ideological but technological. We know how to raise agricultural output in tropical areas with adequate rainfall or access to irrigation water, but arid lands have low yields, and in the absence of water do not respond to fertilisers or to the potential of high yielding varieties. Somewhere between 500,000,000 and 600,000,000 live in these arid lands, on the fringes of the great Asian and African deserts. This is where the real poverty is in LDCs, and the numbers are increasing rapidly. When people say "there has been such rapid growth of output, coupled with such rapid growth of poverty" they are putting together two half sentences which have little to do with each other. Rapid growth has contributed to the rise of unemployment in the towns but this is a fraction of the poverty into which the people of the arid lands are locked. To unlock this prison is the greatest challenge to development.

II The Abundance of Labour

In this model labour moves from the traditional to the modern sector with an infinite elasticity of supply. The potential rate of expansion of the modern sector depends on how much labour is still left in the traditional sector. It can grow rapidly if there are still plenty of farm labourers, handicraft workers, domestic servants, petty traders and such to recruit; if not, it can expand only by increasing capital per head. Pressure is then applied to profits, and the "mature" economy will find itself exporting capital rather than investing it at home. If labour is abundant the profits ratio moves in the opposite direction.

[8]There was also wide support for protecting traditional Asian handicrafts, and a good deal of government effort to this end in South and Southeast Asia.

Real wages are constant; so the annual increase in productivity accrues to profits; so the product-wage is falling; so the investment ratio is rising and the rate of growth of the modern sector is accelerating. Rapid growth of employment in the modern sector has the further pay-off of high productivity. For a modern sector which has doubled in size in ten years will have a higher ratio of the latest machinery than one which has doubled in twenty years, and will be more productive, given that each year's vintage of machines is more productive than that of the year before. The size of the reservoir of cheap labour and the ease or otherwise of its absorption into the modern sector are therefore central to our understanding of the speed of development. But we need not make a fetish of "infinite" elasticity; "very large" would do just as well for our present purpose, which is not to examine the mechanics of the model, but to consider what we know about the availability of labour to modern sectors.

We know, to begin with, that most countries have started with an abundance of land rather than of labour—even though in some cases one may have to go back several centuries to find it. This is only another way of saying that the world's population was very small until recent times, so that in say A.D. 1800 the number of countries where population was pressing on the cultivable land was rather small. It was then extremely difficult to get labour for "modern" sectors, which developed slavery, serfdom and numerous other tricks to keep themselves supplied with labour. The infinite elasticity model is therefore only for countries which have passed through this stage and reached a demographic situation where, at the current level of wages in the modern sector the supply of labour to the modern sector exceeds the demand. To arrive at this point the country will have endured much cultural and sociological change, into which we need not enquire.

As the preceding analysis implies, population growth is at the core of labour abundance. A farm population is forced to react to population growth in one way or another, since its immediate impact is to reduce output per head, and to reduce the average size of farm bequeathed from one generation to the next. The problem can be solved in the countryside if more land can be brought into cultivation; it is still today solved in this way in the less populated parts of Africa. But if there is not enough new cultivable land, or if access to it is restricted, people will emigrate— to the towns, across the ocean, five thousand miles if need be—to wherever work is rumoured to be available. If population growth is the cause of the disequilibrium, migration is the mechanism of adjustment. (See the pioneering study by Thomas, 1954.)

It does not take high rates of population growth to set the mechanism in motion. In the second half of the nineteenth century European populations were growing at just over one per cent per annum, and this rate created an abundance of labour in most of them, judging by the fact that there was no shortage of labour at home, despite huge emigration. The outstanding exceptions were France, where population growth had almost ceased by 1880, and Germany, where the urban population was growing at 2.5 per cent per annum, and where after 1890 emigration slowed to a trickle. ("Urban" is not conterminous with "modern" but will serve as an indicator.) In Britain the population grew at the same natural rate, but the urban population grew only at 1.8 per cent per annum and emigration continued vigorously until 1914.

Since migration is the adjustment mechanism[9] we must note that the expansion of the modern sector is not necessarily tied to the population of the traditional sector in the same country, since migrants may come from outside. Thus something approaching one hundred million people migrated from heavily settled to sparsely settled lands between 1850 and 1929—about a half of them European and a half Asian. In all this time labour was abundant in the Eastern seaboard towns of the United States, and though wages were higher than in Europe, the rate of growth of real wages in manufacturing was no higher than in Germany or Britain. Labour was equally abundant in Guyana or Ceylon or other countries recruiting in India or China. In countries with heavy immigration the neo-classical assumptions about the labour supply are clearly irrelevant.

Of particular interest is the situation in Western Europe between 1950 and 1973. As we have just seen, none of these countries experienced scarcity of labour before 1914, except France and Germany; in all the others the modern sector was not growing fast enough to absorb all the rural migrants. This situation changed after the second world war, when low population growth combined with rapid industrialisation to create a shortage of labour. The shortage was felt not so much in the better paid as in the less well paid jobs. The demand for more workers in the better paid jobs was met by recruiting people from the less well paid jobs, and it is these that ran short of labour. Employers in these categories reorganised the work, with new equipment and self-service. Homes were filled with domestic machinery, and housewives joined the labour market. But with industrial employment growing

[9]Movement from the traditional to the modern sector need not involve migration, but in practice most of it does.

by 2 per cent and the natural increase in the labour force less than 1 per cent the labour market continued to be tight. So Western Europe opened its doors to immigration, especially from Mediterranean Europe.

The results of this tightening of the labour market were magical. These countries experienced full employment for the first time in industrial history (except briefly during wars). They liquidated the *lumpenproletariat*. Collective bargaining negotiations about introducing new machines or restrictive practices ceased to be dominated by fear of redundancy. Tariffs could be reduced against a background of rapid expansion; even tariffs on manufactures from LDCs. Women could be allowed into non-traditional jobs, without a sense of deprivation.

The United States offers a striking contrast. Over this period its labour force grew at 2 per cent per annum, and the number of jobs barely kept pace. From 1969 onwards the growth rate of well paid jobs fell below 2 per cent and the reservoir of cheap labour, including black labour and female labour, has ever since been filling instead of emptying.

Abundance of labour is not a condition to be desired. Emigration apart, the way to get rid of it from a developed country is to have the modern sector grow at least one percentage point faster than the labour force.[10] (The modern sector includes modern services as well as industry.) The surest way to run into trouble is to have "de-industrialisation" (industrial employment growing more slowly than the labour force), since this means that the reservoir of cheap labour will be filling instead of emptying. The political and social health of the community, no less than its economic health, requires a continual transfer from the reservoir to the more productive sectors, rather than the relative expansion of the reservoir.

Unfortunately abundance of labour is very much the condition of the average LDC. Population now grows at 2 to 3 per cent per annum, so it would be surprising if these countries did not suffer from abundance of labour and high migration rates, internal and external. There is still leeway for rural settlement in parts of Latin America and Africa, and this is why agricultural output has just about kept up with population growth. The flow to the towns—growing at from 5 to 10 per cent per annum—is everywhere larger than it needs to be because

[10]The modern sector of an LDC is small, and must therefore grow much faster than the labour force if the reservoir of cheap labour is to begin to empty itself. See below.

development is (wrongly) concentrated in the towns at the expense of the countryside, and because the wage differentials are too wide. But short of physical force to hold people in the countryside, as in China and in Kampuchea, there is no way that a population can grow at 3 per cent per annum without experiencing an abundance of labour in its modern sector.

Another twentieth century phenomenon which augments the labour supply is the presence of married women in the labour market. In the U.S.A. in 1890 only 3 per cent of married women living with their husbands also had jobs outside the home; now that figure is about 40 per cent, and still rising. LDCs are still at the beginning of this change. It will be delayed in Muslim countries, but with the rapid spread of education may be expected soon to be in full swing everywhere else. One must also add that a longer life span has increased the proportion of persons over 45 years of age who are still in the labour force. On the other hand the proportion of children in the labour force has diminished.

Karl Marx, who predicted an ever-increasing reservoir of unemployed persons, was not relying on demographic factors. He argued that capitalism creates its own labour force, by undermining the handicraft workers in the first instance, and then by use of labour saving innovations which create unemployment. We looked at these possibilities in our preceding section, and saw that theory permits any outcome. History shows that in Europe the undermining of handicraft workers was a stage; once this was over and the factory system fully established the reinvestment of profits created more jobs than were lost by invention (as Ricardo had prophesied). Europe's abundance of labour at the end of the century was created by population growth and not by shrinkage of jobs.

In practice the question is not whether the modern sector will contract, but whether it will grow fast enough to absorb those who wish to leave the traditional sector, in the twentieth century demographic situation. Working against such an outcome are first, the size of the traditional sector, secondly, the pervasiveness of labour-saving innovations, and thirdly, the vulnerability of small scale enterprise.

First as to the size of the traditional sector. When the industrial revolution began in Western Europe the agricultural population was already down to about 50 per cent of the labour force. Moreover the technology which would make it possible for 5 per cent of the labour force to grow enough food for the whole population had not yet been created. The current LDCs have started with from 70 to 80 per cent in agriculture. Moreover, the recent green revolution in Asia shows farmers—even on 5 acres—anxious to adopt tractors and other labour saving devices, as one of their first reactions to relative affluence. We may therefore expect the exodus from agriculture to be large and prolonged.

The other side of this is the smallness of the modern sector, which means that even relatively fast growth adds a small number of people. For example, if the modern sector is expected to absorb all the increase in population, and is 30 per cent of the labour force with population growing at 3 per cent per annum, the modern sector would have to grow at 10 per cent per annum, which it cannot do.

The second constraint on labour absorption by the modern sector is the transformation of that sector by labour saving devices. In the nineteenth century the expansion of factory employment was paralleled by expansion of shop assistants, clerks, accountants, hotel workers, restaurant workers and so on. All these occupations have been rendered less labour-intensive; office work by the typewriter, the copier and the computer; shop assistants and restaurant workers by self-service; hotel work by cleaning equipment, washing machines and self-service. These innovations have found their way into the LDCs where the effect is to reduce the number of jobs and increase the abundance of labour.

The third difference between then and now is the greater vulnerability of small scale production in the modern sector. To get this into perspective we must first spend a moment with the structure of production. An economy does not divide into a capitalist sector hiring workers for factories and other large units on the one hand, and a small farming sector on the other hand. In between are units of production of all sizes, and in particular a great number of one-to five-man undertakings in manufacturing, transport and a wide range of services —often nowadays called the informal sector. Some of this activity belongs in the modern sector as we have defined it; i.e., it will expand with economic development; the rest—e.g., some of the handicrafts and some of the services—belong to the traditional sector in that they will contract.

The expansion of small scale activity in the modern sector is an important part of the development process. This is not because it is a temporary resting-place for migrants from the countryside seeking jobs in large scale enterprise. In LDCs, no less than in MDCs (as we shall see in our next section) jobs in large scale urban enterprises are not normally awarded to people who have no connections. It is rather because this sector of the economy is useful in its own right, meeting genuine market needs, and providing a lot of employment in the process.

Particularly remarkable is the degree of market integration between large and small firms, with the large sub-contracting to the small for intermediate products, parts and services. Much has been written about this in the context of Japan, but there is plenty of it in any modern industrial economy. There seems, however, to be less of it currently in LDCs than one would expect. An industrialist who built a factory in Birmingham (England) in 1890 could count on purchasing from other firms a very large part of his intermediate requirements, and designed his factory accordingly. In contrast, the same man building a factory today in, say, Monrovia would have to design it to produce for itself a larger part of its requirements. This could be just a temporary phenomenon, with the larger factories becoming relatively less self-sufficent as small scale firms multiply; but it could also be that such multiplication is prevented by factories having been designed to be self-sufficient. We need more evidence, and perhaps better policies in this area. Small scale firms are more likely to use appropriate technology, and will provide more employment per unit of capital than large firms, so they are much to be cherished.

In sum, I have been considering why the employment problem may be more difficult to solve now than it was a hundred years ago. Population pressure is greater, bringing a greater potential for migration from the countryside; while the capacity of modern sectors to absorb people is more restricted.

III Non-Competing Groups

The model does not in its pure form depend on a difference between wages in the modern and wages in the traditional sector; if the supply of labour is infinitely elastic the modern sector will get all the labour it wants at the current wage.

In practice wages are normally higher in the modern sector, for similar work. Rural wages are possibly about the same as informal sector wages, when allowances are made for differences in seasonality, periods of unemployment and family support. The marginal product of very small family farming is somewhat lower than this in the more overpopulated countries, while wages in factories and other large scale employment show a substantial margin over all others.

The model predicts that this margin should remain constant in the early stages of development, given the abundance of labour seeking jobs in the modern sector. It predicts quite well for nineteenth century Europe, on whose experience it was based, but when applied to one hundred LDCs over the past quarter century its performance is spotty. Urban wages have been rising faster than we would have predicted;

this, and not an alleged failure to trickle down, is the real theoretical puzzle of the period.

Economists automatically resist the idea that the same commodity may command different prices in what looks like the same market; the lower price should drive out the higher price. But the co-existence of "non-competing" groups has been recognised in our discipline ever since Alfred Marshall. It is not confined to the labour market. For example, we have often been told of industrial markets in Japan where highly efficient large firms co-exist with much less productive small firms. The large firms have taken their advantage in rents (higher profits, salaries, wages) instead of using it to reduce prices and bankrupt the smaller firms. Economists studying British industry in the 1950s found this a familiar practice. Groups which "ought" to be competing were not doing so; in numerous cases higher efficiency led to higher rents rather than to lower prices. Seen against this background it is not strange for LDC industrial wages to keep rising despite an abundance of labour which "ought" to be keeping them constant.

We shall return in a moment to this entrepreneurial behaviour, but should first look at another manifestation of non-competing groups, this time in the labour markets of developed countries. We owe the full elaboration of this case to Professors Doeringer and Piore (1971) but I shall not be following their schema exactly. (For a bibliography of the subject see Cain, 1976.)

The essence of this theory is that the labour market segments into two classes of jobs, good and bad, which they call primary and secondary. These two classes do not necessarily differ in starting wages —the good may even pay less in initial years than the bad. But they differ in lifetime earnings, because the good jobs pay more for experience, and also have a ladder for training and promotion. One has therefore to start in good jobs at the bottom; one cannot jump at, say, age 40 from the poorly paid into the high paid stream. The poorly paid stream pays little for experience and has no provision for training. Workers who enter this stream have little incentive to improve themselves. Turnover is high, and work habits are poor. Low wages and unemployment also cause malnutrition.

The question is: why does not the abundance of labour in bad jobs bring down the earnings of labour in good jobs? Insofar as the difference is due to skills which are learnt without cost after entry, the influx would compete away the difference in pay. The maintenance of the differential is defended by arguing that the people in the bad jobs have lower productive capacity. The evidence of high turnover, poor physical condition and poor work habits is cited, but this is irrelevant insofar as it results from the nature of the bad jobs. A stronger case is made if selection for the good jobs is based on objective tests and examinations, but even this is not persuasive. We know that the performance of children in examinations correlates closely with the occupation of their parents, and we suspect that this has more to do with limited horizons and with the intellectual environment of the home than it has to do with potential ability at birth. To the extent that this is so, selection by examination tends to keep the poor poor, rather than to expand their economic opportunities.

We are not in any case dealing only with the poor. The bad job sector of the market includes a very large proportion of the women in the labour force, and while many of these are the sole support of their families and are poor, a large proportion are bringing home a second income. Also, since women in the mass labour market are at least as well educated as men, education cannot explain why they are concentrated in the bad job sector. Neither can education explain the concentration of U.S. blacks in this sector, since at least half the black population earns less than is earned by whites of comparable education.

The superior earning power of the good job set is due not to superior innate capacity of those selected for it, but to strict control of entry. Trade unions are strongest in the good job industries, and have used their power to maintain wages by controlling numbers. In some cases actual selection of recruits is left to the firm, which either makes its own arrangements, or invites its employees to sponsor friends or relatives. In other cases the union itself selects recruits.

Discrimination is built into these processes, for and against whom depending on the local mores. This does not have to be so; given control of entry the favoured workers could select new recruits on a random basis. However one's cohesion to share monopoly power is strengthened when those who share perceive other common bonds. Perhaps the narrowest discrimination would be that of an association that admitted only sons of existing members. The basic distinction in the British labour market is between the "aristocracy of labour", which is represented by the old craft unions, and the rest of the labour force, whose unionisation started at least a generation later; control of entry is central to the craft unions. In the United States job discrimination is used against women, blacks and other ethnic minorities. Outside pressures may break this discrimination at entry level; it then moves to the stage inside the firm where workers are being chosen to receive training, with a view to promotion. If this level is cleared, it moves up to promotion itself. So discrimination is not easily uprooted.

The number of workers allowed into the better job stream is not fixed, but depends on the state of prosperity. As in Western Europe in the 1950s and 1960s, when the good job sector is expanding rapidly firms give more training to their junior workers, move them up into positions requiring skill, and recruit new ones at the bottom. There is no shortage of workers in good jobs, or of applicants, since workers gladly pass from the bad to the good jobs market. The shortage shows in the bad jobs market. So prosperity tends to narrow the differential rather than to widen it. Similarly in bad times the good jobs market curtails recruiting, and the reservoir of cheap labour fills up. In some distant future, through cessation of population growth and of immigration, the duality of the labour market is ended. This will be because prosperity pulls the bottom layer up to the top, and not because competition pulls the top layer down to the bottom. Prosperity is the real friend of the women, the ethnics and the *lumpenproletariat;* with it demand begins to catch up with supply in their market, and the jobs they do are modernised; without it they drown in menial tasks at subsistence wages.

Let us return to the entrepreneur; why does he allow himself to be squeezed in this way? Three possible answers will be considered.

First, he may not realise that he is being squeezed. When he compares his own efficient set of workers with the inefficient poor work habits of the cheap labour market he may feel that the wage differential is amply justified. The extent to which work habits reflect the work escape his attention, and he may genuinely believe that the differences are all rooted in innate ability and in personality.

Secondly, even if he believes that ability is randomly distributed between the two job markets, he cannot alter the situation by creating a new establishment using only labour from the cheap labour market. By definition he needs workers with a combination of skills, training and experience. All such workers are employed in the good labour market. It is part of their creed not to work with other craftsmen who have not come through the proper channels. Unless the entrepreneur can persuade enough of them to violate their creed he cannot get started.

Thirdly, even if he could start a new enterprise with a lower wage and price level, he may not wish to do so. It may be easier to follow established practice and not get into bitter disputes with the unions and his fellow employers. "A quiet life with reasonable profits" may seem more attractive than profit maximisation with a heart attack. And he may persuade himself that it is best to build up a staff of long-service employees, loyal to the firm, and appreciative of his leadership.

In LDCs the outcome will depend in each product line on whether there are economies of scale. If there are no significant economies of scale, a vigorous class of small businessmen will scour the cheap labour market for its best talents, and will prevent the trade unions and the large capitalists from joining together to create restricted entry systems. If there are significant economies of scale the large firms are not being pressured by the small. What they face is pressure from within, to create promotion ladders, training systems, pension schemes, and above all "orderly" entry—all of which translates into a higher life-cycle income, financed from non-competing rents.

This is no doubt an element in those LDCs where wages of large scale employers have been rising rapidly despite abundance of labour. The urban labour market is settling down into a favoured and a competitive sector. There are other elements. One such is pressure of civil service unions raising government pay, which is an important item where the wage-earning labour force is small (because most people are small farmers). Another element is pressure of governments on foreign employers. Given such forces we may expect an aristocracy of labour to emerge, which will protect itself by treaty with those large scale employers who can withstand small scale competition—while population pressures and migration from the countryside keeps the cheap labour reservoir full.

Finally, what determines the levels of wages in this model? The theory of distribution is the No Man's Land of economics. Let us build a small trench in it, taking off from a suggestion of Phelps Brown (1968) that whereas in the early stages of development the supply of labour may be infinitely elastic, in the later stages of development it is the supply of capital that is infinitely elastic. This means that the rate of return to capital (after allowing for taxes and expected inflation) stabilises at a particular level (over the long run). If investment is more profitable, people will save more, banks will lend more to industry, less capital will be exported and more will come in. And if the rate of return is below that level, people save less, banks create less credit, and net capital export is larger.

It follows that in the developed economy wages in the good jobs market are determined by productivity. Workers get their output minus other costs, including the standard rate of return to capital. These wages rise every year in proportion to productivity.[11] This fits the facts over the past hundred years or so.

What happens to wages in the bad jobs market? Productivity has no meaning here because of the dominance of service outputs. This

[11]In civil service pay the dominant influences are political.

wage level lies between two extremes, those of great prosperity and of great depression. Continuous great prosperity would pull the bad job level up to the good job level. In great depression bad job wages would fall to the market clearing point, if permitted to do so. There must be a market clearing point because if wages were low enough everybody would keep a servant—even the servants would have servants. Wages are not allowed to fall to this level, so the minimum is determined by minimum wage laws, by trade unions or by the subsistence level. In practice, in the developed countries the bad job level has kept a steady distance below the good jobs level, yielding that unchanging degree of inequality in wage payments with which we are familiar (see Thatcher, 1968).

The newly developing economy differs in that most of the labour force is on the lower level, where the agricultural wage and the informal sector wage cannot differ very substantially from small farmer productivity. Wages in the good job sector are determined in the first instance by productivity in its own sector. Productivity gives both a lower and an upper limit; upper for obvious reasons; lower because if workers are paid less than their productivity new capital will be attracted into the sector which will (in the long run) pull wages up. Because productivity rises fast as workers acclimatise to the industrial system (including eating more and better food), large scale industrial wages rise fast in the early stage. However, another upward limit to good level wages is set by the stability of the system, in the sense that if the gap between good and bad level wages widens too greatly, employers in the informal sector will put extra effort into organising the same product lines using cheap labour, and may succeed. As the system approaches this limit firms in the good jobs sector will resist paying higher wages, even if they can afford to do so, and will reduce their selling prices instead.

Dualism will continue to be the appropriate mode of analysis until cessation of population growth and immigration create a single market for labour.

REFERENCES

Cain, Glen G. (1976). "The Challenge of Segmented Labour Market Theories to Orthodox Theory: A Survey", *Journal of Economic Literature*, Vol. XIV, No. 4, pp. 1215-1257.

Cornwall, John. (1977). *Modern Capitalism*, London, Martin Robertson.

Doeringer, P.B. and Piore, Michael J. (1971). *Internal Labour Markets and Manpower Analysis*, Lexington, Mass., Heath & Co.

Kindleberger, Charles P. (1967). *Europe's Postwar Growth*, Cambridge, Mass., Harvard University Press.

Lewis, W. Arthur. (1969). *Aspects of Tropical Trade 1883-1965*, Stockholm, Almqvist.

——————(1978). *The Evolution of the International Economic Order*, Princeton, N.J., Princeton University Press.

Perroux, François. (1955). "Note sur La Notion de 'Pôle de Croissance'", *Economie Appliquée*, Vol. 8, No. 2, pp. 307-320.

Phelps Brown, E. H. (1968). *Pay and Profits*, Manchester, Manchester University Press.

Thatcher, A. R. (1968). "The Distribution of Earnings of Employees in Great Britain", *Journal of the Royal Statistical Society*, Series A, Vol. 131, Part II, pp. 133-180.

Thomas, Brinley. (1954). *Migration and Economic Growth*, Cambridge, Cambridge University Press.

Young, Allyn. (1928). "Increasing Returns and Economic Progress", *Economic Journal*, Vol. XXXVIII, No. 152, pp. 527-542.

PART FOUR

EDUCATION

[20]

EDUCATION AND ECONOMIC DEVELOPMENT[1]

W. ARTHUR LEWIS

INTRODUCTION

Poor countries cannot afford to pay for as much education as richer countries. They have therefore to establish priorities in terms both of quantity and of quality.

The requirements of economic development help in setting priorities, but they are not overriding. Education was not invented in order to enable men to produce more goods and services. The purpose of education is to enable men to understend better the world in which they live, so that they may more fully express their potential capacities, whether spiritual, intellectual or material. Indeed, through the centuries the traditional attitude of 'practical' men towards education has been that it unfits its recipients for useful work. Certainly, most people would agree that education is desirable even if it contributed nothing to material output.

From the standpoint of economic development, one may distinguish between types of education which increase productive capacity and types which do not. Teaching an African cook to read may increase his enjoyment of life, but will not necessarily make him a better cook. Education of the former kind I have called 'investment education', while the latter kind is called 'consumption education'. From the standpoint of economic development, investment education has a high priority, but consumption education is on a par with other forms of consumption. The money spent on teaching cooks to read might equally be spent on giving them pure water supplies, or radios, or better housing, and must therefore compete in the context of all other possible uses of resources. In this perspective the needs of economic development help to determine the minimum amount which must be spent on education. How much to spend above this minimum depends on how rich the society is, and on competing claims. This article is confined to seeking to discover the nature and limits of investment education.

1. This is a substantially revised and extended version of a paper presented to the Unesco Conference on the Educational Needs of Africa, held at Addis Ababa from 15 to 25 May 1961.

ABSORPTIVE CAPACITY

It is fundamental to this approach that the amount of education which 'pays for itself' in a poor country is limited. Some confusion has been caused by applying to these countries the conclusions of statisticians who try to measure the yield of education in rich countries, and who emerge with such conclusions as that the yield of investment in humans exceeds the yield of investment in physical resources. In the first place, investment in humans is not to be equated with education, as normally conceived in institutional terms. Human capacity is improved by education, public health, research, invention, institutional change, and better organization of human affairs, whether in business or in private or public life. To attribute all improvements in productivity to education would therefore be more than a little naïve. Secondly, rich countries have a greater capacity to absorb the products of schools than have poor countries; so even if we could isolate the average yield of various types of education in rich countries, this would throw no light on the marginal yield of similar types in poor (or for that matter in rich) countries.

An over-supply of educated persons is a familiar feature in poor countries: e.g., the over-supply of university graduates in India in the 1930's, or the over-supply of primary school graduates in some West African countries today. An education system may very easily produce more educated people than the economic system can currently absorb in the types of job or at the rates of pay which the educated expect. This is a short-period phenomenon. In the long run the educated learn to expect different jobs and to accept lower rates of pay. But the long run may be very long, and the jobs accepted may gain very little from the education received.

Part of the difficulty of absorption is because the education system produces the wrong kinds of education. The balance between primary, secondary and higher education; between general and vocational studies; between humanities and sciences; or between institutional and in-service training—all these need to be blended in the right proportions if education is to be a help rather than a hindrance to economic development. Because the pattern of education was formed many centuries before the modern technological revolution occurred, most education systems give too little weight to the natural sciences and technology, whether at primary, secondary or higher levels, so that a surfeit of persons trained in literary studies, side-by-side with an acute shortage of persons trained in scientific, biological or mechanical arts, is a feature of several countries. Careful survey and planning are needed if the education system is to produce the balance of skills which the community exactly needs at its particular stage of development.

Nevertheless, the problem is not wholly or even mainly one of balance. The main limitation on the absorption of the educated in poor countries is their high cost, relative to average national output per head. In a country where most people are illiterate, the primary school graduate, whose only skills are reading and writing, commands a wage much higher than a farmer's income. A university graduate who, in a rich country, commences at a salary about equal to a miner's wage, may in a poor country receive five times a miner's wage. In consequence all production or provision of services which depends on using educated people is much more expensive, in relation to national income, in poor than in rich countries. The poor countries may need the educated more than the rich, but they can even less afford to pay for or absorb large numbers of them.

In the long run the situation adjusts itself because the premium on education diminishes as the number of the educated increases. Either the educated have to accept less, or else they are unable to resist the pressures which cause the wages of the less educated to rise faster than their own. The grumbling of the middle and lower middle classes as their privileges diminish is a universal phenomenon, and not infrequently has political consequences. Upper classes based on land or capital have always favoured restricting the supply of education to absorptive capacity, because they know the political dangers of having a surplus of educated persons.

The situation is particularly acute in Africa, where senior administrative salaries have been considerably above similar salaries in Europe, in order to attract European recruits. In consequence, the range of personal incomes is wider than anywhere else in the world; much wider than in Asia, where senior salaries are only about half of their European equivalents. Now that Africans are taking over the top administrative jobs, they are asking, in the name of the sacred principle of non-discrimination, to be paid the same salaries as Europeans, as if it were necessary to spend 50 per cent more on them to attract them away from positions in Europe. Many African politicians have condemned this ridiculous proposition, which handicaps development by making it unnecessarily expensive and places an unnecessary burdan on the mass of the population. The ultimate outcome cannot be in doubt, but much passion will be expended on the way.

As the premium on education falls, the market for the educated may widen enormously. Jobs which were previously done by people with less education are now done by people with more education. The educated lower their sights, and employers raise their requirements. Primary school teaching illustrates this admirably. In the poorest countries, the requirement is completion of a primary school education. At the next level, it is completion of a secondary education. In most American states it is now completion of a college education; and in one or two American cities one cannot become a primary school teacher without an M.A. degree. Similarly, ten years ago, people wondered what the United States would do with its flood of college graduates; but as the premium on college graduates has diminished, business men have decided to hire increasing numbers even for jobs requiring no special skill.

As a result of this process an economy can ultimately absorb any number of educated people. It follows that it is erroneous, when making a survey of the need for skilled manpower, to confine one's calculations to the numbers that could be absorbed at current prices. One ought to produce more educated people than can be absorbed at current prices, because the alteration in current prices which this brings about is a necessary part of the process of economic development. On the other hand, this adjustment is painful, and fraught with political dangers. Like all social processes, it requires time for relative smoothness.

PRIMARY EDUCATION

To give eight years of primary education to every child would cost at current prices about 0.8 per cent of national income in the United States, 1.7 per cent in Jamaica, 2.8 per cent in Ghana and 4 per cent in Nigeria. The main reason for this wide difference is that, while the average salary of a primary school teacher is less than one-and-a-half times the *per capita* national income in the United States, a primary school teacher gets three times the *per capita* national income in Jamaica, five times in Ghana, and seven times in Nigeria. If the cost of education is to be kept within taxable capacity, widespread provision of education belongs to a stage of development where the premium on education has already diminished to reasonable proportions.

Apart from its cost, universal primary education, if attained with speed, raises problems of absorption. In a community where only 20 per cent of children enter primary school, and only 10 per cent finish the course, the demand for primary school graduates is such that they command considerable salaries in white-collar jobs. If the number entering primary school is pushed up from 20 to 80 per cent of the age group within ten years, as has happened in some West African countries, the result is frustration. The children pouring out of the primary schools look to the town for clerical jobs, and are disappointed when they do not find employment. The towns fill up with discontented youths, faster than houses, jobs, water supplies, or other amenities can be provided, and urban slums and delinquents multiply while the countryside is starved of young talent.

The situation is sometimes blamed on the failure of rural schools to adapt their curricula in such a way as to orientate rural children to rural life. This, however, is only part of the problem. The primary school leaver's expectations derive not from the curriculum but from the status which his immediate predecessors have enjoyed. In a developed economy the wage of an unskilled labourer (which is all that primary education produces) is about one-third of the average income per occupied person; but a primary school leaver in Africa expects about twice the average income per occupied person. Obviously, if literacy became universal it would be impossible to pay every literate person twice the average income. If the primary school leaver is to get twice the average income, he can fit only into those parts of the economy which yield twice the average income, and the rate of absorption of primary school leavers then depends on the rate at which these modernized sectors of the economy are expanding. He will fit into a revolutionized agriculture, with modern practices and equipment, but it is useless to expect him to fit into the three-acres-and-a-hoe farming of his father. Any good primary school will widen a child's horizon and create expectations which primitive farming cannot fulfil. So even if rural schools concentrate on rural life, their products are bound to suffer frustration unless the whole social fabric of agriculture is being modernized at the same time.

Cutting the cost of education by reducing the length of the primary course makes absorption still more difficult. Several African countries have now adopted a six-year primary course. This means that hordes of youngsters are turned on to the labour market, aged twelve, with high expectations and low skills. In part this is a borrowing from British, French or American systems, where universal six-year primary education is followed by universal schooling of some secondary type for at least a further three years. In the absence of this secondary stage, African countries would do better, from the standpoint of absorption into the economy, if they gave primary education to fewer children for a longer period of, say, eight or nine years.

The limited absorptive capacity of most West African economies today —especially owing to the backwardness of agriculture—makes frustration and dislocation inevitable if more than 50 per cent of children enter school. This, coupled with the high cost due to the high ratio of teachers' salaries to average national income, and with the time it takes to train large numbers of teachers properly, has taught some African countries to proceed with caution; to set the goal of universal schooling twenty years ahead or more, rather than the ten years ahead or less associated with the first flush of independence movements. Such a decision is regarded as highly controversial by those for whom literacy is a universal human right irrespective of cost, or who feel that it is better to be taught by untrained teachers than not to be taught at all, or who see in the frustrations generated by the incapacity of the current social fabric to absorb, the very stuff which will promote needed change rapidly. On the other hand, considering that in most African territories less than 25 per cent of children aged six to fourteen are in school, a goal of 50 per cent within ten years may be held to constitute revolutionary progress.

SECONDARY EDUCATION

If the poorer countries tend to expand primary education too rapidly, their failure to make adequate provision for secondary education is a major handicap to economic development.

The products of secondary schools are the officers and non-commissioned officers of an economic and social system. A small percentage goes on to university education, but the numbers required from the university are so small that the average country of up to five million inhabitants could manage tolerably well without a university of its own. Absence of secondary schools, however, is an enormous handicap. These schools supply the persons who with one or two more years of training (in institutions or on the job) become technologists, secretaries, nurses, school-teachers, book-keepers, clerks, civil servants, agricultural assistants and supervisory workers of various kinds. The middle and upper ranks of business consist almost entirely of secondary school products, and these products are also the backbone of public administration. To have to import large numbers of people at this level, paying them in salaries and allowances two to three times more than what they could get in rich countries, is a blow to most development schemes. In industry it makes production costs absurdly high. In public administration it puts many desirable schemes—such as agricultural extension or nursing services—beyond the range of taxable capacity. While, as for democratic social life, the absence of a good sprinkling of educated people, serving voluntarily in public agencies (local government, co-operative societies, etc.) and acting as an informed public opinion, exposes society too easily to deception and corruption.

When one compares the countries which have become independent since the second world war, there is a clear difference between those whose business and public affairs are still run mainly by expatriates, under ministers of the country, and those which are really competent to run their affairs at all levels, because their secondary schools have supplied streams of people for intermediate and higher posts in business and administration.

The proportion of the population needed in secondary schools is a function of the level of development. If we include nurses, secretaries and school-teachers, the proportion of the adult population holding jobs for which a secondary grammar school education is now normally considered an appropriate preliminary is about 5 per cent in Jamaica. This is higher than the proportion who have actually completed secondary education. It represents the number of jobs for which a secondary education would now be expected. In African countries the current proportion is very much smaller, because the subsistence sector is so much greater. The number who have received secondary education is only a fraction of 1 per cent, while the number holding jobs for which a secondary education is considered appropriate is probably between 1 and 2 per cent.

One can calculate the percentage of the age cohort who should receive secondary education from the formula

$$x = \frac{n\,(a + b + c)}{m}$$

where x = proportion of age cohort to be recruited; n = ratio of number of secondary-type jobs to adult population; m = ratio of number in age cohort to adult population; a = normal percentage wastage of nationals of the country; b = abnormal wastage due to replacement of expatriates; c = percentage rate of growth of the number of secondary-type jobs.

Of these c is the most difficult factor to assess. In a community such as the United States, which is already nearly saturated with secondary-type jobs, the rate of growth of numbers cannot much exceed the rate of growth of population. In a community like Jamaica, where the modernized sector of the economy employs only about half the population, and is still making inroads into the numbers engaged in subsistence farming, petty trading and domestic services, secondary-type jobs probably grow slightly faster than the normal rate of growth of national income, since they depend mainly on the growth of the public sector, and of other service industries. The current growth rate in Jamaica is probably about 6 per cent per annum. In West Africa, where the modernized sector is still smaller, its expansion relative to the whole economy is still faster (especially as public services are growing rapidly) and secondary-type jobs may be growing by as much as 8 per cent per annum. In this area too, the proportion of expatriates in secondary-type jobs is abnormally high, and a large wastage figure may be expected; say, 15 per cent of that proportion in each year. One may thus guess that the percentage of the age cohort required in secondary grammar schools is:

In Jamaica
$$x = \frac{0.05\,(0.02 + 0 + 0.06)}{0.04} = 10.0 \text{ per cent}$$

In Nigeria[1]
$$x = \frac{0.01\,(0.025 + 0.005 + 0.08)}{0.045} = 2.4 \text{ per cent}$$

These ratios are just about consistent with the demand for secondary education on the part of parents. In most of the poorer countries at present, parents of about 8 to 12 per cent of the children who start primary education want these children to go on to secondary education of the grammar school type; and where government schools are not provided, many private schools of very poor quality, charging low fees, spring into existence to meet the demand. If good grammar schools are provided for 10 per cent of children entering primary school, this will just about meet both parental demand and also absorptive capacity.

The obstacle to providing secondary education in West Africa is not so much recurrent cost as capital cost. Recurrent cost is abnormal, for reasons already given. Cost per teacher is thirty times *per capita* national income in Nigeria, compared with twelve times in Jamaica, and with only twice in the United States. Nevertheless, even in Nigeria to provide grammar school education for 5 per cent of the age group costs a little less than 1 per cent of national income. The fantastic burden is the cost of building schools. One can build a good secondary school in England for £50,000; but the cost of a school for a similar number of pupils in Ghana may be £250,000. This is because many West Africans have persuaded themselves that only boarding schools are appropriate to Africa. The argument runs as follows. 'To get a fully specialized staff, a school must have twenty teachers. Therefore it must have 500 pupils. Therefore,

1. This is an average for the whole country. The situation differs widely in the three regions.

assuming 5 per cent schooling, it must draw from a population of 70,000. Since very few African towns have a population exceeding 10,000, it follows that most African towns cannot support a day secondary school. Therefore the solution has to be boarding schools.' A boarding school, complete with dormitories and staff houses, costs £250,000. The argument can be attacked at either end. Must a secondary school have twenty teachers? If, instead, it started with only six teachers, one could build a series of day schools in three times as many small towns. Even when the school has to be large, the British solution is boarding, but the American solution is the school bus, which is hardly known in Africa. Some financial sense is badly needed in planning secondary schools in Africa. It is obviously absurd to take the line that Africa's way to secondary education must be through building 'Etons' for the majority of African children.

Grammar schools are not by any means the only, or in numbers even the chief, form of secondary education. If one follows some authorities in reserving the term 'primary' for education up to age twelve, and in using the term 'secondary' for all education between twelve and eighteen, then some secondary education should be provided for all children who complete primary education, since such children are not ready for the labour market at twelve. Children who do not go on to grammar school pass into secondary schools with a practical bias, known as 'middle', 'intermediate', 'central', or 'modern secondary', or into the practical streams of 'comprehensive' schools, or again, in the French system, into the 'first cycle' of secondary schooling. Except in the United States of America, the great majority of children end their schooling here.

A few of these children are ready, at about age fifteen, to pass into vocational schools, for full-time technical training. It is hard to judge how large this group should be. People possessing the skills taught in such schools—building, metal working, engineering—comprise from 2 to 8 per cent of the working population in less developed countries, but it does not follow that 8 per cent of children should enter such schools. The traditional training for these trades is a system of apprenticeship. In the United States of America, where nearly 70 per cent of children are kept in school until age seventeen, vocational schooling has had to be a substitute for on-the-job training up to that age. Elsewhere, it is probably cheaper and more effective to rely on apprenticeship; to put not more than 2 per cent of the age cohort through full-time courses, and to arrange part-time courses for the rest.

Actually, in poor countries half the age cohort should enter agriculture. Primary and intermediate schools in rural areas have an agricultural bias, but they see the child through at most to age fifteen. Governments provide farm schools to train agricultural assistants for government service, but very few provide courses for students who wish to farm. Probably the ideal is for the child to start farming at fifteen, and then around age eighteen to go to a practical farm school for about six months to observe modern techniques. It is true that agricultural extension can be done on farms by peripatetic agricultural assistants, but this is not an adequate substitute for an intensive course for bright young farmers, any more than 'training-within-industry' is a complete substitute for vocational schools.

When the grammar school children leave school, between sixteen and eighteen, they are ready for specialized training. The great majority will go straight into employment, and receive on-the-job training as clerks or technical assistants. Others need preliminary training of, say, from six months upwards to become secretaries, medical technicians, nurses, agricultural assistants, primary school teachers, junior engineers, or as the case may be.

Very few of the poorer countries make adequate provision for this specialized but sub-professional training. This is because the supply of educational facilities is not properly planned in relation to the needs of economic and social development. The making of 'manpower surveys' is spreading as a remedy for this defect. The technique of making such surveys is still rudimentary. Asking employers how many people they intend, or would like, to employ in various categories yields interesting answers, but these answers do not necessarily add up to absorptive capacity. It should be possible, from examining the manpower statistics of different countries in different stages of development, to produce some coefficients which would act as a check on the results yielded by questionnaires. But basic work of this kind is only just starting in the universities. Meanwhile it is clear that even rudimentary manpower surveys help governments to appreciate the need for specialized training facilities for people between ages sixteen and twenty, so greater use of such surveys is certainly to be commended.

ADULT EDUCATION

The quickest way to increase productivity in the less developed countries is to train the adults who are already on the job. Education for children is fine, but its potential contribution to output over ten years is small compared with the potential contribution of efforts devoted to improving adult skills.

This field is almost wholly neglected. In the government hierarchy it belongs not to the ministry of education but to the ministries of trade, agriculture, mining, health, communications, community development and others. Most of these ministries are too busy making new regulations and processing forms, to regard adult education as a major part of their functions.

Yet there is ample testimony to what adult education can achieve, whether in the form of training-within-industry, evening classes, or sandwich courses in urban centres; or in the form of agricultural extension, health programmes, or community development in rural areas.

Experience shows that the secret of success is to make adult education into a popular mass movement. There is not much point in offering adult classes if adults do not wish to attend classes. The Danish folk movement, or the Russian literacy campaign or any other adult education movement has been successful in so far as it has stirred the imaginations of the people, and created a mass desire to learn. Some popular African leaders, such as M. Sékou-Touré of Guinea, understand this very well, and are therefore likely to succeed in getting adult education, in one form or another, to contribute substantially to economic and social development. Elsewhere, adult education languishes as much for want of understanding as it does for lack of funds.

UNIVERSITY EDUCATION

The number of university graduates who can be absorbed at low levels of economic development is relatively small. The proportion of jobs in Jamaica for which a university education is now considered normal corresponds only to about five per thousand of adult population; and the corresponding figure for Nigeria, according to Professor Harbison's count[1], is only around one per thousand of adult population. We can apply to these figures the same formula and the same rates of growth as for secondary education (leaving out the coefficient for expatriate wastage, since the number of expatriate graduates does not decline with independence; there are fewer pensionable civil servants, but more expatriates on contract). We may thus guess that the proportion of the age cohort who should graduate from the university is:

In Jamaica $$x = \frac{0.005\ (0.022 + 0.06)}{0.035} = 1.17 \text{ per cent}$$

In Nigeria $$x = \frac{0.001\ (0.028 + 0.08)}{0.04} = 0.27 \text{ per cent}$$

The answer we get for Nigeria corresponds to about 2,200 students leaving the university each year, and is not far from Professor Harbison's estimate. The answer for Jamaica, if generalized for the area served by the University College of the West Indies, gives an output of 900 students a year, or a total undergraduate body, allowing for wastage, of about 3,300 students, compared with the current total of 980 students at UCWI.[2]

1. Cf. *Investment in Education* (Ashby Report), Lagos, 1960.
2. The total number of West Indians in universities is about 4,000 of whom 3,000 are in British, American or Canadian universities. Allowing for the longer degree courses in North America, and for the fact that a very large proportion of the students in North America are part-time students, the annual output of West Indians from universities is now probably about 900. The current shortage of graduates is due to the fact that a large proportion of those who qualify in

The postulated increase of 6 per cent per annum would bring this figure up to 5,500 students by 1970.

Most of the new African countries do not at present have enough students to justify building a university; it is cheaper for them to send their students abroad. In a country with a population of two million, putting say 0.5 per cent of the age cohort into university, the total student number comes only to 700. This is quite uneconomic for a university with the broad range of faculties which is usually sought. A liberal arts school of the American type is economic with 500 students, but to be economic a British-type combination of faculties of arts, science and social science needs about 1,200 students; medicine needs 300 students, and agriculture and engineering need 200 each. This makes about 2,000 students in round figures. All the universities founded in Africa since the war have been costing from three to five times as much per student as it costs to run a university in Europe.

In so far as these exorbitant costs are due to abnormally high staff/student ratios, ranging upwards from one to three, as against one to eight in Britain, or one to twenty in liberal arts colleges, they are temporary, and will pass as student numbers expand. But this is by no means the only cause. In British universities the average cost per teacher is about £4,000 a year. In universities in British tropical Africa the cost per teacher exceeds £6,500 a year. This is mainly because the teachers, two-thirds of whom are recruited in Britain, have to be paid higher salaries and given better allowances then they get in Britain, and cost the African universities, including passages, at least £1,500 a year more than they would cost in Britain. Even the African teachers are paid about £1,000 a year more than the African civil servants of equivalent education. On top of this, these universities are not sited in towns, where they could use public facilities (and contribute the maximum amount to public life) but have in every case been sited away from towns, where they have to maintain their own police, telephone exchange, electric power station, sewerage disposal, transport and other services, and have therefore to carry a service organization about five times as large as is carried by an urban university. For the same reason the capital cost, in terms of student hostels and houses for the teaching staff, is abnormally high, largely owing, no doubt, to the extravagant housing standards which have been traditional for Europeans in tropical Africa.

As it happens, the capital cost of African universities seems likely to be met mostly by grants from the treasuries of Britain, France and the United States; but the recurrent cost is an immense burden, except to the

North America do not return to the West Indies: there is also considerable imbalance as between faculties. The West Indian university problem is not to have more students enter university (apart from the postulated increase of 6 per cent per annum) but to provide more university facilities in the West Indies, both to fill the gap of the students who do not return, and also because UCWI has more to offer to West Indians than they can get in foreign universities, in terms of suitable curricula as well as of emotional balance.

extent that it is met by France in the former French territories. (Costs in the West Indies are similarly extremely high.) The situation is very different in India, or in Egypt, where university lecturers are recruited locally, and cost no more than other nationals of equivalent education. Just as African educators want to build 'Etons' for every secondary school child, so also they have loaded on to the backs of their tax-payers, who are among the poorest in the world, the most expensive universities in the world outside North America.

However, even if the cost per student were no higher in Africa than in Britain, the cost to Africa of training a student in Africa would still exceed the cost to Africa of training him in Britain. This is because an African student in Britain pays only a small fraction of the cost of his training; the rest is met by the British tax-payer's grant to the universities. So long as tuition fees in Europe are negligible, it will always cost an African economy more to train students at home than it would do to send them to similar universities in Europe. (One can send a student for £600 a year, whereas even with utmost economy the tuition and maintenance cost at a British-type African university will not fall below £1,000 a year.) It is not possible for a large country to place all its students overseas, but this is feasible for a small country, especially while the percentage of students for university training is still small. From the economic point of view, therefore, one must ask: why should a small African country (or the West Indies) have its own university, when two, three or four times as many students could be sent abroad for the same money?

The chief reason why it is worth while, from the economic point of view, to have a university at home, even though it costs more than sending students abroad, is that the function of a university is not confined to teaching students. If it were merely a question of teaching, there could be no doubt about the answer. For though one can argue on either side in terms of the atmosphere of a home university, or the suitability of its curricula, or the advantages of foreign travel, the net result of such argument fades into insignificance beside the possibility of sending five students abroad for every three who might be trained at home (assuming the most economical arrangements). Only if foreign aid provides all the capital and a third of the running expenditure can a purely teaching university justify itself on economic grounds.

Apart from teaching, a university contributes to its community through the participation of its teachers in the life of the country, and through its research into local problems.

A poor country has very few educated people. To have in its midst a body of one or two hundred first-class intellects can make an enormous difference to the quality of its cultural, social, political and business life. This, however, depends on participation. If the university is built in the bush, and isolates itself as a self-contained community, it misses a tremendous opportunity of service. Countries rich in income and talent can afford to have their universities in the countryside. But the universities of poor countries should be in the heart of urban centres, where they can do most good. The opportunities for participation are immense: membership of public boards and committees; contributions to professional societies; guidance of teacher-training colleges; availability for consultation by administrators and business people; membership of musical, dramatic, artistic and other groups; journalism and radio work; adult education classes. If the staff of the university is not giving active leadership in all these fields, it would be cheaper to close the place down, unless it is also doing excellent research.

A country needs to have some research institutions, whether it has a university or not. If the same people do teaching and research, only a part of the university cost should be charged against teaching. The question therefore arises whether teaching and research should be combined.

The British theory that every university must regard itself as primarily a research institute with students, doubles the cost per student. A research institute type of university has a staff/student ratio of one to ten (excluding medicine) with a maximum teaching load of ten hours a week; whereas a university where the staff are not expected to do research can have a staff/student ratio of one to twenty, with a teaching load of twenty hours a week. A university which adopts the British ratios must insist that any staff member who does not make significant research contributions must be fired. For a poor country in Africa or elsewhere to load itself up with the expense of a British-type university, and accept from its teachers that they should be judged primarily by research results, would be folly of a high order.

One can argue persuasively that the first university in any poor country should be of the research institute type, provided that the research test is rigidly applied to its staff. However, as student numbers expand, it becomes progressively harder to justify the multiplication of these expensive structures in poor countries. The great majority of those entering a university are not research students, and do not need to be brought to the frontiers of knowledge. What they need is a broad education, to fit them for administration, commerce, or teaching up to fifth-form level. For this, the American conception of a liberal arts degree (which combines science, humanities and social studies) is much more relevant than the British Honours degree. There should be at least one university engaging in high quality research, and offering high quality Honours degrees, on the basis of high entrance standards. But, as numbers expand, the majority should be diverted into liberal arts colleges.

Here the teacher/student ratio can be halved, and since one does not need top-flight researchers, teacher salaries can be more in line with salaries in the public services.[1] If in addition most of the students live at home, one can get the cost of a student down to perhaps two-thirds of what it would

1. The British practice of paying all university teachers according to a single scale would not be appropriate to a country which has different kinds of universities.

cost to send a student abroad. To mitigate the prejudice which exists in British circles against such conceptions, one can add that, as in the United States, any graduate of one of these liberal arts colleges who displayed special talents could go on to the major university for postgraduate training.

Similar principles could be applied to professional training, but with less justification. In every profession there are at least three layers; top-flight researchers, professionals and sub-professionals. In agriculture, there are specialists, general agronomists, and agricultural assistants trained in farm schools. Medicine has specialists, general practitioners, and a third layer of nurses, dispensing chemists and medical technologists. Engineering has its scientists, its professional engineers, and its third layer of technologists.

The proportions in which these layers are combined are different in rich and poor countries. The rich countries can afford to spend much more proportionately on research than the poor countries, so the need for top-flight scientists and specialists is proportionately greater. Such men also need long periods of stimulating work in first-class laboratories abroad, so the universities of poor countries should not try to put too much of their resources into superior training of first-class men. The bulk of their work must be the training of the second layer.

The ratio of numbers in the second to numbers in the third layer is also smaller than in rich countries. Because of the high cost of engineers, doctors and agronomists, one employs fewer of these and more technologists, nurses and agricultural assistants, who therefore carry greater responsibilities. This is reflected in the ratio of jobs for which a degree is currently considered necessary to jobs for which a grammar school education is considered appropriate, which is more like one to ten in poor countries, compared with one to five in Europe.

Because of the high cost of training graduates, it is sometimes suggested that the universities in poor countries should lower the standards of professional training, on the grounds that it is better to have, say, a hundred three-quarter trained doctors, who can be spread over the countryside, rather than seventy well-trained doctors, leaving 30 per cent of the population without a doctor. This has been done in some places. The alternative policy is to mass-produce not the second layer, but the third, and in the process even to up-grade the training of the third layer. One then floods the countryside not with low-grade dentists, but with high-grade dental assistants; not with poorly trained agronomists, but with well-trained agricultural assistants. If this policy is adopted, the corollary is to up-grade the training not only of the third layer, but also of the second layer. For the second-layer professional now has many more third-layer people working under him; he assigns to them more of the routine work, and concentrates to a greater extent on the more difficult tasks. His administrative responsibilities are also greater. From this it follows that he needs an even sounder training than his professional colleague in Europe. It is indeed quite arguable that, what with language difficulties, greater administrative responsibilities, and the need to work in isolation from specialist advice and laboratory analysis, professionals require at least one more year of training in poor countries than they do in rich countries.

I have written at some length on university education because the economic aspects of this subject are very different in poor countries from what they are in rich countries, and are nevertheless so seldom considered. It tends to be assumed that what is right in Britain must also be right in Nyasaland. Even in Britain, university people are not good at seeing themselves in their social context; most of the best of them are too busy teaching and doing research to worry about such an abstraction as the social and economic context of a university, and when such people arrive in the tropics, it is easier for them to continue old patterns than to invent new ones. The subject is fraught with difficulty, and merits widespread informed discussion.

[21]

W. ARTHUR LEWIS

Education for Scientific Professions in the Poor Countries

THE POOR COUNTRIES need three types of persons trained scientifically beyond the high-school level: technicians, basic scientists, and professionals. By professionals we mean those trained in agriculture, medicine, dentistry, veterinary science, engineering, architecture, and similar arts. Such courses of education have this in common, that they borrow materials from a number of basic sciences, which they use as a foundation for specialized work. This raises a number of problems, to which this paper is devoted.

The capacity of a country to absorb university graduates is an index of its development. If we take graduates in all subjects, including the humanities, the absorptive capacity measured in terms of the annual intake of graduates seems to range from as low as 20 to as high as 3,000 per million inhabitants. Frederick H. Harbison has recently assessed the absorptive capacity of Nigeria at 50 per million; in recent guesses for the West Indies, I have been using a figure of 300 per million. The concept of absorptive capacity is not a precise one, however. As the number of graduates increases, the possession of a degree becomes a condition for jobs for which it was not previously required, for example, in agricultural extension, dentistry, or teaching in high schools. Also, the gap between the salaries of graduates and nongraduates diminishes as graduates become available for more types of jobs. In other words, the absorptive capacity increases *pari passu* with the supply of graduates and cannot be determined independently. It may still be possible to produce from historical or contemporary data a curve relating the absorption of graduates per million inhabitants to the per-capita national income, but this has not yet been done.

All one can say at present is that, in the sense there are vacant jobs, in nearly every poor country there is a shortage of persons trained in the scientific professions. This is all one needs to say. Most poor countries could substantially increase their output of professionals without any danger of the supply exceeding the absorptive capacity during the next two decades.

In the United States a number of universities consider that professional courses should be undertaken only after a student has already acquired a first degree. This can be defended on two grounds: the student needs to have a good general education before embarking on professional study; or he needs to know a great deal of science before embarking on a scientific profession. The first ground is emphasized, rather than the second, though the second may be included in the first.

In Great Britain the professions we are dealing with can all be studied for a first degree. Before entering the university, however, the student will usually be required to have specialized in science in the high school, as evidenced by his having passed certain science subjects (specified separately for each profession) at the Advanced Level (formerly the Higher School Certificate), equivalent to or slightly beyond what a junior college in California requires. In short, whether professional courses should be postgraduate or not depends on the university requirements for enrolling in basic science, which in turn depend on the standard reached in the high schools. The high schools in Great Britain teach two years more of science than a public high school in New York City does, and as this is the level of university entrance, professional courses may be taught as training for first degrees.

The poor countries vary widely in the standards to which their high schools aspire. In Africa the British and the French have sought to establish standards at their metropolitan levels, and, in so far as they have succeeded, most of Africa should be able to follow the British or French patterns. In some other countries (for example, Egypt or India), in which the numbers of high-school students have swollen more rapidly than funds or trained teachers have, high-school standards are lower, and both entrance and exit levels into and out of universities are substantially lower than in Western Europe. Faced with low standards of entry, the universities in such countries must either lower the professional standard or else lengthen the course (of which the extreme form is to make the professional course postgraduate).

The question as to whether there should be less basic science is a difficult problem. A number of arguments point toward reducing the amount of basic science in professional courses in the poor countries. The students have less practical work in their backgrounds than do the students of rich countries, and therefore they need more time for this aspect. They have less practical experience because in their societies it is offensive for a middle-class person to do manual work instead of employing a servant to do it for him. (This is a form of share-the-wealth which custom has decreed in areas that do not have social insurance.) Students also have less experience with mechanical devices, since they do not live in a mechanical civilization and therefore do not become familiar with mechanical devices from an early age, as do children in the rich countries. Consequently, more time is needed in their professional training to accustom them to using their hands.

Because technicians are not as well trained and not as reliable as in the rich countries, professionals have to spend more time supervising them; the professionals must be able to show their technicians just what to do. The professional, therefore, needs the technician's training as well as his own. This also means relatively more time for practical work. Since professionals are scarce and therefore work in greater isolation from one another, each must have more of an all-round competence. For example, an engineer sent to look after public works in an isolated rural area should be able to turn his hand to civil, mechanical, and electrical tasks; hence he must be given relatively more "know-how" of the various sides of his profession, and he has relatively less time for basic science. The same argument tells in general against providing opportunities for specialization in the undergraduate professional course. Most universities require the student to familiarize himself with every aspect of his profession (if we count civil, mechanical, and electrical engineering as three separate professions) and to postpone specialization until postgraduate courses. A medical student is not allowed to choose between pediatrics and surgery. In the rich countries, however, there are some exceptions: an agricultural student may choose between, say, chemistry and entomology, and an electrical engineer may choose between power generation and electronics. Specialization usually involves more basic science. It is arguable, therefore, that universities in the poor countries should be less willing to permit specialization at the undergraduate level.

In some professions the need of using local materials for teaching purposes increases the factual burden of the course and thus reduces the time available for theoretical principles. This situation occurs wherever the local material has to be an auxiliary to, not merely a substitute for, the material used in teaching in temperate countries. For example, the medical student in the tropics has to know about all the diseases that occur in temperate zones, since these also occur in the tropics, and in addition he has to know about tropical diseases. In adapting any syllabus for use in a poor country, one has to decide how much of the factual framework taught elsewhere can be scrapped in favor of local conditions and how much must be retained. In some cases the result must be a net increase in the facts to be studied.

The professional must learn more social science in the poor countries, since social change is occurring more rapidly there than in the rich countries, and therefore the professional is more deeply involved. His own work is one of the important forces causing social change. Moreover, his status in society is continuously being affected by the changes taking place. Some room, therefore, should be found in his course for instruction in the sociology of change. One cannot class this problem with other aspects of general education and dismiss it by saying, "This should be done in the high schools before the student reaches the university." Students of high-school age are not ripe for sociology.

So much for the arguments for reducing courses in basic science. A strong case can also be made for maintaining the amount of basic science taught. This argument would begin with the premise that the professional is isolated and consequently needs to be able to turn his hand to many things. To do this, he must have a sound training in basic principles rather than a superficial training in techniques. In his isolation he will meet many new problems which he can solve only by taking thought and by returning to basic principles. He needs both more science and more technique, and if one has to be sacrificed, it is not obvious that it is the science that should be curtailed.

The correct answer to our question is probably this: if the professional standard is to be as high in the poor as in the rich countries, professional courses should be a year or so longer in the poor ones, to allow for an inferior background in high schools, the need for more practical work, an increase in the syllabus because of the incorporation of local materials, and the need for a greater emphasis on social studies. But should the professional standard be as high in the poor as in the rich countries? There are several arguments for a lower standard. Even in the rich countries most professionals are overtrained for the work they actually have to do. University syllabuses tend to be framed with an eye on the student who will become a university teacher or research worker, whereas the great majority go into jobs they could do just as well with a year less of academic training. The poor countries need proportionately even fewer research workers, and separate provisions can be made for their training. To maintain equal standards requires a longer and correspondingly more expensive training in the poor countries, which they cannot afford. Many such nations have abandoned the attempt to maintain equal professional standards, even if they once tried to do so. Given the great shortage of professionals, especially in rural areas, such a nation is better off with four three-quarters trained professionals than with three fully trained.

Although many countries have abandoned the attempt, many others still strive to maintain their professional standards at European levels, not only out of national pride but also for other reasons. The routine portion of professionals' work is usually passed over to technicians, whose numbers can be multiplied more easily. This practice makes it all the more important that the relatively small number of professionals who supervise technicians should be thoroughly trained.

The psychological effects of inferior standards are bad. A poor country is likely to employ a number of well-trained foreign professionals, and it is embarrassing if its own professionals are admittedly of inferior quality. This is especially true when the better paid or more responsible jobs are held only by people with foreign qualifications. The local universities are downgraded in the public eye, and students try to go abroad for education rather than to their home institutions. The latter are discouraged and find it hard to recruit or keep good staffs. This further reduces their quality by adversely affecting their capacity to do useful research. For such reasons, a number of countries have abandoned the inferior professional qualifications they previously offered (for example, Nigeria has dropped medicine, and Trinidad, agriculture) and have substituted qualifications intended to equal similar qualifications in Europe.

Although the great majority of the graduates of professional schools are required for jobs that demand competence but not brilliance, a significant number are needed to undertake fundamental research. The biological sciences and the professions based on them demand much more fundamental research than do the physical sciences. Whereas the physical structure of the earth is much the same in temperate as in tropical zones, the living organisms differ considerably. An engineer can transfer from a temperate to a tropical environment with only small adaptations; but an agriculturist has to spend a year or more relearning his job.

How fundamental is "fundamental"? Some research requires scientific training and imagination of the highest order; in the process, new scientific truths of universal application will be discovered. In the biological sciences, it is hardly profitable to distinguish between pure science and research of the kind the poor countries need—for example, research in animal and plant genetics, leading to the breeding of new useful types; human and animal physiology in hot climates; pests and diseases, animal, plant, and human; or plant and animal nutrition. Basic principles already worked out in temperate countries will be applied, but since the animals, the plants, the insects, and the microbes are different, the research has to start almost from scratch; it demands the highest qualities, and is likely to yield new universal principles.

The situation in the physical sciences is rather different. Here the main research task is to devote known principles to making inventories of economic resources: discovering minerals or underground water supplies; assessing soils; recording river flows and meteorological data. Such work demands professional competence rather than scientific imagination. The principal scope for fundamental research is in such fields as these: climatology; methods of combating the effects of torrential rain, earthquakes, or months of continuous sunshine on such structures as roads, dams, and buildings; the utilization of local resources, such as crops, forests, building materials, sources of energy; the conversion of sea water; the invention of new engineering processes that use less capital. Some of this research (especially on the exploitation of materials) can be done in the laboratory in temperate countries, but virtually all the biological research, and nearly all that part of the physical research that is concerned with the effects of the local environment, have to be done on the spot.

There ought, therefore, to be a large number of fundamental research stations strung round the globe between the Tropics of Cancer and Capricorn. Actually, there are very few such stations. The tropics are not yet adequately equipped even to make routine inventories of their resources; and they are far from coming to grips with fundamental research. It is not necessary that each country establish a battery of high-quality research stations. For example, there are now twenty countries in West and Equatorial Africa between the ex-Belgian Congo and the Sahara Desert, but most of them have less than 2,000,000 inhabitants and could not support expensive research institutes. Asia fares better, having fewer and larger countries, of which several could maintain their own scientific establishments, as indeed India already does to a very considerable extent. It is true even of Southeast Asia, however, as of Africa and Latin America, that the necessary stations for fundamental research will not be established on a substantial scale until groups of countries learn to combine for this purpose, with or without the United Nations or other international assistance. There have been some good beginnings, for example, sugar-cane breeding in the West Indies, cocoa research in West Africa, or rubber research in Malaya, as well as outstanding work on tropical diseases (done mainly in the laboratories of temperate countries). Nevertheless, an immense scope for expansion remains.

Since the professionals depend on basic science, their research work depends on a supply of persons with a first-class training in science, whether educated in the professional or in the science schools. The science schools, like the professional ones, mainly produce persons who need to be competent rather than brilliant. Most of their graduates go into high-school teaching or into routine jobs in commerce or administration. There is little manufacturing industry, and such as there is generally does not engage in research or else it conducts its research in parent establishments in the rich countries. The universities themselves are the largest market for highly trained scientists capable of good research. Nevertheless, every university science school is under pressure to do some research and keep up its standards, partly to make its own teaching lively, partly to contribute to knowledge, and partly because good scientists cannot be retained unless they are given opportunities for research. Many universities are therefore able to produce some men who, given further training, would do well in research.

In the professional schools, professors interested in research tend to feel badly handicapped by not having learned enough basic science in their own undergraduate days, and this prejudices them in favor of putting more and more basic science into the undergraduate syllabus, even at the cost of lengthening the course. This is hardly necessary, since the small number of professional men who go on to research can learn the extra basic science they need during their postgraduate training.

What seems important is that, whereas the undergraduate course can be taught adequately in a professional school that has very little basic science, postgraduate training and research in professional subjects can be done adequately only in close association with strong science schools. Thus, while undergraduate teaching can be dispersed over a number of schools, postgraduate teaching must be concentrated in a small number of institutions in which both basic science and professional study are highly developed. It is all the better if these postgraduate teaching institutions can be linked with the fundamental institutes.

Study in foreign countries has many attractions that study at home lacks. Standards are usually higher, the qualification carries more prestige, and its monetary value may exceed that conferred by the local school. Also, travel provides valuable experience. If the students go to foreign universities whose costs are met principally out of public funds and not out of student fees, it becomes much cheaper to send them abroad than to educate them at home. For example, for what it costs to run the University College of the West Indies, we could send one and a half times as many students to universities in Great Britain. This argument applies to small countries like the West Indies or Ghana, but not to large countries like India. Professional schools are especially costly to small nations, because they need a minimum complement of staff to teach each aspect of the course. For example, Nigeria has been advised that to run a veterinary school economically requires an output of about seventy students a year, and she is finding this a stumbling block. The remedy would be for countries in this situation to group together to run professional schools; but this is not always politically possible.

On the other hand, the provision of professional schools at home has several advantages which may outweigh the higher cost. In so far as the syllabus is based on local materials and on research into local problems, what the student learns in the home university is more relevant to the job he will have to do. This is particularly important in the biological professions. The teachers do not merely teach: if doctors, they look after patients, inside and outside the hospital; if engineers, they do consulting work. The teachers play a part in the life of the community, they sit on boards and participate in private and public decision-making. If they are of adequate scientific caliber, they also carry on useful research of a kind worth paying for, even if there were no students. A large proportion of students who do go abroad do not return home, and the cost of educating them, therefore, is lost to their country, except in so far as they make remittances.

A good compromise is to give students their first degree at home and then to send the better ones away for postgraduate training in large, well-staffed and well-equipped institutes. As we have seen, however, the poor countries need a few of their own such institutes to do fundamental research into the problems of their regions. Where such institutes exist, a student can do effective postgraduate work there before he goes abroad.

[22]

Secondary Education and Economic Structure[a]

By

W. Arthur Lewis

In an earlier article in this journal[1] I argued that a country can over a period of years absorb any level of output from schools — whether primary, secondary or university — but that in the short run absorptive capacity depends on

(a) the conventional educational pre-requisites for entering each occupation; and

(b) the salary premium associated with each level of education.

These barriers are both flexible. Historically they have moved continuously in the direction of increasing absorptive capacity, since time raises educational requirements and reduces salary differentials.

If absorptive capacity is so flexible, one cannot associate it precisely with economic structure, unless one finds that countries which have the same economic structure have also the same conventions and differentials. The investigation on which this paper reports was undertaken to find out whether economic structure and the number of persons who have received secondary education can be linked statistically.

Economic structure is here defined by taking the number of persons (male and female) engaged in all industries other than agriculture, forestry and fishing, and dividing by the number of persons aged 15 and over. This is called, for short, the ratio of persons in non-agriculture. Country comparisons are more usually made in terms of per capita national income, but the difficulty of equating to a common price level usually leaves strange results. The ratio of persons in non-agriculture is specially relevant to this study, since agriculture absorbs relatively much less secondary manpower than other industries. The number of persons aged 15 and over is taken as base, rather than the occupied population, because different countries define the occupied population differently.[2]

Education is measured by taking males aged 25 and over who left school at age 15 or later, and expressing this as a percentage of all males aged 25 and over. The stock is used rather than the enrolment percentage since, if there is a relationship with economic structure, what matters must be the stock rather than enrolment in any one year. I have found only two

aI have benefited from discussions with Professors William Bowen and Frederick Harbison.

1"Education and Economic Development", *Social and Economic Studies*, June, 1961.

2As is well known, the problem is the treatment of women who work at home. This arises mainly in agriculture, but it also exists in non-agriculture, and adjustments have had to be made to the Census figures for Jamaica and for Ecuador on this account. See Statistical Appendix.

Censuses which show age on leaving school; others show the number of grades of secondary education achieved; or the number of persons who have completed secondary education; or just the number who have received some secondary education, without specifying grades. Adjustments, listed in the Statistical Appendix, have had to be made in order to arrive at figures representative of those who remained in school to age 15. Most Censuses contain no information on education achieved; some standardization of practice would be helpful.

Females are excluded, because of differences in the extent to which secondary-educated females remain in the occupied population.

The exclusion of persons under 25 at the time of the Census carries on a UNESCO tradition, which is designed to facilitate comparisons of the numbers who have completed higher education. However, in this study the category is defined as those who left school at age 20 or later, because of difficulties in comparing the products of "completed" higher education.

The Censuses are those taken around 1950: 22 of the 27 are between 1948 and 1953; 2 are earlier and 3 are later.

Given the nature of the available figures, and wide differences in what is meant by "completing" secondary education, it seemed best to define the secondary education category as those who left school at age 15 or later. Such an early age as 15 would create difficulties if used to measure secondary education since the second World War, but data collected in 1950 from persons aged 25 and over, reflect mainly the educational policies of the 1920's and 1930's, when primary education nearly everywhere ceased at 14 or earlier. There was also very little vocational education at that time. Except for France and England, the figures we have charted refer almost exclusively to persons who have received secondary education of the traditional grammar school kind. Japan, Canada, and the U.S.A. are not included in the chart because their figures are not comparable.

II.

The results are shown in Table 1 and in the accompanying chart. Countries fall into three groups. The largest number lie near a straight line relating secondary education to economic structure. We shall refer to this group as "traditional". A small number have a larger stock; we call these "liberal"; and another number have a small stock; we call these "elitist".

The formula for the traditional line is

$$x = .68y - 11.3 \qquad (1)$$

$$x \nless 3.0$$

where x = the percentage of males aged 25 and over who left school at 15 or later; and

y = ratio of persons in non-agriculture to persons aged 15 and over.

The restriction on the formula indicates that there is a minimum below

TABLE 1. RATIO OF EDUCATED MALES AGED 25 AND OVER

Country	Economic Structure A	Still in School at Age 15 B	Still in School at Age 20 C
Honduras, 1950	13.5	1.4	...
Thailand, 1960	14.1	4.0	0.6
Haiti, 1950	15.2	2.7	0.3
Nicaragua, 1950	17.7	2.8	0.9
Guatemala, 1950	18.9	2.3	...
El Salvador, 1950	22.1	2.8	0.4
Brazil, 1950	23.0	5.0	1.5
Mexico, 1950	23.4	4.3	...
Philippines, 1948	23.7	9.2	...
Jamaica, 1943	24.8	2.9	...
Paraguay, 1950	25.4	6.4	...
Costa Rica, 1950	26.9	6.2	...
Colombia, 1951	26.9	6.8	1.3
Greece, 1951	27.0	13.6	...
Ecuador, 1950	28.2	5.4	1.1
Hungary, 1949	28.3	10.0	...
Puerto Rico, 1950	30.1	11.3	2.6
Cuba, 1953	31.1	5.2	1.7
Venezuela, 1950	34.2	4.2	...
Chile, 1950	40.5	16.1	...
Cyprus, 1960	40.5	15.9	1.6
Japan, 1950	40.5	29.0	4.8
Argentina, 1947	43.7	6.3	1.7
France, 1954	43.7	18.5	...
Canada, 1951	44.1	41.1	6.1
U.S.A., 1950	48.1	42.3	8.5
England and Wales, 1951	50.2	17.9	2.0

A. Percentage of persons (M and F) aged 15 and over who are occupied in non-agricultural industries and services.
B. Percentage of males aged 25 and over who left school at age 15 or later.
C. Percentage of males aged 25 and over who left college at age 20 or later.
... Not available.

which the stock of educated persons should not fall. This appears to be about 3 per cent.

This line is drawn by inspection, and not by calculation. Its justification is the number of countries which lie close to it, and what we know about those countries. There is not much doubt where it should run at the bottom end, and where it begins to rise is narrowly delineated by Brazil, Mexico, Paraguay, Costa Rica and Colombia. There is leeway at the top end, since the line could run anywhere between France and England and Wales; it has been drawn through France, partly because it then runs through Chile and Cyprus too, and partly because it is generally agreed that the English proportion is below the traditional level. The weakness of the line is paucity of data for countries whose non-agriculture ratio lies between 30 and 40; these are mainly European countries, whose Censuses do not give educational qualifications.

Paradoxically, the validity of the line is also supported by those who lie above and below it. The "liberals" are the Philippines, Greece, Hungary and Puerto Rico. The Philippines and Puerto Rico have modelled their

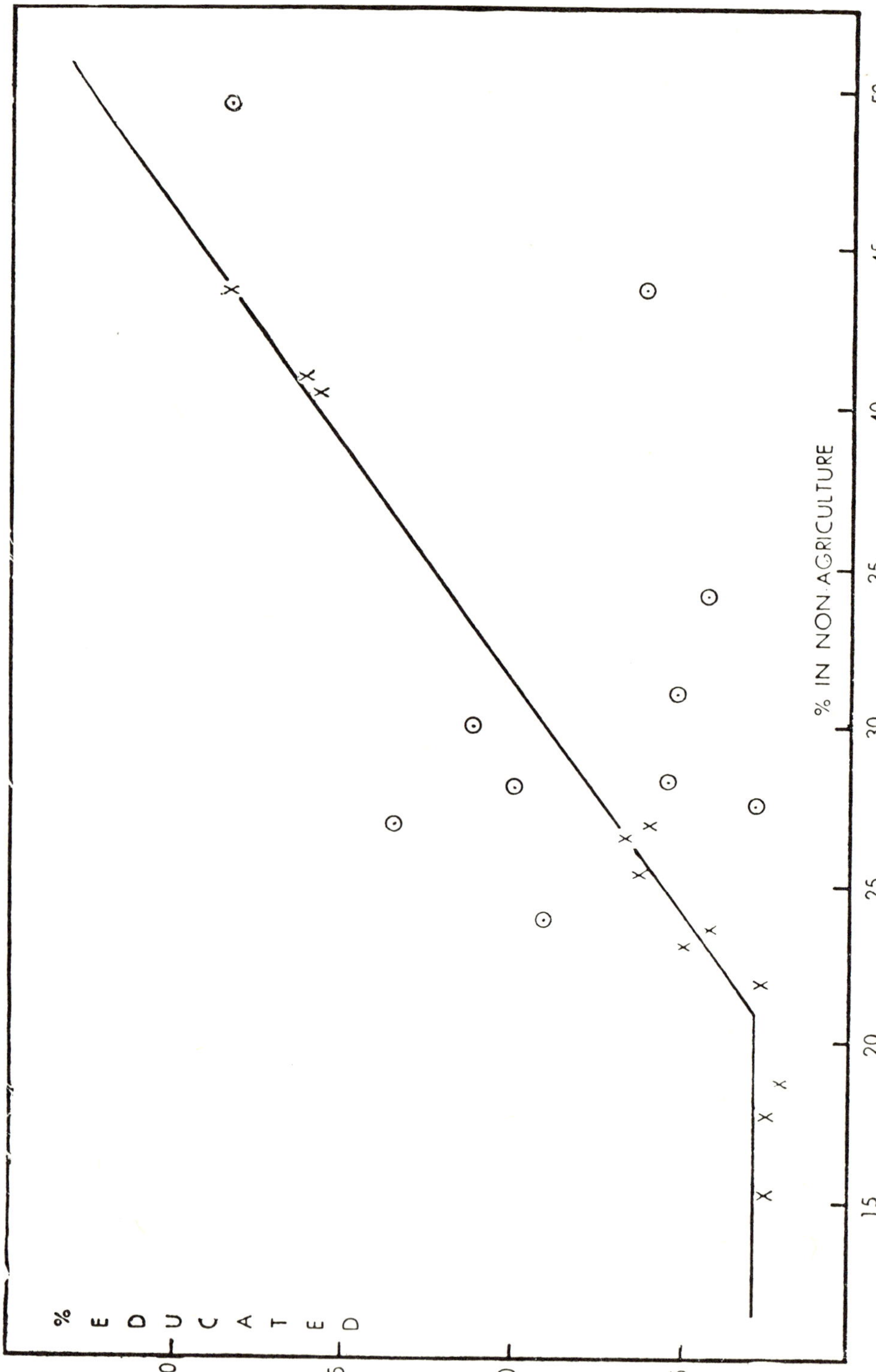
% IN NON-AGRICULTURE
15
20
25
30
35
40
45
50
% EDUCATED
5
10
15
20

educational policies on the United States; and Hungary is well known as an exporter of educated talent. The traditional line must lie below these three. Equally we are not surprised to find that it lies above Jamaica, Ecuador, Cuba, Venezuela and Argentina, who are known for their "elitist" policies.

As an exercise in regression analysis, this investigation is clearly a non-starter. But when the figures are examined in the light of what is generally believed about these countries, the line we have drawn inspires a moderate degree of confidence. If a traditional relationship exists between education and economic structure, this is probably it.

From the traditional formula (1) to the required annual enrolment percentage is a straight step if one can estimate the rate at which y, the proportion in non-agriculture, is changing. Intuition tells us that the enrolment percentage must be the same percentage as the stock, plus an adjustment for any growth in the proportion of persons in non-agriculture. The problem is slightly more complicated than this, and full treatment brings in many more factors. But for practical purposes we can return to a simplified version. For full treatment we need the following symbols:

a = adjustment for accelerated education.
b = "birth rate", $n \div N$.
d = death rate of educated males aged 25 and over.
m = absolute change in y from one year to the next.
n = number of males aged 25.
N = number of males aged 25 and over.
p = rate of growth of N
s = proportion required in school at age 15.

The most important of these factors is m, the absolute amount by which y changes in one year. This is a function both of the rate of growth of the economy, and also of the amount of change which has already taken place. By the time y has reached 50, the relative share of agriculture has already fallen so low (to around 9 per cent of the occupied population) that any further change in y must be very small. The change is also small at the other end of the scale of development, for though non-agriculture may have a high rate of growth, the absolute change cannot be large. The U.S. Census[3] shows m rising from 0.1 at the beginning of the nineteenth century to a maximum of 0.36 at the end of the century, and falling back to less than 0.2 in the 1950's. Western European rates have been lower than the American. However, in these days higher rates than the American are achieved by a number of developing countries, so a rise in the non-agriculture ratio from say 30.0 to 30.5 ($m = .5$) in one year is not inconceivable.

Apart from the change in y, some pupils must be enrolled to replace

[3]In *The Conditions of Economic Progress* Colin Clark has assembled historical data for several countries. Percentage of the occupied population is here converted to percentage of persons aged 15 and over by multiplying by .55.

educated who die, and others to keep the ratio of the stock constant as population grows. The rate of growth of the number of males aged 25 and over ranges between 1.0 and 2.5 per cent; so p ranges between .01 and .025. The death rate of the educated is lower than the death rate of all males of 25 and over, because the educated are concentrated more in the younger than in the older age groups. If this were not so, we would have $b = p + d$. (It should be noted, incidentally, that b exceeds the birth rate of the population).

A further adjustment is needed if it is desired to increase the ratio of the educated by more than is required merely to keep pace with the change in y; for example, if the actual stock is below the traditional level, or if one wishes to increase the ratio beyond the traditional level. There are limits to the rate of increase. For example, if the stock is low because jobs which the educated could do are being done by the uneducated, one can normally replace the uneducated only as they die, so the limit of the possible is equivalent to treating d as the death rate of all males over 25 and not just of educated males. Faster change is possible if one is creating new jobs, and not merely substituting people in old jobs. To increase the stock by more than 2 per cent a year, over and above the increases due to changes in economic structure and in population would prove difficult for under-developed countries, where the relatively high price of secondary school graduates keeps absorptive capacity low. So a may range up to .02.

The proportion to be enrolled is the number required to have been in school at 15 divided by the number of males in one year's age group, n. This is

$$s = \frac{0.68mN\ (1+p)\ +\ (p+d+a)\ xN}{n}$$

$$= \frac{0.68m\ (1+p)\ +\ (p+d+a)x}{b} \qquad (2)$$

which, in the special case where $(p+d+a) = b$, further reduces to

$$s = \frac{0.68m\ (1+p)}{b} + x \qquad (3)$$

Both (2) and (3) are subject to the restriction $x \nless 3.0$. This means that the formula should not be used below the level appropriate to $y = 21$, at which point, assuming $m = 0.35$, enrolment would be 8.4 per cent. The enrolment rate should never be below 4 per cent.[4]

By making reasonable assumptions we can prepare a table showing what the enrolment rate should be at traditional levels, for different levels of economic structure. First we assume that any deficiencies in the size of the present stock are met by using the death rate of all males of 25 and over,

[4]This formula is derived on the same principles as the formula in my earlier article (*op. cit.*). The difference is that whereas the earlier formula required for each country a separate estimate of the desirable stock of educated and of the desirable growth of the stock, the present formula incorporates both these quantities at traditional levels, and requires only an estimate of the annual change of the proportion of persons in non-agriculture — a figure whose past history is easily calculated from the Census.

instead of educated males only. We thus use formula (3). We also assume that national income per head is growing by 2.5 per cent per annum. The values of m, b and p used with different values of y are shown in tabular form:[5]

y	m	b	p
25	.35	.045	.025
30	.40	.045	.025
35	.40	.040	.020
40	.35	.035	.015

In Table 2 a column has been added for required enrolment in higher education, defining this as the proportion of persons aged 25 who should have been in college at age 20. Inspection shows that the ratio of the stock of secondary to the stock of higher educated males is about 6 to 1. Table 2, which relates to males and females together, assumes that the traditional ratio of males to females is 1:1 in secondary and 2:1 in higher education. The higher education column is therefore obtained by multiplying the secondary education column by .125.

Table 2 also translates the proportion of the population aged 15 and over into the proportion of the occupied population, by assuming that the occupied population is .55 of those aged 15 and over. This column must be used with care, since the definition of occupied population which the Census uses may be quite different.

TABLE 2. PERCENTAGE OF AGE GROUP REQUIRED FOR ENROLMENT

Percentage Non-Agric. 15+.	At Age 15	At Age 20	Percentage Agriculture Occup. Pop.
20	8.4	1.1	64
25	11.1	1.4	55
30	15.3	1.9	45
35	19.4	2.4	36
40	22.8	2.9	27

The assumed rate of growth of national income per head makes a big difference. The enrolment rates in Table 2, which may seem high at the less developed end of the scale, are due to the assumption that national income per capita is growing by 2.5 per cent per annum, whereas nineteenth century European rates were nearer 1.5 per cent per annum. If per capita national income is assumed not to grow at all ($m = 0$), the figures in the second column become 3.0, 5.7, 9.1, 12.5 and 15.9 instead of 8.4, 11.1, 15.3, 19.4 and 22.8. The assumption of rapid rates of growth is valid for some of the less developed countries, but not for others.

Given the assumption of 2.5 per cent per capita growth, Table 2 actually understates the required enrolment percentage. First, since the ratio of the educated is increasing, the ratio of persons now 15 and at school needs to be higher than the ratio of persons now 25 who were in school at 15.

[5]Relating m to per capita income growth is difficult. I have arrived at the values in the table by examining the data in Colin Clark, *op. cit.*, and similar sources.

More important, to arrive at the percentage who should start secondary education at 12, one must allow for wastage, which in less developed countries often exceeds 25 per cent in the first three years. The figures in Table 2 are better interpreted as the percentages who should complete secondary education.

Finally, if one were to assume that what the traditional line shows is the demand for education by families, rather than the demand for the educated by employers, one could link this investigation to studies of the elasticity of demand for education. For example, assume population constant, income per capita rising by 2.5 per cent, and the proportion in non-agriculture rising in one year from 30 to 30.40. From (3) we calculate that enrolment (and therefore, with a short time lag, the school population) will increase by 1.2 per cent. So the income elasticity of demand is 0.48. If m is as high as 0.5, income elasticity is 0.52.

Expenditure increases faster than demand because cost per pupil rises faster than the general price level. Productivity increases less rapidly in education than in the rest of the economy; if educational productivity does not increase at all, but teachers' salaries keep pace with other incomes, cost per child will rise as fast as real income per capita. The salary of a teacher of given qualifications does not keep pace with other incomes (blue collar incomes rise faster than white collar incomes), but this is more than offset by the continuous upgrading of qualifications, as the ratio of secondary school teachers who are college graduates increases. Schultz[6] calculates that in the U.S.A. secondary school cost per pupil, deflated by the G.N.P. price, increased by 93 per cent between 1930 and 1956. Since productivity in the whole economy increased only by 65 per cent, one may deduce that average teacher salary increased by more than other incomes. Presumably one should count the upgrading of qualifications as an improvement of the product.

To return to our assumptions, if per capita income increases by 2.5 per cent, demand by 1.2 per cent, and cost per child by 3.0 per cent, income elasticity is 0.5, but the ratio of the increase in expenditure to the increase in income is 1.7 Schultz[7] quotes estimates ranging from 0.7 to 3.5, but some of these are income elasticities and some are expenditure ratios. Strictly speaking, if the upgrading of qualifications does improve the product, then that part of the increase in cost which is due to this factor should be included in measuring income elasticity.

III.

Most of the countries at the top of the development scale now have enrolment ratios substantially above what the traditional formula requires; partly because the 1950's have seen an upward movement from the traditional relationship to more liberal levels, but mainly because their secondary

[6]T. W. Schultz, *The Economic Value of Education*, p. 34.
[7]*Ibid.*, p. 9.

education now includes an increasing proportion of vocational and decreasing proportion of grammar school streams. It is still the case, however, that most of the countries at the bottom, and many in the middle of the scale, are significantly below the traditional level. The writer's interest in this subject began in Africa, where the colonial powers' idea of their self-proclaimed preparation for self-government was enrolment ratios significantly less than 1.0 per cent of the age group.

This investigation throws no light on whether the traditional level is the right level. It is the right level given the traditional educational requirements for various jobs, and given the traditional salary differentials; but, given time, both these factors adjust to any level of secondary enrolment. In countries where enrolment is significantly below the traditional level, the salary of a secondary school graduate is fantastically high, when compared with average national income per head; and economic development is clearly hampered both by the shortage of educated persons and also by their relative cost. There is no doubt that it is in the social interest (though not necessarily in the interest of the secondary school class) to raise enrolment to traditional levels.

How far beyond this, in the liberal direction, it pays to go, in a productivity sense, is not clear. Attempts to measure the yield to society of investment in secondary education founder on the difficulty of separating out the various reasons why the average secondary school graduate earns more than the average primary school graduate. In any case the exercise is hardly necessary in rich countries, since however little difference it may make to productivity, few people doubt that any country should keep nearly all its children in school up to age 16 if it can afford to do so. And whether a rich country can afford to do so is a question not of economics but of social values. Poor countries are a different matter. However, the current situation in those south Asian countries which are pouring out secondary and university graduates far in excess of the traditional proportions, seems to confirm that, while education helps to change economic structure, it is also true that the structure of the economy imposes its own limits to what education can achieve.

IV.

Since sending the above to the printer, I have received from the Director of Statistics, Jamaica, materials relating to the Census for Jamaica for 1960, which enable further light to be thrown on the absorption of secondary school graduates as economic development proceeds.

Using the Census cross-classification by Industry and by Occupation, I have constructed a table relating Industry and Education. The Census does not relate Occupation and Education; this I have done on my own responsibility, using my own experience as to the degree of education required for different occupations.

The table is based on what is now considered in Jamaica to be the appropriate education for a given occupation. Many persons now in the occupation have less education than this. So the table shows not how many educated people there are, but how many there would be if everybody had the education now considered appropriate to his occupation. For example, it is assumed that all primary school teachers, stenographers, nurses and employers of 20 persons or more should have a secondary education, and all lawyers, clergymen and secondary school teachers should have a university education. We choose as basis what is now considered appropriate because the main use of figures of this kind is in manpower budgeting, where the object is to discover how many people have to be recruited at the educational level now considered appropriate: in other words these are the figures required for making calculations at the margin.

From the same materials I have derived the proportion of skilled labour used in each Industry. This refers to occupations which are normally entered not from secondary but from primary schools, and for which at least one year's intensive training or apprenticeship is required. Motor mechanics, painters and printers are included; dressmakers and shoemakers are not. Again the principal use of such figures is in manpower budgeting, where one is interested only in occupations where a shortage might hold up development because of a long training period.

TABLE 3. EDUCATIONAL REQUIREMENTS, BY INDUSTRY.

Per Cent.

	University	Secondary	Skilled	Other	**Total**
Agriculture, large scale	0.4	2.0	3.5	94.1	100.0
Agriculture, small scale	..	0.6	0.1	99.3	100.0
Mining	4.0	10.0	25.0	61.0	100.0
Manufacture, complex	4.0	10.0	25.0	61.0	100.0
Manufacture, simple	2.0	5.0	15.0	78.0	100.0
Manufacture, workshop	0.1	1.0	12.0	86.9	100.0
Construction	0.2	1.7	50.0	48.1	100.0
Communications	1.5	6.0	10.0	82.5	100.0
Commerce	1.5	11.0	1.0	86.5	100.0
Domestic service	..	..	..	100.0	100.0
Other service	4.5	35.0	2.0	58.5	100.0

For the Jamaican economy as a whole the percentages are: university 0.9, secondary 6.0 and skilled 7.0 These figures are based on aspirations rather than on achievement. Thus, against the secondary and university requirement of 6.9 per cent we must set the fact that the proportion of the population over 20 which had actually completed secondary or higher education was only 3.4 per cent; on the other hand the proportion that had received some secondary schooling was 6.4 per cent, the drop-out rate being very high.

It is possible to study changes in these ratios by comparing Jamaica's situation at the time of the 1943 Census with the aspirations of 1964 and the British census of 1950.

The 1943 Jamaica Census cross-classifies occupations with education, making possible an almost exact analysis of the distribution of the educated in

1943 (actual, not aspirations). The difference between 1943 and 1964 is very substantial, mainly because it was not then assumed that nurses or primary school teachers should go through secondary school; and the educational requirements for supervisory staff were also lower. The actual ratios in 1943 were: university 0.3 per cent, secondary 2.0 per cent. (These figures include only those who had *completed* secondary education, and are therefore a little smaller than the number who were still in school at age 15).

The British Census does not cross-classify occupations with education, but similar results can be achieved by assuming that the occupations for which a secondary or higher education is required are "Administrators and Managers", "Professional and Technical" and "Clerks", as shown in the reclassification by Mr. H. S. Parnes[8]. This result gives 19.5 per cent of the occupied population of England and Wales as holding jobs requiring secondary education, which is more than finished but less than started secondary education.

The change in proportions of secondary graduates absorbed at different levels of economic development is due partly to changes in economic structure (proportions of different industries) and partly to increases in minimum qualifications (higher ratios in each industry). Table 4 shows the ratios in each industry at three different levels. Level I gives the actual ratios in Jamaica in 1943. Level II is based on Jamaican aspirations in 1964, and Level III gives the actual ratios in England and Wales in 1950.

TABLE 4. SECONDARY AND HIGHER REQUIREMENTS.

Per Cent.

	Level I	Level II	Level III
Agriculture	0.6	1.0	1.0
Mining	7.0	14.0	5.0
Manufacture, complex	12.0	14.0	22.0
Manufacture, simple	5.0	7.0	12.0
Manufacture, workshop	0.8	1.1	2.0
Construction	0.8	1.9	9.1
Communications	3.8	7.5	14.4
Commerce	6.2	12.5	20.4
Domestic service	..	..	..
Other services	15.6	39.5	41.3

TABLE 5. OCCUPIED POPULATION.

	Level I	Level II	Level III
Agriculture	65,000	50,000	5,000
Mining	2,000	3,000	3,800
Manufacturing, complex	500	1,500	21,600
Manufacturing, simple	1,500	2,500	14,000
Manufacturing, workshop	8,000	10,000	5,000
Construction	3,000	5,000	6,300
Communications	4,000	5,000	7,800
Commerce	6,000	9,000	14,400
Domestic service	4,000	4,000	2,300
Other services	6,000	10,000	19,800
	100,000	100,000	100,000

[8]H. S. Parnes, *Forecasting Educational Needs for Economic and Social Development*, Organisation for Economic Cooperation and Development, Paris, 1962, pp. 92-93.

To distinguish between the effects of changes in structure and changes in qualifications, we show in Table 5 the structure of the occupied population at three different levels. Level III is England and Wales in 1950. For the other two we do not use Jamaican figures because Jamaica has abnormally large numbers in large-scale agriculture and in domestic service. We have therefore invented two structures, corresponding to a country where 65 per cent of the occupied population is in agriculture, and a more advanced country where this ratio is down to 50 per cent.

Table 6 is constructed by multiplying the populations in Table 5 by the ratios in Table 4. The first column shows the number of secondary or higher education graduates at Level I. Similarly columns II and III show the number of secondary educated at Levels II and III. The purpose of column I/III is to discover how much of the change between Levels I and III is due to change in economic structure, and how much to higher qualifications in each industry. This column is found by multiplying the structure of Level III (Table 5) by the ratios of Level I. The answer it yields is that only 33 per cent of the change is due to structure, the rest is due to higher qualifications.

TABLE 6. Secondary and Higher per 100,000

	Level I	Level II	Level III	Level I/III
Agriculture	390	500	50	30
Mining	140	420	190	266
Manufacturing, complex	60	210	4,752	2,592
Manufacturing, simple	75	175	1,680	700
Manufacturing, workshop	64	110	100	40
Construction	24	95	573	50
Communications	152	375	1,123	296
Commerce	372	1,125	2,938	893
Other services	936	3,950	8,177	3,089
	2,213	6,960	19,583	7,956

These tables help to explain why it is not possible to draw a simple straight line relating secondary education to economic growth. Even at the lowest levels, 60 per cent of the educated are in commerce and services (especially government service). Shortage of secondary educated workers is not likely to be a bottleneck to the expansion of other sectors of the economy; if agriculture or manufacturing wish to expand, their relatively small needs can be met without great difficulty from the reservoir in commerce and services. The "industry" most likely to be handicapped by shortage is services, especially as many of its employees require special training (e.g. nurses, agricultural assistants). But even here one can fall back on the reservoir in commerce; the ratio of secondary educated people in commerce is fairly flexible since a secondary education is not absolutely essential to a clerk or a salesgirl.

The flexibility of all the ratios, and especially that of commerce, also explains why it is easy to absorb a "surplus" of secondary educated in countries pursuing a "liberal" policy, without any significant effect on economic structure, or for that matter, on the standard of living. As more secondary graduates become available, a larger percentage of sales staff and of clerical workers have secondary education. Despite sophisticated calculations, the real effect of this on per capita output is probably negligible. In choosing between "liberal", "traditional" and "conservative" policies, governments are not likely to get much help from economic statisticians. The statistician can calculate how many more people are required to cope with expected changes in economic structure, given current qualifications, but the flexibility of qualifications always leaves considerable leeway for decisions based on non-economic grounds.

STATISTICAL APPENDIX

These figures are all derived from Censuses taken at dates shown in Table 1. The United Nations *Demographic Yearbook* for 1956 has collected the data together for all the countries included here except Thailand, Hungary, Colombia, Cyprus, France and England and Wales.

Honduras. Males completing secondary grade 3. The Census does not show males over 25 years separately. Ratio of such males to all males completing grade 3 is .71 in Costa Rica, and .67 in Nicaragua. Here assumed to be .7 in Honduras.

Thailand. Males completing secondary grade 5, or three years of higher education, respectively.

Haiti. Males completing secondary grade 3 shown in column B, and males completing 3 years of higher education shown in column C.

Nicaragua. Same as Haiti.

Guatemala. Same as Haiti.

El Salvador. Same as Honduras.

Brazil. Same as Haiti.

Mexico. Males completing grade 10, plus one-third of those completing grades 7-9.

Philippines. Males completing grade 2 of senior high school.

Jamaica. Males who have reached the fifth form, plus one quarter of those who left secondary school in earlier forms. According to the Census, the ratio of persons occupied other than in agriculture to persons aged 15 and over is 35.3, which is misleadingly high. Because Jamaica has a system of plantation agriculture, the surplus women are not in agriculture, but are attached to urban households in domestic capacities. It is here assumed that the ratio of women occupied other than in agriculture to women aged 15 and over is the same as in Cuba. (This incidentally also brings the ratio of occupied population to population aged 15 and over into line at .54).

Paraguay. Census shows the number and ages of those who have attended secondary school, but not by grades completed. Wastage in grades 1 and 2 is 26 per cent in Costa Rica, 27 per cent in Ecuador and 29 per cent in Colombia. Wastage in Paraguay and in Chile assumed to be 27 per cent.

Costa Rica. Same as Haiti.

Colombia. Same as Haiti.

Greece. Same as Haiti.

Ecuador. Same as Haiti. Census shows more women than men engaged in manufacturing, since it counts women making straw hats in their homes. It is here assumed that the ratio of women to men in manufacturing is the same as in Colombia (.52).

Hungary. Males who have completed grade 5 of secondary or grade 1 of technical education.

Puerto Rico. Males who have completed grade 2 of senior high school, or 3 years of higher education respectively.

Cuba. Same as Haiti, except that column C includes those with five years of higher education plus half of those with four years or less.

Venezuela. Same as Haiti, plus half those whose grade of secondary education is not stated.

Chile. Same as Paraguay.

Cyprus. Same as Haiti.

Japan. Same as Haiti; column C shows males completing 4 years of higher education plus half those completing only 2 or 3 years.

Argentina. Census does not show age group 25-59 separately. Ratios given here are half way between ratio for males over 20 and ratio for males over 30 (the difference is small). One third of males completing only 3 years of secondary education assumed to have completed in third year; same assumption for higher education.

France. Males terminating education at age 15 or later.

Canada. Males completing 9 and 14 years of education respectively. It is assumed that half of those who completed only 13 to 16 years completed only 14 or 15 years.

U.S.A. Same as Puerto Rico.

England and Wales. Same as France.

W. Arthur Lewis

[23]

Economic aspects of quality in education

Quality is a vague word which embraces several characteristics. This paper will group them into three categories, called even more vaguely: breadth, pyramid and success.

Breadth refers to the choice between the vocational and the general in the school curriculum. This choice exists at all levels, from primary to professional.

Pyramid is concerned with proportions in school at different ages, and with the different combinations of general and vocational at each age.

Success refers to the extent to which the school actually achieves with the child what it sets out to do.

Most of these qualities can be measured. We do not have much difficulty in recognizing whether one curriculum is more specialized than another, or in counting the numbers in different types of education or in comparing the effectiveness of two schools which teach to the same curriculum. The problem is not how to measure but how to evaluate. Would a less specialized curriculum be more appropriate? Should one restrict higher education in order to spend more at the primary level? If one can hire more teachers should one use them to improve the student/teacher ratio or to bring more students to school? The vagueness of our measuring rods seems insignificant when compared with our blankness in evaluation.

The market gives some guidance, but not enough. Employers can choose between school leavers with a general education and those with a technical education, and in so far as they know what they are doing we can deduce from differences in pay how they evaluate the differences in education. Different schools working to the same curriculum do a better job than other schools. We can compare the difference between the cost of two schools (if more and better teachers and equipment are the main explanation of quality) with the difference between the average earnings of their pupils. But this is not enough.

In the first place, what the market tells us is whether the schools are producing the type of people who fit into the current social situation. But education cannot always fit the young for what they will have to do after leaving school. What kind of schooling would prepare a youngster to work in a mine at an 18-inch seam in water with only a pickaxe? Or what is the appropriate schooling for spending one's life cultivating two acres with a hoe? The assumption that the school must prepare the child for his environment is not always valid. Many progressive children and parents look to the school not to fit them for their environment, but on the contrary as a window through which they may escape from the job or the village or the social class which is otherwise ordained for them. Modern education fits modern societies. When modern education is introduced into backward societies, backward politically (e.g. feudal) or backward technologically (e.g., hoe agriculture) the consequences can be revolutionary. This is one reason why reactionary governments limit education. But even well-meaning governments may have to limit education if they cannot achieve social change at the pace they would like. Thus in much of rural Africa, where modern education is incompatible with the current agricultural system, how rapidly to expand primary education is a real problem. One alternative – adapting the education to the agriculture – is undesirable (at issue is not merely the curriculum but also the approach to life); and the other alternative – adapting the agriculture to the curriculum – has to proceed relatively slowly. Since it is important for education to change society as well as to adjust to it, one cannot evaluate education simply by the market price which its products can command.

A second difficulty is that market prices measure value only if they are determined by the equation of demand and supply. Now the scale of salaries in under-developed countries is not freely determined. The government is the largest employer of certain groups, and fixes their salaries arbitrarily. Neither is the market cleared by prices; many shortages and surpluses exist. Calculations based on the average earnings in a certain occupation do not justify a larger output if a surplus already exists at current prices. The economist handles this problem conceptually by using 'shadow prices' which clear the market, instead of actual prices. Conceptually these shadow prices may be determined by mathematical programming. Models have been made combining input-output analysis (to take account of the fact that education consumes a significant proportion of its own output) with linear programming. If one knows the educational requirement of each job in the economy, or alternatively knows the relative values of different types of education, the model will determine exactly how many people should receive each type of education. In practice we do not have this information. Even if we had, the appropriate model would be not linear but non-linear, and we would probably not be able to solve the problem. So while conceptually the problem yields to economic analysis, in practice exercises of this kind are founded on guesses.

A third problem is that even accurate market evaluation would not be enough. The market measures some benefits but not others. If we educate a deaf child his earnings go up; so we can measure both the cost of schooling for deaf children and also the difference between the earnings of representative samples of educated deaf and uneducated deaf. But there are also unmeasured economic benefits – the educated deaf are less of a material burden to their families and friends. And there are also uneconomic benefits – first the extra personal satisfactions which the deaf derive from having received an education, and secondly the extra satisfaction which all society derives from knowing that its deaf members have been given the same chance for education as anybody else. All attempts to measure the value of education come up against the fact that education has values which are not reflected in the market-place.

This is where the distinction between education as an investment good and education as a consumer good ceases to be useful. Suppose that every member of the community could benefit by receiving a college education up to the age of 22, and desired such an education. And suppose that only half the jobs to be done actually needed or benefited from such a long period of education. Could one deduce that only half the population should receive a college education? In a poor country, which could not afford college education for all, calculations of this kind would be highly relevant in making decisions. But in a rich country, where the alternative might be to produce more television sets or other knick-knacks, education would be valued for its own sake, irrespective of its contribution to productivity. The economist belongs in a land of scarcity, but not in a land of plenty.

This paper confines itself to the problems of poor countries, where the cost and productivity of education cannot be neglected, but it makes no claim that these are the decisive considerations. Its main task is to define the various aspects of quality, and note the issues which arise as each aspect is considered. Judgements are offered from time to time, unsupported by statistical evidence. The paper should be read mainly as a list of topics about which we need to have more information or analysis.

Breadth

In preparing people for life, education has to perform several functions.

1. Socialization; teaching the child to live with others; teaching social roles; culture patterns; rules of behaviour; history, and so on.
2. Teaching needed facts about the physical world; some science, some geography.

3. Imparting some understanding and appreciation of our artistic heritage; literature, music, art, drama.
4. Providing intellectual tools; reading, mathematics, languages, logical analysis and so on.
5. Training the body; physical exercise, co-ordination of hand and eye, athletic sports.
6. Teaching specialized skills for use in adult life; whether in the home, such as cooking, or in the market-place.

Everybody agrees that the school must do all these things; the argument is only about proportions. In this paper we confine ourselves to the discussion about the relative weight to be given to specialized skills, as against all the other functions.

The first factor which determines the relative proportions of general and specialized education is the length of time available for schooling. If children spend only five years in school, the emphasis is likely to be put on general education rather than on specialized skills. Girls will be taught to read rather than to sew. One defence is that this will be their only opportunity to learn to read, while they can learn to sew later. But one's attitude to the general values of education, as distinct from specialized skills, will also influence the decision. Bigoted employers have always preferred that the schools should concentrate on skills rather than on general education, both because they attach more importance to skills and also because they fear that general education may not be compatible with the kind of social framework which they wish to preserve.

But any educational institution anywhere, at any level, feels that it could do a better job (give a better background and also more specialized knowledge) if only it had its students for just one more year.

Next, it is not easy to agree where to draw the line between specialized training in school and on-the-job training. This line varies with almost every job and every community. The longer the period of schooling the more the school programme eats into what could otherwise be done by on-the-job training. Since schooling is expensive, poor countries give, through shorter schooling followed by apprenticeship, forms of training which richer countries tend to take into formal establishments, not merely because they (the richer) can afford it, but also because, having decided to lengthen the period of schooling, they have to put more specialized training into the curriculum. However, cost apart, the appropriate division between schooling and apprenticeship is always subject to debate. The medical practitioner used to be trained almost exclusively on the job. Then came a phase in which he was trained exclusively in medical school, and could practise immediately after passing his examination. Now a period of compulsory on-the-job training after examination has been restored, and beyond this young doctors tend to spend longer and longer in 'residences' before starting general practice. The schools also have their prejudices. Since the theorist has more snob prestige than the practitioner, the schools tend to be snobbish towards teaching practical subjects. The current pressure of engineering schools to teach science rather than engineering is supported by many good arguments, but it is not without influences of this kind.

From the point of view of the student, early specialization can be a disadvantage. A child of 12 or 14, or even an adult of 18, is not well placed for choosing his life's work, and may try to postpone choice as long as possible. In general the best-paid occupations are those whose specialized training starts latest. Hence ambitious parents and children want to stay in general education as long as possible. This is one reason why vocational programmes often come to grief. Secondary grammar schools may be packed, while secondary technical schools have vacant places. Or if the students go into the vocational courses (train to be teachers, agricultural assistants, laboratory technicians and the like) they use them only as a substitute for general education, and as a stepping-stone to more remunerative jobs. Philosophers may thunder that the schools are not preparing the students for life, but what philosophers want from the schools and what students and parents want from the schools are not necessarily the same.

Actually, the student's desire for flexibility is matched by society's need in those economies where the nature of the jobs to be done is subject to change, whether because jobs change their relative importance, or because the technique of doing any particular job changes with time. Education precedes a working life which may last fifty years. It ought to lay a foundation which will enable a worker to change his skills as opportunities change. A stable society can afford high specialization in its school curriculum (a caste system is the extreme form of a stable society), but a rapidly changing society must put its emphasis instead on general education.

The foregoing points all stress the claims of general education, but, since the problem is one not of absolutes but of relative proportions, they do not destroy the equally strong case for formal specialized training. Speaking historically, as the schooling period lengthens, general education increases; while, as the relative numbers receiving education grow, the schools take over more and more of the specialized training which was previously done on the job. In the United States of America, where the goal is to remain in school until the age of 25, specialized training has been pushed into graduate schools. In the United Kingdom children with similar ambitions begin to specialize at 14 and have considered it normal to leave school at 21 with a bachelor's degree; this is now altering on the United States pattern as the period of education lengthens. As the net widens, more vocations come into the schools. Sometimes this improves the craft; technique is changed because the technician has a better general education. More often, this is merely a matter of convenience. If the children are to stay in school, and do not want to absorb any more general knowledge, they may as well be instructed in useful crafts. Hence historically education tends to become both more general (vertically) and more specialized (horizontally).

Pyramid

Since the relative weight given to specialization depends on the length of the school course and the width of the net, it is directly related to the pyramid, which is the relative proportions in school at each age. These two aspects may now be considered together.

One's attitude to the angle of the pyramid tends to be related to what one wants of an educational system. Those who value education mainly for its non-economic attributes want to spread it as widely as possible. They would rather spend money giving everybody some general education than spend the same amount to give a few a better and more specialized education. Those who emphasize more the economic aspect of education are impressed with the superior contribution of the most highly educated. They tend to call for more students at the top of the pyramid rather than at the bottom. A third group say that their desire is that each child should have the education for which it is capable. This would produce a pyramid similar to the distribution of native ability. For example, this is the basis used by the Robbins Committee report for calculating how large the university population should be in the United Kingdom; no attempt is made to relate these numbers to job opportunities. As we have seen, this basis is more relevant to a rich than to a poor society.

If one starts from job opportunities, the angle of the pyramid depends on the degree of economic development, and more especially on the size of the subsistence sector of the economy. The subsistence sector has little use for highly trained university graduates, apart from doctors, and cannot afford to pay even those whom it could use. The capacity to absorb the highly trained increases steadily as the subsistence sector diminishes. Hence, in an underdeveloped country it is as easy to be producing too many (in terms of absorptive capacity) at the top (e.g., the United Arab Republic) as it is to be producing too few (e.g., Malawi).

Many countries have made manpower studies assessing their needs for high-level skills. Using rough bench marks, African countries show a need for about 10 per cent of the age cohort to be receiving secondary education at the age of 16, and about one per cent to be receiving higher education at about 21. However, these or any other figures are subject to the important qualifications that absorptive capacity is not a fixed concept. As the numbers at high levels increase, they take over jobs formerly done by people with lower levels of education, who in turn drive out people from still lower levels. An economy can therefore absorb any number of educated people, given time for job qualifications to be adjusted upward and relative salaries to be adjusted downward. As in the United States, when the number with top-level education grows, it is the people with the lowest level of education (or none) who find it hardest to get a job.

Manpower surveys, therefore, do not tell us what the pyramid should be. They tell us how many the market will absorb given current job qualifications and relative salaries. If we produce more they will find work sooner or later, even if in less prestigious jobs than they expected, and for lower pay. Since upgrading the qualifications for jobs is one of the major sources of growing productivity, one should always produce more skilled people than the manpower survey shows to be needed at current levels of expectation. As we have seen, conceptually we could find out just how many more by non-linear programming, but this is not practicable.

Manpower surveys have also to make some allowance for desired imports or exports of skills. Most countries will prefer to train their own people (whether at home or abroad is a separate question) rather than to import foreigners, but this is not always practicable within the relevant time span. As for exporting, the 'brain drain' is not always unintended. Some countries have for a long time educated more persons than they could absorb, and supplied their neighbours (e.g., U.A.R., Dahomey, Sierra Leone). Overpopulated countries from which people are migrating (e.g., Puerto Rico, Malta) may well decide that it is better to educate their people before exporting them - this is indeed tending to become one of the conditions on which countries will take immigrants.

Though one can make some case for educating substantially more high-level people than the manpower survey requires, the argument cannot be pressed far in a poor community. Since it would clearly be inequitable to ignore the majority of children while spending lavishly on the few, one can make more persuasively the opposite case for limiting the output at the upper ends of the pyramid within the neighbourhood of the figures indicated by the manpower survey, so that additional sums can be spent at the bottom of the pyramid.

The case for a wide base does not rest only on equity. The future of any country depends on finding its best brains and educating them. Since natural ability is randomly distributed, the only way to find the best brains is to give everybody a chance. Hence, even if the top is very narrow, the bottom should be wide – the age distribution of education in a very poor society should then look more like a rectangular hyperbola than like the side of a pyramid. Universal primary education may not be practicable, for reasons we shall come to in a moment, but the search for the best brains justifies heavy spending at that level.

The quality of the pyramid depends not only on its shape but also on the system for choosing the students at each level. Ideally, the choice should depend only on the child's ability to profit by education, with the most able chosen at each stage. In practice, many other factors intervene (class, religion, income, race, political affiliation, and so on). Universalistic societies seek the ideal, devise 'objective' tests of ability, and provide scholarships and bursaries so that income may not be a barrier to education. Since the achievement of excellence depends on the quality of the students no less than the quality of the teachers, the importance of this point needs no emphasis.

Primary-level education, to, say, the age of 12. How big should the base of the pyramid be in an under-developed country with a large subsistence sector? This subsistence sector is the problem. There is no tenable argument against primary education for children who will earn their living outside the subsistence sector. This gives a minimum goal of 50 per cent of children in primary school just as rapidly as teachers and schools can be mobilized for this purpose. For the rest, the economy needs a simultaneous approach; building rural schools while simultaneously reforming the agrarian structure so that it can absorb and hold the products of the schools. Thus one would expect the passage from 50 to 100 per cent of children entering schools to take at least thirty years. Those West African states which have moved from 30 to 90 per cent in the past ten years are now beginning to observe the results. Educators will hope that the benefits of education (however rudimentary) may triumph over the costs of rural dislocation.

Secondary level. According to manpower budgeting, in countries at low levels of development about 10 per cent of the population should, at the age of 16, still be receiving mainly a general education. Ten per cent of these will go on to university, perhaps a quarter to post-secondary vocational schools, and the rest straight into employment. Most African countries have not yet reached this goal of 10 per cent in general secondary education; many Asian countries have already gone far beyond it, while allowing their primary education to lag.

The other children who stay in school beyond the age of 12 need a substantial vocational mix. This is the stage where the school garden, the workshop, and the domestic science unit can be helpful. The drop-out rate is high. It would probably be better to spend money on improving the vocational facilities at this stage (quality before quantity) than to spend it on trying to increase the number of children staying in school. In British African terminology this means that it is now more important to improve the facilities of the 'middle' schools than to increase the number of their students. The justification for this judgement is the state of the market. Thirty years ago there was a shortage of candidates for clerical jobs, and only a small market for craftsmen, and so efforts to attract students to vocational studies were unsuccessful. Today the clerical jobs go to products of the 'grammar' schools, and the market is crowded with unskilled primary school leavers. At the same time, the progress of public and private investment creates a demand for skills of many kinds. Low levels of skill induce employers to install expensive automated machinery in substitution for skill. As a result, in many under-developed countries high levels of investment are now associated with abnormally low increases in employment. To spend more on vocational education is one of the better remedies for unemployment.

Post-secondary vocational. In all under-developed countries this is the weakest link in the chain. At this stage much that is now done by on-the-job training would be done better institutionally. This means more schools for training technicians, practical engineers, junior agronomists, teachers, secretaries, book-keepers, public service clerks, police officers, and so on. Some of these schools will be run by employers (government, mining companies, etc.) for their employees only (e.g., police), while others will be open to students before making employment contracts. There is room for varied arrangements between government and employers as to who finances or manages these schools. The importance of having adequate facilities of this sort is underlined by the fact that the shortage of people suitable to be foremen and supervisors is one of the marked characteristics of under-developed countries.

The ease with which these sub-professional schools can recruit students depends on the alternative opportunities for schooling. In countries where general secondary education is under-developed, these schools cannot insist on full secondary education as a minimum standard of entry; they have to recruit some primary school leavers, and to adjust their curricula accordingly. They then tend to attract some very bright students, who use them only as a substitute for secondary education on their way to higher things. As the opportunities for general education improve, this situation reverses itself. These schools can then raise their entrance requirements, but have difficulty in competing with the university for good students. It is not uncommon for the university to be flooded with students of the humanities, law, and commerce while the technical schools have empty places, and industry is short of skills. The problem can be tackled in various ways; by raising the pay of technicians; by bringing the technical schools within the university system to give them prestige (an American solution which horrifies the British mind); by limiting the number of students accepted by overcrowded university faculties; or by offering more generous scholarships and bursaries to students in the technical schools than to those who go to the university.

The university. Universities can operate at four different levels: the junior college and technical training level, the liberal arts level, the highly specialized level, and the professional level. Where to site and how to mix these levels are problems which different countries tackle differently.

The British have so far kept the technical and junior college level out of the university (except for the teachers, who broke in after the second world war). The junior college work is added to the secondary schools, giving the 'sixth form' a character of its own. The technical colleges operate on their own. There is pressure in under-developed countries to put both the technical college and the sixth form into the university; partly because the university has usually the best administrative talent for supervising higher education; partly, in the case of the technical colleges, to give them prestige; and partly, in the case of the sixth forms, because it is thought to be easier and cheaper to centralize this work in a few centres than to try to add it separately to each secondary school. (Cost figures on this issue would be welcome.)

Putting all this work into the universities also has disadvantages. The university becomes enormous, and problems of administration, morale, discipline and self-government multiply. Then there is the fear of the effect on standards; if entry and exit standards are lowered to accommodate this work, a downward pull is exerted on all the rest of the university's work. Finally, the universities fear the effect on their costs. The staff required to teach the highly specialized and the professional courses are very expensive, both because they compete in a world-wide market, and also because they require expensive research facilities. They cost more than the people required for liberal arts courses, who in turn cost more than the people required to teach in junior college. It is difficult for a university to make appropriate distinctions between these different grades of teaching staff, especially if it is using public funds, and is required to operate in accordance with published salary scales. The wider the university system the greater the probability that it will pay too little at the top and too much at the bottom.

Despite these disadvantages, the pressure in under-developed countries to put all post-secondary education under university control will probably prove irresistible. Presumably the best administrative solution will then be to have under the university umbrella nearly autonomous administrations for the different levels, keeping programmes and teachers quite separate from each other.

Liberal arts. About half the students who will reach the level of a bachelor's degree will go into jobs which require only a general education; the other half will go into jobs which require a specialized or a professional education. United Kingdom higher education runs these three side by side, but United States education is pushing specialized and professional education into graduate schools, thereby lengthening the period for completion of specialized studies, and requiring a prior general education. The United Kingdom, on the contrary, demands some degree of specialization from all university students, even those who take a 'general' degree. Thus the one approach makes a general education the core of higher education, while the other approach locates the core in specialization. As we have already seen, the length of the course and the width of the educational net are the keys to this dispute. It is not *necessary* to stay in school until the age of 26 to become a good doctor or a good physicist, but if a country can afford to keep its professionals and specialists studying for that long, then it is *feasible* to require a great deal of general education for them. (The two systems differ more in general than in specialized content.) The width of the net determines the character of the general education. The greater the proportion of young people completing college, the wider will be the range of jobs for which a college degree will be the requirement, and therefore the more general the general education must be. Also, since the average intellectual quality must fall as the percentage entering college reaches double figures, it ceases to be feasible to demand of every student that he must 'reach the frontier of knowledge' in some subject. One may predict that United Kingdom university education will follow the United States pattern, while believing that the United Kingdom pattern of running general, specialized, and professional courses simultaneously is more appropriate for poor countries at this stage. However, having regard to the high cost of specialized and professional courses, these countries would probably do better at this stage to establish separate colleges for their 'liberal arts' or 'general' or 'pass' degrees, with cheaper staff, lower staff/student ratios, and longer teaching hours than apply in the colleges for 'honours', specialization, and professional courses.

The high cost of specialized and professional courses raises the question whether poor countries would not do better to send as many of their students abroad for these courses as proves feasible. Their own colleges could thus be confined to liberal arts and general degrees, which can be done relatively cheaply. The specialized and professional courses are expensive because the first-rate teachers needed for such work operate in an international market; their salaries, allowances and travel costs tend to raise the cost per student beyond the cost in developed countries. Moreover, if students can find places abroad, the tuition fees they pay are normally only a fraction of the cost; and there are plenty of scholarships and opportunities for working one's way through college. Against this, there are three points in favour of educating at home rather than abroad. First, a large proportion of those who go abroad do not return home; the economics of this point depends on whether cheapness is offset by numbers. Secondly, a country benefits from having a corps of highly specialized teachers living in its midst, studying its problems, and contributing to its public and cultural life. And thirdly, in some courses what the student learns abroad is not as relevant as what he might learn in his own university. This is particularly relevant to professional training.

The professions. African professions still model themselves on British curricula, but will sooner or later face the same problem as professions in other under-developed countries. From some points of view the training in the subjects of the profession should be more intense. The doctor or engineer in a rural district needs to know more than his counterpart in New York, where there are laboratories and specialists who can be consulted within minutes. At one end he needs the intellectual equipment of the specialist; at the other he also needs the expertness of the technician, since the juniors under him are not well trained, and need his guidance and training. This argues for more detailed knowledge of his profession. At the same time, he needs a broader background knowledge. He needs more knowledge of the disciplines which underpin his subject, for he will meet many unfamiliar problems which he must solve for himself by returning to first principles. He also needs more knowledge of society, since he moves in and out of different cultures, and is himself playing a role – that of the intellectual – which is novel in his society. This is the kind of situation where the educator's reaction is 'if only we had them for another year'.

The financial pressure, however, is in the reverse direction: to cut the length of the course and concentrate on the specialist skills, so that more professionals can be produced for the same money. When such a large countryside has to be covered, two half-trained professionals do more good than one fully trained professional.

The best remedy may be to adopt both solutions: reduce the proportion of fully trained professionals (say, doctors) and greatly multiply the number of technicians at the lower level (say, medical assistants). Simultaneously, upgrade the training of each; of the technician because he will be sent into the countryside on his own and therefore needs to know more; and of the professional because the technician will now take over much of his routine work, making the professional more a consultant and supervisor than a general practitioner. Thus the number of 'half-trained' people is greatly increased, but not at the cost of debasing the training of the professional, which is, on the contrary, stiffened. This difficult problem needs more informed discussion than it has received.[1]

Controlling the pyramid. We have been considering the 'ideal' shape of the pyramid. Even when the authorities know what shape they would like, they are still far from achieving it. The proportions in which students offer themselves are not the proportions which the authorities wish to adopt. At the primary level, developed countries may have to enforce attendance; the under-developed tend to be flooded by more boys than they can cope with, and far too few girls. The demand for general secondary education everywhere exceeds the capacity of public secondary schools; so very many children are in private schools some of which hardly deserve the name. Technical schools tend to have empty places. In the universities, law, economics and humanities are overcrowded, while science, engineering and agriculture do not have enough students.

Since money is a magnet, it is always possible to devise schemes for getting more students into parts of the system which are undermanned. Keeping them out of overcrowded parts is more difficult, for political reasons. Many fine secondary school systems and universities have been ruined in recent years, especially in Asia, because the government did not feel able to control the pyramid.

Success

The third aspect of a system's quality is how effectively it achieves its goals. Given the pyramid and the curriculum, how successful is the teaching?

Success depends partly on how tough the problem is, and partly on the resources devoted to it.

The problem is particularly tough when the culture of the school and the culture of the home are at odds with each other. In western Europe school and home have a common culture, except for children who are moving upward in social class. This is not so in under-developed countries. In such countries all educated people tend to be more scientific, secular, libertarian, and disposed towards change than are the members of the traditional establishment, and the thought patterns of the teachers will be different from those of the parents of most of the children. In Africa there is also a

[1] I have discussed this subject much more intensively in an article 'Education for scientific professions in the poor countries', *Daedalus*, Cambridge, Mass., spring 1962

difference of language even at the primary level. One reason for the prevalence of learning by rote in such countries is the child's difficulty in grasping the full meaning of texts written by members of a different culture in a different language.

The problem is also tough when the students are not well chosen. A university which takes all comers cannot reach the same standard of excellence as a university which selects its students carefully. Hence quality of performance depends on the students being selected appropriately at all levels, and matched with appropriate curricula.

Given the task, success depends on resources. The ideal in education is to tailor the teaching to the capacities and interests of the individual child; to let the genius and the slow proceed each at his own pace; to offer a wide choice of subjects; to make special (though not necessarily separate) provision for the deaf, the blind, and those handicapped in other ways. The ideal is unattainable, if only because it is too expensive. How far one gets will depend on how much is made available.

It will depend on the quality of the teachers and how much education they have themselves received; this will be governed largely by what salaries they are offered. It will depend on the number of teachers, which determines the staff/student ratio, and therefore how much attention each child receives; on the quantity and quality of the physical resources: buildings, laboratories, libraries, workshops, playing fields, musical instruments, and so on. And much also depends on whether the children live at home or at school. This is not just a question of separating the child from the home environment in order to put the school's stamp on him. It may also make a difference to the amount of studying the child can do after school hours, if home conditions (lack of light, space, quiet, or co-operation) do not favour study. And in sparsely populated rural areas availability of dormitories may determine the size of the school, and therefore the variety of its curriculum.

Efficient use of these resources is tested in various ways. Some students indicate their dissatisfaction by dropping out of their courses. The educational testers devise examinations for the student to take. The administrator looks for waste, and must also consider the best allocation of funds as between different factors of production. Finally, there is the social test, which evaluates the competition between quantity and quality.

The drop-out test may not indicate the student's dissatisfaction; he may drop out for financial or family reasons. Even if he drops out for educational reasons, the teacher may welcome his departure and may even have been responsible (by failing him) for bringing it about. Some drop-out rate is necessary for the health of an educational system, just as a bankruptcy rate is necessary for the health of an economic system; it indicates that a misallocation of resources is being terminated. Many state institutions are not allowed to select their students properly, and defend their standards by having a high drop-out rate. Use of the term 'wastage' in this connexion is misleading. If the educational system is planned for some students to leave after six years, some after nine years, some after twelve years and so on, and all students act according to plan, we get a step pyramid; if instead some of the students leave at the end of each year we get a regular pyramid. A step pyramid is not necessarily better than a regular pyramid. It may be desirable to design the system to take in everybody at the bottom, to keep only one per cent at the top, and to have a hyperbolic decline. To give every child two years of primary education is not necessarily bad in comparison with giving 50 per cent of children four years of primary education. This is the kind of problem to which the market gives an answer, since we can compare the average earnings of people according to number of years of education. If the authorities decide that they want a wide base and narrow top, the system should be planned in a series of short self-contained steps, so that students do not disappear halfway through a long programme (thus it is better to have some two-year junior colleges than to have a high drop-out from a four-year college course).

If the ideal is to tailor the course to each child, standard examinations do not exactly measure success. Many teachers resist having their students take tests set by outside bodies. Nevertheless, the case for outside examinations, to test effective use of public funds, is overwhelming. Countries which do not have country-wide examinations tend to have many very poor schools.

The administrator's task, to root out waste, is more difficult than the examiner's. The core of his work is comparative costing, which reveals how each school differs from its fellows in expenditure under each category. However, differences merely suggest that one should seek special circumstances; they do not necessarily prove either waste or economy. Choosing the proper combination of resources is not easy. Given an increase in the budget for a particular school, with number of children constant, is it better to spend on hiring better teachers, on improving the building, on buying more equipment, or in building a dormitory for some of the students? The answer will vary from school to school. Teachers are not much help in solving this problem; they ask for more of everything, starting with salary increases. One sees so many obvious mistakes when travelling from place to place that it seems doubtful whether administrators have as yet devised for themselves a system for evaluating marginal adjustments in factor proportions.

Finally comes the choice between quantity and quality. How important is quality? One can keep down the cost of secondary education by many means; having a high ratio of non-graduate teachers for the lower forms; keeping down the range of subjects; having smaller schools and cutting out dormitories; and so on. Learning is to a considerable extent a function of time; is it better to give more students an opportunity to spend more time in school at a reduced cost per student year? Do the larger numbers made possible by multiple teaching systems (monitors, programmed learning, television) more than compensate for what is lost through reducing the teacher/student ratio?

Every educational system meets the situation by having some institutions which operate at very high levels of quality, along with others at lower levels. Even the poorest country needs some high-level institutions, partly because some jobs demand the highest level of training, and partly because the maintenance of standards in the educational system itself demands the presence of some institutions which reach high levels. So there is a 'pyramid' of quality as well as of quantity. To some extent, this is even institutionalized. If there is pressure to have more doctors, one keeps the medical standard, but invents a new lower category of medical assistants. If students press at the door of the university, one establishes junior colleges. If the demand for secondary places threatens the secondary schools, one invents the 'modern secondary school'. This is a good solution, but it is not final. However many levels one may create, at each level there will be better and worse, and the choice will pose itself. Is it better to have a large number of poor institutions, whose standards one hopes eventually to raise, or to concentrate resources on a smaller number of students in fewer schools of higher quality? Or rather, since it is inconceivable that we need to have all institutions at the same standard of excellence, what is the appropriate shape of the pyramid of quality?

As we have seen, the free market gives answers to this sort of question, since it prices students taught in different schools. If one can agree on tests of quality, one can compare the average earnings of students of similar average intelligence quotient and social class, taught in different schools and going into similar occupations. Such tests could be (either separately or in some weighted combination): average performance of the school at examinations, qualifications of teachers, staff/student ratio, quantity of buildings and equipment, or any other kind of school rating which educational testers may devise. If the differences in prices corresponded exactly to the differences in costs, we would conclude (with the usual assumptions) that the pyramid was right. This kind of statistical exercise is always open to debate, but is nevertheless suggestive.

The market's answer is important but not final, since we value quality in education and its opposite – the opportunity given to large numbers – more than the difference which either makes to productivity. Ultimately this kind of argument has always to be settled at the political level.

Conclusion

From the economist's point of view, it is not difficult to define what one seeks in a school system – the right combinations of general and specialized education, of numbers at different age levels, and of different proportions of competence. Neither is there conceptual difficulty in defining what is right by comparing costs with the market values of different combinations. Data are scarce, but could be collected, and despite the imperfections of the price mechanism could be given some meaning. The biggest obstacle is that even the economist does not believe that market prices are the appropriate values to use. We cannot therefore avoid handing the problem over to those philosophers who deal in more fundamental values.

Summary

1. Quality can be subdivided into breadth, pyramid, and success. Each of these can be measured, costed, and priced in the market. But the market price is not decisive: (a) because education is meant to change society and not merely to adapt it, (b) because market price does not reflect the true scarcity of resources, and (c) because there are other values in education with which the market is not concerned.
2. It is in the social interest, and the interest of the child, to keep education general rather than vocational for as long as is practicable, but this is subject to: (a) how long a period of schooling the community can afford; the longer the schooling, the more general the curriculum, (b) the dividing line between on-the-job training and formal schooling in vocational skills, and (c) the width of the educational net; the wider the net, the greater the proportion of students in vocational programmes.
3. One can calculate how many students are required at different educational levels. Overproduction at the top probably helps to increase productivity. But in the interest of equity, and of searching for talent, it is probably better to universalize education at the bottom before beginning to overproduce at the top.
4. Even the poorest society should pass 50 per cent of its children through primary schools. Progress from 50 towards 100 per cent should be phased with the reconstruction of agriculture.
5. Currently in Africa it would be better to improve the quality of middle schools than to increase their student numbers.
6. Post-secondary vocational training is grossly under-developed. It is necessary to raise the prestige of the institutions which offer such training,

and to offer generous scholarships, so that they may compete with the universities for students. Whether to include such work under the university umbrella is largely a practical question.

7. In the interest of keeping down costs, liberal arts training should be kept separate from more specialized and professional training. How much of the latter to do at home, rather than abroad, is a matter for calculation. Poor countries cannot afford to require that a liberal arts training be taken before proceeding to specialized or professional study.
8. Professional courses need adaptation to local circumstances. The ratio of professionals to assistants should be smaller than in developed countries, but this requires that the training of both be upgraded.
9. Given the curriculum, the success of the educational system depends partly on the extent to which school and home share a common culture, partly on care in the choice of students, and partly on the quantity of resources (teachers, equipment, buildings, hostels) available per student.
10. Educational experts test the efficient use of resources by testing the students in various types of examination. Educational administrators compare the amount of resources used by different schools to get the same results, and check the effect of substituting one factor of production for another at the same total cost.
11. A high drop-out rate is not necessarily a sign of inefficiency; but if the authorities want a pyramid of this shape, they should plan the curriculum in short steps.
12. There is a pyramid of quality, just as of quantity. Any system has a few first-class institutions and many of lower quality. The question whether to increase the number or improve the quality of the lesser institutions can be answered by the market, since one can calculate whether the earnings of graduates from different institutions correspond to differences in the cost of teaching. However, the market's answer is not decisive.

[24]

The University in Less Developed Countries

W. Arthur Lewis

I am both flattered and puzzled by your invitation to introduce your discussion of this topic, and have approached the task with no little apprehension. My experience of universities in less developed countries is brief and episodic. I am not a philosopher of this subject, or a regular student of its literature, to which in any case I have not had access while preparing in Barbados for this ordeal. I see my role therefore as not much more than that of the pampered dignitary whom the professional teams invite to start their play, with the privilege of throwing the first ball.

Let me start by telling you how I have divided the subject, so that as from time to time you are awakened from your reveries you may recognize how far I have gone, and estimate how much more is to come. "Divided the subject" is too pompous a phrase, since it implies that I have tried to be comprehensive. The subject cannot be exhausted in a brief introduction, or by an amateur speaker. More precisely let me give you the four headings under which have been marshalled the various topics which will pop up as I try to assess the special problems of the university in a less developed country (LDC).

These headings are:

The University as the Bearer of the Culture.
The University as the Trainer of Skills.
The University on the Frontiers of Knowledge.
The University as a Service Agency.

The University as the Bearer of the Culture

The relative stress on the role of the university as the bearer of the culture and its role as the trainer of skills is not everywhere the same. In a country where only one percent of the age cohort goes to university, the stress is on training for the jobs which are waiting for them. But in the United States with 40 percent admission, most of the graduates will go into jobs requiring no special training of university type. They are going to sell insurance, or be executives in television studios, or sit in government offices. Hence comes the American emphasis on higher education as first and foremost the transmitter of the culture; the maker of the intelligent citizen, the good American, or as we used to say in the nineteenth century, the cultured gentleman.

The American literature on this subject is large but is not helpful to us. The British, it used to be said, designed their public schools and universities in the nineteenth century in the belief that they were the inheritors of Periclean Athens; their role was to make the cultured gentleman, knowing something about every aspect of human knowledge, well-mannered, and an active participant in public discussion. This inheritance has now passed to the American educators, who are forthright in articulating it.

The situation in less developed countries is complicated. For there are senses in which the university, far from transmitting the culture, is rather part of the forces that are eroding traditional society. Much that the traditionalists weep over, and think so special to their own geography, is really no more than the universal culture of poverty, which could not possibly survive development. But the university is one of the destructive agents so, despite the small ratio of the cohort which it gets, it has inescapably to define its creative cultural role, and to make its contribution to the evolving patterns.

Let us treat separately two different aspects of "culture," namely social relations and aesthetics.

Traditional social systems are breaking down fast in LDCs. Extended kinship is giving way to the nuclear family. Religion is losing its authority. Tribal, princely and other political allegiances have been overthrown. The youngster has to find a new code defining his rights and obligations and modes of behavior in relation to other categories of persons. He needs a new code of social ethics.

The students who pass through our hands are particularly bereft of signals because they are joining a new class, which has not previously existed in LDCs, and for which no traditional code exists within their own cultures. They are creating a new middle class of professionals, managers, scientists, artists and so on. When this class emerged in Western Europe, slowly from the fifteenth century onwards, it inherited the code of the medieval guilds: pride in the craft, honest workmanship, honest dealings with the client, the goal of "zero defect." This same code exists in all countries which have a tradition of fine handicrafts, especially in Asia, where sometimes the handicraft workers have been as much as 15 percent of the labor force. Latin America and Africa also have their handicraftsmen but, except in Sudanese West Africa, these are a small part of the labor force. The new middle class has therefore to grow into an ethical code which is not a part of its tradition. It is the old ethical code common to all those religions and philosophies which are social-oriented, rather than spirit-oriented; but it has to be articulated in new circumstances.

LDC universities have done this part of their job poorly, mainly because we have not recognized its urgency, and have not set up our programs to deal with it. Our graduates, however much admired for their technical proficiency, tend to be scorned in their own countries for their lack of social conscience, their desire to get rich quick, and their lack of responsibility in dealing with their clients. Some of this scorn derives from expecting too much from ordinary human material; but there is a hard core of truth in the complaint.

Our governments are much concerned with this, and are adducing their own remedies. The current favorite is to impose some form of national service on all university graduates. Some think, like the Chinese, that it should be done before university entrance, and that it must be manual work, with preference for farming. This is hard on those disciplines, like music or mathematics, where an interruption of intellectual excitement may hamper intellectual growth. Other governments prefer service after graduation and may be content that the graduate then practice his profession, whatever it may be. Some form of national service may indeed be the only way of getting teachers and professionals to work in the isolation of rural areas. Whether it also achieves the objective of giving the graduate a greater social conscience, I do not know.

The traditional approach of the university to its role in developing the social conscience is to emphasize the value of teaching the humanities and the social sciences to all students, because these are the subjects where the great problems of man's relationship to man have been intensively debated over three thousand years. The Americans, recognizing that most of their 40 percent do not have a middle class or professional family background, make these subjects compulsory for all their students. I shall therefore leave this topic by crystallizing it in the following questions: should an LDC university require all its undergraduates to take some courses in the humanities and social sciences? How would this indoctrination, which normally emphasizes the democratic values and independence of mind, fit into the political framework which LDCs seem to be adopting? And is it really possible to teach to 20 year olds in college basic ethics which they should have learned in secondary school at 15 or at home at 12?

Arts and the University

Now turn to aesthetics, where the solutions are a little easier. Universities have not prescribed music or literature or painting or other arts as compulsory subjects of study. But good universities have always promoted those activities, and tried to make them part of the students' environment; whether by maintaining concert halls and performances, theaters, art galleries and the like on the ordinary budget of the university or also by subsidizing the students' own societies for the enjoyment of the arts.

Unfortunately our universities tend to be particularly barren in these respects. This is mainly because the arts are the special interest of the middle and upper classes, and most of our students do not have such backgrounds. By contrast, today there are relatively few working-class students in the English universities. English students arrive from homes where they have been introduced to the arts at an early age, and from secondary schools which have made some effort in these directions. Most LDC students on the other hand come from homes which do not have a book, and the parents of a large proportion are illiterate. However, we know what our universities have to do; our chief problem is how to persuade our Senates and Councils to allocate more money for aesthetic activities, at the expense of departmental budgets.

LDCs have, however, a problem which most developed countries escape, namely, disagreement as to what culture is to be transmitted. Western universities at home have no doubt that their task is to promote Western music, Western painting, Western literature, and so on. As the Western university spread into India, 115 years ago, it also assumed that it should promote Western culture in India, although India has its own superb traditions of music, painting, sculpture, architecture and so on. A similar assumption in other continents has produced a violent reaction, and now everywhere LDCs emphasize the desirability of teaching and developing their own artistic traditions.

This is easier in some places than in others. My own West Indies, for instance, has no aesthetic traditions of its own, the original inhabitants, the Arawaks, having died out 300 years ago. We have, of course, since then developed a popular music of our own, but when it comes to classical styles, whether in dancing, music, painting or theater, our aesthetic background includes large elements from Western Europe and India, with trace elements from China and various parts of Africa. Our most aggressive spokesmen demand that we should reject everything except what comes from Africa, and students have, for example, gone so far as to disrupt a performance of Mozart on our university campus, claiming that "Mozart is not a part of our culture." What line is the university to take in such circumstances?

My own prejudice is simple: I think that the whole human achievement, whatever its geography, is part of the heritage of each one of us, wherever he may be, and that the "cultured gentleman" who neglects the opportunity of benefiting from all nationalities of aesthetic experience is the poorer for doing so. However, I do not want to answer questions about the directions in which each country should develop its arts, beyond suggesting that variety is the spice of life. I want only to emphasize that the university which does not devote substantial sums to these purposes is neglecting one of its more important obligations.

Dilemmas of Plural Societies

Now, when one is talking about culture, whether aesthetics or social relations, LDCs have an additional complication; namely the fact that, especially in Africa and Asia, our countries are not homogeneous, but are deeply divided by race, religion, language, or tribe. Our political scientists used to think that the basic political division in all societies is between the haves and the have-nots. Bitter experience has shown that in our countries, as seen by our own politicians, this "vertical" division has trivial political significance when compared with the "horizontal" rifts.

(It is true that even in European societies some demand is made to preserve and dignify a separate working-class culture, or various regional, folk, or immigrant cultures; but most Anglo-American universities do not take this seriously; even separate dormitories for women are disappearing, let alone the cultivation of "feminine interests.")

In nineteenth century England, the University of London led the way in creating the tradition that the horizontal differences do not matter within the university walls, and in this was ultimately followed by Oxford and Cambridge and the others. This is a recent and insecure tradition, which has not easily taken root in LDCs. Instead, our universities are subjected to one of two pressures. The first is to have separate universities for different racial, tribal, or religious groups. Our university spokesmen have always resisted this, asserting that the communities will quarrel less if their young people are educated together. But even when this point is conceded, we are faced with the tendency of the students to segregate themselves within the university, just as black students in the United States, having clamored for admission into white universities, are now demanding separate curricula, teachers, halls of residence, and recreation facilities.

The other pressure on us, where there is only one university, is to impose quotas, for each race or what you will. This we have resisted even more vigorously, on the ground that it is wrong to exclude a well-qualified applicant of race A in order to admit a less-qualified applicant of race

B; our attitude is rather that there should be enough places for all who qualify. This is not, however, so simple, even leaving aside the fact that one may not be able to afford enough places for all who qualify. It is simple enough if all the students have equal opportunities to prepare for admission; then quotas are needed only where it is necessary to combat prejudice, such as that against admitting women to medical schools, or tribal favoritism of various kinds. But it is also a fact that our basic principle—that the prizes should go to those who win in competitive tests—is not always applicable in plural societies. One's ability to pass the competitive tests depends not only on innate intelligence, but also on family and social background. If the appropriate background is already monopolized by members of another group, the competitive test serves only to solidify an existing social structure, in which racial etc. inequality is embedded. One cannot break this vicious circle except by insisting on quotas reserved to the underprivileged.

I have said that it is part of our tradition to resist pressures for separate treatment, but where these matters are felt keenly, we are not likely to succeed.

One's attitude toward these matters depends on what one thinks to be the future of plural societies. Pessimists, reading largely from history, assert that they have no future. Sooner or later one group will become dominant economically and politically, and will suppress the religion, language, and culture of all the others, thus enforcing homogeneity within the borders of the nation-state. Others think that the bitterness of these divisions is a passing historical phase, and that just as Protestants and Catholics have learned to tolerate each other in most of Europe (except the Netherlands, Belgium and the United Kingdom of Great Britain and Northern Ireland) so also in due course men will wonder that their ancestors used to fight each other over questions of language or skin color. If you hold to this latter view, however great the pressures, you will keep your university as open as you can, and will make every effort to cooperate closely with other universities of different complexion.

Personally I incline to the view that this is a passing historical phase, for two reasons. First, the spread of a universal youth culture. For example, Japan used to be held up as an example of a country which had absorbed Western science and technology without affecting the rest of its traditions. But Japan is now rapidly Westernizing itself; its rich are buying up and grossly inflating the prices of French wine (to my great disgust) and European painting and sculpture and other treasures; and its young are modelling themselves upon the young people of California, whose dress, drugs, music, dances, religions and attitudes toward parents and teachers now set the fashion for young people throughout the rest of the world. If the young of all tribes make themselves a common culture, then all other cultures will die out.

Even more important is an element which derives from what the universities themselves are doing. The graduates we all turn out are of a single pattern, quite different from that of their parents; more logical, scientific, open-minded, with fewer allegiances and a different set of superstitions; essentially, all children of the French Enlightenment. Our product is managing the world, whether in the public or the private sectors. A Russian physicist, an American physicist, an Indian or a Nigerian physicist, have more in common with each other, whether in outlook or in life style, than any of these has with a bus conductor from his own country. The university is educating a middle class which is homogeneous throughout the world, and which, within any country, must ultimately scoff at the barriers which are now so divisive. Is this not why our various brands of separatists are so vociferous in denouncing "middle class values"? I may be wrong; there is no lack of highly educated racists. But if I am right, then nothing is more important than for us to keep our

13

universities as free from sectional division as our political bosses will permit.

The University as the Trainer of Skills

One has to begin by recognizing the revolt in some student quarters against the university as a place for "training fodder for capitalist employers." This is largely an American phenomenon. When 40 percent of the age cohort is in college, it is inevitable that what most of them do there will have little bearing on the jobs they ultimately get. Hence the university is not for them a place for training. It is a place for spending four years as enjoyably as one can; choosing only such subjects as interest one, and abandoning them as soon as one reaches into fundamental theories or models which demand too much intellectual exercise; skipping exams, or at least examination grades. The college is seen as a young people's Eden, which they may regulate as they please, without interference from adults, whose only duty is to pay the bills. The advantage to the adults is that the young are shut away in institutions while they grow up, especially as their preference for inelegance offends our sense that form ranks equally with substance. It is also thought (but incorrectly) that to keep them off the labor market reduces unemployment. I need hardly add that the number of serious American students is greater than it ever was; all that has happened is that the non-serious have multiplied even faster, and have become shamelessly strident.

Echoes of this disturbance are heard in our LDC universities, since, as I have remarked, everything that starts in California ultimately comes to all of us. It has some relevance to overpopulated LDC universities, such as those of India, where the struggle between the students and their universities has already had such devastating effects on higher education. But in Africa and the Caribbean, where the demand for trained graduates still exceeds the supply, hardly any serious person doubts that one of the principal functions of the university is to train the middle class for the jobs it has to do. This attitude is fortified by the fact that the cost per student is such a large multiple of national income per head; though this would not matter so much if students were paying the cost of their education out of loans, as they should be, since one could then provide all the places for which there was demand.

Now come to the perennial question of which skills are fit to be taught in a university and which are not. The traditional answer is that the university skills are only those which have a major intellectual content.

In practice, however, our universities are asked to teach (or to supervise other schools which teach) many skills which do not pass this traditional test, for two reasons.

The first is administrative capacity. LDCs are short of administrative talent; we have reached a stage of modernization where we have learned the tricks of managing things and ideas (science, power stations, open heart surgery, pianos) but not the tricks of managing people. So when you get a university with a good Vice-Chancellor, a good Registrar and a good Bursar, you ask them to take responsibility for as much postsecondary education as they will swallow (medical technologists, agricultural assistants, primary school teachers, technical institutes, etc.). This makes sense if the university does indeed have a first-class administration; but when it has not (as is more often the case in LDCs) it is easily overburdened.

The second reason for trying to bring as much postsecondary education as possible under the wing of the university is to give this kind of training social status and intellectual prestige. Any ambitious student who gets good O' Levels wants to take a university degree. Also people with degrees get higher salaries than people without. Hence all the non-university institutions are starved of good talent, and in many LDCs the crucial shortage is not of university graduates but of intermediate personnel. In a free market the salaries of technicians would rise relatively to those of skill-less and mediocre graduates in Arts, but since the government, which is the principal buyer, bases relative salaries on tradition rather than on scarcity, the market situation cannot right itself.

Faced with these problems I have never been able to get hot under the collar about what is properly or not properly a university subject. I am even willing to accept mortuary science, which you can study in such highly respectable American institutions as the University of Minnesota, Wayne State University and Temple University. Each community should settle such issues in accordance with its circumstances.

A much more serious problem is that of the number to be trained. This depends first on the structure of the economy. The biggest user of graduates is the services sector, followed by industry and mining, and lastly by agriculture. Since services employ more than 50 percent of the labor force in the USA, and agriculture only about 5 percent, the demand for graduates is enormous, and anything less than 20 percent of the age cohort would produce a serious shortage. Whereas in LDCs, where agriculture employs half the labor force or more, even 1 or 2 percent of the cohort can produce a glut of graduates.

Apart from structure, the economy's capacity to absorb graduates depends also on their salaries, relative to per capita national income. This ratio is very much higher than in developed countries, making the cost of services too high for the economy to afford as much as it needs. As educated numbers increase, the ratio falls and absorptive capacity automatically increases, so the way to create demand is to flood the market; but this is a painful and politically dangerous process.

Most LDC universities admit too many undergraduates, and then have high dropout rates (not to speak of those which have too many students, but are prevented by their governments from failing more than x percent). This relates to the desirability of giving other postsecondary schools a higher status, and deflecting more students there. Another issue is the desirability of establishing community colleges of a comprehensive kind, offering 2- or 3-year courses from O' Level in both technical and academic subjects, so that only the tested move on into the university. This would mean that the university could raise its admission level, and take fewer students.

Universities try to insist on determining for themselves what their entrance level should be, but this position is hardly tenable. The university has to relate to other educational institutions. For example, rural secondary schools have difficulty in attracting and holding the kind of teachers required for sixth forms, so if, in the absence of community colleges, the university insists on entrance only at A' Level, it is discriminating against half the secondary school population. On these matters university senates tend to be reactionary; so inevitably the government, which pays the bill, will want to have a say in determining university entrance levels. And this in turn will react on the demand for student places.

Besides the total number of students, there is the question of the relative numbers in different subjects. Usually there are not enough in mathematics or the scientific professions, while there are too many in social sciences (especially the "soft" social sciences) and in law. Humanities also tend to be starved, relative to the need for secondary school teachers.

Here again the government may be expected to take a hand, by fixing maximum quotas for social science and for law. It is true that the basic solutions are rather to teach more and better science and mathematics in the secondary schools, and also for the government in its own salary structures to pay more for graduates in the subjects which are in short supply. A quota probably does not help much in deflecting students toward the highly scientific subjects, but at least it cuts down on the cost of producing a lot of low grade social "scientists" and may also push some students toward the more practical kinds of training which they now avoid.

Universities claim autonomy in determining what subjects they will teach, but they seldom deserve it. Senates are reactionary, and are slow to admit new subjects even of a highly scientific nature. LDC governments are everywhere involved in deciding what subjects shall be taught, at their expense, and this is inevitable.

(I have not asked whether our professionals are too highly trained; the answer is that we need all sorts.)

The University on the Frontiers of Knowledge

To advance the frontiers of knowledge is rather a recent function of universities; knowledge used to be advanced rather by gentlemen scholars outside the universities. Nowadays, though, all the best universities claim that the advancement of knowledge is their pride and joy. From this it follows that they must hire only staff with first-class creative minds, use them in teaching only for 8 to 10 hours a week, enforce "publish or perish." However, the number of first-class creative minds is small; they get better job satisfaction working in the well-equipped laboratories and libraries of U.S. institutions (not to speak of better pay); and frequently don't much care for teaching undergraduates. So many of our LDC universities, clinging to the research ideal and its corollaries, get the worst of both worlds; they have to pay salaries competitive with Oxford and Cambridge, and to limit teaching hours, without getting much creativity for the money.

This is a British trap; the United States is not caught in it. The United States has 1,500 degree-granting institutions, of which less than a hundred expect to advance the frontiers of knowledge. The rest hire teachers at lower salaries and work them 20 to 25 hours a week. The 100 or so are supplemented by a great many research institutions, public and private, which have no students, or have only graduate students. India is travelling the same way. The money now goes increasingly into wholly postgraduate institutions, like the new Jahawarlal Nehru University, or into research institutes which have no teaching function.

At the University of the West Indies, I became convinced that we had started on the wrong track in adopting the English pattern. We would have done better to have had two separate institutions; one offering undergraduate degrees, and the other concentrating on graduate and professional studies. They would have had two entirely different staffs, with different pay, different teaching loads, and different objectives. The cost per undergraduate place in our university is much too high in relation to per capita national income, and would be smaller if we had started from more appropriate staff/student ratios and from salary scales more closely akin to those of civil servants.

The current situation in most of our countries is not tenable. Our governments are beginning to see through the pretense that we are advancing the frontiers of knowledge (some staff do, of course, but not enough of them for the money), and the unruly behavior of our undergraduate students has not increased our popularity with the public. I expect a shift of government emphasis away from university research toward the establishment of separate research institutes; these latter, I would hope, would have provision for graduate students, since I agree that the skepticism of the good student spurs the teacher toward a clearer understanding of his own thesis.

I am not arguing that universities should not do research, or that research institutes should not be under the sponsorship of universities. My sole point is that as the number of students increases, we should restrict the number of research-dominated universities and increase the proportion of essentially teaching institutions, on the American rather than the British pattern, which is simply too expensive for us.

The University as a Service Agency

When once a university has started in a new community, its collection of relatively high-powered people can make an enormous contribution outside their walls, and are normally expected to do so. They create scientific societies embracing practicing professionals; they serve on public committees; accept offices of various kinds; and serve as consultants to the private sector as well as to governments. More formally, the university organizes extramural teaching, and perhaps school examinations. It sponsors concerts, lectures, exhibitions and sporting spectacles, which it opens to the public. Well-endowed private universities in the United States are now expected to spend on improving their neighborhoods, even to the point of slum clearance; but universities on the public payroll escape this imposition.

Performance of functions for the whole community, financed from the public treasury, involves some element of political neutrality. It is inappropriate for your one and only heart surgeon to be a prominent member of some political party, since members of other parties may fear that his knife may inadvertently slip when he performs for them. It is equally inappropriate for your one and only professor of economics, whose salary is paid by all, so to conduct himself that he has only the confidence of and is consulted only by the Chamber of Commerce, or the trade unions, or the government or the opposition. Such conduct does not matter in a developed country where professors are two a penny and available in every hue. But in our countries with one university only, or only one per province, the political professor fails in his duty as a public servant.

Some of our professors have gone to the limit of the obnoxious. We have professors who are leaders of political parties (even the official leader of the opposition in Parliament) and who publish political tracts which are way below normal intellectual standards. Some see their salaries and their eight-hour week merely as a means of financial support for their political activities, doing no research to justify their pay. Some LDC universities are sanctuaries for subversive movements pledged to overthrow society by violence. All of this is defended in the name of academic freedom.

Of course our governments retaliate. If public funds are going to be used to support political activity, they wish to choose the politicians. So the right of the university to choose its own teachers is challenged, and the government seeks a hand. Actually this right, which Anglo-American universities see as fundamental to their autonomy, is by no means universal; it is quite common for those who put up the money, whether it be the state or the church or the private benefactor, to insist on the right to veto teaching appointments. In France, university teachers are appointed by the Minister. Universities on the public payroll may be permitted to exercise autonomy of appointment if they keep out of politics; if they become havens for political activity they must not be surprised if the politicians take over the appointment of their staffs.

This is not a simple matter. I would like to see our professors practice both less party politics and also more participation in political life.

As for the first half, I think that in an LDC with only one university per province, professors in publicly financed universities should not identify themselves with political parties, and should even try to make it clear that their advice is available to clients of all religions, languages, or tribes. I recognize that this is a limitation on academic freedom, as traditionally understood in British and American private universities. Academic freedom, however, has two parts. The more important part, which I fully accept, is the right, or rather the duty, of the academic to publish the considered results of research, study, or reflection without regard to their effect on existing interests or opinions. On this we cannot compromise without embedding hypocrisy at our core. The lesser part of academic freedom, which I would limit in the before-mentioned circumstances, is the right to participate in party politics. This limitation would put professors into the same category as civil servants, which is what they essentially are in these circumstances. Academic freedom in this latter sense is of recent vintage and narrow geographical extent.

At the same time I should like to see professors participating more freely in debates on public issues than they now do in most of the third world. Good government depends on the existence of a well-informed and articulate public opinion; and the teachers in the university, with their free time for study and research, are better placed than almost any other group to raise the level of public discussion by communicating information and criticism, from a nonpolitical party standpoint. We do not get as much of this in LDCs as we need, because most of our politicians do not want an independent public opinion; their motto is that "he who is not with me is against me." Universities should insist on this right (nay, duty) of free comment, but will win and hold it only insofar as they scrupulously steer clear of party entanglements.

I should emphasize that my image of the LDC professor as voluntarily non-partisan, yet active in public affairs, applies only to countries which are trying to maintain a democratic framework, including political opposition. The professor is not needed in party politics when there are plenty of other people for that role. My prescription could not work in a society where opposition is suppressed. In such a society some professors who feel very strongly about government wrongdoing will inevitably become involved in organized anti-government activity, as will some of their students. The freedom and neutrality of a university can be maintained only in societies with a democratic atmosphere; in oppressive societies the freedom of the university almost always disappears in conflict between its members and the government. The essence of my point is that even in democratic developing societies, the freedom of the government-financed university depends on its trying to maintain political neutrality.

Coda

So far I have spoken only of the obligations of the university to society, as you asked me to do, and not about the obligations of society to the university. Let me just sketch three aspects of this side.

First, recognizing as we do the right of the government to infringe on university autonomy in so many ways, we are entitled to demand that what it does be done with due care, after proper consultation and advice. The government will nominate to many committees and institutions affecting the university: its Council; some form of University Grants Committee; Appointments committees; the Scientific Research Council, and others. Let its nominees be men of substance, accustomed to disciplined thought and behavior. Several confrontations have occurred not between the university and the government, but within the university itself, between the academic Senate and the government appointees to the Council.

Second, the university is entitled to financial support adequate for agreed programs. The university is not entitled to determine by itself either the program or its cost. But once the appropriate machinery has agreed on these matters, its decisions should be carried out. This has to be said because, alas, some of us have to deal with governments which agree and promise, but do not eventually pay up.

Third, we need the support of government and society in our efforts to lead students along disciplined paths. The students of these days are confused as to why they are in the university; where supply exceeds demand they are terribly frustrated, and worried about jobs; also they live in an era where respect for law, authority, and non-violent persuasion is no longer fashionable. So they do things which horrify their elders—from burning down the property to preventing freedom of speech. University authorities cannot cope unless their attempts to enforce discipline are supported by the government and other responsible opinion, including that of the great majority of the student body itself. If not, a minority of students reduces the university to a shambles, as has already happened in many parts of the world.

The university cannot fulfill its obligations to a society which does not, in its turn, fulfill its obligations to the university. But to explore this further would outrun my mandate.

PART FIVE

OTHER DEVELOPMENT ISSUES

[25]

Journal of Agricultural Economics. 3

THOUGHTS ON LAND SETTLEMENT.

By W. ARTHUR LEWIS.

These thoughts are occasioned by my wanderings around the under-developed countries of the world, either in person, or through the medium of books and reports. In practically all these countries land settlement is a major activity. Their populations are growing rapidly, and they are having to bring large new areas of land into cultivation—perhaps I should speak of " colonisation " rather than " land settlement," though in some countries the breaking up of estates for the settlement of small farmers is also occurring, and the problems are in any case much the same. There is great enthusiasm for this work, and much money and effort are going into clearing forests, or controlling river systems, or other preliminaries of settlement. But there is also everywhere some disillusionment. The expense is very heavy; or it proves unexpectedly difficult to get settlers for the land; or if settlers are found, to prevent them from abandoning their settlements within two or three years; or, if they stay, to prevent them from ruining the fertility of the soil. It is the universality of these problems which causes me to ask whether enough experience of land settlement has accumulated, in the various countries of the world to enable us now to lay down a set of rules for the success of land settlement. I have visited areas of recent settlement in the West Indies, in Nigeria, and in Malaya, for the purpose of investigating these problems in the field, and I have also read a great deal about experience in some other parts of Africa and of Asia, but I claim no real expertise, and am hoping rather to stimulate you to give of your experience by opening this discussion tonight.

It seems that success depends on the following factors: (a) choosing the right place; (b) choosing the right settlers; (c) physical preparation of the site before the settlers arrive; (d) settlers' capital; (e) the organisation of group activities; (f) the acreage per settler; and (g) the conditions of tenure. I propose to go systematically through each of these factors, but I shall dwell lengthily only upon those which seem to me to raise the more difficult questions.

(*a*) *The Place.* It is pretty obvious that settlement must fail if the place chosen is unsuitable, whether because of poor soil, or uncertain rainfall, or its unhealthiness, or for other such reason. This, though obvious enough, has not always been taken into account, and many elaborate plans have been frustrated for no better reason. The place must also be reasonably accessible, so that settlers can hope to get their produce out cheaply. Such things are easily said. The trouble with most land settlement is that the best lands are already settled, so that land settlement officers are almost by definition working with areas which the people have rejected for centuries, because of the difficulty of making a reasonable living there. Sometimes the area can be transformed: you can suddenly wipe out the malaria from the dry zone of Ceylon, or you can irrigate what was previously uncultivable for lack or uncertainty of water. But you cannot always make these transformations, and if population is doubling every forty years, as it is in many places, people just have to move on to lands which were formerly sub-marginal. One cannot therefore say, settle only good lands; all one can say is do not settle lands which are on the face of the matter not suitable for settlement.

I have been impressed, particularly in West Africa, with the large areas of land between the forest belt and the desert, which are now sparsely settled, which will have to be fully occupied one day, and in which contemporary efforts at settlement are frustrated more by our not knowing what to do with such lands than by anything else. For example, the Colonial Development Corporation and the Nigerian government have started a settlement scheme at Mokwa, in the middle belt of Nigeria, which I have visited. The problems there are as much problems of pioneering in agriculture as of pioneering in settlement. There is a complete lack of knowledge as to what crops can be grown there economically; what the soil requires by way of fertilisers; what rotations are appropriate; what protections the soil needs against the sun, wind, and rain, and so on. One cannot help feeling that such questions ought to be decided on pilot farms before the expense is undertaken of clearing laıge areas for colonisation. But the British taxpayer knows to his cost how seldom this is done. In all the under-developed countries governments are anxious to get a move on with opening lands up for settlement, and it is almost universal practice to settle the lands first and find out what they will grow economically afterwards.

(*b*) *The Settlers*. To say that one must choose the right settlers for colonisation violates the principle on which most of the world has been brought into cultivation in the past—namely that anyone who wished to clear and farm virgin land was welcome to do so, either freely, or on payment of a small price or rent for the land. It is still reasonable, I think, that if there is unlimited land available, it should be had for the asking. In most of these countries, however, settlement is possible only on lands on which a great amount of money has been spent to make them cultivable. Such lands are scarce and valuable, and it is only common sense to restrict their use to the best persons whom one can find for the purpose. One can list the principles most often violated. First, preference should be given to agriculturists of experience. In the nineteen thirties in this country there was a curious doctrine that you could take unemployed men from towns and turn them easily into successful farmers, and the same doctrine is still applied in such places as Jamaica, where land settlement is thought of as a means of reversing the drift from the land into the towns (I should say "was thought of" since much more careful selection of settlers was started in 1950). All "back to the land" movements are economic nonsense. As productivity per head grows, every country needs a smaller proportion of its population in agriculture, to feed itself, the proportion falling from around 75 per cent. in the most backward to around 15 per cent. in the most advanced agricultures. The purpose of colonisation is not to remove people from the towns to the land, but to make more land available to those who are already in agriculture. I do not deny that individual townsmen should be permitted to qualify for settlement; but they should do this by first going to work in training centres or on other farms, and demonstrating that they have acquired sufficient skill, and are attuned to the rural way of life. Ideally, no person should be accepted until his record as an agriculturist has been checked and found satisfactory; but this is a counsel of perfection, for it is not always easy to make this kind of check in the under-developed countries, where the agricultural officers are spread very thinly on the ground and cannot possibly know or report upon all applicants for land.

A second principle of settlement is to choose for each new area people of similar social background, i.e. speaking the same language, if there are language differences, or belonging to the same tribe, or coming from the same group of villages. Thus sources of social tension are reduced to a minimum, and a new community life is quickly built. Settlers depend very much on each other's co-operation, especially in the early stages, and this is helped if they are acquainted even before arriving on the settlement.

A third and more debatable principle is to choose only settlers who have some capital of their own. This also may seem a counsel of perfection. All the same, new settlement requires an immense amount of capital, and a settler who has no capital of his own to start with is gravely handicapped. It is true that the settlement agency can lend him capital, or provide him with tools or livestock—if it has the money, but it seldom has enough to be able to provide him with all the capital he needs. One way out of this proved very successful in Indonesia before the war. New recruits for settlement were transported from Java to the Outer Islands just before the harvest. They were lodged with established settlers, and they helped with the harvest, for wages. The money thus earned, plus the experience, the period of acclimatisation, and the formation of new friendships, all proved invaluable when the recruit moved on to start his own farm. You will no doubt recognise the resemblance of method, if not of objective, to the proposals formulated by Edward Gibbon Wakefield over a century ago.

(*c*) *Preparing the Site.* In the good old days each settler had to prepare the land himself. He cut the forest, or diverted streams, or built tracks, or built his house, or whatever was required. Millions emigrated from Europe to people the Americas on this basis in the nineteenth century, and millions of shifting cultivators are doing this to this very day, say in the African forests or in Sumatra. At the other extreme we can find today, say in Wisconsin, or in Ceylon, settlement agencies which not only clear the ground, lay in water, build roads, and build houses before the settlers arrive, but also stock up the place with equipment or cattle or other needs. Where should the line be drawn ?

In the first place, some preparations are better done by a central agency than by the individual settlers, and there is no doubt that these should be done by the agency. Making the land accessible by roads or otherwise is one of these. Controlling or diverting rivers, building irrigation channels, or piping water, supplies (if feasible) is another. So would the provision of electricity supplies if this were feasible, as it usually is not. On the other hand, the settler can often clear his own land, build his own house, or dig his own wells just as economically as the agency. This is not always so. Where modern bulldozing techniques are appropriate, the agency may be better at clearing the land, cleaning it of stumps, and preparing it, though our African experience shows that mechanical clearing is not always effective or cheap. Digging tube wells is also a specialised occupation which is probably best done by an agency. I confess to peculiar doubts about housing. In all my travels I have never found a government agency which could build cheap rural houses. Their houses cost more than the house the settler would build for himself, and only too often become a burden round his neck and that of the Minister of Finance. So in under-developed countries I always feel that there is much to be said for leaving the rural people to put up their own houses, at any rate until government agencies solve the problem of cheap rural housing.

The advantage of doing as much as you can for the settler before he arrives—including clearing the land and building his house—is that it makes the settlement more attractive, and therefore makes it easier to get and to hold settlers. If the settler has to do these things for himself after he arrives, it will be some time before he can get down to the business of farming, and he may have to spend two or three years on the land before he gets a self-sufficient crop. A good compromise, from his point of view, is for the agency to employ him for wages to do the preparatory work, so that when he eventually gets his farm, he starts with some accumulated savings. On the other hand, the more the agency does for the settler, the greater is the financial cost of settlement, and the smaller is the number of new areas which it can afford to open up. Moreover, we want to be able to rely on the spirit of " Community Development " as much as we can, to get the settlers to give their own free labour for communal works of general advantage (though the community spirit may not be very strong in the initial stages of creating a new community). In practice it is necessary to balance the advantage of getting and holding settlers against the disadvantage of cost. In those areas where there will be plenty of settlers even if the agency does little more than provide roads; the emphasis should be on opening up as much land as possible, at low initial cost; whereas in other countries, where the people are reluctant to move from their villages despite congestion, it is necessary to tempt them by making the new settlements very attractive.

(*d*) *Settlers' Capital.* What we have just discussed is in effect how much fixed capital the agency should sink in the settler. Much the same considerations apply to working capital. The settler needs tools, seeds, fertilisers, food until the first harvest, livestock, and so on. Many settlements have failed not because of lack of fixed capital—for the settler can rig up a temporary hut, or cut a track to the main road—but because the settler did not have enough working capital to cultivate the land economically. This is why the settlers' own capital is so important; why recruits who have capital are preferable to those who have not (*ceteris paribus*); and why it is useful to have the recruits work for wages before taking over their farms, whether working for other settlers, or working for the agency on preparing the land, or on a demonstration or experimental farm (if the agency runs one). Nevertheless, it is most unlikely that settlers will have all the capital they need, and the difference must be provided by or through the agency, since there is no security to offer to other lenders (neither the land nor the house can be mortgaged, at any rate at the beginning).

On the other hand, the settlement agency is bound to be short of money, and simply cannot afford to supply the settler with all the capital he is likely to require. I would say that the absolute minimum is to ensure what is necessary to make production economic—main roads, water, seeds, fertilisers, tools, livestock—these the settler must have if he is to make a success of the settlement. As for the rest—housing, clearing the land, schools, hospitals, side roads—experience shows that he can make do with rudimentary facilities for a start, which can be improved later, as the returns of farming begin to come in. If the agency is short of money, it should not bother to provide the latter unless it has difficulty in attracting settlers. But in any case it should assure itself that the former are available to every settler, either from his own resources, or from the loans it makes to him. I have the distinct impression that many settlement agencies fall down on their minimum obligations in the sphere of providing working capital.

(*e*) *Group Activities.* It is now necessary to enquire whether people should be settled on large units, or whether each settler should have his own farm; and in the latter event, what facilities should be organised on a communal basis. This question has to be faced because of the economies of large scale organisation.

The large plantation has well known economic advantages over the family size unit (employing no labour at all); its disadvantages are as a social unit. Large organisations have to be administered on a hierarchial basis, and this gives rise to conflicts and tension between the few who command and the many who have to obey. These tensions are at their greatest if the plantation is owned by private capitalists, but they are not much less if it is owned by the state, or owned by the workers themselves collectively. It used to be thought, in the nineteenth century, that government ownership would abolish exploitation (real or imagined) and unrest, but this myth is now thoroughly exploded. For instance, when the Government of Puerto Rico bought out several large American sugar plantations, there was no noticeable improvement in industrial relations. The myth that all would be well if the workers owned the means of production collectively is even older, but it has never—except temporarily in the peculiar conditions of Palestine—proved possible for a group of workers (say 100 or more) to run a large organisation collectively (I am not referring to co-operatives with a dozen or two members, which are relatively easy to work, though not by any means always so) and democratically (by which I rule out collectives in the U.S.S.R.), without coming to grief either through internal dissension and lack of discipline, or else through capital consumption—and there have been many attempts at this in the history of the world. There is still colonisation going on in large units, whether in private plantations, or in government plantations (of which there are interesting examples in British West Africa) or in collectives. But most of the under-developed countries have now turned their backs upon the large unit. Their ideal in colonisation is the family size farm, or something rather like it. They may establish a plantation for pioneering purposes, to discover what crops or agricultural methods are appropriate, or to introduce a new crop or new methods to surrounding peasants, but this is a special function.

If the family size farm is to be economic, some central agency must organise on its behalf all those matters which are best done on a larger scale—mechanical operations, irrigation, pure seed farms, research, technical advice, processing the crop, marketing the crop, credit, purchasing supplies, and so on. These may be done by private firms, by co-operative action, by the land settlement agency, or by some other government agency. I do not want to raise here the question who should do these things, which is a subsidiary question well covered in the literature. Rather I would like to emphasise that if small scale farming is to be efficient, it is absolutely necessary to have a framework of centrally organised services doing each of these things on a large scale. If one examines small scale farming in under-developed countries, what sticks out a mile is the inadequacy of this framework, especially in the spheres of water, seed farms, research, extension and credit.

The other question I would like to raise is whether the settler should be under the control of a central agency in these matters, and compelled to follow their advice, or whether he should be free to use or reject their services as he wills. The classical example of control is the well known Gezira scheme, where the farmer's land is ploughed for him, and where he has to plant the seed he is given in the rotations he is told, to fertilise and cultivate as recommended, and to hand over the crop for processing and marketing—for all of which operations he has of course to foot the bill. The case for compulsion is that it ensures ever-increasing efficiency, whereas if the service were voluntary many farmers would plant inferior seeds and cultivate or market in inferior ways. Compulsion combines the advantages of the plantation with the advantages of family size; on the other hand it does this only by partly reducing the status of the settler from that of independent farmer towards that of labourer acting under orders. Despite the success of the Gezira scheme, it has not often been imitated. As far as I know, the imitations can be counted on one's fingers, and none of them is so clearly successful. Probably the best answer is to apply compulsion in those cases where the advantages of plantation type are known to be considerable—of which sugar cane is probably the most outstanding example at present—but not to use it where the advantages are not so clear—as in rice, or cotton, or rubber.

Some compulsions are probably desirable in any case, even without going the whole hog of Gezira. For example, in rice cultivation, control of movement of water on and off the land may make it desirable for the irrigation authority to lay down a planting calendar to which all settlers must adhere. Or, in the case of cotton, it may be desirable, in the interest of preventing hybridisation, to insist on all farmers planting only the pure lines of seed provided by the agency. Or there may be compulsory measures in the interest of soil conservation; compulsory crop rotations in the interest of soil fertility; or compulsory disease controls, to prevent the spread of plant or cattle epidemics. Compulsory marketing through designated agencies has also become very popular, for many reasons, good and bad. All these compulsions represent a compromise designed to combine the social advantages of small scale operation with the economic advantages of large scale control. My own belief is that it is a good compromise, and that land settlement agencies do not make sufficient use of such compulsions.

(*f*) *Acreage per Settler.* Two principles determine how much land the settler should have: (a) it must be enough to make a living; (b) it must not be more than he can cultivate. Most settlement agencies make the mistake of thinking that the latter is more important than the former; accordingly they do not give the settler enough land on which to make a living, and so after a while he quits.

In fact the latter is no principle at all. The amount of land a family can cultivate depends on the equipment it has; perhaps three arable acres, if it has only a hoe; 10 to 15 acres with a plough and draught animals; 50 acres and upwards with a tractor. It is no use giving the settler less land than he needs in order to make a living. One must first determine what this area is, and then adjust the equipment accordingly.

By " to make a living " I mean to be able to earn as much on the land as he could earn if he went to town and did the sort of work which men of his education and ability can get. In these days this sets rather a high standard. For, in the under-developed countries, wages in the towns are tending to rise continually, through the pressure of trade unions, or of inflation. Let me give an example. An intelligent wage earning family in a Nigerian town could earn at least £60 a year. If the alternative is to grow sorghum, yielding 10 cwt. an acre at £15 a ton, it needs to have 8 acres under cultivation (not allowing for fallows or for rent or other costs) to get the same income. It is not necessary to have quite the same income—a differential of 30 per cent. or more between town and rural incomes seems to be acceptable. All the same, wherever one makes this calculation, the conclusion seems to be that in the under-developed countries the family needs around a dozen acres of arable land. There are many examples of land settlement schemes, especially in Africa, where the settler is getting twelve acres or more of arable land, but there is also a marked tendency elsewhere to give the settlers only about five acres of arable land per family or even less (e.g. the West Indies, Malaya, Ceylon, Indonesia).

I am fully aware of the complications in this kind of calculation: the different sizes of families, the different yields of different crops, the need to have some non-arable land, complications of shifting cultivation, non availability in some areas of sufficient draught animals and so on. I do not stick to any particular figures. But I do stick to my impression that in some of these schemes one of the causes of failure is that the settler is not given enough land to keep him from drifting into other employments. I admit that there are important exceptions. Market gardening can be extremely profitable on as little as two acres—but this is irrelevant to the colonisation schemes we are discussing, which are seldom near to big towns. More important is the fact that at current prices five acres in sugar cane, in rice, in cotton or in cocoa may yield a pretty large income by local standards (how long these prices will last no one knows). I admit also the political difficulty of settling a few people on twelve acres when most of their compatriots have to make do with five or less; as well as the financial difficulty of doing this if it means equipping the farmers with ploughs and animals or arranging for mechanical assistance, in countries where their compatriots are still at the stage of the hoe. I admit that it may be politically or financially impracticable to give the settler more than five acres, and that it may also in some cases be unnecessary. All I am saying is that if he cannot make a living on five acres, it is a waste of effort to try to establish him on an acreage which will not be large enough to hold him.

In those countries where settlement is associated with mechanical cultivation by a central agency, the settler gets around 30 to 50 acres (e.g. Sudan, Nigeria). Mechanical cultivation, however, belongs to countries where land is abundant relatively to labour. In countries where there is already surplus labour in the countryside its introduction is justified only in those marginal cases where it makes possible increased yields *per acre*. Mechanised land settlements have a future in Africa, or in parts of Latin America or the Middle East, but not much future in the West Indies or in South East Asia (except Burma and Siam).

(*g*) *Tenure*. There has been a tremendous battle of words over the relative merits of freehold and leasehold tenures in land settlements. Since these tenures are not absolutes, but overlap widely, it does not matter, I suggest, what name the tenure is given, provided that certain principles are observed. On the one hand the settler must have security of tenure, and must be free to pass the farm to his heirs. These are characteristics of a freehold system. On the other hand, tenure must be subject to certain restrictions. He must live on the farm and cultivate it. He must not subdivide it between his heirs. He must not mortgage the farm. He cannot sell except to approved purchasers—or may even not be allowed to sell at all, in which case he must be guaranteed compensation for improvements if he surrenders his holding to the agency. He may also be subjected to a number of the compulsions referred to in section (e), relating to what, when, or how to plant, to soil conservation, to rotations, to disease control, or to the sale of his crop. These restraints can be called covenants, if we choose to refer to the system as freehold tenure, or clauses if we prefer to call it a leasehold contract. It is the thing, and not its name that matters.

Difficult problems arise in connection with the rent, or whatever name we give to the annual payment which the settler must make to recoup the agency for the investment it has made on his behalf. First there is the question whether this should be a fixed annual sum, or whether it should be a proportion of the harvest. Like most other economists, I do not like proportional rents because of their disincentive effects. On the C.D.C.'s settlement in Nigeria, the farmers were being asked to pay two-thirds of their crop to the company, and though this was a very fair proportion in terms of the company's costs as well as in terms of what was earned by the farmer, there was evidence of its disincentive effect. In the United Kingdom, where people like both work and money, it may not make much difference if the Chancellor takes two-thirds of marginal income (a much disputed point), but in some under-developed countries where the preference for leisure is high and the opportunities for spending income are restricted, proportional rents may damage incentive. On the other hand, proportional rents are easier on the farmer in circumstances where income fluctuates widely from year to year. Probably the best compromise is a combination: a basic rent fixed in money or in kind plus a small proportion of the crop (say ten per cent.), plus separate charges for specific services (mechanical ploughing, marketing, seeds, fertilisers, etc.).

The next question is how large the annual payment should be, and, in particular, should it be large enough to reimburse the agency completely for its investment ? Some of these settlement schemes are frightfully expensive, especially where they involve great expenditure on irrigation or on drainage. Costs in Ceylon are running out at well over £1,000 per settler, which is a frightful sum for five acres of irrigated and three acres of dry land. Translated into a 30 year annuity at 5 per cent. it would work out as an annual charge of over £12 per irrigated acre, a charge which a yield of perhaps 12 cwt. of rice per acre can bear only for so long as rice maintains its currently inflated price.

Clearly we cannot say that the annual charge must equal the cost. It must be determined, rather, in relation to yields on the one hand, and to what the farmer could earn in alternative occupations on the other. Obviously this itself depends on the number of acres allocated to the settler, since the amount of rent he can afford to pay per acre increases as the number of acres increases, and this is a part of the case for giving the settler more land rather than less. Where land can be brought into cultivation cheaply, the cost may well be less than the rent which the farmer can bear. But where land settlement is expensive the cost per acre is almost always much greater than the farmer could afford to pay, unless it is feasible to grow crops with extraordinarily high money yields per acre. In these circumstances the question that arises is not whether to fix the charge at a level that covers the cost, but whether to undertake settlements which will cost more than the farmers will be able to pay. The answer to this question is an exercise in the theory of surplus resources. If labour is abundant and unemployed, there is little real cost in employing people to build irrigation systems, and this is eminently worth doing even if the cultivable land which results therefrom cannot be sold or rented at a remunerative price. In all such cases one has to peer behind the veil of money, and ask what are the real costs, and what addition to real national income results. When the veil is replaced the Minister of Finance may be extremely embarrassed to find that what is good economic sense is very difficult in financial terms. This is a very important problem in under-developed countries; they have idle resources, especially labour, which commonsense urges them to use for capital formation, but which cannot be so used without the embarrassment of budget deficits, or balance of payment deficits or inflation at home. This is not the place to elaborate this enormous practical problem, and its possible solutions. Its relevance to my present theme is merely the fact that much land settlement has to be subsidised, and deserves to be subsidised, and that this will be a brake on the rate of colonisation unless Ministers of Finance are extraordinarily clever, not only as economists, but even more so as politicians.

Conclusion. I hope I have said enough to stimulate an evening's discussion. My final plea is that some agricultural economists should do a lot more empirical research into this subject, not only because of its intrinsic interest, but also because of its current practical importance in the under-developed world. At present, the literature is very fragmentary, and scattered in out of the way places. If I succeed in stimulating one or two of my listeners to work and publish in this field, I shall feel amply rewarded.

[26]

Patterns of Public Revenue and Expenditure[1]

I. Introduction.

This article compares the revenues and expenditures of sixteen countries at different levels of economic development. Its main purpose is to see how patterns of expenditure and sources of revenue vary with economic development, in the hope of discovering in this process what patterns are appropriate to different levels of development.

The basic statistics are set out in six tables at the end of the article, which are described more fully in the Statistical Appendix. Except in the case of Colombia, the material is for a year overlapping with 1953 or 1954. The figures have been classified according to the categories of expenditure and the sources of revenue. They are all shown as proportions of Gross National Product at factor cost.[2] Current expenditure is distinguished from capital expenditure, but no distinction is made between transfer expenditures and expenditures on goods and services. The figures are consolidated for all public authorities (central state, and local authorities), except in Tables VIII, IX, XIII, XIV and XV, which relate to state and local finance exclusively.

Comparisons of this kind are subject to several criticisms. First, different countries classify the same expenditure in different ways. We have tried to meet this by going through the budgets and classifying expenditures according to a common pattern ; hence the figures for each country appear according to our classification, which is not necessarily the same as that used in the country's budget.

Secondly, expenditures which appear in the budgets of some countries are left to other agencies in other countries. For example the expense of medical care falls mainly upon the government in the United Kingdom, but is left to private

[1]Some of the material of this paper was used for the Sidney Ball Lecture delivered in the University of Oxford by Professor W. A. Lewis on 4th May, 1956.

[2]Except in two cases, where we have had to use other national income concepts. See Statistical Appendix.

individuals in the United States of America. The figures are not intended to show how much a *country* spends on a service, but only how much its *governments* spend. Public undertakings and nationalised industries are the most difficult case. We are concerned with these only in so far as they affect the budgets of the public authorities. For example, if their profits are paid into the Treasury, or their losses met by the Treasury, they (*i.e.* the surpluses or deficits only) are included in our accounts ; but if their surpluses or deficits are not in the government's accounts they are excluded. Similarly, if the government has to find capital for them, this will appear in our figures of capital expenditure ; but if they borrow in the capital market or finance capital expenditure out of their own profits, these sums are not shown in our figures.

Thirdly, comparisons of the Gross National Product of different countries are always shaky. We escape most of the usual problems, since our tables do not require G.N.P's to be compared directly Nevertheless the structure of G.N.P's differs, especially in the respective proportions of monetary and of subsistence income, and also in the different ways in which subsistence income is valued, and these differences need to be taken into account in making comparisons. Despite the difficulties inherent in using G.N.P. as a base, we have preferred to use it instead of using "Total Expenditure" or "Total Revenue," because we find it more illuminating. For example, general administration as a proportion of current expenditure is 13 per cent. in Sweden and 35 per cent. in India. We find it more illuminating to note that general administration costs 3·07 per cent. of G.N.P. in Sweden and 3·09 per cent. in India, but any reader who prefers to convert our tables into proportions of total revenue and expenditure can do so for himself.

Section II of the article deals with expenditure, distinguishing current and capital expenditure. Section III is concerned with the sources of revenue, excluding loans. Section IV is a brief note on the finances of "local" authorities, using this term to include not only municipal and rural authorities, but also states, provinces and other units in federal structures.

II. Expenditure.

When we began this investigation we expected to find that public expenditure rises relatively to national income as income grows. This is very broadly true, as far as total expenditure goes. Table I shows current expenditure of the sixteen countries, in order of G.N.P. per head. Column *A* shows total current expenditure, while Column *B* shows the total excluding expenditure on social insurance, food or agricultural subsidies, defence and public debt.

TABLE I

CURRENT EXPENDITURE AS % OF G.N.P.

	A	B		A	B
Tanganyika ...	11·91	10·68	Colombia ...	11·80	8·42
Uganda	12·26	10·78	Italy	24·58	12·79
India	8·84	6·15	Trinidad	15·54	12·42
Nigeria	4·98	4·34	France	25·76	10·79
Ceylon	14·42	11·59	U.K.	34·00	11·52
Gold Coast ...	12·20	10·43	New Zealand ...	30·12	13·77
Jamaica	13·08	10·38	Sweden	23·49	13·26
British Guiana ...	14·29	11·44	U.S.A.	27·43	7·24

It will be seen from Column *A* that there is a rough relationship between total expenditure and G.N.P. per head. The mean of the first four figures is 9·50 per cent., the mean of the second four 13·50 per cent., the mean of the third four 19·42 per cent., and the mean of the last four 28·76 per cent.

This relationship does not, however, extend so clearly to Column *B*. The great differences between the richer and the poorer countries are in the amounts spent on defence, on the public debt (which reflects past defence expenditure), on social insurance schemes, and on food or agricultural subsidies. Expenditure in these four categories is excluded from Column *B*, so that what is left—the civilian administrative services, health and education—comprises the major expenditures of the poorer countries, suitable for comparison with similar expenditure in the richer countries.

(*a*) *"Basic" Expenditure.*

Let us begin by comparing only this "basic" expenditure, which is common to countries at all levels of development. The figures in Column *B* show only a slight correlation with income per head. The mean of the first four is 7·99 per cent. ;

of the second four 10·96 per cent. ; of the third four 11·11 per cent. ; and of the last four 11·45 per cent. The coefficient of rank correlation is only 0·46.

If we confine ourselves for the moment to the services included in "basic" current expenditure, it is appropriate to ask why anyone should expect the proportion of G.N.P. spent on these services to be a function of G.N.P. per head. There are three reasons for expecting the proportion to grow with G.N.P., and one reason for expecting it to fall.

The first reason for expecting the proportion to grow turns out to be fallacious : it is that the proportion has in fact grown in Europe and in North America during the past hundred years, during which G.N.P. per head has also grown. This is the fallacy of *post hoc propter hoc.* The main reason why these countries now spend relatively more on their public services than they did a hundred years ago is not that they are richer, but that they have a different conception of the duties of the state. The citizens did not take it for granted a hundred years ago that public authorities must pay for schooling for every child, that they must pave and light the streets of every village with a thousand inhabitants, or that they must maintain those public services which have brought the infant mortality rate down from 250 to 30 per thousand. But this change in ideas is not confined to the richer countries, and is not proportional to income per head. It has affected the poorer countries just as much, and it shows up in just as great an increase in the ratio of public expenditure in poor countries as in rich countries.

A second reason why we might expect the proportion spent on public services to rise is the relatively slow growth of productivity in this sector of the economy. This is best illustrated by making the extreme assumptions. Suppose that the number of policemen required varies directly with the output of commodities. Suppose also that while the total population, the number producing commodities, and the productivity of policemen remain constant, the productivity of those making commodities doubles, and so therefore does the output of commodities. It will follow that the number of policemen required will double. And if a policeman is paid the same as a producer of commodities it will also follow that the percentage share of commodities received by policemen will double. It is hard to measure the productivity of services. Thanks to the typewriter, the telephone, the mechanical computer and other inventions, it has undoubtedly increased. But it is generally believed to have increased less than productivity in manufacturing or in agriculture, and to this extent the share of national income spent on public services would rise if these services were a function of output.

This brings us to the third point. Is the need for public services a function of output? To revert to our previous example, if the number of policemen needed is a function not of the output of commodities but of the number of men making commodities, and if the number of men is constant, and if policemen are paid the same as others, then the percentage share of policemen in commodity output will be constant whatever may happen to productivities, absolutely or relatively. Similarly if teachers are paid the same as other people, and if the ratios of teachers to children and of children to adults are constant, then the percentage share of teachers in the national income will be constant whatever may happen to productivity. Actually the ratio of children to adults is greater in poor countries, so if other things were equal the proportion of the national income spent on education would fall as productivity increased.

Assuming for the moment that public servants are paid on the average the same as other people, we can cut through this tangle by asking our question in the form : does the proportion of the population required in the public services vary with output per head? Different answers may be given for different services. As far as justice, police, and administration (narrowly defined) are concerned, there is no obvious reason why the proportion of men required should vary significantly with output per head, though there is possibly less voluntary public service in the richer communities, and correspondingly more people on the public payroll. (Cf. the amount of administration and of judical work done by the "squire" in eighteenth century England). There is also greater expenditure on foreign missions, and on other representation in foreign countries—though the cost of this may be as much a function of size and of status as it is of income. As for the economic services, the proportion of men required should on balance grow with income per head. The proportion required as agricultural extension workers should diminish as the farmers become more educated (and decline relatively in numbers) ; but the proportion engaged in maintaining roads, or water supplies or public works may be expected to increase. In the social services, the proportion required in education and in health is primarily a matter of policy. In one sense backward countries need relatively more spent on health and education because of the leeway to be made up, but in practice the numbers engaged in these services are relatively larger in rich than in poor countries.

It follows that we should expect the proportion of the population engaged in the basic public services to increase with income per head. Column *B* in Table I, however, shows that the difference in the proportion of national income spent on these services is relatively insignificant. Probably the main explanation of this paradox is the fact that a public servant usually costs more in relation to average income per head in poor than in rich countries. In Britain or the U.S.A., government employees receive an average income not very different from the average in the country. This is not so in the poorer countries. It is not merely that the higher civil servants and scientists cost relatively more, especially when these are imported from richer countries. There is also the mass of clerks, nurses, teachers and other subordinate grades. An elementary school teacher in Britain earns a salary about equal to that of an industrial worker, but an elementary school teacher in most poor countries (India is a notable exception) earns two or three times as much as the average farmer. As output grows and education spreads, the skills commanded by public servants become relatively less scarce, and their share of the national income would decline sharply but for the factors already mentioned which bring about a relative increase in numbers.

The importance of these factors comes out more clearly when we split "basic" expenditure into sub-groups, as is done in Table II. The exact meaning of the terms used can be found by reference to Table X and to the Appendix. Broadly speaking,

"Administration" excludes the economic departments—Agriculture, Commerce, Labour, etc.—which are included with public works and roads in "Economic."

TABLE II

"BASIC" CURRENT EXPENDITURE AS % OF G.N.P.

	Administration (1)	Economic (2)	Education	Health	Total
Tanganyika ...	3·87	3·83	1·70	1·28	10·68
Uganda ...	3·17	4·16	2·39	1·06	10·78
India	3·09	1·85	·77	·44	6·15
Nigeria ...	1·42	1·61	·78	·53	4·34
Ceylon ...	2·77	3·81	2·94	2·07	11·59
Gold Coast ...	2·56	3·58	3·06	1·23	10·43
Jamaica ...	2·89	3·44	1·99	2·06	10·38
British Guiana	3·24	4·08	2·19	1·93	11·44
Colombia ...	3·26	2·64	1·68	·84	8·42
Italy	3·76	3·96	2·99	2·08	12·79
Trinidad ...	3·23	4·49	2·24	2·46	12·42
France ...	3·32	3·88	1·97	1·62	10·79
U.K.	2·36	2·41	3·47	3·28	11·52
New Zealand	2·92	4·75	2·68	3·42	13·77
Sweden ...	3·07	3·35	4·27	2·57	13·26
U.S.A. ...	2·40	1·52	2·40	·92	7·24

(1) Row 1 in Table X.
(2) Rows 4 to 16 in Table X.

Table II shows that the proportions spent on administration and on economic services are relatively constant, while the proportions spent on education and on health vary considerably.

In the sub-group administration, 10 out of the 16 countries spend between 2·77 and 3·32 per cent. of G.N.P. The four which spend less than this include two poor ones (Nigeria and Gold Coast) and two rich ones (U.K. and U.S.A.) ; and the two which spend more are also widely separated (Tanganyika and Italy).

In both Nigeria and the Gold Coast much administration is done by chiefs, whose major source of income is from trade or farming or other payments which do not enter into the public accounts, so the figures do not fully measure the real resources used in administration. On the other hand, considerable expenditures on colonial development are hidden in the French figure for administration, which would otherwise be nearer to those of other countries at the richer end of the table.

In the economic sub-group, nine out of the sixteen countries spend between 3·35 and 4·16. New Zealand and Trinidad spend even more, in both cases because of much more than average expenditure on roads. On the other hand, in the cases of India, Nigeria, the U.K. and the U.S.A. some part of the relatively low figure is due to expenditure on ports, railways and other works either being done by private companies, or else appearing in separate budgets which are not incorporated in the general budget.

It is notable that, apart from housing subsidies (which are included in "Economic") the U.K. and the U.S.A. spend almost exactly the same proportions of G.N.P. on administration (2·36, 2·40) and on economic services (1·73, 1·52). The great differences between these two nations are to be found in their social services and in the categories excluded from Table II. Also, one must remember that the Federal Government finds it easier to finance some essentially civilian expenditures on the defence vote (*e.g.* research) so "basic" civil expenditure is rather larger than these figures show.

The fact that the Colombian figures are for 1947 should be borne in mind, since this was before the governments of under-developed countries got into the swing of their post-war development programmes. Unfortunately we have not had access to later Colombian figures, which are probably much higher, and which would be more fully comparable with the other figures in this article.

The expenditure on health varies most widely. Four countries spend less than 1·0, five spend between 1·0 and 2·0, five between 2·0 and 3·0, and two over 3·0. In general it is the richest countries which spend the most, but the fact that the U.S. spends less than 1·0 while Ceylon spends more than 2·0 emphasises that in this field policy is as important as income per head. The doctrine that it is the duty of the state to provide an adequate health service for all the citizens is very recent, and different countries have responded to it in widely differing degrees.

The duty to provide education is of much older recognition, and this expenditure varies less than health, though more than administrative or economic expenditure. The ten countries which spend more than 2·00 include six of the seven richest, as well as British Guiana, Gold Coast, Ceylon and Uganda. India's expenditure is specially low because the average income of teachers is much closer to average national income in India than it is in other poor countries, but even with this allowance the figure is a reminder that India's large output of university graduates rests on a rather narrow base of primary and secondary education.

In all these figures India and Nigeria stand out for the poverty of their public services. Their expenditures are so small when compared with those of poorer countries (Tanganyika, Uganda) or of countries not so very much richer (Ceylon, Gold Coast) that they cannot possibly be explained in terms of national income per head. These low figures are due to large portions of these two countries having been governed until fairly recently by rulers who had low standards of public service. What they have in common is that they have both been ruled through native princes, who were left to decide for themselves what public services were required, and who remained steeped in mediæval notions of the functions of government. Outside the Indian States and the Nigerian Emirates the British Raj busied itself creating a modern framework of government, but in these two great areas the initiative was left to native rulers. The resulting figures for India and for Nigeria are the clearest proof that the proportion of national income spent on public services is a function not mainly of national income per head but of how "backward" or "progressive" are the rulers of the state.

(*b*) *Other Current Expenditure.*

The four items we have so far excluded are far more important in the budgets of the richer than of the poorer countries. These items are defence, public debt, social insurance and agricultural subsidies. If we exclude New Zealand, the U.S.A. and the countries of Europe, the total of these four items averages only 2·26 per cent. of G.N.P. in the remaining ten countries, whereas in New Zealand it is 10·23 per cent., and in the rest it ranges up to 22·48 per cent., which is twice as much as "basic" current expenditure.

There is least variation between countries in the cost of the public debt. It is less than 1·0 per cent. of G.N.P. in the African countries, in India and in Sweden (thanks to absence of wars). At the other extreme there is a big gap between the largest figure, the U.K.'s 4·77, and the next largest, New Zealand's 2·76. The U.S.A. has not fought such long wars as has the U.K., and is not so socialistically inclined as New Zealand; she escapes with 2·16 per cent. Italy and France have fought lengthy wars, but with less care to prevent inflation, so their debt costs only 1·97 per cent. of G.N.P. in each case.

One important conclusion is that several of the poorer countries have such small debt burdens that they could afford to finance much development by borrowing. Much the same conclusion was reached by Dr. Finch, who approached the matter via the balance of payments.[1]

The leading country in the field of social insurance is New Zealand, which spends 7·98 per cent. of G.N.P. in this way. The U.K. and Sweden spend significantly less, respectively 5·84 and 5·59 per cent. Italy comes next with 4·33 per cent., followed by France 3·51 and the U.S.A. 3·49 per cent. Clearly policy is as important as degree of industrialisation in determining how much is spent in this way.

Finally, defence. This is an insignificant item in the British colonies and in Ceylon (0·50 per cent. of G.N.P. or less). It absorbs 1·43 per cent. in Colombia, 1·91 per cent. in India, 3·74 per cent. in New Zealand and also in Sweden, 5·33 per cent. in Italy, 9·49 per cent. in France, 9·89 per cent. in the U.K., and 13·90 per cent. in the U.S.A. Probably the U.S.A. figure for defence includes some civilian expenditures which the administration finds it convenient to classify under this head for political reasons.

Comparison between the U.S.A. and the U.K. will interest those U.K. taxpayers who are groaning under the burden of current expenditure totalling 34 per cent. of G.N.P. The U.K. spends roughly the same as the U.S.A. on administration and on economic services (apart from housing subsidies) and 4·0 per cent. of G.N.P. less on defence. It spends 1·1 per cent. more

[1]D. Finch, "Investment Service of Under-developed Countries," *International Monetary Fund Staff Papers*, September, 1951.

on education, 1·3 per cent. more on food or agricultural subsidies, 2·4 per cent. more on health, 2·4 per cent. more on social insurance, and 2·6 per cent. more on public debt. Significant cuts in these expenditures are unlikely outside the fields of food subsidies and defence.

(c) *Capital Expenditure.*

Capital expenditure is less easy to compare than is "basic" current expenditure, because the extent to which governments provide for capital formation through the budget varies more widely. In Table III the expenditure is grouped under four sub-heads. "Departmental" in this table covers a wider range than "Administration" in Table II ; it includes education, health and social insurance, and also economic departments, with the exception of those otherwise specified. "Transport" includes roads, and the whole of public works. "Finance" includes agriculture, water, industry and housing, which are the services where there is greatest variation in the extent to which finance is privately or publicly supplied.

TABLE III.

CAPITAL EXPENDITURE AS % OF G.N.P.

	Departmental (1)	Transport (2)	Finance (3)	Defence	Total
Tanganyika ...	1·27	1·24	1·45	·02	3·98
Uganda ...	2·37	2·17	2·17	·10	6·81
India	·21	·59	1·40	·10	2·30
Nigeria ...	·62	1·19	·49	·10	2·40
Ceylon ...	·98	1·91	4·30	·26	7·45
Gold Coast ...	1·80	4·03	2·28	·13	8·24
Jamaica ...	·60	1·48	1·96	—	4·04
British Guiana	1·62	1·58	2·76	—	5·96
Colombia ...	*	2·66	·55	—	3·21
Italy	·67	1·62	3·26	—	5·55
Trinidad ...	1·06	2·03	2·42	—	5·51
France ...	1·01	1·90	4·02	1·18	8·11
U.K.	1·24	·68	2·99	·46	5·37
New Zealand	1·56	2·40	4·31	—	8·27
Sweden ...	2·64	4·69	3·76	2·90	13·99
U.S.A. ...	1·18	·99	·71	1·38	4·26

(*) Included in Transport, which also includes some items of Finance.
(1) Rows 1, 2, 3, 13, 14, 15 and 17 in Table XI.
(2) Rows 4, 5 and 6 in Table XI.
(3) Rows 7, 8, 9, 10, 11, 12 and 16 in Table XI.

It is at once apparent from Table III how wide is the range of capital expenditures by governments—from 2·3 per cent. of G.N.P. in India to 14·0 per cent. in Sweden. The figures are misleading because they exclude the expenditures of those public agencies which do not appear in the budget, and these vary from country to country. For example, the capital expenditures of publicly owned railways, harbours or electric power stations are included in some cases and excluded in others, so the figures do not accurately state the total spending of public agencies. What they do state is the total spending for which the Minister of Finance holds himself responsible, in so far as his decision to include these figures in the budget indicates that he regards the financing of their expenditures as a part of his responsibility. They are therefore a good measure of the extent of the fiscal problem as he sees it.

The smallness of the "Departmental" and "Transport" expenditures is remarkable. The expenditures listed under "Administration," "Health" and "Education" in Table II account for about 70 per cent. of basic current expenditures. Yet these three together are slightly narrower than the category listed as "Departmental" in Table III, which takes typically much less than 2 per cent. of G.N.P. Basic current expenditures are mainly on administration, education, and health, but it is economic services which make the large drafts on capital expenditure.

The smallness of the capital expenditures on education and on health is particularly remarkable. The mean capital expenditure on education (the mean of row 2 in Table XI) is 0·5 per cent. of G.N.P. while the mean current expenditure (the mean of row 2 in Table X) is 2·3 per cent. of G.N.P. Similarly the mean capital expenditure on health is 0·3 per cent., whereas the mean current expenditure is 1·7 per cent. The capital expenditure may be understated, since some budgets hide expenditure on schools and health buildings under "public works," but this is probably not very significant. In making public expenditure programmes one of the maxims is that it is not safe to plan only in terms of capital expenditure because some of the items which look attractive because of their small capital requirements are in fact very expensive because of the heavy commitment of current expenditures which they carry. The figures in Table III cannot be used to prove this by comparison with Table II, since Table III shows only gross additions to capital, while Table II shows current expenditures associated with all existing capital. But the maxim is undoubtedly relevant to education and to health.

Expenditure on roads is also remarkably small. The mean capital expenditure is 0·73 per cent. of G.N.P., and the mean current expenditure is 0·71 per cent. The largest combined expenditure is 2·69 per cent., which occurs in Sweden.

It is therefore clear that the extent of government capital expenditures depends mainly on how far the "productive" sectors of the economy—agriculture, transport, and industry—lean on the government for finance (and also on how much government finance goes into housing). This is not primarily a question of the extent to which these sectors are publicly owned, since publicly owned industries may raise their own finance privately in the capital market, while privately owned industries may be financed by loans from government sources.

The idea that the government should be a source of saving is relatively new. It follows from three policy objectives. First, the amount of private saving in under-developed countries is relatively small, and so also is the amount available through international investment. Hence, if a large investment programme is to be financed it must be through forced saving, and this is more equitably achieved through taxation than through inflation. Secondly some developed countries have exactly the same problem of a tendency for investment to exceed saving, and the prescription of a budget surplus to counter inflation in these circumstances is exactly the same solution reached by a different road. Thirdly, socialistic governments are anxious that new capital be created on public rather than private account, and since all capital is created out of saving the only way to prevent private fortunes from growing *pari passu* with capital formation is to finance capital out of public rather than private saving. Public ownership is not the antithesis of private wealth if, through dependence on private saving, all increase in publicly owned capital is matched by an increase in privately held government bonds.

The extent of public saving can be deduced by subtracting the total of current expenditures shown in Table X (row 21) from the total of current revenue shown in Table XII (row 12). This yields the results in Table IV.

TABLE IV.

PUBLIC SAVING AS % OF G.N.P.

Tanganyika	0·32	Colombia	1·07
Uganda	4·88	Italy	−1·05
India	−0·56	Trinidad	0·19
Nigeria	3·43	France	3·14
Ceylon	4·93	U.K.	3·09
Gold Coast	10·00	New Zealand	3·06
Jamaica	0·20	Sweden	9·82
British Guiana	3·38	U.S.A.	1·88

The figures in Table IV indicate the extent to which a country is "socialistic" in the sense of believing in public *ownership* (rather than in the sense of believing in public *control,* or in *equality* of income or of opportunity) since they show how much new capital is being created in the community without a corresponding increase of private wealth. On the other hand they somewhat understate the amount of public saving because they omit sinking fund contributions (which are in any case a small percentage of G.N.P.), investment by publicly owned enterprises financed out of their own savings, and, in the case of the African territories, grants from the statutory Marketing Boards for general development purposes (which are substantial).

Here again the range is remarkable. Even in 1953 there were two governments not raising enough revenue to cover even their current expenditures. The Gold Coast and Sweden stand out as the most "socialistic governments" with Ceylon, Uganda, Nigeria, British Guiana, France, U.K., and New Zealand following a long way behind.

(*d*) *A Frame of Reference?*

Does this analysis help to answer the question : what is the appropriate level and distribution of public expenditure in under-developed countries? The question cries out for an answer, if not in rigid quantitative terms, but at least in terms of some principles which may be used in judging government programmes. Throughout the world Ministers and officials are busily engaged in working out five-year plans for public expenditure, and they look anxiously to economists and to others for guidance as to what is appropriate. Neither is there any lack of advice offered. The United Nations International Bank has sent out a succession of missions which have produced reports tendering such advice. Also many economists have sat on fiscal or other commissions reviewing public expenditure, and they seem usually to have been able to decide what levels were appropriate. But in none of the mass of published reports can one discover how the authors have decided what level or pattern of public expenditure was appropriate. Judgments in this sphere of public finance boil down to little more than personal assertions.

This analysis can make only one small contribution to the present situation—that of providing material with which to make comparisons. Such material does not enable the planner directly to answer the question: "Is my pattern right?", but it does enable him to answer the question: "How does my pattern differ?", and thereby sets him to seek the reasons for difference.

This contribution is most usefully summarised in a table showing the median and upper quartile expenditures of our sixteen governments in each category of expenditure. As we have already seen, the basic current expenditure of governments does not vary significantly with national income per head, so the median expenditures can be used as an indication of "standard" practice by a government seeking to achieve no more than "average" performance. Upper quartile expenditures indicate a more than average performance, though not the best (or most extravagant). However, since no government wishes to show more than average performance in every sphere of activity, the sum of the upper quartiles (13·18 current and 8·23 capital in Table V) exceeds the upper quartiles of total expenditure (12·01 current and 7·78 capital), and only Sweden and New Zealand surpass the upper quartile totals of spending.

TABLE V

COMBINED EXPENDITURE AS % OF G.N.P.

	Median			Upper Quartile		
	Current	Capital	Total	Current	Capital	Total
Administration ...	3·08	·42	3·50	3·25	·57	3·82
Education	2·32	·50	2·82	2·97	·73	3·70
Health	1·78	·27	2·05	2·27	·42	2·69
Water Supplies ...	·16	·31	·47	·29	·75	1·04
Public Works ...	·65	·39	1·04	·82	·45	1·27
Roads	·73	·68	1·41	·90	1·00	1·90
Transport	·64	·53	1·17	·85	1·03	1·88
Agriculture (1) ...	·98	·49	1·47	1·21	1·10	2·31
Industry (2) ...	·29	·31	·60	·44	·73	1·17
Housing	·11	·72	·83	·18	1·45	1·63
	10·74	4·62	15·36	13·18	8·23	21·41
Social Insurance ...	...	... ...	1·29			
Defence	...	... ...	1·09			
Public Dept. ...	...	... ...	1·10			
			18·84			

(1) Rows 7, 8, 10 and 11 in Table X and corresponding rows in Table XI. Irrigation is included but agricultural subsidies are excluded.

(2) Rows 12, 13, 14 and 15 in Table X and corresponding rows in Table XI.

Let us reiterate that Table V does not claim to show how any particular country must distribute its expenditure. For example, the appropriate expenditure on roads is probably relatively larger in a sparsely settled than in a densely settled country. The table is intended merely to stimulate enquiry into differences.

Table V shows that average performance takes 15·4 per cent. of G.N.P. for basic and capital expenditure, plus 3·5 per cent. for social insurance, defence and public debt, making a total of roughly 19 per cent. of G.N.P. Among the under-developed countries analysed here, this level of expenditure is attained by Uganda (19·1), British Guiana (19·8), Gold Coast (20·0), Trinidad (20·3) and Ceylon (21·8).[1] It seems not unreasonable to conclude that the governments of countries making a special development effort will find themselves spending between 19 and 22 per cent. of G.N.P.

[1]These totals exclude agricultural subsidies.

As a by-product of this analysis, we can compare the expenditures proposed under India's Second Five-Year Plan with the figures in Table V. To do this we have to deduct development expenditure under the First Five-Year plan from the figures we have been using, and to add development expenditure under the Second Five-Year plan. The distribution of development expenditure in the year 1953-4 it given in the *Five-Year Plan Progress Report for* 1953-4, page 300. We have deducted this, and have added one-fifth of the proposed expenditure under the Second Five-Year Plan, as set out on page 35 of the *Draft Outline of the Second Five-Year Plan.*[1] The result gives the average public expenditure (ordinary plus development) contemplated under the Second Five-Year Plan. This is shown in Table VI as a percentage of the 1953/4 G.N.P. and compared with the Median expenditure taken from Table V.

TABLE VI

INDIA'S SECOND FIVE-YEAR PLAN AND MEDIAN COMPARED

	India	Median	Difference
Administration	3·34	3·50	− ·16
Education	1·35	2·82	−1·47
Health and Water	·94	2·52	−1·58
Agriculture and Irrigation ...	2·30	1·47	+ ·83
Industry	2·80	·60	+2·20
Roads, Works and Transport ...	3·19	3·62	− ·43
Housing	·18	·83	− ·65
	14·10	15·36	−1·26

Two comments can be made on this comparison. First, there is furious debate in India on the question whether the total expenditure envisaged under the Plan is not too large. The answer to this question is "Obviously not." The proposed expenditure will merely bring India into line with such

[1]In classifying the expenditure shown on page 35 of the *Draft Outline* it is assumed that half the expenditure on the Backward Classes and on Rehabilitation should be credited to Education. The other half is credited to Agriculture in the first case, and to Industry in the second case. But in making deductions from the 1953/4 figures it is assumed that the half which is here credited to Education was originally credited to Administration in the source from which we took the figures. Power is included in Industry.

countries as Tanganyika and Jamaica, and will leave her still far behind other progressive governments in Asia, in Africa and in the Caribbean. If it is contended that the expenditure is too large for the revenue-raising capacity of the Indian governments, the answer is simply that it is ridiculous for a government in the middle of the twentieth century to be raising less than 10 per cent. of G.N.P. in taxation, or to be claiming that it would be an intolerable burden or an insuperable task for the fiscal administration to raise as much as 15 per cent. But elaboration of this answer must wait for Section III of this paper.

The second feature which the comparison throws up is the great difference between the proportions in the Median and in the Indian proposals. India proposes to spend very much less on the "social" services, education, health and housing, and very much more on agriculture and industry. The proposed expenditure on industry is large only in the sense that in the countries included in our survey a larger part of the financing of industry is usually left to private enterprise. But the total capital investment in industry by public and private sources is not remarkable. The figures given in the draft outline amount to about 2·6 per cent. of G.N.P. for large scale industry (excluding power), to which one might add another 1·0 per cent. per annum for cottage industry. Comparable gross investment in the U.K. is consistently above 4 per cent. of G.N.P. Apart from industry, agriculture and the railways receive substantial provision, but the proposed expenditure on roads is almost incredibly small.

India's small expenditures on health and education distinguish her sharply from other progressive governments, and especially from the programmes of the new nationalist governments in Ceylon, in the Gold Coast, and in Nigeria.[1] In reply to the contention that economic expenditures should precede social service expenditures, politicians in these countries reply both that health and education expenditures are necessary for increasing the output of commodities, and also

[1]The Nigerian figures in these tables are for 1952/3. The constitutional changes of 1953 have resulted in a very large increase of public expenditures, especially on health and on education.

that it is just as important to get rid of illiteracy and of disease as it is to provide more steel or cloth. Some West African politicians explain the difference mainly in terms of political structure. India, they say, is ruled by her upper classes, in a situation where caste and class differences are pronounced. Her rulers do what they think is best for the masses of her people, but they do not have to take much account of what the masses themselves think they want. West African society, on the other hand, is nearly classless. The masses have great political influence, and they make it clear that they value expenditures on health and education more than any other kind of government expenditure. In the final analysis there is no "model" which can show what government expenditure ought to be, without taking account of differing political pressures.

III. Revenue.

We have seen that the government of an under-developed country needs to be able to raise revenue of about 17 to 19 per cent. of G.N.P., according to the extent of its defence burden, in order to give a not better than average standard of service. How it can be done, and is done, is the subject of this section.

Table VII summarises the information in Table XII by classifying the sources of revenue in three groups only. "Direct taxes" consists of income tax, poll tax, social insurance tax, land tax, rates and death duties. "Taxes on foreign trade" are shown separately, because it is much easier to raise large sums by way of import and export duties in countries where exports account for as much as 40 per cent. of G.N.P. than it is in those, such as India, where exports account for less than 10 per cent. of G.N.P. The remaining category consists of excise taxes, motor licences, earnings of government departments, interest and miscellaneous fees. Grants-in-aid and loans are not included in the table.

(*a*) *Direct Taxes.*

Much the most important direct tax is the income tax, with a yield ranging from 1·61 per cent. of G.N.P. in India to 13·52 in the U.K., 15·86 in the U.S.A. and 16·75 in Sweden.

TABLE VII

REVENUE AS % OF G.N.P.

	Direct Taxes	Taxes on Foreign Trade	Other Revenue	Total
Tanganyika	6·11	2·81	3·31	12·23
Uganda	3·71	10·36	3·07	17·14
India	2·51	1·53	4·24	8·28
Nigeria	1·94	4·51	1·96	8·41
Ceylon	5·49	10·80	3·06	19·35
Gold Coast	3·47	14·72	4·01	22·20
Jamaica	4·31	4·39	4·58	13·28
British Guiana ...	7·56	6·19	3·92	17·67
Colombia	4·22	1·99	6·66	12·87
Italy	7·09	1·27	15·17	23·53
Trinidad	6·87	3·60	5·26	15·73
France	9·47	1·99	17·44	28·90
U.K.	20·99	6·92	9·18	37·09
New Zealand ...	20·12	2·44	10·62	33·18
Sweden	19·63	1·68	12·00	33·31
U.S.A.	21·82	·18	7·31	29·31

(That the U.S. figure is larger than the U.K. is worth noting. Personal income tax rates are higher in the U.K., but taxes on profits, not set off against personal income tax, are much higher in the U.S.A. Paradoxically, in any debate on the alleged greater enterprise of business men in the U.S.A. most business men or economists offer the explanation that it is due to higher taxation of profits in the U.K.—a piece of inaccuracy which merely underlines how little we know about the effect of taxation on incentives).

Compared with the richer countries, the fundamental reason for the difficulty the poorer countries have in raising public revenue is their reluctance to levy adequate sums through the income tax. This reluctance is based on certain misconceptions.

First, it is sometimes believed that a poor country would have to tax relatively more people in order to raise the same proportion of the national income, but this is true only if the distribution of income is more equal in the poorer country. Income is probably more evenly distributed in West Africa than in Western Europe, because in West Africa the farmers all have access to land free of rent, or at negligible rents. On the other hand, in the overcrowded parts of Asia a handful of landlords takes up to 50 per cent. of the farmers' output in rents, and the distribution of income is as uneven or more uneven than in Europe. The top 10 per cent. of the population receives as much or more of the national income, so an income tax falling on the top 10 per cent. should be capable of yielding just as large a percentage of the national income if comparable rates were charged.

Income tax yields much less because comparable rates are not charged, especially in the middle ranges of the income scale. The rates in the upper ranges are often quite high—for example in India, where nevertheless the income tax (including agricultural income tax) brings in only 1·61 per cent. of G.N.P. Taxes on profits may also be very high—for example, the standard rate is as high in British West Africa as in the U.K. The general practice in the poorer countries is to have high exemption limits for personal incomes, with generous allowances, so that even if the sum payable at £10,000 a year may be very substantial, the sum payable at £1,000 a year is usually only a token amount, compared with what would be paid in the U.K. The man earning £200 a year usually escapes altogether.

Now, in a country like India or Nigeria, a man earning £200 a year is extremely well off in comparison with the average income of the population, which is only about £60 a year per person gainfully occupied. Even the £100 a year man is definitely "middle-class," and a cut above his neighbours. The effect of present policies is to exempt practically the whole of the "middle-class" from paying income tax, and so the yield of the tax is bound to be small. In the U.K. the number of people paying income tax is equal to just over 30 per cent. of the population. In the U.S.A., where the allowances are greater, and where the gainfully occupied are relatively fewer, the number paying income tax equals 25 per cent. of the population. The percentage in Jamaica is 2·1, in Trinidad 1·8, in British Guiana 1·4, and in Ceylon 0·6.

Present policies also have the effect that the middle-class pays proportionally less of its income in taxation than the poorer classes, on whom the incidence of indirect taxation is relatively heavier. The Colwyn Committee showed that this was happening in the U.K. in 1925, when U.K. allowances were similarly generous.[1] According to Dr. Das Gupta this was also the situation in Ceylon in 1942, though the difference is not now so pronounced.[2] There is also evidence that it is the situation in urban areas in India.[3] Such a policy is particularly inequitable in under-developed countries since in these countries the £100 to £500 a year man benefits more from public expenditure than the rest of the population. It is his children who get educated in the state schools, and his family that uses the hospitals. Most of the poorer people in the countryside are outside the reach of these services, and most of the richer use private schools, private nurses and private doctors. It is therefore quite unjustifiable morally to exempt this class from paying direct taxation.

Objection is sometimes made on the ground that it is costly to collect small sums from large numbers of persons, but the importance of this is grossly exaggerated. It is traditional in Asia and Africa to levy a direct tax upon nearly every adult —the land tax in Asia and the poll tax in Africa—and the cost of collection has been small. The average sum paid by each taxpayer is smaller than in Europe, but so also is the average salary of the tax collector. It is not differences in the cost of collection that explain why only 0·6 per cent. of the population pays income tax in Ceylon, compared with 25 per cent. in the U.S.A.

Apart from the income tax, the yield of other direct taxes is bound to be small in under-developed countries, though it might be larger than it is. Death duties are bound to be small because the ratio of capital to income is low. Assuming that the country's capital (including land) is worth 1·5 times its G.N.P., the amount becoming liable for death duties in any year (which depends on the death rate) would be only 3 or 4 per cent. of G.N.P., so even rates of duty comparable to those of the U.K. would not yield much more than 0·8 per cent. of G.N.P. The

[1] *Report of the Committee on National Debt and Taxation, Cmd.* 2800, 1927, p. 96.

[2] *Report of the Taxation Commission*, Colombo, 1956, page 52. This Report quotes Dr. Das Gupta's conclusion.

[3] *Report of the Taxation Enquiry Commission*, New Delhi, 1955, Vol. I, p. 69.

case for higher death duties in these countries must rest on political and equity considerations rather than on the prospect of raising revenue. The land tax used to raise 1·25 per cent. of G.N.P. in India before the war, but now raises only 0·66 per cent., inflation having proceeded faster than re-assessment. If it were politically acceptable to classify all rural land into four or five rough grades of potential fertility, the process of assessment would be greatly simplified and accelerated, without grave injustice. But such a simple reform is contrary to a tradition of making a lengthy, detailed, and expert assessment of every acre. Finally, there is the social insurance tax, which yields as much as 6·4 per cent. of G.N.P. in New Zealand. However, since social insurance payments usually grow faster than the yield of this tax, it does not contribute towards the cost of "basic" services in any of our sixteen countries. Unless the income tax rates are sharply increased in the middle income ranges, the poorer countries will have to continue to rely mainly on indirect taxation.

(*b*) *Taxes on Foreign Trade.*

Taxes on foreign trade are popular with governments because of the ease with which they can be collected, and because they are a means of levying taxation even upon the poorest citizens. Their protectionist function, which is considered important in developed countries, is seldom significant in the less developed.

Import duties raise on the average 3·59 per cent. of G.N.P. in the nine poorest countires in our survey. The lowest figure is 1·14 per cent. in India, where imports are only 5·7 per cent. of G.N.P., and the highest is 5·77 per cent. in the Gold Coast, where imports are 35·6 per cent. of G.N.P. The average rate of the tax is therefore 20 per cent. in India, and 16 per cent. in the Gold Coast.

Heavy taxation of exports is entirely a post-war phenomenon, and is confined to Ceylon, Uganda and the Gold Coast, where export duties raise respectively 5·78, 7·02, and 8·95 per cent. of G.N.P. (not including the profits and reserves of statutory marketing agencies). In the remaining six of the nine poorest countries the average is only 0·55 per cent. of G.N.P.

The purpose of levying these high duties has been to take advantage of some extraordinary increases of prices. For example, in the Gold Coast before the war a price of £30 per ton for cocoa was considered good. Allowing for the average trebling of commodity prices, a post-war price of £100 a ton would have been considered good. Actually the post-war price soared for a time as high as £500 per ton, and even now, when it is thought to be low, it exceeds £200 per ton. Essentially the governments' object has been to siphon off some of these windfall profits into the public purse.

This policy has been criticised on the ground that it is unfair to pick on a small section of the farming community for such heavy taxation ; but it is equally arguable that the man most able to bear taxation is he who has received a sudden windfall increase in his profits. It is also objected that this high taxation has diminished private saving. This is true, but it has also much more than correspondingly increased public saving. Much money which the farmers would otherwise have spent on Cadillacs and on other forms of conspicuous consumption has gone instead into water supplies, electric power stations, and schools.

More serious is the possible long-term effect of such high taxation of a few commodities. It would be foolish to keep the net price to the farmer so low that he finds other crops more profitable—the Gold Coast has avoided this error, but Uganda has not. In the long run one may expect the prices of these commodities in the world market to come into line with the prices of other commodities, so that there is no longer a windfall margin to be taxed. It is a sensible policy to tax away part of the windfall while it lasts, but the governments in this favoured postion ought to be preparing to cultivate other sources of taxation, since it is improbable that they will for long be able to rely on such substantial contributions from a few favoured exports.

One permanent legacy of these interludes is that they have shown the value of basing export duties upon a sliding scale varying with the commodity's price. The value of this system does not lie mainly in its contribution to the public revenue, since it makes export duties a very unstable source of revenue, and since what is gained in the boom may well be lost in the slump. Its value lies rather in that it helps to stabilise the economy internally. In the absence of such arrangements the internal price levels of these countries are dragged up and down in the wake of external prices, which may move 50 per cent. in either direction within twelve months, and the strain of pushing up wages and trying to get them down again does considerable unnecessary harm to industrial relations.

(*c*) *Other Revenue.*

The only other large source of revenue is excise duties, raising an average of 1·94 per cent. of G.N.P. in the nine poorest countries, and an average of 6·28 per cent. in the seven richest, with France achieving the peak of 12·09 per cent. The main reason for this big difference is the adoption of sales and purchase taxes in many of the richer countries, a form of taxation which is now spreading into the under-developed countries.

If an under-developed country needs to raise some 15 to 20 per cent. of G.N.P. in revenue, and cannot rely on a large yield from taxing foreign trade, the adoption of some form of sales tax is inevitable. A general sales tax is not as difficult to collect as one might think. One begins by registering all the people who have to pay it—manufacturers, wholesalers, and retailers. The larger units have in any case to submit their accounts for income tax purposes, so it costs little to extract the sales tax from them. One draws a line below which small traders are not assessed individually—say a turnover of £1,000 a year—and levies instead on these traders a lump sum tax of say £5 a year if the sales tax is one-half of one per cent.

If a commodity passes through several hands before reaching the final consumer, a sales tax levied each time it changes hands must encourage vertical integration. Such a tax is known as a multi-point sales tax, whereas a tax which is paid only once is known as a single-point sales tax. A multi-point sales tax is attractive because the opportunities of evading it are less than the opportunities of evading a single-point sales tax, since the single-point sales tax has to distinguish between sales which are taxed and sales which are not taxed, and this opens up loopholes for evasion. On the other hand, a multi-point sales tax would be a pronounced encouragement to vertical integration unless it were small, so in effect a multi-point sales tax can hardly be more than 0·5 per cent. This in turn means that it cannot yield much revenue. If one needs to raise 4 or 5 per cent. of G.N.P. through a sales tax, as India will have to do, one must choose instead a single-point sales tax of around 10 per cent. The problem is then to prevent evasion. The system works by keeping a register of all those who are liable to pay the tax, and by taxing all their sales except sales to other people on the register. Some sellers then produce false receipts purporting to be from other people on the register, and some fraudulent evasion is inevitable, however busy the tax inspectors may be. But, in a country which has little foreign trade, what is the alternative to taxing domestic trade? The answer implicit in India's *Draft Outline of the Second Five-Year Plan* is: "Inflation." But most economists would agree that a proper exploitation of available sources of taxation should have priority.

(*d*) *A Frame of Reference?*

When we were dealing with expenditure it was easy to construct a tentative frame of reference for under-developed countries by taking the medians and upper quartiles, since the differences between countries at different levels of development were not large. This cannot de done on the revenue side since the difference here is tremendous owing to differences in the burden of defence.

The frame of reference for expenditure gives some indication of the revenue required. Assuming median levels of expenditure, it is 18 to 20 per cent. of G.N.P., according to the burden of defence. Some of the capital formation can be financed by borrowing, but having regard to the low availability of international loans; and to the fact that private domestic saving is itself inadequate to finance an appropriate level of private investment; and to the fact that the private sector leans on government agencies for some finance, especially for agriculture, for factories and for housing; the minimum target of the government of an under-developed country should be to save enough to finance its own capital expenditures. Of course, if these governments receive substantial grants-in-aid from other countries their fiscal task will be lightened, but the immediate prospect for substantial international aid is not bright.

Assuming that a government needs to raise 20 per cent. of G.N.P., and is not able to rely on taxing windfalls in export trade, the following "model" is tentatively suggested :

Income tax	8·0
Land tax, rates	1·5
Death duties	0·5
Export duties	1·0
Import duties, excise, sales tax	7·0
Earnings, fees, interest	2·0
	20·0

This division is based on one of Mr. Gladstone's canons of finance : that the revenue should come about equally from direct and from indirect taxes. Our goal for consumption taxes, 7·0 per cent. of G.N.P., is not far removed from current practice, since the mean sum raised by the nine poorest countries in import duties and excise taxes is already 5·53 per cent. In fact this goal is already nearly reached by Ceylon (6·12), by Colombia (6·18), and by Trinidad (6·84), and is passed by the Gold Coast (7·29), by Jamaica (7·46) and by British Guiana (7·55). The big increase in our "model" is in the income tax, since our goal of 8·0 per cent. compares with a mean of 3·59 per cent. raised by the nine poorest countries. The three under-developed countries nearest to this goal are Tanganyika (5·21), Trinidad (6·08) and British Guiana (6·97).

IV. Local Government Finance.

The people of under-developed countries will not willingly pay higher taxes unless they can see the fruit in additions to those categories of public service which they value, which are more especially roads, water supplies, medical services, schools and electric power. They will also pay more willingly if they can play a part in planning the services of their own locality, instead of depending on plans made in a distant capital city. Hence it is important to have the right balance of central and local expenditures, and also of central and local taxation. In another context the difficulties produced by an inappropriate balance can be seen in acute form in India, where the initiative to step up the expenditure programmes comes from the centre, but where the three taxes which could add most to the revenue (the agricultural income tax, the sales tax and the land revenue) are controlled by the states, who are reluctant to increase taxation.

(*a*) *Expenditure.*

Table VIII summarises the information given in Tables XIII and XIV. Current and capital expenditure are combined in this table. The categories are the same as in Table II, except that an additional column "other" is added for expenditure on social insurance,. defence, and public debt. The expenditure of the regions in Nigeria and of the states in India and in the U.S.A. is included.

TABLE VIII

LOCAL GOVERNMENT EXPENDITURE AS % OF G.N.P.

	Administration	Economic	Education	Health	Other	Total
Tanganyika ...	1·18	·20	·31	·31	—	2·00
Uganda ...	·71	1·01	·45	·12	·03	2·32
India	2·59	2·93	·72	·42	·38	7·04
Nigeria ...	·73	1·42	·74	·55	·31	3·75
Ceylon ...	·40	·37	—	·07	·04	·88
Gold Coast ...	·77	·49	·36	·40	·03	2·05
Jamaica ...	·33	·46	—	·27	·56	1·62
British Guiana	·30	·95	—	·20	·10	1·55
Colombia ...	1·65	1·70	1·09	·41	1·23	6·08
Italy	1·54	2·14	·51	1·13	1·06	6·38
Trinidad ...	·27	·67	—	·44	—	1·38
France ...	1·49	2·66	·36	1·02	·75	6·28
U.K.	1·16	4·24	3·38	·38	·93	10·09
New Zealand	1·11	2·66	—	·22	·30	4·29
Sweden ...	3·06	5·53	3·60	2·68	1·17	16·04
U.S.A. ...	1·44	2·16	2·83	·96	1·59	8·98

The figures must be treated with reserve. It is not possible to be certain that one has got hold of the figures of each of several thousands of local authorities, and in several cases expenditures on capital account have not been obtainable (whether because there are no such expenditures, or because they are included in the current accounts or because we could not find a source). Errors here make little difference to the aggregates in Tables II and III, but they are of course of greater significance for Table VIII.

The main conclusion, however, is not obscured by the shakiness of some of the figures. This is : that the weakness of local government in relation to central government is one of the most striking phenomena of under-developed countries. In Ceylon, in Africa and in the West Indies the central government directly controls the major part of the public service. This weakness of local government is particularly marked in relation to education. Only in the U.K., Sweden, and the U.S.A. do local authorities play a significant role in the education system ; in five countries they play no role at all. On the other hand, except in Nigeria (where the powers of the regional governments were substantially increased in 1953 under a new federal constitution) the countries where the local governments spend less than 6 per cent. of G.N.P. are all small, and the fact that New Zealand is included among them suggests that the absence of strong subordinate authorities may be due to their size rather than to their state of development. Nevertheless one retains the impression that the size of some of these countries, especially in Africa, would justify greater regional devolution, and it is interesting to note that this has become a major political issue in some of them.

(*b*) *Revenue.*

To construct Table IX we have first arranged countries in order of the percentage of G.N.P. accruing as revenue to subordinate authorities (including grants), and we have then averaged the receipts of the first four, the second four, and so on. For example, the first four (*i.e.* those receiving least) are Ceylon, Trinidad, Jamaica and British Guiana. They receive in land tax and rates respectively 0·32, 0·27, 0·78 and 0·43 of G.N.P. The average of these figures, 0·45, is entered in row one, column one of Table IX.

TABLE IX

SOURCES OF LOCAL REVENUE AS % OF G.N.P.

	First Four	Second Four	Third Four	Fourth Four
Land tax, rates	·45	·70	·52	2·07
Income and poll tax	·19	·47	·63	1·75
Excise duties	—	·10	1·55	·91
Grants from centre	·33	·61	1·11	1·79
Other revenue	·43	·62	·66	2·73
Total	1·40	2·50	4·47	9·25

A tax on land or houses is the most popular source of local revenue; it is the only tax which is levied at the local level by all the sixteen countries in our survey. It is usually also the largest single source of revenue. Next in popularity (with governments if not with taxpayers) is a local income tax, levied by nine of our countries. Local excise duties do not normally bring in a substantial revenue. Grants from the central government usually account for between 20 and 25 per cent. of the revenues of subordinate authorities.

ALISON MARTIN
W. ARTHUR LEWIS

University of Manchester.

	Tanganyika	Uganda	India	Nigeria	Ceylon	Gold Coast	Jamaica	Br. Guiana	Colombia	Italy	Trinidad	France	U.K.	New Zealand	Sweden	U.S.A.
1. Administration	3·87	3·17	3·09	1·42	2·77	2·56	2·89	3·24	3·26	3·76	3·23	3·32	2·36	2·92	3·07	2·40
2. Education	1·70	2·39	·77	·78	2·94	3·06	1·99	2·19	1·68	2·99	2·24	1·97	3·47	2·68	4·27	2·40
3. Health	1·28	1·06	·44	·53	2·07	1·23	2·06	1·93	·84	2·08	2·46	1·62	3·28	3·42	2·57	·92
4. Roads	·71	·74	·22	·23	·51	·92	·82	·87	·39	·55	1·13	·78	·70	1·18	1·05	·63
5. Transport	·59	·37	·12	·31	·83	·41	·68	1·09	1·00	·75	·89	·86	·10	·72	·45	·27
6. Public Works	·74	·96	·53	·53	·55	·55	·50	·35	·79	1·01	·80	·82	—	·94	—	·03
7. Agriculture	1·09	·86	·41	·23	·43	·80	·58	·46	·23	·61	·55	·23	·24	·54	·72	·23
8. Drainage	—	·02	·24	—	·24	—	·05	·55	—	—	·13	—	·08	·10	—	—
9. Water Supplies	·14	·44	—	·07	·16	·27	·09	·32	—	—	·20	·05	·32	·14	·23	·08
10. Land Settlement	·33	·35	—	·10	·57	·18	·30	·28	—	·38	·34	·25	—	·45	·24	—
11. Co-operatives	·03	·07	·06	·01	·14	·03	·02	·03	—	—	·04	—	—	—	—	—
12. Industry	—	·05	·27	·05	·20	·11	·04	—	·12	·16	·12	·29	·16	·21	·17	—
13. Commerce	·02	·05	—	·06	·02	·12	·07	—	—	·36	·09	·37	—	—	—	·02
14. Mining	·09	·08	—	·02	·02	·04	·01	·06	·03	—	·02	—	—	·01	·06	·01
15. Labour	·07	·12	—	—	·13	·05	·04	·05	·08	·14	·08	·12	·12	·28	·30	·08
16. Housing	·02	·05	—	—	·01	·10	·24	·02	—	—	·10	·11	·69	·18	·13	·17
17. Agricultural Subsidies ...	·13	—	—	—	·04	·46	·14	·50	—	·16	·79	—	1·98	1·87	·09	·64
18. Social Insurance	·50	·60	·18	—	1·24	·43	1·07	1·26	·56	4·33	1·17	3·51	5·84	7·98	5·59	3·49
19. Defence	·27	·45	1·91	·50	·49	·48	·14	·06	1·43	5·33	·03	9·49	9·89	3·74	3·74	13·90
20. Public Debt.	·33	·43	·60	·14	1·06	·40	1·35	1·03	1·39	1·97	1·13	1·97	4·77	2·76	·81	2·16
21. **Total**	**11·91**	**12·26**	**8·84**	**4·98**	**14·42**	**12·20**	**13·08**	**14·29**	**11·80**	**24·58**	**15·54**	**25·76**	**34·00**	**30·12**	**23·49**	**27·43**

TABLE XI.—CAPITAL EXPENDITURE AS % OF GROSS NATIONAL PRODUCT

	Tanganyika	Uganda	India	Nigeria	Ceylon	Gold Coast	Jamaica	Br. Guiana	Colombia	Italy	Trinidad	France	U.K.	New Zealand	Sweden	U.S.A.
1. Administration	·40	·81	·20	·01	·16	·42	·21	·60	—	·44	·35	·41	·57	·52	·65	·24
2. Education	·53	1·15	—	·46	·39	·69	·32	·15	—	·15	·24	·48	·52	·76	1·13	·66
3. Health	·32	·34	·01	·09	·36	·58	·06	·64	—	·05	·47	·06	·13	·14	·36	·27
4. Roads	1·02	·97	·02	·30	·43	1·29	·60	·46	1·02	·37	1·24	·54	·09	·76	1·64	·90
5. Transport	·12	·19	·29	·47	1·09	2·49	·43	·76	·46	·82	·24	·96	·59	1·29	2·89	·08
6. Public Works	·10	1·01	·28	·42	·39	·25	·45	·36	1·18	·43	·55	·40	—	·35	·16	·01
7. Agriculture	·38	·80	·02	·06	1·15	1·00	·54	·74	·34	·87	·06	·57	·04	·59	·32	·24
8. Drainage	—	·03	·32	—	1·55	—	·22	1·01	—	·47	·21	—	·10	·09	—	—
9. Water Supplies	·80	·46	·68	·17	·12	·75	·30	·10	—	·18	1·81	·15	·36	·10	1·57	·31
10. Land Settlement	·03	·09	—	·01	·15	·03	·09	·08	—	·44	·13	—	—	·45	—	—
11. Co-operatives	—	—	—	—	—	·01	·01	·11	—	—	—	—	—	—	—	—
12. Industry	—	·03	·38	·25	1·04	·49	·09	—	·21	·58	—	1·48	·11	1·70	·35	—
13. Commerce	—	·02	—	—	·01	·09	—	—	—	—	—	—	—	—	·38	·01
14. Mining	·02	·05	—	·06	—	·01	·01	·23	—	·03	—	·06	—	·14	—	—
15. Labour	—	—	—	—	·01	·01	—	—	—	—	—	—	—	—	—	—
16. Housing	·24	·76	—	—	·29	—	·71	·72	—	·72	·21	1·82	2·38	1·38	1·52	·16
17. Social Insurance	—	—	—	—	·05	—	—	—	—	—	—	—	·02	—	·12	—
18. Defence	·02	·10	·10	·10	·26	·13	—	—	—	—	—	1·18	·46	—	2·90	1·38
19. **Total**	**3·98**	**6·81**	**2·30**	**2·40**	**7·45**	**8·24**	**4·04**	**5·96**	**3·21**	**5·55**	**5·51**	**8·11**	**5·37**	**8·27**	**13·99**	**4·26**

TABLE XII.—REVENUE SOURCES AS % OF GROSS NATIONAL PRODUCT

	Tanganyika	Uganda	India	Nigeria	Ceylon	Gold Coast	Jamaica	Br. Guiana	Colombia	Italy	Trinidad	France	U.K.	New Zealand	Sweden	U.S.A.
1. Income Tax	5·21	3·34	1·61	1·75	4·72	2·73	3·24	6·97	2·78	4·54	6·08	7·82	13·52	10·41	16·75	15·86
2. Social Insurance	·07	—	—	—	·26	·04	·07	—	—	·37	—	·48	3·39	6·40	·53	2·78
3. Land Tax	·78	·35	·90	·19	·42	·70	·87	·48	1·15	1·22	·56	·97	2·92	2·19	2·18	2·84
4. Death Duties	·05	·02	—	—	·09	—	·13	·11	·29	·96	·23	·20	1·16	1·12	·17	·34
5. Export Duties	·12	7·02	·39	2·07	5·78	8·95	—	·66	·04	1·07	·04	·08	—	—	·56	—
6. Import Duties	2·69	3·34	1·14	2·44	5·02	5·77	4·39	5·53	1·95	·20	3·56	1·91	6·92	2·44	1·12	·18
7. Excise Duties	1·37	1·26	2·14	·76	1·10	1·52	3·07	2·02	4·23	9·07	3·28	12·09	4·82	4·43	5·25	5·05
8. Motor Licences	·23	·09	·12	·12	·20	·16	·16	·13	·11	·26	·29	·08	·49	·88	·52	·44
9. Govt. Dept. Earnings ...	·50	·81	·86	·40	·27	·42	·32	·52	·48	3·02	·36	·98	2·13	2·62	2·02	·45
10. Miscellaneous Fees ...	·97	·57	1·02	·29	1·23	·93	·96	1·06	1·84	2·53	1·14	3·21	·60	1·70	3·64	1·14
11. Interest	·24	·34	·10	·39	·26	·98	·07	·19	—	·29	·19	1·08	1·14	·99	·57	·23
12. **Total**	**12·23**	**17·14**	**8·28**	**8·41**	**19·35**	**22·20**	**13·28**	**17·67**	**12·87**	**23·53**	**15·73**	**28·90**	**37·09**	**33·18**	**33·31**	**29·31**

TABLE XIII.—LOCAL CURRENT EXPENDITURE AS % OF GROSS NATIONAL PRODUCT

	Tanganyika	Uganda	India		Nigeria		Ceylon	Gold Coast	Jamaica	Br. Guiana	Colombia	Italy	Trinidad	France	U.K.	New Zealand	Sweden	U.S.A.	
			States	Local	Regions	Local												States	Local
1. Administration...	1·18	·71	1·96	·37	·42	·31	·40	·55	·33	·24	1·65	1·54	·27	1·38	·97	1·03	2·41	·31	·95
2. Education ...	·31	·39	·56	·16	·47	·10	—	·26	—	—	1·09	·51	—	·08	2·91	—	2·65	·40	1·79
3. Health	·31	·05	·32	·09	·32	·14	·07	·29	·27	·20	·41	1·13	·44	1·02	·36	·22	2·32	·29	·45
4. Roads	·11	·18	—	—	·05	·10	·09	·25	·29	·18	·07	—	·64	·78	·62	·66	·62	·20	·41
5. Transport ...	—	·01	·03	·05	—	—	—	·01	·07	·07	·10	—	—	·20	—	·08	·45	·01	·08
6. Public Works ...	—	·18	·48	·14	·17	·10	·15	—	·01	—	·47	·62	—	·82	—	·32	—	·01	·02
7. Agriculture ...	·09	·06	·38	—	·16	·05	—	·02	—	·01	—	—	—	—	·01	·11	—	·13	·05
8. Drainage ...	—	—	·23	—	—	—	—	—	—	·11	—	—	—	—	·08	·11	—	—	—
9. Water Supplies ·	—	·02	—	—	·03	·03	·13	·08	·07	·32	—	—	—	—	·32	·17	·23	·01	·03
10. Land Settlement	—	·01	—	—	·05	·03	—	—	—	—	—	—	—	·25	—	—	·24	—	—
11. Co-operatives ...	—	—	·06	—	·01	—	—	—	—	—	—	—	—	—	—	—	—	—	—
12. Industry ...	—	—	·15	—	·01	·03	—	—	·02	—	—	1·52*	—	·26	—	·01	—	·06	—
13. Housing ...	—	—	—	—	—	—	—	—	—	·02	—	—	·01	—	·15	·03	—	—	·03
14. Social Insurance	—	·03	·15	—	—	—	·04	·01	·38	·02	·46	·90	—	·52	·12	—	1·12	·88	·50
15. Defence ...	—	—	—	—	·22	·09	—	—	—	—	—	—	—	—	—	—	—	·02	—
16. Public Debt. ...	—	—	·21	·02	—	—	—	·02	·18	·08	·77	·16	·02	·23	·81	·30	·05	·05	·14
17. **Total** ...	**2·00**	**1·64**	**4·53**	**·83**	**1·91**	**·98**	**·88**	**1·49**	**1·62**	**1·25**	**5·02**	**6·38**	**1·38**	**5·54**	**6·35**	**3·04**	**10·09**	**2·37**	**4·45**

* Appears as "Economic and Productive." In Table X it has been split between 4, 5, 7 and 10.

TABLE XIV.—LOCAL CAPITAL EXPENDITURE AS % OF G.N.P.

	Uganda	India States	Nigeria		Gold Coast	Br. Guiana	Colombia	France	U.K.	New Zealand	Sweden	U.S.A.	
			Regions	Local								States	Local
1. Administration	—	·26	—	—	·22	·06	—	·11	·19	·08	·65	·03	·15
2. Education	·06	—	·13	·04	·10	—	—	·28	·47	—	·95	·09	·55
3. Health	·07	·01	·06	·03	·11	—	—	—	·02	—	·36	·07	·15
4. Roads	·05	·01	·09	·04	·10	·16	·20	·08	·08	·48	·59	·63	·26
5. Transport	·01	—	—	—	—	—	·06	—	·03	·01	·50	·01	·01
6. Public Works	·45	·13	·16	·10	—	—	·70	·27	—	·39	·16	·01	·01
7. Agriculture	·01	·01	·04	·01	—	—	·10	—	—	·08	—	·02	—
8. Drainage	—	·32	—	—	—	—	—	—	·10	·09	—	—	—
9. Water Supplies	·01	·63	·15	·01	·03	·08	—	—	·36	·11	·78	—	·01
10. Industry	—	·31	—	—	—	—	—	—	·10	—	·53	—	—
11. Housing	·02	—	—	—	—	—	—	—	2·39	·01	1·43	—	·16
12. **Total**	**·68**	**1·68**	**·63**	**·23**	**·56**	**·30**	**1·06**	**·74**	**3·74**	**1·25**	**5·95**	**·86**	**1·30**

TABLE XV.—LOCAL REVENUE SOURCES AS % OF GROSS NATIONAL PRODUCT.

	Tanganyika	Uganda	India		Nigeria		Ceylon	Gold Coast	Jamaica	Br. Guiana	Colombia	Italy	Trinidad	France	U.K.	New Zealand	Sweden	U.S.A.	
			States	Local	Regions	Local												States	Local
1. Income Tax	·74	1·14	·58	·01	·06	·68	·07	—	—	·68	—	1·18	—	—	—	—	6·44	·54	·03
2. Social Insurance	—	—	—	—	—	—	—	—	—	—	—	—	—	—	—	—	—	·75	·09
3. Land Tax	·39	·03	·67	·22	·03	·09	·32	·59	·78	·43	·49	·59	·27	·44	2·93	1·98	2·06	·15	2·68
4. Death Duties	—	—	—	—	—	—	—	—	—	—	—	—	—	—	—	—	—	·07	—
5. Excise Duties	—	·37	1·34	·05	·01	—	—	·03	—	—	2·99	1·80	—	1·49	—	—	·08	1·87	·21
6. Motor Licences	—	—	·12	—	·09	—	·06	—	·11	—	·11	·07	—	—	—	·20	—	·29	·15
7. Govt. Dept. Earnings... ...	—	—	·68	—	·05	·10	—	·03	·01	·14	·48	·04	·01	—	1·31	·23	1·40	·30	—
8. Miscellaneous Fees	·30	·27	·50	·28	·03	·18	·16	·36	·24	·34	1·02	·54	·35	2·56	—	·86	2·90	·34	·70
9. Interest	—	·04	·08	—	·09	—	—	·01	—	·01	—	·22	—	—	·04	—	—	·04	—
10. Grants from Central G. ...	·47	·44	·43	·17	2·59	·05	·37	·93	·40	·09	·36	·82	·76	1·45	2·75	·59	2·08	·77	·09
11. „ „ States	—	—	—	—	—	·16	—	—	—	—	—	—	—	—	—	—	—	—	1·62
12. „ „ Local Gov. ...	—	—	—	—	—	—	—	—	—	—	—	—	—	—	—	—	—	·06	—
13. **Total**	1·90	2·29	4·40	·73	2·95	1·26	·98	1·95	1·54	1·69	5·45	5·26	1·39	5·94	7·03	3·86	14·96	5·18	5·57

STATISTICAL APPENDIX

Tables I to VII and X to XII show the combined expenditures and revenues of central and local governments, excluding inter-governmental transfers. Tables VIII, IX and XIII to XV are for "local" authorities only, including states and other constituent units of federations.

I. Expenditure Classification.

Public utilities are excluded unless their accounts appear in government budgets. They are then included net ; deficits appear in the expenditure tables (posts and telecommunications in Transport, electricity in Industry, etc.), and surpluses in the revenue tables.

Refunds of revenue which appear as expenditure in the budgets are here excluded from expenditure and deducted from revenue.

Administration includes all administrative and legislative expenditure except the administrative expenditure of the education, health and economic departments specified below. It includes tax collection and accounting, prisons, police, printing, fire service and miscellaneous expenditure not elsewhere specified. Pensions are shown in Social Insurance.

Education includes universities, technical colleges (not agricultural) and adult education.

Health includes hospitals, sanitation, and medical services, but not health insurance.

Roads includes public lighting.

Transport includes railways, civil aviation, mercantile marine, harbours, posts and telecommunications. Current accounts include only deficits on these services, unless they are organised as separate agencies, in which case the administrative expenditures of the departments responsible for supervising them are also shown. Capital expenditures are shown only in so far as the budget provides for them.

Public Works includes buildings and works not elsewhere specified. Where several categories are included in the budget of a "Public Works Department" the administrative expenditure of the department is divided proportionally between them.

Agriculture includes fishing, veterinary services, and tsetse control, but excludes subsidies and grants to farmers ; these are shown separately.

Drainage includes irrigation and coast protection.

Water supplies includes sewerage, but excludes irrigation and power.

Land settlement includes forestry, lands and surveys.

Industry includes electricity and gas.

Commerce includes expenditure on trade promotion.

Mining includes geological surveys.

Labour includes employment services, but not unemployment insurance.

Housing includes rehabilitation measures.

Agricultural subsidies includes all food subsidies and all grants or subsidies to farmers or losses on farm support programmes.

Social insurance includes all civil and military pensions, public assistance, and social security benefits.

Defence includes all military expenditures, but not police.

Public debt includes interest and sinking fund payments, but not repayment of debt.

The term *Basic Expenditure* is applied to all categories except the last four named above.

2. Revenue Classification.

Reimbursements of revenue are excluded ; so are loans ; and so are grants received from other countries

Income tax includes personal and company taxes, excess profits tax, education tax, agricultural income tax, and poll tax.

Social insurance includes contributions to pensions, and superannuation.

Land tax includes rates, land revenue.

Death duties includes legacy duty.

Export duties includes cesses on exports, but excludes profits of statutory marketing boards in Africa. These profits do not appear in these tables.

Import duties includes "customs duties" where these are not specifically divided between import and export duties.

Excise duties include sales tax, purchase tax, turnover tax, and minerals duties.

Motor licences includes vehicle licences, but not purchase taxes on vehicles, or petrol taxes.

Government department earnings includes trading profits and surpluses of government departments, revenue of state monopolies, revenue of government owned land and buildings, miscellaneous fees of government departments.

Miscellaneous fees includes stamp duties, licences except motor vehicle licences, fines, fees for specific services, miscellaneous revenue not elsewhere specified.

Interest : receipts on government investments.

3. Tanganyika.

Sources for central government : *Estimates of Revenue and Expenditure for the Year Ending June 30th*, 1955, Dar es Salaam. The figures are for the calendar year 1953 in the case of current expenditure and revenue, but for 1954-5 in the case of capital, since 1953 was not found in this source. The European, Indian and Other Non-Native (including Goan) Education Funds are included in full because they are financed entirely by the government ; contributions to Non-Native Education Authorities and loans to European Education Authorities are therefore excluded. No details are given for the 1953 Public Works Extraordinary expenditure or the 1953 Township Authorities expenditure, so they are both divided proportionately to their 1954-55 expenditures. Subventions and Contributions to the East Africa High Commission are included under the appropriate heads. Schemes financed from the Agriculture Development Reserve are included, and also the Capital Works Expenditure, which is financed from C.D. and W. grants, the Development Plan Reserve, Loan Funds, and the Lint and Seed Marketing Board Loan.

Source for local authorities : *Tanganyika Statistical Abstract*, 1955. The figures are for 1953. The revenues of the Native Treasuries are shown in total, but no details of sources are given other than their share of the Hut and Native Poll tax ; it is assumed that the other sources are distributed in the same proportions as the Dar es Salaam revenue.

The *Report of the Royal Commission on East Africa* estimates the money product of Tanganyika at £62 million in 1952. This is impossibly low, since the same source gives exports as £47 million and government expenditure as £16 million. We have estimated the gross national product (including subsistence) by rough methods at £121 million. A statistician in East Africa, who wishes to remain anonymous at present, arrived independently at £125 million, using more ample information. For 1953-4 we have assumed £121 million, equivalent to £15·0 per head.

4. Uganda.

Source for central government : *Estimates for the Uganda Protectorate for the Year Ending, June 30th, 1956.* The figures are for 1954-5 in the case of current expenditure and revenue, but for 1955-6 in the case of works financed through the capital budget, since the earlier figures were not available. Subventions and Contributions to the East Africa High Commission are included under the appropriate heads. The Price Assistance Funds are not included in the revenue.

Source for local authorities : *Annual Estimates for the Buganda Kingdom, Eastern Province, Northern Province and Western Province.* The figures are for 1953, the latest year available.

The gross national product is from *Background to the Budget*, Uganda Protectorate, April, 1955. Export taxes are added to the figure given in this source. We have used the figure for 1954, which is £109 million, equivalent to £20·1 per head.

5. India.

Source : *Report of the Taxation Enquiry Commission*, Vol. I. The figures are revised estimates for 1953-4. The source gives consolidated estimates as well as estimates for each level of government, but does not include capital expenditures by minor authorities. Community Development is included under Agriculture. Receipts in aid of superannuation are included in Miscellaneous Fees.

The same source estimates *net* national product for 1953-4 at 105,000 million rupees, equivalent to 282·5 rupees or £21·1 per head. We have used this *net* figure.

6. Nigeria.

Source : *The Economic Development of Nigeria*, a report by the International Bank. The figures are for 1952-3. The Public Works figure includes the whole establishment cost of the Public Works Department, some of which should be included under Roads, Water Supplies, etc. Expenditure on the public debt interest is excluded from the Administration figure but the latter still includes expenditure on pensions and gratuities which should be shown separately under social insurance. Revenue from Customs and Excise has been divided in accordance with information given in the 1953 *Annual Colonial Report for Nigeria*. Extra-budgetary receipts are included under interest, being interest receipts of the Revenue Equalisation Fund and other funds, and reimbursement receipts from Marketing Boards and similar institutions. Other non-Tax Receipts are divided between land tax, government department earnings and reimbursements in proportion to the 1953-54 expenditure on them by the Regional governments. "Other Local Receipts," which includes all receipts from public services, are divided equally between Government Department Earnings and Miscellaneous fees. The figures include expenditure from renewals funds held by the central and regional governments ; from the central government Highways Capital Account, the Cameroons Development Fund, the distributed profits of the Cameroons Development Corporation, the Northern Region Capital Development Account, the Loan Development Fund and expenditure by the central and regional governments reimbursed by Marketing Boards or Regional Production Development Boards. Also, Development and Welfare expenditures are divided between the federal and regional governments, according to the administering authority, despite the fact that payments originate in, or pass through, the federal government.

This source estimates gross national product in 1952-3 as £677·4 million, equivalent to £21·7 per head.

7. Ceylon.

Source for the central government : *Estimates of Revenue and Expenditure for the year ending September 30th*, 1956. Also, *Estimated Capital Outlays of the Ceylon Government*, 1955-6. The figures are for 1954-5. Food subsidies, manure subsidies and refunds of fuel tax on tractors are included in Agricultural Subsidies. Eradication of plant pests is included in capital expenditure. The capital expenditures of the railways and other public utilities are included.

Source for local authorities : *Statistical Abstract of Ceylon*, 1955. These figures are for 1953. Details are not given for Town Councils or Village Committees ; the totals given have been allocated in the same proportions as Urban Councils.

The *Statistical Abstract of Ceylon*, 1955, estimates gross national product for 1954 at 4,772 million rupees, equivalent to 569·2 rupees or £42·5 per head.

8. Gold Coast.

Source : A special analysis of the budgets of central and local authorities was made for us by the Gold Coast Statistical Department, to which we are most grateful. The data supplied have been slightly re-arranged. Figures are actuals for 1953-4.

In their *Report on the Financial and Physical Problems of Development in the Gold Coast*, 1952, Seers and Ross estimated the national income for 1950-51 at £152 million, including food sales of £30 million but excluding food consumed on farms. According to the *Economic Survey of the Gold Coast*, food produced in 1953 was worth £73 million, and prices were the same as 1951. This brings the Seers and Ross estimate up to £195 million for 1950-51, all-inclusive. Allowing for changes in output and prices, we have estimated gross national product in 1953-4 at £208 million, equivalent to £50·4 per head.

9. Jamaica.

Source for central government : *Annual Estimates for the year ending March* 31*st*, 1956, and *Development Estimates for* 1954-5. The figures used are for 1954-5.

Source for local authorities : *Annual Estimates for the parishes and for the Kingston and St. Andrew Corporation*. These figures are for 1953-4.

In *Social and Economic Studies*, Supplement to Vol. 4, No. 4, Alfred P. Thorne estimates gross domestic product at £105 m. in 1953. Income from overseas amounted to about £1 million. We have used a figure for gross national product of £106 million, equivalent to £71·3 per head.

10. British Guiana.

Source for central government : *Annual Estimates and Development Estimates for* 1955. The figures are for the year 1953. The land settlement schemes, processing factory, produce depot and transport services are included net. Expenditure under Public Works Miscellaneous, "roads, rivers, creeks and portages" is allocated to roads. Public Works Extraordinary is distributed proportionally to the 1955 expenditure, since only the total is given for 1953. Only the total for the Cost of Living Allowances for 1953 is given, so the 1954 proportions have been used.

Source for local authorities : *Annual Report of the Commissioner of Local Government for* 1953 ; also *Statement of the Funds of the City of Georgetown for* 1953. The figures are for the year 1953. Only totals were available for New Amsterdam, so the distribution of revenue and expenditure was presumed to be proportionately the same as Georgetown. Total local expenditure in 1953 is given in the *Annual Colonial Report*, so the expenditures of Village and Country Districts were obtained by difference. Their distribution was assumed to be the same as in 1951, using the details given by Percival and D'Andrade in *The National Economic Accounts of British Guiana*, 1948-51. The revenues of the districts are given in the Commissioner's Annual Report.

The *Annual Colonial Report for British Guiana*, 1954, estimates net national product at factor cost at $170 million in 1953, basing itself on earlier estimates by Percival and D'Andrade. We have added $8 million for depreciation, making gross national product $178 million, equivalent to $387·4 or £80·7 per head.

11. Colombia.

Source : *The Basis of a Development Programme for Colombia*, a report by the International Bank for Reconstruction and Development, 1950 ; with several mimeographed appendices. The figures are for 1947. The classification used in this report is not always the same as ours, and we have not had the budgets to make our own classification. These figures are therefore not strictly comparable with the others.

This source estimates gross national product in 1947 at 3,367·5 million pesos. Colombia's position in the tables, however, is determined by her gross national product in 1953, estimated at 7,970 million pesos, equivalent to 658·3 pesos or £93·7 per head.

12. Italy.

Source: *Italian Economic Survey*, May-June, 1955, published by the Association of Italian Joint Stock Companies ; and *Ragioneria Generale Dello Stato, Bilancio di Previsione*, 1953-4. The figures for the central government are for 1953-4. "Grants to public bodies" and "deficits of autonomous concerns" are excluded because no details are given in these sources. The figures for capital expenditure are for assessments and not payments, because the latter include arrears of payments relating to the previous year. Expenditure on war losses is included under Housing. The Investment Fund for the South and investments for autonomous concerns are included.

The figures for the local authorities are for 1953, and relate to the Communes, Provinces and Regions. These sources do not give details for "economic and productive expenditure," so in the combined tables this item, amounting to 1·52 per cent. of G.N.P., has been split between Agriculture, Land Settlement, Roads and Transport.

The United Nations' *Statistics of National Income and Expenditure*, 1955, gives gross national product for 1953 as 10,177 billion lire, equivalent to 214,500 lire or £122·1 per head.

13. Trinidad.

Source for the central government : *Annual Estimates for Trinidad and Tobago for* 1955. The figures are for 1954.

Source for local authorities : *Annual Statistical Digest for* 1953, and *Annual Colonial Report for Trinidad*, 1953. The figures are for 1953. In the municipalities, "public services expenditure" is divided between health and roads in the same proportions as central government expenditure. In the County Councils the total revenue is divided between rates and miscellaneous fees in the same proportion as central and municipal revenues combined.

In *A Fiscal Survey of the Caribbean*, A. R. Prest estimates gross *domestic* product *at market prices* in 1953 at $400 million, equivalent to $590 or £122·9 per head. We have used these figures.

14. France.

Source : Ministère des Finances, *Statistiques et Etudes Financières*, No. 52 April, 1953, Supplement 74, February, 1955, No. 76, April, 1955 ; and *Le Budget de* 1954. The figures are for 1953. *Reconstruction et urbanisme* is included under Housing, *affaires économiques* under Commerce. *Subventions aux enterprises d'intérèt national* are excluded because no details are given. *France d'Outre-mer* is included in all the tables. Capital expenditure includes *réparations des dommages de guerre, reconstruction et équipement des services civils, investissements économiques et sociaux exécutés avec le concours de l'Etat*, which are financed from *fonds publics*.

The figures for local authorities exclude Hospital Boards. Expenditure on *assistance* is to a large extent health expenditure, so *dépenses d'assistance, assistance, prévoyance, famille*, and *securité, salubrité, santé* have been divided two to one between health and social insurance respectively. *Acquisitions, travaux neufs et grosses réparations* are included under public works. Local capital expenditure is taken out of the total expenditure to give current expenditure.

The United Nations *Statistics of National Income and Expenditure* gives gross national product for 1953 as 12,321 billion francs, equivalent to 287,500 francs or £292·4 per head.

15. United Kingdom.

Source : *National Income and Expenditure*, 1955. The figures are for 1954. School meals, milk and welfare foods and child care are included under Education. Town and country planning and parks are included under Administration.

The gross national product for 1954 was £15,718 million, equivalent to £309·6 per head.

16. New Zealand.

Source : *Official Year Book for* 1955. The figures are for 1953-4. Expenditure of Hospital Boards is included in central government expenditure. Transfers from the National Development Loans Account to the Electricity Supply Account, the Land Settlement Account, the State Coal Mines Account, the Workings Railways Account and the Post Office Account are included under Capital expenditure.

For local authorities the totals for 1953-4 are allocated in accordance with the proportions for 1951-2, given in detail in *New Zealand Local Authorities Handbook*, No. 28, 1951-2.

Gross national product for 1953-4 was £N.Z.776 million, equivalent to £N.Z. 380·8 or £379·3 per head.

17. Sweden.

Source : *National budget for År* 1955, and *Statistisk Årsbok for Sverige, År* 1955. The figures for the central government are for 1953-4. Capital expenditures are shown separately in detail. Some capital expenditures are, however, shown in the current budget, and though the total amount of these is available, their distribution is not. We have assumed that the distribution of the capital figures in the current budget is the same as the distribution of total capital expenditures. A similar adjustment has been made for the expenditure of the local authorities, which is known in total and in detail, but part of which is financed by transfers from the central government which are not shown separately. It follows that our tables for combined capital expenditure and for local revenues and expenditures are accurate, but the table for combined current expenditure, while accurate in total, is not quite accurate in detail.

Gross national product in 1954 was 41,750 million kroner, equivalent to 5,788 kroner or £398·6 per head.

18. United States of America.

Source for the federal government : *The Budget of the United States for* 1955. The figures are for the year 1952-3. Veterans' services and benefits are allocated to the appropriate categories. Stabilisation of farm prices and incomes is in Agricultural Subsidies. Insurance trusts, revenues and expenditures are included gross.

Source for states and local authorities : *Compendium of State Government Finances in* 1953, *Compendium of City Government Finances in* 1953, *Statistical Abstract of the United States*, 1955. The figures are for 1952-3. For capital expenditures of Townships only the totals were available, and these were divided proportionately to the current expenditures on roads and education. The capital expenditure of Special Districts is allocated to Housing.

Gross national product was $332·2 billion in 1953, equivalent to $2,081 or £740·6 per head.

[27]

THE SHIFTING FORTUNES OF AGRICULTURE

I. THE GENERAL SETTING

W. ARTHUR LEWIS
University of Manchester, England

THE fortunes of agriculturists depend not only upon the prices they receive but also upon their productivity. If real prices halve but productivity doubles, they are no worse off than before. In practice, farmers are interested not only in their own absolute standard of living, but also in how their earnings compare with earnings in other occupations. So, in comparing members of the same community, the terms of trade which matter are not the commodity terms of trade but the factoral terms of trade.

The behaviour of the factoral terms of trade depends on three movements:

(*a*) the comparative rates of growth of demand for agricultural and for non-agricultural products;
(*b*) the comparative rates of growth of productivity in agricultural and in non-agricultural industries; and
(*c*) the mobility of the population into and out of agriculture.

The balance between these different rates of growth is so different in different phases of economic development that it is not feasible to speak in the same breath about the newly developing and the advanced countries. Broadly speaking, the advanced countries produce too much food while the newly developing countries produce too little. I propose, therefore, to speak separately about these two groups. It is not possible in 1958 to say anything about these matters which is both startling and true; I shall make only some random introductory remarks.

The Role of Agriculture in Economic Development

The economic development of most countries is unbalanced, in the sense that not all sectors come alive and show vigorous growth simultaneously. From the point of view of the role of agriculture in economic development we may distinguish three cases:

(1) where development begins outside agriculture, or
(2) where development begins with agricultural exports, or
(3) where development begins with greater productivity in food for the home market.

We can dismiss the third of these cases because it is seldom if ever self-sustaining. Since the elasticity of demand for food is less than unity, an increase in home food production when other sectors of the economy are stationary is almost certain to drive the farmers bankrupt. It is true that at low levels the farmers may eat nearly the whole of their extra production so that they may be better off in terms of food, even though the increase in their marketings causes them to have less of other commodities. It is also true that the rest of the economy benefits from the reduction of food prices; but since this means selling less to the farmers, the effect may be to increase urban unemployment rather than to stimulate non-agricultural production. One can conceive of a case where economic development begins with increased productivity in food and is sustained because farmers move rapidly out of food into other occupations as their productivity rises; but I cannot think of any case in history where the initiative in development (as distinct from the response to development) has been taken by the food farmers and has been sustained. I suspect that Malthus was right in thinking that the only long-term effects would be that more of the farmers' children would live, and that equilibrium would be re-established with a larger population.

The farmers' position is much more hopeful if development begins outside agriculture. This is quite common. Minerals are discovered, or new technologies are applied to manufacturing industry, or a tourist trade develops, or shifts in trade favour a particular port, or some other stroke of fortune stimulates the non-agricultural sector. This in turn generates an increase in demand for agricultural products, and so development spreads from sector to sector. Ricardo believed that this could not sustain itself because the failure of food output to grow adequately would turn the factoral terms of trade against the non-agricultural sector and so stop its expansion. Indeed, I believe that we have here the main reason for the very slow growth of manufacturing industry in India and China during the past century, compared with Japan where increases in agricultural productivity have been spectacular. Similarly, agricultural stagnation helps to explain why French manufacturing industry made so little progress before 1914, compared with the rest of western Europe.

However, Ricardo did not tell the whole story, since he was writing of the closed economy. The open economy can import agricultural products to match an expansion of industrial output and employment. So if one can import food, one can expand the other sectors of the economy even while agriculture stagnates. There is no difficulty in financing imports if the development is for the purpose of expanding exports, visible or invisible, such as the opening up of mines, or of a tourist trade. But if the emphasis is on industrial production for the home market, the resulting increase in agricultural imports produces a balance of payments crisis, as in contemporary England and in contemporary India, and then forces the nation to adopt one or more of three policies: to cut investment, which is the English and the Indian solution and leads back to Ricardian stagnation, or to make a big drive to export more manufactures, which is the German and Japanese solution, or to raise agricultural productivity as rapidly as possible.

The obstacle to the third of these solutions is mainly psychological. We know how to increase agricultural productivity in newly developing areas—by spending on water, on the distribution of high yielding strains, on agricultural extension, and so on—at a cost which is a fraction of what governments spend on their other programmes. Governments are beginning to realize that food production is as important as anything else, but there is still hardly any country in Asia or in Africa where the Ministry of Agriculture is occupied by a senior cabinet minister.

If development begins with an increased supply of agricultural exports, the country does not run into these awful balance of payments difficulties, partly because the supply of output from other home sectors is fairly elastic in response to farmers' demands and, even more importantly, because the exports provide the foreign currency with which to pay for imports. Countries which begin this way will have balance of payments deficits if they live beyond their incomes, especially if they borrow abroad more than their incomes can support; but they have no balance of payments problem if they live within their incomes. On the contrary, since the marginal propensity to import is less than unity, and since there is a time lag in the multiplier, such a country, if living within its means, would always tend to have a balance of payments surplus. This is the main reason why virtually nothing was heard about balance of payments crises during the seventy-five years before the First World War although this was a time of rapid development all over the world; whereas these words are on everybody's tongue today. In the former period development was concentrated in export sectors; whereas nowadays nearly every country plans for home demand, for public utilities, and for public services, but forgets about exports. Since development always increases imports, one of the most important chapters in any development plan is that which tells what is to be done to increase exports, whether of manufactures or of agricultural products or of services.

Though development through agricultural exports works wonders, it has also its disadvantages. A well-known disadvantage is the fact that it discourages manufacturing industry. True, it provides demand, but this demand is easily met by imports. At the same time, it creates the wrong atmosphere for industrialization. Everything is geared to agricultural exports—research, training facilities, public utilities, representation of vested interests in the legislature, and so on. To get money spent in ways that are favourable to manufacturing industry requires a great effort in these circumstances. All this is well known and generally accepted. It is merely an extension of the old 'infant industry' argument.

An even more serious disadvantage, in tropical countries, is the difficulty of getting favourable terms of trade for agricultural exports. Tropical agricultural exports are small in relation to agricultural production as a whole; the main output is of foodstuffs for home consumption. Hence the supply is very elastic. The incomes of farmers producing for export cannot rise significantly above the incomes of farmers producing for the home demand. Naturally there are lags, frictions and some inelasticities which modify the argument and create temporary or permanent gaps between home and export incomes, but the two are chained together. The incomes of farmers producing for export are determined not by their own productivity but by the productivity of the food farmers, which is very low in comparison with the productivity of food farmers in the temperate zones whose incomes are linked in turn to those of industrial producers in the temperate zones. We have then the following relationship. Suppose that temperate farmers earn 60 per cent. as much as industrial workers and produce eight times as much food per head as tropical farmers. It will then follow that the income of tropical exporters of agricultural products cannot be much more than 7½ per cent. of the incomes of industrial workers in the temperate zones. However much productivity may rise in tropical agricultural export crops, the terms of trade will always adjust themselves to keep down the farmer's standard of living.

It follows that tropical countries cannot rely for major development solely on incomes derived from agricultural exports. Neither can they become prosperous simply by producing more food for home consumption since, in the absence of expansion in other sectors of the economy, this would merely bankrupt the farmers. They must look instead to balanced development. If productivity and investment are raised in all sectors, the growing manufacturing and service sectors will absorb both an increasing output of food and also agricultural labour rendered surplus. At the same time the real incomes of agricultural exporters will rise as the gap between food productivities in the temperate and the tropical zones closes.

I do not rule out the possibility that the people of one small country may grow prosperous by raising their productivity and exporting more agricultural products at constant prices; but the tropics as a whole cannot do this, and improvements in the export sector spread fairly rapidly from one tropical country to another. Neither do I neglect the fact that time-lags in supply may bring temporary windfalls, as to the cocoa producers today. But it remains true that a general improvement in tropical terms of trade will occur only when there is an all-round increase in tropical productivity in all sectors for home consumption.

The Role of Mobility in Agricultural Adjustment

This brings me to the problems of the advanced economy since, from the point of view of this discussion, the distinction between the undeveloped and the advanced country is that in the latter one can normally expect a substantial increase in agricultural productivity per man from one decade to the next. The starting-point of farmers' troubles in these countries is the fact that the demand for food tends to grow less rapidly than the supply; whereas the starting-point of the planners' troubles in newly developing countries is that the demand for food grows more rapidly than the supply.

It is a well-established proposition that consumers' expenditure on food rises less rapidly than income. There is a little doubt about this in poor countries, but no doubt in wealthier countries where the average daily intake per person exceeds, say, 2,500 calories. Farm receipts rise even less rapidly than consumers' expenditure on food. As incomes rise, consumers want their food prepared and served more elaborately; it must be processed, or preserved and served out of season, or brought from the far corners of the earth, or served in restaurants with music. Hence the 'value added' after it leaves the farm becomes an increasing proportion of the whole, to the increasing disgust of the farmer. The farmer's only consolation is that as incomes grow the wastage of food by the average household seems to grow even more.

The reverse happens to the agricultural raw materials; they are more and more carefully economized. The income elasticity of demand for manufactures exceeds unity in the poorer countries, though it is probably not greater than unity in the richer countries where increases in income go much more to services than to purchasing further knick-knacks. This high income elasticity is favourable to agricultural raw materials, but it is not decisively favourable. In the first place, since raw materials for industry are only a small part of agricultural production, the elasticity of supply is high, and prices are determined more by what is happening to food prices than they are by the demand for raw materials. Secondly, there is continuous economy in the use of raw materials and especially in the utilization of by-products. And thirdly, raw materials are menaced all the time by synthetics, which are a means of substituting cheaper and more abundant raw materials for more expensive ones. The only thing the farmer can say in praise of synthetics is that they tend to stabilize his market. For these synthetics are often made by monopolistic industries which hold prices more or less constant through boom and recession. Thus the price of rubber is now fairly stable after two decades of wild confusion; and the emergence of detergents seems similarly to have reduced the fluctuations in the prices of vegetable oils.

If the demand for food grows slowly while productivity grows rapidly, the terms of trade must move against the farmer unless the proportion of the population engaged in agriculture contracts. Poets and other romantics have always deplored this change but it is inevitable in the arithmetic. So far as the agricultural economist is concerned, the main remedy for the farmer's ills must always be to have fewer farmers.

The speed with which the proportion must contract depends entirely upon the rate of growth of consumption per head of population and the rate of growth of productivity per person in agriculture. The required contraction is greater in rich than in poor countries. Thus if consumption per head grows by 0·5 per cent. per annum and productivity by 3·0 per cent. per annum over twenty years, the proportion must contract by 37 per cent., i.e. the proportion of the population in agriculture must fall from, say, 20 per cent. to 13 per cent. On the other hand, in a poor country, where consumption can grow by 1·0 per cent. per annum, and productivity, say, by 2·0 per cent. per annum, the proportion contracts over twenty years by only 18 per cent., or, say, from 60 per cent. to 49 per cent. of the population.

Moreover, the difficulty of making this contraction depends upon how rapidly population is growing (though this does not affect the required proportions). If population is growing only by 1·0 per cent.

in the wealthier country, to reduce the proportion in agriculture from 20 to 13 per cent. in twenty years means that the absolute number in agriculture must be reduced by 24 per cent. Whereas, in the poorer country, if population is increasing by 2·0 per cent. per annum, a fall in the proportion in agriculture from 60 to 49 per cent. is consistent with an increase in the absolute number by 22 per cent.

These calculations illustrate the point that in a closed economy the farmers would have a harder time in a rich country than in a poor one, because of slower population growth, smaller increases in food consumption per head, and faster increases in farm productivity. However, there is no closed economy. In practice most of the world's farmers, with the notable exception of North American farmers, would stay reasonably prosperous if imports of food were prohibited. What troubles them is neither the slow growth of demand in their countries nor the speed with which their own productivity is rising, but the rising tide of supplies in a very few other countries.

The international division of labour requires that countries which are short of arable land should import food and export manufactures. Thus Britain, Germany, Japan, India, China, Java, and one or two other countries should export manufactures, while North America, Africa, S.E. Asia (excluding Java), and others should import manufactures and export food. Alas, the international division of labour does not have its way.

The main reason why the international division of labour does not have its way is that food is too cheap, i.e. at current prices farmers' real incomes are substantially lower than the real incomes of other occupations. This causes food-exporting countries to be anxious to industrialize rather than continue exporting food, and causes food-importing countries to try to keep imports down for the sake of their own farmers.

Now food is too cheap because farmers are not sufficiently mobile; agriculture contracts too slowly. In the poorer countries of the world this is primarily due to lack of opportunities outside agriculture. Not enough investment is occurring in manufacturing industry or in other sectors to draw off the rural surplus. However, neither Asia nor Africa suffers from a surplus of food. In the over-populated parts of Asia the rural surplus should be drawn out of agriculture; but not in order to reduce the food supply, which would, by definition, not be affected. The problem of these countries is simultaneously to increase food supplies while finding other work for the rural surplus. Africa has no rural surplus, except in a few small areas; but neither has Africa, at present, a surplus of food. The African problem is to start an upward movement of productivity, so that other sectors of the economy can be expanded, without running short of food.

It is in the other continents, especially in North America and in Europe, that the immobility of farmers is keeping down farm prices, and here the cause is not failure of other sectors to expand, but the unwillingness of farmers to move. Investment proceeds so rapidly in these parts of the world that even the largest conceivable exodus from farms to towns would be snapped up in a very short time, just as Western Germany has absorbed millions of refugees. It is true that demand does not grow steadily; there are Kitchin, Juglar, Kuznets, and even possibly Kondratieff cycles. Farmers are used to having a decade of prosperity succeeded by a decade of poverty. Nevertheless, in times of prosperity the non-agricultural sector can absorb all who want to leave farming. If there are still too many farmers, it is because too many people want to be farmers.

I doubt whether this problem is capable of solution. There will always be occupations which attract too many people—farming, teaching, shop-keeping, music, acting, and many others—and the economy will always retaliate by paying people in these occupations less than they could earn in others. They, in their turn, resenting this, will do whatever they can to get higher rewards, by restricting entry to their trades, by tariffs and quotas, by parity-price formulas, or by any other regulative device for which they can win acceptance. Their philosophers—in our case the agricultural economists—will wrangle among themselves over these devices, some supporting, others denouncing, and yet others confining themselves to measuring. This is what we have assembled here to do, and I hope that you will find enough material in this paper to make a start.

[28]

PART ONE

OPENING ADDRESSES

Commonwealth Address

by Dr. W. Arthur Lewis

THE EARLY decades of industrialization are always a time of troubles, presenting the paradox that though society is growing richer, it simultaneously grows angrier, and most angry at the points where most development is taking place. The contrasts today are remarkable. On the one hand, the developed countries of Western Europe and North America present a remarkable spectacle of social peace. At election time people vote, with little passion and less violence, to choose between parties whose programmes can hardly be distinguished from each other. Strikes are few, and are quickly settled. People worry about the young, and about crime, but these are minor worries when compared with the great antagonisms of class, religion, and nationality, which shook the first half of the twentieth century, and which now play so small a role.

When we turn to the underdeveloped countries, we turn to an angry world. Whether we look in Asia or Africa, the Middle East, Latin America, or the Caribbean, conflict is more bitter today than at any time in the past half-century. Race, religion, language, tribe, class, and every other division known to man play havoc with these countries, accompanied by riots, strikes, political imprisonments, and communal murders on an unprecedented scale. And yet the underdeveloped countries are richer today than they have ever been before. Real output has been growing rapidly, and social services improving.

The anger and the development are connected with each other. The early stage of rapid economic growth is a turbulent transition from one period of social stability to another period of social stability. Early industrialization is always a time of troubles, but the same forces which create disturbance also, in due course, restore relative tranquillity. Our problem is how to survive in between. What I wish to say can therefore be divided into three parts. First I will consider why industrialization causes so much strife in its early stages; then why, as it develops, its later stages automatically become more peaceful. And finally, what prospects we have of surviving in between, without our societies tearing themselves to pieces.

A TIME OF TROUBLES

Pre-industrial societies are kept stable and peaceful by general acceptance of certain patterns of rights and obligations adhering to family, class, caste, tribal, religious, or political status. The key word is status. The young are trained to recognize status, and to play their role in the status accorded to them. So long as these ideas are accepted, social peace prevails. By peace I do not mean a total absence of social conflict. I mean only that, comparatively speaking, the social tensions are minor.

Industrialization destroys this peace by destroying the status ideas on which it rests.

First, it creates four new classes which do not exist, or exist only insignificantly, in pre-industrial societies; namely, the wage-earner, the capitalist employer, the middle class, and the professional politician. Each of these new classes has to find itself a niche in society, and, in so doing, to alter the status of former dominant groups, including chiefs, kings, landed aristocrats, priests, and farmers. It would be surprising if these adjustments were effected without strain.

To be a wage-earner, one of hundreds or thousands employed for wages by a large corporation, is a novel status, which does not exist in pre-industrial societies. The employee finds himself working with strangers, not colleagues of his choosing, and not necessarily of the same family, tribe, religion, or language; he has to learn a new code of behaviour towards fellow wage-earners. He has a new type of job which must be done at times and in ways prescribed for him by others, and the purpose of which, because of the division of labour, he may not even know. And he has to learn a new employer-employee relationship, which is based on cash and contract, without the overtones of paternalism and feudal protection to which he has been accustomed. He is therefore bewildered, and bewildered men are easily angered. The passage of time, counted in generations, permits employers and employees to establish and learn new codes of behaviour towards each other – codes embodied not just in the formal words of collective contracts or of labour laws, but, more profoundly, in unwritten conventions of factory life, which anthropologists are now studying with the same methods as they have studied kinship in rural areas, and with the same excitement.

Capitalists are people who buy labour or commodities in order to sell at a profit. Capitalists exist even in the most primitive societies, but their status in pre-industrial societies is low. They are fair game for kings, priests, and landed barons, who keep capitalists much as we keep cows, to tax, borrow, confiscate, or otherwise exploit them whenever money is needed. Industrialization begins when money-making is given its head. Capitalists challenge the old rulers. They insist on making new laws to protect persons and property. They demand administrative reforms. They seize a share, even the dominating share, in the government. They change even the national ideology. Profit-making, which in most religions is slightly immoral, comes to be sanctified as a reward for enterprise. The production of material goods becomes one of the principal aims of society, under the title of economic development, and is sanctified as a means of abolishing poverty – poverty which again in most religions carries some flavour of holiness.

A rising working class and a rising capitalist class are notoriously aggressive. The rising middle class, by contrast, is notoriously timid. The middle classes are the products of the secondary schools and universities, the demand for whom increases enormously with industrialization. The middle class has no need to be aggressive in early industrialization, because the shortage of trained people ensures very high premiums for education. For example, on starting his career, a primary school teacher in the United States or Great Britain gets a salary about twice the national income per head, but in Nigeria a primary school teacher gets seven times the national income per head. It is in the second stage of industrialization that the middle classes become sullen and aggressive. For, as the schools expand and pour out more and more trained people, the gap between middle-class and working-class incomes closes swiftly. Then we begin to get strikes of doctors, nurses, teachers, civil servants, and other middle-class categories, who find that they can no longer maintain their economic distance. Ultimately, the middle class learns to substitute machinery for domestic servants, and to measure status by personal achievement rather than by possessions; but in many underdeveloped countries the middle class is now just entering its angry phase.

These disturbances of status, associated with the rise of new social classes, take place against a background of economic disturbance which I must now describe.

In economic terms, the principal reason why industrialization provokes unrest even at the same time as it increases output is the fact that its benefits are not spread evenly over all members of the community, but are confined to a few patches of the economy.

Economic growth does not begin throughout the economy simultaneously. Here some corporation opens a mine, employing 500 people. Somewhere else a port is built. Somewhere else a merchant begins to buy a commodity for export. Wherever this happens it brings prosperity to a few – high wages, good salaries, high profits, good prices for produce or services. But these benefits do not necessarily spread throughout the community. In the early stages of industrialization, what happens is that a few people become more prosperous, with high wages and salaries and profits, while the great majority of the people remain in their poverty, and some are even impoverished by the new prosperity of the others. Ultimately, the developing sectors will grow until they embrace the whole economy, but intermediately, the patchiness of development produces social problems. Let me put this another way.

Industrialization raises the incomes of all those who participate in it. This causes two kinds of strife. First, those who participate argue about the division of the proceeds. Wage-earners strike for higher wages, and peasants organize to secure higher prices for their produce. We are familiar with disputes of this kind, and we now have elaborate machinery for publishing information and for arbitrating between the parties. Much more difficult is the second kind of strife, arising from the protests of those who do not participate in the expanding industries, especially those whose incomes fall in consequence of industrialization, whether because the cost of living rises, or because they become unemployed. This is more difficult because expanding industries can settle their disputes out of expanding income, but industries which are not expanding do not have this easy way out.

Economic development does not inevitably raise the cost of living, but it frequently does so. Take for example the opening of the bauxite mines in Jamaica. Naturally, when a new mine is opened up to export bauxite, the community as a whole is that much richer. However, the money earned in the mines is used to buy local foodstuffs, services, and commodities, whose prices tend to rise. The people who work in the bauxite mines can afford these prices, and the people from whom they buy food or services are also richer; but the rest of the community is adversely affected, and may be expected to strike or to protest in other ways. Besides, the bauxite mine, or other new industry, will probably pay workers twice as much as is paid in older employments. If your brother is getting six pounds a week in the new mine, the three pounds a week which you have been receiving on the cocoa plantation no longer seems adequate, and trouble may be expected. Much of the industrial unrest in the developing countries today is due to the efforts of people in one sector of the economy to keep up with price increases generated by economic development in another sector of the economy.

Then there is the unemployment created by development. Labour-saving devices put people out of work; for example, the West Indies now produces much more sugar than before the war, but employs a much smaller labour force. Cheap imports of textiles and shoes destroy handicraft production. Supermarkets drive the small traders bankrupt. Bulldozers reduce the demand for unskilled building labour. Moreover, as wages rise, everybody uses labour more economically. Offices have fewer clerks and messengers; housewives substitute machines for domestic servants, and a considerable number of people who were being carried along at subsistence wages in marginal employments find themselves thrown onto the labour market.

This is one of the reasons for the explosion of towns, which is one of the more horrid features of the early stages of industrialization. Since employment grows faster in the cities than in the countryside, the cities attract the displaced, and those who hope to better themselves. They attract especially the young, flowing out of the primary schools, whose expectations have been stimulated beyond the absorptive capacity of the rural areas. If the migration to towns merely kept pace with expanding opportunities in the towns, we need hardly worry, but this is not so. The fact that the towns are prosperous brings to them more labour than they need, and so paradoxically creates the greatest unemployment in the very places where employment is expanding more rapidly. In Jamaica, for example, the more jobs you create in Kingston, the more unemployment you have in Kingston. Once the towns start to expand, they attract labour faster than they can provide jobs, houses, buses, water, or other amenities. Crime and juvenile delinquency spread, and the soul is seared. The rapid growth of slums is one of the worst features of the early phase of industrialization.

Yet even the explosion of towns is only a phase. In Europe and North America, if you define a city in terms of the geographical space it occupied thirty years ago, most cities now have a smaller population than they had thirty years ago. The movement is no longer inward to city centres, but outward to suburbs. Population density, which increased viciously in early industrialization, now decreases rapidly, since suburbs are planned at low densities. And, most important from our point of view, whereas the peasants who pour into cities in early industrialization move from conservatism to radicalism, their descendants who move out to the suburbs are moving back from radicalism to relative political indifference.

RESTORATION OF SOCIAL PEACE

Karl Marx, who grew up during the early stages of rapid industrialization in Western Europe, described with penetrating eye the various kinds of trouble which early industrialization produces. But he made one major error. He failed to see that this was only a transitional phase. He expected conditions to get worse in every decade. He could not predict that economic development would itself eliminate the major causes of unrest and so lead us back into a period of relative calm. Let us consider why this happens.

First, if the rate of capital accumulation is sufficiently high, unemployment must ultimately vanish. We must distinguish sharply between capital accumulation and technical progress. Technical progress sometimes creates more employment, by creating sources of income which did not exist before; but technical progress also frequently creates unemployment by means of labour-saving devices. Capital accumulation, on the other hand, as distinct from technological change, must always create more jobs. Two shoe factories of the same type and size must create twice as many jobs as one shoe factory – that is capital accumulation. But a new shoe factory of improved type may reduce the number of jobs – that is a technological improvement of the labour-saving kind. So, on the one hand we have capital accumulation creating more jobs, while on the other hand technological innovations may be reducing the number of jobs, and the growth of population increasing the numbers looking for jobs. One cannot prove theoretically that the positive forces must exceed the negative, or, as Marx tried so hard to do, that the negative forces must exceed the positive. All we can say, looking back, is that rapid capital accumulation creates sufficient jobs to bring about full employment even in the most adverse circumstances. Given net investment of, say, fifteen per cent of national income every year, the demand for labour will eat into unemployment, and a shortage of labour must sooner or later develop.

A shortage of labour raises wages, so it follows, again contrary to Marx's prediction, that the standard of living will rise continuously. Industrialization abolishes one of the causes of social strife by abolishing economic misery. In face of rising national output per head, slums, famine, early mortality, ignorance, and other great social evils are rolled away. In the early phase of industrialization men worry about whether their children will die of hunger; in the later phase their worry is about whether they can maintain their payments on the television set; and these two kinds of worry are so different in magnitude as to be different in kind.

Next, economic development restores social peace by reducing the number of significant human differences. In societies which live on the margin of subsistence, it is important to have patrons and protectors. Affiliations matter more than personal qualities. Society is built on patronage, and one's chances of progress, or even of survival, depend on ties of family, class, caste, religion, race, tribe, or political affiliation. Successful industrialization, on the other hand, depends mainly on competence at the bench, so the economic forces work strongly in favour of 'the career open to the talents'. This substitution of merit for status and affiliation has now eliminated the major sources of human conflict, short of international war. We have only to consider the ease with which men still murder each other, in some underdeveloped continents, for speaking a different language or for attending a different church, to realize how much the developed countries owe to the evolution of an economic system which rewards primarily by performance and not by affiliation, and which, in doing so, has reduced conflicts of race, religion, and tribe to the significance of children's games.

By the same token, industrialization promotes equality. Status has no place in a competitive market economy. You take a man as you find him. You recognize that merit exists potentially in any class, and with this recognition begins equality of opportunity. Capitalists have developed the philosophy of equality before the law, and the protection of all from arbitrary treatment. Wage-earners have established equality of bargaining power, through their trade unions, which farmers emulate through their co-operatives. Once launched, the idea of equality reaches into every aspect of social life, removing causes of frustration and bitterness, which otherwise poison social relations. Tax systems are reformed, so that the rich pay proportionately more than the poor; whereas in pre-industrial societies it is the poor who pay taxes to the rich. In pre-industrial societies the poor have neither respect nor rights. They appear in the courts by favour. If they seek interviews, they must expect to wait endless hours before they are admitted to the presence, if at all. They must never answer back. This is how the poor still live in Asia and Africa, subjected to constant humiliation by men of their own race and religion. Industrialization takes the humiliation out of the lives of the masses of the people.

It does this, finally, by abolishing social classes and making us all middle class. This is not an accident. Industrialization demands educated use of mechanical power. Education floods the market with skilled people, and thus reduces the relative wealth and status of the professional classes. Mechanical power abolishes the jobs which required mere brawn, and so abolishes the classes which lived by hard manual labour. Everybody comes to spend at least ten years in school and so acquires a common culture. Because of the growth of mammoth corporations, the capitalist is replaced by the manager, whose outlook is essentially middle class. Less and less of the corporation's profit goes to private pockets and more and more to pay for the welfare state. One Western European country prides itself that it is now a community where everybody, from the messenger up to the Sovereign, now pretends to be just middle class. And when we are all just middle class, we can live in mutual toleration.

All this is hateful to politicians. Throughout Western Europe and North America the heat has gone out of politics, and old hands lament that the younger generation seems so little interested in ancient feuds.

POLITICAL FOUNDATIONS

The problem of the countries now starting to industrialize is how to get themselves through their present time of troubles into the easier times which lie ahead, without in the meantime tearing themselves to pieces.

The tensions of early industrialization produce aggressive leaders who find it easy to exploit and ride to power on the resentments of workers, peasants, and members of other classes who are displaced by economic change. Their anger is matched by that of aggressive capitalists and stubborn landlords, reluctant to give up their exploitation of peasants and of landless workers. Where, in addition, the country is divided among peoples of different race, language, religion, or tribe, the opportunities for sectional leadership are irresistible, and the call to national leadership is faint.

In all times of troubles leaders divide into two main groups: those who think that social problems can and should be solved by persuasion, negotiation, and compromise, on the one hand, and those who think, on the other hand, that social problems can be solved effectively only by force. The compromisers we call democrats, while those who believe in force may be called, for short, authoritarians.

Authoritarianism in its various forms has great attractions in a time of troubles. Times are hard and tempers short. Sectional interests are seen to prevail over the national interest. Patience and compromise seem to result only in defeat. By contrast, authoritarianism seems to offer swift and easy solutions, always at the expense of other groups in society, whose liquidation seems imperative. And yet, oddly enough, even at the height of a time of troubles most men reject authoritarianism. Only very rarely does any dictator come to power by winning fifty per cent of the popular vote. Most men believe that human affairs must be regulated by compromise, and will vote democratic rather than authoritarian if given the chance.

It cannot be denied that situations exist which cannot be solved by compromise because of the obstinate clinging to power of a ruling, propertied class. Marx asserted that the evils of capitalism were insoluble without revolution, because of the entrenched power of the capitalists; but he was clearly wrong. Capitalists are aggressive in the early stages of industrialization, but thereafter they are always on the run. In this they differ markedly from an entrenched landowning class. Landowners are able to control the thoughts, actions, and votes of the peasants, serfs, and landless labourers who depend upon them, in a way that capitalists cannot control the loyalties of industrial workers. Marx saw correctly that the industrial worker was easily organized for political and industrial action, and was therefore essentially an aggressive class. Even the most reactionary landowners can command the votes of their dependents in a way that even progressive capitalists cannot achieve. Hence Marxist revolution may be a necessary prelude to reform in countries dominated by reactionary landlords, as, for example, in one or two Latin-American countries; but it is not a condition for social progress in countries where capitalists are the dominant class, since capitalists can be made to yield by other pressures.

In this respect the countries of the British Commonwealth are extremely fortunate. Africa has relatively few landlords, and in most parts of Asia the power of the landlords is already broken. Most political parties now in power in the British Commonwealth are leftist parties, more or less, whether they call themselves Conservative, Liberal, Labour, National, People's Movement, or what you will. We do not have the situation which you find in some of the underdeveloped countries, where the state is run by powerful reactionary landowning interests, who are determined to keep the mass of the rural population in subjection. All our leading political parties are dedicated to economic and social progress. Whether in Britain or Canada, in India or Ghana or Jamaica, compromise solutions are clearly possible.

The menace to democracy in some of our countries is a surfeit of politicians unwilling to compromise with each other. I use the term politician here in a wide sense, to include all those who acquire income, power, or prestige, by championing the interests of groups – and therefore I mean not only members of parliament, but also leaders of chambers of commerce or trade unions or religious or other groups. The professional politician is a new phenomenon; he did not exist in pre-industrial society, in India or Africa. He is one of the new classes created by industrialization. Our societies have sprouted an abundance of politicians, because we have such an abundance of groups. The countries of Europe are relatively homogeneous, and therefore their politics are relatively simple. But, fragmented as we are by tribe, and religion and language and economic interest, each of our countries can easily throw up a dozen different groupings, warring passionately over one or other of our many divisions. This shows itself acutely in the political atmosphere. One can live in London or New York and hardly notice what the politicians are saying. Not so in Africa or Asia. Our newspapers carry little else but reports of political speeches, strikes, lockouts, ultimatums, and the ceaseless cries of politicians shouting abuse at each other. And it is most exciting. If one misses the wireless news at midday one can hardly wait until the evening to hear what one has missed that day.

It is now often said that the transition of social peace cannot be effected in Asia or Africa except by dictatorial leadership. This transition was effected democratically in Europe, but many centuries went into making each European nation, and by the time industrialization began in Europe, countries were more homogeneous than they now are in Asia or in Africa. Europe had learnt religious toleration before rapid industrialization began, and was left only with class antagonisms to resolve; while Asia and Africa will have as well to cope with tribe and caste and religion and language. In this situation it is argued that only a dictator can keep the peace; the democratic right of each section to advance its claims is held to be inconsistent with peaceful transition to a state of toleration. So we are invited to give our confidence to generals, or to the leaders of monolithic and totalitarian parties.

I do not believe that we can solve our minority problems by denying the right of minorities to political expression. The kind of social peace which we seek to reach is one where people accept their political system because they have hope and confidence that their aspirations can be met within that system. If their aspirations cannot be met within the political system, they have no alternative but subversion and rebellion. It follows that a parliamentary system is useless unless it is of the kind where minorities are fully represented, and their rights fully respected. Electoral systems which distort the vote by giving seventy per cent of the seats in parliament to a party which has won only thirty-five per cent of the votes, and parliamentary procedures which enable a majority utterly to ignore the rights of a minority, are certain to kill respect for democracy in countries where democracy is just beginning. Yet most of the new countries in the Commonwealth are trying to make do with unsuitable constitutions of this kind.

Nevertheless, while I believe that a proper choice of constitutional systems is important, I do not suggest that this alone can safeguard social peace. We need two other ingredients; namely, real democratic leadership and a devoted administrative class.

We need democratic leaders who will rise above sectional interests. This is difficult in a time of troubles. Our societies are disturbed and tense. They are fragmented into hostile groups, each of which welcomes aggressive leadership. Men who speak compromise are not welcome. It is easy to achieve power by unrestrained championship of sectional demands, and difficult to win recognition by counselling moderation and restraint. And yet it can be done, and has been done. Both inside and outside the Commonwealth, Africa and Asia have already produced some great statesmen who are held in affection as national leaders even by those of their fellow countrymen who vote against them. The idea of mutual toleration and respect is not really so difficult to grasp. The newly industrializing countries are not really in this respect much worse off than early-nineteenth-century Europe. Our societies are more fragmented, but Europe, on the other hand, had to pioneer. All the egalitarian ideas which modern man now takes for granted had to be fought over bitterly during Europe's time of troubles. Africa and Asia are emerging into a modern world which takes it for granted that it is absurd for reasonable men to murder each other over languages or tribal or racial differences, and, though it will take a couple of decades for this idea to penetrate to the vast masses to whom it is still strange – including backward Europeans – I expect it to spread as rapidly as other Western inventions, such as radio, penicillin, or jazz, as soon as the masses of the people make contact with it. In the not distant future, public opinion will tame our politicians by shaming them into respectable behaviour.

Not every small country can hope to throw up a political leader of world stature – but we do not need to ask for as much as this. In most cases it would suffice if the democratically-minded sectional leaders would sink their differences enough to enter into coalitions with each other against the authoritarians. There are many cases where an authoritarian manages to win an election on a minority vote, because his democratic opponents failed to unite; and, having won the election, simply proceeds to liquidate both them and democracy. An electoral system which permits this is bad, but democratic politicians who let this happen are bad too. In the British Commonwealth we have a horror of coalitions. This may be justified in Britain or in Canada, but it makes no sense at all in our highly fragmented countries, where democratic government is often not possible without coalition. In any case, all good government anywhere is coalition government, whether the members of the coalition seek a single name for their union – like the Labour Party or the Republican Party – while retaining separate names for their various factions or wings, or whether, as in most of Western Europe, they dispense with the common name and openly recognize that they are a coalition, doing their best on common ground. If we had more frank recognition in the British Commonwealth that coalition and compromise is the secret of political stability, we would not always be looking for a Great Man to be our saviour, and our chances of retaining democracy would be stronger.

The other factor which will reduce the bitterness in our societies is an inevitable growth in the importance of administration in contrast to politics. In newly independent countries we look to politics and politicians to solve our problems; any time of troubles puts a premium on the emotions. In contrast, the older, developed countries rely for smooth operation on building up a sound administration. This applies in every sphere. Their government is based on a well-trained civil service rather than on parliamentary speeches. The church relies on a well-trained clergy rather than on charismatic prophets. Business is carried by well-trained managers, rather than relying on capitalistic flair. If all the cabinet ministers in London or Paris or Ottawa were to disappear, good government would continue all the same, and six months might pass before their absence was noticed. We are passing through our time of troubles towards this happier state, and the sooner we can reach it the better.

This is not to say that the administrative class, the managers and the civil servants, is necessarily sound. In Western Europe the middle class is steeped in a long tradition of public service, based on a long tradition of Christian morality and a long intellectual tradition. Our middle class, on the other hand, is new. It is growing rapidly, as our schools and universities pour out their graduates, but, by very virtue of its rate of growth, most of its members come from families which have not themselves received a modern education or faced the responsibilities of modern management. Our universities and schools therefore face a special challenge, for they are not merely turning out trained minds; they have also, in the few years at their disposal, to try to get their students to understand the social upheaval through which they are passing, and to appreciate that they will be stepping into a role where the maintenance of the traditional values of service, fairness, and industry is more important than counting the amount of money in one's bank at the end of the month. Most of our universities, let us face it, simply fail to meet this challenge. We try, more or less, but we ourselves do not understand the problem sufficiently well as yet to have much impact. Fortunately, men learn from their experience even more than from their teachers. Responsibility is forcing our managers and administrators to assume their traditional task, and to learn to carry the burdens of discipline and compromise and respect for fellow men.

These are trying times for the new Commonwealth members. In each of our countries democracy is on trial, and men doubt it can be preserved. I do not share this doubt. I believe that our troubles are temporary, and that the very forces which have created them, the forces of economic development, will also take us through the relative calm. Our problems can be solved, if only we can substitute patience and compromise for vanity and anger.

[29]

2. CLOSING REMARKS

W. Arthur Lewis

I.

It was originally decreed that Dr. Prebisch and I were to share this session with you. Having regard to your desire that the conference should in this final session receive a balanced summing up of its problems, I told my speechwriter, "Just find out what Dr. Prebisch is going to say, and say the exact opposite." Unfortunately both Dr. Prebisch and my speechwriter have defected, so I am left to do the best I can for all three of us.

Thinking back over the mass of papers and speeches with which we have been entertained during the past nine days, what stands out most clearly in my mind is the importance of distinguishing between factors which cause prices to start to rise, and spiral processes which keep prices rising on and on far beyond any level that you can justify in terms of the original cause. Our economics have become much more unstable since 1945 than they ever were before. I use the word unstable in the technical sense, to indicate that if for any reason prices move from what may in some sense be an equilibrium level, there are no forces to bring them back. On the contrary, powerful forces at once take over to send prices rising and rising and rising to levels for which there is no justification in the original cause which started them off.

The mechanism is familiar to us all, and is not confined to Latin America. Every country in the world, including the Soviet bloc, has either experienced it, or views it with apprehension. It has three contributing parts: wages, budgetary deficits, and devaluation, and it runs somewhat as follows. First comes the original cause, which starts the mechanism working. This may be a rise in the price of domestic foodstuffs, or a rise in import prices, or an increase in the quantity of money, or a rise in the price of exports, or anything you like, provided it is something which raises the cost of living. Then the mechanism starts. Wages rise, and this raises prices more, wages more, prices more, and so on. Secondly, in those countries where the marginal ratio of government receipts to national income is below the average ratio, the price rise opens up a budget deficit, because government costs rise faster than government revenues. This gives an extra twist to the spiral. Then thirdly the rise in prices forces devaluation, and this raises import prices proportionately to the devaluation and domestic prices in somewhat smaller proportion, so a third twist is given to the spiral. So what with wage pressures, budget deficits, and devaluation, prices may rise continuously and at a high rate for reasons which have nothing to do with the original cause.

Failure to distinguish between the original cause and the spiral mechanism can only cause confusion. If one asks why prices rise by 25 percent per annum in Chile, it is confusing to be told that this is because agricultural output is growing less rapidly than the demand for agricultural products. Chile is only one of 50 countries where agricultural demand is growing more rapidly than supply. The difference between Chile, where prices increase by 25 percent per annum, and India, where prices increase by only 2 percent per annum, is not a difference in the elasticity of supply of agricultural output, which is equally low in both countries, nor a difference in the rate of growth, which is higher in India than in Chile. The difference is that Chile is in the grip of the spiral processes to a much greater degree than India.

The spiral is not confined to Latin America; all the world's continents are having to cope with it. Yet it seems to have gotten much more out of hand in some Latin-American countries than in the rest of the world. If during 1963 the cost of living were to rise by, say, 10 percent in, say, Nigeria or Ceylon, one could not confidently predict that this would set off spiral processes which would raise the general price level in Nigeria or Ceylon by 30 percent in three years. But it seems that one could safely predict such a result in some Latin-American countries. Some Latin-American economists assert that this is because their people have acquired expectations of continuously rising living standards which make them more aggressive than the peoples of Asia or Africa. I do not believe this to be so. I do not think that Latin-Americans are more anxious to have a rising standard of living than Nigerians or Ceylonese. The difference is in the expectations, not about the standard of living, but about how prices will behave. A Nigerian is used to seeing prices rise, and then fall again; in fact, if you ask a Nigerian farmer what is likely to happen to agricultural prices, he is even now more likely to predict that they will fall than to predict that they will rise. This is in sharp contrast to those Latin-American countries where today no person under 40 years of age can remember any time when prices fell continuously over a period of two years. A country's expectations depend on its history, and the intensity of the spiral depends on its expectations. Prices rise much faster in Chile or Brazil than they do in Nigeria or Ceylon mainly because Chileans and Brazilians expect prices to rise much faster.

I think we are all agreed that this is a terrible state to be in, because this kind of inflation is quite pointless. One can argue for an inflation which sets out to achieve a deliberate purpose, such as to acquire more resources for a government which is engaged in military operations, or to bring about a change in the distribution of income such that proportionately more resources will be devoted to productive investment. I shall examine such inflations later in this paper. But the spiral has neither these purposes nor these effects. Once the whole community has been subjected to a high rate of inflation over long periods, nobody is caught by inflation any more. There are no unprotected contractual incomes any more. Even pensioners and professors of economics learn to keep up. So the spiral has all the usual evil effects of inflation without achieving anything useful. I think we are all agreed that, whatever may be the original fundamental causes which start prices rising, the spiral itself adds nothing and should be eliminated if this is at all possible.

Now, in order to eliminate the spiral you have to get at its fundamental cause and stop wages chasing prices. But you must also deal with its secondary contributor, the budgetary deficit.

A budget deficit is not a necessary part of a spiral and does not, in fact, contribute to the spiral as it is experienced in the advanced industrial countries. In most of those countries a rise in the general price level leads, on the contrary, not to a budgetary deficit, but to a budgetary surplus. This is because the marginal ratio of government receipts to national income exceeds the average ratio. These governments take 25 to 35 percent of national income, but their marginal rates of direct taxation exceed 50 percent, and many of their indirect taxes are well over 50 per cent on the goods for which demand rises most rapidly. Hence, as national income increases, their revenues rise faster than their civilian expenditures, and, in the absence of increases in military expenditures, the Minister of Finance is every year in the happy position of having to announce tax cuts in order to avoid an ever-increasing budget surplus. Most underdeveloped countries are in the opposite situation. Their marginal tax rates are too low; too many taxes are fixed in money, instead of being on a proportionate basis; and prices of public utilities are slow to adjust. So a general increase in prices raises the government's cost faster than its revenues, and the resulting deficit makes the spiral worse than it would otherwise be. This seems to be of enormous importance in the bigger Latin American inflations. Without the budgetary deficit the wage spiral by itself might raise prices by 5 or even 10 percent per annum. Increases of 20 percent per annum and more over long periods must mainly be due to the secondary contribution of the budgetary deficit.

To explain how the spiral can produce a budgetary deficit is not to explain why these large budgetary deficits are tolerated year after year. This seems to be a specifically Latin-American phenomenon. Public opinion in India or Nigeria would be shocked by the idea of a large budget deficit every year, financed by creating new money, but public opinion in many Latin-American countries seems to accept the right of the government to print money as it likes. Here again these psychological differences must have largely historical explanations. Whenever I find myself tempted to generalize about Latin-American opinion, I draw back hastily. After all I was chosen to give this talk, I am informed, mainly because I know almost nothing about Latin America, and am therefore neutral. Moreover, my Latin-American friends seem to hold as widely differing opinions as my friends of any other nationality. Indeed, usually when I take any particular opinion as being typically Latin-American, or in some sense the expression of *the* Latin-American point of view, the typical Latin-American who has expressed this idea turns out to be Mr. Dudley Seers. But I cannot foist upon Mr. Seers any *laissez passer* attitude to budgetary deficits, since in one of his papers he goes out of his way to attack budgetary deficits and argues for budgetary surpluses. All one can safely say is that in a number of Latin-American countries the government gets away with printing money to an extent which is puzzling to visitors from any other continent, and one cannot help feeling that the people deserve better governments than they get.

If one eliminated the budgetary deficits, prices would not rise so fast, but the wage-price spiral could still be there, just as it exists in many of the advanced industrial countries which have no budget deficit. This problem cannot be solved without the consent of the trade unions. Monetary weapons are inappropriate. By reducing the quantity of money, one may stop prices from rising, at the expense of employment and growth, but this is not even certain since the wage spiral may be continued even in face of much unemployment.

The spiral may stop temporarily, but unless the consent of the trade unions has been gained, it is likely to start again as soon as the deflationary pressures are removed. A lasting solution requires trade union consent, which can be secured only on two conditions.

First, the cost of living must cease to rise, and stability of prices must be maintained for a period sufficiently long enough to convince the unions that the government means to control the cost of living and has the means of doing so. At the technical level this requires a combination of means: price controls, subsidies, use of foreign exchange reserves to bring in wage goods and dampen domestic prices, even perhaps an upward revaluation of the currency. But behind these technical means must lie the will to achieve price stabilization. The other condition for winning the confidence of the trade unions is political sympathy between the unions and the government, such that the unions are not striving all the time to embarrass the government by every means in their power. Such sympathy exists in Communist countries, but it is not confined to Communist countries. It is found also in many of the new nationalist states, even in those which are quite democratic, like India or Nigeria. The basis for this sympathy is a belief, on the part of the union leaders, that they and the government leaders have pretty well the same objectives, and that these objectives are dominated by the interests of the common man. As far as one can gather, conditions for this sympathy do not exist in most Latin-American countries. The reasons for this lie in political theory. Of all social classes the most reactionary is the class of great landowners. As Marx himself recognized, the industrial capitalists are a progressive liberalizing class. Moreover, face to face with powerful unions living in urban centers, industrial capitalists have relatively little power when compared with the control which great landowners are able to exercise over the lives and votes of those who live in the countryside. Nowadays the power of great landowners has been broken all over the world except in the Middle East and in Latin America, and so Latin America is the most politically reactionary of all the continents. It is, for this reason, the angriest continent and therefore about the last place where the trade unions are likely to agree to any kind of wage control. In this sense the wage spiral in Latin America is fundamentally political and cannot be eliminated without fundamental political change. Whether the cooperative efforts of the Alliance for Progress can succeed in bringing about such fundamental change is more than I would know. On the other hand, one reads that Latin-American trade unions are pretty weak. So a combination of firmness with progressive policies might possibly bring the spiral to a stop.

II

So far, I have really said nothing about the relationship between economic growth and inflation, since the spiral is not essentially a phenomenon of growth. This spiral is, in the last analysis, a political phenomenon, arising out of political tensions in society and aggravated by poor fiscal policies. You could expect to find it in any economy, whether growing or stagnant. I began with the spiral in order to get it out of the way, since it seems largely irrelevant. If prices are increasing by 25 percent or more every year over several decades, this is because the society is sick rather than because it is developing.

When we turn to examine the relationship between inflation and economic growth, the subject matter breaks into two parts: inflation as a by-product of growth and inflation as an instrument of growth. We cannot, of course, entirely escape the spiral, since any inflation can set the spiral off. But it is important to distinguish between what sets the spiral off and how the spiral itself works, especially since, with good management, one can have price increases associated with growth which nevertheless do not spiral because the spiral itself is under control.

Economic growth will cause the general price level to rise through the effects of the expansion of some sectors of the economy on other less responsive sectors. The classical case is where extra income derives from an increase of exports. Part of the proceeds of these exports is spent on other sectors, and insofar as the output of these other sectors is inelastic and not completely substitutable by imports, prices rise in these other sectors. Prices will rise if demand puts pressure on supplies, but prices may also rise sympathetically, without such pressure. In the classical case, the price of rubber or cocoa or some other primary product rises on world markets, and one follows through the effect on other prices in Malaya or Ghana as the extra income of the farmers works its way through the system. Let me take instead the case of Jamaica, where, in the newly opened bauxite industry, the trade union is extracting a wage of £8 per week for unskilled work for which the normal Jamaican wage is £3 a week. This sets up two different strains. First, as the workers spend their extra incomes, they put pressure on the prices of wage goods. But, secondly, even if they consumed only imports and bought no domestically produced wage goods, there is a sympathetic upward movement of all other wages. If your cousin is getting £8 per week working on a bauxite mine, or reaping £8 per week because the price of rubber or cocoa has risen, you are no longer willing to accept £3 per week for working on the roads. The £8 a week serves as a challenge to all other unions to try to get increases in all other wages. In this conference we have heard a good deal about the direct pressure of demand on the output of stagnating sectors, but I think that in practice the sympathetic upward movement of incomes is just as important a source of rising prices. We have heard a good deal also about food, but the pressure of demand may affect all domestic output, including manufactures, raw materials, and services, such as the price of haircuts. From the angle of the spiral, any price which enters into the cost of living matters, not excluding the price of haircuts.

Since *de minimis non curat les,* let us concentrate on food. If the supply of food does not keep pace with growing demand, food will put a brake on growth unless one imports more food, in which case one must either export more of something, or import less of something else. This is very familiar territory, so familiar that it is puzzling to learn that this proposition now forms the basis of a new school of structural economics. The British economy met this problem head on as the economy developed in the nineteenth century. Its solution was to increase its propensity to export. Germany followed suit, and so did Japan. Other economies, faced with the same problem, have reduced their propensity to import: the Soviet Union, India, and Egypt are spectacular examples of import substitution. All these countries take this particular structural change in their stride. Why do we hear such pessimistic cries from those Latin American countries which now face the same problem?

Adjustment can be made either by increasing the propensity to export or by reducing the propensity to import. Particularly puzzling are those cries which seem to be founded on the belief that it is particularly difficult to expand exports because the world is buying fewer and fewer exports. The opposite is true. World trade has never grown faster. Between 1950 and 1960 the quantum of world trade in primary products increased at an average rate of 5½ percent per annum, and the quantum of world trade in manufactures by 7 percent per annum. The terms of trade for primary products could not retain the heights to which they were raised by the speculative fever of the Korean War and the heavy American stockpiling in the early fifties; nevertheless, the average terms of trade for the decade of the 1950's were better than for any previous decade in all the preceding 100 years. I do not know whether it is in fact true that in the 1950's Latin America had difficulty in keeping her exports growing at the same rate as national income, but if this was so, it cannot possibly have been due to failure of world demand to grow adequately, since the quantum of world trade was growing by about 6 percent per annum throughout the 1950's. Taking the continent as a whole, rather than individual countries, failure on this score can only have been a failure of effort.

Undoubtedly success in achieving major sectoral change, whether a fall in the propensity to import, or an increase in the propensity to export, or agricultural reform, creates pressures which will show up in rising prices. This is a temporary growing pains phenomenon, which should cease as the economic structure adjusts itself in the required direction, as the economy learns greater flexibility, and as increasing productivity takes effect on prices. One may note, incidentally, that this phenomenon is not confined to individual countries but exists for the world economy as a whole. Looking back over the past 90 years for which we have figures, we can see that whenever world manufacturing production has accelerated, or risen faster than 4 percent per annum, both the money prices and the terms of trade of primary products entering into world trade have risen, and whenever world manufacturing production has decelerated, prices have fallen. The world economy as a whole has the same difficulty with the inelasticity of primary production as have individual countries. But the associated changes in prices are relatively moderate: big changes can occur only if the wage-price spiral is set in motion.

In practice, in an open economy which has its spiral under control, the cost of living is determined more by price movements in the international markets for primary commodities than by domestic pressures. Every country both imports and exports primary products, whose prices enter directly or indirectly into its cost of living, and most other prices seem to take their cue from these international prices. If wage costs get out of line with international price movements, there are repercussions on employment and on the balance of payments, so most open economies pursue policies which are set, in the last analysis, by the direction of international commodity prices. Since the early stages of growth involve some increase in domestic prices, it is easiest to keep an economy open if its period of growing pains coincides with a period of general upward movement in international commodity prices; and one will find historically that periods when international commodity prices are rising secularly, whether à la Kuznets or à la Kondratief, are also the periods when development is occurring most widely over the whole world economy. If by misfortune one's period of growing pains occurs during one of the periods when international commodity prices are moving downwards, one must look out for trouble in the balance of payments.

III

From price increases as a by-product of growth, I turn to consider inflation as a deliberate instrument of growth.

One may decide to open the monetary tap to promote growth in two situations: if the propensity to invest is too low, or alternatively and paradoxically, if the propensity to save is too low.

In speaking of the propensity to invest being too low, one has in mind sluggish economies where investment is low, not because of a shortage of saving potential, but because entrepreneurs are too easily satisfied. For example, it is said of British entrepreneurs that the proportion who will invest for the sake of innovation is too small, and the proportion who will invest only because demand presses on capacity is too large. By contrast, it is said that German or Japanese entrepreneurs are driven by a devil which makes them invest in any circumstances whatever. If people invest not primarily to innovate but primarily because demand presses upon capacity, then a policy of keeping demand and supply exactly equal results in low investment and slow growth. The remedy is to keep the tap slightly open—just 1 or 2 percent per annum. One does this not to increase profits, or to redistribute income, but simply to keep order books slightly overfull. I think there is some evidence that Britain and France and the United States now fall into this category of needing just a little monetary stimulus if they are to keep at full stretch.

The case where the propensity to save is too low is very different. Here the object of opening the monetary tap is to divert income from those who spend on consumption to those with a greater propensity to spend on long-term improvement. In the typical underdeveloped country 80 percent or more of gross national product is spent on personal consumption, and the remaining 20 percent on capital formation and on public services, some of which, such as education and health services, may do as much for economic growth as is done by capital formation. One wants to get the 80 percent spent on personal consumption down to 70 percent, and investment and public services together up to 30 percent of national income. When inflation is used for this purpose it is only temporary; the object is to effect a permanent structural change in the distribution of income in favor of government and of savers. When this change is achieved, the inflation stops, and prices are stable at a higher level of growth. This kind of inflation is therefore self-liquidating.

Self-liquidating inflation is quite different from spiral inflation. Spiral inflation goes on forever, but self-liquidating inflation comes to a stop when the share of personal consumption has been reduced permanently to the new equilibrium level.

Large changes in the distribution of income, whether as between one class and another, or as between the public and the government, are not possible without inflation if they are to be accomplished over a short period of time. This is the proposition which inflation theorists have invited the statisticians to test. Instead we are inundated with diagrams relating the rate of inflation to the rate of economic growth itself, instead of to the rate of increase of the rate of economic growth. Nobody argues that a high rate of growth must be associated with a high rate of inflation. On the one side, we know that spiral inflation does not cause growth; and on the other side, you can have any rate of growth without inflation if the propensities to save and to pay taxes are already adjusted to that rate of growth. The proposition in which we are interested is that acceleration in the rate of growth causes inflation because the proportionate fall in consumption which this requires is resisted by the public, which therefore maneuvers to get higher money incomes. Will statisticians please note, and stop boring us with irrelevant comparisons between rates of inflation and growth in different countries?

Since the distinction between spiral inflation and self-liquidating inflation is so crucial, it is important to recognize the conditions which are necessary if inflation is to succeed in being self-liquidating.

The first condition is that it should result in an increase in the output of wage goods. You can get consumption down from 80 to 70 percent of national output if at the same time it is rising in absolute terms from 80 to 100, but not if it is falling in absolute terms, because the public will always fight to keep its absolute standards up. The corollary of this is that the purpose of the inflation must be to secure resources for investment in productive enterprises which yield a quick increase in the output of wage goods. Consumers then get something, and if their standard of living is rising absolutely, they are not so concerned about the fact that it is not rising as fast as productivity. However a rapid increase in the output of wage goods itself requires certain favorable factors: there must be natural resources capable of quick development; there must be enough foreign exchange to spare for importing equipment, and enough skilled labor to get on with the job. Giving the government money to spend does not necessarily result in increased output.

The second condition for success is that the inflation should redistribute income to the right people. Insofar as the purpose is to increase the government's share, this is relatively easy. One sets the marginal rates of taxation well above the average rates, so that government revenues automatically increase faster than incomes. A shift toward industrial profits is not so easy, because in economies dominated by cost accountants, industrial prices tend to be fixed on a cost-plus basis, which keeps gross profit a constant proportion of industrial prices. If left to themselves, farm prices will rise as fast as other prices, so farmers can be milked only by special measures, such as price controls, or collectivization, or using some foreign exchange to subject farm prices to international competition. The most likely result of inflation is to shift income from the nonunionized classes to get-rich-quick types of capitalists in retail or wholesale trade, and it is by no means certain that these will use their profits for productive investment. Inflation equilibrates most satisfactorily when its purpose is to increase the share of the government in national income, or when it originates, Schumpeter style, with entrepreneurs (whether private or public) actually increasing the amount of resources used in productive investment and so forcing the economy to accept a shift toward profits used productively. (Incidentally, as a social democrat I prefer the increase to be in public saving rather than in private profits.)

The third and final condition for success is command over the loopholes, command over the foreign exchanges, over flight of capital, over luxury consumption, luxury building, and such. But all this goes without saying if we are talking about successful inflations.

The size of the inflation depends on how big a proportionate change one is trying to achieve, and how soon. If the annual rate of exchange is large, the annual rate of inflation will also be large, and prices must rise, say, threefold to fivefold in ten years. A big inflation cannot go on for long without turning into spiral inflation, because in a big inflation everybody soon gets the point, and learns to protect himself by demanding higher money income. In this sense, by having prolonged large spiral inflations, which have achieved nothing, Latin America has already wasted her inflationary potential, and barred herself from turning now to useful self-liquidating inflations. If one takes a longer period in which to achieve the proportionate fall in consumption, one can get the same result with much smaller increases in prices. If, for example, the share of consumption falls each year by only one half of 1 percent of national income, while in absolute terms per capita consumption continues to rise by 1 percent per annum, some sluggish classes of the community will never get around even to trying to protect their position, and this, with the unsuccessful attempts of some others, will keep the rise of money incomes low.

For examples of self-liquidating inflation we must look, not at what is happening in Latin America today, but to other parts of the world where the gap between output and consumption has actually been widened. I think the satisticians will find, once they stop chasing hares and come to the real point, that virtually all take-off periods, which by definition are short periods of rapid acceleration of the rate of growth, have been periods of self-liquidating inflation. The so-called Lewis model was constructed to show how the share of profits and savings in national income can rise over a long period without inflation, but in practice there is usually a period when change is fairly swift. The classical examples in our day are provided by the Communist countries. For example, starting in 1928, when personal consumption was taking 80 percent of national product, Stalin succeeded in reducing the proportion to about 60 percent in 1939, at the cost of a tenfold increase in prices. His task was specially difficult because there was no significant increase in the quantity of wage goods. With better agricultural policies he might have achieved his end with only, say, a fourfold increase in prices. Anyway, by 1939 equilibrium had been reached, and price stability could thereafter have been maintained, with consumption at only 60 percent of national product, but for the outbreak of the war.

Now since any rapid increase in prices, even fourfold in ten years, is a pretty horrible process, one must also ask whether the same results cannot be achieved less painfully. Rapid growth can, of course, be achieved without this process if it is financed by foreign capital, as for example, in Puerto Rico or in Northern Rhodesia, but this is beside the point, partly because there isn't all that foreign capital to go round, and partly because our question is whether a rapid increase can be financed domestically by widening the gap between output and consumption without getting involved in inflation. I think the answer must be negative. It is fashionable to say that the gap can be widened by sharp increases in taxation, and to put forward such increases as an alternative to inflation, but this is misleading if it is exaggerated. A large increase in taxation is bound to be inflationary, if its purpose is to reduce mass consumption, because people will always try to get their incomes raised if their purchasing power is reduced, whether by taxation or in any other way. Taxes which fall on savings will not have this effect, but they are irrelevant to our present purpose, which is to reduce the share of consumption in national income. Taxes which fall squarely on the consumption of the rich, such as the great landowners, may also be noninflationary, and there is much scope for such taxes in Latin America. A drastic reduction in consumption cannot, however, take place only at the expense of the rich, because there are not enough rich. So far as I know, all attempts in recent years to effect a drastic reduction in consumption by means of taxes have been followed by industrial strife, even to the point of riot and bloodshed. Whether one proceeds via taxation or via turning the monetary tap, attempts to reduce sharply the share of consumption in the national income will always be inflationary.

For my part I do not believe that any country is wise to try for a sharp and swift reduction in the proportionate share of consumption, whether by taxation or otherwise, because I believe that a big inflation is a horrible experience and is too heavy a price to pay for achieving in five to ten years changes which could be achieved in fifteen to twenty years with only a moderate increase in prices. I believe that there should be a steady fall in the share of consumption, but that this should be within the limits set by the need to increase real per capita consumption all the time and should therefore not much exceed a relative fall of one half of 1 percent of national income per year. So, after one has squeezed what one can out of the landowners, taxes and savings taken together should not rise in real terms faster than about 6 percent per annum, when national income is rising by 3 or 4 percent. This, however, is a very personal judgment, based on my belief that civilization is pretty fragile and that if it gets torn apart in violent social conflict, it is hard to put together again. I do not want to force on the man in the street economic progress at a rate faster than he is willing to bear, defining this rate not in terms of individual savings, as the laissez-faire economists do, but in terms of the rate of change which the man in the street finds politically tolerable.

Since I am ending on this personal note, I may as well add that my highest preference is for rapid growth financed not solely as a bootstrap operation but also by massive foreign aid. But this is clearly outside my present terms of reference.

[30]

RICHARD T. ELY LECTURE

A REVIEW OF ECONOMIC DEVELOPMENT

By W. Arthur Lewis
Princeton University

The underdeveloped countries did reasonably well during the 1950's. According to the United Nations' statisticians,[1] gross domestic product increased at an annual rate of 4.6 percent in Latin America, 4.2 percent in the Far East (excluding Japan and mainland China), 5.2 percent in Southern Asia, and 4.1 percent in Africa. At the beginning of the decade economists were concerned about whether these countries could make the minimum critical effort needed to exceed population growth, then thought to be 2 percent, now accelerating disquietingly to 2½ and 3 percent. Growth rates exceeding 4 percent have shown that capital, entrepreneurship, skill, and foreign trade are not such formidable obstacles as they were thought to be. In reviewing each of these categories, I shall use the occasion to consider some of the concepts which economists have been using to analyse the problems of economic growth.

I. *Capital*

Capital has not been as scarce as expected, first because the capital-output ratio turned out to be unusually low, second, because more foreign aid became available, and, third, because some of these countries are managing to save more.

In 1950, economists thought that the capital-output ratio was around 4 (net); actually in the 1950's it has often been even between 2 and 3, both in developed and in underdeveloped countries. We do not yet know why, or whether the change is permanent. Let us note four possible explanations. First, Western Europe has been exploiting a backlog of technological progress, accumulated during the interwar stagnation. The underdeveloped countries may be reaping a similar harvest—will certainly do so as soon as they tackle their agriculture properly. Second, expenditure on infrastructure may be abnormally low; underdeveloped countries are putting a lot of money into transportation and power, but they are still starving housing and the public services. Third, the high growth rates of industrial production

[1] *World Economic Survey, 1963,* p. 19. The figure for Africa is probably too high. On the other hand an earlier estimate by the Economic Commission for Africa (*Industrial Growth in Africa,* p. 3) that commodity output grew by 2.1 percent per annum is too low, since it assumes that the growth rate of agriculture was only 1.4.

(ranging between 6 and 10 percent) and of services have effected considerable transfers from less to more productive sectors of the economy. And, finally, high rates of growth of population, in countries where land is abundant, produce a proportionate growth of agricultural output, using little capital. The question whether in some other countries, such as India or Egypt, the marginal productivity of labor in agriculture is zero seems to arouse fierce passions, though the answer does not seem to be relevant to any practical problem.

When we turn to the transfer of capital from the developed to the underdeveloped world, we are on firmer ground. The United Nations[2] estimates that the net flow increased from about 2 billion dollars in 1950 to about 6 billion dollars in 1960. Six billion dollars was about 3½ percent of the national incomes of the underdeveloped world and was therefore associated with about a quarter of their rate of growth at the end of the decade. This is a very considerable achievement for those of us who have made ceaseless propaganda for foreign aid.

It would be pleasant to be able to report a universal increase in domestic ratios of saving, resulting from these high rates of growth and of aid, but alas only a minority of countries have risen to their opportunity. The best documentation is for Latin America, where if the Economic Commission for Latin America[3] is right, the ratio of gross domestic savings to gross domestic product fell, for the continent as a whole, from 16.8 percent in 1950-54 to 15.6 percent in 1955-61, or 15.2 percent in 1960. Fragmentary evidence suggests that the rest of the underdeveloped world did not do much more than maintain domestic savings ratios (e.g., Philippines from 9.0 percent in 1950 to 9.5 percent in 1960; Nigeria from 8.3 in 1951 to 8.6 in 1957) but there were also spectacular exceptions, such as India, from about 6 percent (net) in 1950 to about 8 percent in 1960, and Jamaica, from 12.2 (gross) in 1950 to 16.1 percent in 1960.

Some of the countries which failed to improve their savings ratios nevertheless increased the take of public expenditure, which can be just as important for growth. The 1950's were a good decade for education, for public health, and for roads. Since both savings and public expenditure come out of the surplus of output over private consumption and improve future productive capacity, they should be considered together when measuring achievement. Availability of foreign capital enabled some governments to put improvement of the public services ahead of improvements in the savings ratio during the 1950's.

[2] *The International Flow of Long-Term Capital and Official Donations, 1959-1961*, and earlier publications in this series.

[3] *The Development of Latin America in the Post-war Period*, p. 10. Domestic saving equals investment minus the surplus on current account in the balance of payments.

We do not have enough evidence to test theories of how income distribution and the propensity to save change as per capita income increases. The fall in export prices relatively to domestic costs was important, since the export sector saves more and is more highly taxed than the rest of the economy. ECLA estimates that adverse terms of trade cost Latin America 3.6 percent of national income, comparing 1960 with 1950, but one would still have expected the savings ratio at least to be maintained, since per capita real output increased by 19 percent. Presumably significant changes in private saving require longer periods and bigger per capita changes.

The slow rate of change of private savings is one reason why more importance is now attached to increasing public saving. This, however, is not easy. First, the marginal rate of taxation is lower than the average in most of these countries; so the percentage share of public revenue falls as national income increases. Radical reforms are required in tax structures if public revenue is even to keep up with public expenditure. Second, where public services are rudimentary, rapidly increasing expenditures on these services are just as important as increased savings and will for some time absorb most of the increase in revenues. Third, the rate of change must inevitably be slow. Attaining self-sustaining growth means reducing the ratio of private consumption to gross domestic product from around 80 to say around 70 percent. Any attempt to reduce the ratio of consumption faster than by about one-half-of-one percent of gross domestic product per year will defeat itself, and also create political unrest. It defeats itself because output cannot be increased without increasing consumption, since growth requires incentives. And it creates unrest because rapid economic growth produces social turbulence, which can be contained only by devoting increased resources to welfare and consumption. My limit of one-half-of-one percent assumes that per capita consumption must grow at least 60 percent as fast as per capita output, in the relevant ranges. Attempts to move faster than this, whether through taxation, inflation, or rationing, are likely to end in riots.

International economic aid is supported by different people for many different reasons. Insofar as its object is to give the big push which creates the opportunity for self-sustaining growth, its success must be measured by the extent to which countries do indeed increase their investment in men and resources faster than current consumption. And if this is the test, then there is something to be said for tying the distribution of foreign aid to actual performance. In another place[4] I have produced a formula for this, making the amount of aid a

[4] "Allocating Foreign Aid to Promote Self-Sustaining Economic Growth," in *Motivations and Methods in Development and Foreign Aid,* Proceedings of the Sixth World Conference of the Society for International Development, 1964.

country receives a multiple of

$$\frac{S_{-1}}{GDP_{-1}} - \frac{S_{-4}}{GDP_{-4}}$$

where $S =$ expenditure on gross investment (minus foreign aid) plus current government expenditure (minus defense and welfare transfers), and subscripts refer to years.

Nobody wants to be governed by a rigid formula, but if we want foreign aid to show results in promoting progress towards economic dependence, it should be more closely linked to performance. These issues can no longer be evaded, because the future of foreign aid is now critically in doubt, not only in the United States, but even in France, where aid has hitherto been sacrosanct. Most aid is given for political reasons, and much of the current disillusionment springs only from belated discovery that political aid cannot achieve all that is expected of it. Nevertheless, it has to be admitted that the nonpolitical aid is also distributed haphazardly, whether by bilateral or multilateral agencies; better criteria and better results might win wider support.

II. *Entrepreneurship*

Growth rates exceeding 4 percent suggest that the shortage of entrepreneurship cannot have been the major obstacle it is normally thought to be. It is well known that these countries have no shortage of small-scale entrepreneurship; the desire to make money and the willingness to gamble are endemic. What lacks is the experience of organizing large-scale businesses. Assuming that this lack of experience springs from lack of desire, or from institutional inhibitions, historians have devoted much paper to considering what social and ideological climate spawns successful large-scale enterprise; and the social psychologists have now joined them. The last fifteen years have thrown little light on their theories, except, perhaps, to question the quantitative importance of their problem. Perhaps, too, those politicians were right who said that the end of imperialism and racial subjugation would spark a surprising release of energy.

Meanwhile the shortage of large-scale domestic entrepreneurship has been met to some extent by foreign enterprise. Here the 1950's saw a marked change in the attitudes of governments. During the 1930's and 1940's the air resounded with diatribes against foreign investors, but in the 1960's newspapers in Europe and North America are full of advertisements in which the governments of newly independent states offer foreign investors innumerable incentives, including exemption from taxes. Foreign entrepreneurs have not been allowed to do much for agriculture or for trade, but their contribution in mining and manufacturing is a major explanation of the high rates of growth of industrial production.

The shortage has also stimulated governments to assume some of the attributes of entrepreneurship themselves. The governments of underdeveloped countries do not command either the capital or the administrative skills necessary to play any significant role as managers of industrial or agricultural enterprises, though some have tried, often for ideological reasons. They can play a more important role in creating a favorable climate for private entrepreneurship, helping with improved infrastructure, market research, feasibility studies, technical advice, and financial aid. Development theory makes a great deal out of external economies, whether in explaining the low level of investment, or assessing the advantages of geographical concentration, or tracing the history of growth through linkages, or arguing the case for the government as a promoter of interdependent investments. The analysis has been influential, though factual evidence remains scarce.

Governments have done better at stimulating the private sector than at controlling it, not surprisingly, since both the statistics and the personnel for efficient control are lacking. Many controls have hindered more than helped, especially by restricting the smaller businessmen, some of whom are the hope for the future. Also, the new states often begin with hostility between politicians and administrators, and need to find a new equilibrium which will reduce corruption and arbitrary decisions. The record is spotty even in the public sector. Most governments have made development plans, but few take their own plans seriously, although planning could undoubtedly help to bring more order into public sector programs. Governments have first to learn to control the public sector before they can hope usefully to control the private sector.

The sector to which government initiatives could contribute most is agriculture, which has, alas, been the most neglected. Everybody talks about the necessary framework for agriculture—the agricultural research stations, the extension agents, farm institutes, animation, water supplies, fertilizers, land reform, and so on—but little gets done. Prime ministers have had their minds on other things: on political questions such as neutralism, Pan Africanism, Afro-Asian unity and the like, or in the economic realm mainly on industrialization; and since most great men can achieve no more than one or two things at a time, agriculture has had to content itself with occasional lip service. Agriculture will have to be seen to be important before any considerable progress will be made.

This change is beginning in countries where agricultural stagnation is the obvious cause of the shortage of foreign exchange. But the crucial role of agriculture is also obvious in the elementary arithmetic of economic growth. For it is easy to show that national income cannot attain a rate of growth of 5 percent in Asian and African conditions. At present none of these countries is able to increase agricultural output faster than 3 percent per annum. Assume optimistically that industrial output increases by 10 percent per annum. Then, if agriculture contributes 50 percent of gross national product and industry 12 percent, the growth of commodity output averages out, initially, at 4.4 percent. Output of services grows slightly faster than output of commodities; so gross domestic product as a whole would grow at a maximum rate of 4.6 percent. Given the failure to reform agriculture, the rates of growth actually achieved in the 1950's are a matter for congratulation. One must assume that the United Nations call for 5 percent in the 1960's is mainly a call for a massive assault on agricultural stagnation, without which such a target is impracticable. Also, the call should not be mixed in with the discussion of foreign aid, since it is with the governments of the underdeveloped countries that the initiative lies in agriculture.

III. *Skill*

Shortage of skills has been even less of a bottleneck than shortage of entrepreneurs. In part this has been due to the large international flow of technical assistance. Despite the break-up of the colonial empires, there are now more European and American technicians in Asia and in Africa than there were in 1950, and the numerous channels through which this movement is organized are an achievement in which the world can take some pride.

Nevertheless, technical assistance is marginal. Leaving aside for the moment the agricultural sector, the amount of skill which these countries can currently absorb is relatively small, mainly because their non-agricultural sectors are relatively small. Where half the population is in agriculture, the number of jobs requiring a secondary education does not exceed 10 percent of the occupied population, nor do the jobs requiring university education exceed 2 percent[5]. The majority of countries in Asia and Latin America (but not all) have as many secondary educated people as they need for strictly economic purposes, and many of them have many more such people than they can absorb in current market conditions. There are shortages of particular types. In general there is too much literary education and not enough technological, but this defect is easily remedied. The number of technical

[5] For amplification of this statement see my articles "Education and Economic Development," *Social and Economic Studies,* June, 1961, and "Secondary Education and Economic Structure," *ibid.,* June, 1964.

institutes and special training institutions has multiplied quite rapidly in underdeveloped countries. What most of the Asian and Latin-American countries need is better quality rather than more quantity.

Africa's situation is quite different. There in 1960 less than 1 percent of the population had received a secondary education and less than 10 percent primary education. This situation is now changing rapidly since these countries have become independent and have made education a first priority.

There is no evidence to suggest that economic development is accelerated by supplying more educated people than the market can absorb. India is one of the best educated underdeveloped countries, but not conspicuously the most successful in economic development. An oversupply of educated people creates great frustrations, stimulates excessive migrations to the towns, and results in political turbulence. All this makes the political situation more exciting; but though the long-run effects of political excitement on development may be positive, the short-term effects seem to be zero, or even negative.

The biggest problem in education is the relation of schooling to agricultural improvement. The problem does not arise in plantation agriculture, since the planters, who are the decision-makers, can adopt the latest techniques whether their workers are literate or not. We cannot doubt that literate farmers are likely to absorb new technology more rapidly than illiterate farmers. Illiterate farmers can be taught the most obvious things and have made important decisions, such as changing from subsistence to commercial crops. But it must be a goal to have as soon as feasible an agricultural system in which every farmer is literate.

The problem is the transition. Putting the children into school, which costs a great deal of money (as much as 3 or 4 percent of national income) does not guarantee that one will have literate farmers. Much depends on the speed with which one moves from 10 percent of rural children in school towards 100 percent, for when the figure is only 10 percent, that 10 percent knows that it will get jobs off the farms, at wages from two to three times as high as the average farmer's income. If one raises the proportion to 60 percent within ten years, as some West African countries have done, the 60 percent also expect to get jobs off the farms at high incomes. They cannot be attracted by three acres and a hoe; only a modernized agriculture capable of high yields per man could hope to hold them. Hence the only way to effect a smooth transition is to keep the rate of modernization of agriculture and the rate of expansion of rural schooling in step with each other. This is not a case for less schooling so much as a case for faster modernization of agriculture—for greater expenditure on research, agricultural credit, water supplies, and so on.

Given the time it takes to organize the right kind of agricultural framework for small farming, expenditure on adult education in the countryside, including short courses for farmers at residential centers and other forms of community development, will probably at this stage prove more productive in Africa than money spent on getting all rural children into primary schools, desirable as that is for innumerable reasons, political and social no less than economic.

IV. *Foreign Trade*

Foreign trade has played its customary role as the engine of growth in most of these countries but not in all. Both the terms of trade and the rate of growth of trade have been high by comparison with prewar statistics.

The terms of trade for primary as against manufactured products averaged higher in the 1950's than at any time in the preceding eighty years. The first half of the 1950's was especially good because of the Korean war and heavy stock-piling in the United States and elsewhere. The terms of trade deteriorated in the second half of the decade and on till 1962, since when they have moved upwards. However, even in 1962 they were 5 percent above 1929, which preceded the Great Depression.

The volume of exports from underdeveloped countries increased at an annual rate of 3.6 percent, which is also much higher than before. But this rate is lower than the growth of national income because of the important part played by import substitution, especially in Latin America.

We are being deluged with literature arguing that the underdeveloped countries cannot grow at an adequate rate if the developed countries increase their demands for the exports of underdeveloped countries at an annual rate as low as 3½ percent. Such literature ignores the important part played by import substitution in economic development. Most of the calculations assume rates of growth of national income, consumption, industrial production, and imports which are not mutually consistent. A little arithmetic shows that if one assumes continuance of the current rate of growth of industrial production, the underdeveloved countries must soon be supplying themselves with nearly all the manufactures they need.[6] They have the necessary minerals

[6] Currently these countries use manufactures equal to about 30 percent (including raw materials) of national income, of which about one-third are imported. If national income grew at 5 percent per annum, use at 6 percent, and production of manufactures at 8 percent, net imports of manufactures would fall to zero in twenty-two years. If the growth rate of production of manufactures is assumed to be lower, so must the growth rate of national income, and therefore of use of manufactures. Considering how slowly agriculture is growing, national income cannot grow by 5 percent if manufacturing is growing by less than 8 percent.

and fuels, and the skills are not hard to learn. It is better that they should not be forced into autarky since comparative advantage demands that, even if net imports be low, this be only because large imports of some manufactures are matched by large exports of others. Recent international discussion has focused rightly on the market for the manufactures of underdeveloped in developed countries; this is likely to be much more important in future than the never ending talks on primary products. Some of us believe even that the time is not far off when the underdeveloped will be net importers of primary products and net exporters of manufactures. This is not only because of high population growth, which the new techniques of family limitation will soon begin to control. More fundamentally, it is arguable that the real competitive advantage of temperate countries is in agriculture, since their temperate climates are more favorable to the retention of soil fertility than the harsher climates of the tropics.

To the individual underdeveloped country, import substitution offers less opportunity for growth with diminishing trade than it does to the group taken as a whole. Only the largest countries (possibly China, India, the U.S.S.R. and the United States) have that wide variety of climates and minerals which is a necessary condition for development as a closed economy. Everywhere else a rise in real income must increase the imports of some commodities. These imports have to be paid for either by expanding exports or by releasing foreign exchange through import substitution. In the nineteenth century, growth was sparked by exports, which generated incomes and so also stimulated production for the home market. In the second half of the twentieth century, import substitution has offered some countries an easy path to growth, without dependence on increasing exports. However, once the limits to import substitution are reached, the rate of increase of exports sets a ceiling to the rate of growth of output, since natural resource limitations make it impossible to have balanced growth for the home market only.

Economists have produced a turgid literature on balanced growth. Most writers do not make clear whether they are concerned with the balance between production for the home market and production for export or are concerned only with production for the home market.

If one assumes a closed economy, the pattern of production must obviously be related to the pattern of domestic demand. The original Rosenstein-Rodan proposition was to the effect that in a closed economy with unemployment, an entrepreneur could employ some of the unemployed with greater confidence if he knew that other employers were simultaneously offering employment in other industries; for his workers would spend some of his outlays on buying their goods, but their workers would spend some of their incomes on buying his. A parallel proposition in the two-sector model says that if the two sectors trade with each other, the expansion of the one can be brought to an end by the stagnation of the other. These propositions have not been upset by any of the subsequent writing, most of which has merely demonstrated that, while demand and supply are linked, the link is not absolutely rigid. Some production can take place in advance of demand; innovating suppliers create demands which did not previously exist; in other sectors it is safe for capacity to lag behind demand; the availability of entrepreneurial talents will decide where demand may lag, and where it may go in advance; inventions usually bunch in a few industries, in response to shortages, rather than spread all over the economy; and so on. Much controversy has raged around such propositions, not because they are controversial, but because economists like to be controversial.

Maintaining a proper balance between production for the home market and production for export is a much more important subject, because failure to do this has serious consequences for the balance of payments, for prices, and for the growth rate of the economy. Attempts to increase output faster than the growth rate of exports will support give rise to what the Latin Americans now call "structural inflation." This literature, too, is much obscured by irrelevancies. Structural inflation is not due to being underdeveloped, to having a high rate of population growth, to exporting mainly primary products, or to having difficulty in raising taxes; the British economy is the clearest contemporary example of structural inflation, and it has none of these characteristics. Neither is structural inflation due to investing more than is saved, or to running a budget deficit; these cause demand-pull inflations, whereas structural inflation is a cost-push phenomenon.

A simple example illustrates the species. Suppose that a country produces only two commodities, motor cars and wheat, and consumes only these two commodities. Suppose also that through technological progress the output of cars is increased, but structural barriers hold down the output of wheat. The increase in real income increases the demand for wheat. This is met by importing wheat. Thus income generated in the production of cars is used to buy imports; there is a deficit in the balance of payments, and deflation in the home market, represented by a surplus of cars. This structural deflation is turned into structural inflation by the measures taken to right the balance of payments. Devaluation or tariffs or import controls will raise the price of wheat and therefore the cost of living, and so a cost-push inflation spiral will start. Four solutions are possible. One solution would be to reduce the output of cars to the level of home demand. This reduces employment and damps the rate of growth of national income. We can call this the British solution, since this is what Britain has done regularly over the past fifteen years; it is also what Latin-American economists accuse the International Monetary Fund, rightly or wrongly, of wanting them to do. The second solution would be to go out into the world market and sell more motor cars. This is the Japanese solution. The rate of growth of the economy is then set by the degree of success in exporting. The third solution would be to break the agricultural bottleneck and have balanced growth in the narrow sense of patterning domestic production on domestic demand. This is the Mexican solution. The fourth solution would be to force the public to consume what is being produced; namely, more cars rather than more wheat, whether by subsidizing cars, or by taxing wheat, or by some system of rationing. This was the old Russian solution.

Only two of these solutions appeal to economists; namely, either to sell more exports or to break the bottleneck. Nothing in economic science can tell us a priori which is preferable, but great passions have been aroused by our prejudices. Economists reared in the free-trade tradition tend to look first for the opportunities for increasing trade; whereas a later generation, which learnt in the interwar years to be wary of dependence on exports, prefers to explore first the opportunities for increasing the productivity of home supplies. Inefficient governments chose neither of these solutions. They either damp down growth or try to push ahead despite imbalances. The latter policy has produced its full crop of foreign exchange shortages, devaluations, and inflations. The process is cumulative; persistent cost-inflation discourages both exports and import substitution, so aggravating the foreign exchange shortage, and giving the spiral another push. Whatever merits a policy of persistent inflation may or may not have in a closed economy, in an open economy it can work havoc with employment and growth, by causing a country to price itself persistently out of world markets. A perpetually overvalued currency can be the chief cause of economic stagnation.

One of the advantages of input-output analysis is that it puts these problems into their proper framework. A projected increase in national income results in projected increases in final demands. In balancing demand and supply for each commodity separately, the law of comparative costs is invoked (perhaps in the form of linear or preferably nonlinear programming) to decide the appropriate balance between imports, exports, and production for the home market. Economists are asking whether the new "indicative planning" has really contributed anything to the rate of growth of the French economy. In less developed countries the making of such projections could not but improve existing planning procedures, so long as good statistics are available and so long as projection is not confused with prophecy. I suspect that if such exercises were done correctly, most of the countries which have been concentrating on the home market would find that a shift to exports would pay, and most of those now concentrating on exports could do better by giving more attention to import substitution.

V. *Unemployment*

One disturbing factor must be set against the high rates of growth of output and investment on which we have been congratulating ourselves; namely, the rising levels of unemployment in the underdeveloped countries[7]. This cannot be documented because there are no reliable statistics of unemployment, but it is everywhere a cause of concern. The phenomenon is unexpected, since rapid growth and high investment ought not to increase unemployment but to reduce it.

This unemployment is not due in the first instance to rising populations. In a well-organized society, surplus population shows itself in disguised unemployment on family farms and in other traditional places, whereas what we are now talking about is unemployment of people working for wages and living in big towns.

The simplest approach to understanding the causes of unemployment is through the model which divides the economy into a growing modern capitalist sector and a traditional subsistence sector which feeds labor to it as required. Unemployment is growing rapidly for two reasons: first, because the traditional sector is expelling labor too rapidly; and, second, because the modern sector is taking in too few because it is too highly capital intensive.

One reason why the traditional sector is discharging labor too rapidly is the unusually large differential between wages in the modern sector and earnings in the traditional sector. We are used to assuming a differential of about 50 percent, and to assuming that the modern sector can grow at a constant wage level. This seems to have happened in the nineteenth century, but in the twentieth century trade-union pressure, nationalistic governmental pressure on foreign enterprises, and the new social conscience of big entrepreneurs are combining to raise wages very sharply in the modern sectors of the developing economies, and it is now not unusual to find some unskilled workers in the modern sector earning three or four times as much as the average small farmer. This causes a sympathetic increase in wages in traditional occupations, and since productivity is very low in these occupations, employers

[7] I have treated this subject more fully in "Unemployment in the Developing Areas" in *Proceedings of the Third Biennial Midwest Research Conference on Underdeveloped Areas* (Chicago, 1965).

get rid of domestic servants and of the surplus clerks and messengers whom their businesses have traditionally sheltered. The high wages in the modern sector also attract people out of the countryside into the towns, where they manage to live by doing a few hours occasional work per week.

Imbalance between the modern and the traditional sectors is not confined to wages. An important factor in Africa is the rapid acceleration in the output of rural schools, which are now producing more primary school graduates than the rural economy is able to absorb at the wages they expect. So young people are flooding into African towns. The excessive rate of growth of a few towns is a problem throughout the underdeveloped world. This is compounded by errors of policy in industrial location and by concentrating development expenditures on these few large towns, making them much more attractive than the villages and the small country towns in terms of water supplies, transportation, schools, hospitals, electric light, and opportunities for unemployment relief. Holding the surplus in the countryside until required has always been a problem in developing economies. The British poor relief authorities gave it much attention at the end of the eighteenth century and the beginning of the nineteenth, and tried to prevent people from coming into the towns if work was not available.

The other aspect of this problem is the high capital intensity of the new investment, not in the sense of the ratio of capital to output, which we have seen is low, but in the sense of the proportion of the national income invested which is required to provide additional employment for one more man. Most of these countries are surprised at how few people have found employment in the growing sectors of the economy, especially manufacturing, mining, and transportation, despite the high investment which has been taking place.

High capital intensity is appropriate when it embodies greatly superior technology, without demanding very high skills. The Ohlin approach to comparative costs puts us against high-capital intensities, but Ohlin's model assumes that countries have the same technology and differ only in the relative scarcity of resources. In comparing developing with underdeveloped countries, it is more appropriate to use the Ricardian version of the law of comparative costs, which stresses instead relative differences in productive efficiency. Now there is no a priori reason for developed countries to have a comparative efficiency advantage in capital intensive industries, and one can easily construct cases where the comparative advantage remains with the underdeveloped country, even when the relatively higher cost of capital is taken into account. Since this result is unfamiliar, I am attaching an arithmetical example as an appendix to this paper.

Economic theory offers no reason why development must increase rather than reduce employment. Capital investment as such must increase employment in a system with an infinitely elastic supply of labor, since it cannot pay in such a system to increase the ratio of capital to labor. Just as important as capital investment, however, is the introduction of new technology. This may operate in either direction, but on balance tends to be laborsaving. Karl Marx asserted that the employment-destroying effects of new technology must more than offset the employment-creating effects of capital investment, but he produced no arguments in favor of this proposition, and proved to be wrong in the nineteenth century. It does not follow that he must be wrong in the twentieth century. The underdeveloped economies lag so far behind in technology, that the opportunities for introducing laborsaving methods are immense, and it could well happen that the new employment created in the factories, in modern forms of transportation, and in modern services could be more than offset by the employment destroyed in handicrafts, traditional forms of transportation, and old-fashioned types of personal service.

This possibility is heightened by the tendency of wages to rise sharply in the modern sector. The higher wages are, the more it pays to import cheap machinery from the developed countries, and therefore the less employment investment creates. Not only are the newest industries highly capital intensive, but some of the well-established older export industries, such as mines and plantations, are finding themselves squeezed by their inability to pay the wages that are being demanded and offered by more profitable enterprises; and the opportunities for import substitution are also diminished. Professors Liebenstein and Galenson have urged upon us the desirability of high capital intensity in underdeveloped countries as a source of profits and therefore of savings and investment. Unfortunately, that policy would be feasible only if the labor surplus remained disguised and could therefore be ignored; it is not practicable when the unemployed are roaming the streets and burgling your houses. Most developing countries have to give the highest priority to providing employment now rather than to maximizing consumption or income or employment in ten years time.

Economists have also developed a theory of the desirability of assessing the real social value of a project by calculating with shadow factor prices differing from the actual factor prices. In the situation described, they would recommend calculations in which the existence of unemployment is recognized by attributing a low wage to labor, below the actual wage. This is arguable on paper, but how does one translate it into practice? Investment decisions are made, not by economists making calculations in government offices, but by private decision-makers and by civil servants, all of whom are under pressure to produce at minimum costs in money terms, and the government does not possess the resources with which to subsidize labor so as to bring the wage down to the shadow price, or the administrative capacity to substitute an effective licensing system for the price system of the market. The only way to achieve decision making on the basis of a low shadow wage is to have a low actual wage.

Recognition of the connection between wages and employment has opened up a gulf between trade-union leaders and political leaders in new states, especially where the government is the chief employer of labor, or is concerned about the adverse effects of high wages on exports, import substitution and employment, or even prefers high profits to high wages because it can tax profits more easily than wages. Governments have therefore begun to think in terms of an incomes policy. Minimization of unemployment requires that wages should be tied to average agricultural incomes at a level sufficiently high to produce the labor required by the expanding nonagricultural sector, but not so high as to produce a great outflow which the towns cannot yet absorb. If at the same time vigorous measures are raising agricultural productivity, mass consumption will rise sharply, not merely because people are transferring from the lower level of the traditional sector to the higher level of the modern sector, but also because both levels are rising. Without some such policy, development must result in sharply increasing unemployment.

We are back in the political sphere. Trade-unions are not likely to accept an incomes policy from governments in which they have no confidence, whether because the politicians are corrupt, indifferent, reactionary, or inefficient. Economists in the twentieth century usually call upon governments to redress the imperfections of the market, just as their forebears in the nineteenth century looked to the market to replace the imperfections of the government. The last fifteen years have lengthened the list of things which governments can usefully do and improved the statistical and theoretical tools for making decisions, but only a handful of governments show promise of rising to their opportunities. Here the economist must hand the development problem over to his colleagues in the other social sciences.

Appendix

1. Assume that before "Libya" adopts new technologies, the position is that one man produces

in "Germany"	20 steel	or	3 baskets
in "Libya"	1 steel	or	1 basket

Therefore "Libya" specializes in baskets.

2. Now introduce new technology to Libya. Assume that the factor proportions are the same in both countries, in physical terms, namely

in steel	1 man + 1	capital
in baskets	1 man + 0.25	capital

3. Suppose, however, that capital makes much more contribution to steelmaking than to basketmaking. The former is a simple operation, which Libyans can do as well as Germans, given the capital; but the latter (basketmaking) is a skilled occupation, in which the Libyan output is still far short of the German, even with capital. The position is now that one man, with the appropriate capital produces

in Germany	20 steel or 3	baskets
in Libya	16 steel or 1.75	baskets

4. The difference is now smaller in steel than in baskets, but we cannot tell which should specialize in which without the relative prices of labor and capital. Suppose that labor costs one mark in Germany, one franc in Libya. Suppose that a unit of capital costs, on a rental basis, 2 marks in Germany and 3 francs in Libya. The relative cost of capital is higher in Libya because (*a*) it takes more labor to make a unit of capital, (*b*) capital maintenance is more expensive, (*c*) capital has a shorter life, and (*d*) the rate of interest is higher.

5. Costs per unit can now be calculated. They are

Germany,	steel 0.15 marks;	baskets 0.50 marks
Libya,	steel 0.25 francs;	baskets 1.00 francs

Hence steel is relatively cheaper in Libya than in Germany.

6. The moral is that the Hecksher-Ohlin test (relative scarcity of factors) gives the answer by itself only if the production functions are the same (i.e., if Ricardian differences are absent). In normal cases one must combine Ricardo and Ohlin to get the right answer.

7. The right answer will favor capital intensity in the countries which are short of capital if capital can be used without skill. As Leontief says, the real superiority of developed countries is not in capital intensive but in skill intensive industries, and though these two categories overlap, they are not identical.

[31]

SOCIALISM AND ECONOMIC GROWTH

Economic growth played little or no part in the blueprints of socialism which were drawn in the nineteenth century or earlier; no part in fact in the writings of any leading socialist before the 1920's. This is not strange. The idea of unlimited progress is itself relatively new in human history; it emerges significantly only in the eighteenth century. Eighteenth-century economists were aware that one nation was richer than another, and the reasons for this were the principal subject of their inquiry; but their context was that every country has a limit which it can reach with full exploitation of its natural resources; so they were only asking how to reach this limit. The Ricardian system, in the nineteenth century, saw each country developing up to a limit, and then stagnating. The self-styled socialist, John Stuart Mill, writing in the middle of the nineteenth century in elaboration of Ricardo's ideas, even goes so far as to argue that it is more pleasant to live in a stationary state than in one where economic growth is occurring, a proposition which attracts some L.S.E. economists even now. Karl Marx was in the same tradition. He was convinced that society, once liberated from the constraints of private property, would move swiftly to abundance. However, Marx's idea of abundance was rather limited, since his personal needs were very small; his Utopia which, to avoid alienation, dispensed even with the division of labour, was not much more productive than Mill's stationary state. Economic growth is not elevated to be a topic for serious thought in socialist circles until the era of Stalin, who realized early in his regime that the blueprints he had inherited were not compatible with the economic objectives he sought to attain, and he therefore promptly discarded the blueprints. Socialists no longer write blueprints, those long treatises in which every aspect of social relations is prescribed in detail. Instead, they now define their system in terms of its objectives, rather than in terms of any particular set of institutions. The basic objectives of democratic socialists remain unchanged, namely to combine

> political democracy, meaning representative government and civil rights, with

> economic equality, involving especially the elimination of an unequal distribution of private property.

Any system of institutions which meets these two tests is democratic socialism, and the variety of institutions which could do so is fairly wide.

One can state equally simply, but with less hazard, what an economic system requires in order to promote economic growth: namely

> conditions which promote the growth of new knowledge and its application; combined with
> economic incentives;
> adequate savings; and
> adequate foreign exchange.

The requirements for economic growth do not conflict with the objectives of democratic socialism, but they undoubtedly conflict with many cherished socialist blueprints, dogma and slogans. Hence the last fifty years have seen much discarding of ways of thought which are not compatible with the new objective of economic growth. For example, two of the most famous socialist slogans have gone: 'from each according to his ability to each according to his need', which is clearly incompatible with incentives; and 'the right of the worker to the whole product of his labour', which in addition to conflicting with distribution according to need, would also clearly result in inadequate savings. A philosophical system which is purging itself of ancient dogma, as socialism is, as it grapples with economic growth, is bound to give an appearance of confusion, as socialists clearly do today. So it is impossible to say what is or is not essential socialist practice unless one goes back to the original intentions of the faith.

In this short talk it is not necessary, and I do not have the time, to match the whole range of socialist prescriptions of the past against the requirements for economic growth. I shall not, for example, examine the problems connected with the creation and diffusion of knowledge, although the clash between egalitarianism and the economics of education is currently a lively and exciting issue. I shall instead concentrate on the two crucial issues which have given democratic socialists the biggest headaches, namely those questions associated with what the level of wages should be and how it should be determined, and those other questions associated with the management of industrial property.

WAGES

Professional anti-socialists make a great issue of the need for adequate wage differentials as an incentive, and claim that this makes socialism incompatible with economic growth. Actually socialist economists have never objected to wage differentials. The socialist hostility to inequality fastens not on earned income but on the unearned income from property, which is even more unequally distributed. Socialists do object to too wide a range of earned income, and try through welfare payments, minimum wages and surtax levies, to clip off both the bottom and the top. But this is a peripheral issue.

The core issue is what the average level of wages should be, whether in real terms or in money terms. In real terms we are concerned with the proportionate share of wages in the national income, while in money terms we are also concerned about inflation and its effects both at home and in the foreign exchanges.

Let us take first real wages. The proportionate share of wages matters to economic growth because of the low propensity to save out of wages. Socialists who desire rapid economic growth have therefore to keep a wide gap between the average wage and the average output per head.

What the desire for economic growth has done is to turn Ricardian socialism on its head. In the Ricardian system wages are determined at a conventional subsistence level, arbitrarily adopted. The surplus over wages is thus equally arbitrary. Ricardo, who was a humanitarian, wished that wages could be higher and the surplus smaller. This was the origin of modern socialism, since to writers like Bray and Marx, who started from Ricardo, an arbitrary surplus was obviously robbery and exploitation. They wanted to abolish the surplus and give the worker the whole product of his labour. Nowadays the good socialist is preoccupied rather with how to increase the surplus, so as to have the resources for capital formation and public expenditure. What was robbery in the stationary state becomes prudence when socialism makes its marriage with economic growth.

What is the right ratio of wages to output per head? The question of course has no economic answer. Even if we ignore the proposition, nurtured in some quarters of L.S.E., that there is little relationship between capital formation and the rate of economic growth, we are still left with no means of determining what the rate of economic growth ought to be. Stalin's answer was in effect that it should be just about as high as you can make it, and most of the so-called communist countries have followed his example. But most democratic socialists would not accept this answer because of the obvious dislocations created by rapid growth.

These dislocations are even more obvious in the less developed than in the industrially advanced countries. One of these dislocations, paradoxically, is that rapid industrial growth produces a rapid growth of unemployment, because the more jobs you create in the towns, with good wages, the more people will come streaming in from the countryside. There is a break-even point, but it is determined among other things by the rate of population growth. If population is stagnant, and the rural population is already small, you can easily industrialize faster than the towns can grow; but it is almost impossible to do this if population is growing by 3 per cent. per annum, and the rural reservoir is large. So we get the paradox that though industry is growing faster in less-developed countries than it ever has in the advanced countries—with growth rates of 10 to 15 per cent. being common—these countries are tending to be strangled by mounting unemployment. When this happens governments are forced to think more about welfare than about growth; resources are devoted to making work, both in the towns and in the countryside; and though some of this work results in productive capital there is almost certainly a net diversion of resources from activities which make national income statistics grow fast to activities which keep people from riot and starvation.

The conflict between welfare and growth was equally obvious in early industrial capitalism, when the great urban slums were being laid down. It is not now so startling in the industrially advanced countries, but it is real enough. Today's most popular subject is the deterioration of the environment. Even if there were no such problem, the general public does not accept the Stalin view that the most desirable growth rate is the highest which is feasible. The ordinary individual tends to care more about what he gets today than about what he is promised for five years from now.

From this situation the liberal economist deduces that the level of saving is a matter for individual determination. Let each save as much as he likes out of his income, and let total saving be no more than the sum of individual saving. Socialist economists, on the contrary, recognize that individuals may want their society to do compulsorily some things which few members would do voluntarily—such as to fight in a war. They list the level of national saving among the things for collective decision—like how many years of compulsory education to impose on children, or how large the navy should be—thus breaking decisively with liberal economics, which is not, as it pretends, a science, but is merely a by-product of individualist philosophy.

Now if the volume of saving is a matter for collective decision, and if the volume of saving also varies inversely with real wages, it follows automatically that the level of real wages has to be determined by those who determine what the level of savings should be. To put it bluntly, the level of real wages has to be determined by the government, that is to say, by some system of peaceful compromise acceptable to the whole society, and not by the trade unions, nor by the employers, nor by the trade unions and the employers acting together. The whole apparatus of collective bargaining and striking to determine the level of real wages is incompatible with a socialist economy in which the rate of saving is to be collectively determined. I have said that economic growth forces socialists to discard traditional patterns; this has been the hardest discard for socialist parties, especially given their traditional ties with parts of the trade union movement.

Actually if it were not for the repercussions on the foreign exchanges, governments could control real wages and savings without being directly involved in fixing money wages. They could, for example, simply set *ad valorem* indirect taxes at whatever level is required to produce an adequate budget surplus, or public saving. But then, the higher money wages rose, the higher prices would have to rise, with adverse repercussions on the balance of payments and the foreign exchange rate.

Nowadays socialists write a lot about foreign exchange rates, but foreign exchange rates are hardly mentioned in the traditional socialist literature, and innocence in this sphere has already ruined three British Labour governments. I have nothing special to say about this subject. Everyone now knows that a nation which has to trade cannot afford to let its prices get out of line, and cannot therefore live with a perpetual tendency for money wages to rise faster than productivity to a greater extent than is occurring in its chief competitors. The foreign exchange constraint has been a major brake on the rate of growth of numerous economies, especially in Latin America.

It is also increasingly recognized that wage inflation does not result only from the aspirations of trade unionists; it can also be inherent in the structure of the economy itself. As any economy grows, its demand for imports grows, and it will get into trouble unless its exports, visible and invisible, grow at the corresponding rate. Equilibrium between import and export rates of growth may require continual readjustment of the exchange rate. This is one of the results of growth economics which runs counter to the conventional wisdom of the economics of stationary states, whether socialist or otherwise. If a country has rich natural resources, or the propensity for continual technological change, or the drive to export—like Germany—its exports may tend continuously to outrun its imports. Or if, like Britain, it is deficient in all these respects, economic growth will tend to push up imports faster than exports. Continual devaluation then becomes inevitable, even if money wages are held constant. Since, in fact, devaluation will push up money wages via rising import costs, and so cause more devaluation in a continual chain, the fundamental remedies have to be sought elsewhere—in the British case in tackling the backwardness in technology and in export salesmanship which is the fundamental cause. Continual devaluation may become a necessary palliative, like applying heat to an aching back, but it is not an ultimate cure.

That inflation cannot be controlled, now that we have largely abolished the trade cycle, without controlling money wages is now generally recognized. Trade union power is now just about a century old in Europe, and we have come to the end of that century. Already trade union power has been abolished in the communist countries; and has in the Third World very widely been prevented by law from coming into existence; the struggle over guidelines and incomes policies suggests that it is merely a matter of time before the unions are deprived of their collective bargaining functions in Western Europe and North America. This will probably happen before 1980. The decade of the 1970's seems likely to be the decade of the backlash—against blacks, against students and against militant unionism—and the social democratic governments, backed by popular resentment against the militants, will be as active in clipping their wings as will governments of more conservative bent.

The problem of wage control is at its most difficult in those less-developed countries where foreign companies are making a lot of money out of some resource, such as oil or copper. In the past, militant unionism in such industries has had popular national support. For the government to fix money wages would be a gift to the rich foreigner and would do nothing to increase domestic savings. On the other hand, these industries are often a menace to the economy. The oil industry employs very few people at very high and constantly rising wages. This pulls up all other wages in the economy, beyond the level which other industries can afford to pay. The sugar industry is killed. Domestic service becomes too expensive. Import substitution is unable to get off the ground. So the effect of rising wages in oil is rising unemployment in everything else. Several Third World governments have found themselves compelled to end this spiral by controlling wages in these very profitable industries, even when they could clearly afford to pay higher wages. They get at the super-profits of these industries in other ways—essentially by taxation and by raising rents. Then, once the governments have got their hands into the companies' pockets they also have a direct interest in keeping wages down, since anything which reduced profits would also reduce the government's cut.

PROPERTY

Developed capitalist economies have essentially the same problem. To keep down the share of wages in the national income is to keep up the share of other income—and especially the share of unearned income from property, since the distribution of earned income is pretty stable. The justification for keeping up this surplus income, to use the classical term, is that it is the major source of saving, and therefore of the creation of new wealth. But who is to own and control this new wealth? The early capitalist answer made no distinction between ownership and control. Capital formation proceeded through a small number of capitalists making very large fortunes, which they also controlled. Nowadays control and ownership are divorced, since the great corporations have come to be managed by a bureaucratic class; but ownership continues to be highly concentrated in a few private fortunes.

For socialists the ownership and management of property are at the core of their concern, since it is the unequal inheritance of private property which is at the base of the class system. This attitude clearly separates the socialists from non-socialists. The world is full of people who still believe it desirable for a man to be able to make a fortune, and found a family to which he bequeaths his riches. This appeals to the very large number who would like to do it themselves. But it also appeals to others who think it good for incentives, or healthy for the support of private foundations or, by some strange process of reasoning, necessary for the preservation of democracy. It is simply not true that 'we are all socialists now.' The majority of people still admire, envy, cringe before or excuse the man who makes a million, whereas the true socialists, who are in a minority, abhor the creation and even more the inheritance of private fortunes.

In social democracies the remedy is seen as nationalization of private property, paying compensation to the owners. It is at once evident that this is no remedy. Control of the physical assets passes to the state, but the rich are as rich as before, now holding government securities. That much is generally realized; to reduce the wealth of the rich would need some form of what is euphemistically called a 'capital levy'. I am not, however, in this paper concerned with existing wealth; my concern is with growth, and therefore with new capital formation. Nationalization by itself does nothing to ensure that private wealth will not continue to grow even as nationalized industry itself grows. But I shall come to this in a moment.

Nationalization has also caused some disillusionment because it has not ended industrial strife. Not all socialists agree that management or physical control of industrial assets should pass to the state. Socialists divided early in their history between those who wanted property to be owned and managed by the workers and those who wanted property to be owned and managed by the state. Worker management has a long tradition, including some anarchists, the Guild socialists, the kibbutzes, and perhaps most importantly the new economic system in Yugoslavia. But Marx submerged the anarchist tradition, and his successors' elevation of the state to be our holiest institution was reflected in Fabianism, Stalinism and the nationalization programmes of Western Europe. Now Marxism is dying and philosophical anarchism is being resurrected all over the world.

Worker management is obviously an excellent idea if it is compatible with economic growth. Its opponents have attacked it on various grounds. The two which concern us here are that it would be inefficient, and that it would not save enough. It would be inefficient because management would be too kind to inefficient workers; and it would not save enough because the workers would want to consume as nearly as possible the whole product of their labour. The system would therefore be incompatible with economic growth. Yugoslav economists deny that this is so. They say that this might happen in a planned economy but that the competitive market economy, which their system incorporates, exerts just as much pressure on worker managements as it does on capitalist managements to be efficient, to innovate and to save, since worker enterprises which fail in these respects go bankrupt. They also deny that modern industry has to be run in great centralized trusts which dominate the market, and this is surely not a matter for simple generalizations. It is too early to judge the Yugoslav case. Undoubtedly the worker managements save and innovate, but it is not clear to what extent this is due to market pressure, and to what extent to the pressures of the Communist Party within factory counsels.

Nationalized industry, as practised in Western Europe, is not so vulnerable on the score of management, but it has in many countries failed on the score of saving.

The cardinal error has been the failure to make adequate profits. Business profit is one of the larger sources of saving for industrial investment. If nationalized industries just break even, or make a loss, then every extension of nationalization reduces the community's propensity to save. The extension of the public sector over the last fifty years is one of the chief reasons for the low propensity to save in Britain. If socialism were inevitably of this kind, it would certainly be incompatible with adequate economic growth.

How do nationalized industries finance their expansion if they are not saving enough? By borrowing from the private sector, or from the government which is borrowing from the private sector. This means that private wealth, even if only in the form of ownership of securities, has to be growing *pari passu* with the increase of the publicly owned physical assets. Nationalization has not then effected a change in the distribution of wealth. The original property owners were paid the value of their property, leaving them equally rich. And if also every extension of nationalized property is matched by issuing more securities to private holders of wealth, instead of by savings (including sinking fund payments), then nationalization does nothing to alter the ratio of private to public wealth. It gives control of property to the state, but private wealth is growing as fast as public property.

If nationalization is to be compatible with economic growth, and is also to reduce the growth of private wealth, it must be accompanied by public saving. This is a fairly obvious proposition. All new investment, whether private or public, is financed by saving, whether private or public. If public saving is low, investment will have to be financed largely by private saving, and so private wealth will continue to grow. What matters to the growth rate of private wealth is not whether enterprises are privately or publicly owned, but whether *saving* is private or public. Whether industry is nationalized or not is irrelevant to the growth rate of private wealth. The nineteenth-century socialists could not think in terms of a distinction between ownership and control since this was before their time, so all their blueprints assume that ownership and management must go together in socialism. Twentieth-century socialists have been rather slow in grasping the significance of the distinction.

One socialist who grasped the distinction was Mr Hugh Gaitskell. He saw that the crux of socialist economic growth is not in nationalization or public management, but in public saving. If public saving were adequate to finance economic expansion, private wealth would cease to grow whether industry was nationalized or not. One could thus consider separately the problems of industrial management and the problems of ownership. Public ownership and public financing of production could be combined with private management, or worker management, or consumer management, or state management, or any other industrial form, without violating the socialist concern to restrain the growth of private wealth. In the British case he thought that the best combination would be public ownership with private management; and he proposed that the government buy shares in business enterprises. He favoured this combination because he thought that British industry, which has to live by innovation and by exporting in a highly competitive world, needs much flexibility and capacity to experiment. It was all right to put British electricity generation under a single national management, or even the production of steel, but he did not want to do this to the 100 other trades on which Britain's export survival depends. But this is only the British case. Grant that public saving will provide the finance for economic growth, and you can choose any kind of management, worker, co-operative, private or public; if it is also consistent in the particular industry with economic efficiency, it will also be consistent with economic growth. The idea of private management of publicly owned enterprise sounded strange in Britain, but the practice is quite common in the Third World, and not uncommon in communist countries, as the Soviet Union's recent contract with Fiat Motors reminds us. Mr Gaitskell was hounded by many of his followers for dropping nationalization; and attacked just as fiercely by Conservatives, who were quicker to see that public saving without nationalization is a greater danger to the growth of private wealth than is nationalization without public saving.

The economist who opened the way to the marriage of private enterprise with socialist ownership was Alfred Marshall, when he liberated the word 'profit'. Up to his time economists divided the national income into wages, rent and profit. Profit was the remuneration of capital, and so if you were against private capital you automatically denounced profit. By inventing a fourth factor of production, organization, Marshall split profit into two parts, earnings of capital and earnings of management. Some managers are paid fixed salaries; others, even in the Soviet Union, are remunerated on a residual basis, out of and in proportion to profits. Socialists no longer fear the word 'profit' as such, do not worry about small profit makers like shopkeepers or farmers, except in doctrinaire countries, and have no difficulty in seeing managers working for profits, using capital which belongs to the state; or, perhaps I should say, have only a slight emotional difficulty, which is a throwback to ancestral memories.

Let me be a little more specific on public saving. Public saving is the difference between the government's revenues and expenditures on current account, plus the gross profits of public enterprises, or for short the budget surplus plus the public profits.

I have already mentioned that to have an adequate level of public saving one must arrange for public enterprises to make substantial profits—no less than is made by private firms if the extension of public enterprise is not to reduce the propensity to save. One must also have an adequate budget surplus, which is attained by keeping taxes up and current expenditure down. Neither of the British political parties conforms to this prescription; the Conservatives want to keep taxes down, while the Labour Party wants to keep current expenditure up. In fact if the British Labour Party wanted to become truly socialist it would have to change its whole fiscal approach. It would have to urge nationalized industries to make profits, and it would have to keep strict curbs on public expenditure on current account. The latter is particularly hard to swallow. The fiscal history of the left is one of continually thinking up new targets for social and welfare expenditure; whereas what socialist economic growth requires is to produce a bigger budget surplus every year to finance the expansion of public property. Actually, there is already some socialist retreat from the proposition that everything is for everybody, which puts an immense burden on the budget, to the original proposition that welfare is only for those who need it, which makes possible more generous benefits. Free welfare services for all are on the way out, even in socialist literature.

Another necessary change in socialist thinking which is imposed by the need to finance some capital formation out of taxes is to recognize the limits of a progressive tax on earned incomes; one cannot keep on raising income tax rates on earned incomes, without damaging incentives. It is possible to devise a system of indirect taxes which is nearly as progressive as an income tax, if not equally so, and which is not resented so much because people are not so much aware of it, and pay only as they spend. Indirect taxes are the principal source of revenue in the communist countries. Again, if one wishes to tax the business corporations very heavily this cannot be done by taking taxes in cash, since this weakens their power and incentive to invest. It would be better to take a substantial proportion of the corporation tax in shares, voting or non-voting. Management and saving would be unaffected thereby, but the wealth of the government would grow instead of that of the private shareholder. This is feasible only when one is taxing to raise public savings rather than to increase public expenditure.

If one were to set out to abolish private saving altogether and substitute public saving, a sharp increase in taxes would be required. The government budget and the profits of public enterprises would have to take between them say 30 per cent. of the national income, for civil expenditure and gross capital formation—not in these days a startling figure, if it were not for the added burden of defence. But it is neither feasible nor desirable to abolish all private saving. Neither is it necessary to attain full socialism in one year; the relative proportions of private and public saving can be altered gradually over ten or twenty years without calling for drastic changes in tax rates from one year to the next.

Once one grasps that the core of socialist economic growth is in public saving rather than in any particular form of asset control, socialists can look at industrial organization with a new eye. I have just pointed out that even private enterprise is consistent with socialism if it is mainly financed by public rather than by private saving. More importantly, one can take another look at the clash between the worker management socialists and the nationalization socialists. Each rides a good horse, the Guild socialists emphasizing the right of the worker to control his own conditions, while the nationalizers emphasize that the property belongs to the state. But if socialism is not tied to the old blueprints, then Guild socialism can no longer be rejected on the ground that saving would be too low—since public saving would look after that—or on the ground that it would be inefficient—since the competitive market economy would look after that. Socialists could say goodbye to most of nationalized industry, with its industrial strife, its contempt for the consumer and its administrative rigidities. I do not want to be caught plugging any particular blueprint, least of all one like Guild Socialism that is seventy years old. But I shall be very surprised if Bakunin does not submerge Marx throughout the socialist movement over the next decade or two.

Let me end by turning to the less-developed countries. Most Afro-Asian political parties in power style themselves socialist, but they are necessarily even further from socialism than the parties in Europe. Less-developed countries, like industrial countries, can grow on socialist lines only through public saving; but how are they, with their rudimentary tax administrations and their hunger for government services, to achieve the necessary budget surpluses? Most of these parties do not yet even understand the significance of public saving in the socialist plan; they believe, as Western European socialists believed until very recently, that the mark of good socialism is to spend lavishly on social and welfare services, and are puzzled by the suggestion that the basic socialist objective, viz. capital formation without private wealth, is attainable only through public saving.

Less-developed countries (LDCs) need a large increase in public saving whether or not they are socialistically inclined, since a large increase in private saving is most unlikely at current levels of income and expectations. The alternative would be to rely mainly on foreign capital, but no country wishes to be permanently dependent on foreign capital. The correct strategy for using foreign capital is to use it only to prime the pump. Bringing in foreign capital and enterprise will raise the national income. There is thus an opportunity to raise the dometic savings ratio rapidly, without hardship. For example, a marginal savings ratio of only 0·25 with income growing by 5 per cent. per annum will raise gross domestic saving from say 12 to 20 per cent. in twenty years. The current wave of resentment against foreign enterprise in the LDCs is due to the governments having failed to use their opportunity to raise domestic savings. Some of these countries save hardly more today than they did twenty years ago, although their *per capita* incomes are up by 50 per cent. This is a failure of public will, rather than of private foreign investment.

The LDCs cannot become both wealthy and economically independent without exercising fiscal restraint for the purpose of public saving. It is popularly believed that socialism itself speeds up the rate of economic growth, much of the credit being given to centralized economic planning. The Third World shows no evidence of this; the self-styled socialist economies in the Third World have been the slowest growing—Guinea, Mali, Burma, Indonesia and even Cuba, whose phenomenal expansion of social services does not seem to be matched by any extraordinary expansion of productive capacity. The reason is of course that central planning has little to do with economic growth. The economies of Eastern Europe grow rapidly not because they are socialist or planned, but because they have high saving and investment ratios combined with high investment in education and training. Their capacity to restrain personal consumption is the key to their success.

Now if LDCs are driven to public saving, even if only because private saving grows too slowly, it follows that they will automatically develop on more socialist lines than did Western Europe or North America. They will neither need nor have great private fortunes, and will thus by-pass the robber-baron stage. They may have a wide variety of enterprises—consumer co-operatives, Yugoslav-type worker managements or plain private firms—working to a considerable extent with funds lent or invested by the state. The reality of socialism will lie in the absence of large private fortunes, rather than in the forms of industrial management.

This is fortunate for the less-developed countries since, if socialism lay in public management, their socialism would have to be long delayed. In many of them public management is notoriously inefficient, if not also corrupt, and its losses are a drain on the savings of the economy. An efficient system of public administration is one of the prerequisites of managerial socialism, but it takes a long time to reach this stage of political sophistication. What such countries have to do at present is to build up public saving, but contract out management in various forms of mixed contract.

Socialism sounds somewhat confused in these days because it is in the process of adjusting itself to the requirements of economic growth as well as to a world-wide demand for more decentralization of decision-making. The basic objectives of socialism remain the same, but the institutions must change continually to reflect new fiscal policies, new welfare policies or new forms of industrial organization. The anti-socialists are just as confused, since their philosophy is also founded in outdated early nineteenth-century forms of competitive family capitalism, which makes no sense in today's world of faceless industrial giants. Confusion is the bread and butter of intellectuals; we make our living trying to clear it away, and in the process usually make nearly as much as we remove. I am happy to have had this opportunity of plying our trade today.

[32]

The Evolution of Foreign Aid
by Sir W. Arthur Lewis

It is a great privilege to give this lecture in memory of David Owen. My assignments with the United Nations during the 1950's and 60's brought us into close contact, and it was always a pleasure to work with him. David combined clarity of objectives with hard work and a wonderfully pleasant personality, which helped him to keep things moving. He created and developed the technical assistance activities of the United Nations, from nothing to the great edifice which is today that organisation's most outstanding achievement. We who believe in creating an international framework for the peace and prosperity of mankind will always be in his debt.

When David Owen first went into the field of foreign aid and technical assistance, it hardly existed. Most of what we now call the third world was still in a colonial state, and though some colonial powers were making subventions towards the upkeep of colonial governments, these were rather small, except for the French subventions, which were just then beginning to build up. In 1948 the total amount being transfered by the governments of Western Europe and North America cannot have exceed five hundred million dollars a year; now it exceeds seven thousand million dollars a year.

Not only was the effort small; but there was also widespread doubt whether larger effort would be worthwhile. Many doubted that the less developed countries were currently capable of development; they seemed to have inappropriate attitudes to economic effort; restrictive social customs, religions and institutions; even also intractable climates. Money spent pursuing development would almost certainly be wasted, if indeed it did not merely end up in pockets of corruption. Those who like David, threw themselves into the struggle to create a large and universal flow of foreign aid and technical assistance were thought to be starry-eyed, and certainly had a hard persuasive task.

Since nothing succeeds like success, the main problem of foreign aid supporters has always been to show that aid can be effective when well regulated. Hence much thought has been given to creating institutions and formulating strategies for effective aid, resulting in the evolution which is the subject of this lecture. But before I come to this, let us first see what has actually happened in the developing countries.

i

The most important change over the past two decades has been in our understanding of what is possible in the developing countries. Twenty years ago we were influenced by the newly emerging historical statistics of national income, which showed growth rates for the United States and Western Europe for the half-century before the first world war of between 1 and 2 per cent per head per year. If that was the best that these rich countries could achieve, during their period of fastest growth to date, then 2 per cent per head would be an optimistic target for the less developed countries. Death rates were still high in the 1940's, so population was growing only by about 1½ per cent. Putting population and per capita growth together, the optimists then hoped for overall growth of national income at about 3½ per cent. This was a minority view; the majority of informed people thought 2 per cent much more likely.

When around 1960 the United Nations fixed a growth target for the decade of the 60's, it soared as high as its imagination could go, and named 5 per cent, not because anybody thought that feasible, but because it was a star to follow.

In the event, the developing countries taken as a whole grew at an average rate exceeding 5 per cent per annum during the 1960's. The growth rate per head was up to 2½ per cent, exceeding that of the United States over the past century. The United Nations has now fixed for the 1970's a target 6 per cent per annum. And Mr. Edwin Martin, the American Chairman of the Development Assistance Committee of the OECD (the Organisation for Economic Co-operation and Development, which is the organisation of the donor countries) has now written in his annual report, reviewing the development situation, that

> "it may turn out that the 6 per cent growth target for the Second Development Decade will be rather easy to achieve."

Anybody who has been around these countries knows that these are not mere figures. Apart from the obvious signs of industrialisation, there has also been a major improvement of infrastructure and of service industries. Incredible change has occurred in such features as the number of miles of paved road, the number of villages with water supplies, the proportion of children attending schools, the prevalence of electricity, the death rates from malaria, small-pox and dysentery, the number of hospital beds, and other such indicators of modernisation. The service industries, as they are called, have been growing by around 6 per cent per year.

There are weak spots. Some countries are doing very much better than others, differing according to their natural resources and their own internal economic policies. Countries with rich mineral resources have done particularly well – especially oil, copper, bauxite and iron ore. At the other end countries with poor or unreliable rainfall, which also cannot be trapped for irrigation, are not able to take advantage of the "green revolution," the name given to the new agricultural techniques which are doubling agricultural yields in more favoured places. This is especially the problem of India, where about 40 per cent of the area under cultivation lacks adequate water.

Besides these differences in natural resources, some countries are better governed than others, from the economic standpoint. Several handicap themselves, just like their more developed neighbours, by clinging to over-valued exchange rates; by keeping agricultural prices too low; or by tying themselves up in badly administered licensing systems. Economic administration is improving as more bright young men enter the civil service and acquire strategic positions, but all have still a long way to go in learning to pursue sound economic policies.

Many problems still lie ahead: the rapid growth of population and of urban unemployment; the rising social and political tensions associated with uneven distribution of income and wealth; the uncertain future of foreign trade; the accumulating debt burden; and so on. The developing world has not solved all its economic and political problems in two decades. But it has demonstrated that it responds to economic stimuli; to capital investment, to opportunities for foreign trade; to new technical innovations; and so on. It has shown that foreign aid is not money down the drain, but is potentially a valuable investment in human beings all around the world. Those who have laboured to make it possible can take some pride in the fact that the developing countries have more than justified their hopes.

ii

How much of this economic achievement is due to foreign aid? The question is unanswerable. One can see clearly the relevance of that part of foreign aid with which David Owen was primarily concerned, namely technical assistance, which is the transfer of skilled people; but the effect of the monetary flows is not so easily assessed.

7

Technical assistance has been a star performer, and David could look back with great pride on the rapid expansion and undoubted contribution of this part of foreign aid. During this period the colonial relationship was liquidated, and the number of independent countries belonging to the United Nations more than doubled. Very many of these new countries simply did not have the technical personnel to man their public services, and had therefore to rely on getting people from abroad to come and work for them. The number of people working abroad for governments under technical assistance arrangements, bilateral and multilateral, is now about 112,000 of whom about a half are teachers or in education, and the other half are widely spread in agriculture, health and so on. Technical assistance also brings people to the developed countries for training. In 1970 the number on government schemes was about 38,000 university students and 28,000 others for shorter technical courses.

The role of technical assistance over these two decades is hard to exaggerate. Facilities for secondary and higher education and technical training were totally inadequate two decades ago. Since then they have expanded very rapidly, with the help of technical assistance, and the supply of trained people is fast catching up with the demand. The numbers in technical assistance are already stabilising, and will probably not grow very much during the 1970's. But the international community can take real pride in the achievement of the past two decades.

iii

Now let us turn to the monetary flows. I shall not attempt to answer the question how much of the economic growth was due to foreign aid because there is no global answer. If one goes country by country one can find case after case where foreign aid financed crucial activities which clearly fostered development. But one can also find examples, especially where bilateral aid was given for purely political reasons, where aid has disappeared without trace. What rather distinguishes these two decades is the evolution of institutions and policies designed to ensure the effectiveness of aid, and it is these which I more particularly wish to consider.

Five major developments have to be noted:

First, the emergence of huge departments administering foreign aid;

Secondly, the shift from project to programme aid;

Thirdly, the multilateralisation of bilateral aid;

Fourthly, the expansion of multilateral aid; and

Fifthly, the search for criteria of allocation as between countries.

Let me say a word about each of these.

Beginning briefly with the public service. The first concern of donors is that their money will be used for the specific purposes for which it is granted, and not simply be diverted into corrupt pockets. So every donor government now has a special department with a large staff and many complicated rules and systems of inspection to keep track of its transfers. We can I think be fairly satisfied that most foreign aid is used for precisely the purposes for which it has been approved, though not absolutely certain since, even inside the best countries some domestic expenditure goes astray, but certain enough to agree that this is not a major problem.

In trying to ensure the effectiveness of aid, the first approach of the donor country was to tie his contribution to a particular project, such as the building of a particular port. The applicant country had to submit detailed engineering drawings and an elaborate cost-benefit analysis justifying the project. It had to call for open tenders; and after the contract was awarded, consultants hired by the donor country would have to certify progress before the donor country would make payments.

This is still the standard way of administering foreign aid, but the second development of the past two decades has been the big shift from project aid to programme aid. Project aid proved to be restrictive because not enough suitable projects could be found to meet the rules. One of the rules, which is still with us, is that foreign aid finances only those parts of the project which have to be imported. Suppose then that the project is to build a school. No aid will be given towards the cost of labour employed on the project. Aid will be given for cement or glass or roofing materials if these are imported. But suppose that the country manufactures its own building materials. Then the project does not qualify for foreign aid, because it has no direct foreign exchange costs. This is obviously absurd. If labourers are paid wages they go into shops and markets and buy goods, many of which are imported. The building of a school uses up resources whether it is built with local materials or with imported materials; so foreign aid is equally helpful in either case.

In countries which manufacture very little for themselves, it is easy to find projects to which to tie one's aid; but scarcity of projects needing foreign imports soon became a problem in India, as that country became more self sufficient in manufactures, so it was in India that the passage was first made from project aid to programme aid. In programme aid one recognises that as a country develops, its need for imports of all kinds will increase – for raw materials, consumer good

9

manufactures and so on. One looks at the foreign trade balance as a whole, without trying to identify individual projects which give rise to it; and one then makes a grant to the developing country to help cover the gap in its balance of payments. The grant will be tied to particular purchases, but not necessarily to particular projects.

How does the donor country in these circumstances ensure the effectiveness of its aid? The gap in the balance of payments is due to the whole pattern of development in the country, and the policies pursued by its government. Some policies will keep the balance of payments deficit down; others will inflate it. If a donor country merely undertook to meet a deficit in the balance of payments it would be encouraging many poor programmes and policies of which it strongly disapproved. It is therefore only natural that countries which are willing to give programme aid will want to have a look at the whole programme, and will be reluctant to pick up the tab unless they approve it.

Here we slide off into rough water. The poor countries are proud and independent. They do not welcome having rich countries bring pressure on them to adopt particular programmes, as a condition of foreign aid. Their attitude may be summed up as "give us the money and shut up".

iv

Now we come to the third development in foreign aid. A receiving country is more likely to take criticism if it comes from a multilateral source than if it comes from a single government. Most official foreign aid is bilateral, i.e. from one government to another. About 10 per cent is multilateral, that is, handled by an international organisation such as the United Nations or the World Bank. The new development may be called multilateralisation of bilateral aid.

This began to take shape in 1958 because in that year, when India was in very serious balance of payments difficulties, the World Bank organised a consortium for India in the major European and North America states, who were given data showing the size of India's need, and asked to pledge contributions. This was the genesis of the programme rather then the project approach. The governments did not at this first meeting take it upon themselves to criticise Indian policies. But the World Bank began to do an annual report on the Indian economic situation and to summon the consortium to meet every year; and inevitably this meeting led into discussions of Indian economic policy.

The idea of a mulilateral meeting caught on fast. Receiving countries liked it, because they hoped to get more by having all their potential donors sit around a table, and by using the more generous ones to put pressure on the less generous. Donor countries welcomed the opportunity to discuss the programmes of the recipients, in a multilateral atmosphere, on the basis of an independent and critical annual report by the World Bank. They did not like the opportunity which it gave the receiving country to pressure them into making higher contributions. So after the first four consortia, organised as pledging sessions, they asked the World Bank to arrange the next set of countries under the title of "consultative groups" rather than "consortia". A consultative group does not hold pledging sessions, but does have the World Bank's report on the country, and the regular meeting to review the country's progress and programmes. There are now twelve of these consultative groups, in Asia, Africa and the Mediterranean.

This principle was further strengthened by the signing of the Charter of the Alliance for Progress in 1961. Here the United States was pledged to give substantial aid to Latin American countries who, in return, undertook to adopt certain policies spelt out in great detail in the document, such as land reform, progress towards universal primary education, and so on. A committee of nine wise men was set up, and each Latin American country was required to submit its plans to this committee. The wise men criticised these plans, and the amount of aid was supposed to be related to the response to these criticisms. The system was stregthened in 1963 by the creation of the Committee of the Alliance for Progress (CIAP) with a staff, which writes an annual report on each country, much like a World Bank report. The Committee meets representatives of each country each year to discuss the report, and to this meeting go representatives of the United States and of any other country giving foreign aid to Latin America, and also representatives of the international organs like the World Bank.

This is multilateralisation of bilateral aid in the sense that the donor is still the individual country – the U.S.A. or the U.K. or West Germany – which decides how much to give. But the annual meeting of the consortium or consultative group or the Committee of the Alliance for Progress, with the independent World Bank or CIAP report, provides a multilateral framework within which pressure can be put on the receiving countries to modify their economic policies.

V

Multilateralisation of bilateral aid makes the pressure more respectable, but does not eliminate all the objections to bilateral aid. In particular, the amount that any donor country gives to any recipient country continues very largely to be influenced by political considerations. Britain gives to former British colonies, the United States gives to countries bordering Russia and China, France gives to

Francophone Africa, and so on. The result, when you look at a table showing how much each of the one hundred countries receives in foreign aid, is a distribution which cannot be defended on any principle of need, size of population, absorptive capacity or any economic test. For example, at the end of the 1960's the per capita aid to India averaged $2.10 a year; Liberia received $21.50; and the global average was $5.50. Politics was the chief determinant of aid.

The desire to take politics out of foreign aid dominated the discussions of the less developed countries in the early 1950's and led them to press for multilateral aid under United Nations auspices, which would presumably be distributed fairly all round without political strings. They were supported by the smaller European donor countries, especially those without ex-colonies to favour, for whom it would be simpler to use a multilateral agency than to build up their own foreign aid programmes. This battle was not exactly lost, since multilateral aid has expanded very considerably. But it was not exactly won either, since bilateral aid has expanded too, and the geographical distribution of aid remains as arbitrary as before.

The leading donor countries, especially the United States, set their faces against a United Nations capital aid programme, which would inevitably they thought be controlled by the recipients, and therefore they argued, be distributed without stringent administrative checks or economic tests. They agreed eventually to a large expansion of United Nations technical assistance, but to this day have not provided funds to the United Nations for capital transfers. Instead they compromised by expanding the resources of the World Bank, an institution which is under the firm control of the donor countries, since voting power is more or less propotional to how much money each country puts in. They have also cooperated in establishing the regional development banks, especially the Inter-American and the Asian Development Banks, where also their large contributions, plus the fact that these Banks have to borrow in the donor capital markets and must conduct themselves acceptably, again gives heavy weight to the views of the developed countries.

Much of the heat has gone out of the multilateral vs. bilateral argument, partly because India, who was the leader, turned inward after the death of Mr. Nehru. Nevertheless, the demand for more multilateral aid continues, and the Pearson Commission supported it, with a recommendation that the proportion of aid given multilaterally should rise from 10 to 20 per cent.

vi

The assumption underlying this pressure is that multilateral aid will be distributed more fairly than bilateral aid. So one must ask, what would be a fair distribution of aid? The question becomes more urgent as the amount of aid given by the World Bank and the regional development banks on soft terms grows. The ordinary commercial lending of the World Bank does not raise the question of fairness since the World Bank has always been willing to lend on hard terms for any project which meets its criteria. But when you are lending money at 2 per cent or less for 40 years, the demand is unlimited and some system of rationing becomes urgently necessary. What is a fair distribution of soft aid?

Let us note first that fairness depends on the purpose of aid. On this subject the consensus has been through a considerable evolution over the past two decades. We have, to begin with, sorted out the difference between aid to consumption and aid to capital formation. It is now generally agreed that the main purpose of aid is to increase productive capacity; we set out not to give people food but to help them to grow enought food to feed themselves. There are exceptions, such as special programmes for children, health programmes and disaster relief, but in the main the intention of foreign aid is to increase in the first instance not consumption but capital formation, and proof that this is intended is one of the conditions of eligibility.

It seems to follow that one should give aid not in accordance with consumption need but in accordance with capacity to invest. This is obviously a controversial conclusion. These two criteria, need and capacity, tend to clash, because those with the best capacity to invest tend to be those who are already well on the way to development; while the poorest countries, who in some sense need aid most, tend to be, with the notable exception of India, those which are least able to use it effectively. Some reconciliation is effected by defining "capital formation" to include expenditure on education and on institution building designed to raise administrative capacity; but the pay-off tends to take a long time. The conflict between helping the poor and helping the capable can never be entirely resolved. The Lord himself is required to help both those who help themselves and those who need help most, and if He cannot resolve this conflict, neither can we.

For the most part theorists of foreign aid have tried to settle this controversy by concentrating on what they call absorptive capacity. The discussion went through a phase in the early 60's of trying to measure the absorptive capacity of each developing country, and to calculate from this how much aid it should receive. Professor Rosenstein-Rodan did this by estimating how much capital each country could usefully invest, and how much it might reasonably be expected to save; the difference between these two it should receive as aid. Professor Chenery forecast instead each country's deficiency of foreign exchange. Without stopping to ask how these two bases can be reconciled, we note that they are both vunerable to the same two objections, which diminish their usefulness. First they are highly subjective. Since no good economist making a prediction will offer a single figure, we may deduce that five economists, each making any one of these calculations independently, would produce at least ten different solutions. Secondly, these formulae tend to reward the bad and penalise the good. The country which already has a high savings rate, or which is already pursuing good export policies, tends to come out on such calculations as needing little aid; while countries which emphasise domestic consumption rather than savings or exports are highly rewarded.

For this reason people interested in finding a reasonable basis for allocating foreign aid shifted the focus of their interest from absorptive capacity to performance Those countries should receive most help which did most for their productive capacity. Aid, they argued, should be based not on the absolute level of savings, but on the rate of increase of saving; in recent years; and not on the size of the balance of payments gap, but on the rate of progress being made towards closing the gap. This has the further advantage of eliminating discrimination against the poorer countries, since the poor have lower absolute levels than the less poor developing countries, but their potential rate of change seems to be about the same.

Now if countries raise their savings and export ratios they are well on the way to becoming self-sufficient. The Pearson Commission pointed out that if the target was to raise national income by 6 per cent per year, and if each less developed country saved a little over 20 per cent out of marginal income – which is not too much to ask – then the need for foreign aid would disappear altogether by the end of this century, since every country would by then be saving for itself as much as one needs for 6 per cent per annum growth. The Pearson Commission rejoiced that foreign aid could be regarded as self-liquidating within one generation, and, writing in the United States, with an eye especially on American opinion, saw this as an extra reason why we should not hesitate to put our shoulders to the wheel: the burden of foreign aid was temporary, and had an early date for termination.

However, we can decide to reward countries for saving more without also demanding that they become self-sufficient. The 6 per cent growth target is for the 1970's only. As absorptive capacity grows, the target growth rate can be raised towards that which Japan has been achieving over the last two decades (8 to 10 per cent). The less developed countries would then be saving more and more, but they would then also be investing more and more, if the international community were willing to support these higher targets.

vii

In the Report of the Pearson Commission the distribution of foreign aid is tied to performance. At the financial level this refers to levels of taxation, increases in the ratio of savings, and efforts to stimulate exports. But economic development does not depend solely on finance; one can make a long list of programmes and policies which governments should adopt in the interest of development - ranging into education, health, land reform, and so on. The treaty of the Alliance for Progress contains a very long comprehensive list of all liberal and progressive measures to which the Latin American countries were supposed to be committing themselves in return for financial aid.

Actually, performance by itself cannot tell you how much aid a country should get; it is only one element in a formula for allocating aid. Suppose that a country is given full marks for performance, 100 per cent. Does that mean $50 million or $500 million? It means that the country should get the full amount to which it is entitled according to the criteria the donors are using; one is still left to determine what the criteria should be.

The Pearson Commission decided to recommend that each developing country should get the same amount of aid per head, subject to performance tests, which would give it slightly more or slightly less. An alternative egalitarian precept would be to give each country the same proportion of its national income, but the same amount per head has the advantage over this that it gives proportionately more to the poorer countries.

The desire for greater equality in aid was the chief reason for the Pearson Commission recommending greater multilateral aid; specifically that the proportion of multilateral aid be doubled. The World Bank, in particular, was asked to concentrate on the countries which were getting relatively little bilateral aid, so as to even up the score: this would be a sharp reversal of World Bank practice, which has tended to favour the same countries as are favoured by the bilateral donors. In moving towards an egalitarian distribution the World Bank would also take performance into account. It would be a plus or minus factor, adding to or subtracting some percentage from the amount of aid the country would get solely on the basis of equality per head. Performance would be assessed not by figures, but against the broader background of a generally accepted code of behaviour.

What would be the principal items in such a code? So far our experience in this area has been over-ambitious. In practice, what aid administrators, bilateral or multilateral, have tended to expect of aid recipients falls into three groups: economic, social and international.

On the economic side countries have been advised, by the World Bank or the IMF for instance, to arrest inflation by reducing the monetary supply, to raise their tax levels and reduce government expenditures, to give greater scope to the free market in place of administrative licensing, or to bring their balance of payments into equilibrium. These are all highly controversial policies, as people in the United Kingdom know only too well from their own encounters with the so-called gnomes of Zurich.

On the social side countries have been advised to pursue land reform, to deflect more of the national income from rich to poor, to encourage population control, to extend educational facilities even to the point of creating unemployment of the educated, and so on.

And countries are also enjoined to practise good international behaviour, of which the most important ingredient turns out to be not to nationalise the property of foreign companies without paying prompt and adequate compensation. But additionally also countries which get involved in fighting their neigbours or in major civil wars also find pressure applied to them to agree to peaceful solutions, if foreign aid is not to be curtailed.

This is a formidable list of economic, social and political criteria, and it is not surprising that attempts by foreign aid administrators to take them into account in one case or another have produced bitter protests. Much of the economic advice given by the international institutions has clearly been erroneous, since it gave too high a priority to price stability. Both the IMF and the World Bank have come under heavy criticism for this, and have in response somewhat modified their positions. In any case these are not the only multilateral institutions; we now have also the regional development banks, with the majority of the voting power in the hands of the less developed countries themselves, and their influence somewhat offsets the orthodoxy coming out of Washington. They should play a much larger role than they now do in administering aid.

Still, the basic situation cannot be evaded. It is inevitable that donor governments will resist giving foreign aid to countries which they believe to be wasting it, or to be pursuing policies unfavourable to economic development. Those who accept and use other people's money must expect that further assistance will be conditional on how they act.

The core of the problem is to adopt a code of behaviour which is mutually acceptable to the great bulk of donor and recipient opinion, and to create and preserve a multilateral framework within which this code can be applied. We have already had one shot at writing the code; namely the charter of the Alliance for Progress which set out in detail what was expected of the Latin American participants. This code was too elaborate. Conceivably, no effective code could be agreed unanimously around a table; yet in the process of discussion within consultative and similar multilateral groups a set of precedents could be created which had the same effect - just as a legal system can be enshrined in statutes or may evolve through the common law. This is the more likely case.

The beginnings of the multilateral framework we already have in the consortia, the consultative groups, CIAP and the World Bank's regular reporting on the economic progress and problems of each of its developing members. Within this framework a developing member whose policies are being criticised can defend itself openly and seek support from other countries, both developing and developed. Since it is going to be criticised anyway, and subjected to bilateral pressures, it is much better off within the multilateral framework, where everything can be brought to the surface. This is the context in which the Pearson Commission recommended that all the less developed countries should be covered by a multilateral network of the consultative kind.

When talking about a code of behaviour for recipient countries, which is a heated subject, it is important to note that even greater effort has gone into trying to create a code of behaviour for donor countries. Several items figure in this code: the attempt to get unanimous commitment that each developed country will contribute one per cent of its national income to foreign aid; the pressure on these countries to commit themselves to recipient countries for four or five years ahead, instead of only for one year at a time; the attack on tied aid, which nearly succeeded; the agreement to increase the grant element in loans by reducing interest rates and giving longer grace periods. For the most part the developing countries pressure for such a code has been made through the United Nations Conference on Trade and Development. The developed countries have not been willing to use the United Nations for such negotiations, but inside the OECD, where they confer by themselves, the more generous have raised such issues continually, bringing pressure to bear on the less generous. The result is that there is consensus within that group on how donors ought to behave, even though not every country has made the formal commitment. We do not have international treaties governing the aid relationship, but we have made great progress in two decades in nearing detailed consensus on what it ought to be.

viii

Unfortunately the consortia and the consultative groups have themselves been in the doldrums for the last two or three years, despite the fact that the developing countries, recognising their advantages, keep asking for more and more consultative groups to be created. This setback results from the decline in American aid; the American aid authorities have been less anxious to participate in international gatherings when they know that they will have to announce arbitrary cuts rather than increases in their contributions. The situation is rather anomalous. All the other members of the OECD have now accepted the target of transferring one per cent of their national income as foreign aid, and several have stated the precise steps which they are taking to reach this level within the next three years. At this point the Americans have repudiated the one per cent target, and are cutting back.

We have thus got into a vicious circle. Americans are cutting aid, partly because they believe, erroneously, that it has not been effective. They are doing this just as we are building up the international institutions which can monitor and bolster effectiveness. And the result of their doing this is to undermine these very institutions.

Fortunately it is now possible to take a further step in the multilateralisation of aid which would also free it from direct dependence on the will of individual parliaments. The recent dollar crisis has brought consensus among the monetary authorities of both deveolped and less developed states that the new international currency, the Special Drawing Rights issued by the IMF, must now play a much larger role than before, and must be created in expanding amounts to meet the needs of world trade. It has for a long time been urged that instead of this new money going mainly to the large industrial nations, as it now does, it should in part be used to finance foreign aid. This could easily be done by the IMF giving a significant part of this new money directly to the World Bank and to the regional development banks (in proportion to the regional subscriptions to these banks). This would be foreign aid without pain, since it would cost the individual industrial country nothing. The industrial country would sell goods to a developing country for SDR's which it could use to finance imports, or could hold in its reserves. The time to move in this direction has certainly arrived.

The theme of what I have been saying is that in so far as the current pause in the expansion of foreign aid derives from American suspicions that such aid is not effective, there is no justification for such attitudes. The less developed countries are growing with unexpected and unprecedented speed. They are capable of reaching self sustaining growth within a generation. Their policies are monitored by the World Bank, and are the subject of exchanges within the framework of multilateral consultations. We are set to make a real assault on poverty on a global scale. To turn back at this stage would be as illogical as it would be tragic.

[33]

17 Objectives and Prognostications

W. Arthur Lewis
PRINCETON UNIVERSITY

I. OBJECTIVES

Assignment to such a title as this affords an author little scope for systematic investigation; it seems rather to invite rambling reflections, appropriate to a closing session. I shall take it in this sense, though lacking the advantage of reading the preceding papers.

I have never been much impressed by 'the revolution of rising expectations', or 'the demonstration effect', or 'the importance of closing the gap', so these remarks will concentrate on the prospects of the less developed countries, without reference to what may happen simultaneously to the living standards of the more developed.

The central objective is taken to be to raise the level of living of the masses of the people in L.D.C.s as rapidly as is feasible, with all the problems hidden in the word 'feasible'. One will thus begin by studying those constraints which make it desirable to keep the growth rate lower than is technically possible; the second half of the paper will reflect on what is technically possible.

(1) *Present v. Future Consumption*

Economists' formulae for deriving the optimal growth rate of consumption assume (subject to discounting the future) that a man at time *n* equals a man at time zero; that my son and I are the same person. The assumption is of course false. I may wish to save most of my income to make my children rich; or, expecting that the continuous increase in productivity will inevitably make them richer than I, I may feel that it is they who should mortgage their future for my present rather than I my present for their future. Economics has no basis for calculating an optimal rate of savings, or of economic growth.

Three factors counsel restraint. One is current poverty, especially in some overpopulated rural areas and some metropolitan slums. Some part of current output should be devoted to relieving these miseries now, rather than (via saving) in the future. A second restraining factor is the political dislocation created by rapid social change, which makes some absolutely poorer and others relatively poorer for reasons which they may neither understand nor accept. A wider spreading of the benefits of growth is to be desired, even at the expense of reducing the rate of growth.

The third factor emphasises that a high rate of growth of *commodities* is not all that important in the public's sense of well being. If asked what they most need from the economic system, those at the bottom of the ladder seem almost everywhere to concentrate on a few simple needs: (a) continuous employment, (b) a somewhat higher income[1], (c) more or better schooling for the children, (d) better medical services, (e) pure water at hand, and (f) cheap transport.[2] This list does involve greater output of some commodities, whether for direct use by their producers, or indirectly to supply the men who produce the services; but an economic plan which gave more emphasis to the wants listed here would devote relatively less resources to commodity production. It would have less saving, more taxes and a relatively slower rate of growth, as national income statisticians measure growth.[3]

These arguments do not run against increasing the ratio of savings, which is still too low in most L.D.C.s. They run against setting too high a target for the marginal ratio of savings. A ratio of 0·2 would be comfortable, whereas 0·4 would be excessive, except in an economy which was already growing very rapidly. One must raise the average savings ratio, but gradually.

Some economists have argued for very high savings in order to promote rapid industrialisation and so solve the unemployment problem. But unemployment can be eliminated without industrialisation (via public works, higher agricultural output, expansion of public services, housing programmes, national wage policies, restrictions on capital intensity, etc.). The level of employment is indeed tied to the availability of wage goods, which requires some capital; but the availability of wage goods is only rather loosely tied to the expansion of modern factory industry, which anyway eats up so much capital and employs so little labour. The need to cope with unemployment is one of the reasons why it may be desirable to keep taxes high and investment in industry low.

(2) *Economic Independence v. Neo-Colonialism*

One would like to have the most of both – consumption and investment. This is possible if one uses foreign funds and personnel. Leaving aside foreign aid and public borrowing, a word is in order here about foreign private investment.

[1] I have read, but cannot trace the reference, that when people are asked how much more income they would need to make them really comfortable, the modal demand is only for about 20 per cent more.

[2] Surprisingly, better housing is low on the list of L.D.C. felt needs; if one gets more housing space, one is likely to take in more tenants or relatives. Housing space is, like whisky, an acquired taste.

[3] In valuing goods and services at cost, they pass over the fact that those which are in short supply (e.g. hospital service in L.D.C.s) are valued by the poor at more than cost.

One reason for the unexpectedly high growth rate of manufacturing in L.D.C.s since the war has been substantial private foreign investment. In the thirties and forties African and Asian political leaders were very hostile towards foreign investment. This attitude relaxed notably in the fifties and sixties, but there are signs that the atmosphere is again changing.

Relaxation was associated with mutual adjustment. Governments passed a series of new laws – licensing investment, regulating inflows and outflows of funds, controlling immigration so as to enforce hiring of local personnel, and so on. Investors in their turn learned to accept controls and tried to accommodate to new political leadership.

Nevertheless hostility is reviving, especially among the young generation coming out of schools and universities, and demanding to pass beyond the political independence won by their fathers to what they call economic independence. The new term 'neo-colonialism' has many meanings; in one it describes a society which has political independence, but whose economy is controlled by foreign shareholders. They argue that it is better for the economy to grow slowly than to succumb to neo-colonialism.

Economic independence also has many meanings, in some of which it is unattainable – all modern economies are interdependent through international trade. But in the limited sense of absence of foreign ownership, any L.D.C. could become independent if it were willing to save more or to grow less rapidly. There are a few cases where foreign firms have a monopoly of advanced technology which they will share only if allowed to invest. But for the most part L.D.C.s can buy technology and management, and can grow with independence at the rate determined by their own willingness to save.

Whether the fears of neo-colonialism are justified on economic or political grounds has no doubt been investigated in earlier papers, so the exercise is not needed here. Even if there were no grounds – and there are some – nationalist feeling is still a factor that cannot be ignored. It will probably significantly restrain the level of private foreign investment in the 1970s; and since those who advocate such restraints are not noticeably forward in promoting domestic savings, the net result will probably be a lower rate of economic growth than would otherwise be possible.

(3) *Growth v. Equality*

During the period when a traditional economy is transformed into a modern economy, a few people inevitably benefit more than the general mass. This is so even when the engine of growth is in small farm agriculture (e.g. cocoa), for usually the profitable crop flourishes only in some regions of the country and not in others. It is still more the case when the transformation occurs through the establishment of a new sector (e.g. factories, mines) which grows by attracting labour from the rest, since the smallness of that sector will ensure it labour with an almost infinite elasticity of supply; and most of the benefits of the new technology will accrue to profit and 'rent' receivers in the new sector. In a modern economy income seems to grow at the same rate at all levels (i.e. distribution remains unchanged), but in the transforming economy most of the poor stay poor while the rich get richer.

Several aspects of this attract particular attention. One is that the transforming economy spawns a middle class (professional, administrative and managerial) whose earnings tend to be rather high in relation to per capita income, when compared with the similar relationship in advanced economies. Where this middle class also holds the potential power, it accumulates privileges for itself (e.g. taxes the farmers to give its own children free university education) without effective political opposition. But where politics is dominated by groups suspicious of 'the establishment' (e.g. Tanzania) the tensions between the government and the middle class can easily erupt into constraints on the rate of economic expansion. Indeed a significant part of the so-called brain drain results from the unwillingness of traditional societies to adjust to men with modern education – not merely in the sense of paying salaries, but rather in the sense of giving them the freedom to exercise their talents which they could expect to find in more modern environments.

The problem is compounded when the society is divided into tribes or races or religious groups, one of which is more successful economically than the rest (e.g. Ibos in Northern Nigeria, Indians in Kenya, Chinese in Malaysia). Left exclusively to market forces, such situations tend to get worse rather than better. The superiority of the advanced group resides in its culture, which gives greater emphasis to the factors that ensure economic success (e.g. education, saving, attention to detail, responsibility and reliability in fulfilling contracts or meeting obligations). For the same reason members of such a group prefer to hire or do business with each other. The disadvantaged groups do not therefore get the opportunity to learn and resent their exclusion from superior opportunities for employment and business. The situation can be righted only by deliberate action to break the monopoly (reserving special educational, financial or business opportunities for the disadvantaged) but it is hard to do this without in the interim restraining growth.

It used to be argued that economic growth required the emergence of large personal fortunes to yield the savings for new investment, but the socialist countries have demonstrated that this is not so. If the state is well managed, it can raise all the required savings through budget surpluses and the profits of public enterprises. There is in many L.D.C.s a yearning to develop through socialist institutions and bypass the robber baron stage. One of the chief obstacles between the L.D.C.s and development on socialist lines is the fact that they are not well managed. Inept administration is not the major problem since, if the governments could save the capital, they could contract with foreign firms to manage the government enterprises until a domestic cadre was formed. The obstacle is rather inability to save; government current expenditure tends to outrun revenue and public enterprises make losses instead of profits. In these circumstances the drift towards socialism in L.D.C.s will restrain economic growth until they learn the principles of sound socialist finance.

(4) *Conclusion*

Availability of foreign aid – grants and cheap loans – makes all these problems easier, but they persist at any reasonably likely level of aid. They explain why politicians do not see the development process quite as economists see it, and do not always give it top priority. They know the disadvantages of development, and will sometimes deliberately stand in its way. The growth rates of L.D.C.s show a wide range over the past fifteen years. A substantial part of this is explained by the differing degrees of priority accorded to development by different governments.

It follows that the rate of economic growth would be faster if governments were more ruthless. However, ruthlessness does not identify with ideology; the Ivory Coast grows rapidly, with indifference to the charge of neo-colonialism; but despite their ideologies, Burma, Mali and Guinea have lagged. Neither does ruthlessness identify with administrative competence, lack of which constrains the effectiveness of most L.D.C. governments, whatever their ideologies may be; to this we shall return.

II. POSSIBILITIES

In this part of the paper I consider what is technically possible given adequate savings (or foreign aid) and top priority for development.

On this subject the climate of opinion has changed drastically over the past decade. When 5 per cent growth was chosen as the target for the first development decade, it was chosen as an almost unmeetable challenge. It was then assumed that such a high growth rate (higher than the now developed countries had ever achieved before 1950) would not be possible in L.D.C.s without major changes in attitudes, social institutions and land ownership. That this rate has been achieved still comes as a surprise to economists when they first hear of it. Now Professor Tinbergen has informed us that a 6 per cent growth rate is a feasible target for the second development decade, and most of the dissent comes from younger members of our profession who wish to accelerate the pace. What are the technical constraints?

(1) *Population*

Growth of population is a constraint on the growth of output per head. Traditionally economists have worried about food supplies, but we are not at the moment in that mood; on the contrary some of our number are asking whether the 'green revolution' is not about to bankrupt the farmers of the L.D.C.s (especially in Asia). It looks as if the next decade should be free from worries about food; beyond that we cannot guess.

There is a new worry about exhaustible raw materials, especially fuels and metals. We are warned that it will not be possible for all countries in the world to consume that at the same per capita rate as the U.S.A., and this is seen as a constraint on growth. If we take refuge in scientific progress, which is bound to produce some substitute materials (not to speak of nuclear fission) we are accused of burying our heads in the clouds. Suffice it to say that if a shortage of materials is going to constrain growth, this is still some years ahead.

When we worry about population today we worry not about natural resources but about the drain on savings. It is very expensive to provide houses, schools, hospitals, water supplies and factory space and equipment for a population which doubles every twenty-five years – even if one is merely keeping up with numbers. A lower population growth makes possible more capital per head.

Progress is being made in population control. The problem is not in popular attitudes; the proportion of L.D.C. women who wish to plan their families is already much larger than the resources available to help them. One of the problems is that the technologies we now use are either expensive (like pills) or not entirely reliable (like I.U.D.s). Birth rates are coming down, but rather slowly, except in countries which have legalised abortion. Population growth will continue to be a major constraint on per capita growth for at least the rest of this century.

(2) *Agriculture*

Balance of payments pressure has moved agriculture from low to top priority. The need to earn foreign exchange has promoted concern for agricultural exports, while the need to save foreign exchange on food imports for swiftly rising populations has given equal urgency to domestic food production. Still more recently the relevance of agriculture to unemployment has begun to stand out. Rising urban unemployment seems likely to be the most intractable problem of the 1970s. It is due in part to excessive development of the towns relatively to the countryside, with the higher wages and greater amenities of the towns attracting more young people than the towns can absorb even in casual employment. It is easy to demonstrate that the towns cannot grow fast enough even to absorb the annual increase in the population,[1] let alone also to reduce the

[1] If non-agricultural occupations are 30 per cent of the labour force, and grow by 5 per cent a year, they can take in 1·5 per cent of the labour force in any year. So if the rate of natural increase is 3 per cent, half the natural increase must be added to the agricultural population.

absolute numbers in agriculture. Hence agricultural prosperity is an essential part of any programme for reducing the growth of urban unemployment.

Thanks to the 'green revolution', the current prospect is good. Our pessimism about L.D.C. small farmers has proved unfounded; we do not have to chivvy them into vast communes, or to control by edict what they may plant and when, or to abandon them in favour of opening up new lands with highly capital-intensive techniques. The solutions to their problems lie more in biology than in capital or organisation, though these last two will also help.

The green revolution, however, is a phenomenon of the wet tropics, or areas which can be irrigated. Vast millions, however, live in the dry tropics, especially in parts of India and in Africa. The comparative advantage of such areas does not lie in agriculture. West Africa's response to this problem, during the first seventy years of this century, was a vast migration from north to south, from the dry savannahs to the wetter coastlands; but the enforcement of national boundaries is now reducing this migration.

The immediate prospect is then that agriculture is not likely to be a constraint on growth in the wet L.D.C.s; on the contrary such countries may need at least a 6 per cent growth of domestic product to keep their agriculture prosperous. But agriculture will continue to lag in the drier L.D.C.s, and their growth rates will continue to be below the average.

(3) *Industry*

Contrary to expectation, industrial production now grows more swiftly in L.D.C.s than it does in developed countries. Problems of management and of productivity are solvable, especially if use is made of foreign managerial skills. Developed countries, from traditionally sneering at the industrial incompetence of L.D.C.s, are now hastily erecting barriers to keep out L.D.C. manufactures.

In many L.D.C.s, industry has been growing by more than 10 per cent per annum. Since the growth rate of domestic use of manufactures does not exceed 7 or 8 per cent, output can maintain a rate of 10 per cent only if it is eating into imports or spilling over into exports. Import substitution kept industry buoyant during the 1960s, but in much of Asia and Latin America the limits of import substitution have already been reached in light consumer goods. To continue at a 10 per cent rate for industry one must do one of three things: (1) raise the growth rate of G.D.P. as a whole to 8 per cent – this would require an impossibly high growth rate for agriculture; (2) move over into import substitution of capital goods; or (3) export manufactures (with a growth rate for exports exceeding 10 per cent).

Only two L.D.C.s have made substantial inroads into producing capital goods – India and Brazil. In most L.D.C.s the market is too small, but one can think of another dozen or so which ought to be further advanced than they are, and which are likely to become substantial producers of capital goods both for themselves and for their neighbours.[1] The rest will retain their high growth rates of industrial production only if they move over into exporting light manufactures.

In fact, manufactures have been the fastest growing export of L.D.C.s over the past decade, even when metals are excluded. About a dozen countries have participated, showing that it is quite possible to beat the developed countries at their own game. The list would be larger if so many Latin American countries were not continuously pricing themselves out of the market with high rates of continuous inflation. And the volume would be larger still if the developed countries were willing to play the game, and refrained from discriminating against the exports of manufactures from L.D.C.s.

(4) *Trade*

This brings us to trade, a crucial constraint on growth. One reason why L.D.C.s grew so rapidly in the 1960s was the fact that the prosperity of the developed countries caused world trade to grow faster than at any time in the preceding century.

Even so, there were weaknesses. The demand for the 'traditional' agricultural exports from L.D.C.s now grows relatively slowly – by 3 per cent per annum or less. These can no longer support the import requirements of L.D.C.s. If L.D.C. income grows by 6 per cent, L.D.C. imports will grow at about the same rate[2] and L.D.C. exports must grow at about the same rate.[3]

It follows that if L.D.C. growth is not to be constrained by the balance of payments, L.D.C.s must

(a) sell more non-traditional exports to developed countries;
(b) become individually more self-sufficient; or
(c) sell more to each other.

As to the first, L.D.C. exports of fuels, minerals, metals and manufactures to developed countries have been mounting swiftly. Unfortunately the concentration of manufactures on textiles and clothing makes difficulties in those markets, which invite restrictions. The situation calls both

[1] For figures relevant to this paragraph and the next see my Wicksell Lectures, *Aspects of Tropical Trade, 1883–1965* (Stockholm, 1969).

[2] Imports grew faster than income over the past two decades because investment was accelerating, and investment has a higher import content than consumption. Imports cannot grow faster than income permanently.

[3] This assumes that net foreign aid and investment grow as fast as imports; exports must grow even faster if the net transfer grows only as fast as the G.D.P. of developed countries.

for greater understanding in the developed countries and also for a wider range of exports of manufactures from the L.D.C.s.

As to the second, L.D.C.s now import from the developed countries over $4 billion of food in a good year and over $7 billion of light manufactures. There is clearly room for more import substitution both in agriculture and in industry. The larger L.D.C.s could also make more of their own capital goods.

Thirdly, L.D.C.s must trade more with each other. If the income of the developed countries grows by 4 per cent per annum, they are not likely to be wanting to increase their imports from L.D.C.s by 6 per cent per annum, especially if this includes manufactures growing by 12 per cent per annum. So if the imports and exports of L.D.C.s are to grow by 6 per cent per annum they must buy and sell more from and to each other. The green revolution should make it possible to eliminate altogether the current food import from the developed countries, and there are also immense possibilities for exchanging exports of manufactures.

Trade is the main potential obstacle in the way of achieving the 6 per cent target of the second development decade. This almost certainly must be a decade in which L.D.C.s trade much more with each other. But this development requires new patterns – new tariff structures, new institutions for financing inter-L.D.C. trade, new selling organisations, etc. (ground doubtless covered in earlier papers). Progress in creating these patterns has been slow, and one cannot confidently predict that it will henceforth be adequate. The growth of Latin America is especially tied to greater exploitation of the opportunities presented by foreign trade; a prerequisite for this is greater stability of the prices of exportable manufactures.

(5) *Commitment*

The rate of economic growth depends to some extent on the degree of government commitment – on willingness to raise taxes, willingness to create infrastructure, treatment of entrepreneurs, incentives offered, amount of administrative delay, control of inflation, and so on.

Commitment to development has generally been low, if measured by actions rather than by words. The first half of this paper gave one reason for this: awareness of the disadvantages of growth, which led to caution. But beyond this the commitment of L.D.C. governments is constrained by their low average quality. Some Ministers are deeply interested in the affairs of their departments, which they labour to promote, but a high proportion are more interested in other matters.

The quality of economic administration has been much improved by the creation of planning agencies, usually staffed by enthusiastic and well-educated young men and women. They have experimented a lot with planning, going through a phase of vast statistical documentation, and another phase of over-licensing of private activity, but we have all learnt a great deal about these matters during the past two decades, and a moderate consensus is coming to be the mode.

One cannot write with equal confidence about the political situation. There is a crisis of legitimacy in nearly every L.D.C., whether in Asia, Africa or Latin America. These countries are so divided by tribe, religion, language, race or class that it is hard to establish a government which the majority of the politically active will regard as having the right to rule. So they are subject to a succession of political takeovers which create uncertainty, even in the cases where the administration of economic affairs is not actually changed. This has to be listed as one of the constraints on growth.

III. CONCLUSIONS

I see no reason to doubt that 6 per cent is a feasible growth target for the 1970s, at any rate for the wetter tropics. It is on the margin of what is possible without excessive acceleration of savings ratios; with reasonable priority for public services and for relieving current poverty; without too much dependence on private foreign investment; and without too uneven a distribution of income, if adequate reliance is placed on public saving. It corresponds reasonably to the potential growth rates of industry and of agriculture, and is menaced only by need for considerable changes in the pattern of trade if the balance of payments is not to be a major constraint.

A growth rate of 6 per cent reduces to about 3·5 per cent per head. This is without historical precedent. Continued for only sixty years it would bring income per head in the average L.D.C. (say Ghana or Ceylon) to about the present level in Great Britain (assuming the current real difference to be about 8 : 1). To those with a sense of history this would seem to be a remarkable achievement, but a sense of history is not widespread and is also a conservative bias.

I cannot answer the question whether a higher rate of growth would be possible if the developed countries gave aid more generously than the 1 per cent of G.D.P. which this 6 per cent growth rate assumes. I doubt that it would be possible in the 1970s; although if 6 per cent were achieved in the seventies, 7 per cent might become feasible in the eighties, with the kind co-operation of further biological change in agriculture.

What will happen to the gap between the rich and the poor countries? This could not be answered without a paper of equal length on the prospects of the rich countries. I do not know the answer and, to end where I began, since I think what matters is the absolute progress of the L.D.C.s and not the size of the gap, I do not care.

[34]

The Less Developed Countries and Stable Exchange Rates

Sir Arthur Lewis

Mr. Chairman, ladies, and gentlemen: It is an honor to be asked to give a Per Jacobsson lecture, and it is a special privilege and pleasure to be asked to share it with Wilfried Guth, who is an old colleague. At the same time, I was somewhat frightened by the invitation because I wasn't sure what I would be able to talk to you about. I am, alas, not a banker, and I have no day-to-day connections with the international monetary system. So what I have done is what most aging economists do: I have taken refuge in talking about history.

It is now the conventional wisdom that the currencies of the developed countries should float, but the currencies of the less developed countries (LDCs) should not; that is to say that each LDC should choose a more developed country (MDC) as a partner--or the SDR--and tie itself in a fixed relationship. It is quite an advance in our thinking to recognize that in the international monetary sphere the LDCs may require different treatment from the MDCs. Members of the Group of Ten used to assume, rather in the spirit of General Motors, that whatever solution was best for them would also be best for all, and were surprised when the LDCs insisted on having the wider Group of Twenty. The purpose of my paper is to explore aspects of the special problems of LDCs.

One has to begin by confirming the General Motors proposition, up to a point. LDCs require two things of MDC currencies, and neither of these is fixity in relationship to each other. The first requirement is that they be freely convertible into each other, so that what LDCs earn in one market they can spend in another. And the second requirement is a regime within which MDCs feel comfortable, in the sense that they have no urge to restrict their imports from the rest of the world. In this limited sense, any regime that is good for the MDCs is also good for the LDCs. Any individual LDC that wishes to keep its currency relatively stable in terms of floating MDCs can tie itself to the SDR and can hold its reserves in an appropriate basket of currencies. It will suffer inconveniences from other countries' fluctuations, but these are a minor nuisance compared with a possible breakdown of world trade occasioned by MDC currencies operating within an inappropriate regime.

However, my main concern is with what LDCs should do, and not with what MDCs should do.

It is quite clear why the experts advise the LDCs that they should be stable even though the others float. Note four powerful reasons.

In the first place there are forward markets for MDC currencies but not for LDC currencies. This is a particular nuisance for LDCs trading with each other and is one of the obstacles to regional integration and, more generally, to the expansion of inter-LDC trade. (It applies also to LDC trade with MDCs, but the behavior of other LDC currencies is perhaps somewhat less predictable.)

Secondly, fear of devaluation inhibits investment--not portfolio investment denominated in external currencies, but direct investment, whether of foreign or of domestic capital, since there is no certainty that capital values will rise by as much as the currency depreciates.

Thirdly, frequent changes in the value of an LDC currency add to the uncertainty of holding it and increase its instability. If the government is known to be ready to let the currency depreciate whenever it runs into balance of payments problems, nobody is willing to hold it, since the prospect of depreciation is always on people's minds. The onset of every minor difficulty then leads to a rush to sell and an exhaustion of the country's foreign exchange reserves.

Fourthly, the instruments of monetary control are perhaps more fragile in LDCs than in MDCs. When an LDC devalues, forces are set in motion that it may not so easily control. Our theories of these matters were framed in the eighteenth century, when food was a small proportion of imports, and when trade unions had not yet acquired the power to keep real wages rising in all situations. An economy with weak control over its internal prices is likely to find itself on a treadmill, where devaluation raises domestic money incomes and prices, so setting off further devaluation, *ad infinitum*. Firm control over the level of money incomes is a precondition for successful floating.

For such reasons it is easy to understand why the representatives of LDCs at IMF meetings have always expressed their preference for stability of currencies, and also why LDC central banks have shown so much reluctance to devalue over the past thirty years, even in situations where there was clearly no other viable alternative.

I shall proceed from the assumption that an LDC desires to keep its foreign exchange value constant in terms of SDRs, and that it is pursuing reasonably orthodox fiscal and monetary policies, which need not be defined for this purpose. I have also to assume that the rate chosen *ab initio* is the right rate, which again need not be defined for this purpose, but which I nevertheless will define, in order to spice the discussion, not as the rate which balances imports and exports, since any rate can do that via employment and income effects, but as the exchange rate which produces the rate of growth of exports appropriate to the targeted rate of growth of output; say, the exchange rate that is required for exports to grow by 6 per cent a year.

My question is then what external conditions must be met if the country is to be able to maintain exchange stability. Our literature focuses rather on what the country's internal policies should be. And if exchange stability cannot be retained we tend to assume automatically that this is the fault of the LDC's government. I, on the other hand, assume a well-behaved government--which you may define in any way you wish--and am in effect asking what cooperation it is entitled to expect from an international monetary system in its effort to hold exchange rates steady.

My paper originates in a suggestion that I should approach this question historically: What in fact have been the main problems menacing exchange stability in the less developed countries, other than those arising from their own disregard of orthodox financial canons; and how can an international monetary system help to reduce such stresses?

For this we do not need to go back beyond the 1870s, the decade in which Western Europe and the United States adopted the gold standard. At that time most of the countries of Latin America, Eastern Europe, and Asia were on silver. In the 1870s the price of silver started to fall, and it halved over the next twenty years, taking their exchange values with it. What were the silver countries to do? After long hesitation the majority moved to gold (or a gold exchange standard) and had accomplished this by 1900. From 1900 to 1929 the consensus of economists was that all countries, whether more or less developed, should maintain fixed exchange rates. However, from 1930 to 1965 it was increasingly felt that primary producing countries (even rich Australia) had special problems. Our current consensus that the developed should float while the less developed peg is the exact opposite of what had nearly become the consensus only a dozen years ago.

The debate between gold and silver in the 1880s and 1890s raised all the problems, though the context in which it was then set--the merits and demerits of bimetallism--obscures the matters of interest to us. The challenges to exchange stability which surfaced in the 1880s and 1890s can be grouped, with some overlap, under three heads:

- Long-run price movements
- The trade cycle
- The debt problem.

These challenges all arose again in the 1930s and, with some modification, in the 1950s and 1960s.

The World Price Level

A long period of falling commodity prices affects the LDCs' capacity to maintain fixed exchange rates in three ways:

(1) it tends to be deflationary, and so to discourage exports;

(2) it raises the real burden of debt; and

(3) it tends to be associated with adverse terms of trade for agricultural commodities.

We have had three of these long secular declines over the past hundred years. First, from 1873 to 1895; the British index of wholesale prices fell 36 per cent from 1871-75 to 1891-95. Then in the 1920s and the 1930s, the price index of tropical agricultural exports fell by 43 per cent between the two peak dates of 1925 and 1937. And thirdly in the 1950s and the 1960s. In the developed world we tend to think of the whole period since 1945 as one of inflation, but in fact tropical agricultural prices fell 20 per cent between the first half of the 1950s and the second half of the 1960s.

Those developing countries that remained on silver in the 1880s and 1890s escaped the first consequence of the secular decline of prices (deflation), but not the second and third consequences (the debt burden and the adverse terms of trade).

Prices were falling in the countries on gold, but rising in the countries on silver. The argument that the countries on gold were repressed depends on what happened to relative prices; they were deflated if export prices fell by more than domestic prices and wages. On the other side, the countries on silver were stimulated if the prices of export crops rose faster than food prices, encouraging the small farmers to switch; or if plantation wages failed to keep up with export prices. The planters of Ceylon, which was on silver, seem to have been unanimous that the price of tea in silver was rising faster than wages, and that continual depreciation therefore stimulated production for export. Indian data bear this out. Between 1880-84 and 1890-94 Indian agricultural wages rose by 2 per cent, while wholesale prices rose by 21 per cent;[1] over the same period the export price of tropical agricultural commodities, excluding freights, fell in gold by 15 per cent.

The Indian literature of the day was not much concerned with the effects of inflation or deflation on output. Majority opinion was strongly in favor of switching to gold, because the rupee burden of India's fixed commitments in sterling was magnified as silver depreciated. Here it is important to distinguish the two influences at work. Since prices were falling in gold, the real burden of fixed commitments, such as debt charges, increased whether the rupee depreciated or not. The further burden imposed by rupee depreciation was an internal shift within the country, of the kind which economists love to ignore as "mere transfers," but which statesmen cannot neglect. The depreciation of the rupee, with its accompanying rise of internal prices, did not affect all classes equally. Specifically, the incomes of civil servants lagged, because the Government found it hard to keep raising taxes every year. And since India was ruled by civil servants, the authoritative view was that India should switch to gold. The possibility that continual depreciation had the merit of counteracting any deflationary tendencies inherent in what we now call the Kondratiev downswing finds little mention in the Indian literature of the day.

It is hard to know whether the depreciation of the silver currencies stimulated development, but there is no doubt that the continual fall of prices in gold aggravated the debt burdens of the LDCs of the day, contributing to the massive defaults on debt obligations of the 1870s and 1890s; just as an earlier long Kondratiev downswing contributed to the massive defaults of the 1820s and the 1840s, and a later one to the

1/ Calculated from M. Mukherjee, *National Income of India* (Statistical Publishing Society, Calcutta, 1969), pp. 91 and 94.

defaults of the 1930s. The troubles of Argentina and Australia in 1890 did not even wait for a recession; seventeen years which took a third off the price of wool made the accumulated debt intolerable.

I shall return to debt in a moment. The third menace of a falling price level is that it is associated with adverse terms of trade for agriculture. Thus the terms of trade moved against the agricultural countries in the 1880s and 1890s, in the 1930s, and again in the 1950s and 1960s. In the first two periods both industrial and agricultural prices fell, whereas in the 1950s and 1960s industrial prices rose while agricultural prices fell; this is why these last two decades seem inflationary in the developed but deflationary in the less developed countries.

The mechanism which causes these long Kondratiev swings in world agricultural prices is controversial. The Victorians thought that it was changes in gold supply; Schumpeter that it was changes in the level of investment in major industrial innovations; others, including myself, that it is primarily changes in the relative growth rates of world demand and supply of foodstuffs. Whatever the cause may be, the effect seems to be that the terms of trade move in the same direction as agricultural prices.

In sum, long periods of falling prices put pressure on the exchange rates of agricultural countries, whether by discouraging production for export, by increasing the real burden of debt, or by moving the terms of trade adversely. It is therefore easy to understand the appeal to these countries of proposals for commodity price stabilization, whether through a commodity reserve currency, or through international buffer stocks. Such measures would not guarantee the terms of trade (might indeed work adversely in inflationary times), but would at least evade the other two burdens (the discouragement of exports and the aggravation of debt). They belong in the same category as the domestic agricultural programs by which the governments of developed countries have now set minimum levels to the prices received by their own farmers; and they would make the same kind of contribution to the stability of the world economy, by maintaining purchasing power at times of general cyclical recession and stimulating developed country exports too. It is in the joint interest of both developed and developing countries that the prevention of secular decline of commodity prices in world trade be a declared objective of an international monetary system, ranking equally with the maintenance of full employment in the minds of the system's governors.

The Trade Cycle

Quite apart from the question whether to peg to gold or to silver, if one were to peg, the question whether to peg to anything or to float was already at issue before the first world war. An ordinary Kitchin or even a Juglar recession might be taken in one's stride, but Kuznets' great depressions, both deep and prolonged, put an intolerable burden on foreign exchange. The relevant dates in world trade are 1873-76, 1891-95 and after the war, 1929-33.

These depressions created both an exchange problem and also an output problem. The output problem originated in the fact that as exports declined, domestic income would decline by more than the original fall in foreign exchange. This could be mitigated by depreciating the currency to the extent of the fall in export prices, since this would keep constant the domestic money incomes of those producing for export. The case of the United States is particularly interesting. The United States was caught in a foreign exchange jam in the first half of the 1890s, partly because the prices of its agricultural exports fell, and partly because the British had cut their lending. It held on to the gold standard through six difficult years. But the considered judgment of Milton Friedman is:

> It should perhaps be noted explicitly that we do not intend to suggest that the alternative involving abandonment of the gold standard was economically undesirable. On the contrary, our own view is that it might well have been highly preferable to the generally depressed conditions of the 1890's. We rule it out only because, as it turned out, it was politically unacceptable.[2/]

The check to output could of course be mitigated through internal stabilization schemes for keeping domestic money income constant irrespective of changes in international prices. This is more difficult for the developing than for the developed countries. Fluctuations in the developed originate mainly in domestic investment, which is presumably susceptible to control by domestic monetary and fiscal policies. Whereas fluctuations in the developing originate mainly in exports, which the government cannot control, and can only adjust itself to. The timing is also difficult, because the industrial countries have their balance of payments difficulties in the boom, while the developing have theirs during the slump. Measures to revive the economy in the slump are constrained by shortage of foreign exchange in the agricultural but not in the industrial countries. Nevertheless, in theory, internal stability could always be achieved by such internal measures as maintaining buffer stocks or varying export taxes inversely with prices. But to stabilize income would be to stabilize imports (or even to increase them as their prices fell), and this would not be feasible unless one had large reserves of foreign exchange. In this sense the output problem resolves into the exchange problem.

In theory the less developed countries could ride the trade cycle simply by holding large enough foreign exchange reserves, but the problem is more difficult for them than it is for the developed, for three reasons.

First, the recession dries up not just the earnings on current account, but also the long-term capital inflows. International investment was particularly vulnerable to the Kuznets great depressions. Borrowers could not meet their commitments, and a string of defaults was inevitable, or as we would now call them "requests for rescheduling of debt." We tend to be shocked by such requests, but they are an old and intrinsic part of international investment. There were heavy defaults in the 1820s, the 1840s, the 1870s, the 1890s, the 1930s, the 1950s, and we are now

---

2/ Milton Friedman and Anna Jacobson Schwartz, *A Monetary History of the United States, 1875-1960* (Princeton University Press, Princeton, N.J., 1963), p. 111.

holding our breath for the heavy defaults of the end of the 1970s. The European capital market took such defaults in its stride. It knew that the borrowers would have to come back for more money, and could then be made to recognize outstanding obligations before becoming eligible for new borrowing. But the United States lost its temper when caught in the defaults of the 1930s, and with its "blue sky" laws effectively closed its long-term capital market to foreign governments, with unfortunate consequences for our day, which we shall come to in a moment. All the same, although the defaults had no long-term effect on European lending in the nineteenth century, the immediate short-term effect was a cyclical drying up of foreign investment, coinciding with the reduction in current earnings. Paradoxically, we have done better at the cyclical level since 1950, because the bilateral and multilateral lending agencies, unlike the private lenders, have maintained their lending without cyclical fluctuations.

The second element distinguishing the developing countries is that they cannot use short-term capital inflows and outflows, responding to changes in their discount rates, to meet temporary shortages of foreign exchange. On the contrary, an LDC which raises its discount rates is signaling a crisis which is more likely to drive money out than to bring money in. It is true that some of the developed countries have now become more like underdeveloped countries in this respect; but the central banks of the industrial countries help each other out in time of trouble--a tradition which goes back to Bank of England reliance on the French and German central banks in 1890 and 1907.

Thirdly, taking these elements into account, the magnitude of the foreign exchange reserves that an LDC would have to carry in order to ride out a Kuznets cycle would simply be beyond its means. It is not unusual for the price of one's principal commodity export to fall by one third, producing over the course of, say, four below-average years a deficit of 50 per cent of one year's exports. One must also anticipate some decline in private foreign lending or investment during the slump. So, if committed to stabilizing domestic money income through the cycle, the government would have to approach the slump with reserves equal to at least 75 per cent of a year's exports. This would be very expensive, since a debtor country which keeps large foreign reserves is in the position of a man borrowing money at 6 per cent to put it in the bank at 3 per cent.

In the 1890s most of the currencies of the agricultural countries were already tied to one or other of the precious metals, gold or silver. Those on gold, such as Australia and New Zealand, took a terrible beating, as agricultural prices dropped to previously unimagined levels. Those on silver were partly shielded by the sharp decline in the price of that commodity. India chose the year 1893 to abandon silver, fortunately for it only a couple of years before prices in gold reached their lowest levels and started their upward climb. There were very few countries on a floating paper standard in the 1890s; such behavior was held in the deepest contempt by the monetary experts of the day. The two most important were Argentina and Brazil. Their floating was a calculated policy. It paid the agricultural classes to let the peso fall as prices fell in gold. This kept up their incomes in pesos, and by preventing the urban community from enjoying the lower gold prices of imports, also moved the terms of trade in favor of the agricultural classes.[3/] When prices began moving upwards again, Argentina joined the gold standard, for the same reasons in reverse.

Australia and New Zealand were caught in the 1890s, but not in the 1930s. When this depression arrived, Argentina was the first country to leave the gold standard, Australia the second, and New Zealand not far behind. British and French colonies on gold again took a beating. International investment collapsed altogether, and by 1933 most of the leading countries in the world had abandoned the gold exchange system.

By 1939 it was clear to all that the foundation of any new international monetary system must be a lender of last resort, and this was built into the International Monetary Fund. Unfortunately, the magnitude of the LDCs' problem was not then, and still is not now fully comprehended. I earlier hazarded that fully to ride a Kuznets depression would require access to reserves equivalent to 75 per cent of a year's exports. Oil importing country exports last year amounted to US$118 billion. If the LDCs keep three months' reserves on their own, they need stand-by facilities of, say, US$60 billion over four years. Now the original quotas of the oil importing LDCs amounted to less than US$7 billion, carrying a right to borrow of only US$13 billion. These quotas are about to be increased, and one must also add SDRs, the IMF buffer stock scheme, and funds available under the export compensation schemes, both of the IMF and of the European Community.

The net potential stand-by need from the IMF will not be clear until some decision is reached on the international buffer stock proposals which, if successful, would considerably reduce the need for individual country reserves. But it is quite clear that the IMF has not helped significantly to reduce the required reserves of the LDCs, and that while adequately provided for a small slump, it could not now cope with a large one. It is also clear that if LDC trade is to grow by 6 per cent a year, doubling every dozen years, the IMF armory of quotas, SDRs, and compensation schemes should be doubled at least as often or sooner (to allow for rising prices).

Long-Term Finance

The developing countries have to invest more than they can save, and must therefore borrow. If they cannot borrow long, they will either borrow short or inflate. Either of these leads to a shortage of foreign exchange, and therefore menaces exchange stability.[4/]

It is not because they are poor that LDCs have to borrow. In the last quarter of the nineteenth century the biggest borrowers, the United States, Canada, Australia, and Argentina, were richer than the principal lenders, the United Kingdom, France, and the Federal Republic of Germany.

3/ The Argentinian strategy is analyzed in A.G. Ford, *The Gold Standard--1880-1914, Britain and Argentina* (Oxford University Press, Oxford, 1962).

4/ This section overlaps with the corresponding section of my forthcoming book, *The Evolution of the International Economic Order* (Princeton University Press, Princeton, N.J., 1978).

They borrowed not because they were poor, but because they were urbanizing rapidly. In the lending countries the urban population was growing by less than 3 per cent per annum (France 1.0, the United Kingdom 1.8, and the Federal Republic of Germany 2.5), while in the rich borrowers the urban population was growing by more than 3 per cent (Australia 3.5, the United States 3.7, Canada 3.9, and Argentina 5.3). Nowadays, population is growing more than twice as fast in LDCs as it ever grew in Europe, and urbanization is also twice as fast. And there is also a drive, sparked by recent independence, to build roads, schools, health facilities, and water supplies in rural areas. So the pressure on LDC governments for large capital budgets is inescapable.

Seen through the historian's eye, dependence on borrowing has created two problems for developing countries. One is its liability to wide fluctuations, which we have already considered, and the other is the speed with which the debt charges build up, to which I now turn.

Domar has given us the formula for the ratio of debt charges to new annual lending.[5] It rises asymptotically to a limit

$$\frac{D}{F} L = \frac{a + i}{a + g}$$

where a is the annual repayment ratio (on the diminishing balance principle), i is the rate of interest, and g is the rate of growth of annual lending. Thus, if the rate of interest if 5 per cent, and annual lending grows by 5 per cent, the debt charge will mount until it exactly equals the annual lending. If lending is to contribute net resources to the borrower, it must grow faster than the rate of interest.

In the British case in the last quarter of the nineteenth century, lending grew less rapidly than the rate of interest. So from 1890 onwards, new lending was less than the sum of repayments, interest, and dividends. The average difference in favor of the United Kingdom was £42 million a year, from 1890 to 1907. Only in the final prewar spurt between 1908 and 1913 did average lending exceed the average inflow, and then only by an average of £3 million a year.

In consequence, the debt situation in 1913 was incredible. For comparison let us look at the situation of developing countries in 1972, just before the explosion of oil prices affects the situation. Outstanding debt of developing countries was than 1.8 times annual exports. (Government debt was US$85 billion, private investment US$53 billion, and trade US$75 billion.) This ratio of 1.8 was already thought to be very high; people were worrying about it, and calling for debt cancellation. By comparison, ratios of debt to exports (not debt charges but outstanding debt) were enormous in 1913. The lowest ratios, those for India, Japan, and China, were around 2 1/4. Australia's ratio was 4.8, Latin America's 5.2, and Canada's 8.6. (Canada tops this list, since its annual borrowing had been averaging 7 per cent of national income.)

How does one meet debt charges on obligations which are 8.6 times exports? If the debt charges were 10 per cent of the debt, they would absorb 86 per cent of exports. Argentina's debt charges in 1890 were

5/ E.D. Domar, "Foreign Investment and the Balance of Payments," *American Economic Review*, December 1950.

indeed 60 per cent of its exports. Still, after the troubles of the first half of the 1890s, the borrowers met their obligations during the next twenty years preceding the outbreak of the first world war, without much difficulty.

They managed for three reasons. First, prices moved upwards after 1895, eroding the burden of debt. As we have seen, prices for LDCs moved downward in the 1950s and 1960s, increasing the burden of debt. But the turnaround of the prices of tropical exports has been so marked since 1969, and more so since 1974, that in spite of the huge borrowings of the last three years, the oil importing LDCs had at the end of 1976 a ratio of public debt to exports which was still less than two to one.

The second reason why a high debt ratio was manageable in the early part of this century is that the borrowers' exports were rising 50 to 100 per cent faster than their national incomes, in contrast with the 1950s and 1960s, when national income and the purchasing power of LDC exports rose at the same rate (about 5 per cent a year). Various factors have closed the gap. For one, LDC growth was spurred in the nineteenth century only by exports, whereas since the second world war it has responded also to domestic demand (services and import substitution). For another, the developed countries have built formidable obstacles to LDC trade, whether in agricultural products or in manufactures. Estimates of how much more the LDCs could export without such obstacles start from US$10 billion a year upwards.

The ability of LDC governments to meet their debt obligations depends on how rapidly their trade is growing. It is not enough that an economy be buoyant, and that its government be able to raise the money through domestic taxation; the proceeds must also be convertible into foreign exchange. This two-gap problem did not surface in the nineteenth century because in the developing countries of the day exports were growing much faster than national income. Imports therefore lagged, and there was no pressure on foreign exchange. The situation is reversed when the growth rate of exports drags behind that of income. Some LDCs are much better placed than others for rapid growth of exports; LDCs are far from being all alike. It is true that any individual country can speed up its exports and decelerate its imports by adopting appropriate policies; but even so, the fallacy of composition reminds us that the capacity of all LDCs taken together to increase their exports is much smaller, since what they do at each other's expense cancels out. Exports of the group as a whole depend to a large extent on the willingness of the developed countries to buy more from them. LDCs will not be able to maintain a 6 per cent growth target and meet all their debt obligations unless the developed countries now make more space for them in world trade, by dismantling some of the barriers to LDC exports.

The third reason why a high ratio of foreign obligations was more manageable before 1913 is that it really was less of a burden. In the first place, the ratio of equities to bonded debt was larger. Private investors built a lot of infrastructure (railways, etc.), as well as the factories, plantations, and mines, so the profits to be transferred fluctuated *pari passu* with foreign exchange earnings.

In the second place, the ratio of short-term to long-term debt was negligible, and it was the heavy charges on short-term debt that started forcing LDCs into bankruptcy already in the 1950s and 1960s although the ratio of outstanding debt to exports was still small. In 1913 the United Kingdom's outstanding short-term loans were only about £300 million, in contrast with long-term lending of nearly £4,000 million. But the developing countries have been shut out of the long-term capital markets of the United Kingdom, France, and the United States by the foreign exchange restrictions of the first two and by the "blue sky" laws of the third. This exclusion of LDC governments from private portfolio borrowing is a major change in the international economic order, with major adverse consequences. Government-to-government lending is a partial but insufficient substitute. So LDC governments have been driven into short-term borrowing; through suppliers' credits in the 1950s and the 1960s, and Eurocurrency loans in the first half of the 1970s. Already at the end of 1972 about 30 per cent of LDC obligations were short term, and the oil crisis is pushing this figure higher and higher.[6/] A curtailment of short-term borrowing, with corresponding expansion of access to long-term lending, is the biggest financial requirement of LDCs.

The third reason why foreign obligations were easier to manage before 1913 is that debt could be rolled over. In 1913 a government could borrow in Europe for unspecified purposes, or even specifically to pay off old debt or the interest thereon, whereas nowadays the World Bank and the bilateral government agencies insist on tying new loans to new projects. The only good thing one can say of today's large debt to European and American bankers is that it can be rolled over, thus increasing the flexibility of debt management. But it would be better still for LDC governments to regain access to long-term capital markets, with some capacity to borrow for roll-over purposes. This would at least diminish the frequent unpleasantness of asking the Paris Club to reschedule short-term obligations.

In sum, LDCs have a continuing need for long-term finance for capital development, in the absence of which they will be driven either to more short-term finance, or to inflation, at the expense of exchange stability. What is wrong in the current situation is not that debt ratios are high--they are low by historical standards. What is wrong is the structure of the debt: too short and too much tied to projects. What we need is an adequate flow of long-term finance, of various kinds, through all conceivable channels, including a long-term capital market reopened to good borrowers, supplemented by the multilateral and bilateral government agencies and by private foreign investment, on terms ranging from market rates to grants to the poorest countries. This has been agreed by governments ever since the beginning of the 1960s. Members of the Organization for Economic Cooperation and Development are pledged to an annual net flow of not less than 1 per cent of their national incomes and have further agreed that the average rate of interest on the government-to-government part of this flow should not exceed 3 per cent. If the developed countries actually honored these commitments, which are not particularly burdensome, the flow of long-term finance on reasonable terms would be adequate; we could reduce the

---

6/ I need not pursue here the implications of the oil crisis. It is clear that what the oil importing LDCs need for this is a special medium-term (say, 15-year) security, producing about US$10 billion a year (the amount by which their oil bills were increased) and tapering off over 10 to 15 years. Short-term finance will probably have to be rescheduled in numerous cases.

short-term borrowing and would not have to bother about the burden of debt. The problem, then, is how to get the developed countries to keep their commitments, but this is outside my present terms of reference (apart from the fact that I do not know the answer).

Conclusion

Putting together the various sections of this paper, the answer of the historical record is that the exchange stability of developing countries is menaced by secular decline in world prices (which depresses the economy, increases the debt burden, and worsens the terms of trade); by cyclical fluctuations (which call for larger foreign reserves than can be afforded); by an excessive offer of short-term relative to long-term finance; and by developed country barriers which retard the growth rate of LDC exports. Since all these forces were in operation in the 1950s and 1960s, it is not surprising that there was a record number of devaluations and defaults, though of course a substantial number of these also resulted from human error.

If this list seems to take us beyond the confines that are normally considered to be appropriate for an international monetary institution, this itself underlines the difference between developed and developing countries in this sphere. International monetary problems derive from the entire network of international economic relations and cannot be solved within the walls of any single institution. In fact, the developed countries, with stronger economies, less dependence on international inflows, and easy fraternal relations between central bankers, could get along fairly well without an international monetary institution; and having one, could manage quite well if its function was confined to discussing changes in exchange rates. To the LDCs, on the other hand, an institution which did not look beyond exchange rates to the wider context which determines international monetary flows could be a menace rather than a help. Given the difference in their immediate interests, the instinct of the developed countries will be to narrow the discussion, while the instinct of the developing will be to widen it. In the long run, our salvation lies in the General Motors proposition: What is good for the developing countries is also good for the developed.

* * * *

BIBLIOGRAPHY

Book reviews, newspaper articles and the other short pieces are excluded.

Books

Economic Problems of Today (London: Longmans, 1940).

Economic Survey, 1919–39 (London: George Allen & Unwin, 1949).

Overhead Costs (London: George Allen & Unwin, 1949).

The Principles of Economic Planning (London: D. Dobson and George Allen & Unwin, 1949).

The Theory of Economic Growth (London: George Allen & Unwin, 1955).

Politics in West Africa (The Whidden Lectures) (London: George Allen & Unwin, 1965).

Development Planning (London: George Allen & Unwin, 1966).

Some Aspects of Economic Development (The Aggrey Memorial Lectures) (Accra: Ghana Publishing Company, 1969).

Aspects of Tropical Trade 1883–1965 (The Wicksell Lectures) (Stockholm: Almqvist & Wiksell, 1969).

Editor, *Tropical Development 1880–1913* (London: George Allen & Unwin, 1970).

Growth and Fluctuations 1870–1913 (London: George Allen & Unwin, 1978).

Monographs, Pamphlets

Labour in the West Indies (London: Fabian Society, 1939).

Monopoly in British Industry (London: Fabian Society, 1945).

Aspects of Industrialisation (Cairo: National Bank of Egypt, 1953).

Economic Problems of Jamaica (Kingston: Daily Gleaner, 1964).

The Agony of the Eight (Bridgetown: Barbados Advocate, 1965).

Reflections on Nigeria's Economic Growth (Paris: OECD, 1967).

Socialism and Economic Growth (The Annual Oration) (London: LSE, 1971).

The Evolution of Foreign Aid (The David Owen Memorial Lecture) (Cardiff: University of Wales, 1972).

Development Economics: An Outline (Morristown, New Jersey: General Learning Press, 1973).

Dynamic Factors in Economic Growth (Tata Memorial Lectures) (Bombay: Orient Longman, 1974).

The University in Less Developed Countries (New York: International Council for Educational Development, 1974).

The Evolution of the International Economic Order (Janeway Lectures) (Princeton, New Jersey: Princeton University Press, 1978).

LDCs and Exchange Stability (Per Jacobsson Lecture) (Washington, D.C.: IMF, 1978).

Economic Inequality in the United States: An Analysis of Racial Differences in Earnings and Employment (New York: The Rockefeller Foundation, 1981).

Articles

'The inter-relations of shipping freights', *Economica,* vol. 8, no. 29 (1941), pp. 52–76.

'The two-part tariff', *Economica,* vol. 8, no. 31 (1941), pp. 249–270.

'The economics of loyalty', *Economica,* vol. 9, no. 36 (1942), pp. 333–348.

'Monopoly and the law', *Modern Law Review,* vol. 6, no. 2 (1943), pp. 97–111.

'An economic plan for Jamaica', *Agenda,* vol. 3, no. 4 (1944), pp. 154–163.

'Competition in retailing', *Economica,* vol. 12, no. 48 (1945), pp. 202–234.

'Spare time activities of employees', *Modern Law Review,* vol. 9, no. 4 (1946), pp. 280–283.

'Fixed costs', *Economica,* vol. 13, no. 49 (1946), pp. 231–258.

'The prospect before us', *The Manchester School,* vol. 16, no. 2 (1948), pp. 129–164.

'Colonial development', *Transaction of the Manchester Statistical Society,* Session 1948–1949 (12 January 1949), pp. 1–30.

'Whither prices?', *District Bank Review,* 1949.

'The British Monopolies Act', *The Manchester School,* vol. 17, no. 2 (1949), pp. 208–217.

(With F. V. Meyer) 'The effects of an overseas slump on the British economy', *The Manchester School,* vol. 17, no. 3 (1949), pp. 233–265.

'Developing colonial agriculture', *The Three Banks Review,* no. 2 (1949), pp. 3–21.

'Sur quelques tendances seculaires', *Economie Appliquée,* Vol. 2, nos. 3–4 (1949), pp. 374–391.

'The price policy of public corporations', *The Political Quarterly,* vol. 21, no. 2 (1950), pp. 184–196.

'Food and raw materials', *District Bank Review,* no. 99 (1951), pp. 1–11.

'The future of world trade', *Scope: A Magazine for Industry,* Annual Review (1952).

'World production, prices and trade, 1870–1960', *The Manchester School,* vol. 20, no. 2 (1952), pp. 105–138.

'Reflections on South East Asia', *District Bank Review,* no. 104 (1952), pp. 3–20.

'United Nations primer for development: A comment', *Quarterly Journal of Economics,* vol. 67, no. 2 (1953), pp. 267–275.

'Thoughts on land settlement', *Journal of Agricultural Economics,* vol. 11, no. 1 (1954), pp. 3–11.

'Economic development with unlimited supplies of labour', *The Manchester School,* vol. 22, no. 2 (1954), pp. 139–191.

'Trade drives', *District Bank Review,* no. 112 (1954), pp. 1–15.

(With P. J. O'Leary) 'Secular swings in production and trade, 1870–1913', *The Manchester School,* vol. 23, no 2 (1955), pp. 113–152.

'Investment policy', *Bulletin of the Oxford Institute of Statistics,* vol. 17, no. 1 (1955), pp. 57–58.

(With A. Martin) 'Patterns of public revenue and expenditure', *The Manchester School,* vol. 24, no. 3 (1956), pp. 203–244.

'International competition in manufactures', *American Economic Review,* vol. 47, no. 2 (1957), pp. 578–587.

'Recent controversies over economic policy in the British Labour Party', *World Politics,* vol. 10, no. 2 (1958), pp. 171–181.

'Unlimited labour: Further notes', *The Manchester School,* vol. 26, no. 1 (1958), pp. 1–32.

'Employment policy in an underdeveloped area', *Social and Economic Studies,* vol. 7, no. 3 (1958), pp. 42–54.

'On assessing a development plan', *Economic Bulletin of Ghana,* vol. 3 nos. 6–7 (1959), pp. 2–11.

'Education and economic development', *Social and Economic Studies,* vol. 10, no. 2 (1961), pp. 113–127.

'Education for scientific professions in the poor countries', *Daedalus,* vol. 91, no. 2 (1962), pp. 310–318.

'Secondary education and economic structure', *Social and Economic Studies,* vol. 13, no. 2 (1964), pp. 219–232.

'A review of economic development' (Richard T. Ely Lecture), *American Economic Review,* vol. 55, no. 2 (1965), pp. 1–16.

'Unemployment in developing countries' (Stephenson Memorial Lecture), *World Today,* vol. 23, no. 1 (1967), pp. 13–22.

'World trade since the War', *Proceedings of the American Philosophical Society,* vol. 112 (1968), pp. 362–366.

'Black power and the American university', *University: A Princeton Magazine,* no. 40 (Spring 1969), pp. 8–12.

'The economic profile of the American Black', *Journal of Religion and Health,* vol. 9, no. 4 (1970), pp. 323–330.

'Summary: The causes of unemployment in less developed countries', *International Labour Review,* vol. 101, no. 5 (1970), pp. 547–554.

'The dual economy revisited', *The Manchester School,* vol. 47, no. 3 (1979), pp. 211–229.

'Rising prices: 1899–1913 and 1950–1979', *Scandinavian Journal of Economics,* vol. 82, no. 4 (1980), pp. 425–436.

'The slowing down of the engine of growth', *American Economic Review,* vol. 70, no. 4 (1980), pp. 555–564.

Chapters in Books

'Recent British experience in nationalisation', in *Monopoly and Competition and their Regulation,* ed. E. H. Chamberlin (London: Macmillan, 1954), pp. 459–470.

'The Economic development of Africa', in *Africa in the Modern World,* ed. C. W. Stillman (Chicago: University of Chicago Press, 1955), pp. 97–112.

'The economic and social council', in *The United Nations,* ed. E. A. Wortley (Manchester: Manchester University Press, 1957), pp. 34–46.

'The shifting fortunes of agriculture', in *Agriculture and its Terms of Trade: Proceedings of the Tenth International Conference of Agricultural Economics* (London: Oxford University Press, 1960), pp. 27–34.

'Sponsored growth: Challenge to democracy', in *Problems of Economic Growth,* ed. M. K. Haldar and E. Ghosh (Delhi: Congress for Cultural Freedom, 1960), pp. 107–120.

'Economic conditions for greater agricultural output', in *Report of the Annual Meeting of the British Association for the Advancement of Science* (1960).

'Depreciation and obsolescence as factors in costing', in *Depreciation and Replacement Policy,* ed. J. L. Meij (Amsterdam: North Holland, 1961), pp. 15–45, revised and reprinted in *Studies in Accounting,* ed. W. T. Baxter and S. Davidson (London: The Institute of Chartered Accountants in England and Wales, 1977), pp. 210–233.

'The emergence of West Africa', in *The Promise of World Tensions,* ed. H. Cleveland (New York: Macmillan, 1961), pp. 87–100.

'Science, man and money', in *Science and the New Nations,* ed. R. Gruber (New York: Basic Books, 1961), pp. 24–33.

'Competition and regulation in the West Indies', in *Economic Systems of the Commonwealth,* ed. C. B. Hoover (Durham, North Carolina: Duke University Press, 1962), pp. 501–518.

'Tensions in economic development', in *Restless Nations,* ed. L. B. Pearson (New York: Dodd, Mead, 1962), pp. 68–98.

'Industrialisation and social peace', in *Conference Across a Continent,* Report of HRH The Duke of Edinburgh's Study Conference (Macmillan of Canada, 1963), pp. 46–60.

'Social services in development planning', in *Planning for Economic Development in the Caribbean,* Report of a Carribean Organization Conference (Puerto Rico: Caribbean Organization, 1963), pp. 156–167.

'Closing remarks', in *Inflation and Growth in Latin America,* ed. W. Baer and I. Kerstenetzky (New Haven: Yale University Press, 1964), pp. 21–33.

'Economic development and world trade', in *Problems in Economic Development,* ed. E. A. G. Robinson (London: Macmillan, 1965), pp. 483–497.

'African economic development', in *Africa: Progress Through Co-operation,* ed. J. Karefa-Smart (New York: Dodd, Mead, 1966), pp. 115–130.

'Planning public expenditure', in *National Economic Planning,* ed. M. F. Millikan (New York: National Bureau of Economic Research, 1967), pp. 201–227.

'Unemployment in developing areas', in *A Reappraisal of Economic Development,* ed. A. M. Whiteford (Chicago: Aldine, 1967), pp. 1–17.

'International trade and economic growth', in *Fiscal and Monetary Problems in Developing States,* ed. D. Krivine (New York: Praeger, 1967), pp. 350–358.

'Development planning', in *International Encyclopedia of the Social Sciences,* vol. 12 (Macmillan & The Free Press, 1968), pp. 118–125.

'Economic aspects of quality in education', in *Qualitative Aspects of Educational Planning,* ed. C. E. Beeby (Paris: UNESCO, International Institute for Economic Planning, 1969), pp. 71–88.

'On being different', in *Speeches made at the 1971 Graduation Ceremonies of the University of the West Indies* (Kingston: University of the West Indies, 1971).

'Objectives and prognostications', in *The Gap Between Rich and Poor Nations,* ed. G. Ranis (London: Macmillan, 1972), pp. 411–420.

'Reflections on unlimited labour', in *International Economics and Development* (Essays in Honour of Raoul Prebisch), ed. L. E. diMarco (New York: Academic Press, 1972), pp. 75–96.

'The development process', in *The Case for Development: Six Studies* (New York: Praeger, 1973), pp. 52–84.

'Development and distribution', in *Employment, Income Distribution and Development Strategy,* ed. A. Cairncross and M. Puri (London: Macmillan, 1976), pp. 26–42.

'The diffusion of development', in *The Market and the State,* ed. T. Wilson and A. S. Skinner (Oxford: Oxford University Press, 1976), pp. 135–156.

'The rate of growth of world trade, 1830–1973', in *The World Economic Order, Past and Prospects,* ed. S. Grassman and E. Lundberg (London: Macmillan, 1981), pp. 11–74.

Official Papers

Industrial Development in the Caribbean (Port-of-Spain, Trinidad: Caribbean Commission, 1949).

Land Settlement Policy (Port-of-Spain, Trinidad: Caribbean Commission, 1950).

(With others) *Measures for the Economic Development of Under-Developed Countries* (New York: United Nations, 1951).

(With others) *Report on National Fuel Policy* (London: UK Government, 1952).

Report on Industrialisation and the Gold Coast (Accra: Gold Coast Government, 1953).

Eastern Caribbean Foundation (Trinidad: Government of the West Indies, 1962).

Proposals for an Eastern Caribbean Federation of Eight Territories (Trinidad: Government of the West Indies, 1962).

(With others) *Partners in Progress* (''Pearson Commission'') (New York: Praeger, 1969).

Presidential Address on Unemployment to the Board of Governors, Caribbean Development Bank (Barbados: Caribbean Development Bank, 1972).

Some Constraints on International Banking (Barbados: Caribbean Development Bank, 1972).

Presidential Address on the Shortage of Entrepreneurship to the Board of Governors, Caribbean Development Bank (Barbados: Caribbean Development Bank, 1973).

Author Index

Subject Index